MATHEMATICS PLUS

HBJ

Harcourt Brace Jovanovich, Inc.

Orlando   Austin   San Diego   Chicago   Dallas   New York

Printed in the United States of America
ISBN 0-15-300145-3
2 3 4 5 6 7 8 9 10   048   95   94   93   92

ACKNOWLEDGMENTS

Some computer lessons in this book are based on AppleWorks® by Claris Corporation. © 1989 by
Claris Corporation. All rights reserved. Claris is a registered trademark of Claris Corporation. AppleWorks is a registered
trademark of Apple Computer, Inc. licensed to Claris Corporation. Apple is a registered trademark of Apple Computer, Inc.

Logo lessons in this book present the Terrapin Logo version. Terrapin is a registered trademark of
Terrapin Software, Inc.

A U T H O R S

Grace M. Burton
Professor, Department of Curricular Studies
University of North Carolina at Wilmington
Wilmington, North Carolina

Jerome D. Kaplan
Professor of Education
Seton Hall University
South Orange, New Jersey

Martha H. Hopkins
Associate Professor
University of Central Florida
Orlando, Florida

Leonard Kennedy
Professor Emeritus
California State University at Sacramento
Sacramento, California

Howard C. Johnson
Chair, Mathematics Education
Professor of Mathematics and Mathematics Education
Syracuse University
Syracuse, New York

Karen A. Schultz
Professor, Mathematics Education
Georgia State University
Atlanta, Georgia

S E N I O R   E D I T O R I A L   A D V I S O R

Francis (Skip) Fennell
Professor of Education
Western Maryland College
Westminister, Maryland

A D V I S O R S

Janet S. Abbott
Curriculum Coordinator
Chula Vista Elementary School District
Chula Vista, California

Don S. Balka
Professor
Saint Mary's College
Notre Dame, Indiana

Gilbert Cuevas
Professor of Education
University of Miami
Miami, Florida

Michael C. Hynes
Professor
University of Central Florida
Orlando, Florida

Genevieve M. Knight
Professor of Mathematics
Coppin State College
Baltimore, Maryland

Charles Lamb
Associate Professor
University of Texas at Austin
Austin, Texas

Marsha W. Lilly
Mathematics Coordinator, K–12
Alief Independent School District
Alief, Texas

Sid Rachlin
Professor
University of Hawaii
Honolulu, Hawaii

Steven Tipps
West Foundation Professor
Midwestern State University
Wichita Falls, Texas

David Wells
Retired Assistant Superintendent
for Instruction
Pontiac, Michigan

▶ ▶ ▶ ▶ ▶ ▶ ▶ ▶

Contents

INTRODUCING
◀ *Mathematics Plus* ▶

Welcome to **Mathematics Plus** **xvii**
How Do You Use Math Every Day? **xviii**
Solving Problems **xx**
How Will You Learn Math? **xxv**

1
Using Whole Numbers and Decimals **I**
THEME: *Entertainment*

Using Place Value **2**
Rounded Numbers **4**
Using Estimation **6**
Properties **8**
   Mixed Review **9**
Using Addition and Subtraction **10**
Problem Solving • Multistep Problems **12**
Using Multiplication and Division **14**
Review and Maintenance **16**
Spotlight on Problem Solving **17**
   Restate the Problem
Dividing Decimals by Decimals **18**
Interpreting Remainders **20**
   Mixed Review **21**
Powers and Exponents **22**
Order of Operations **24**
Problem Solving Strategy • Find a Pattern **26**

Chapter Review   **28**
Chapter Test   **30**
Teamwork Project • Make Movie Products   **31**
Math Fun • Extend Your Thinking   **32**
   Boomerang: A Game for Two, Palindromic Numbers, Logical Reasoning
Cumulative Review • Chapter 1   **33**

Algebra • Expressions and Equations   **34**
THEME: *Spending Money*

Language of Algebra   **36**
Expressions: Addition and Subtraction   **38**
Addition Equations   **40**
Problem Solving Strategy • Guess and Check   **42**
Subtraction Equations   **44**
   Mixed Review   **45**
Review and Maintenance   **46**
Spotlight on Problem Solving   **47**
   Identify Relationships
Expressions: Multiplication and Division   **48**
Multiplication Equations   **50**
Division Equations   **52**
   Mixed Review   **53**
Two-Step Equations   **54**
Solving Inequalities   **56**
Problem Solving Strategy • Write an Equation   **58**
Chapter Review   **60**
Chapter Test   **62**
Teamwork Project • Write a Newsletter   **63**
Math Fun • Extend Your Thinking   **64**
   Historical Note, Logical Reasoning, Visual Thinking
Cumulative Review • Chapters 1–2   **65**

3

Number Theory and Fractions   66
THEME: *Careers*

Primes and Composites   **68**
Using the GCF and the LCM   **70**
Problem Solving • Making Choices   **72**
Equivalent Fractions and Mixed Numbers   **74**
Problem-Solving Practice   **77**
Comparing and Ordering   **78**
    Mixed Review   **79**
Review and Maintenance   **80**
Spotlight on Problem Solving   **81**
    Analyze Information
Estimating Sums and Differences   **82**
Adding Fractions and Mixed Numbers   **84**
Subtracting Fractions and Mixed Numbers   **86**
    Mixed Review   **87**
Problem Solving Strategy • Draw a Picture   **88**
Chapter Review   **90**
Chapter Test   **92**
Teamwork Project • Take a Survey   **93**
Math Fun • Extend Your Thinking   **94**
    Historical Note: Unit Fractions, Number Sense, Number Sense
Cumulative Review • Chapters 1–3   **95**

4

Using Fractions   96
THEME: *Gardening*

Estimating Products   **98**
Multiplying Fractions   **100**
Multiplying Mixed Numbers   **102**
    Mixed Review   **103**

Estimating Quotients **104**
Review and Maintenance **106**
Spotlight on Problem Solving **107**
   Discuss the Process
Dividing Fractions **108**
Problem Solving Strategy • Solve a Simpler Problem **110**
Dividing Mixed Numbers **112**
Equations with Fractions **114**
   Mixed Review **117**
Decimals for Fractions **118**
Fractions for Decimals **120**
Problem Solving • Choose a Strategy **122**
Chapter Review **124**
Chapter Test **126**
Teamwork Project • Plan a Garden **127**
Math Fun • Extend Your Thinking **128**
   Continued Fractions, Number Sense, Patterns
Cumulative Review • Chapters 1–4 **129**

5   **Geometric Relationships and Constructions** **130**
       THEME: *Construction*

Basic Ideas in Geometry **132**
Angles and Angle Pairs **134**
Constructing Congruent Segments and Angles **138**
Exploring Parallel Lines and Transversals **140**
Constructing Parallel and Perpendicular Lines **142**
   Mixed Review **143**
Bisecting Segments and Angles **144**
Problem Solving Strategy • Find a Pattern **146**
Polygons **148**
Exploring Triangles **152**

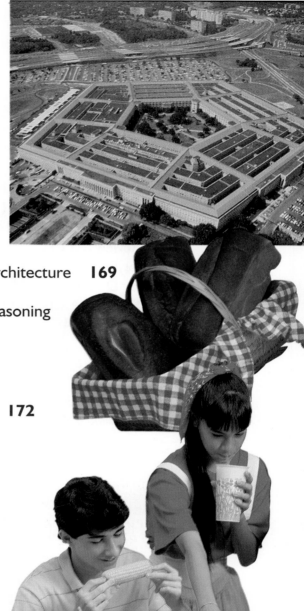

Review and Maintenance **154**
Spotlight on Problem Solving **155**
    Visualize the Results
Congruent Polygons **156**
Constructing Congruent Triangles **158**
Circles **162**
    Mixed Review **163**
Problem Solving • Making Choices **164**
Chapter Review **166**
Chapter Test **168**
Teamwork Project • Find Geometry in Architecture **169**
Math Fun • Extend Your Thinking **170**
    Tessellations, Number Sense, Logical Reasoning
Cumulative Review • Chapters 1–5 **171**

6 Ratio, Proportion, and Percent **172**
THEME: *Food and Nutrition*

Ratios and Rates **174**
Proportions **176**
Scale Drawings **178**
Problem Solving • Use a Map **182**
Understanding Percent **184**
Percents, Decimals, and Ratios **186**
Exploring Percent Problems **188**
Finding a Percent of a Number **190**
    Mixed Review **191**
Review and Maintenance **192**
Spotlight on Problem Solving **193**
    Decide When to Estimate
Finding the Percent One Number Is of Another **194**
Finding the Number When the Percent Is Known **196**
Estimating Percents **198**

Exploring Percent of Increase and Decrease   **200**
Percent of Increase and Decrease   **202**
Simple Interest   **204**
    Mixed Review   **205**
Problem Solving Strategy • Use Estimation   **206**
Chapter Review   **208**
Chapter Test   **210**
Teamwork Project • Make a Table   **211**
Math Fun • Extend Your Thinking   **212**
        Who's the Greek Mathematician?, Logical Reasoning, Number Sense
Cumulative Review • Chapters 1–6   **213**

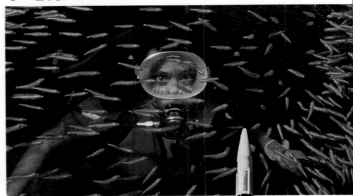

7   **Integers   214**
    THEME: *Exploration*

Understanding Integers   **216**
Adding Integers   **218**
Subtracting Integers   **220**
Multiplying Integers   **222**
Problem Solving Strategy • Make a Table   **224**
Dividing Integers   **226**
    Mixed Review   **227**
Review and Maintenance   **228**
Spotlight on Problem Solving   **229**
        Collect and Analyze Data
Properties of Integers   **230**
Integers as Exponents   **232**
Exploring Products and Quotients of Powers   **234**
Scientific Notation   **236**
    Mixed Review   **237**
Problem Solving Strategy • Write an Equation   **238**
Chapter Review   **240**
Chapter Test   **242**

Teamwork Project • Make a Scale Drawing **243**
Math Fun • Extend Your Thinking **244**
    Matching Integers: A Game for Two, Logical Reasoning, Number Sense
Cumulative Review • Chapters 1–7 **245**

Real Numbers 246
THEME: *Science and Technology*

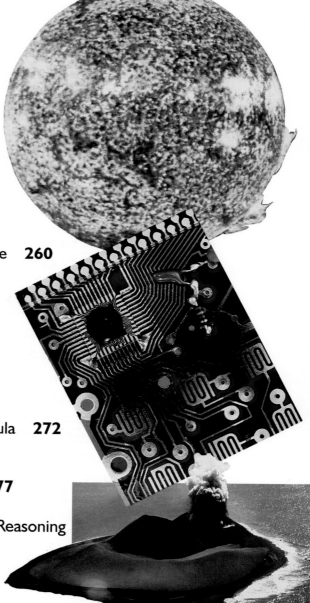

Rational Numbers **248**
Squares and Square Roots **250**
Finding Square Roots **252**
Exploring Irrational Numbers **256**
Adding and Subtracting **258**
    Mixed Review **259**
Problem Solving Strategy • Make a Table **260**
Multiplying and Dividing **262**
Review and Maintenance **264**
Spotlight on Problem Solving 265
    Determine Reasonable Solutions
Solving One-Step Equations **266**
    Mixed Review **267**
Solving Two-Step Equations **268**
Solving Inequalities **270**
Problem Solving Strategy • Use a Formula **272**
Chapter Review **274**
Chapter Test **276**
Teamwork Project • Write an Article **277**
Math Fun • Extend Your Thinking **278**
    Twin Solutions, Number Sense, Logical Reasoning
Cumulative Review • Chapters 1–8 **279**

9   **Algebra • Graphing Relations and Functions**   **280**
THEME: *Sports*

Graphing Ordered Pairs   **282**
Relations and Functions   **284**
Equations with Two Variables   **286**
Graphing Equations   **288**
   Mixed Review   **289**
Problem Solving • Use a Graph to Estimate   **290**
Exploring Slope of a Line   **292**
Review and Maintenance   **294**
Spotlight on Problem Solving   **295**
   Recognize Multiple Solutions
Systems of Equations   **296**
Graphing Inequalities   **298**
Transformations   **300**
   Mixed Review   **303**
Problem Solving Strategy • Guess and Check   **304**
Chapter Review   **306**
Chapter Test   **308**
Teamwork Project • Exercise and the Heart   **309**
Math Fun • Extend Your Thinking   **310**
   Equations for Image Points, Logical Reasoning, Number Sense
Cumulative Review • Chapters 1–9   **311**

10   **Statistics and Graphing**   **312**
THEME: *School Life*

Analyzing Data: Mean, Median, and Mode   **314**
Frequency Tables and Histograms   **316**
Line Graphs   **318**
Problem Solving • Sufficient and Insufficient Data   **320**

▶▶▶▶▶▶▶▶▶▶▶▶

Bar Graphs   **322**
   Mixed Review   **323**
Review and Maintenance   **324**
Spotlight on Problem Solving   **325**
   Analyze Misleading Graphs
Circle Graphs   **326**
Stem-and-Leaf Plots   **328**
Quartiles and Extremes   **330**
   Mixed Review   **331**
Box-and-Whisker Graphs   **332**
Making Inferences   **334**
Exploring Scattergrams   **336**
Problem Solving • Choose an Appropriate Graph   **338**
Chapter Review   **340**
Chapter Test   **342**
Teamwork Project • Choose a Field-Trip Destination   **343**
Math Fun • Extend Your Thinking   **344**
   Use a Stem-and-Leaf Plot to Find the Mean, Number Sense, Number Sense
Cumulative Review • Chapters 1–10   **345**

Probability   **346**
THEME: *Games*

Fundamental Counting Principle   **348**
Permutations   **350**
   Mixed Review   **353**
Combinations   **354**
Probability   **356**
Exploring Pascal's Triangle   **358**
Problem Solving • Use a Diagram   **360**
Random Numbers   **362**
Predictions   **364**
   Mixed Review   **365**

Review and Maintenance **366**
Spotlight on Problem Solving **367**
    Understand the Question
Independent Events **368**
Dependent Events **370**
Venn Diagrams **372**
Problem Solving Strategy • Act It Out **374**
Chapter Review **376**
Chapter Test **378**
Teamwork Project • Batting Averages **379**
Math Fun • Extend Your Thinking **380**
    Number Patterns, Patterns and Relations, The Fibonacci Sequence
Cumulative Review • Chapters 1–11 **381**

Plane Geometry and Measurement **382**
THEME: *School Projects*

Selecting an Appropriate Unit **384**
Estimating Measures **386**
Precision: Greatest Possible Error **388**
    Mixed Review **391**
Significant Digits **392**
Problem Solving Strategy • Make a Model **394**
Perimeter of Polygons **396**
Review and Maintenance **398**
Spotlight on Problem Solving **399**
    Check the Reasonableness of a Solution
Circumference of Circles **400**
Area of Rectangles and Parallelograms **402**
Area of Triangles and Trapezoids **404**
    Mixed Review **405**
Area of Circles **406**

Problem Solving Strategy • Use a Formula   **408**
Chapter Review   **410**
Chapter Test   **412**
Teamwork Project • Just the Facts Brainteasers   **413**
Math Fun • Extend Your Thinking   **414**
    Conversion Factors, Number Sense, Patterns
Cumulative Review • Chapters 1–12   **415**

Solid Geometry and Measurement   **416**
THEME: *The Environment*

Solid Figures (Polyhedra)   **418**
Cylinders, Cones, and Spheres   **420**
Drawing Three-Dimensional Figures   **422**
    Mixed Review   **423**
Problem Solving Strategy • Make a Table   **424**
Surface Area of Prisms and Pyramids   **426**
    Mixed Review   **427**
Review and Maintenance   **428**
Spotlight on Problem Solving   **429**
    Choose a Method for Solution
Exploring Surface Area of Cylinders and Cones   **430**
Volume of Prisms and Pyramids   **432**
Volume of Cylinders and Cones   **434**
Capacity   **436**
Problem Solving Strategy • Use a Formula   **438**
Chapter Review   **440**
Chapter Test   **442**
Teamwork Project • Recycle Containers   **443**
Math Fun • Extend Your Thinking   **444**
    Spheres, Cylinders, and Cones; Visual Thinking, Number Sense
Cumulative Review • Chapters 1–13   **445**

Indirect Measurement **446**
THEME: *Design*

Exploring Right Triangles   **448**
Using the Pythagorean Property   **450**
Special Right Triangles   **452**
Problem Solving • Making Choices   **454**
Similar Figures   **456**
   Mixed Review   **457**
Review and Maintenance   **458**
Spotlight on Problem Solving   **459**
   Visualize the Results
Trigonometric Ratios   **460**
Using the Tangent Ratio   **462**
Using the Sine and the Cosine Ratios   **464**
   Mixed Review   **465**
Problem Solving Strategy • Draw a Picture   **466**
Chapter Review   **468**
Chapter Test   **470**
Teamwork Project • Design a Youth Center   **471**
Math Fun • Extend Your Thinking   **472**
   Enlargements from Unit Figures, Logical Reasoning, Visual Thinking
Cumulative Review • Chapters 1–14   **473**

Computer Connection
LOGO: Geometry Review   **476**
LOGO and BASIC Random Numbers   **478**
Spreadsheet: Sale Discounts and Taxes   **480**
Spreadsheet: Solving Equations   **482**
Spreadsheet: Business Application   **484**
Word Processing: Adding and Replacing Text   **486**
Data Base: Conducting a Survey   **488**
Idea Bank   **490**

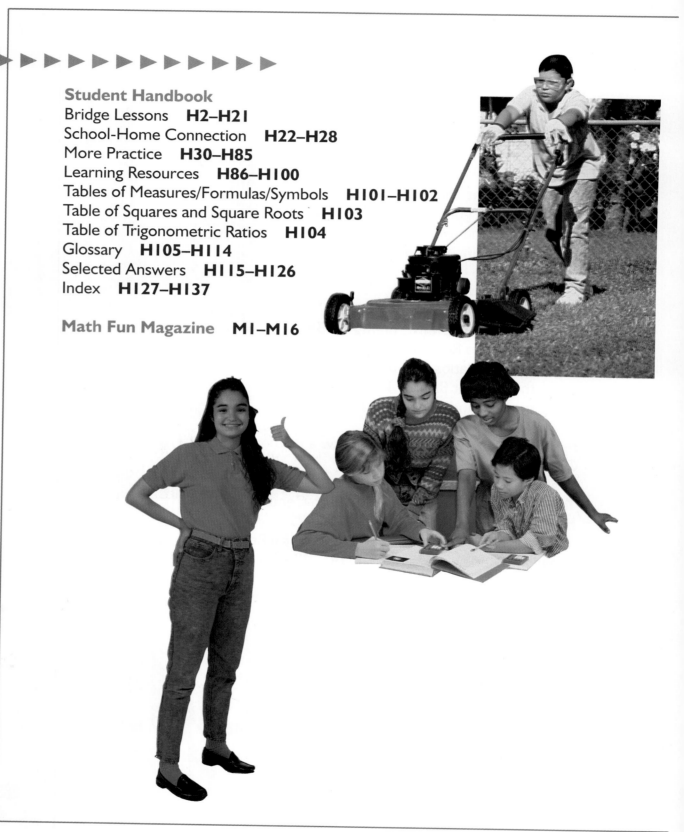

Student Handbook
Bridge Lessons   **H2–H21**
School-Home Connection   **H22–H28**
More Practice   **H30–H85**
Learning Resources   **H86–H100**
Tables of Measures/Formulas/Symbols   **H101–H102**
Table of Squares and Square Roots   **H103**
Table of Trigonometric Ratios   **H104**
Glossary   **H105–H114**
Selected Answers   **H115–H126**
Index   **H127–H137**

Math Fun Magazine   **M1–M16**

Welcome to MATHEMATICS PLUS

Mathematics is an important part of your daily life. You use it at school, at home, and everywhere you go. As you study math this year, think about how the ideas you are learning help you with other school subjects and with your everyday activities.

This year you are going to use ideas you have already learned in interesting, new ways. You will learn more about how to solve problems. You will use the calculator and the computer as problem-solving tools. You will use whole numbers, decimals, fractions, and integers to solve problems. You will explore ideas about rational and real numbers. You will learn more about solving equations and inequalities. You will explore many new ideas in algebra. You will use probability ideas to solve problems. You will learn more about collecting, organizing, and analyzing data. You will learn more about geometric figures and measurement of these figures.

Math is fun! You will work in groups to share what you are learning. You will have fun solving the puzzles and problems in the **Math Fun Magazine** at the back of this book.

This year
you can make mathematics
a learning adventure!

The Authors

How Do You Use Math Every Day?

People use math in their everyday activities in many ways. Here are some of the things people do that involve math.

shop	weigh
count	measure
share	save
build	cook
travel	tell time
compare	keep score
estimate	predict

Talk about how the people in these photographs are using math. Share with your classmates some of the ways you use math at school, at home, and everywhere you go.

Solving Problems

You use math every day to solve problems. In this book you will learn how to solve problems by asking yourself questions. These questions will help you

- UNDERSTAND the problem.
- PLAN a solution.
- SOLVE the problem.
- LOOK BACK and check your solution.

Lashonda has a problem to solve. Read her problem slowly and carefully.

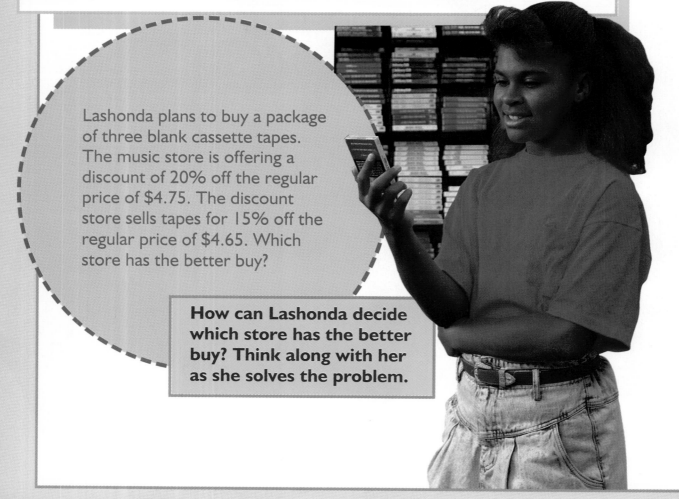

Lashonda plans to buy a package of three blank cassette tapes. The music store is offering a discount of 20% off the regular price of $4.75. The discount store sells tapes for 15% off the regular price of $4.65. Which store has the better buy?

How can Lashonda decide which store has the better buy? Think along with her as she solves the problem.

Understand the Problem

First, Lashonda must UNDERSTAND the problem.

She restates the problem to herself. She wants to be sure she knows what the problem is about. Then she asks herself these questions.

What must I find?
I must find whether the music store or the discount store has the better buy on tapes.

What facts do I have?
The music store's price is 20% off $4.75. The discount store's price is 15% off $4.65.

How would you restate Lashonda's problem in your own words?

Then, Lashonda must PLAN how to solve her problem.

She thinks about the ways she solves problems. She chooses one of these strategies.

- Draw a diagram
- Make a model
- Work backward
- Guess and check
- Make a table, chart, or graph
- Write a number sentence

Then she makes a plan by asking herself this question.

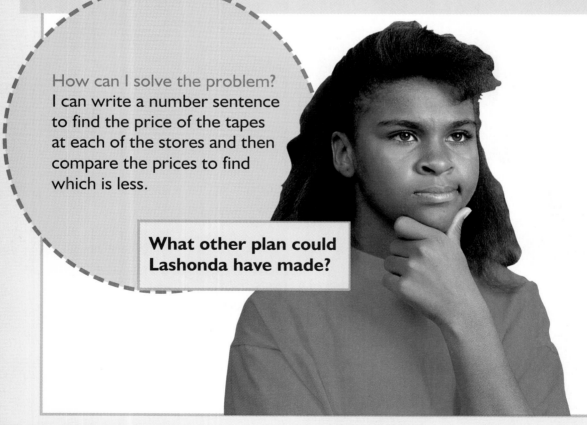

How can I solve the problem? I can write a number sentence to find the price of the tapes at each of the stores and then compare the prices to find which is less.

What other plan could Lashonda have made?

▶ ▶ ▶ ▶ ▶ ▶ ▶ ▶

Solve the Problem

Next, Lashonda must SOLVE the problem.

She must decide how to solve the problem. She can choose paper and pencil, a calculator, or mental math to find the answer.

Lashonda thinks about the best method to use to find the price of the cassettes at each store.

I can use a calculator to find the price of the cassettes at each store.

price at
music store   4.75 ⊟ 20 %   3.8

price at
discount store   4.65 ⊟ 15 %   3.9525

$3.80 < $3.95

So, the music store has the better buy on cassette tapes.

Why do you think Lashonda used a calculator to solve the problem? What method would you choose?

Look Back

Last, Lashonda can LOOK BACK and check to see whether her answer is correct.

She thinks about a way to check her answer. She thinks about whether her solution answers the question.

She asks herself these questions.

How can I check my answer?
I can add the amount of the discount to the sale price to see if that equals the regular price.

	amount of discount		sale price		regular price
music store	$0.95	+	$3.80	=	$4.75
discount store	$0.70	+	$3.95	=	$4.65

So, my solution is correct.

Does my solution answer the question?

Since I determined which store has the better buy, my solution answers the question.

How else could Lashonda check her answer?

Lashonda solved her problem. She used math to determine the better buy.

In Mathematics Plus you will learn to be a problem solver!

How Will You Learn Math?

In **Mathematics Plus you will learn math in different ways.** All of the ways to learn involve *thinking*.

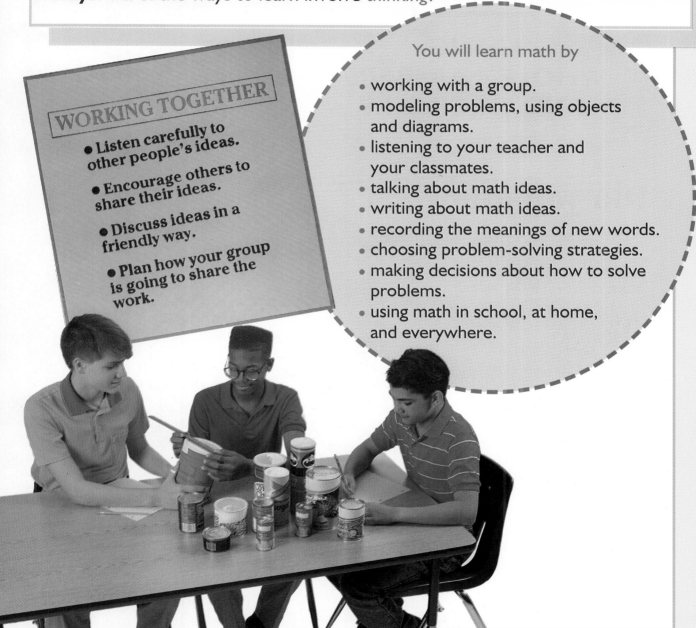

WORKING TOGETHER

- Listen carefully to other people's ideas.
- Encourage others to share their ideas.
- Discuss ideas in a friendly way.
- Plan how your group is going to share the work.

You will learn math by

- working with a group.
- modeling problems, using objects and diagrams.
- listening to your teacher and your classmates.
- talking about math ideas.
- writing about math ideas.
- recording the meanings of new words.
- choosing problem-solving strategies.
- making decisions about how to solve problems.
- using math in school, at home, and everywhere.

USING WHOLE NUMBERS AND DECIMALS

Did you know . . .

. . . that there are stores where you can make your own music video?

Suppose you want to make a video that will cost $30.00. You earn $4.25 per hour. How would you find the number of hours you need to work to pay for the video?

WARM UP...

What is the place value of the digit 3 in 134,725.6?

Jason used a calculator to multiply two numbers. This is the product the calculator displayed. How can you make this number easier to read?

To make the number easier to read, use commas to divide it into periods.

$$3165735.3 = 3,165,735.3$$

Read: 3 million, 165 thousand, 735 and 3 tenths
or 3 million, 165 thousand, 735 point 3

Talk About It

▶ Why do we often say "point 3" instead of "and 3 tenths"?

▶ How does the place value of the digit 1 in 3,165,735.3 compare to the place value of the digit 6?

In many tables large numbers are shortened so they are easier to read. In this table, for example, the column for the number sold is labeled "in millions." This means that in 1987, 19.3 million (19,300,000) color television sets were sold.

● How many home VCR's were sold in 1987?

● How many camcorders were sold in 1987?

● How would you show 19,300,000 if the column for the number sold were labeled "in thousands"?

1987 VCR and TV Sales	
Item	**Number Sold (in millions)**
Color television	19.3
Black-and-white television	3.5
Home VCR	13.3
Camcorder	1.6

Check for Understanding

Tell how you would read each number.

1. 45678.8
2. 708923.43
3. 145897.69
4. 60043220
5. 432.126
6. 1264.125
7. 2006401
8. 400.04

Write the standard form of each number.

9. 4.5 million
10. 8.65 thousand
11. 22.1 billion
12. 981 thousand

Practice

Write each number in words.

13. 30091　　　　**14.** 80876.1　　　　**15.** 3074389.32　　　　**16.** 101106.34

Name the place of the underlined digit.

17. 1<u>7</u>8,430.9　　　　**18.** 423.1<u>0</u>9　　　　**19.** 1<u>9</u>,376,452.9　　　　**20.** 345.198<u>7</u>

Write the standard form of each number.

21. 24.56 million　　**22.** 7.81 billion　　**23.** 1.03 thousand　　**24.** 7.08 million

Write in shortened form using the word *million*.

25. 13,456,000　　　　**26.** 5,876,000　　　　**27.** 124,060,000　　　　**28.** 324,156

Compare. Use $<$, $>$, or $=$.

29. 12.3 ● 13.2　　　　**30.** 456.708 ● 456.7080　　　　**31.** 156,321 ● 156,231

Mixed Applications

32. In 1989, 87.3 million homes in the United States had color television sets. Write the number of homes in standard form.

33. Write a five-digit number with a 4 in the hundreds place and a 9 in the hundredths place.

34. Mental Math A store sold 35 radios and 65 cameras for $50 each. What were the total sales?

35. Use the table on page 2 to find how many more home VCR's than camcorders were bought in 1987.

36. Find Data Use an almanac to find the five all-time top television programs.

CHALLENGE • LOGICAL REASONING

37. A five-digit number contains the digits 1, 2, 3, 4, and 5. Use the following clues to find the number.

Clue 1: The number is less than 40,000.
Clue 2: The 4 is next to the 2.
Clue 3: The 2 is not next to the 1 or 3.
Clue 4: The 5 is not next to the 1 or 3.
Clue 5: The 4 is next to the 3 or 5.

I can use the strategy *guess and check*.

Explain how you can use multiplication to write 12.5 million in standard form.

WRAP UP . . .

ROUNDED NUMBERS

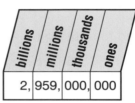
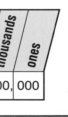

Most statistics given in newspapers and magazines are rounded numbers. For example, a newspaper report stated that in a recent year, recording manufacturers shipped 2,959,000,000 cassettes. This is not the exact number of cassettes shipped, but an estimation.

● Why do you think that many of the reported numbers in newspapers and magazines are rounded numbers?

The numbers in the table have been rounded.

billions	millions	thousands	ones
2,	959,	000,	000

Talk About It

▶ To what place does it appear the numbers have been rounded? Explain how you can tell.

▶ Which would be closer to the exact amount, a number rounded to the nearest million or a number rounded to the nearest thousand?

▶ The greatest number of CD's that could have been shipped was 1,593,499,999. Explain why this is a true statement.

▶ What is the least number of CD's that could have been shipped? Explain your answer.

Recordings Shipped	
Type	**Number**
Single	203,000,000
LP	793,000,000
CD	1,593,000,000
Cassette	2,959,000,000

The numbers in the table can be written in shortened form.

Examples 1,593,000,000 can be written as 1.593 billion.
203,000,000 can be written as 203 million.

Check for Understanding

Name the place to which each number appears to be rounded.

1. 340   **2.** 1,200   **3.** 540,000   **4.** 34.2

An exact number has been rounded to the given number. Name the greatest whole number and the least whole number that the exact number can be.

5. 34,000   **6.** 18,100   **7.** 605,000   **8.** 1,230,000

Practice

Name the place to which each number appears to be rounded.

9. 270   **10.** 252.1   **11.** 1,500   **12.** 12,300

13. 1.04   **14.** 424,000   **15.** 7,000,000   **16.** 9,000.1

An exact number has been rounded to the given number. Name the greatest whole number and the least whole number that the exact number can be.

17. 120   **18.** 3,400   **19.** 16,000   **20.** 210

21. 4,500,000   **22.** 12,400,000   **23.** 90   **24.** 140,000,000

25. An exact number has been rounded to 12. The least number that the exact number can be is 11.5. Is it possible to name the greatest number it can be? Explain.

Round each number to the nearest hundred thousand. Then write the rounded number in shortened form using the word *million*.

26. 5,092,713   **27.** 64,372,110   **28.** 394,876,243

29. 1,434,699,600   **30.** 3,517,400,520   **31.** 9,990,099,632

Mixed Applications

32. In 1991, ABC Records sold about 3,430,000 cassette tapes. What is the least number of cassette tapes ABC Records could have sold?

33. If the largest whole number that can be rounded to 400 is 449, what is the largest whole number that can be rounded to 4,000,000?

34. While doing research on the recording industry, Paul finds this sales information.

ABC Records: $12,435,144
Rocket Records: $13.6 million

To what place should Paul round the sales amount for ABC Records so that it is similar to the amount for Rocket Records? How can he write the rounded amount for ABC Records in shortened form?

35. Number Sense Use these facts to find the three-digit number.

- If the number is rounded to the nearest ten, the result is 10.

- If the number is rounded to the nearest whole number, the result is 12.

- The tenths digit is 2 more than the ones digit.

In your own words, state the rules for rounding a number to any given place.

WRAP UP...

WARM UP...

Is it possible to give more than one estimate for 346×12? Explain.

USING ESTIMATION

Walter is in charge of ordering programs for a concert at school. The auditorium has 51 rows of seats, with 32 seats in each row. Walter is responsible for making sure there is a program for each person who attends the concert. To determine how many programs are needed, Walter estimates.

$51 \times 32 \longrightarrow 50 \times 30 = 1,500$ estimate

So, Walter decides to order 1,500 programs for the concert.

Talk About It

▶ Is Walter's estimate an overestimate or an underestimate? Explain.

▶ If every seat in the auditorium is filled, will every person have a program? Why or why not?

▶ What numbers could Walter have used to get an overestimate?

▶ Which overestimate would be closer to the actual answer, 50×40 or 50×34? Explain.

The closer the numbers you use to estimate are to the actual numbers, the closer the estimate will be to the exact answer.

Examples

	A. 24×4	**B.** $178 + 261$	**C.** $5,234 - 1,588$
estimate:	$20 \times 4 = 80$	$200 + 300 = 500$	$5,000 - 2,000 = 3,000$
closer estimate:	$25 \times 4 = 100$	$180 + 260 = 440$	$5,200 - 1,600 = 3,600$

● Is the closer estimate in Example **C** an overestimate or an underestimate? Explain.

Throughout this book, you can use a combination of estimation methods and number sense to find estimates.

6

Check for Understanding

Write *overestimate* or *underestimate*.

1. A truck must cross a bridge that is weight-restricted. The truck driver should __?__ the weight of his loaded truck.

2. You are taking a trip. You should __?__ the amount of money you will need.

Choose the estimate that is closest to the actual answer. Choose **a**, **b**, or **c**.

3. 48×22 **a.** 40×20 **b.** 45×20 **c.** 50×20

4. $122 - 78$ **a.** $100 - 80$ **b.** $120 - 80$ **c.** $100 - 100$

Practice

Choose the overestimate. Write **a** or **b**.

5. $332 + 248$
   a. $300 + 200$
   b. $350 + 250$

6. $835 - 672$
   a. $850 - 650$
   b. $800 - 700$

7. 52×8
   a. 52×10
   b. 50×8

8. $72 \div 7$
   a. $72 \div 8$
   b. $77 \div 7$

Give two estimates for each problem. Tell which is the closer estimate.

9. $155 + 722$ 10. $4,569 + 2,543$ 11. 23×15 12. 965×220

13. $543 - 223$ 14. $163 \div 8$ 15. $49.9 + 27.6$ 16. $1,055 \times 18$

Mixed Applications

17. Terry has a job interview early tomorrow morning, and she must be on time. In determining when she should get up, should she overestimate or underestimate the time needed to dress and eat breakfast?

18. The Video Tech Company had expenses of $4,322, $8,104, and $6,450 this month. Is $18,000 an overestimate or an underestimate of the total expenses? Explain.

19. **Mental Math**   Jason Keller paid $75.25 for 25 floppy disks. How much did he pay for each disk?

20. **Number Sense**   For the problem $355 \div 6$, the estimate $360 \div 6$ is an overestimate. What type of estimate do you think $355 \div 10$ is? Explain.

Explain why 30×25 is a closer estimate than 30×20 for 32×24.

WRAP UP...

PROPERTIES

Is $(20 \times 5) + (4 \times 5)$ equivalent to 24×5? Explain.

Recall that addition and multiplication have similar properties.

Addition	Multiplication
Commutative Property $a + b = b + a$ $12 + 6 = 6 + 12$	**Commutative Property** $a \times b = b \times a$ $8 \times 2 = 2 \times 8$
Associative Property $(a + b) + c = a + (b + c)$ $(3 + 2) + 8 = 3 + (2 + 8)$	**Associative Property** $(a \times b) \times c = a \times (b \times c)$ $(5 \times 1.2) \times 9 = 5 \times (1.2 \times 9)$
Identity Property (Property of Zero) $a + 0 = a$ $24 + 0 = 24$	**Identity Property** (Property of One) $a \times 1 = a$ $54 \times 1 = 54$

The Distributive Property can be used with multiplication and addition or multiplication and subtraction.

$$a \times (b + c) = (a \times b) + (a \times c) \qquad r \times (s - t) = (r \times s) - (r \times t)$$
$$4 \times (6.4 + 2) = (4 \times 6.4) + (4 \times 2) \qquad 3 \times (8 - 2) = (3 \times 8) - (3 \times 2)$$

These properties for addition and multiplication can be used to help you compute mentally.

Examples

A. $25 \times 14 = 25 \times (10 + 4)$
$= (25 \times 10) + (25 \times 4)$
$= 250 + 100$
$= 350$

B. $(14 + 18) + 6 = (18 + 14) + 6$
$= 18 + (14 + 6)$
$= 18 + 20$
$= 38$

● What property was used to solve Example **A**?

● What properties were used to solve Example **B**?

Check for Understanding

1. State in your own words the meaning of the Commutative and Associative Properties of Addition.

2. State in your own words the meaning of the Distributive Property.

Complete.

3. $4 \times 24 = 4 \times (\blacksquare + 4) = (4 \times 20) + (\blacksquare \times 4) = 80 + 16 = 96$

4. $64 + (13 + 6) = 64 + (\blacksquare + 13) = (64 + 6) + 13 = \blacksquare + 13 = \blacksquare$

Practice

Name the property shown.

5. $20 + (75 + 5) = (20 + 75) + 5$

6. $2.5 + 8.3 = 8.3 + 2.5$

7. $1 \times 89 = 89$

8. $4 + (7 + 5) = (7 + 5) + 4$

9. $45 \times 6 = 6 \times 45$

10. $78 + 0 = 78$

11. $14 \times (5 + 9) = (14 \times 5) + (14 \times 9)$

12. $1.3 + 8 + 2.7 = 8 + 1.3 + 2.7$

13. $(8 \times 7) + (2 \times 7) = (8 + 2) \times 7$

14. $43 = 43 + 0$

Complete.

15. $145 + \blacksquare = 145$

16. $115 \times \blacksquare = 115$

17. $6 \times 24 = 6 \times (\blacksquare + 4) = (6 \times 20) + (\blacksquare \times 4) = 120 + 24 = 144$

18. $65 + (7 + 15) = 65 + (\blacksquare + 7) = (65 + 15) + 7 = \blacksquare + 7 = \blacksquare$

19. $31 \times 12 = (30 + 1) \times \blacksquare = (30 \times 12) + (\blacksquare \times 12) = 360 + \blacksquare = \blacksquare$

Mixed Applications

20. Philip bought 16 stickers for $0.25 each. Use the Distributive Property to determine how much he paid for the stickers. Show your work.

21. Trish bought 6 pencils for $0.12 each and 6 erasers for $0.08 each. Use the Distributive Property to determine how much she paid. Show your work.

22. Number Sense Can you subtract two numbers in either order? In other words, is subtraction commutative? Give two examples to explain your answer.

23. Show how to rewrite 32×16 using the Distributive Property. Write one example using addition and another example using subtraction.

MIXED REVIEW

Write the standard form of each number.

1. 1.6 thousand　　**2.** 3.44 million　　**3.** 0.5 million　　**4.** 12.2 billion

Round to the nearest tenth.

5. 235.154　　**6.** 8.9084　　**7.** 0.9802　　**8.** 76.2133

Compare. Use $<$, $>$, or $=$.

9. $8.52 \bullet 8.25$　　**10.** $256.01 \bullet 265.01$　　**11.** $3,485 \bullet 3,489$

Explain why $(63 + 37) + 98$ is easier to compute mentally than $63 + (98 + 37)$.

WRAP UP...

USING ADDITION AND SUBTRACTION

A survey was taken in a town for an evening news show. The table shows the number of people of various ages that watch the show. How many people over the age of 11 watch the show?

Survey Results	
Ages of Viewers	**Number (in thousands)**
Women 18 and over	10.083
Men 18 and over	7.42
Teens 12–17	1.537
Children 2–11	0.042

Step 1
Estimate the sum.

10,083	10,000
7,420	7,400
+ 1,537	+ 1,500
	18,900

Step 2
Find the exact sum.

10,083
7,420
+ 1,537
19,040

Since 19,040 is close to the estimate of 18,900, the answer is reasonable. So, 19,040 people over the age of 11 watch the evening news show.

● In the computation, why was the number of men 18 and over written as 7,420 instead of 7.42?

Another Example

Jerome is buying a new VCR that costs $319.49. He makes a down payment of $63.89. How much does he still owe on the VCR?

$319.49	→	$320
− 63.89	→	− 60
		$260 estimate

Use a calculator.

319.49 ⊖ 63.89 ⊜ [255.6]

So, Jerome still owes $255.60 on the VCR.

Check for Understanding

Tell whether you would add or subtract to solve. Then solve.

1. Mr. Hart bought an entertainment center priced at $1,235.89. He traded in his old stereo, and the store took $213.50 off the price of the entertainment center. What was the new price?

2. A school survey shows that 565 students watch Channel 8 news, 838 watch Channel 3 news, and 345 do not watch the news. How many students were surveyed?

Practice

3. In the past three months, Debra spent $24.80, $15.95, and $18.72 for records and cassettes. How much did she spend in all?

4. Andre has saved $178.24. He wants to buy an amplifier that costs $262.99. How much more money does he need to buy the amplifier?

A news report on the U.S. Treasury Department gave the information shown in the table. The table shows the values of the $100, $20, and $10 bills in circulation in a recent year.

Use the table for Exercises 5–8.

U.S. Bills in Circulation	
Currency	**Value**
$100 bills	$114,602,020,000
$20 bills	$ 63,316,206,660
$10 bills	$ 11,823,664,200

5. What is the difference between the value of the $20 bills and the value of the $10 bills?

6. What is the total value of the $100 and $20 bills?

7. To the nearest million dollars, what is the total value of the $100, $20, and $10 bills?

8. To the nearest billion dollars, what is the difference in the value of the $100 and $10 bills?

9. In 1989 there were 8,573,470,000 pennies produced. In 1988 there were 11,346,550,443 pennies produced. What was the total number of pennies produced in 1988 and 1989?

10. On June 30, 1989, there was $249,182.7 million in circulation. On June 30, 1910, there was $3,148.7 million in circulation. How much more money was in circulation on June 30, 1989?

Mixed Applications

11. Notice in the table that the value of the $20 bills in circulation is almost six times the value of the $10 bills. Does this mean that there are almost six times as many $20 bills in circulation as $10 bills? Explain.

12. **Make Up a Problem** Use the information in the table to write a problem that can be solved by using addition or subtraction. Exchange with a classmate and solve.

Rewrite Exercise 5 so it can be solved by using addition.

WRAP UP...

PROBLEM *Solving*

Multistep Problems

The table shows the types of television programs that are watched by teenagers who are 13 to 17 years old. How many more teenagers watch situation comedies than watch dramas and mysteries?

Television Programs Watched	
Program Type	Number of Teenage Viewers
Drama	1,160,000
Mystery	1,200,000
Situation comedy	2,470,000
Adventure	1,830,000

Sometimes, you need to use more than one step or operation to solve a problem. Such problems have information that you must find before you can answer the question.

▶ **UNDERSTAND**

What are you asked to find?

What facts are given?

▶ **PLAN**

What steps will you follow to solve the problem?

Step 1: Find the total number of teenagers that watch dramas and mysteries.

Step 2: Find the difference between the number that watch situation comedies and the total number that watch dramas and mysteries.

▶ **SOLVE**

What operations will you use to solve the problem? You add to find the total for dramas and mysteries.

Step 1: 1,160,000 ⊞ 1,200,000 ⊟ 2360000.

You subtract to find the difference.

Step 2: 2,470,000 ⊟ 2,360,000 ⊟ 110000.

So, 110,000 more teenagers watch situation comedies than watch dramas and mysteries.

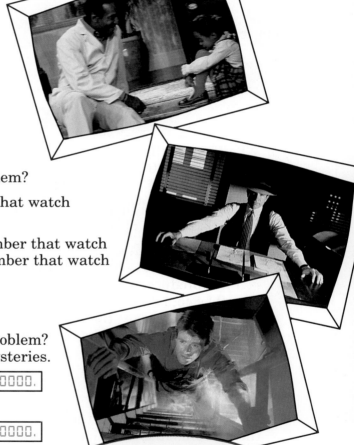

▶ **LOOK BACK**
How can you check your answer?

. . . the total number of teenagers that watch television movies is 4,340,000? Which is greater, the number of teenagers that watch movies or the number of teenagers that watch adventures and dramas?

Apply

Write the steps for solving the problem. Then solve.

① In June Cassie spent $24.25 on movie rentals, $10.60 on movie tickets, and $6.36 for a new videocassette. In July she spent $8.32 less on these items than in June. How much did she spend in July?

② Tom paid $135.98 more for his compact disc player than Julian paid. Julian paid $298.42 plus $17.91 in sales tax for his new player. How much did Tom pay?

Mixed Applications → **STRATEGIES**   • Guess and Check • Write a Number Sentence • Work Backward • Use Estimation

Choose a strategy and solve.

③ Each week Amy spends $10.25 at the movies. She buys a ticket for $5.50, a bottle of fruit juice for $1.75, and 2 boxes of popcorn. How much does she pay for 1 box of popcorn?

④ Jeff was paid $52.00 for his two after-school jobs. His job at the music store paid $5.00 an hour. The other job paid $4.50 per hour. He worked fewer than 8 hours at each job. How many hours did he work at each job?

⑤ Than had $245.60 in her checking account. She wrote one check for $24.65 and another check for $50.48. Then she made a deposit of $100.00. What is her new balance?

⑥ Darrin is a cameraman for a local TV station. In a 3-day period he shot 3,420; 2,752; and 5,775 ft of film. About how much film did he shoot in the 3 days?

⑦ Joseph bought two tickets for a play. The cost of each ticket was $12.75. If Joseph gave the cashier $40.00, how much change did he receive?

WRITER'S CORNER

⑧ Write a word problem that has more than one step in the solution. Exchange problems with a classmate and solve.

A movie production studio rented 37 cars last week at the rate of $151.98 per week for each car. How much did the studio pay for the cars?

Step 1	**Step 2**
Estimate the product.	Find the exact product.

Step 1
Estimate the product.

$$\begin{array}{rr} \$151.98 & \$150 \\ \times \quad 37 & \times \quad 40 \\ \hline & \$6{,}000 \end{array}$$

Step 2
Find the exact product.

$$\begin{array}{r} \$151.98 \\ \times \quad 37 \\ \hline 1063\ 86 \\ 4559\ 4 \\ \hline \$5{,}623.26 \end{array}$$

Since $5,623.26 is close to the estimate, the answer is reasonable. So, the studio paid $5,623.26 for the cars.

Another Example The members of the Portsmith High School Cinema Club paid $55.60 to rent a van for a field trip to the new movie studio. If the 8 members of the club divided the cost equally, how much did each pay?

Step 1
Estimate the quotient.
Use compatible numbers.

$$8)\overline{\$55.60}$$

$$\begin{array}{r} \$\ 7 \\ \hline 8)\overline{\$56} \end{array}$$

Step 2
Find the exact quotient.
Use a calculator.

55.6 ÷ 8 = ⟨ 6.95 ⟩

So, each member paid $6.95.

Check for Understanding

Tell whether you would multiply or divide to solve. Then solve.

1. The movie production company paid $1,334.40 for 24 extras in one movie scene. How much did each extra receive for the scene?

2. The Cinema Club put 12 gallons of gasoline in the rental van. The gasoline cost $1.33 per gallon. What was the total cost of the gasoline?

Practice

3. The Big Star Movie Studio bought 12 new cars. They paid a total of $108,540 for the cars. What was the average cost of each car?

4. Sam paid $4.55 per day to rent a video camera. He rented the camera for 12 days. How much did he pay in all?

5. Sara works at a concession stand at the movie studio. She earns $6.76 per hour. Each week she works 38 hours. How much does she earn each week?

6. Steven has a part-time job washing cars at the movie studio. He earns $76.50 each week for 18 hours of work. How much does Steven earn per hour?

7. The Big Star Limousine Service pays $1.52 per gallon for gasoline. Yesterday the company's gasoline bill totaled $583.68. How many gallons were bought?

8. Mrs. Medina paid $1.34 per gallon for gasoline last week. She bought 12.5 gallons. How much did she pay in all for the gasoline?

Mixed Applications

9. **Making Choices** One option Paul has for renting a car is to pay $129.90 for a 5-day rental and $27.50 for each additional day. Another option is to pay $27.50 per day. Which option will cost less if Paul rents a car for 7 days?

10. Julie bought some oil for $0.89 per can and some oil for $0.94 per can. She paid $14.54 for a total of 16 cans of oil. How many cans did she buy for $0.89?

11. **Mental Math** The Big Star Movie Studio hired 100 extras for 10 days at $78.65 each per day. How much money did the studio pay in all for the extras?

12. **Number Sense** Since $15 \times 12 = 180$, what number would you multiply by 5 to get 180?

$$5 \times \blacksquare = 180$$

CHALLENGE • NUMBER SENSE

Suppose that the ⑤ key does not work on your calculator. Show how you might use the calculator to do these problems.

13. $125 + 350 + 521$

14. $5.678 - 2.45$

15. 52×12

16. $528 \div 4$

Look back at Exercise 7. Explain how you know whether to multiply or divide to solve.

WRAP UP...

1. Kim and Jay built a tree house. The ladder to the tree house has 11 rungs, with 10 in. between rungs. The bottom rung is 10 in. from the ground, and the top rung is 10 in. from the floor of the tree house. How high is the floor of the tree house?

2. Kim and Jay used 15 boards to make the floor of the tree house. Each board was 4 in. wide and 8 ft long. How many inches wide is the tree house? How wide is it in feet?

3. Beth and her family are spending a weekend at a theme park 276 miles from their home. The camper they drove to the theme park averaged 13.7 miles per gallon of gasoline. About how many gallons of gasoline did they use in traveling to the park?

4. Beth's father asks her to buy soft drinks for the family. He gives her $5.00 and says she can have the change. If she buys 5 drinks at $0.75 each, will she have enough left for a book that costs $1.25?

5. On Monday through Friday, Jack runs 5.8 miles each day. On Saturday and Sunday, he runs 4.6 miles each day. About how far does Jack run in a week?

6. Phil earned $26.20 in wages and tips for 4 hours of work. His hourly wage was $4.50. How much did he earn in tips?

Compare. Write $<$, $>$, or $=$.

7. 5.0210 ● 5.021   8. 6,123 ● 6,132   9. 0.0064 ● 0.011   10. 300.21 ● 300.2

11. 100.09 ● 10.100   12. 568 ● 547   13. 405.6 ● 400.68   14. 30,245 ● 32,045

Give an underestimate and an overestimate for each problem.

15. $187 + 93$ 16. $927 - 645$ 17. 62×8 18. $985 \div 9$

19. $1.89 + 9.7$ 20. 109×12 21. $7,314 - 2,199$ 22. $1,122 \div 11$

Find the sum or difference.

23. $\begin{array}{r} 1,863 \\ + 1,329 \\ \hline \end{array}$ 24. $\begin{array}{r} 243.77 \\ + 280.95 \\ \hline \end{array}$ 25. $\begin{array}{r} 932.26 \\ - 194.359 \\ \hline \end{array}$ 26. $\begin{array}{r} 16,247 \\ - 11,682 \\ \hline \end{array}$

Find the product or quotient.

27. $\begin{array}{r} 67 \\ \times 54 \\ \hline \end{array}$ 28. $\begin{array}{r} 142.5 \\ \times 8.3 \\ \hline \end{array}$ 29. $1,029 \div 49$ 30. $0.8288 \div 0.8$

Spotlight ON PROBLEM SOLVING

Understand
Plan
Solve
Look Back

Restate the Problem

The first step in solving a problem is to understand it. To help yourself understand a problem, you can restate it in your own words.

Talk About It

Work with a classmate. Read the problem.

Calvin and his family bought a dozen compact discs at $13.35 each. They paid for the discs with $200.00. Was any money left after the purchase? If so, how much?

a. Restate the problem in your own words.

b. Did you both agree on a restatement of the problem?

c. Solve the problem and answer the questions.

d. What information did you have to find before you solved the problem?

e. How many steps were needed to solve the problem?

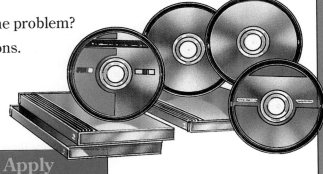

Apply

Restate each problem in your own words. Then solve.

1. A video store was renting 3 movies for $5.25. Lena decided to rent 6 movies. How much did she pay?

2. Andrea rented a car for a business trip. The odometer read 34,002.6 when she started and 34,315.4 when she returned. How many miles did she drive the car?

3. Over a 3-month period, the Hatfields spent $103.50, $82.96, and $32.30 for entertainment. What was the average amount spent on entertainment per month?

4. Kirsten has a part-time job at a TV station. The first three weeks she earned $65.20, $45.38, and $55.60. How much did she earn in the three weeks?

DIVIDING
Decimals by Decimals

Marshall has a small part in a surfing movie. This
week he worked 8.5 hours and earned $129.54.
How much did Marshall earn per hour?

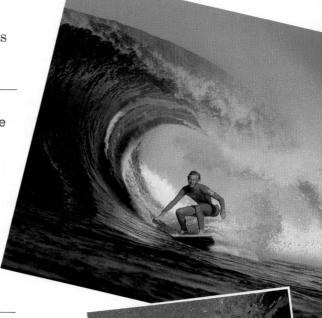

Step 1	**Step 2**	**Step 3**
Estimate the quotient.	Multiply the divisor and the dividend by 10.	Divide. Place the decimal point in the quotient.
$8.5 \overline{)\$129.54}$	$85 \overline{)\$1295.4}$	$\begin{array}{r} \$15.24 \\ 85\overline{)\$1295.40} \\ -85 \\ \hline 445 \\ -425 \\ \hline 204 \\ -170 \\ \hline 340 \end{array}$
$\begin{array}{r} \$15 \text{ estimate} \\ 8\overline{)\$120} \end{array}$		

Since $15.24 is close to the estimate, the answer is
reasonable.

So, Marshall earned $15.24 per hour.

Sometimes, it is useful to round a quotient to a given
decimal place.

Examples Find the quotient to the nearest hundredth.

A. $3.2 \overline{)56.432}$ $56.432 \div 3.2 =$ | 17.635 | ← 17.64

B. $1.03 \div 0.07$ $1.03 \div 0.07 =$ | 14.714285 | ← 14.71

Talk About It

▶ If you multiply the divisor and the dividend by 10 in Example **A**
before dividing, will the quotient be the same as that shown?
Explain.

▶ When you use a calculator to divide by a decimal, is it necessary
to make the divisor a whole number first? Explain.

▶ How can you check the quotient in Example **A**? How can you
check the quotient of any division problem?

Check for Understanding

Rewrite the problem so that the divisor is a whole number.

1. $0.32\overline{)20.224}$
2. $1.9\overline{)1.14}$
3. $0.043\overline{)1.108}$
4. $0.91\overline{)29.575}$

Find the quotient.

5. $0.5\overline{)4.75}$
6. $0.04\overline{)2.968}$
7. $0.24\overline{)13.152}$
8. $0.57\overline{)0.1881}$

Practice

Find the quotient.

9. $0.4\overline{)3.6}$
10. $0.8\overline{)10.4}$
11. $2.4\overline{)3.24}$
12. $1.6\overline{)9.632}$

13. $4.2\overline{)15.12}$
14. $9.8\overline{)4.116}$
15. $0.71\overline{)0.3692}$
16. $0.009\overline{)0.846}$

17. $0.7\overline{)0.0455}$
18. $1.2\overline{)3.648}$
19. $0.32\overline{)8.128}$
20. $1.15\overline{)7.475}$

Find the quotient to the nearest tenth.

21. $0.6\overline{)3.216}$
22. $0.08\overline{)2.57}$
23. $1.8\overline{)13.464}$
24. $0.034\overline{)0.106}$

Find the quotient to the nearest hundredth.

25. $0.3\overline{)1.2795}$
26. $0.06\overline{)0.2175}$
27. $8.4\overline{)0.388}$
28. $2.04\overline{)5}$

Mixed Applications

29. Marshall earned $129.54 for one week. The star of the movie earned $1,554.48 for one week. How many times greater were the star's earnings than Marshall's earnings?

30. The Surf Time Shop bought 12 surfboards for $1,875.90. To the nearest cent, what was the average cost of each surfboard?

31. **Mental Math**   Look for a pattern in the completed problems. Then use the pattern to find the missing factors.

    $9 \times 2 = 18$ $9 \times \blacksquare = 1,999.8$
    $9 \times 2.2 = 19.8$ $9 \times \blacksquare = 19,999.8$
    $9 \times 22.2 = 199.8$ $9 \times \blacksquare = 199,999.8$

32. **Logical Reasoning**   A cardboard strip is 1 in. wide and 46 in. long. It is cut with scissors at 1-in. intervals, making 46 squares. If one cut takes 1 second, how long will it take for all the cuts?

Since $36 \div 3 = 12$, $0.36 \div 0.03 = 12$. Explain why this is true.

WRAP
UP...

A roll of dimes has 50 dimes. Roger has 112 dimes. How many full rolls can he make?

INTERPRETING REMAINDERS

Sometimes, when you divide to solve a problem, there is a remainder in the answer. You must decide how to interpret this remainder in terms of the problem situation and the question asked.

Example The photographer for *Entertainment Magazine* is planning to take 204 photographs for the new issue. She can take 24 photographs with each roll of film.

Use this computation to answer the questions that follow.

$$\begin{array}{r} 8.5 \\ 24\overline{)204.0} \\ -192 \\ \hline 120 \\ -120 \\ \hline 0 \end{array}$$

120 ← The whole-number remainder is 12.

- How many rolls of film will the photographer use?

- How many rolls of film should the photographer buy?

- How many rolls of film will the photographer completely use?

- How many more photographs will she be able to take with the film that is left?

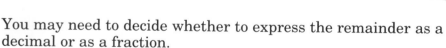

You may need to decide whether to express the remainder as a decimal or as a fraction.

Use a decimal to express a remainder of money.

How much does 1 roll of film cost if 3 rolls sell for $9.63?

$9.63 \div 3 = \boxed{3.21}$

So, one roll of film costs $3.21.

Use a fraction to express a remainder as part of a whole.

Mark and James shared 5 apples equally. How many apples did each boy get?

$$\begin{array}{r} 2\frac{1}{2} \\ 2\overline{)5} \\ -4 \\ \hline 1 \end{array}$$

So, each boy got $2\frac{1}{2}$ apples.

Check for Understanding

Solve. If the remainder is used in the solution, explain how it is used.

1. There are 126 people who are going to ride a bus to the game. Each bus can hold 40 passengers. How many buses are needed?

2. Brason Music has 290 tapes to pack in boxes. Each box holds 12 tapes. How many full boxes can be packed?

3. A nursery is selling shrubs for $4 each. If Bob buys as many shrubs as he can with the $135 he has, how much money will he have left?

4. Casey has a 10-ft board that he needs to divide into 3 equal pieces. How long will each piece be?

Practice

5. Rob and Joe worked together on a job and earned $58.25. Will they be able to divide the money equally between themselves?

6. Travis owns 329 baseball cards. He wants to put 9 cards on each page of an album. How many pages will he need in the album?

7. Mrs. McGhee needs 33 ft of wood to complete a fence. The wood is sold in 8-ft sections. How many sections must she buy?

8. Super Grocery is selling grapes at 4 lb for $3.50. Find the cost for 1 lb of grapes. Round to the nearest cent.

9. Julian has 190 in. of fabric to make banners. Each banner will be 20 in. long. How many banners can Julian make? How much fabric will he have left?

10. The music store is selling tapes at $4.50 each. Robin has $30.00 to spend. How many tapes can Robin buy? How much money will she have left?

Mixed Applications

11. Eric has 17 cookies to share with 3 of his friends. If each person gets an equal share, how many cookies will each have?

12. Super Grocery sells tomato juice at 4 cans for $2.37 or 1 can for $0.60. How is the price for 1 can rounded? Why does the store do that?

MIXED REVIEW

Compare. Use $<$, $>$, or $=$.

1. 45.7 ● 45.70

2. 6,735 ● 6,753

3. 90.2305 ● 902.305

Find the quotient to the nearest tenth.

4. $0.6\overline{)0.741}$

5. $1.2\overline{)2.855}$

6. $0.07\overline{)2.267}$

7. $0.013\overline{)0.0067}$

Can the remainder in a division problem be greater than the divisor? Why or why not?

WRAP
UP...

More Practice, Lesson 1.9, page H32

21

WARM UP...

Show how you can use multiplication to find $15 + 15 + 15 + 15 + 15$.

POWERS AND EXPONENTS

Just as some addition problems can be written in a shortened form using multiplication, some multiplication problems can be written in a shortened form using exponents.

Addition as multiplication	Multiplication using exponents
$3 + 3 + 3 + 3 = 4 \times 3 = 12$	$7 \times 7 \times 7 \times 7 = 7^4 = 2{,}401$

In the expression 7^4, 7 is the **base** and 4 is the **exponent**.

$7^4 \leftarrow$ exponent

base $\rightarrow$

You can use exponents to show powers of any number.

Exponent Form	Read	Value
2^2	2 to the second power, or 2 squared	4
7^3	7 to the third power, or 7 cubed	343
12^5	12 to the fifth power	248,832

$(1.035)^6

With powers of 10, you can see a relationship between the exponent and the number of zeros in the value.

$10^5 = 100{,}000 \leftarrow$ 5 zeros $\qquad 10^2 = 100 \leftarrow$ 2 zeros

$10^4 = 10{,}000 \leftarrow$ 4 zeros $\qquad 10^1 = 10 \leftarrow$ 1 zero

$10^3 = 1{,}000 \leftarrow$ 3 zeros $\qquad 10^0 = 1 \leftarrow$ no zeros

Note that $10^1 = 10$ and $10^0 = 1$. In general, any number to the first power equals that number. Any number (except zero) to the zero power equals 1.

$$12^1 = 12 \qquad 8^1 = 8 \qquad 5^0 = 1 \qquad 15^0 = 1 \qquad (1.6)^0 = 1$$

Talk About It

▶ Why does 7^6 equal 117,649 and not 42?

Check for Understanding

Tell the number you would use as an exponent to write each in exponent form.

1. 2×2

2. $14 \times 14 \times 14$

3. $9 \times 9 \times 9 \times 9 \times 9 \times 9$

Tell how each would be read.

4. 2^3 **5.** 9^2 **6.** 10^7 **7.** $(6.3)^1$ **8.** 8^0 **9.** 7^4

Practice

Write in exponent form.

10. $4 \times 4 \times 4$ **11.** $7 \times 7 \times 7 \times 7$ **12.** $10 \times 10 \times 10 \times 10 \times 10$

13. $3 \times 3 \times 3 \times 3$ **14.** 3.2×3.2 **15.** $5 \times 5 \times 5 \times 5 \times 5 \times 5$

Find the value. You may use your calculator.

16. 3^4 **17.** 7^3 **18.** 11^0 **19.** 2^6 **20.** 10^5

21. $(1.3)^2$ **22.** $(5.6)^1$ **23.** 9^3 **24.** 8^6 **25.** $(0.5)^4$

Complete.

26. $2^\blacksquare = 8$ **27.** $3^2 = \blacksquare$ **28.** $\blacksquare^2 = 36$ **29.** $\blacksquare^2 = 81$

30. $4^3 = \blacksquare$ **31.** $5^\blacksquare = 625$ **32.** $\blacksquare^4 = 1$ **33.** $\blacksquare^6 = 1,000,000$

Mixed Applications

34. Jill has a job that pays 2¢ on the first day of work. Then, for each day after the first, she receives double the preceding day's wage. Using exponent form, write the number of cents she would receive on the sixth day of work.

35. Because of inflation, a hamburger that costs $1.00 today may cost $$(1.035)^6$ in 6 years. Using standard form, write the future cost of the hamburger. Round the cost to the nearest cent.

36. The formula for the area of a square is $A = s^2$ where A is the area and s is the length of each side of the square. Find the area of a square whose sides are each 15 in. long. Write the answer in square inches.

37. The formula for the volume of a cube is $V = s^3$ where V is the volume and s is the length of each side of the cube. Find the volume of a cube when the length of each side of the cube is 4.5 cm. Write the answer in cubic centimeters.

38. To find the value of 5^4 on some calculators, you can use the key sequence shown.

Now look at the second key sequence. Does the sequence equal 8^6? Why or why not?

5 $\boxed{\times}$ $\boxed{=}$ $\boxed{=}$ $\boxed{=}$

8 $\boxed{\times}$ $\boxed{=}$ $\boxed{=}$ $\boxed{=}$ $\boxed{=}$ $\boxed{=}$ $\boxed{=}$

$2^4 = 4^2$. Does $2^3 = 3^2$? Why or why not?

WRAP UP...

ORDER OF OPERATIONS

You know you must follow an order of operations when solving problems that involve more than one operation. Recall these rules.

Order of Operations
1. First, do the operations within parentheses or the computations above or below a division bar. Also, find the value of any numbers in exponent form.   **2.** Then, do multiplication and division from left to right.   **3.** Finally, do addition and subtraction from left to right.

Before you use a calculator to solve problems with more than one operation, you need to know whether the calculator follows the rules for order of operations.

Example Roger uses two different calculators to evaluate the expression $6 + 3 \times 5$. Which answer is correct?

Calculator 1: 6 ⊞ 3 ⊠ 5 ⊟ ⟨ 45. ⟩

Calculator 2: 6 ⊞ 3 ⊠ 5 ⊟ ⟨ 21. ⟩

Calculator 1 performed the addition first and then the multiplication. Calculator 2 performed the multiplication first and then the addition, following the rules for order of operations. So, 21 is the correct answer.

If the calculator you use does not follow the rules for order of operations, you will need to rewrite the problem or use the calculator memory keys.

More Examples

A. $5 \times (6 + 2.4) + 8 = (6 + 2.4) \times 5 + 8$

6 ⊞ 2.4 ⊠ 5 ⊞ 8 ⊟ ⟨ 50. ⟩

B. $7^2 + 15 - \dfrac{18}{2}$

18 ⊞ 2 M⁺ 7 ⊠ 7 ⊞ 15 ⊟ MRC ⊟ ⟨ 55. ⟩

Talk About It

▶ How can you tell if a calculator follows the rules for order of operations?

▶ Since you know that $\frac{18}{2}$ is 9, what other key sequence can you use on a calculator for Example **B**?

Check for Understanding

Tell what you would do first to compute the value of each expression.

1. $(30 + 35) \times 2$ **2.** $3 \times 2^3 - 5$ **3.** $4 + 6 \times 5$ **4.** $\dfrac{14 - 4}{2}$

April used a calculator to compute the value of $24 + 7 \times 2$.
The answer she got was 62.

5. Is 62 the correct answer? Explain.

6. Show how the problem can be rewritten so that a calculator that does not follow the rules for order of operations can be used to compute the answer.

Practice

Compute.

7. $6 \times 5 + 3$ **8.** $6 \times (5 + 3)$ **9.** $5.4 \times 8 \div 4$

10. $32 - 2^3 + 10$ **11.** $(5 + 12) \times (51 - 17)$ **12.** $10 \times 4 + 15 - 6$

13. $6 \times (3 + 8) - 12$ **14.** $5^2 \times 8 \div 16$ **15.** $2.5 + 4 \times 1.2$

16. $120 - 2^3 \times 5 + 9$ **17.** $(4.3 + 1.4) \times 1.4$ **18.** $32 \div 0.4 + 6.4 \times 3$

19. $\dfrac{13 + 12}{5}$ **20.** $\dfrac{(9 - 4) + 15}{(12 - 8)}$ **21.** $7 \times 2^2 + 6 - \dfrac{18}{2}$

22. $(24 + 15 \div 3) - 6$ **23.** $\dfrac{12 + 8}{4} + 7^2$ **24.** $\dfrac{3.4 + 3^2}{2.1 + 10.3}$

Write the key sequence you can use to compute the value on a calculator that does not follow the rules for order of operations. Then compute.

25. $18 + 5 \times 2.2$ **26.** $24 + 16 \div 2$ **27.** $4.2 \times (16.8 - 5)$

28. $9 + 27 - \dfrac{120}{15}$ **29.** $45 + 6^2$ **30.** $16 + 5^2 - \dfrac{24 - 6}{9}$

Mixed Applications

For Exercises 31–32, write the expression. Then compute.

31. Multiply the difference between fourteen and eight by three.

32. Add twelve to the sum of two squared and ten.

33. Using the numbers 3, 5, 7, and 9 and the operation signs $-$ and $\times$, write an expression that has a value of 8.

34. **Visual Thinking** Draw a circle. Then divide the interior of the circle into seven regions, drawing just 3 straight lines.

John said that $3^2 + 4 \times 6 = 78$.
Explain what he did wrong.

PROBLEM *Solving*

Karen's teacher gave Karen this number sequence and asked her to find the next two numbers, or terms, in the sequence.

$$1, 4, 8, 13, 19, \ldots$$

What are the next two terms in the sequence?

You can often solve a problem by finding a pattern.

▶ **UNDERSTAND**

What are you asked to find?

What facts are given?

▶ **PLAN**

How will you solve the problem?

You must first identify the pattern in the sequence that Karen was given and then use the pattern to find the next two terms.

▶ **SOLVE**

What is the pattern in the sequence?

First term: 1
Second term: $1 + \mathbf{3} = 4$
Third term: $4 + \mathbf{4} = 8$
Fourth term: $8 + \mathbf{5} = 13$
Fifth term: $13 + \mathbf{6} = 19$

Pattern: The numbers you add to the terms increase by 1.

To find the sixth term, add 7 to 19. $19 + 7 = 26$
To find the seventh term, add 8 to 26. $26 + 8 = 34$

So, the next two terms in the sequence are 26 and 34.

▶ **LOOK BACK**

How can you check your answer?

WHAT IF... . . . Karen wants to find the term that comes after 34 in the sequence? What number should she add to 34 to find that term?

Apply

Write the next two terms in the sequence.

(1) 2, 4, 6, 8, 10, 12, . . .

(2) 1, 4, 16, 64, 256, . . .

(3) 4, 8, 7, 14, 13, 26, . . .

(4) 2, 3, 6, 7, 14, 15, 30, . . .

Find the pattern. Then solve the problem.

(5) The Radical Recording Company must reduce its work force over the next five months. There are now 2,215 employees. Next month there will be 1,415 employees. For the following three months, the totals will be 1,015, 815, and 715. How many employees will the company have in the fifth month?

(6) The utility bills for the Music Shop for the past four months were $260, $264, $269, and $275. If the utility bills continue to increase at the same rate, what will be the utility bill this month?

| Mixed Applications | STRATEGIES | • Write a Number Sentence • Make a Table • Draw a Picture • Find a Pattern |

Choose a strategy and solve.

(7) At a neighborhood picnic, Eric came in first in a footrace. At the end of the race, Julie was 6 yards behind Eric and 12 yards in front of Kay. Stan was 8 yards behind Eric, and Jim was 3 yards behind Stan. Who came in fourth?

(8) The Binter Company has an electric bill for $345.67, a phone bill for $365.24, a copier bill for $176.53, a paper bill for $368.90, and a water bill for $130.67. How much more is the highest bill than the lowest bill?

(9) Tom counted the washers, nuts, and bolts in two bins. In bin A he counted 1,800 washers, 1,350 nuts, and 1,200 bolts. In bin B he counted 960 washers and 720 nuts. If the items in bin B follow the same pattern as the items in bin A, how many bolts did he count in bin B?

(10) Carla worked as a salesclerk earning $7.80 per hour. She was promoted to assistant manager, earning $9.15 per hour. If she works 40 hours per week, how much more should she earn per week as an assistant manager than as a salesclerk?

CHAPTER REVIEW

Vocabulary Check

Choose a word or words from the box to complete each sentence.

Associative
base
Distributive
exponent
overestimate
underestimate

1. When the estimate for an answer is greater than the exact answer, the estimate is an __?__ . *(page 6)*

2. The number sentence $8 \times (5.4 + 6) = (8 \times 5.4) + (8 \times 6)$ is an example of the __?__ Property. *(page 8)*

3. In the expression 36^6, the number 6 is the __?__ and the number 36 is the __?__ . *(page 22)*

4. The number sentence $(3 + 2) + 4 = 3 + (2 + 4)$ is an example of the __?__ Property of Addition. *(page 8)*

Concept Check

In which place is the underlined digit? *(page 2)*

5. 13,9<u>7</u>8,365
6. <u>5</u>67,439
7. 0.896<u>4</u>
8. 12.<u>3</u>067

Write each number in words.

9. 500712
10. 44192.3
11. 672841.12
12. 0.911

Write the standard form of each number. *(page 2)*

13. 3.2 million
14. 4.6 thousand
15. 82.4 billion
16. 100 million

Name the place to which each number appears to be rounded. *(page 4)*

17. 3,500
18. 120,000
19. 160
20. 14,000

Identify as an *overestimate* or *underestimate*. *(page 6)*

21. $453 + 94 \rightarrow 450 + 90$
22. $1{,}015 - 86 \rightarrow 1{,}000 - 90$
23. $435 \times 26 \rightarrow 440 \times 30$
24. $175 \div 9 \rightarrow 180 \div 9$

Tell how many times the factor 2 is used when computing the value. *(page 22)*

25. 2^3
26. 2^6
27. 2^1
28. 2^{12}

Tell what you would do first to compute the value of each expression. *(page 24)*

29. $3 \times 4 + 9$
30. $8 \times (6 + 13)$
31. $5^3 + 1.095$
32. $6 + \frac{15}{3} - 4$
33. $\frac{18 - 3}{5} \div 3$
34. $32 \times 7 - 8 \div 2$

Skill Check

Write in shortened form using the word *thousand*. *(page 2)*

35. 124,000   **36.** 61,700   **37.** 1,250   **38.** 900

An exact number has been rounded to the given number. Name the greatest whole number and the least whole number that the exact number can be. *(page 4)*

39. 450   **40.** 2,000   **41.** 71,000   **42.** 160,000

Give two estimates for each problem. Tell which is the closer estimate. *(page 6)*

43. $109 + 62$ **44.** 72×18 **45.** $456 - 122$ **46.** $330 \div 12$

Complete. *(page 8)*

47. $182 + \blacksquare = 182$ **48.** $6.2 + 1.4 = 1.4 + \blacksquare$ **49.** $(9 + 8) + 2 = \blacksquare + (8 + 2)$

Find the quotient to the nearest hundredth. *(page 18)*

50. $1.9\overline{)4.455}$ **51.** $0.7\overline{)14.108}$ **52.** $0.16\overline{)50.34}$ **53.** $0.012\overline{)0.145}$

Find the value. *(page 22)*

54. 9^3 **55.** 3^4 **56.** 23^2 **57.** 8^5 **58.** 10^0

Compute. *(page 24)*

59. $8 \times 7 + 15$ **60.** $4 \times (18 - 9)$ **61.** $\frac{35}{7} + 3 \times 2$ **62.** $6^3 \times 5 - 8$

Solve. *(pages 10, 14, 20)*

63. Wilma is paid $4.24 per hour at her part-time job. She worked 21.5 hr last week. How much did she earn for the week?

64. Michelle has $35.75 to spend on computer games. The games are on sale for $12.95 each. How many games can she buy? How much money will she have left?

Problem-Solving Check

65. Mr. and Mrs. Cornwall and their children, ages 9, 11, and 15, are going to an amusement park. Admission to the park is $17.95 for each adult and $13.50 for each child under 12 years of age. How much will the Cornwalls pay for admission? *(page 12)*

66. The cost of a movie ticket at the Regency Theater for the past three years was $4.55, $4.75, and $4.95. This year the cost is $5.15. If the cost continues to increase at the same rate, what will be the cost for a ticket next year? *(page 26)*

Write in shortened form using the word *million*.

1. 3,170,000   **2.** 85,000,000   **3.** 324,000,000   **4.** 620,000

An exact number has been rounded to the given number. Name the greatest whole number and the least whole number that the exact number can be.

5. 75,000   **6.** 30   **7.** 8,000   **8.** 2,000,000

Give two estimates for each problem. Tell which is the closer estimate.

9. $623 + 419$ **10.** $1,013 \times 51$ **11.** $915 \div 3.06$ **12.** $1,415 - 287$

Complete. Name the properties shown.

13. $8 \times (43) = 8 \times (\blacksquare + 3) = (8 \times 40) + (\blacksquare \times 3) = 320 + 24 = 344$

14. $23 + (9 + 67) = 23 + (\blacksquare + 9) = (23 + 67) + \blacksquare = 90 + 9 = 99$

Find the quotient to the nearest hundredth.

15. $0.3\overline{)0.176}$ **16.** $1.4\overline{)4.77}$ **17.** $0.28\overline{)0.015}$

Find the value.

18. 2^6 **19.** $3^3 + 4 - 2$ **20.** $(4.5)^2$ **21.** $(9 - 2) + 3 \times 8$

Solve.

22. For the past four weeks, Wilma made deposits of $6.00, $7.50, $9.00, and $10.50 in her savings account. If she continues to increase the amount of her deposits at the same rate, how much will she deposit in her account this week and next week?

23. Before he starts working, Robb has to count the money in the cash register. Today he has 2 $10 bills, 4 $5 bills, 18 $1 bills, 9 quarters, 18 dimes, 15 nickels, and 35 pennies. How much money is in the cash register?

24. Noah studies for an average of 2.8 hr a night, Monday through Friday. He also studies for 1.5 hr on Sunday. How many hours does he study each week?

25. Each term in a number sequence is 3 less than 2 times the one before. The first term in the sequence is 4. Find the next five terms in the sequence.

Make Movie Products

O ver the years there have been movies that were popular at the box office. Many of these movies were also popular away from the box office because stores sold millions of dollars' worth of movie-related products such as games, toys, and clothing.

Suppose that you and your teammates own a company that creates and sells products related to movies.

DECIDE

As a team, choose a movie for which a product could be made. Discuss the types of products that could be made for the movie. Choose one product for this project. Discuss whether you will make a drawing or a model of your product to present to the class. Consider the time it will take to make the drawing or model, and the cost of the supplies you will need.

DO

As a team, make the drawing or model of your product.

SHARE

Compare your team's product with the products of other teams. Tell why you think your product will be popular and profitable.

TALK ABOUT IT

- Why did you choose to produce this product?
- Why do you think the selling price of an item is an important part of its popularity?

- Would you consider associating your product with another company, such as a fast-food chain, a clothing manufacturer, or a toy-and-game company? Explain.
- What arithmetic operations did you use in planning this product?

MATH FUN

extend your thinking

BOOMERANG: a game for two

MATERIALS

Paper, pencil, number cube

OBJECT OF THE GAME

- Start with a two-digit decimal between 1 and 10 and then return to that decimal by using the operations numbered 1–12.

1	Multiply by 20.	7	Divide by 100.
2	Multiply by 15.	8	Divide by 10.
3	Multiply by 9.	9	Divide by 4.
4	Multiply by 8.	10	Divide by 3.
5	Multiply by 5.	11	Divide by 2.
6	Multiply by 1.5.	12	Divide by 0.9.

- A player selects a two-digit decimal and rolls the number cube. The number cube determines the first operation to use on the decimal.

- The player then chooses the next operations to use. An operation cannot be repeated.

- If the last answer is the same as the first decimal, the player earns one point for each correct computation. If the last answer is not the same as the first decimal or if the player makes a mistake, the player does not earn any points.

- The players take turns. After three turns each, the player with the most points wins.

Example Player **A** chooses 1.4 and rolls 5. The player then decides to follow operation 5 with operations 1 and 7.

5 $\quad 1.4 \times 5 = 7$
1 $\quad 7 \times 20 = 140$
7 $\quad 140 \div 100 = 1.4$

The player earns 3 points.

CHALLENGE

Palindromic Numbers

A palindromic number is a number that reads the same backward and forward.

Example 121

1. Find the palindromic numbers between 100 and 200.

2. Find the palindromic numbers between 1,000 and 2,000.

Logical Reasoning

Write plus signs and decimal points between the digits to make each statement true.

Example $\quad 3 \ 4 \ 1 \ 2 \ 5 \ 6 \ = 12.72$
$\quad\quad\quad\quad 3 + 4.12 + 5.6 = 12.72$

1. $9 \ 1 \ 4 \ 6 \ 7 \ 3 = 164.46$
2. $5 \ 0 \ 8 \ 2 \ 6 \ 3 \ 7 = 11.38$

CUMULATIVE REVIEW

CHAPTER 1

Write the letter of the correct answer.

1. Which is the standard form of nine and seventeen thousandths?

   A. 9.017   **B.** 9.17

   C. 9,017   **D.** 917,000

2. Which is a shortened form for 56,800,000?

   A. 568 thousand   **B.** 56.8 million

   C. 56,800 million   **D.** not here

3. Find the value of 2^5.

   A. 10   **B.** 25

   C. 32   **D.** 64

4. Which is an overestimate for $88 + 173 + 39$?

   A. 150   **B.** 200

   C. 250   **D.** 350

5. $6 \times (100 + 25)$

   A. 131   **B.** 250

   C. 625   **D.** not here

6. $5 \times 7 + 9 \times 3$

   A. 62   **B.** 132

   C. 240   **D.** 945

7. Which is the quotient rounded to the nearest tenth?

   $34.5 \div 0.7$

   A. 0.0202898   **B.** 4.93
   C. 49.2   **D.** 49.3

8. A number n is rounded to 7,600. What is the greatest number n can be?

   A. 7,500   **B.** 7,549

   C. 7,649   **D.** 7,650

9. Which is the correct exponent form for $5 \times 5 \times 5$?

   A. 5^3 **B.** 3^5

   C. 5^5 **D.** not here

10. In which place is the digit 3 in the number 123,987.42?

    A. tenths   **B.** tens

    C. hundreds   **D.** thousands

11. Matt is buying a hat that costs $24.50. He must also pay a sales tax of $1.47. If he gives the cashier $40.00, how much change will he receive?

    A. $14.03   **B.** $15.50

    C. $16.97   **D.** $25.97

12. The first term in a sequence is 2. Each term in the sequence is 3 more than the term before. Which shows the second and third terms in the sequence?

    A. 6 and 18   **B.** 4 and 6

    C. 5 and 7   **D.** 5 and 8

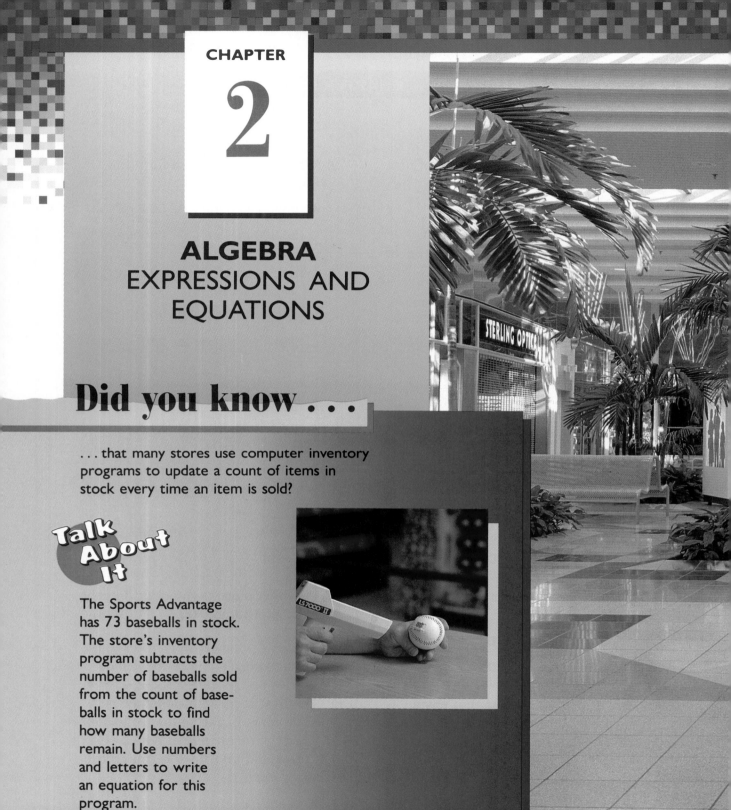

ALGEBRA
EXPRESSIONS AND EQUATIONS

Did you know . . .

. . . that many stores use computer inventory programs to update a count of items in stock every time an item is sold?

Talk About It

The Sports Advantage has 73 baseballs in stock. The store's inventory program subtracts the number of baseballs sold from the count of baseballs in stock to find how many baseballs remain. Use numbers and letters to write an equation for this program.

LANGUAGE OF ALGEBRA

One of the main applications of algebra is translating an everyday problem into a mathematical sentence so that it can be solved. Learning some of the vocabulary of algebra will help you to do this.

These are examples of **numerical expressions.**

$$3 + 4 \qquad 26 - 16 \qquad 19.5 - 6.5 \qquad 3\tfrac{1}{2} \times 8$$

These are examples of algebraic expressions.

$$n + 5 \qquad t - \tfrac{4}{5} \qquad 4.5 - a \qquad 12.3a$$

An **algebraic expression** is an expression that is written using variables. A **variable** is a letter that represents one or more numbers.

An **equation** is a mathematical sentence that uses an equals sign to show that two quantities are equal. These are examples of equations.

$$6 + 2 = 8 \qquad 90 - 6 = 84 \qquad t + 12 = 35 \qquad \tfrac{x}{2} + 4 = 9$$

Some equations may contain one or more variables.

● Which of the equations shown above contain one or more variables?

In algebra there are also mathematical sentences that show quantities that are not equal. These sentences are called **inequalities.** An inequality uses the symbol $<, >, \le, \ge,$ or $\ne$ instead of $=$.

These are examples of inequalities.

$$5 + 4 > 6 \qquad x + 12 < 15 \qquad a - 40 \ne 0 \qquad b - 7 \ge 49$$

Check for Understanding

Name the variable in each.

1. $t - 24 = 15$ **2.** $r \ge 121$ **3.** $2s + 17 = 19$ **4.** $8.3 + h^2 - 3$

Tell whether each is a *numerical expression,* an *algebraic expression,* an *equation,* or an *inequality.*

5. $3 < 6 + 9$ **6.** $x + 4 = 12$ **7.** $3 + f$ **8.** $8 - g = 6$ **9.** $24 - 16$

Practice

Write *expression, equation,* or *inequality* for each.

10. $35 + 19$

11. $35 - 16 \leq 20$

12. $b + 40 = 80$

13. $21 + 3 = 24$

14. $105 - 15 = c$

15. $\frac{2}{3} + 3 \leq 4$

16. $190 - t + 3^2$

17. $15 = 48 - 3t$

18. $15 + x + 3$

19. $2y - 4 > 9$

20. $a + 4 = 27$

21. $32 \neq 7 + 15$

22. $x + 2 > 5^3$

23. $2c - 8$

24. $d - 4.6 \leq 19$

25. $7 + a^2 - 1.5$

Write an example of each.

26. equation

27. algebraic expression

28. inequality

Complete. Write $<$, $>$, or $=$.

29. $18 \times 5 \bullet 80$

30. $23 \times 7 \bullet 161$

31. $28 \bullet 14 + 12$

32. $45 - 8 \bullet 39$

33. $3^3 \bullet 27$

34. $0.65 + 1.3 \bullet 2$

35. $4.5 \bullet 3.2 + 1.4$

36. $45 \div 15 \bullet 4$

Use the expression to write an equation.

37. $225 + 15$

38. $15.4 - 0.12$

39. $34 \times 5 + 8$

40. $18 \div 2 + 6$

41. $x + 4$

42. $c - 32$

43. $2t + 4$

44. $\frac{a}{4} - 5$

Use the expression to write an inequality. Use $<$, $>$, $\leq$, $\geq$, or $\neq$.

45. $24 - 6$

46. $18.9 + 4.3$

47. 121×12

48. $4 \div 2 + 3$

49. $b - 6$

50. $3t + 5$

51. $x + 7$

52. $c - 3.4$

Mixed Applications

53. Write a numerical expression using addition that shows the number of days in 2 weeks.

54. Write a numerical equation using multiplication that shows the number of quarters in 5 dollars.

55. Susan's teacher asked Susan to write an equation that shows the sum of 13 and 25. This is what Susan wrote:

$$13 + 25 = 39$$

Did Susan write an equation? Explain your answer.

56. Visual Thinking Write a numerical expression that shows the sum of the numbers of triangles in the squares.

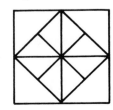

57. In the equation $t + 5 = c + 5$, what do you know about the values of t and c? If $t = 6$, what is the value of c?

What is the difference between an expression and an equation?

WRAP
UP...

Write the numerical expression
5 + 8 in words.

EXPRESSIONS
Addition and Subtraction

An algebraic expression can be written
for a word expression.

Example   Mike and Joey bought
flowers for their mothers. Mike spent
$10 more than Joey. Write an algebraic
expression that represents the amount
of money Mike spent.

Let n = the amount Joey spent.
Then $n + 10$ = the amount Mike spent.

The same algebraic expression can be
used for several word expressions.

Word Expression	Algebraic Expression
8 more than the number of kites, n The sum of a number, n, and 8 The cost, n, increased by $8	$n + 8$
4 meters less than d meters The distance, d, decreased by 4 feet The difference between the weight, d, and 4 pounds	$d - 4$

To **evaluate** (find the value of) an expression, substitute a
number for the variable, and then perform the indicated
operation or operations.

Example   Evaluate $c - 6$ for $c = 25$.

$c - 6$ ← Write the expression.
$25 - 6$ ← Replace c with 25.
19 ← Subtract.

Talk About It

▶ When the expression $c - 6$ is evaluated, the result is 0.
What is the value of c?

▶ What information must you have before you can evaluate
an algebraic expression?

▶ Is the expression $d - 4$ the same as the expression $4 - d$?
Explain. Give an example to support your answer.

Idea Bank, page 490, Exercise 1

Check for Understanding

Choose from the box the algebraic expression
that represents the word expression.

$$
\begin{array}{l}
n + 6 \\
n - 6 \\
6 + n \\
6 - n
\end{array}
$$

1. 6 more than a number, n
2. 6 less than a number, n
3. 6 decreased by a number, n
4. the sum of a number, n, and 6

Evaluate the expression for $b = 14$.

5. $b + 12$
6. $b - 4$
7. $b + 2.3$
8. $b + 9.6$
9. $18 - b$
10. $53 - b$

Practice

Write an algebraic expression for each word expression.

11. 12 more than the number of banks, b
12. 8.6 feet less than the depth, d
13. the sum of 23 hits and the total hits, t
14. the number of miles, m, increased by 12.3 miles
15. the difference between the number of airplanes, a, and 30
16. the number of pounds, p, decreased by 16.7 pounds

Write two word expressions for the algebraic expression.

17. $p + 9$
18. $t - 5$
19. $1.3 - r$
20. $z + 9.5$
21. $438 - x$

Evaluate the expression for $b = 5$, $n = 2.5$, and $x = 12$.

22. $n + 18$
23. $7 + b$
24. $x - 9$
25. $5.4 - n$
26. $56 - b$

27. $b + 4.5$
28. $x - 8.4$
29. $3.7 - n$
30. $122 - b$
31. $n + 3.5$

32. $x + 91$
33. $7.43 - b$
34. $5^2 + n$
35. $b + n$
36. $x - b - n$

Mixed Applications

37. Ben paid $1.50 less for a compact disc than he had expected. Write an expression that represents how much Ben paid. Let c represent the amount he had expected to pay for the disc.

38. Gwen bought a new lawn mower. The cost of the lawn mower, c, was increased by a sales tax of $9.18. Write an expression that represents the total cost of the lawn mower.

39. **Number Sense** Using the signs $+$ and $-$, complete the expression so that it has a value of 60.

$$44 \; \bullet \; 17 \; \bullet \; 5 \; \bullet \; 38$$

40. **Logical Reasoning** If the value of $x + 12$ is 21, what is the value of $x + 16$?

Is the expression $b + 5$ the same as the expression $5 + b$? Explain.

WARM
UP...

Subtract 5 from each side of
$6 + 5 = 11$. What is the result?

ADDITION EQUATIONS

Recall that an equation is a mathematical sentence containing an equals sign (=).

$$n + 12 = 19 \leftarrow \text{equation}$$

To **solve** (find the solution of) an equation, you get the variable alone on one side of the equation. Since addition and subtraction are inverse operations, you can solve an equation that shows addition by subtracting the same number from each side of the equation.

Example   Solve and check. $n + 12 = 19$

Step 1 Subtract 12 from each side of the equation.	**Step 2** Check the solution. Replace n with 7.
$n + 12 = 19$ $n + 12 - 12 = 19 - 12$ $n = 7 \leftarrow \text{solution}$	$n + 12 = 19$ $7 + 12 = 19$ $19 = 19$

Many word problems can be solved by writing and solving an equation.

Example   Marla paid $8 more for a watch than she paid for a hat. She paid $23 for the watch. How much did she pay for the hat?

Step 1 Choose a variable. Let t = the amount paid for the hat. Then $t + 8$ = the amount paid for the watch.	**Step 2** Write an equation. $t + 8 = 23$
Step 3 Solve the equation. $t + 8 - 8 = 23 - 8$ $t = 15$	**Step 4** Check the solution. Replace t with 15. $t + 8 = 23$ $15 + 8 = 23$ $23 = 23$

So, Marla paid $15 for the hat.

Talk About It

▶ Can the variable in $t + 8 = 23$ have more than one value? Why or why not?

Check for Understanding

Tell what number you would subtract from each side of the equation to solve the equation. Then solve the equation.

1. $b + 23 = 41$ **2.** $17 + h = 26$ **3.** $9.8 = 2.5 + x$ **4.** $y + 1.24 = 12$

Practice

Tell whether the given value is the solution of the equation. Write *yes* or *no*.

5. $3 + x = 45, x = 48$ **6.** $t + 2 = 9, t = 7$ **7.** $3.5 + n = 8.7, n = 5.2$

Solve the equation. Check your solution.

8. $20 + x = 52$ **9.** $16 + a = 31$ **10.** $b + 13 = 72$ **11.** $18 + y = 100$

12. $6.4 = 2.9 + d$ **13.** $3.7 + e = 8.4$ **14.** $s + 3 = 29$ **15.** $95 + x = 115$

16. $2.3 = y + 1.74$ **17.** $d + 94 = 106$ **18.** $0.2 = n + 0.02$ **19.** $30 + r = 75$

20. $20 + y = 36$ **21.** $a + 2.1 = 5.6$ **22.** $0.6 = 0.15 + d$ **23.** $245 + t = 352$

First, choose a variable and tell what it represents. Then, write an equation for the word sentence.

24. Six hours more than the number of hours worked is 45 hours.

25. The cost of a new car plus $630 in options is $9,875.

26. The cost of a bat increased by $24.45 for a glove equals $37.95.

27. The sum of the deposits and a balance of $455.32 equals $565.33.

Mixed Applications

For Exercises 28–29, write an equation. Then solve.

28. Margaret sold her surfboard for $13 more than she paid for it. She sold her surfboard for $62. How much did she pay for the surfboard?

29. John spent $2.13 more for a spinning reel than he had planned. He paid $22.80 for the reel. How much had he planned to pay?

30. In the formula $l = s + d$, l represents the list price, s represents the sale price, and d represents the discount. Find the sale price when the list price is $35.50 and the discount is $9.85.

31. **Make Up a Problem**   Write a word problem that can be solved using the equation $x + 5 = 24$. Exchange with a classmate and solve.

Explain how to find the value of *n* in $4.5 + n = 55.4$.

W R A P
U P . . .

Alphonso spends $2.98 on postage for a total of 12 postcards and letters. It costs $0.19 to mail one postcard and $0.29 to mail one letter. How many postcards and how many letters can Alphonso mail?

Sometimes you can solve a problem by using the strategy of *guess and check*.

► **UNDERSTAND**

What are you asked to find?

What facts are given?

► **PLAN**

What strategy will you use?

You can use the strategy of *guess and check*. First, you make a reasonable guess. Then, you check your answer against the conditions stated in the problem. If your guess does not satisfy the conditions, guess again.

► **SOLVE**

How will you solve the problem?

Guess 1: 7 postcards and 5 letters
Check 1: ($0.19 × 7) + ($0.29 × 5) = $1.33 + $1.45
                                   = $2.78

Since $2.78 is less than $2.98, this guess uses too many postcards.

Guess 2: 6 postcards and 6 letters
Check 2: ($0.19 × 6) + ($0.29 × 6) = $1.14 + $1.74
                                   = $2.88 ← still too many

Guess 3: 5 postcards and 7 letters
Check 3: ($0.19 × 5) + ($0.29 × 7) = $0.95 + $2.03
                                   = $2.98 ← correct

So, Alphonso can mail 5 postcards and 7 letters.

► **LOOK BACK**

What other strategy can you use to solve the problem?

WHAT IF... . . . Alphonso mails a total of 10 postcards and letters for $2.40? How many postcards and how many letters does he mail?

Apply

1 Alphonso paid the $2.50 for postage with nickels and dimes. He gave the postal clerk 10 more dimes than nickels. How many dimes did he give the postal clerk?

2 Marge mailed a total of 24 letters and postcards. She mailed 6 more letters than postcards. How many postcards did she mail?

Mixed Applications ➤ **STRATEGIES** • Guess and Check • Find a Pattern • Write a Number Sentence • Work Backward

Choose a strategy and solve.

3 Mrs. Martin mailed 3 packages. The postage for each of 2 packages was $8.25. The postage for the third package was $4.25. How much did she pay in all?

4 Jake bought a card for $1.25, a book for $3.75, and 4 pencils. He spent a total of $5.80. How much did he pay for each pencil?

5 Jessica is sending a 10-lb package of books and magazines to a friend. The box she is using weighs 1.4 lb. She wants one half of the remaining weight to be for books. How many pounds of magazines can she send?

6 April bought some 29-cent stamps and some 3-cent stamps for a total of $1.72. She bought a total of 14 stamps. How many 29-cent stamps did she buy?

7 For the past three months, the Secure Fence Company paid $65.25, $66.50, and $67.75 for postage. If the amount paid for postage continues to increase at the same rate, how much will the company pay for postage this month?

8 The postage for a first-class letter in the United States is $0.29 for the first ounce and $0.23 for each additional ounce or part of an ounce. Find the postage for a 2.5-ounce letter.

9 There are 78 cars in the parking lot of the main post office. There are twice as many compact cars as full-size cars. How many compact cars are in the parking lot?

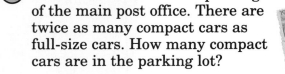

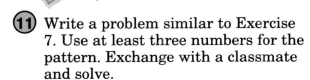

WRITER'S CORNER

10 Write a problem similar to Exercise 6. Use a total of 16 stamps in your problem. Exchange with a classmate and solve.

11 Write a problem similar to Exercise 7. Use at least three numbers for the pattern. Exchange with a classmate and solve.

SUBTRACTION EQUATIONS

Carole paid $31 for hiking boots.
The boots were on sale for $19 off
the regular price. What was the
regular price of the boots?

To find the regular price of the boots,
you can write an equation. Then solve
the equation for the variable.

WORK TOGETHER

- What are you asked to find? What variable can you use to
  represent this amount?

- Use the variable to write an algebraic expression for the sale
  price. What is the sale price given in the problem?

- Use the algebraic expression and the sale price to write an
  equation for the problem.

- What operation can you use to solve the equation? Explain.

- Solve the equation. What is the value of the variable?

- What was the regular price of the boots?

- How can you check your solution?

Add 10 to both sides
of the equation.

Another Example   Often, operations should be
performed on just one side of an equation before
the equation is solved.

$$15 = x - (6 + 4) \longleftarrow \text{Find the sum of 6 and 4.}$$
$$15 = x - 10 \longleftarrow \text{Solve the equation.}$$
$$15 + 10 = x - 10 + 10$$
$$25 = x$$

Check for Understanding

Tell whether the given value is the solution of the equation. Answer *yes* or *no*.

1. $t - 7 = 35, t = 28$ **2.** $100 = x - 87, x = 177$ **3.** $b - 9 = 9, b = 18$

Solve the equation. Check your solution.

4. $h - 9 = 6$ **5.** $m - 14 = 25$ **6.** $8 = s - 5.3$ **7.** $n - (9 + 14) = 27$

Practice

Solve the equation. Check your solution.

8. $w - 7 = 54$ **9.** $x - 11 = 21$ **10.** $60 = y - 34$ **11.** $z - 103 = 262$

12. $m - 83 = 111$ **13.** $8.09 = w - 4.9$ **14.** $710 = q - 200$ **15.** $u - 29 = 40.23$

16. $p + 34 = 115$ **17.** $m + 9.2 = 16$ **18.** $44 = n - 8$ **19.** $y - 1.3 = 1.35$

20. $17 = x - (6 + 5)$ **21.** $t - (3 \times 8) = 62$ **22.** $(19 - 6) + h = 33$

23. $b - 4^2 = 92$ **24.** $(14 + 18) = k - 9$ **25.** $s + 3^2 = 32 - 5$

First, choose a variable and tell what it represents. Then, write an equation for the word sentence.

26. The total of 39 cars decreased by the number of cars sold today equals 14 cars.

27. The difference between 4,333.7 gallons and the number of gallons pumped is 3,687 gallons.

28. Eight less than the number of radios in stock is 78 radios.

29. The number of pounds decreased by 35.6 pounds is 125.6 pounds.

Mixed Applications

For Exercises 30–31, write an equation. Then solve.

30. Mary paid $124 for an airline super-saver ticket. This was $38 less than the regular price of the ticket. What was the regular price of the ticket?

31. The price of a new bicycle sprocket is $38.00. This is $8.45 more than the amount of money Ted has in his wallet. How much money is in his wallet?

32. Write a Question Vera has 198 baseball cards. This is 43 less than the number of baseball cards Robbie has. Write a question for this situation.

33. Tom's age decreased by the age of his five-year-old sister is 8. Tom's age increased by his father's age is 58. How old is Tom's father?

MIXED REVIEW

Compute.

1. $4 + 8 \times 6$ **2.** $2^2 + (18 - 6)$ **3.** $8 + 12 \div 6 - 3$ **4.** $\dfrac{(4.5 + 3.2)}{28 \div 4}$

Solve the equation.

5. $x + 3 = 15$ **6.** $72 = 5 + b$ **7.** $2.5 = t + 1.7$ **8.** $35 + y = 35$

Write a word problem that can be solved by using the equation $n - 20 = 75$.

WRAP UP...

REVIEW AND MAINTENANCE

Solve.

1. Colleen wants to buy an electric piano that costs $195.00. She works 18.5 hours per week for $4.60 an hour. She is paid once a week. She plans to save all her money until she has enough for the electric piano. How many weeks will that take?

2. Tim saved $12 the first week he worked, $15 the second week, $19 the third week, and $24 the fourth week. If Tim continues to save at the same rate, how much will he save the sixth week he works?

3. The shop class made 3-legged stools and 4-legged stools. The class used a total of 24 legs. How many 3-legged stools and how many 4-legged stools did the class make?

4. Pam worked 22.5 hours last week. She was paid $6.24 an hour. Roger worked 31.25 hours for $5.48 an hour. Who earned more money? How much more?

5. The sum of two numbers is 24. The difference of the two numbers is 10. Find the two numbers.

6. Write the next three numbers in this sequence.
1, 1, 2, 6, 24, 120, . . .

Give an underestimate and an overestimate for each problem.

7. 422×8
8. $528 + 676$
9. $62.4 + 36.8$
10. 882×17

Find the quotient to the nearest hundredth.

11. $0.6\overline{)2.54}$
12. $3.6\overline{)705.2}$
13. $1.4\overline{)99.7}$
14. $0.34\overline{)0.35}$

Find the quotient to the nearest tenth.

15. $0.5\overline{)0.62}$
16. $1.2\overline{)3.913}$
17. $0.72\overline{)1.15}$
18. $0.14\overline{)7.34}$

Find the value.

19. 2^4
20. 12^0
21. 8^1
22. 6^3
23. $(1.2)^2$

Compute.

24. $4 + 3 \times 12$
25. $8^2 - 12 + 6$
26. $\frac{1.5}{3} \times (6 + 5)$
27. $32 \div \frac{24}{6} - 2^2$

Evaluate the expression for $c = 5$ and $d = 8.5$.

28. $c + 13$
29. $20 - d$
30. $c + d$
31. $d - 1.23$
32. $4^2 + c + d$

Solve the equation. Check your solution.

33. $a + 12 = 17$
34. $24 = x - 8$
35. $c - 4.3 = 1.9$
36. $s + 3.7 = 9.8$
37. $9.4 = n + 3.1$
38. $k - 2.6 = 0.8$
39. $13 = n + 5.4$
40. $b - 7.9 = 6.3$

46

Spotlight ON PROBLEM SOLVING

Understand
Plan
Solve
Look Back

Identify Relationships

To solve a problem, look for the relationship between what you are given and what you are to find. Then determine the format that can be used.

Sandra bought a skirt for $24.95 and a pair of shoes for $29.00. Her total bill including the sales tax was $56.65. How much was the sales tax?

Skirt price + shoe price + sales tax = total

__ + __ + __ = __

Talk About It

a. How can you find how much Sandra paid for the skirt and shoes?

b. What operation would you use to find the amount of sales tax?

c. How much was the sales tax?

Apply

Choose the format that can be used to solve the problem. Write a, b, c, or d. Then solve.

a. __ − __ = __

c. (__ + __) × __ = __

b. (__ ÷ __) × __ = __

d. __ + (__ ÷ __) = __

1. Don, Jorge, and Jenna work at a diner on Saturdays. Each earns $20.00 and an equal share of the tips received. How much does each earn if the tips total $63.48?

2. Randy had 4.5 gallons of gasoline in his car. He bought 10 gallons more. How far can he drive if his car travels an average of 24 miles per gallon of gasoline?

3. Lois reupholsters furniture. She buys decorating tacks in boxes costing $4 each. What is the cost of 1,500 tacks if one box contains 250 tacks?

4. Vera has saved $75.60. She wants to buy a bicycle that costs $120.00. How much more does she need to save in order to buy the bicycle?

47

Write the expression *twelve divided by four* using numbers and an operation sign.

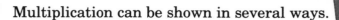

EXPRESSIONS
Multiplication and Division

Multiplication can be shown in several ways.

$$7 \times 6 \qquad 7 \cdot 6 \qquad 7(6) \qquad (7)(6)$$

When a variable is used in an expression with multiplication, the multiplication sign is usually omitted. An expression such as $4 \times n$ is written as $4n$.

Example Ian and Chris bought several cassette tapes. Ian bought 3 times as many as Chris. Write an algebraic expression that represents the number of tapes Ian bought.

Let t = the number of tapes Chris bought.
Then $3t$ = the number of tapes Ian bought.

The table shows how algebraic expressions can be used to represent word expressions involving multiplication and division.

Word Expression	Algebraic Expression
7 times the number of boats, b The number of hours, h, multiplied by 6.3 Twice the cost, c	$7b$ $6.3h$ $2c$
The diameter, d, divided by 4	$d \div 4$, or $\dfrac{d}{4}$
The quotient of a number, n, and 2.3	$n \div 2.3$, or $\dfrac{n}{2.3}$
The quotient of 16 and t weeks	$16 \div t$, or $\dfrac{16}{t}$

Recall that when the value of the variable is known, you can evaluate an expression.

Example Evaluate $\dfrac{b}{4}$ for $b = 24.8$.

$\dfrac{b}{4}$ ← Write the expression.

$\dfrac{24.8}{4}$ ← Replace b with 24.8.

6.2 ← Divide.

Talk About It

▶ In what ways other than $2c$ can 2 times c be expressed?

▶ Can you write the expression 7×6 as 76? Why or why not?

48

Check for Understanding

Choose from the box the algebraic expression that represents the word expression.

$$5t$$
$$\frac{t}{5}$$
$$\frac{5}{t}$$

1. 5 times a number, t

2. a number, t, divided by 5

3. the quotient of 5 and a number, t

4. the product of a number, t, and 5

Evaluate the expression for $n = 5$.

5. $5n$

6. $7.3n$

7. $28n$

8. $\frac{30}{n}$

9. $\frac{145}{n}$

10. $\frac{n}{5}$

Practice

Write an algebraic expression for each word expression.

11. twice the distance, d

12. four times the perimeter, p

13. the quotient of the number of gallons, g, and 12

14. the number of hours, h, divided by 4.5

Write two word expressions for the algebraic expression.

15. $8n$

16. $\frac{4.5}{k}$

17. $b \div 6$

18. $4.8a$

19. $132y$

20. $\frac{x}{42}$

Evaluate the expression for $a = 4$, $b = 6.5$, and $c = 10$.

21. $7a$

22. $3.2c$

23. $\frac{48}{a}$

24. $\frac{c}{2}$

25. $\frac{a}{4}$

26. $4.6a$

27. $100b$

28. $\frac{c}{100}$

29. ab

30. $\frac{b}{c}$

31. bc

32. ac

33. $\frac{a}{c}$

34. $\frac{c}{a}$

35. abc

36. $2a + 6$

37. $3b - 4$

38. $\frac{c}{2} + 13$

39. $2(c - 4)$

40. $16 + \frac{a}{4}$

Mixed Applications

41. Juan bought t apples that cost $0.35 each. Write an expression that represents the total cost of the apples.

42. The Turner family spent $1,500 on a vacation that lasted d days. Write an expression that represents the average cost per day.

43. Peaches are on sale at 3 pounds for n dollars. Write an expression that represents the cost of 2 pounds of peaches.

44. The sum of two numbers is 80. Their difference is 48. One number is 4 times the other. What are the two numbers?

Evaluate $\frac{n}{5}$ for $n = 5$, $n = 10$, and $n = 20$.
Describe the value of $\frac{n}{5}$ as n increases.

WRAP UP . . .

More Practice, Lesson 2.6, page H35

49

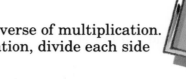

You have learned that division is the inverse of multiplication. To solve equations that show multiplication, divide each side of the equation by the same number.

Example   Solve and check. $6c = 132$

Step 1 Divide each side of the equation by 6.	**Step 2** Check the solution. Replace c with 22.
$6c = 132$	$6c = 132$
$\frac{6c}{6} = \frac{132}{6}$	$6 \times 22 = 132$
$c = 22$	$132 = 132$

You can apply what you know about writing a multiplication expression to writing an equation for a word problem.

Example   Miguel owes a balance of $270 on a loan. His monthly payment on the loan is $15. At that rate, for how many more months must Miguel pay on the loan?

Step 1 Choose a variable. Let m = the number of months. Then $15m$ = the amount owed.	**Step 2** Write an equation. $15m = 270$
Step 3 Solve the equation. $15m = 270$ $\frac{15m}{15} = \frac{270}{15}$ $m = 18$	**Step 4** Check the solution. $15m = 270$ $15 \times 18 = 270$ $270 = 270$

So, Miguel must pay on the loan for 18 more months.

A calculator is very useful when you are solving equations.

Example $14.6x = 189.8$

$$\frac{14.6x}{14.6} = \frac{189.8}{14.6}$$

$$x = 13$$

189.8 ÷ 14.6 = [13.]

Check for Understanding

Tell whether the given value is the solution of the equation. Answer *yes* or *no*. If the value is not the solution, solve the equation.

1. $6x = 18, x = 3$ **2.** $9t = 72, t = 12$ **3.** $2.5y = 15, y = 37.5$

Practice

Solve the equation. Check your solution.

4. $6t = 36$ **5.** $75 = 5h$ **6.** $4n = 40$ **7.** $8a = 296$

8. $52,000 = 200y$ **9.** $0.25k = 0.5$ **10.** $7d = 490$ **11.** $3w = 762$

12. $774 = 6v$ **13.** $4 = 8k$ **14.** $5m = 0.5$ **15.** $1.8 = 0.6n$

16. $x + 4 = 15$ **17.** $b - 14 = 12$ **18.** $9n = 3^3$ **19.** $6p = (3.6 \times 5)$

Mixed Applications

Solve. Write an equation for Exercises 20–21.

20. Peter owes a balance of $320 on a loan. He has 20 more equal monthly payments to make. How much is each monthly payment?

21. Sonia made monthly payments of $35.80 for a stereo. She paid a total of $286.40. For how many months did she pay for the stereo?

22. Mental Math Complete: If $3t = 6$, then $3t + 4 = \blacksquare$.

23. Mental Math Complete: If $7x = 21$, then $7x - 5 = \blacksquare$.

24. Leah works at the Pizza Place. She earns $4 per hour plus tips. Last week she earned $184, $60 of which was tips. How many hours did she work?

SCIENCE CONNECTION

The formula $d = rt$, where d = distance, r = rate, and t = time, can be solved as an equation if the values for two of the variables are known.

Example During a landing the space shuttle orbiter travels a distance of 22.4 km in 4 min. Find the rate of speed in km/min.

$d = rt \;\longleftarrow d = 22.4, t = 4$
$22.4 = 4r$
$\dfrac{22.4}{4} = \dfrac{4r}{4}$
$5.6 = r \;\longleftarrow 5.6$ km/min

25. Use the formula to find the time the orbiter takes to travel 19.6 km ($r = 5.6$ km/min).

Explain why you divide each side of the equation $4n = 12.4$ by 4 to solve for n.

WRAP
UP...

DIVISION EQUATIONS

Emilia is going to buy a new keyboard for her computer. She wants to be able to buy the keyboard in 8 weeks. To find how much she must save each week, she divides the price of the keyboard by 8. She finds that she needs to save $17 each week. What is the price of the keyboard?

To find the price of the keyboard, write an equation.

Step 1 Choose a variable.	**Step 2** Write an equation.	**Step 3** Solve the equation. Multiply each side by 8.	**Step 4** Check the solution. Replace k with 136.
Let k = the price. Then $\frac{k}{8}$ = the amount saved each week.	$\frac{k}{8} = 17$	$\frac{k}{8} = 17$ $\frac{k}{8}(8) = 17(8)$ $k = 136$	$\frac{k}{8} = 17$ $\frac{136}{8} = 17$ $17 = 17$

So, the price of the keyboard is $136.

More Examples

A.
$$\frac{a}{2.4} = 15$$
$$\frac{a}{2.4}(2.4) = 15(2.4)$$
$$a = 36$$

Check: $\frac{a}{2.4} = 15$
$$\frac{36}{2.4} = 15$$
$$15 = 15$$

B.
$$4 = \frac{m}{27}$$
$$4(27) = \frac{m}{27}(27)$$
$$108 = m$$

$$4 = \frac{m}{27}$$
$$4 = \frac{108}{27}$$
$$4 = 4$$

C.
$$\frac{x}{3} = 2.5$$
$$\frac{x}{3}(3) = 2.5(3)$$
$$x = 7.5$$

$$\frac{x}{3} = 2.5$$
$$\frac{7.5}{3} = 2.5$$
$$2.5 = 2.5$$

Check for Understanding

Tell whether the given value is the solution of the equation. Answer *yes* or *no*.

1. $\frac{z}{7} = 5$, $z = 35$

2. $\frac{w}{16} = 8$, $w = 2$

3. $4 = \frac{r}{1.3}$, $r = 6.5$

Solve the equation. Check your solution.

4. $\frac{x}{4} = 13$

5. $\frac{t}{15} = 8$

6. $2.5 = \frac{z}{8}$

7. $17 = \frac{s}{9.2}$

Practice

Write the operation you would use to solve the equation.

8. $\frac{r}{8} = 10$ **9.** $3h = 2.3$ **10.** $120 = p - 5$ **11.** $h + 3.5 = 22.8$

Solve the equation. Check your solution.

12. $41 = \frac{w}{2}$ **13.** $\frac{a}{11} = 23$ **14.** $\frac{b}{1.75} = 100$ **15.** $\frac{r}{20} = 18$

16. $\frac{z}{3} = 7.3$ **17.** $\frac{n}{0.5} = 6$ **18.** $2.5 = \frac{v}{3.1}$ **19.** $\frac{b}{62} = 9$

20. $75.6 = \frac{s}{3}$ **21.** $\frac{r}{14} = 4$ **22.** $\frac{b}{0.3} = 30$ **23.** $\frac{t}{0.5} = 14$

24. $\frac{x}{2.3} = 12.4$ **25.** $\frac{t}{10.8} = 40$ **26.** $9^2 = \frac{k}{3}$ **27.** $\frac{t}{5} = (4 + 9)$

Mixed Applications

Solve. Write an equation for Exercises 28–29.

28. The Pep Club divided a shipment of pep ribbons equally among 32 members. Each member received 15 ribbons. How many ribbons were in the shipment?

29. When the total cost of a dinner was divided equally among 6 people, each paid $7.80. Find the total cost of the dinner.

30. Analyze Data The table shows how the owner's cost for an item and the price of the item are related. Copy and complete the table.

Owner's cost, c	$8	$10	$12	$14	$16	$18	$20
Price, p	$13	$15	$17	$19	▪	▪	▪

31. Write a formula that shows how the owner's cost and the price are related. Let c represent the cost, and let p represent the price.

32. Use the formula you wrote in Exercise 31 to find the price of an item when the owner's cost is $45.75.

MIXED REVIEW

Solve the equation. Check your solution.

1. $18 + x = 32$ **2.** $5.5y = 110$ **3.** $4.65 = b - 2.8$ **4.** $5b = 32$

5. $75 = 73 + a$ **6.** $9k = 639$ **7.** $t - 35.5 = 17.2$ **8.** $(40 + 7) + r = 100$

Write an equation and solve.
The cost, c, divided by 6 is $1.24.

WRAP
UP...

WARM

UP...

Write an equation for "Four less than two times t is six."

TWO-STEP EQUATIONS

Allen joined a health club three years ago. Reuben joined the same health club this year. Reuben paid $50 more than twice the amount Allen paid to join the club. Reuben paid $300. How much did Allen pay?

You can write a two-step equation to solve this problem.

Let c = the amount Allen paid.
Then $2c + 50$ = the amount Reuben paid.

Equation: $2c + 50 = 300$

To solve a two-step equation, first do addition or subtraction, and then do multiplication or division.

$$2c + 50 = 300$$
$$2c + 50 - 50 = 300 - 50 \quad \longleftarrow \text{ Subtract 50 from each side.}$$
$$2c = 250$$
$$\frac{2c}{2} = \frac{250}{2} \quad \longleftarrow \text{ Divide each side by 2.}$$
$$c = 125 \qquad \text{So, Allen paid \$125 to join the club.}$$

More Examples

A. $3p - 6 = 9$ Check:

$3p - 6 + 6 = 9 + 6$ $3(5) - 6 = 9$
$\frac{3p}{3} = \frac{15}{3}$ $15 - 6 = 9$
$p = 5$ $9 = 9$

B. $\frac{b}{6} + 3.6 = 9.2$ Check:

$\frac{b}{6} + 3.6 - 3.6 = 9.2 - 3.6$ $\frac{33.6}{6} + 3.6 = 9.2$
$\frac{b}{6} = 5.6$ $5.6 + 3.6 = 9.2$
$\frac{b}{6}(6) = 5.6(6)$ $9.2 = 9.2$
$b = 33.6$

Talk About It

▶ Can you solve the equation $3p - 6 = 9$ by dividing first and then adding? Explain.

Check for Understanding

Tell what operation you would use first to solve the equation. Then solve the equation.

1. $2x + 3 = 7$ **2.** $5b - 9 = 11$ **3.** $6 = \frac{c}{2.4} - 8$ **4.** $\frac{h}{7} + 5 = 10$

Practice

Name the two operations you would use to solve the equation in the order you would use them.

5. $2c + 5 = 15$ **6.** $\frac{m}{4} - 7 = 13$ **7.** $\frac{x}{1.2} + 3 = 10$ **8.** $11 = 6f - 4$

Solve the equation. Check your solution.

9. $\frac{e}{5} - 2 = 7$ **10.** $\frac{d}{4} + 5 = 13$ **11.** $4m - 5 = 27$ **12.** $7z + 3 = 59$

13. $2a + 9 = 17$ **14.** $\frac{h}{6} + 8 = 15$ **15.** $\frac{r}{9} - 2 = 7$ **16.** $2k - 6 = 8$

17. $4g + 8 = 32$ **18.** $6w - 9 = 9$ **19.** $15 = 3n - 3$ **20.** $6 = \frac{m}{3} - 2$

Write an equation for the word sentence.

21. Five more than the product of 9 and a number, d, is 32.

22. Three less than the quotient of a number, s, and 6 is 8.

Mixed Applications

Solve. Write an equation for Exercises 23–24.

23. The price of a hammock is $12 more than one half of the price of a tent. The price of the hammock is $50. Find the price of the tent. (HINT: $\frac{1}{2}n = \frac{n}{2}$)

24. The length of a garden is 4 ft shorter than 3 times the width. The length is 32 ft. What is the width?

25. Make Up a Problem Write a word problem that can be solved by using the equation $3x - 6 = 15$. Exchange with a classmate and solve.

26. Show the calculator key sequence you can use to solve the equation $3.5a + 8.25 = 45.98$.

MATH CONNECTION

When you solve an equation such as $2x + 3x - 4 = 36$, you must first combine (add or subtract) like terms. In this equation, $2x$ and $3x$ are **like terms.**

Example
$$2x + 3x - 4 = 36$$
$$5x - 4 = 36$$
$$5x = 40$$
$$x = 8$$

Solve the equation. Check your solution.

27. $12r + 8r + 3 = 103$

28. $10b - 7b + 6 = 18$

29. $14t - 8t - 3 = 15$

30. $44 = 7s + 8 + 2s$

Explain the steps that you would use to solve the equation $2x - 8 = 32$.

SOLVING INEQUALITIES

Recall that an **inequality** is a mathematical sentence that uses the symbol $<$, $>$, $\leq$, $\geq$, or $\neq$.

$x + 3 > 4$ ← x plus 3 is greater than 4.
$n - 5 \leq 2$ ← n minus 5 is less than or equal to 2.
$2n + 1 \neq 6$ ← $2n$ plus 1 is not equal to 6.

Solving an inequality is similar to solving an equation. NOTE: The replacements for the variables in these inequalities are whole numbers.

Solve. $x + 3 \geq 4$
$\quad x + 3 - 3 \geq 4 - 3$ ← Subtract 3 from each side.
$\quad\quad\quad x \geq 1$

So, the solution is all whole numbers greater than or equal to 1, or 1, 2, 3, 4, . . . ← The dots stand for all whole numbers after 4.

- Is 6 a solution of $x + 3 \geq 4$?

More Examples

A. $3n < 15$

$\quad \dfrac{3n}{3} < \dfrac{15}{3}$

$\quad n < 5$

$\quad n = 0, 1, 2, 3, 4$

B. $\quad 2c + 1 > 9$

$\quad\quad 2c + 1 - 1 > 9 - 1$

$\quad\quad\quad \dfrac{2c}{2} > \dfrac{8}{2}$

$\quad\quad\quad c > 4; c = 5, 6, 7, . . .$

Some word problems can be solved by writing inequalities.

Example Alex has 6 more baseball cards than football cards. He has fewer than 175 baseball cards. How many football cards does he have?

___

Step 1 Choose a variable.
Let s = the number of football cards.
Then $s + 6$ = the number of baseball cards.

Step 2 Write an inequality. $\quad s + 6 < 175$

Step 3 Solve the inequality. $\quad s + 6 - 6 < 175 - 6$
$\quad\quad\quad\quad\quad\quad\quad\quad\quad\quad\quad s < 169$

___

So, Alex has fewer than 169 football cards.

Check for Understanding

Tell whether the given value is a solution of the inequality.
Answer *yes* or *no*.

1. $n + 3 > 4, n = 5$

2. $x - 4 \leq 3, x = 8$

3. $b + 5 \neq 8, b = 4$

Solve. Write the whole numbers that make the inequality true.

4. $a + 3 < 6$

5. $x - 2 > 5$

6. $2r \leq 10$

7. $\frac{b}{8} \neq 8$

Practice

Solve. Write the whole numbers that make the inequality true.

8. $n + 6 < 10$

9. $b + 8 \leq 13$

10. $a + 5 > 8$

11. $5k \geq 30$

12. $4f \neq 8$

13. $\frac{s}{3} < 4$

14. $3z \leq 24$

15. $2t > 28$

16. $9n \leq 63$

17. $\frac{w}{4} < 9$

18. $\frac{c}{6} \leq 2$

19. $n - 7 > 0$

20. $5m + 8 < 28$

21. $5s + 1 \leq 31$

22. $\frac{x}{3} - 4 \geq 1$

23. $4t + 2 > 30$

Mixed Applications

Write an inequality for the problem. Then solve.

24. Liz deposited $20 in her savings account. After the deposit she had more than $250. How much did she have in her savings account before the deposit?

25. The cost of renting a vacation house was less than $795. The cost was shared equally by 5 people. Could the amount each paid have been $175? Why or why not?

Assume that the given statement is true. Write *true, false, possible,* or *cannot tell* for each conclusion that follows the statement. Explain each answer.

Statement: The Sandlot Hitters played more than 20 games last season.

26. Conclusion: The Sandlot Hitters had a winning season last year.

27. Conclusion: The Sandlot Hitters played at most 20 games last season.

28. Conclusion: The Sandlot Hitters played exactly 21 games last season.

29. Conclusion: The Sandlot Hitters played between 21 and 28 games last season.

30. Conclusion: The Sandlot Hitters won 20 games last season.

How is an inequality different from an equation?

WRAP
UP...

PROBLEM *Solving*

Kyle rented 682 surfboards in June. This was
15 surfboards fewer than he rented in July.
How many surfboards did Kyle rent in July?

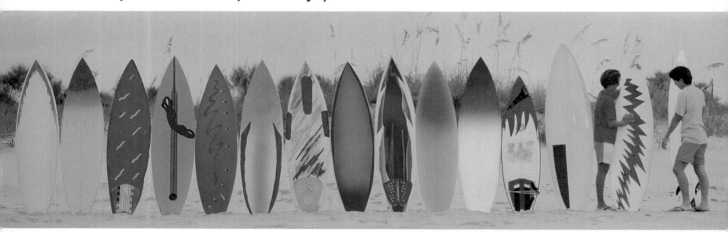

To use an equation to solve a problem, you must write an equation
that represents the information given in the problem.

▶ **UNDERSTAND**

What are you asked to find?
What facts are given?

▶ **PLAN**

What strategy will you use?
Write an equation is a good strategy to use. First, decide what
operation to use in the equation. Then, write and solve the equation.

▶ **SOLVE**

How will you solve the problem?

Write an equation showing subtraction. Let s = the number of surfboards
Kyle rented in July. Then $s - 15$ = the number of surfboards rented in
June.

$$s - 15 = 682$$
$$s - 15 + 15 = 682 + 15 \longleftarrow \text{Use addition to solve.}$$
$$s = 697$$

So, Kyle rented 697 surfboards in July.

▶ **LOOK BACK**

How can you check your answer?

 WHAT IF... . . . Kyle rented 17 more
surfboards in June than in July?
What equation can you use to
find the number of surfboards
he rented in July?

Apply

Write an equation for the problem. Then solve.

① The regular price of a beach raft was reduced by $5. The sale price was $16. Find the regular price of the raft.

② The price of a pair of swimming trunks is 3 times the price of a beach towel. The trunks cost $24.36. Find the price of the towel.

Mixed Applications ➤ **STRATEGIES**

- Write an Equation • Guess and Check
- Find a Pattern • Use Estimation
- Draw a Picture • Work Backward

Choose a strategy and solve.

③ Kyle rented 12 beach chairs on Monday, 14 on Tuesday, 18 on Wednesday, and 24 on Thursday. If the number of chairs rented continues to increase at the same rate, how many chairs will Kyle rent on Friday?

④ Tasha has a total of 15 quarters and dimes. The value of the coins is $2.85. She has more quarters than dimes. How many of each coin does she have?

⑤ A concert will be held on the beach to raise money for charity. The sponsors hope to raise more than $20,000. The tickets will cost $11.50 each. About how many tickets will have to be sold to make the goal?

⑥ The lifeguards are putting a fence around an area that is 18 ft wide and 30 ft long. The fence posts will be 3 ft apart. How many fence posts will be needed?

⑦ Yesterday Elena played volleyball 15 min less than she played today. She played for 35 min yesterday. How long did she play today?

⑧ The Snack Stand sold 104 tacos at $0.75 each and 185 fruit drinks at $0.55 each. About how much did the Snack Stand receive in all for tacos and fruit drinks?

CHAPTER REVIEW

Vocabulary Check

Choose a word from the box to complete each sentence.

algebraic
equation
inequality
multiplication
subtraction

1. To solve an equation that shows division, use __?__ . *(page 52)*

2. The expression $6 + p$ is a(n) __?__ expression. *(page 36)*

3. The mathematical sentence $3p = 18$ is a(n)__?__ . *(page 36)*

4. The mathematical sentence that uses the symbol $<$, $>$, $\leq$, $\geq$, or $\neq$ is called a(n)__?__ . *(page 36)*

5. To solve an equation that shows addition, use __?__ . *(page 40)*

Concept Check

Choose the algebraic expression that matches the word expression.
(pages 38, 48)

$n + 4$	$n - 4$	$4n$	$\dfrac{n}{4}$

6. 4 less than a number

7. the product of a number and 4

8. a number increased by 4

9. a number divided by 4

Tell what operation you would use to solve the equation. *(pages 40, 44, 50, 52)*

10. $x + 3 = 14$

11. $2y = 32$

12. $\dfrac{b}{8} = 3$

13. $c - 12 = 8$

14. $15 = t - 4$

15. $4 + k = 16$

16. $\dfrac{a}{9} = 3.2$

17. $7x = 4.9$

Tell whether the given value is the solution of the equation. Write *yes* or *no*.
(pages 40, 44, 50, 52, 54)

18. $3 + x = 18, x = 6$

19. $n - 4 = 21, n = 25$

20. $6a = 2.4, a = 0.4$

21. $\dfrac{b}{6} = 36, b = 6$

22. $2p + 4 = 14, p = 5$

23. $3y - 9 = 9, y = 3$

Tell what operation you would use first to solve the equation. *(page 54)*

24. $2x + 6 = 100$

25. $\dfrac{n}{3} - 4 = 12$

26. $3a - 5 = 4$

27. $7 = \dfrac{k}{4} + 5$

Tell whether the given value is a solution of the inequality. Write *yes* or *no*. *(page 56)*

28. $n + 3 < 12, n = 5$

29. $c - 9 \geq 5, c = 13$

30. $2r - 4 > 6, r = 61$

Skill Check

Write an algebraic expression for each word expression. Use the variable n. *(pages 38, 48)*

31. the sum of a number and 12

32. the product of 8 and a number

33. 9.5 less than a number

34. the quotient of a number and 5

Evaluate the expression for $t = 4$. *(pages 38, 48)*

35. $t + 8$

36. $t - 2.5$

37. $5t$

38. $\dfrac{t}{0.2}$

39. $3.2t$

40. $2t - 3$

41. $\dfrac{t}{4}$

42. $3t + 1$

Solve the equation. Check your solution. *(pages 40, 44, 50, 52, 54)*

43. $n + 8 = 19$

44. $a + 16 = 20$

45. $2.4 = d + 1.9$

46. $p + 13 = 31$

47. $g - 6 = 10$

48. $b - 8 = 2$

49. $c - 4.5 = 14.2$

50. $140 = c - 4$

51. $6n = 24$

52. $5m = 10.5$

53. $3t = 9.9$

54. $12k = 96$

55. $\dfrac{n}{2} = 12$

56. $\dfrac{x}{8} = 4$

57. $4.5 = \dfrac{b}{3}$

58. $\dfrac{c}{1.2} = 4.6$

59. $\dfrac{t}{2} + 3 = 7.5$

60. $\dfrac{a}{4.2} - 4 = 10$

61. $2t + 1 = 9$

62. $5m - 3 = 17$

63. $2 = 11p - 9$

Solve. Write the whole numbers that make the inequality true. *(page 56)*

64. $n + 6 < 10$

65. $b + 2 \geq 115$

66. $4n - 1 > 15$

Problem-Solving Check

Solve. *(pages 42, 58)*

67. A bicycle shop has a total of 120 three-speed bicycles and ten-speed bicycles. There are twice as many ten-speed bicycles as three-speed bicycles. How many are there of each type?

68. Joan bought some 10-cent stamps and 29-cent stamps for $3.31. She bought a total of 16 stamps. How many 29-cent stamps did she buy?

69. Jerome's weight is 3.5 kg less than Mark's weight. Jerome weighs 47.6 kg. How much does Mark weigh?

70. Miriam earned 3 times the amount Jenny earned. Miriam earned $354. Find the amount Jenny earned.

CHAPTER TEST

Write an algebraic expression for the word expression. Use the variable a.

1. 5 less than three times a number

2. 24 divided by a number

3. the product of 6.3 and a number

4. the sum of a number and 4.15

Evaluate the expression for $b = 3$.

5. $4b + 6$

6. $\frac{b}{1.5}$

7. $b - 0.25$

8. $\frac{18.6}{b}$

9. $10.4b$

Solve the equation.

10. $q - 6.5 = 3.7$

11. $4d + 3 = 35$

12. $\frac{n}{4.4} = 2.1$

13. $22 = x + 6$

14. $2.5t - 5 = 10$

15. $\frac{c}{7} = 33$

16. $p + 0.3 = 5.2$

17. $9.5n = 19$

18. $a + 72 = 103$

19. $b - 9.9 = 17$

20. $8.1 = \frac{x}{2.75}$

21. $12r = 93.6$

22. $3x + 1 = 10$

23. $28 = c - 18$

24. $\frac{t}{3.4} = 7$

25. $5k = 11.75$

Solve. Write the whole numbers that make the inequality true.

26. $n + 2 < 5$

27. $a - 4 > 1$

28. $3x \geq 21$

29. $2p + 1 \leq 11$

Solve.

30. The Sunshine Club has been collecting money for a local charity. The members have collected or donated $90 in $1, $5, and $10 bills. The total number of bills is 26. How many of each bill has the club collected?

31. The club has also collected a total of 66 quarters and dimes. The value of the coins is $12.90. How many of each coin has the club collected?

32. Mr. Schmidt bought a bottle of grape juice. He also bought a 42-oz bottle of apple juice. That amount was 6 oz less than twice the amount in the bottle of grape juice. How much grape juice did he buy?

33. José lives 3.5 miles from school. The distance from José's home to school is 1 mile less than 3 times the distance from Sabina's home to school. How far from school does Sabina live?

WRITE A NEWSLETTER

Many consumer magazines and newsletters are written to give people information about products that they have bought or are considering buying.

Work with your teammates to plan a consumer newsletter that can be given to the students in your school. Your newsletter should be at least two pages long.

DECIDE As a team, discuss what products you will review in your newsletter. Make a list of categories of products. Then choose at least five products that you can evaluate for price, usefulness, and durability.

- Discuss how many lines each review will be and how the five reviews will be arranged in the newsletter.
- Discuss how many copies of the newsletter you will make.
- Discuss how much it will cost to produce the newsletter. Consider the cost of the paper and the cost of making copies.

DO As a team, divide the chosen products among yourselves. Write reviews of the products you have chosen. Type the reviews and arrange them in the form of a newsletter.

- Make copies of your newsletter to distribute.

SHARE Compare your team's newsletter with those of other teams. Tell why you chose each product.

Talk About It

- Did you learn anything that you did not know about a product?
- Suppose you wanted to sell your newsletter. How much would you have to charge for each copy in order to make a profit of $0.05 per copy?

MATH FUN

extend your thinking

HISTORICAL NOTE

About 6,000 years ago, the wheel was invented in Mesopotamia. Later, people in that region used a mixed-number system based on sixty and ten. Who were these people?

To find the answer, solve each equation. Then write the letter that matches the solution to the equation.

2 → A	6 → I	10 → N	14 → S
4 → B	8 → L	12 → O	16 → Y

1. $\frac{t}{0.5} = 8$ ___?___

2. $1 = \frac{w}{2}$ ___?___

3. $d + (2 \times 3) = 10$ ___?___

4. $0.2f = 3.2$ ___?___

5. $\frac{k}{5} + 5 = 6.6$ ___?___

6. $20 = 2p - 4$ ___?___

7. $0 = 3.5y - 35$ ___?___

8. $0.4k - 1 = 1.4$ ___?___

9. $b + (40 - 2) = 40$ ___?___

10. $\frac{d}{0.1} = 100$ ___?___

11. $\frac{s}{2} - 3 = 4$ ___?___

CHALLENGE

Logical Reasoning

On the small island of Ubs, there are some Fubs and some Gubs. Four tenths of Fubs are Gubs. Two tenths of Gubs are Fubs. Six Fubs are not Gubs. How many Gubs are there?

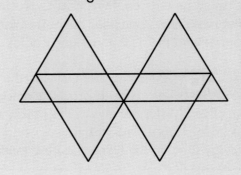

Visual Thinking

How many triangles are in this figure?

Write the letter of the correct answer.

1. Which number is twenty-five and seventeen hundredths?

    A. 25.017   **B.** 25.17

    C. 25,170   **D.** not here

2. Which is the standard form of 23.4 million?

    A. 234   **B.** 234,000

    C. 23,400,000   **D.** 234,000,000

3. Which number is 79.3999 rounded to the nearest hundredth?

    A. 79.30   **B.** 79.39

    C. 79.40   **D.** 790

4. Which is the value of $b + 4$ for $b = 4.3$?

    A. 0.3   **B.** 4.7

    C. 8.3   **D.** 17.2

5. $52 = m + 10$

    A. $m = 5.2$ **B.** $m = 62$

    C. $m = 520$ **D.** not here

6. $0.9\overline{)6.3}$

    A. 0.7   **B.** 7

    C. 70   **D.** 700

7. $14^3 = \blacksquare$

    A. 17   **B.** 42

    C. 126   **D.** 2,744

8. $5 \times 7 + 9 \times 3$

    A. 62   **B.** 132

    C. 240   **D.** not here

9. Which is the best estimate for the product?

$$304 \times 52$$

    A. 1,500   **B.** 15,000

    C. 30,000   **D.** 150,000

10. Which is the best estimate for the quotient?

$$20\overline{)163}$$

    A. 8   **B.** 80

    C. 800   **D.** 8,000

11. Ira and Cami launched rockets for science class. Ira's rocket went 3 times farther than Cami's rocket. Ira's rocket went 177 ft. Which equation would you use to find how far Cami's rocket went?

    A. $n + 3 = 177$ **B.** $3n = 177$

    C. $\frac{n}{3} = 177$ **D.** $n - 3 = 177$

12. Matt is buying a hat that costs $24.50. He must also pay a sales tax of $1.47. If he gives the cashier $40.00, how much change will he receive?

    A. $14.03   **B.** $15.50

    C. $16.97   **D.** $25.97

CHAPTER

3

NUMBER THEORY AND FRACTIONS

Did you know . . .

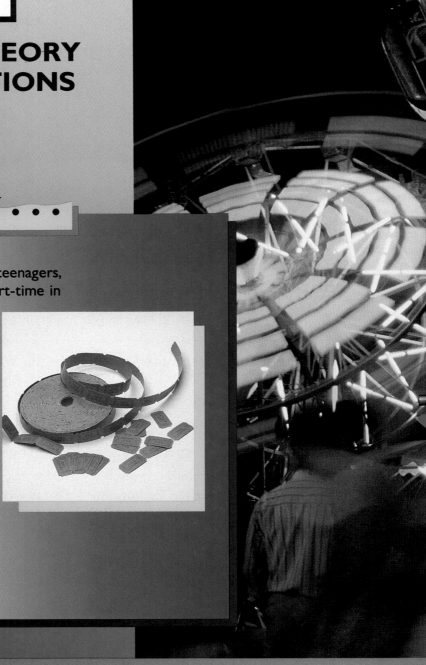

. . . that in 1987 about 4,185,000 teenagers, ages 16 to 19, were employed part-time in the United States?

Robbie collects tickets at a local amusement park. This week his boss asked him to work $6\frac{1}{2}$ more hours than he usually works per week. How can Robbie determine how many hours he will work this week?

Joy Vickers installs tile on walls, floors, and fireplaces. For one job Joy is making a rectangular design with 24 square mosaic tiles. How many choices for the design does she have?

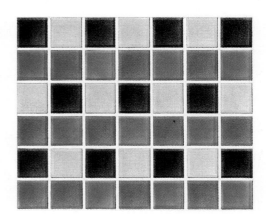

Columns		Rows	Columns		Rows
1	×	24	6	×	4
2	×	12	8	×	3
3	×	8	12	×	2
4	×	6	24	×	1

So, Joy has 8 choices.

The numbers 1, 2, 3, 4, 6, 8, 12, and 24 are factors of 24. **Factors** are numbers that are multiplied to find a product.

A whole number such as 24 is called a **composite number** because it has more than two whole-number factors.

Examples of composite numbers: 4, 10, 20, 35, 86, 104

Suppose one of Joy's tiles breaks. How many choices for a rectangular design does she have with the remaining tiles?

Columns		Rows
1	×	23
23	×	1

A whole number greater than 1 having exactly two whole-number factors, itself and 1, is a **prime number.**

Examples of prime numbers: 2, 3, 5, 7, 11, 13, 17, 23, 29

NOTE: The numbers 0 and 1 are neither prime nor composite.

Every composite number can be shown as the product of prime factors. This product is called the **prime factorization** of the number.

Example   Use a factor tree to find the prime factorization of 72.

The prime factorization of 72 can be written using exponents as $2^3 \times 3^2$.

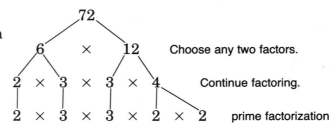

Check for Understanding

List all the factors.

1. 4
2. 12
3. 20
4. 35
5. 100
6. 48

Tell whether the number is *prime* or *composite*.

7. 24
8. 50
9. 37
10. 53
11. 93
12. 83

Complete the prime factorization.

13. $24 = 2 \times 2 \times 2 \times$ ■
14. $50 = 2 \times 5 \times$ ■
15. $36 = 2 \times$ ■ $\times 3 \times$ ■

Practice

Write *prime* or *composite* for the number.

16. 33
17. 57
18. 89
19. 77
20. 67
21. 121

Write the prime factorization, using exponents.

22. 40
23. 28
24. 75
25. 90
26. 56
27. 88
28. 120
29. 125
30. 180
31. 315
32. 420
33. 900

Write the number represented by the prime factorization.

34. $2^3 \times 3^2$
35. 11×2^2
36. $3^2 \times 5^2 \times 7$
37. $11^2 \times 13$
38. $3^3 \times 5 \times 7$
39. $5^2 \times 7^2$
40. $2^3 \times 5 \times 11$
41. $3 \times 7^2 \times 17$

Mixed Applications

42. Joy Vickers has 42 tiles to use for a rectangular design. How many choices for the design does she have?

43. How many choices for a rectangular design does Joy have if she uses 45 tiles?

44. The sum of two prime numbers is 36. Their difference is 2. Find the prime numbers.

45. **Number Sense** A number that is less than 40 has 1, 2, 3, and 5 as factors. What is the number?

Is $2^2 \times 5 \times 9$ the prime factorization of 180? Why or why not?

WRAP UP...

USING THE GCF AND THE LCM

Michelle works at a plant nursery. She is cutting price-tag ties for trees from an 80-in. piece of string and from a 96-in. piece of string. She wants to make all the ties the same length and to cut each piece of string into equal lengths. What is the length of the longest tie that she can cut?

Think: The length of each tie must be the greatest common factor (GCF) of 80 and 96.

Remember that the GCF is the product of the common prime factors.

Prime factorization of 80: ② × ② × ② × ② × 5
Prime factorization of 96: ② × ② × ② × ② × 2 × 3
GCF of 80 and 96: $2 \times 2 \times 2 \times 2 = 16$

So, the length of the longest tie is 16 in.

You can also use the least common multiple (LCM) to solve problems.

Example   Michelle is planting two gardens for a customer. One garden will have 8 rows of plants, and the other garden will have 14 rows of plants. The customer wants each garden to have the same number of plants. What is the least number of plants that can be planted in each garden?

Think: Find the LCM of the number of rows.

Prime factorization of 8: $2 \times 2 \times 2 = 2^3$
Prime factorization of 14: 2×7
LCM of 8 and 14: $2^3 \times 7 = 56$

So, the least number of plants that can be planted in each garden is 56.

Remember that the LCM is the product of the highest power of each prime factor.

Talk About It

▶ For any two numbers that are different, is the GCF or the LCM greater?

▶ Explain how you can find the GCF and the LCM of a pair of numbers without finding the prime factorizations.

Check for Understanding

Tell whether you would use the *GCF* or the *LCM* to solve the problem.

1. Michelle is cutting plant stakes from a piece of wood 120 in. long and from a piece of wood 88 in. long. All the stakes are to be the same length, and each piece of wood is to be cut into equal lengths. What is the length of the longest stake that she can cut?

2. Michelle waters the plants every fourth day, and Dave waters the plants every sixth day. They are both watering plants today. How many days will pass before both will be again watering on the same day?

Practice   Solve.

3. Dave is making two tree displays. One display will have 10 rows of oak trees, and the other display will have 12 rows of maple trees. Each display will have the same number of trees. What is the least number of trees he can use in each display?

4. Michelle divided 300 quarters and 462 dimes among the cash registers at the nursery. She put the same number of coins in each register. What is the greatest number of cash registers that the nursery can have?

5. The nursery has two neon signs. One sign blinks off every 20 sec, and the other sign blinks off every 15 sec. Both signs are turned on at the same time. How many seconds will pass before the signs will blink off at the same time?

Mixed Applications

6. Dave is cutting tags for the trees from a 45-in. strip of paper and from a 126-in. strip. Each tag will be the same length. Each piece of paper will be cut into equal lengths. What is the length of the longest tag he can cut?

7. Jason paid $1.98 each for 6 azalea plants and $3.25 each for 3 rose bushes. What was the total amount Jason paid?

8. **Make Up a Problem**   Write a problem that can be solved by using the LCM. Exchange with a classmate and solve.

The LCM of 4, 5, and 6 is 60. What is the LCM of 8, 10, and 12?

PROBLEM Solving

Making Choices

Wesley is training to be a commercial photographer. To further his training, he needs to buy an enlarger. The price of the enlarger he wants is $450. Wesley is considering these options.

Option 1: buy the enlarger and receive a $40 discount
Option 2: use a rent-to-own plan and buy the enlarger for $12.50 per month for 36 months
Option 3: rent the enlarger for $10 per month

Which option should Wesley choose?

The solution to a problem sometimes depends on the situation and on the available options.

▶ **UNDERSTAND**

What are you asked to find?

What facts are given?

▶ **PLAN**

How will you solve the problem?

You can consider the advantages and disadvantages of each option.

▶ **SOLVE**

What questions should you ask to consider the advantages and disadvantages of each option?

- With which option, Option 1 or Option 2, will Wesley spend the lesser amount of money?

- Will Wesley ever own the enlarger if he chooses Option 3?

- Does Wesley have enough money to consider Option 1?

Which option would you choose?

▶ **LOOK BACK**

What reasons did you use for making your choice?

WHAT IF . . . . . . Wesley knows that a better enlarger will be on the market next year? Would this affect your choice? Why or why not?

Apply

Wesley decides to buy the enlarger. He is considering these options.
Use the options for Exercises 1–4.

Option A: borrow the money from a bank and make payments of
$21.20 per month for 24 months
Option B: take $410 from a savings account to pay for the enlarger

1. How much will Wesley pay for the enlarger if he chooses Option A?

2. How much more is the total paid using Option A than the total paid using Option B?

3. If Wesley chooses Option B, he will not get the $41 in interest that his money would have earned in two years. What is the difference between the amount you found in Exercise 2 and the amount of interest?

4. Which option do you think Wesley should choose? Give reasons for your answer.

Mixed Applications	STRATEGIES	• Use Estimation • Guess and Check • Write an Equation • Draw a Picture

Choose a strategy and solve.

5. Marge has $50.00. She plans to buy a camera for $38.98 and a photography book for $9.97. Does she have enough money for both items?

6. Miles has a total of 18 nickels and dimes. The value of the coins is $1.45. He has more dimes than nickels. How many dimes does he have?

7. Wesley took 45 photographs on Friday. This is 12 more than the number of photographs he took on Saturday. How many photographs did he take on Saturday?

8. The price of a photo album is $4 less than twice the price of a picture frame. The price of the photo album is $16. What is the price of the picture frame?

9. Wesley works at a photo studio. He earns $4.25 per hour. Last week he worked 22 hours. About how much did he earn last week?

10. A photograph is 10 in. wide and 15 in. high. The frame is 1 in. wide. What are the width and the height of the framed photograph?

More Practice, Lesson 3.3, page H38

73

EQUIVALENT FRACTIONS
and Mixed Numbers

Coleen and Jack each baked a small pizza.

Coleen sold $\frac{2}{3}$ of her pizza.   Jack sold $\frac{6}{9}$ of his pizza.

Coleen and Jack sold the same amount of pizza.
The fractions $\frac{2}{3}$ and $\frac{6}{9}$ are equivalent fractions.
Equivalent fractions name the same amount.

To find equivalent fractions, multiply or divide
the numerator and the denominator by the same
number (except zero).

$$\frac{9}{12} = \frac{9 \times 2}{12 \times 2} = \frac{18}{24} \qquad \frac{15}{25} = \frac{15 \div 5}{25 \div 5} = \frac{3}{5}$$

Recall that the greatest common factor (GCF) of
two or more numbers is the greatest factor that
the numbers have in common. When you divide
the numerator and the denominator of a fraction
by their GCF, the resulting fraction is in
simplest form.

Example Write $\frac{16}{24}$ in simplest form.

Step 1	**Step 2**
Use the prime factorizations of 16 and 24 to find the GCF.	Divide the numerator and the denominator by the GCF.
$16 = ②\times②\times②\times 2$ $\quad$ GCF $= 2^3$, $24 = ②\times②\times②\times 3$ $\quad$ or 8	$\frac{16 \div 8}{24 \div 8} = \frac{2}{3}$ $\quad$ simplest form

More Examples Write the fraction in simplest form.

A. $\frac{15}{40} = \frac{15 \div 5}{40 \div 5}$ $\qquad$ **B.** $\frac{35}{28} = \frac{35 \div 7}{28 \div 7}$ $\qquad$ **C.** $\frac{24}{36} = \frac{24 \div 12}{36 \div 12}$

$\quad = \frac{3}{8}$ $\qquad\qquad\qquad = \frac{5}{4}$ $\qquad\qquad\qquad = \frac{2}{3}$

- How can you tell that a fraction is greater than 1?

Recall that fractions greater than 1 can be written as mixed numbers.

Example Write $\frac{14}{4}$ as a mixed number.

Divide the numerator by the denominator. Write the remainder as a fraction in simplest form.

$$3\frac{2}{4} = 3\frac{1}{2}$$

$$4\overline{)14}$$
$$\underline{-12}$$
$$2$$

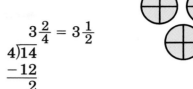

Another Method

You can use mental math to change a fraction to a mixed number.

12 is a multiple of 4.

$$\frac{15}{4} = \frac{12}{4} + \frac{3}{4} = 3 + \frac{3}{4} = 3\frac{3}{4}$$

You can write a mixed number as a fraction by multiplying the denominator by the whole number and then adding the numerator to the product.

Examples **A.** $3\frac{1}{4} = \frac{4 \times 3 + 1}{4} = \frac{13}{4}$ **B.** $2\frac{4}{5} = \frac{5 \times 2 + 4}{5} = \frac{14}{5}$

Talk About It

▶ Why is it helpful to write fractions in simplest form?

▶ When writing $\frac{12}{8}$ as a mixed number, can you write the fraction in simplest form first and then write the mixed number? Explain.

▶ How many fractions are equivalent to $\frac{9}{12}$?

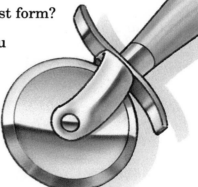

Check for Understanding

Complete.

1. $\frac{2}{3} = \frac{2 \times 6}{3 \times 6} = \frac{\blacksquare}{18}$ 2. $\frac{3}{5} = \frac{3 \times 4}{5 \times 4} = \frac{12}{\blacksquare}$ 3. $\frac{12}{21} = \frac{12 \div 3}{21 \div 3} = \frac{\blacksquare}{7}$

Write the GCF of the numerator and denominator. Then write the fraction in simplest form.

4. $\frac{6}{12}$ 5. $\frac{14}{16}$ 6. $\frac{8}{10}$ 7. $\frac{20}{25}$ 8. $\frac{21}{14}$ 9. $\frac{36}{24}$

Write as a whole number or a mixed number.

10. $\frac{11}{5}$ 11. $\frac{14}{6}$ 12. $\frac{13}{3}$ 13. $\frac{27}{9}$ 14. $\frac{10}{7}$ 15. $\frac{24}{4}$

Write as a fraction.

16. $4\frac{1}{2}$ 17. $2\frac{2}{5}$ 18. $9\frac{3}{4}$ 19. $1\frac{7}{8}$ 20. $21\frac{1}{2}$ 21. $4\frac{3}{7}$

More Practice, Lesson 3.4, page H39

Practice

Write three equivalent fractions for each fraction.

22. $\frac{1}{2}$ **23.** $\frac{2}{5}$ **24.** $\frac{15}{20}$ **25.** $\frac{9}{21}$ **26.** $\frac{3}{8}$ **27.** $\frac{7}{10}$

Write the fraction in simplest form.

28. $\frac{21}{28}$ **29.** $\frac{30}{45}$ **30.** $\frac{12}{15}$ **31.** $\frac{14}{30}$ **32.** $\frac{16}{20}$ **33.** $\frac{50}{70}$

34. $\frac{18}{24}$ **35.** $\frac{60}{25}$ **36.** $\frac{8}{6}$ **37.** $\frac{54}{72}$ **38.** $\frac{33}{55}$ **39.** $\frac{12}{6}$

Write as a whole number or a mixed number.

40. $\frac{21}{20}$ **41.** $\frac{22}{11}$ **42.** $\frac{11}{5}$ **43.** $\frac{162}{8}$ **44.** $\frac{21}{7}$ **45.** $\frac{75}{10}$

Write as a fraction.

46. $3\frac{1}{3}$ **47.** $7\frac{1}{2}$ **48.** $1\frac{2}{5}$ **49.** $9\frac{1}{6}$ **50.** $2\frac{9}{10}$ **51.** $11\frac{1}{5}$

Mixed Applications

52. Jack bought $\frac{3}{4}$ lb of ground beef. Coleen bought $\frac{12}{16}$ lb of ground beef. Who bought more ground beef? Explain.

53. A fraction is equivalent to $\frac{3}{5}$. The sum of the numerator and the denominator of the fraction is 48. What is the fraction?

54. The GCF of two numbers is 12. The sum of the numbers is 60. What are the numbers?

MATH CONNECTION • CHALLENGE

Fractions such as $\frac{3}{x}$, $\frac{4x}{y}$, and $\frac{6d}{8d}$ are **algebraic fractions.** Algebraic fractions can be expressed in simplest form using the same methods as those used for numerical fractions.

Examples **A.** $\frac{2x}{4} = \frac{2x \div 2}{4 \div 2}$ ⟵— GCF = 2 **B.** $\frac{ab}{3a} = \frac{ab \div a}{3a \div a}$ ⟵— GCF = a

$= \frac{x}{2}$ $= \frac{b}{3}$

Write the fraction in simplest form.

55. $\frac{4n}{6}$ **56.** $\frac{12b}{8}$ **57.** $\frac{4}{10b}$ **58.** $\frac{5t}{4t}$ **59.** $\frac{3y}{xy}$ **60.** $\frac{5c}{5cd}$

WRAP UP... Explain how you can determine whether a fraction is in simplest form.

1. Rita and Carlos have part-time jobs at the local grocery store. On Friday Carlos gave Rita a ride to work. He drove 2.5 mi from his house to Rita's house and then 3.2 mi to work. After work Carlos took Rita back to her house and then went home. How many miles did Carlos drive?

2. Rita usually works 22 hr each week. This is 5.5 hr less than the number of hours Carlos works each week. How many hours does Carlos work each week?

3. The first task that Carlos had at work on Friday was to set up a display of soup cans. He put 22 cans in the first row, 19 cans in the second row, and 16 cans in the third row. Carlos continued to decrease the number of cans in each row at the same rate. How many cans did he put in the seventh row?

4. Rita helped out at the cash register on Friday. To pay for a purchase, a customer gave Rita $3.55 in quarters and dimes. There were 3 more quarters than dimes. How many quarters did the customer give Rita?

5. Friday was payday. Rita and Carlos both earn $4.10 per hour. Rita and Carlos worked more than usual this week. Rita was paid for 25 hr and Carlos was paid for 31.5 hr. How much more did Carlos earn than Rita?

6. Rita is saving $30 each week so she can buy a used car. She does not want to spend more than $1,200 for a car. She has saved $300. For how many more weeks does she need to save before she has enough money for a car?

7. After the store closed on Friday, Carlos was asked to hang signs showing Saturday's specials. He needs to put one sign on a window that is 72 in. wide. The sign is 48 in. wide. How many inches should he leave on each side of the sign so that the sign is centered in the window?

COMPARING AND ORDERING

Nat took a survey of his classmates to determine their career goals. His results are shown in the table. Which profession did more of Nat's classmates choose, education or medicine?

You can compare the fractions by writing **like fractions,** fractions that have a common denominator. To find the least common denominator (LCD) of $\frac{2}{9}$ and $\frac{1}{6}$, find the LCM of their denominators.

Survey Results	
Profession	**Part of Class**
Law	$\frac{1}{9}$
Education	$\frac{2}{9}$
Business	$\frac{5}{18}$
Medicine	$\frac{1}{6}$
Military	$\frac{1}{18}$
Athletics	$\frac{7}{36}$

Step 1 Find the LCM of the denominators. This is the LCD.	**Step 2** Use the LCD to write equivalent fractions.	**Step 3** Compare $\frac{4}{18}$ and $\frac{3}{18}$.
$9 = 3 \times 3 = 3^2$ $6 = 2 \times 3$ $LCD = 2 \times 3^2 = 18$	$\frac{2}{9} = \frac{2 \times 2}{9 \times 2} = \frac{4}{18}$ $\frac{1}{6} = \frac{1 \times 3}{6 \times 3} = \frac{3}{18}$	$\frac{4}{18} > \frac{3}{18}$ So, $\frac{2}{9} > \frac{1}{6}$.

So, more of Nat's classmates chose education rather than medicine.

Another Example Order $\frac{3}{4}$, $\frac{5}{8}$, and $\frac{5}{6}$ from least to greatest.

Prime Factorizations
$4 = 2^2$
$8 = 2^3$
$6 = 2 \times 3$

$LCD = 2^3 \times 3 = 24$

Like Fractions
$\frac{3}{4} = \frac{3 \times 6}{4 \times 6} = \frac{18}{24}$

$\frac{5}{8} = \frac{5 \times 3}{8 \times 3} = \frac{15}{24}$ $\quad \frac{15}{24} < \frac{18}{24} < \frac{20}{24}$

$\frac{5}{6} = \frac{5 \times 4}{6 \times 4} = \frac{20}{24}$ $\quad$ So, $\frac{5}{8} < \frac{3}{4} < \frac{5}{6}$.

Another Method

Two fractions may also be compared by using cross multiplication. Multiply the denominator of each fraction by the numerator of the other fraction.

$$\overset{8}{}\quad\overset{6}{}$$
$\frac{1}{2} \diagdown \frac{3}{8}$ $\quad (8 \times 1) > (2 \times 3)$, or $8 > 6$. So, $\frac{1}{2} > \frac{3}{8}$.

Check for Understanding

Find the LCM of the numbers.

1. $6, 9$ **2.** $4, 6$ **3.** $5, 8$ **4.** $6, 20$ **5.** $8, 12$ **6.** $3, 5$

Tell which fraction or mixed number is greater.

7. $\frac{3}{8}, \frac{7}{8}$ **8.** $\frac{3}{6}, \frac{1}{3}$ **9.** $15\frac{2}{3}, 15\frac{5}{9}$ **10.** $1\frac{1}{5}, 1\frac{4}{6}$ **11.** $\frac{3}{5}, \frac{2}{3}$

Practice

Write the LCD of the fractions.

12. $\frac{7}{4}, \frac{3}{7}$ **13.** $\frac{3}{12}, \frac{7}{10}$ **14.** $\frac{4}{9}, \frac{7}{6}$ **15.** $\frac{21}{30}, \frac{14}{15}$ **16.** $\frac{1}{3}, \frac{2}{5}, \frac{5}{4}$

Compare. Write $<, >$, or $=$.

17. $\frac{3}{2} \bullet \frac{8}{9}$ **18.** $\frac{12}{8} \bullet \frac{13}{4}$ **19.** $\frac{3}{6} \bullet \frac{8}{16}$ **20.** $\frac{5}{6} \bullet \frac{3}{4}$ **21.** $\frac{21}{4} \bullet \frac{17}{3}$

22. $5\frac{2}{5} \bullet 5\frac{3}{8}$ **23.** $5\frac{7}{8} \bullet \frac{47}{8}$ **24.** $\frac{17}{3} \bullet 5\frac{1}{4}$ **25.** $3\frac{3}{10} \bullet 3\frac{1}{3}$ **26.** $4\frac{2}{3} \bullet \frac{33}{8}$

Write in order from least to greatest.

27. $\frac{5}{4}, \frac{7}{8}, \frac{2}{3}$ **28.** $\frac{9}{10}, \frac{21}{30}, \frac{13}{15}$ **29.** $3\frac{1}{2}, 3\frac{2}{5}, 3\frac{1}{10}$ **30.** $\frac{8}{3}, 2\frac{5}{6}, 2\frac{1}{4}, \frac{25}{12}$

Mixed Applications

Solve. Use the table on page 78 for Exercises 31 and 32.

31. Which profession was chosen by more of Nat's classmates, education or business?

32. List the fractions for the professions in order from greatest to least.

33. Number Sense Explain what you would do to compare the numbers $2\frac{1}{3}$ and 2.4.

34. Find Data Use an almanac to find the 10 highest-paying occupations for men and women in a recent year.

MIXED REVIEW

Write the prime factorization, using exponents.

1. 25 **2.** 42 **3.** 36 **4.** 72 **5.** 108 **6.** 200

Write the fraction in simplest form.

7. $\frac{3}{9}$ **8.** $\frac{7}{14}$ **9.** $\frac{8}{22}$ **10.** $\frac{36}{20}$ **11.** $\frac{15}{18}$ **12.** $\frac{56}{16}$

Describe two methods you can use to compare $\frac{3}{4}$ and $\frac{7}{10}$.

WRAP UP...

1. Carola plans to wash 11 cars this weekend. This is 3 more than twice the number of cars she washed last weekend. How many cars did Carola wash last weekend?

2. Howard has 15 model airplanes. This is 6 fewer than the number of model airplanes Mark has. How many model airplanes does Mark have?

3. Kevin is decorating boxes to sell at a crafts fair. He spent $19.61 for 20 undecorated boxes, paint, ribbon, and glitter. The paint cost $4.47, the ribbon cost $3.20, and the glitter cost $1.29. What was the cost of the undecorated boxes?

4. Patty has $5.00. She needs to buy 2 notebooks at $1.46 each, 2 pens at $0.89 each, and 6 pencils at $0.14 each. Does Patty have enough money to buy all these items?

5. Kevin sells all 20 of the boxes described in Exercise 3 for $4.00 each. How much greater is the amount he received than the amount he spent?

6. Use the information in Exercise 4 to find how much Patty will spend if she buys 2 notebooks, 2 pens, and 2 pencils.

Find the quotient.

7. $0.6\overline{)3.66}$

8. $1.3\overline{)3.12}$

9. $0.09\overline{)1.098}$

10. $0.25\overline{)1.55}$

Evaluate the expression for $a = 5$ and $b = 12.2$.

11. $2.4a$

12. $\frac{b}{2}$

13. $6b$

14. $3a + 7$

15. ab

Solve the equation. Check your answer.

16. $2p + 7 = 15$

17. $\frac{x}{6} = 3.6$

18. $5.8r = 19.72$

19. $4.9 = n - 67.2$

20. $\frac{c}{12} = 66$

21. $6b - 9 = 15$

22. $z + 48 = 98$

23. $325 = 25m$

Write *prime* or *composite* for the number.

24. 75

25. 53

26. 9

27. 115

28. 101

29. 57

Write as a fraction.

30. $2\frac{1}{3}$

31. $8\frac{5}{6}$

32. $1\frac{2}{3}$

33. $3\frac{3}{7}$

34. $10\frac{1}{2}$

35. $2\frac{5}{8}$

Write as a mixed number.

36. $\frac{7}{2}$

37. $\frac{15}{8}$

38. $\frac{32}{10}$

39. $\frac{17}{4}$

40. $\frac{28}{5}$

41. $\frac{45}{18}$

Analyze Information

When planning how to solve a problem, you need to analyze all the information provided. Some problems contain more information than needed. Such information is **irrelevant.**

Copy this problem. Underline the information needed to solve it. Circle the irrelevant information.

Ben taught a class in glassblowing. His class produced a total of 15 vases and glasses. Each student worked on either vases or glasses, but not both. Three sevenths of the class worked on vases. What part of the class worked on glasses?

- What information is needed to solve the problem?
- What information is irrelevant?

Talk About It

Read and analyze this problem. With a classmate, discuss and identify the information needed to solve the problem. Identify any irrelevant information.

The crafts shop has 12 dozen silver bracelets selling for $79.88 each. The shop also has 55 wooden bracelets selling for $19.98 each. How many bracelets does the shop have in stock?

Apply

Read and analyze each problem. List the steps needed to solve each problem, and then solve. Be prepared to identify any irrelevant information.

1 A bead-making process has 20 steps. Will has completed $\frac{4}{5}$ of the steps. Emma has completed $\frac{7}{10}$ of the steps. Who has completed more steps?

2 Jeremy sold a beaded watchband for $18.24 and a necklace for $24.50. How much did he receive in all for the watchband and the necklace?

3 A silver bead has a diameter of 4.9 mm and costs $0.88. A wooden bead has a diameter of 12.75 mm. Which bead has the larger diameter? How much larger is it?

Which fraction is closer to 1, $\frac{1}{3}$ or $\frac{1}{2}$?

Which fraction is closer to 0, $\frac{1}{4}$ or $\frac{1}{5}$?

Eve makes jewelry. She has designed a gold pendant and hopes to make it out of pieces left over from prior work. She needs a total of 2 oz of gold. Eve has found pieces weighing $\frac{1}{6}$, $\frac{2}{5}$, and $\frac{7}{8}$ oz. When she melts these down, will she have enough gold for the pendant?

Estimate the total weight of the three pieces of gold. You can estimate the sum or difference of fractions that are less than 1 by rounding to 0, $\frac{1}{2}$, or 1.

$\frac{1}{6}$ rounds to 0. $\longleftarrow$ The numerator is much less than the denominator.

$\frac{2}{5}$ rounds to $\frac{1}{2}$. $\longleftarrow$ The numerator is about half the denominator.

$\frac{7}{8}$ rounds to 1. $\longleftarrow$ The numerator is about the same as the denominator.

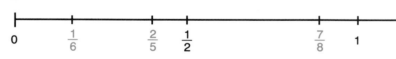

Estimate the sum. $\frac{1}{6} + \frac{2}{5} + \frac{7}{8} \longrightarrow 0 + \frac{1}{2} + 1 = 1\frac{1}{2}$

Eve has about $1\frac{1}{2}$ oz of gold. So, she does not have enough for the pendant.

You can estimate the sum or difference of mixed numbers by rounding to the nearest whole number.

Example   Estimate the sum.

$2\frac{1}{8} \longrightarrow$ 2 $\frac{1}{8}$ is less than $\frac{1}{2}$.

$1\frac{3}{4} \longrightarrow$ 2 $\frac{3}{4}$ is greater than $\frac{1}{2}$.

$+ 2\frac{3}{5} \longrightarrow$ $+ 3$ $\frac{3}{5}$ is greater than $\frac{1}{2}$.

$\overline{\phantom{+ 2\frac{3}{5}}}$ $\overline{}$
   7

Talk About It

▶ What is the advantage of estimating over finding an exact answer?

 Idea Bank, page 491, Exercise 9

Check for Understanding

Tell whether the fraction is closest to 0, $\frac{1}{2}$, or 1.

1. $\frac{1}{5}$ 2. $\frac{2}{9}$ 3. $\frac{4}{5}$ 4. $\frac{11}{20}$ 5. $\frac{7}{13}$ 6. $\frac{1}{8}$

Estimate the sum or difference.

7. $\frac{1}{5} + \frac{2}{4}$ 8. $\frac{7}{10} - \frac{3}{12}$ 9. $5\frac{1}{4} - 3\frac{3}{10}$ 10. $6\frac{2}{7} + 4\frac{3}{8}$

Practice

Choose the best estimate. Write **a**, **b**, or **c**.

11. $\frac{7}{8} + \frac{5}{6}$ **a.** 1   **b.** 2   **c.** $\frac{1}{2}$

12. $\frac{12}{13} - \frac{3}{7}$ **a.** $\frac{1}{2}$ **b.** 0   **c.** 2

13. $5\frac{1}{7} + 3\frac{2}{9}$ **a.** 10   **b.** 8   **c.** 6

14. $8\frac{5}{8} + 4\frac{2}{9} - 3\frac{12}{14}$ **a.** 15   **b.** 7   **c.** 9

Estimate the sum or difference.

15. $\frac{16}{30} + \frac{3}{4}$ 16. $\frac{5}{8} - \frac{1}{5}$ 17. $\frac{7}{15} + \frac{15}{16}$ 18. $\frac{9}{10} - \frac{7}{8}$

19. $9\frac{7}{8} - 4\frac{3}{5}$ 20. $3\frac{3}{4} + 3\frac{2}{3}$ 21. $7\frac{1}{3} + 4\frac{1}{6}$ 22. $5\frac{4}{9} - 1\frac{4}{5}$

23. $\frac{7}{8} + \frac{7}{12} + \frac{8}{10}$ 24. $2\frac{1}{3} + 5\frac{7}{12} + 6\frac{4}{5}$ 25. $10\frac{1}{2} - 3\frac{1}{3} - \frac{3}{4}$ 26. $1\frac{2}{3} - \frac{4}{5} - \frac{1}{4}$

Mixed Applications

27. Eve used $2\frac{1}{3}$ oz of stone for a necklace and $\frac{5}{8}$ oz of stone for a bracelet. About how much more stone did she use for the necklace?

28. Three pieces of jewelry contain $2\frac{1}{3}$ oz, $1\frac{7}{8}$ oz, and $2\frac{3}{8}$ oz of silver. About how much silver is in the three pieces of jewelry?

29. **Visual Thinking** What fraction of the figure is shaded?

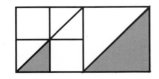

30. **Mental Math** Patrick got the sum $\frac{12}{14}$ when he added the fractions $\frac{7}{8}$ and $\frac{5}{6}$. Was his answer reasonable? Why or why not?

Is an estimate of 6 for $2\frac{1}{5} + 4\frac{1}{4}$ greater than or less than the actual sum? Explain.

ADDING FRACTIONS
and Mixed Numbers

Courtney makes candles. She is working with one candle mold that holds $\frac{2}{3}$ lb of wax and a second candle mold that holds $\frac{1}{2}$ lb. How much wax does Courtney need to fill both molds?

Estimate. $\frac{2}{3} + \frac{1}{2} \rightarrow 1 + \frac{1}{2}$, or $1\frac{1}{2}$

Find the exact sum. Use the LCD to write equivalent fractions.

$$\begin{array}{r} \frac{2}{3} = \frac{4}{6} \\ + \frac{1}{2} = \frac{3}{6} \\ \hline \frac{7}{6}, \text{ or } 1\frac{1}{6} \end{array}$$

Since $1\frac{1}{6}$ is close to the estimate, the answer is reasonable. So, Courtney needs $1\frac{1}{6}$ lb of wax.

Another Example Courtney is going to make red and green candles. She plans to use $2\frac{1}{4}$ lb of red wax and $1\frac{7}{8}$ lb of green wax. How much colored wax does Courtney need in all?

Estimate. $2 + 2 = 4$

Step 1 Use the LCD to write equivalent fractions.	**Step 2** Add the fractions. Add the whole numbers.	**Step 3** Rewrite the sum.
$2\frac{1}{4} = 2\frac{2}{8}$ $+ 1\frac{7}{8} = 1\frac{7}{8}$	$\begin{array}{r} 2\frac{1}{4} = 2\frac{2}{8} \\ + 1\frac{7}{8} = 1\frac{7}{8} \\ \hline 3\frac{9}{8} \end{array}$	$\begin{array}{r} 2\frac{2}{8} \\ + 1\frac{7}{8} \\ \hline 3\frac{9}{8} = 4\frac{1}{8} \end{array}$

So, Courtney needs $4\frac{1}{8}$ lb of colored wax.

Check for Understanding

Find the sum.

1. $\frac{3}{4} + \frac{2}{4}$

2. $\frac{1}{5} + \frac{2}{5}$

3. $\frac{2}{3} + \frac{4}{5}$

4. $\frac{1}{2} + \frac{2}{3}$

5. $\frac{5}{6} + \frac{3}{4}$

6. $1\frac{1}{5} + 3\frac{3}{5}$

7. $2\frac{5}{6} + 3\frac{2}{3}$

8. $1\frac{1}{4} + 2\frac{7}{8}$

9. $6\frac{3}{5} + 2\frac{7}{10}$

10. $5\frac{2}{3} + 3\frac{1}{9}$

Practice

Find the sum. Write the answer in simplest form.

11. $\quad \frac{1}{4}$ **12.** $\quad \frac{7}{8}$ **13.** $\quad \frac{2}{3}$ **14.** $\quad \frac{5}{9}$ **15.** $\quad \frac{4}{7}$ **16.** $\quad \frac{4}{5}$

$\qquad +\frac{2}{4} \qquad\quad +\frac{1}{6} \qquad\quad +\frac{7}{9} \qquad\quad +\frac{2}{5} \qquad\quad +\frac{1}{2} \qquad\quad +\frac{3}{8}$

17. $\quad \frac{3}{8}$ **18.** $\quad \frac{2}{5}$ **19.** $\quad \frac{4}{5}$ **20.** $\quad 7\frac{1}{9}$ **21.** $\quad 4\frac{1}{6}$ **22.** $\quad 3\frac{5}{16}$

$\qquad +\frac{1}{2} \qquad\quad +\frac{1}{3} \qquad\quad +\frac{3}{4} \qquad\quad +5\frac{3}{9} \qquad\quad +2\frac{2}{5} \qquad\quad +11\frac{3}{4}$

23. $\quad 14$ **24.** $\quad 4\frac{2}{5}$ **25.** $\quad 2\frac{6}{7}$ **26.** $\quad 9\frac{2}{3}$ **27.** $\quad 6\frac{1}{4}$ **28.** $\quad 10$

$\qquad +\ 2\frac{5}{6} \qquad\quad +4\frac{1}{4} \qquad\quad +1\frac{1}{5} \qquad\quad +8\frac{1}{4} \qquad\quad +5\frac{5}{6} \qquad\quad +\ 9\frac{7}{8}$

Mixed Applications

29. Marion needs $4\frac{1}{2}$ hr to fill her candle molds and remove the cooled candles. She needs $1\frac{1}{5}$ hr to clean her molds and tools. How long does Marion need for the entire process?

30. Logical Reasoning If the value of $\frac{a}{8} + \frac{b}{8}$ is less than 1, how does the value of $a + b$ compare with 8? Explain.

31. Number Sense Show two ways to find the sum of 3.5 and 4.5, using fractions.

MATH CONNECTION

Some calculators operate with fractions as well as with whole numbers and decimals. The example shows how you can use one of these calculators to add $\frac{5}{6}$ and $1\frac{1}{2}$.

32. Why do you think the (Unit) key was used?

33. What did pressing the (Simp) key do? the (Ab/c) key?

34. What is the sum of $\frac{5}{6}$ and $1\frac{1}{2}$?

35. Show the key sequence you think you would use on this calculator to find $3\frac{1}{3} + 3\frac{4}{5}$.

Keys	Display
5 (/) 6	5/6
(+) 1 (Unit) 1 (/) 2	+ 1ᴜ1/2
(=)	1ᴜ8/6
(Simp) (=)	1ᴜ4/3
(Ab/c)	2ᴜ1/3

Can you use a denominator other than 6 to add $\frac{2}{3}$ and $\frac{1}{6}$? Explain.

WRAP UP...

SUBTRACTING FRACTIONS
and Mixed Numbers

Cary Barnett is a plumber. He needs
a piece of pipe that is $2\frac{3}{4}$ in. long. His
only piece of pipe is $3\frac{1}{2}$ in. long. How
much pipe will he have left after he
cuts off the length that he needs?

Estimate. $3\frac{1}{2} - 2\frac{3}{4} \rightarrow 4 - 3 = 1$

Then find the exact difference.

Step 1 Use the LCD to write equivalent fractions.	**Step 2** Rename $3\frac{2}{4}$ as $2\frac{6}{4}$. Subtract.
$3\frac{1}{2} = 3\frac{2}{4}$ $-\,2\frac{3}{4} = 2\frac{3}{4}$	$3\frac{2}{4} = 2\frac{6}{4}$ $-\,2\frac{3}{4} = 2\frac{3}{4}$ <div align=right>$\frac{3}{4}$</div>

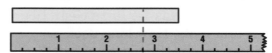

So, Cary will have $\frac{3}{4}$ in. of pipe left.

More Examples

A.
$$\frac{5}{6} = \frac{5}{6}$$
$$-\,\frac{1}{3} = \frac{2}{6}$$
$$\frac{3}{6} = \frac{1}{2}$$

B.
$$6\frac{2}{5} = 6\frac{12}{30} = 5\frac{42}{30}$$
$$-\,2\frac{5}{6} = 2\frac{25}{30} = 2\frac{25}{30}$$
$$3\frac{17}{30}$$

C.
$$12\quad = 11\frac{9}{9}$$
$$-\quad 4\frac{2}{9} = \quad4\frac{2}{9}$$
$$7\frac{7}{9}$$

Talk About It

▶ In Example **B,** why is it necessary to rename $6\frac{2}{5}$?

▶ In Example **C,** why is 12 renamed as $11\frac{9}{9}$?

Check for Understanding

Tell whether you need to rename in order to subtract. Answer *yes* or *no*.
Then find the difference.

1. $3\frac{1}{2} - 1\frac{1}{2}$ **2.** $2\frac{2}{5} - \frac{7}{10}$ **3.** $8\frac{9}{16} - 5\frac{3}{4}$ **4.** $4\frac{3}{15} - 1\frac{3}{5}$

Practice

Find the difference. Write the answer in simplest form.

5. $\dfrac{5}{8}$
$-\dfrac{3}{8}$

6. $\dfrac{9}{10}$
$-\dfrac{3}{10}$

7. $\dfrac{4}{5}$
$-\dfrac{1}{3}$

8. $\dfrac{3}{4}$
$-\dfrac{2}{5}$

9. $\dfrac{9}{10}$
$-\dfrac{3}{5}$

10. $\dfrac{7}{9}$
$-\dfrac{2}{3}$

11. $7\dfrac{8}{16}$
$-2\dfrac{4}{16}$

12. $4\dfrac{7}{8}$
$-1\dfrac{3}{8}$

13. $7\dfrac{2}{3}$
$-5\dfrac{3}{8}$

14. 100
$-16\dfrac{2}{3}$

15. $3\dfrac{3}{4}$
$-1\dfrac{1}{3}$

16. $12\dfrac{1}{9}$
$-8\dfrac{1}{4}$

17. $6 - 3\dfrac{5}{8}$

18. $\dfrac{5}{6} - \dfrac{1}{2}$

19. $32\dfrac{4}{7} - 12$

20. $9\dfrac{3}{7} - 4\dfrac{1}{6}$

Complete.

21. $4\dfrac{4}{5} - 2\dfrac{\blacksquare}{5} = 2\dfrac{1}{5}$

22. $\dfrac{5}{8} + \dfrac{\blacksquare}{8} = 1$

23. $\dfrac{5}{6} - \dfrac{\blacksquare}{\blacksquare} = \dfrac{2}{3}$

24. $1\dfrac{3}{\blacksquare} + 3\dfrac{1}{2} = 5$

Solve. Write the answer in simplest form.

25. $\dfrac{7}{6} - \dfrac{1}{3} - \dfrac{1}{2}$

26. $20\dfrac{1}{3} - 3\dfrac{1}{6} - \dfrac{2}{9}$

27. $\dfrac{2}{3} + \dfrac{1}{6} - \dfrac{1}{4}$

28. $\dfrac{4}{5} - \dfrac{3}{10} + \dfrac{1}{2}$

Mixed Applications

The table shows the number of hours Carl Barnett worked last week.
Use the table for Exercises 29–31.

29. How much longer did Carl work on Monday than on Tuesday?

30. How much longer did Carl work on Thursday than on Wednesday?

31. Carl earns $18 per hour as a plumber. About how much did he earn last week?

Time Worked Last Week	
Day	**Hours**
Monday	$10\dfrac{1}{2}$
Tuesday	$9\dfrac{2}{3}$
Wednesday	$11\dfrac{1}{4}$
Thursday	$12\dfrac{2}{5}$

MIXED REVIEW

Compare. Write $<$, $>$, or $=$.

1. $45.2 \; \bullet \; 45.24$

2. $0.251 \; \bullet \; 0.215$

3. $\dfrac{2}{3} \; \bullet \; \dfrac{5}{6}$

4. $2\dfrac{1}{2} \; \bullet \; 2\dfrac{3}{5}$

Estimate the sum or difference.

5. $3{,}425 + 1{,}836$

6. $3\dfrac{1}{3} + 4\dfrac{4}{5}$

7. $8.56 - 3.14$

8. $9\dfrac{7}{8} - 4\dfrac{4}{5}$

Explain the steps you would follow to subtract $3\dfrac{3}{4}$ from $8\dfrac{1}{3}$.

WRAP UP...

PROBLEM Solving

Melissa works at the Frame Shop. She is making a frame for a painting. The painting is $12\frac{1}{2}$ in. high and $18\frac{1}{4}$ in. wide. The width of the frame is $2\frac{3}{8}$ in. What will be the size of the framed painting?

Sometimes, it is easier to solve a problem if you draw a picture. The picture will help you visualize the solution.

▶ **UNDERSTAND**

What are you asked to find?
What facts are given?

▶ **PLAN**

How will you solve the problem?
You can *draw a picture* of the painting and the frame. Label the picture clearly with the dimensions given in the problem.

What will you do to find the total width and height of the framed painting?

Total width = width of painting + width of frame + width of frame

Total height = height of painting + width of frame + width of frame

▶ **SOLVE**

What numbers will you use to find the total width and height of the framed painting?

Total width = $18\frac{1}{4} + 2\frac{3}{8} + 2\frac{3}{8} = 18\frac{2}{8} + 4\frac{6}{8} = 23$

Total height = $12\frac{1}{2} + 2\frac{3}{8} + 2\frac{3}{8} = 12\frac{4}{8} + 4\frac{6}{8} = 17\frac{1}{4}$

So, the framed painting will be 23 in. wide and $17\frac{1}{4}$ in. high.

▶ **LOOK BACK**

How can you check your answer?

WHAT IF... . . . Melissa uses a frame that is $1\frac{7}{8}$ in. wide? What will be the size of the framed painting?

Apply

Draw a picture to solve the problem.

(1) For a display Melissa is going to hang a painting that is 25 in. wide in the center of a wall that is 97 in. wide. How much wall space should she leave on each side of the painting?

(2) The Frame Shop is putting a new tile floor in the workroom. The workroom floor is 144 in. long and 96 in. wide. The side of each square tile is 8 in. How many tiles are needed?

Mixed Applications ⟩ **STRATEGIES** • Draw a Picture • Guess and Check • Write an Equation • Use Estimation

Choose a strategy and solve.

(3) The owner of the Frame Shop spent $57 for 120 lb of nails. The owner bought some 10-lb bags for $6 each and some 20-lb bags for $9 each. How many 20-lb bags did the owner buy?

(4) During her lunch break, Melissa walked 8 blocks north, 4 blocks east, and 5 blocks south. She then walked 2 blocks west and 3 blocks south. How many blocks west did she walk to get back where she started?

(5) Timothy works part-time at the Frame Shop. He worked $4\frac{1}{6}$ hr on Monday, $5\frac{2}{3}$ hr on Tuesday, and $3\frac{1}{2}$ hr on Thursday. About how many hours did he work in all?

(6) Timothy framed 74 pictures this week. This is 13 more than the number of pictures he framed last week. How many pictures did he frame last week?

(7) The Frame Shop has entered four employees in a charity race. Timothy is 20 blocks behind Melissa, Melissa is 45 blocks ahead of Karen, and Karen is 10 blocks behind Tom. How far behind Timothy is Tom?

(8) A customer gave Melissa $2.75 in dimes and nickels. There were 5 more dimes than nickels. How many of each coin were there?

WRITER'S CORNER

(9) Write a problem similar to Exercise 7. Have a classmate draw and label a picture for your problem and then solve the problem.

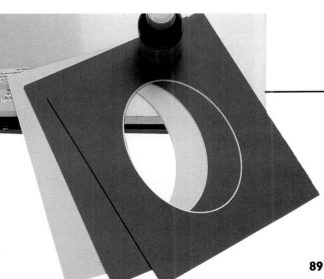

Vocabulary Check

Choose a word or words from the box to complete each sentence.

composite
equivalent
prime
prime factorization
simplest form

1. A whole number that has exactly two whole-number factors, itself and 1, is a __?__ number. *(page 68)*

2. Every composite number can be shown as the product of prime factors. This product is called the __?__ of the number. *(page 68)*

3. A whole number that has more than two whole-number factors is a __?__ number. *(page 68)*

4. Fractions that name the same amount are __?__ fractions. *(page 74)*

5. When you divide the numerator and the denominator of a fraction by their GCF, the resulting fraction is in __?__. *(page 74)*

Concept Check

Write *prime* or *composite* for the number. *(page 68)*

6. 11 **7.** 32 **8.** 41 **9.** 56 **10.** 77

Write the GCF of the numerator and denominator. *(page 74)*

11. $\frac{6}{8}$ **12.** $\frac{12}{15}$ **13.** $\frac{24}{42}$ **14.** $\frac{8}{32}$ **15.** $\frac{45}{21}$

Write two equivalent fractions for each fraction. *(page 74)*

16. $\frac{2}{3}$ **17.** $\frac{5}{8}$ **18.** $\frac{2}{7}$ **19.** $\frac{12}{15}$ **20.** $\frac{20}{8}$

Tell whether the fraction is closest to 0, $\frac{1}{2}$, or 1. *(page 82)*

21. $\frac{4}{5}$ **22.** $\frac{1}{8}$ **23.** $\frac{4}{9}$ **24.** $\frac{8}{10}$ **25.** $\frac{2}{5}$

Tell whether you need to rename in order to subtract. Write *yes* or *no*. *(page 86)*

26. $2\frac{2}{3} - 1\frac{1}{4}$ **27.** $5\frac{3}{9} - 3\frac{4}{5}$ **28.** $8\frac{1}{2} - 4\frac{5}{6}$ **29.** $4\frac{3}{4} - 1\frac{2}{5}$

Skill Check

Write the prime factorization, using exponents. *(page 68)*

30. 12 **31.** 18 **32.** 120 **33.** 81 **34.** 75

Write as a whole number or a mixed number. *(page 74)*

35. $\frac{8}{3}$ **36.** $\frac{17}{5}$ **37.** $\frac{12}{6}$ **38.** $\frac{35}{10}$ **39.** $\frac{62}{8}$

Write as a fraction. *(page 74)*

40. $1\frac{2}{5}$ **41.** $4\frac{3}{8}$ **42.** $7\frac{1}{3}$ **43.** $2\frac{2}{7}$ **44.** $12\frac{3}{4}$

Compare. Write $<$, $>$, or $=$. *(page 78)*

45. $\frac{1}{2} \bullet \frac{3}{5}$ **46.** $\frac{2}{3} \bullet \frac{4}{6}$ **47.** $\frac{3}{8} \bullet \frac{3}{6}$ **48.** $\frac{2}{7} \bullet \frac{4}{15}$

Estimate the sum or difference. *(page 82)*

49. $\frac{1}{4} + \frac{8}{9}$ **50.** $\frac{6}{8} - \frac{7}{12}$ **51.** $4\frac{1}{5} - 1\frac{3}{4}$ **52.** $12\frac{7}{8} + 5\frac{2}{5}$

Find the sum or difference. *(pages 84, 86)*

53. $\frac{3}{5} + \frac{1}{3}$ **54.** $\frac{1}{2} - \frac{1}{8}$ **55.** $3\frac{5}{6} - 1\frac{3}{8}$ **56.** $8\frac{1}{3} + 3\frac{3}{4}$

57. $4 - 2\frac{2}{7}$ **58.** $\frac{4}{5} + \frac{5}{6}$ **59.** $7\frac{1}{4} - 3\frac{3}{5}$ **60.** $5\frac{3}{8} + 4\frac{3}{4}$

61. Mark divided 15 quarters and 27 nickels among his sisters. Each sister received the same number of quarters and nickels. What is the greatest number of sisters that Mark can have? *(page 70)*

62. Lisa works every third day, and Rick works every fifth day. They are both working today. How many days will pass before both will again be working on the same day? *(page 70)*

Problem-Solving Check

Monica drives a six-year-old car to work. The car needs $350 in repairs. Monica is considering these options. Use these options for Exercises 63–64. *(page 72)*

Option 1: have the car repaired and pay for the repairs with savings

Option 2: have the car repaired and pay for the repairs at the rate of $65 a month for 6 months

63. Suppose Monica chooses Option 2. How much will she spend for the repairs?

64. Suppose Monica chooses Option 1. Give one advantage and one disadvantage of this choice.

65. Gordon is putting a fence around his yard. The yard is 100 ft wide and 125 ft long. How much fence will he need for the yard? *(page 88)*

66. In a cross-country race, Mike is 20 m behind John and 6 m behind Sue. Ed is 5 m ahead of Sue. How far behind John is Ed? *(page 88)*

Write *prime* or *composite* for each number.

1. 17   **2.** 24   **3.** 99

Write the prime factorization, using exponents.

4. 42   **5.** 72   **6.** 150

Write the fraction in simplest form.

7. $\frac{10}{15}$ **8.** $\frac{30}{48}$ **9.** $\frac{8}{24}$ **10.** $\frac{40}{25}$

Compare. Write $<$, $>$, or $=$.

11. $\frac{1}{5} \bullet \frac{2}{9}$ **12.** $1\frac{4}{7} \bullet \frac{10}{7}$ **13.** $\frac{1}{3} \bullet \frac{4}{9}$

Estimate the sum or difference.

14. $\frac{5}{8} + \frac{5}{6}$ **15.** $2\frac{3}{4} + 1\frac{5}{6}$ **16.** $7\frac{1}{4} - 3\frac{3}{5}$ **17.** $7\frac{3}{4} - 6\frac{2}{3}$

18. $\frac{2}{3} + \frac{3}{4}$ **19.** $1\frac{1}{8} + 4\frac{1}{3}$ **20.** $\frac{8}{9} - \frac{1}{5}$ **21.** $9\frac{2}{3} - 4\frac{1}{6}$

Find the sum or difference.

22. $\frac{2}{7} + \frac{2}{3}$ **23.** $5\frac{1}{5} + 2\frac{1}{3}$ **24.** $15 - 3\frac{2}{3}$ **25.** $3\frac{1}{4} - 2\frac{2}{5}$

26. $\frac{1}{4} + \frac{2}{3}$ **27.** $2\frac{1}{5} + 3\frac{1}{2}$ **28.** $\frac{7}{8} - \frac{1}{3}$ **29.** $5\frac{3}{5} - 2\frac{9}{10}$

Solve.

30. A 60-ft wire and a 150-ft wire are being cut to make guy wires. Each guy wire is to be the same length. Each wire is to be cut into equal lengths. What is the longest length that can be cut for each guy wire?

31. A truck is $6\frac{1}{2}$ ft wide. It is driven in the center of a bridge that is 8 ft wide. Find the space on either side of the truck.

32. Jason is going to buy some new cassette tapes. He can choose between 4 tapes at Store A for $15.92 and 3 tapes at Store B for $11.55. Which choice will cost him the least per tape?

33. Cami rode her bicycle 3 mi south, 5 mi west, 2 mi north, 4 mi east, and then 1 mi north. How far is Cami from her starting point?

Teamwork P·R·O·J·E·C·T

TAKE · A · SURVEY

What kind of a career would you like to pursue? Imagine becoming an ice cream taster, an animal talent agent, a fragrance sniffer, or a toy tester.

Work with your teammates to prepare a career survey that can be used with the students in your school.

DECIDE

As a team, discuss the careers you want to list in your survey. Decide the number of careers you are going to put on the list.

Discuss how many students will be surveyed. The number of students should be less than 200.

Discuss how you are going to record the responses to your survey, and how you are going to display the data.

SHARE

Compare your team's results with those of other teams.

DO

Make copies of your list of careers so that each member of the team has a copy.

As a team, survey the number of students you decided to use. Record the choices.

When you have finished the survey, combine all the results and display the data.

TALK ABOUT IT

- Did any student choose a career that was not on your list?
- Suppose you wanted to survey 1,000 students. How long would it take?

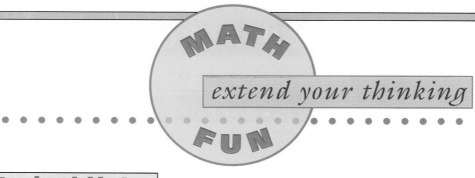

Historical Note

Unit Fractions

The Rhind Papyrus is an ancient Egyptian handbook of mathematics. In the Rhind Papyrus are examples of how the Egyptians expressed all fractions, except $\frac{2}{3}$, as the sums of unit fractions. A **unit fraction** is a fraction with 1 as the numerator.

Using the diagrams, express each unit fraction as the sum of unlike unit fractions, as shown in Exercise 1. Check your answers by adding the fractions.

1. One half of the 2-by-3 rectangle is shaded. The shaded region is separated into parts representing $\frac{1}{6}$ and $\frac{1}{3}$. Check that $\frac{1}{2} = \frac{1}{6} + \frac{1}{3}$.

   $\leftarrow \frac{1}{2} = \frac{1}{6} + \frac{1}{3}$

2. In this 3-by-4 rectangle, $\frac{1}{3}$ of the region is shaded.

   $\frac{1}{3} = \frac{1}{12} + \frac{1}{\blacksquare}$

   $\leftarrow \frac{1}{3}$

3. In this 4-by-5 rectangle, $\frac{1}{4}$ of the region is shaded.

   $\frac{1}{4} = \frac{1}{\blacksquare} + \frac{1}{\blacksquare}$

   $\leftarrow \frac{1}{4}$

4. Draw a 7-by-8 rectangle, and shade $\frac{1}{7}$ of it. Then write $\frac{1}{7}$ as the sum of $\frac{1}{56}$ and another unit fraction.

5. Using your answers to Exercises 1 and 2, write $\frac{1}{2}$ as the sum of three different unit fractions.

☆ ☆ ☆ ☆ ☆ ☆

CHALLENGE

Number Sense

Find two whole numbers, a and b, such that $a \times b = 10,000$ and neither a nor b has zero as a digit.

CHALLENGE

Number Sense

Show how to write twelve thousand, twelve hundred twelve in standard form.

Write the letter of the correct answer.

1. Which expression means 3 times a number?

   A. $3n$ B. $n + 3$

   C. $\frac{n}{3}$ D. $n - 3$

2. What is $\frac{24}{40}$ written in simplest form?

   A. $\frac{12}{20}$ B. $\frac{1}{2}$

   C. $\frac{3}{5}$ D. $1\frac{2}{5}$

3. Solve. $\frac{x}{5} = 35$

   A. $x = 7$ B. $x = 175$

   C. $x = 40$ D. $x = 30$

4. What is $3\frac{2}{5}$ written as a fraction?

   A. $\frac{15}{5}$ B. $\frac{13}{5}$

   C. $\frac{17}{5}$ D. $\frac{5}{17}$

5. Find the value of 12^3.

   A. 144   B. 1,728

   C. 36   D. 177,147

6. Which fraction is less than $\frac{1}{3}$?

   A. $\frac{1}{4}$ B. $\frac{3}{4}$

   C. $\frac{3}{9}$ D. not here

7. Solve. $6.4n = 32$

   A. $n = 204.8$ B. $n = 50$

   C. $n = 0.5$ D. not here

8. $12 + \frac{36}{4} \times 3$

   A. 36   B. 63

   C. 45   D. 39

9. Which is the value of $n + 6$ when $n = 8$?

   A. 14   B. 48

   C. 2   D. $1\frac{1}{4}$

10. Which is an underestimate for $7,560 + 3,256$?

    A. 11,000   B. 13,000

    C. 10,900   D. 10,000

11. Tasha works at a grocery store 3 days each week. The distance from her house to the store is 6.8 mi. How many miles does she travel each week going to and from work?

    A. 20.4 mi   B. 13.6 mi

    C. 81.6 mi   D. 40.8 mi

12. The Cougars have the football on their 10-yard-line. In the next four plays, they gain 13 yd, lose 8 yd, gain 12 yd, and gain 3 yd. Where is the football at the end of the fourth play?

    A. 20-yard-line   B. 46-yard-line

    C. 30-yard-line   D. 36-yard-line

CHAPTER

4

USING FRACTIONS

Did you know . . .

. . . that tomato seeds orbited the earth for $5\frac{1}{2}$ years on NASA's Long Duration Exposure Facility?

Of the tomato seeds brought back from space, 12.5 million were given to students and schools to study. What would you need to know in order to find what fraction of the 12.5 million seeds were given to eighth-grade students?

Explain why you would estimate the product of two fractions.

Rebecca's garden has $3\frac{1}{4}$ rows of lettuce. She wants to plant $1\frac{2}{3}$ times as many rows of tomatoes. About how many rows of tomato plants does Rebecca want to plant?

Estimate the product $1\frac{2}{3} \times 3\frac{1}{4}$.

The same methods that you used to estimate the sum or difference of fractions can be used to estimate a product.

$$3\frac{1}{4} \quad \text{rounds to} \quad 3$$
$$\underline{\times 1\frac{2}{3}} \quad \text{rounds to} \quad \underline{\times 2}$$
$$6 \longleftarrow \text{estimate}$$

So, Rebecca wants to plant about 6 rows of tomato plants.

When you estimate products with fractions and mixed numbers, you can determine whether the estimates are overestimates, underestimates, or close estimates.

More Examples Estimate the product.

A. $1\frac{7}{8} \times 6\frac{5}{6}$

$\downarrow \qquad \downarrow$

$2 \ \times \ 7 = 14$

Both rounded factors are greater than the exact factors. So, the estimate is an **overestimate.**

B. $\frac{3}{5} \times 4\frac{2}{7}$

$\downarrow \qquad \downarrow$

$\frac{1}{2} \times \ 4 = 2$

Both rounded factors are less than the exact factors. So, the estimate is an **underestimate.**

C. $\frac{5}{6} \times \frac{7}{10}$

$\downarrow \qquad \downarrow$

$1 \ \times \ \frac{1}{2} = \frac{1}{2}$

One rounded factor is greater than the exact factor, and the other is less. So, the estimate is a **close estimate.**

Check for Understanding

Estimate the product. Tell whether the estimate is an *underestimate,* an *overestimate,* or a *close estimate.*

1. $\frac{2}{5} \times \frac{5}{6}$

2. $\frac{7}{12} \times \frac{4}{5}$

3. $2\frac{1}{6} \times 3\frac{1}{4}$

4. $4\frac{2}{3} \times 8\frac{7}{8}$

5. $2\frac{1}{4} \times 10\frac{1}{2}$

6. $6\frac{2}{5} \times 7\frac{4}{5}$

7. $1\frac{1}{2} \times 1\frac{1}{3}$

8. $10\frac{1}{5} \times 12\frac{1}{8}$

Practice

Estimate the product.

9. $\frac{3}{7} \times \frac{12}{14}$ **10.** $\frac{5}{6} \times \frac{8}{9}$ **11.** $1\frac{5}{8} \times 2\frac{7}{9}$ **12.** $5\frac{3}{4} \times 1\frac{1}{8}$

13. $4\frac{3}{5} \times 7\frac{3}{8}$ **14.** $\frac{11}{13} \times 12$ **15.** $2\frac{5}{6} \times 6$ **16.** $2\frac{1}{3} \times 5\frac{2}{9}$

17. $\frac{7}{16} \times 3\frac{2}{3}$ **18.** $3\frac{3}{4} \times 2\frac{5}{6}$ **19.** $\frac{1}{3} \times 8\frac{3}{8}$ **20.** $\frac{3}{4} \times 12\frac{1}{6}$

21. $2\frac{1}{5} \times 8 \times 6\frac{2}{3}$ **22.** $1 \times 6\frac{1}{8} \times \frac{7}{16}$ **23.** $3\frac{2}{9} \times 4\frac{2}{3} \times 9\frac{1}{2}$ **24.** $16 \times 2\frac{2}{3} \times \frac{3}{4}$

Estimate the product. Tell whether the estimate is an *underestimate,* an *overestimate,* or a *close estimate.*

25. $\frac{3}{4} \times \frac{8}{10}$ **26.** $1\frac{5}{6} \times 2\frac{6}{8}$ **27.** $9\frac{1}{3} \times 8\frac{7}{8}$ **28.** $6\frac{1}{9} \times 20\frac{3}{8}$

29. $6\frac{2}{9} \times 5\frac{3}{5}$ **30.** $9\frac{6}{7} \times 3\frac{1}{3}$ **31.** $\frac{7}{12} \times 12\frac{3}{7}$ **32.** $2\frac{3}{6} \times 4\frac{3}{9}$

Mixed Applications

33. During the past $9\frac{2}{3}$ months, an irrigation system was used about $\frac{2}{5}$ of the time. About how many months was the irrigation system used?

34. Matt mowed a $340\frac{1}{3}$-ft strip in the meadow. Then he mowed $3\frac{1}{2}$ more strips of the same length. About how long was the total distance that Matt mowed?

35. **Mental Math** Sonia spread mulch for $3\frac{1}{2}$ hr on Friday, $6\frac{2}{3}$ hr on Saturday, and $2\frac{3}{4}$ hr on Monday. She added 3, 6, and 2 to estimate the total number of hours that she worked. Show how she could find a closer estimate of the total number of hours.

36. **Number Sense** Gabriella wants to buy as many tulip bulbs as she can. Last week she bought 50 bulbs for $0.16 each. This week the bulbs are selling at half their former price. Gabriella has $4.00 to spend. How many tulip bulbs can she buy?

Explain how you can find an overestimate and an underestimate for $6\frac{3}{4} \times \frac{2}{3}$.

MULTIPLYING FRACTIONS

Tomasito planted $\frac{3}{4}$ of his garden with watermelons and cantaloupes. Cantaloupes cover $\frac{2}{3}$ of this part of the garden. What part of the whole garden is planted with cantaloupes?

The first fraction square shows 3 one-fourth fraction pieces. The second square shows 2 of those 3 pieces shaded green. This is $\frac{2}{3}$ of $\frac{3}{4}$.

- What fraction of the square is shaded green?

You get the same result when you multiply $\frac{2}{3}$ and $\frac{3}{4}$.

$$\frac{2}{3} \times \frac{3}{4} = \frac{2 \times 3}{3 \times 4} = \frac{6}{12}$$ Multiply the numerators.
Multiply the denominators.

$$= \frac{1}{2}$$ Write in simplest form.

So, $\frac{1}{2}$ of the garden is planted with cantaloupes.

Another Method Sometimes you can simplify before you multiply. You can divide a numerator and a denominator by their GCF.

Examples

A. $\dfrac{3}{\overset{1}{\cancel{6}}} \times \dfrac{\overset{1}{\cancel{5}}}{8} = \dfrac{3}{8}$

B. $\dfrac{\overset{1}{\cancel{2}}}{\underset{1}{\cancel{3}}} \times \dfrac{\overset{3}{\cancel{9}}}{\underset{5}{\cancel{10}}} = \dfrac{3}{5}$

C. $\dfrac{7}{\underset{4}{\cancel{8}}} \times \dfrac{\overset{3}{\cancel{6}}}{1} = \dfrac{21}{4}$, or $5\dfrac{1}{4}$

- What number can you multiply by $\frac{3}{4}$ to get a product of 1? How are $\frac{3}{4}$ and this number related?

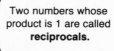
Two numbers whose product is 1 are called **reciprocals.**

- By what number can you multiply any number $\frac{a}{b}$, where a and b are not zero, to get a product of 1?

Check for Understanding

Choose the expression that best describes the circles. Choose **a**, **b**, or **c**.

1.
  a. $\frac{1}{2}$ of $\frac{1}{2}$
  b. $\frac{1}{3}$ of $\frac{1}{2}$
  c. $\frac{2}{3}$ of 1

2.
  a. $\frac{1}{2}$ of $\frac{1}{4}$
  b. $\frac{1}{4}$ of $\frac{4}{6}$
  c. $\frac{1}{2}$ of $\frac{4}{6}$

3. What part of the second circle in Exercise 1 is orange? Write an equation to show the product.

4. What part of the second circle in Exercise 2 is purple? Write an equation to show the product.

Practice

Find the product. Write the product in simplest form.

5. $\frac{6}{8} \times \frac{8}{6}$

6. $\frac{7}{5} \times \frac{5}{7}$

7. $\frac{2}{3} \times \frac{9}{10}$

8. $\frac{9}{4} \times 34$

9. $\frac{14}{5} \times \frac{25}{8}$

10. $\frac{7}{9} \times \frac{9}{7}$

11. $\frac{2}{9} \times 10$

12. $\frac{1}{4} \times \frac{12}{19}$

13. $\frac{2}{9} \times \frac{1}{3}$

14. $\frac{4}{7} \times \frac{8}{9}$

15. $\frac{3}{4} \times \frac{1}{11}$

16. $\frac{2}{3} \times \frac{3}{2}$

17. $\frac{9}{10} \times \frac{35}{36}$

18. $\frac{7}{8} \times \frac{12}{21}$

19. $\frac{2}{5} \times \frac{8}{9}$

20. $\frac{42}{55} \times \frac{25}{28}$

21. $\frac{1}{8} \times \frac{8}{15} \times \frac{5}{3}$

22. $\frac{5}{6} \times \frac{4}{15} \times \frac{2}{3}$

23. $\frac{18}{25} \times \frac{6}{9} \times \frac{15}{24}$

24. $\frac{7}{8} \times \frac{8}{9} \times \frac{9}{21}$

25. Choose the pairs of fractions that have a product of 1.

$\frac{1}{2}$ $\qquad$ $\frac{3}{4}$ $\qquad$ $\frac{8}{9}$ $\qquad$ $\frac{4}{3}$ $\qquad$ $\frac{3}{5}$ $\qquad$ $\frac{5}{1}$ $\qquad$ $\frac{9}{8}$ $\qquad$ $\frac{6}{8}$ $\qquad$ $\frac{2}{1}$

Solve.

26. $\frac{1}{8} \times \left(\frac{3}{4} + \frac{1}{8} \right)$

27. $\frac{3}{10} \times \left(\frac{5}{8} - \frac{1}{2} \right)$

28. $\frac{2}{3} + \frac{1}{2} - \frac{5}{6}$

29. $\frac{4}{10} + \frac{3}{4} \times \frac{1}{2}$

Mixed Applications

30. Crape myrtle shrubs make up $\frac{2}{3}$ of the shrubs in Gwen's yard. Of these, $\frac{1}{3}$ are white. What portion of the shrubs in Gwen's yard are white crape myrtle shrubs?

31. Angela planted $\frac{3}{5}$ of her garden with rosebushes. Of these, $\frac{1}{6}$ were hybrids. What part of Angela's garden was planted with hybrid rosebushes?

32. **Mental Math** Using the numbers 7, 8, 10, 12, 14, 15, 20, and 25, write as many fractions as possible that are equivalent to $\frac{4}{5}$.

33. Look at Exercise 19. What would happen to the product if $\frac{8}{9}$ changed to $\frac{9}{8}$?

MUSIC CONNECTION

In music, the time signature is a fraction that tells how many beats there are per measure and how many beats a whole note gets. In a time signature of $\frac{4}{4}$, there are 4 beats per measure, and a whole note gets 4 beats.

34. In a $\frac{4}{4}$ signature, how many beats does a half note get? (HINT: $\frac{1}{2}$ of $4 = \blacksquare$)

35. In a $\frac{4}{4}$ signature, how many beats does a sixteenth note get?

Explain why you would simplify $\frac{4}{5} \times \frac{7}{8}$ before multiplying.

WRAP UP...

Explain how to change $2\frac{3}{4}$ to a fraction.

MULTIPLYING MIXED NUMBERS

Yesterday Ben watched 5 trailers being loaded with oranges. If each trailer held $2\frac{1}{4}$ tons of oranges, how many tons of oranges were loaded yesterday?

Estimate. $5 \times 2\frac{1}{4} \longrightarrow 5 \times 2 = 10$

Find the exact product.

Step 1 Write each number as a fraction.	**Step 2** Multiply.
$5 \times 2\frac{1}{4} = \frac{5}{1} \times \frac{9}{4}$	$\frac{5}{1} \times \frac{9}{4} = \frac{45}{4}$, or $11\frac{1}{4}$

Since $11\frac{1}{4}$ is close to the estimate, the answer is reasonable. So, $11\frac{1}{4}$ tons of oranges were loaded yesterday.

More Examples

A. $9\frac{3}{5} \times 3\frac{1}{8} = \frac{\overset{6}{\cancel{48}}}{\underset{1}{\cancel{5}}} \times \frac{\overset{5}{\cancel{25}}}{\underset{1}{\cancel{8}}}$

$= \frac{30}{1}$, or 30

B. $7 \times 2\frac{2}{5} = \frac{7}{1} \times \frac{12}{5}$

$= \frac{84}{5}$, or $16\frac{4}{5}$

Another Method You can use a standard calculator to multiply some fractions. The calculator shows the product as a decimal.

Find the product. $\frac{3}{5} \times \frac{9}{10}$

Multiply the denominators.

$5 \boxed{\times} 10 \boxed{=} \boxed{M+} \boxed{^M \quad\quad 50.}$

Multiply the numerators. Divide by the product of the denominators.

$3 \boxed{\times} 9 \boxed{\div} \boxed{MR} \boxed{=} \boxed{^M \quad\quad 0.54}$

$\frac{3}{5} \times \frac{9}{10} = 0.54$

- What is 0.54 written as a fraction in simplest form?

- If you use this calculator procedure to find $\frac{8}{9} \times \frac{3}{4}$, will you get the exact product? Why or why not?

Check for Understanding

Find the product. Write the product in simplest form.

1. $1\frac{1}{2} \times 3\frac{1}{4}$ **2.** $5\frac{1}{6} \times 2\frac{3}{4}$ **3.** $3\frac{3}{4} \times 8$ **4.** $4\frac{8}{9} \times 2\frac{3}{8}$

Practice

Find the product.

5. $1\frac{2}{3} \times 3\frac{1}{2}$

6. $\frac{12}{8} \times 3\frac{1}{4}$

7. $4\frac{3}{4} \times 2\frac{1}{8}$

8. $4\frac{3}{8} \times 8$

9. $\frac{1}{4} \times 6\frac{1}{2}$

10. $2\frac{1}{4} \times 10$

11. $5\frac{1}{2} \times 6\frac{1}{3}$

12. $3\frac{1}{6} \times 12$

13. $3\frac{1}{3} \times \frac{7}{10}$

14. $9\frac{1}{8} \times 4\frac{2}{3}$

15. $\frac{7}{8} \times 6\frac{2}{3}$

16. $8\frac{1}{2} \times 16$

17. $\frac{1}{3} \times 3\frac{3}{5} \times 1\frac{3}{4}$

18. $2\frac{5}{8} \times 2\frac{1}{3} \times 2\frac{2}{7}$

19. $1\frac{1}{9} \times 2\frac{1}{3} \times \frac{15}{21}$

20. $\frac{3}{4} \times 1\frac{2}{3} \times 5\frac{1}{2}$

Use a calculator to find the product for Exercises 21–24.

21. $\frac{4}{5} \times \frac{7}{8}$

22. $\frac{1}{5} \times \frac{3}{4}$

23. $1\frac{4}{5} \times 3\frac{1}{4}$

24. $1\frac{1}{2} \times 2\frac{1}{4}$

25. The product of $4\frac{1}{4} \times 2\frac{1}{2}$ is $10\frac{5}{8}$. Find two other numbers that have a product of $10\frac{5}{8}$.

Mixed Applications

26. Rachel's largest tomato weighs $8\frac{1}{2}$ oz. Steve's largest tomato weighs $1\frac{1}{3}$ times as much as Rachel's. How much does Steve's tomato weigh?

27. Jim worked $2\frac{1}{2}$ times longer on the hybrid plant project than Sarah. Sarah worked on the project for $6\frac{2}{3}$ hours. How many hours did Jim work on the project?

28. **Visual Thinking** Copy the circles below. Then shade the circles to represent $\frac{3}{4} \times \frac{2}{3}$.

29. **Number Sense** Use the Distributive Property to find $6 \times 2\frac{1}{4}$. Do not change the mixed number to a fraction.

30. Find the next term in the sequence: $\frac{3}{5}, \frac{3}{10}, \frac{3}{20}, \cdots$

MIXED REVIEW

Estimate the product.

1. 252×12

2. 12.34×2.88

3. $1{,}106 \times 72$

4. 302×189

5. $3\frac{1}{4} \times 1\frac{1}{6}$

6. $\frac{8}{10} \times \frac{3}{4}$

7. $\frac{7}{9} \times 3\frac{1}{3}$

8. $8\frac{1}{8} \times 7\frac{3}{4}$

Is $3\frac{1}{3} \times 4\frac{1}{2}$ greater than or less than 12? Explain.

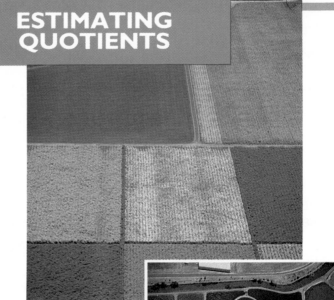

ESTIMATING QUOTIENTS

Recall from dividing with whole
numbers and decimals that when the
divisor is less than the dividend, the
quotient is greater than 1.

$12 \div 6 = 2 \qquad 2 > 1$
$2.5 \div 0.5 = 5 \qquad 5 > 1$

When the divisor is greater than the
dividend, the quotient is less than 1.

$2 \div 5 = 0.4 \qquad 0.4 < 1$
$1.4 \div 7 = 0.2 \qquad 0.2 < 1$

When you divide fractions, you can
use these same rules to determine
whether your exact quotient is
reasonable.

Examples Tell whether the quotient
is less than 1 or greater than 1.

A. $\frac{3}{4} \div \frac{1}{2}$ **Think:** Is $\frac{1}{2}$ less than or greater than $\frac{3}{4}$?
$\frac{1}{2} < \frac{3}{4}$. So, $\frac{3}{4} \div \frac{1}{2} > 1$.

B. $\frac{1}{3} \div \frac{5}{6}$ **Think:** Is $\frac{5}{6}$ less than or greater than $\frac{1}{3}$?
$\frac{5}{6} > \frac{1}{3}$. So, $\frac{1}{3} \div \frac{5}{6} < 1$.

You can use compatible numbers to estimate the quotient of mixed numbers.

Example Katlin plowed $218\frac{1}{2}$ rows in $5\frac{1}{4}$ hours.
About how many rows did she plow in 1 hour?
Estimate the quotient. $218\frac{1}{2} \div 5\frac{1}{4}$

$$200 \div 5 = 40 \quad \text{estimate}$$

So, Katlin plowed about 40 rows in 1 hour.

• What other compatible numbers can you use to estimate $218\frac{1}{2} \div 5\frac{1}{4}$?

More Examples Estimate the quotient.

A. $5\frac{3}{4} \div 2\frac{1}{3}$
$6 \div 2 = 3$

B. $12\frac{5}{8} \div 3\frac{2}{5}$
$12 \div 3 = 4$

C. $3\frac{1}{3} \div 8\frac{2}{3}$
$3 \div 9 = \frac{3}{9} = \frac{1}{3}$

Check for Understanding

Complete. Use $<$ or $>$.

1. $\frac{3}{5} \div \frac{1}{2}$ ● 1
2. $\frac{5}{6} \div \frac{7}{6}$ ● 1
3. $2\frac{1}{2} \div 3\frac{2}{3}$ ● 1
4. $8\frac{1}{6} \div 6\frac{1}{3}$ ● 1

Practice

Tell whether the quotient is less than 1 or greater than 1.

5. $\frac{5}{8} \div \frac{1}{2}$
6. $\frac{3}{4} \div \frac{4}{5}$
7. $\frac{1}{4} \div \frac{1}{16}$
8. $\frac{9}{12} \div \frac{1}{5}$

9. $\frac{7}{9} \div \frac{2}{19}$
10. $\frac{1}{10} \div \frac{4}{5}$
11. $2\frac{1}{3} \div 5\frac{3}{4}$
12. $7\frac{1}{8} \div 3\frac{4}{5}$

Use compatible numbers to estimate the quotient.

13. $7\frac{3}{4} \div 7\frac{2}{3}$
14. $9\frac{5}{6} \div 4\frac{3}{7}$
15. $31\frac{5}{8} \div 15\frac{2}{3}$
16. $18\frac{1}{2} \div 3\frac{4}{5}$

17. $44\frac{3}{4} \div 11$
18. $35\frac{2}{9} \div 9$
19. $7\frac{1}{4} \div 13\frac{8}{9}$
20. $6\frac{2}{5} \div 17\frac{2}{6}$

21. $9\frac{2}{7} \div \frac{7}{6}$
22. $3\frac{2}{3} \div 1\frac{5}{6}$
23. $75\frac{2}{9} \div 24\frac{1}{2}$
24. $4\frac{3}{4} \div 19\frac{1}{8}$

Mixed Applications

25. Tim needs $69\frac{3}{4}$ points in all to win the agriculture award at his school. He has $30\frac{1}{3}$ points now. About how many more points does he need? About how many points does he need to earn in each of the five events left in the competition?

26. Molly thought she used a 1-ft ruler to space some seedlings 1 ft apart in a row that was 5 ft long. However, the ruler she used was 2 in. too short. If she planted a seedling at the beginning of the row, how many seedlings did she plant in all?

VISUAL THINKING

This cube was painted on all sides and then cut into 27 equal-sized cubes. Write as a fraction:

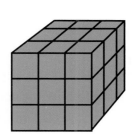

27. the number of smaller cubes painted on only 3 sides.

28. the number of smaller cubes painted on only 2 sides.

29. the number of smaller cubes painted on only 1 side.

30. the number of smaller cubes painted on at least 1 side.

Which is greater, $3\frac{1}{3} \div 2\frac{1}{2}$ or $2\frac{1}{2} \div 3\frac{1}{3}$? Explain.

WRAP UP...

Solve.

1. Celia is hanging wallpaper on one wall of a bedroom. Each strip of wallpaper is 70 cm wide. The wall is 3.8 m wide. How many strips of wallpaper will Celia use?

2. Jamie is fencing a rectangular yard. The length of the yard is 100 m, and the width is 60 m. Each section of fence is 5 m long. How many sections does Jamie need?

3. A bus picked up 2 passengers at the first stop, 4 passengers at the second stop, 7 passengers at the third stop, and 11 passengers at the fourth stop. If the number of passengers picked up continued to increase at the same rate, how many passengers did the bus pick up at the tenth stop?

4. Jose's mother gave him $0.20 for every math homework problem that he did correctly. She took away $0.15 for every problem that he did incorrectly. After he had worked 25 problems, Jose's mother paid him $3.25. How many problems did Jose do correctly?

5. Judy, Ed, and Carmen shared 2 medium pizzas. Judy ate $\frac{3}{8}$ of pizza A and $\frac{1}{4}$ of pizza B. Ed ate $\frac{3}{16}$ of pizza A and $\frac{5}{16}$ of pizza B. Carmen ate $\frac{7}{16}$ of pizza A and $\frac{1}{6}$ of pizza B. Who ate the most pizza?

6. What part of a medium pizza was left after Judy, Ed, and Carmen had finished eating?

Write an algebraic expression for each word expression.

7. twice the number of hours, h

8. three inches more than the width, w

9. the number of dimes, d, divided by 10

10. eight gallons less than the total number of gallons, g

Solve. Write the whole numbers that make the inequality true.

11. $n + 2 < 8$

12. $b - 3 \geq 5$

13. $3p > 27$

14. $\frac{t}{4} < 2$

Compare. Write $<$, $>$, or $=$.

15. $\frac{2}{3} \bullet \frac{3}{4}$

16. $\frac{7}{8} \bullet \frac{5}{6}$

17. $2\frac{1}{3} \bullet \frac{14}{6}$

18. $3\frac{1}{3} \bullet 3\frac{2}{5}$

19. $\frac{1}{4} \bullet \frac{3}{5}$

20. $2\frac{1}{3} \bullet 2\frac{2}{5}$

21. $3\frac{5}{6} \bullet 3\frac{4}{7}$

22. $1\frac{1}{4} \bullet \frac{7}{6}$

Estimate the product or quotient.

23. $\frac{5}{6} \times \frac{6}{7}$

24. $1\frac{2}{3} \times 3\frac{1}{5}$

25. $2\frac{3}{4} \times 8$

26. $\frac{3}{5} \times \frac{9}{10}$

27. $9\frac{3}{5} \div 2\frac{1}{2}$

28. $35\frac{3}{8} \div 3\frac{5}{8}$

29. $2\frac{3}{10} \div 4\frac{1}{6}$

30. $19\frac{2}{3} \div 5\frac{2}{8}$

Spotlight ON PROBLEM SOLVING

Understand
Plan
Solve
Look Back

Discuss the Process

When you are planning to solve a problem, it is often useful to discuss the process used in its solution. Read this problem.

Linda is a floral designer. She wants to use three colors in a particular arrangement of flowers. She has red roses, pink carnations, yellow daisies, blue irises, white chrysanthemums, and green ferns. How many color combinations could Linda use in her arrangement?

Talk About It

Work with a classmate.

a. What is the question?

b. How would you solve the problem?

c. Draw a diagram or make a list to represent the problem.

d. What conclusions can you draw from the diagram or the list?

e. Have you answered the question?

Apply

Brett brought lunch for 35 people at a tree-planting. He has $6\frac{1}{2}$ dozen boiled eggs, 53 hamburger patties, and $3\frac{1}{3}$ dozen hot dogs. The 35 people at the tree-planting shared the eggs, hamburgers, and hot dogs equally.

Discuss the operations needed to solve the problems. Then solve.

1. How many eggs, hamburgers, and hot dogs did each person eat?

2. Was any food left over? If so, how much?

DIVIDING FRACTIONS

Chris has $\frac{3}{4}$ lb of grass seed to spread on the bare spots in his yard. He needs $\frac{1}{8}$ lb of seed for each bare spot. How many spots can Chris cover?

You know that numbers such as 3 and $\frac{1}{3}$ are reciprocals. The table shows that dividing by a number gives the same answer as multiplying by its reciprocal.

Division	Multiplication
$4 \div 2 = 2$	$4 \times \frac{1}{2} = 2$
$9 \div 3 = 3$	$9 \times \frac{1}{3} = 3$
$24 \div 4 = 6$	$24 \times \frac{1}{4} = 6$

When you divide fractions, you can change the division problem into a multiplication problem, using the reciprocal of the divisor.

Find the quotient. $\frac{3}{4} \div \frac{1}{8}$

Think: How many $\frac{1}{8}$'s are in $\frac{3}{4}$?

Step 1	**Step 2**
Write the division problem as a multiplication problem, using the reciprocal of $\frac{1}{8}$. $$\frac{3}{4} \div \frac{1}{8} = \frac{3}{4} \times \frac{8}{1}$$	Multiply. $$\frac{3}{\underset{1}{4}} \times \frac{\overset{2}{8}}{1} = \frac{6}{1}, \text{ or } 6$$

So, Chris can cover 6 spots.

More Examples

A. $\frac{15}{4} \div \frac{3}{2} = \frac{\overset{5}{15}}{\underset{2}{4}} \times \frac{\overset{1}{2}}{\underset{1}{3}}$

$\qquad = \frac{5}{2}$, or $2\frac{1}{2}$

B. $7 \div \frac{4}{5} = \frac{7}{1} \times \frac{5}{4}$

$\qquad = \frac{35}{4}$, or $8\frac{3}{4}$

C. $\frac{3}{8} \div 5 = \frac{3}{8} \times \frac{1}{5}$

$\qquad = \frac{3}{40}$

Talk About It

▶ How can you change $8 \div \frac{3}{4}$ into a multiplication problem, using the reciprocal of $\frac{3}{4}$? Explain.

▶ How can you solve $\frac{15}{4} \div \frac{3}{2}$ without writing a multiplication problem? Explain.

Check for Understanding

Write a multiplication problem for the division problem.

1. $24 \div 3$ **2.** $\frac{3}{9} \div \frac{1}{3}$ **3.** $9 \div \frac{3}{2}$ **4.** $\frac{13}{3} \div 2$ **5.** $\frac{7}{8} \div \frac{1}{3}$

Find the quotient. Write the quotient in simplest form.

6. $\frac{7}{9} \div \frac{3}{4}$ **7.** $\frac{3}{10} \div \frac{7}{5}$ **8.** $\frac{11}{12} \div \frac{1}{6}$ **9.** $\frac{5}{8} \div 10$ **10.** $\frac{6}{7} \div \frac{9}{14}$

Practice

Find the quotient. Write the quotient in simplest form.

11. $\frac{2}{3} \div \frac{4}{5}$ **12.** $\frac{7}{8} \div \frac{3}{4}$ **13.** $\frac{4}{7} \div \frac{7}{12}$ **14.** $\frac{1}{3} \div \frac{5}{9}$ **15.** $\frac{1}{2} \div 2$

16. $18 \div \frac{1}{3}$ **17.** $15 \div \frac{1}{5}$ **18.** $\frac{1}{5} \div 6$ **19.** $\frac{1}{9} \div \frac{8}{21}$ **20.** $\frac{3}{8} \div \frac{3}{8}$

21. $\frac{8}{3} \div \frac{6}{5}$ **22.** $\frac{7}{9} \div \frac{14}{15}$ **23.** $\frac{5}{12} \div \frac{8}{15}$ **24.** $\frac{11}{20} \div \frac{7}{8}$ **25.** $4 \div \frac{2}{9}$

26. Look at Exercise 25. What happens to the quotient if the problem is changed to $\frac{2}{9} \div 4$?

Solve.

27. $\frac{7}{8} - \left(\frac{1}{2} \div \frac{4}{5} \right)$ **28.** $\frac{7}{8} \div \frac{3}{4} \times \frac{6}{7}$ **29.** $\frac{4}{3} \div \frac{4}{5} - \frac{2}{5}$

Mixed Applications

30. How many pieces of twine, each $\frac{5}{12}$ yd long, can be cut from a roll of twine that is 4 yd long? Will there be any twine left over?

31. A threshing machine can thresh $\frac{1}{8}$ of a wheat field in 1 hour. How long will it take the threshing machine to thresh $\frac{6}{10}$ of the wheat field?

32. Logical Reasoning On Monday Terry sold $\frac{1}{2}$ of her tomatoes. On Tuesday she sold $\frac{1}{3}$ of the remaining tomatoes. On Wednesday she sold the 20 tomatoes she had left. How many tomatoes did she sell in all?

33. Number Sense The quotient of $\frac{2}{3} \div \frac{3}{4}$ is $\frac{8}{9}$. Find two other fractions that have a quotient of $\frac{8}{9}$.

Explain how you would find $\frac{2}{3} \div \frac{4}{5}$.

WRAP UP...

PROBLEM Solving

Strategy • Solve a Simpler Problem

There are 12 students planting flower beds. The students work in pairs. Each student is paired with every other student once. How many different pairings are there in all?

Sometimes you can solve a problem that appears to be difficult by solving a simpler problem.

► **UNDERSTAND**

What are you asked to find?

What facts are given?

► **PLAN**

What strategy will you use?

You can use the strategy *solve a simpler problem*. Use a smaller number for the number of students. Then *make a table* to *find a pattern*. Use the pattern to solve the original problem.

► **SOLVE**

How many pairings can be made with 2, 3, and 4 students?

Number of Students	Students Paired	Total Number of Pairings
2	1–2	1
3	1–2, 1–3, 2–3	3, or 1 + 2
4	1–2, 1–3, 1–4, 2–3, 2–4, 3–4	6, or 1 + 2 + 3

What pattern do you see?

Now, use the pattern to solve the original problem.

Number of Students	2	3	4	5	6	7	8	9	10	11	12
Number of Pairings	1	3	6	10	15	21	28	36	45	55	66
Number Added		2	3	4	5	6	7	8	9	10	11

So, there are 66 different pairings for the 12 students.

► **LOOK BACK**

What other strategy can you use to solve the problem?

WHAT IF... . . . there are 14 students planting flower beds? How many different pairings will there be in all?

110

Apply

1 A diagonal of a polygon is a line segment joining 2 vertices that are not next to each other. How many diagonals are in a polygon of 10 sides?

4 sides   5 sides   6 sides

2 There are 7 dots on a sheet of paper. No 3 dots are in a straight line. How many line segments are needed to connect each dot to every other dot?

2 points   3 points   4 points

Mixed Applications   **STRATEGIES**   • Solve a Simpler Problem • Draw a Picture
• Write an Equation • Use Estimation

Choose a strategy and solve.

3 There are 9 people at a garden club meeting. Each person shakes hands with every other person in the room once. Find the total number of handshakes.

4 Jason paid 3 times more for a new garden rake than for a new hose. He paid $16.44 for the rake. How much did he pay for the hose?

5 Martin is putting a fence around a rectangular garden. The garden is 6.2 m wide and 8.7 m long. How much fencing does he need for the garden?

6 Julia paid $45.75 for plants, $12.20 for fertilizer, $68.90 for sod, and $4.52 for flower seeds. About how much did she pay in all?

7 An ant climbs up a pole 5 ft during the day and slides back 4 ft during the night. The pole is 30 ft high. How many days will it take the ant to reach the top of the pole?

8 In how many ways can a group of 10 new players be divided among 3 teams if each team receives at least 1 new player?

WRITER'S CORNER

9 Write a problem needing the same strategy used in Exercise 3. Exchange with a classmate and solve.

10 Write a problem that can be solved by using the strategy *write an equation*. Exchange with a classmate and solve.

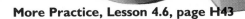

DIVIDING MIXED NUMBERS

Anthony's front yard is $161\frac{1}{2}$ ft wide. He wants to divide this width into $8\frac{1}{2}$-ft sections and plant a maple tree in the center of each section. How many maple trees will he need?

WORK TOGETHER

- What compatible numbers can you use to estimate $161\frac{1}{2} \div 8\frac{1}{2}$? What is your estimate of the quotient?

- To multiply mixed numbers, first change each number to a fraction. Explain why this same procedure should be used when you divide mixed numbers.

- What multiplication problem can you write to solve the problem?

- How many maple trees will Anthony need?

- Is your answer reasonable? Why or why not?

More Examples

A. $15 \div 2\frac{2}{3} = \frac{15}{1} \div \frac{8}{3}$

$\qquad = \frac{15}{1} \times \frac{3}{8}$

$\qquad = \frac{45}{8}$, or $5\frac{5}{8}$

B. $\dfrac{1\frac{3}{5}}{3\frac{3}{4}} = \frac{8}{5} \div \frac{15}{4} = \frac{8}{5} \times \frac{4}{15}$ ◀— $\dfrac{1\frac{3}{5}}{3\frac{3}{4}} = 1\frac{3}{5} \div 3\frac{3}{4}$

$\qquad\qquad\qquad = \frac{32}{75}$

- What compatible numbers would you use to estimate the quotients in Examples **A** and **B**?

- The fraction shown in Example **B** is called a complex fraction. Write Example **A** as a complex fraction.

Check for Understanding

Write a multiplication problem for the division problem, using fractions.

1. $2\frac{1}{2} \div 1\frac{1}{4}$ **2.** $4\frac{2}{3} \div 1\frac{3}{4}$ **3.** $3\frac{5}{6} \div 1\frac{2}{3}$ **4.** $9\frac{2}{3} \div 3\frac{3}{4}$

Find the quotient.

5. $7\frac{1}{3} \div 3\frac{1}{3}$ **6.** $8\frac{1}{2} \div 2\frac{1}{4}$ **7.** $1\frac{7}{8} \div 3\frac{1}{2}$ **8.** $1\frac{5}{6} \div 4\frac{1}{4}$

Practice

Find the quotient.

9. $12\frac{1}{2} \div 8\frac{3}{4}$

10. $5\frac{2}{3} \div 2\frac{1}{4}$

11. $6\frac{7}{8} \div 1\frac{3}{4}$

12. $6\frac{3}{8} \div 4\frac{1}{4}$

13. $2\frac{3}{7} \div 1\frac{4}{7}$

14. $10\frac{1}{20} \div 4\frac{4}{5}$

15. $2\frac{4}{5} \div 6\frac{2}{3}$

16. $5\frac{1}{3} \div \frac{4}{9}$

17. $3\frac{1}{8} \div 2\frac{1}{4}$

18. $2 \div 3\frac{1}{3}$

19. $1\frac{3}{7} \div 5$

20. $1\frac{7}{8} \div 14$

21. $10 \div 4\frac{1}{5}$

22. $24 \div 5\frac{2}{3}$

23. $9\frac{1}{4} \div \frac{1}{8}$

24. $6\frac{9}{10} \div 7\frac{1}{4}$

25. $\dfrac{5}{2\frac{1}{2}}$

26. $\dfrac{10}{3\frac{1}{3}}$

27. $\dfrac{9\frac{1}{3}}{6\frac{3}{5}}$

28. $\dfrac{4\frac{5}{6}}{5\frac{2}{3}}$

29. $\dfrac{1\frac{1}{2}}{4\frac{1}{4}}$

30. $\dfrac{12\frac{3}{4}}{3\frac{1}{5}}$

Mixed Applications

31. Larry bought some plant food that weighed $34\frac{1}{2}$ oz. He divided the plant food into 6 piles of equal weight. How much did each pile weigh?

32. Steffi planted tomato plants in a row that was $5\frac{3}{4}$ ft long. She covered the plants with 5 equal sections of insect netting. How long was each section of netting?

33. **Number Sense** Show the calculator key sequence you can use to find $3\frac{1}{2} \div 1\frac{5}{9}$. (HINT: First write as a multiplication problem.) If you have a calculator that operates with fractions, show the key sequence you can use.

34. **Making Choices** Becca can buy 3 azalea plants at one store for $10.95 or 4 similar azalea plants at another store for $15.80. She wants to buy 12 plants. Where should she buy the plants? Explain.

LOGICAL REASONING • CHALLENGE

35. Fill in each circle with the fractions $\frac{1}{2}$, $\frac{3}{4}$, or $\frac{7}{8}$ so that each row and column forms a true statement. Any of the fractions can be used more than once in any equation. Perform the operations in the sequence given.

$$\bigcirc + \bigcirc - \bigcirc = 1\frac{1}{8}$$
$$+ \quad \times \quad +$$
$$\bigcirc - \bigcirc \div \bigcirc = \frac{1}{2}$$
$$\div \quad \div \quad \div$$
$$\bigcirc \div \bigcirc \times \bigcirc = \frac{3}{7}$$
$$= \qquad = \qquad =$$
$$2\frac{1}{6} \qquad \frac{1}{2} \qquad 2\frac{1}{2}$$

Explain why you change mixed numbers to fractions before you divide.

EQUATIONS WITH FRACTIONS

You can solve equations with fractions and mixed numbers in the same way you solve equations with whole numbers and decimals.

Solve and check. $n + \frac{2}{3} = \frac{5}{6}$

Step 1 Subtract $\frac{2}{3}$ from each side of the equation.	**Step 2** Check the solution. Replace n with $\frac{1}{6}$.
$n + \frac{2}{3} = \frac{5}{6}$	$n + \frac{2}{3} = \frac{5}{6}$
$n + \frac{2}{3} - \frac{2}{3} = \frac{5}{6} - \frac{2}{3}$	$\frac{1}{6} + \frac{2}{3} = \frac{5}{6}$
$n = \frac{5}{6} - \frac{4}{6}$	$\frac{1}{6} + \frac{4}{6} = \frac{5}{6}$
$n = \frac{1}{6}$	$\frac{5}{6} = \frac{5}{6}$

Examples

A.
$$x - 1\frac{1}{4} = 2\frac{1}{3}$$
$$x - 1\frac{1}{4} + 1\frac{1}{4} = 2\frac{1}{3} + 1\frac{1}{4} \qquad \text{Add } 1\frac{1}{4} \text{ to each side.}$$
$$x = 2\frac{4}{12} + 1\frac{3}{12}$$
$$x = 3\frac{7}{12}$$

B.
$$\frac{2}{3}r = 4$$
$$\frac{2}{3}r \div \frac{2}{3} = 4 \div \frac{2}{3} \qquad \text{Divide each side by } \frac{2}{3}.$$
$$r = 4 \times \frac{3}{2}$$
$$r = \frac{12}{2} = 6$$

C. When solving two-step equations, remember that you do addition or subtraction first. Then you do multiplication or division.

$$\frac{b}{4} + 1\frac{1}{5} = 1\frac{4}{5}$$
$$\frac{b}{4} + 1\frac{1}{5} - 1\frac{1}{5} = 1\frac{4}{5} - 1\frac{1}{5} \qquad \text{Subtract } 1\frac{1}{5} \text{ from each side.}$$
$$\frac{b}{4} = \frac{3}{5}$$
$$\frac{4}{1} \times \frac{b}{4} = \frac{3}{5} \times \frac{4}{1} \qquad \text{Multiply each side by 4.}$$
$$b = \frac{12}{5} = 2\frac{2}{5}$$

- **What is the first step in checking the solution of Example C?**

Talk About It

▶ In Example **A** on page 114, would the solution be the same if you changed $1\frac{1}{4}$ and $2\frac{1}{3}$ to fractions with a common denominator in the first step?

▶ In Example **B** on page 114, could you multiply each side by the reciprocal of $\frac{2}{3}$ instead of dividing by $\frac{2}{3}$? Explain.

Remember that you can write equations for some word problems.

Natalie bought fertilizer to use on her tomato plants and squash plants. She used $1\frac{1}{2}$ more pounds of fertilizer on the squash plants than on the tomato plants. She used $2\frac{5}{8}$ lb of fertilizer on the squash plants. How much fertilizer did she use on the tomato plants?

To find the amount of fertilizer Natalie used on the tomato plants, you can write and solve an equation.

Step 1 Choose a variable. Let t = the amount of fertilizer used on the tomato plants. Then $t + 1\frac{1}{2}$ = the amount of fertilizer used on the squash plants.	**Step 2** Write an equation. $t + 1\frac{1}{2} = 2\frac{5}{8}$
Step 3 Solve the equation. Subtract $1\frac{1}{2}$ from each side. $t + 1\frac{1}{2} = 2\frac{5}{8}$ $t + 1\frac{1}{2} - 1\frac{1}{2} = 2\frac{5}{8} - 1\frac{1}{2}$ $t = 2\frac{5}{8} - 1\frac{4}{8}$ $t = 1\frac{1}{8}$	**Step 4** Check the solution. Replace t with $1\frac{1}{8}$. $t + 1\frac{1}{2} = 2\frac{5}{8}$ $1\frac{1}{8} + 1\frac{1}{2} = 2\frac{5}{8}$ $1\frac{1}{8} + 1\frac{4}{8} = 2\frac{5}{8}$ $2\frac{5}{8} = 2\frac{5}{8}$

So, Natalie used $1\frac{1}{8}$ lb of fertilizer on the tomato plants.

Another Example

Mitchell wants to dig a fish pond that will have a length $3\frac{1}{2}$ ft longer than twice the width. He has decided that the length of the pond will be $15\frac{3}{4}$ ft. What will be the width of the pond?

$15\frac{3}{4}$ ft

Step 1 Choose a variable. Let w = the width. Then $2w + 3\frac{1}{2}$ = the length.	**Step 2** Write an equation. $2w + 3\frac{1}{2} = 15\frac{3}{4}$

Step 3
Solve the equation.

$$2w + 3\frac{1}{2} = 15\frac{3}{4}$$

$$2w + 3\frac{1}{2} - 3\frac{1}{2} = 15\frac{3}{4} - 3\frac{1}{2}$$

$$2w = 15\frac{3}{4} - 3\frac{2}{4}$$

$$2w = 12\frac{1}{4}$$

$$\frac{2w}{2} = 12\frac{1}{4} \div 2$$

$$w = \frac{49}{4} \times \frac{1}{2}$$

$$w = \frac{49}{8}, \text{ or } 6\frac{1}{8}$$

Step 4
Check the solution.

$$2w + 3\frac{1}{2} = 15\frac{3}{4}$$

$$2 \times 6\frac{1}{8} + 3\frac{1}{2} = 15\frac{3}{4}$$

$$12\frac{1}{4} + 3\frac{1}{2} = 15\frac{3}{4}$$

$$12\frac{1}{4} + 3\frac{2}{4} = 15\frac{3}{4}$$

$$15\frac{3}{4} = 15\frac{3}{4}$$

So, the width of the pond will be $6\frac{1}{8}$ ft.

Check for Understanding

Tell what you would do to each side of the equation to solve for the variable.

1. $x - \frac{2}{3} = 4$ **2.** $r + \frac{1}{5} = 2\frac{1}{6}$ **3.** $\frac{3}{5}n = \frac{9}{10}$ **4.** $\frac{c}{3} = \frac{7}{8}$

Write the two steps you would use to solve the equation.

5. $2x + \frac{1}{2} = 4\frac{2}{5}$ **6.** $\frac{3}{4}n - 1\frac{3}{5} = \frac{4}{5}$ **7.** $\frac{t}{5} + 2\frac{4}{5} = 5\frac{7}{8}$ **8.** $\frac{d}{\frac{2}{3}} - \frac{3}{8} = 6$

Solve the equation. Check your solution.

9. $b + \frac{2}{5} = 4\frac{3}{5}$ **10.** $a - \frac{3}{4} = 2\frac{7}{8}$ **11.** $\frac{4}{5}n = \frac{3}{8}$ **12.** $3t - 1\frac{1}{2} = 5\frac{2}{3}$

Practice

Solve the equation. Check your solution.

13. $m - \frac{1}{4} = 5\frac{1}{4}$

14. $p + \frac{1}{3} = 4\frac{2}{3}$

15. $5 = r + 4\frac{1}{2}$

16. $v - 7\frac{2}{3} = 12\frac{3}{4}$

17. $\frac{2}{3}p = \frac{1}{6}$

18. $\frac{3}{8}b = 4$

19. $\frac{c}{\frac{2}{3}} = \frac{7}{8}$

20. $\frac{a}{1\frac{1}{4}} = \frac{3}{5}$

21. $n - 9 = \frac{1}{2}$

22. $6a = 2\frac{1}{4}$

23. $\frac{m}{\frac{3}{5}} = 1\frac{1}{9}$

24. $d - 5\frac{3}{5} = 10\frac{2}{3}$

25. $10 = 3\frac{1}{3}t$

26. $4\frac{1}{5} = c + 2\frac{2}{3}$

27. $\frac{r}{4} = 8\frac{3}{5}$

28. $7k = 8\frac{1}{2}$

29. $\frac{3}{5}p + \frac{1}{2} = 5$

30. $\frac{c}{4} + \frac{1}{6} = 2\frac{1}{2}$

31. $\frac{1}{3}c - 1\frac{1}{2} = 4\frac{1}{3}$

32. $\frac{d}{\frac{3}{4}} + 1\frac{1}{4} = 6$

Mixed Applications

Solve. Write an equation for Exercises 33, 34, and 36.

33. Greg picked $3\frac{1}{2}$ more bushels of apples than Ann did. Greg picked $12\frac{1}{4}$ bushels. How many bushels did Ann pick?

34. Judy earned $40 working in Mr. Medina's yard. She worked for $6\frac{1}{4}$ hr. How much did she earn per hour?

35. Find the pattern in this sequence. Then write the next three terms in the sequence.
$2\frac{3}{4}, 2\frac{5}{8}, 2\frac{1}{2}, 2\frac{3}{8}, 2\frac{1}{4}, \ldots$

36. Eric bought 2 bags of corn seed and $3\frac{1}{2}$ lb of grass seed. He bought a total of $15\frac{1}{4}$ lb of seed. How much did each bag of corn seed weigh?

MIXED REVIEW

Compare. Use $<$, $>$, or $=$.

1. 345 ● 354

2. 1.243 ● 1.234

3. 20.4 ● 20.40

4. 9.08 ● 9.8

5. $\frac{2}{3}$ ● $\frac{3}{5}$

6. $4\frac{1}{4}$ ● $4\frac{3}{12}$

7. $2\frac{1}{2}$ ● $2\frac{2}{3}$

8. $1\frac{1}{4}$ ● 1.5

Find the sum or difference.

9. $2\frac{3}{4} + 1\frac{1}{3}$

10. $\frac{3}{8} + \frac{3}{4} + \frac{1}{2}$

11. $10\frac{4}{5} - 6\frac{5}{6}$

12. $\frac{5}{8} - \frac{1}{6}$

13. $1 - \frac{5}{9}$

14. $\frac{2}{7} + \frac{3}{5}$

15. $5\frac{3}{10} + 4\frac{7}{8}$

16. $9\frac{1}{2} - 7\frac{4}{5}$

Explain how you would solve $\frac{2x}{3} + 1\frac{1}{2} = 3\frac{3}{4}$.

WRAP
UP...

DECIMALS FOR FRACTIONS

Tara needs $\frac{3}{4}$ lb of concentrated plant food for her bonsai plants. The packages in the store show decimal weights. What decimal weight of plant food should Tara buy?

To write a decimal for a fraction, divide the numerator by the denominator.

$3 \boxed{\div}\ 4 \boxed{=} \boxed{0.75}$ $\frac{3}{4}$ means $3 \div 4$.

So, Tara should buy 0.75 lb of plant food.

The decimal 0.75 is called a **terminating decimal** because the division terminates and the remainder is 0.

Some fractions cannot be written as terminating decimals.

Example

$\frac{1}{3} \longrightarrow$

$$\begin{array}{r} 0.333 \\ 3\overline{)1.000} \\ -9 \\ \hline 10 \\ -9 \\ \hline 10 \\ -9 \\ \hline 1 \end{array}$$

The division does not terminate. The 3 in the quotient will continue to repeat, and the remainder will never be 0. The decimal 0.333 . . . is called a **repeating decimal.**

A bar is often written over the digit or digits that repeat.

$\frac{1}{3} = 0.333 \ldots = 0.\overline{3}$

More Examples

A. $\frac{3}{5} = 0.6$

B. $\frac{5}{6} = 0.8333 \ldots$
$= 0.8\overline{3}$

C. $1\frac{2}{9} = 1.222 \ldots$
$= 1.\overline{2}$

D. $\frac{3}{8} = 0.375$

Talk About It

▶ Use a calculator to change $\frac{7}{9}$ to a decimal. Does the calculator show 0.7777777 or 0.7777778? Why would a calculator show 0.7777778?

▶ Explain what you would do to compare $\frac{5}{6}$ with 0.85.

118

Check for Understanding

Rewrite the decimal, using a bar over the digit or digits that repeat.

1. 0.8282828 . . .   **2.** 0.1666666 . . .   **3.** 0.222 . . .   **4.** 5.02727 . . .

Write a decimal for the fraction or mixed number.

5. $\frac{1}{2}$ **6.** $\frac{4}{5}$ **7.** $\frac{2}{3}$ **8.** $\frac{4}{9}$ **9.** $3\frac{1}{4}$ **10.** $\frac{7}{8}$

Practice

Write a decimal for the fraction or mixed number.

11. $\frac{3}{20}$ **12.** $\frac{4}{25}$ **13.** $\frac{1}{4}$ **14.** $\frac{7}{10}$ **15.** $\frac{3}{50}$ **16.** $\frac{11}{20}$

17. $\frac{3}{16}$ **18.** $\frac{13}{20}$ **19.** $1\frac{5}{16}$ **20.** $3\frac{3}{5}$ **21.** $\frac{8}{9}$ **22.** $\frac{1}{7}$

Compare. Write $<$, $>$, or $=$.

23. $1.1 \bullet 1\frac{1}{5}$ **24.** $0.8 \bullet \frac{4}{5}$ **25.** $\frac{1}{2} \bullet 0.6$ **26.** $0.7 \bullet \frac{2}{5}$

27. $1\frac{3}{4} \bullet 1.7$ **28.** $2\frac{1}{2} \bullet 2\frac{2}{5}$ **29.** $8.9 \bullet 8\frac{3}{5}$ **30.** $4.8 \bullet 4\frac{4}{5}$

Mixed Applications

The table shows the amount of rain Mr. Franklin recorded in his garden and the amount of rain the local news reported.

Use the table for Exercises 31–32.

31. Write as a decimal the amount Mr. Franklin recorded for Monday. Is this amount greater than or less than the amount the local news reported?

32. Write as a decimal the amount Mr. Franklin recorded for Friday. How much greater than this amount is the amount the local news reported?

Day	Mr. Franklin	Local News
Monday	$\frac{1}{2}$ in.	0.35 in.
Tuesday	$\frac{3}{4}$ in.	0.7 in.
Wednesday	0 in.	0.1 in.
Thursday	$\frac{2}{3}$ in.	0.66 in.
Friday	$\frac{7}{10}$ in.	1.2 in.
Saturday	$\frac{1}{4}$ in.	0 in.

33. Find Data Use an almanac to find the 5 states that had the greatest amount of precipitation during a 24-hour period in a recent year.

34. Number Sense Explain how you can use the fact that $\frac{1}{5} = 0.2$ to find the decimal equivalents for $\frac{2}{5}, \frac{3}{5},$ and $\frac{4}{5}$.

How can you compare two fractions without finding the common denominator?

WRAP UP . . .

FRACTIONS FOR DECIMALS

Margo ordered 0.25 lb of seeds from a catalog. What fraction of a pound did she order?

Any terminating decimal can be written as a fraction or a mixed number by using the place value of the last digit of the decimal.

Read the decimal 0.25 as twenty-five hundredths.

$0.25 = \frac{25}{100} = \frac{1}{4}$ Stated in simplest form, Margo ordered $\frac{1}{4}$ lb.

More Examples

A. $0.125 = \frac{125}{1,000} = \frac{1}{8}$

B. $0.6 = \frac{6}{10} = \frac{3}{5}$

C. $2.36 = 2\frac{36}{100} = 2\frac{9}{25}$

You can also write a fraction or a mixed number for a repeating decimal. You can use these steps to write $0.\overline{6}$ as a fraction.

Step 1
Let $n = 0.\overline{6}$. Since one digit repeats, multiply the equation by 10.
$n = 0.\overline{6}$
$10n = 6.\overline{6}$

Step 2
Subtract the original equation.
$10n = 6.\overline{6}$
$- n = 0.\overline{6}$
$9n = 6.0$

Step 3
Solve the equation.
$9n = 6$
$\frac{9n}{9} = \frac{6}{9}$
$n = \frac{6}{9} = \frac{2}{3}$

So, the decimal $0.\overline{6} = \frac{2}{3}$.

More Examples

A. $0.\overline{45} \rightarrow 100n = 45.\overline{45}$
$- n = 0.\overline{45}$
$99n = 45$
$\frac{99n}{99} = \frac{45}{99}$
$n = \frac{45}{99}$
$n = \frac{5}{11}$
Since 2 digits repeat, multiply by 100.

B. $0.1\overline{3} \rightarrow 10n = 1.3\overline{3}$
$- n = 0.1\overline{3}$
$9n = 1.2$
$\frac{9n}{9} = \frac{1.2}{9}$
$n = \frac{1.2}{9}$, or $\frac{12}{90}$
$n = \frac{2}{15}$
Only the hundredths digit repeats.

Check for Understanding

Complete.

1. $0.8 = \dfrac{8}{\blacksquare}$ **2.** $0.375 = \dfrac{375}{\blacksquare}$ **3.** $0.27 = \dfrac{27}{\blacksquare}$ **4.** $0.1385 = \dfrac{1{,}385}{\blacksquare}$

Write a fraction in simplest form or a mixed number for the decimal.

5. 0.4 **6.** 0.9 **7.** 0.15 **8.** 0.08 **9.** 2.1

10. $0.\overline{4}$ **11.** $0.\overline{3}$ **12.** $1.\overline{7}$ **13.** $0.1\overline{6}$ **14.** $0.\overline{81}$

Practice

Write a fraction in simplest form or a mixed number for the decimal.

15. 0.5 **16.** 0.56 **17.** 0.75 **18.** 0.28 **19.** 5.8

20. 6.25 **21.** 0.006 **22.** 0.17 **23.** 8.028 **24.** $0.\overline{7}$

25. $0.\overline{8}$ **26.** $0.\overline{38}$ **27.** $0.\overline{72}$ **28.** $1.\overline{5}$ **29.** $0.\overline{83}$

Write in order from least to greatest.

30. $\dfrac{1}{2}, 0.\overline{3}, \dfrac{1}{4}$ **31.** $0.\overline{6}, \dfrac{2}{5}, \dfrac{1}{2}, \dfrac{3}{4}$ **32.** $\dfrac{1}{8}, \dfrac{1}{6}, 0.\overline{1}, \dfrac{1}{10}$

33. $0.24, \dfrac{1}{4}, \dfrac{2}{5}, 0.\overline{6}$ **34.** $1.5, 1.\overline{5}, 1\dfrac{4}{9}, \dfrac{16}{9}$ **35.** $0.375, \dfrac{2}{8}, \dfrac{5}{8}, 0.125$

Mixed Applications

36. Julian said that he picked 2.15 bushels of peaches. Rebecca said that she picked $2\dfrac{2}{5}$ bushels. Who picked more peaches?

37. A bag of tulip bulbs weighs 0.625 lb. Write the weight of the bag of bulbs as a fraction.

38. **Number Sense** Suppose you were asked to write a fraction for the decimal $0.\overline{123}$. By what number would you multiply both sides of the equation $n = 0.\overline{123}$? Explain.

39. Mrs. Reed paid $15 to frame a picture that was $2\dfrac{1}{4}$ ft long and $1\dfrac{1}{2}$ ft wide. How much per foot did the framing cost?

Name a situation in which changing a decimal to a fraction would be helpful.

More Practice, Lesson 4.10, page H45

Devon is using recycled railroad ties to build a tiered flower bed. He had the ties drilled so that they could be connected with spikes. It cost $7.50 to drill the first 5 ties and $1.05 to drill each additional tie. Devon paid $13.80 for the drilling service. How many ties were drilled in all?

You can use either the *work-backward* strategy or the *write-an-equation* strategy to solve the problem.

| Understand |
| Plan |
| Solve |
| Look Back |

Strategy: Work Backward

First, subtract the cost of drilling the first 5 ties from $13.80. Then, subtract the cost of drilling each additional tie until the final amount is $0.00.

13.80 ⊟ 7.50 ⊟ 1.05 ⊟ 1.05 ⊟ 1.05 ⊟

1.05 ⊟ 1.05 ⊟ 1.05 ⊟ [0.]

You subtracted $1.05 six times. So, the number of ties drilled was 5 ties + 6 ties, or 11 ties in all.

Strategy: Write an Equation

Let d = the number of additional ties drilled. Then $1.05d$ = the cost of drilling each additional tie. Write and solve the equation.

$$1.05d + 7.50 = 13.80$$
$$1.05d + 7.50 - 7.50 = 13.80 - 7.50$$
$$1.05d = 6.30$$
$$\frac{1.05d}{1.05} = \frac{6.30}{1.05}$$
$$d = 6 \leftarrow \text{additional ties drilled}$$

So, the number of ties drilled was 5 ties + 6 ties, or 11 ties in all.

WHAT IF... . . . the cost of drilling each additional tie was $0.90? What equation would you write to solve the problem?

Mixed Applications

STRATEGIES

- Write an Equation • Work Backward
- Guess and Check • Draw a Picture
- Find a Pattern • Solve a Simpler Problem

Choose a strategy and solve.

1 Jason made 48 wooden plant stands in his woodworking class. The number of stands he made of pine was 3 times the number of stands he made of oak. How many oak plant stands did Jason make?

2 Mr. Thomas is putting a fence around his cornfield. The field is 360 yd long and 225 yd wide. He wants to put a fence post every 3 yd. How many fence posts will Mr. Thomas need?

3 Jessica and Mark collect books about plants and gardening. Jessica has 12 fewer than 2 times the number of books Mark has. She has 38 books. How many books does Mark have?

4 Cheryl has 12 apples left on her apple tree. In how many ways can she divide the 12 apples among 3 of her friends if each friend receives at least 2 apples?

5 At 9:00 A.M. a plane left Boston for Dallas. An hour later an airplane left Dallas for Boston. Both airplanes were traveling at 500 mph. The distance between Boston and Dallas is 1,500 mi. At what time did the airplanes pass each other?

6 There were 13 riders on a bus after the third stop. At each stop, riders got off and on as follows: Stop 1—10 off, 15 on; Stop 2—8 off, 20 on; Stop 3—18 off, 3 on. How many riders were on the bus before the first stop?

7 Mike launches his kayak from Ramp A. At the same time, Julie launches her kayak from Ramp B, 15 miles away. Mike paddles upstream toward Ramp B at 2 mph. Julie paddles downstream toward Ramp A at 3 mph. How many miles from Ramp A will Mike and Julie be when they meet?

8 The Big C Farm is divided into 6 parts. The largest part is 1,100 acres, and the second largest part is 1,050 acres. The third and the fourth largest parts are 950 acres and 800 acres. If the sizes of the other parts of the farm follow the same pattern, what are the sizes of the two smallest parts of the farm?

Vocabulary Check

Choose a word from the box to complete each sentence.

| denominator |
| GCF |
| numerator |
| overestimate |
| reciprocal |
| underestimate |

1. When both rounded factors of a product are greater than the exact factors, the estimate is a(n) __?__. *(page 98)*

2. Dividing by a number gives the same answer as multiplying by its __?__. *(page 108)*

3. It is sometimes possible to simplify fractions before multiplying by dividing a numerator and a denominator by their __?__. *(page 100)*

4. To write a decimal for a fraction, you divide the __?__ by the __?__. *(page 118)*

5. When both rounded factors of a product are less than the exact factors, the estimate is a(n) __?__. *(page 98)*

Concept Check

An estimate is given for each product. Tell whether the estimate is an overestimate or an underestimate. *(page 98)*

6. $1\frac{3}{4} \times 3\frac{5}{8}$; 8

7. $\frac{15}{16} \times \frac{10}{12}$; $\frac{1}{2}$

8. $2\frac{1}{4} \times 15\frac{1}{8}$; 30

Write the reciprocal. *(page 100)*

9. $\frac{3}{4}$

10. $\frac{5}{9}$

11. $\frac{6}{7}$

12. $\frac{1}{4}$

13. $2\frac{4}{5}$

Tell whether the quotient is less than 1 or greater than 1. *(page 104)*

14. $\frac{5}{8} \div \frac{7}{8}$

15. $\frac{7}{5} \div \frac{2}{3}$

16. $2\frac{1}{2} \div 1\frac{1}{3}$

17. $9\frac{2}{3} \div 12\frac{3}{4}$

Tell what you would do to each side of the equation to solve for the variable. *(page 116)*

18. $a + \frac{1}{2} = 3\frac{1}{3}$

19. $\frac{4}{5}b = \frac{6}{9}$

20. $t - 2\frac{2}{3} = 1\frac{3}{5}$

21. $\frac{7}{8} = \frac{r}{9}$

Tell whether the decimal is a terminating decimal or a repeating decimal. *(page 118)*

22. 0.375

23. $0.12222\ldots$

24. $8.\overline{45}$

25. 1.7624

Skill Check

Estimate the product or quotient. *(pages 98, 104)*

26. $\frac{3}{4} \times \frac{8}{9}$

27. $\frac{2}{3} \times \frac{4}{7}$

28. $7\frac{3}{4} \times 1\frac{1}{8}$

29. $1\frac{3}{4} \times 6$

30. $6\frac{1}{3} \div 2\frac{1}{4}$

31. $12\frac{2}{3} \div 5\frac{4}{5}$

32. $18\frac{1}{6} \div 2\frac{4}{6}$

33. $3\frac{4}{9} \div 11\frac{3}{4}$

Find the product. *(pages 100, 102)*

34. $\frac{7}{8} \times \frac{4}{5}$

35. $\frac{5}{6} \times \frac{13}{4}$

36. $\frac{5}{8} \times 24$

37. $\frac{3}{4} \times \frac{8}{9}$

38. $35 \times \frac{11}{15}$

39. $5\frac{7}{9} \times 1\frac{5}{8}$

40. $7\frac{3}{4} \times 1\frac{1}{8}$

41. $4\frac{1}{2} \times 6\frac{1}{3}$

Find the quotient. *(pages 108, 112)*

42. $\frac{3}{4} \div \frac{1}{2}$

43. $\frac{4}{5} \div \frac{3}{2}$

44. $\frac{1}{2} \div \frac{2}{5}$

45. $\frac{3}{5} \div 9$

46. $16 \div \frac{3}{8}$

47. $6\frac{2}{3} \div 8\frac{5}{9}$

48. $5\frac{1}{8} \div 2\frac{3}{4}$

49. $6\frac{1}{4} \div 5\frac{1}{3}$

Solve the equation. Check your solution. *(page 114)*

50. $\frac{3}{4}t = \frac{5}{6}$

51. $\frac{2}{5}b = 1\frac{1}{2}$

52. $\frac{9}{12} = y \div \frac{5}{6}$

53. $\frac{t}{4} + \frac{1}{8} = 2\frac{1}{2}$

Write a decimal for the fraction or mixed number. *(page 118)*

54. $\frac{1}{4}$

55. $\frac{7}{8}$

56. $\frac{2}{3}$

57. $1\frac{5}{12}$

Write a fraction in simplest form or a mixed number for the decimal. *(page 120)*

58. 0.7

59. 1.75

60. $0.\overline{13}$

61. 2.06

Problem-Solving Check

Solve. *(pages 110, 122)*

62. In how many ways can a group of 12 new students be divided among 3 classes if each class receives at least 2 new students?

63. There are 8 people in a room. How many handshakes will there be if every person shakes hands with every other person once?

64. Albert had a total of 14 dimes and quarters. The value of the coins was $1.85. He had 8 more dimes than quarters. How many of each coin did he have?

65. Janell bought a book for $12, a record for $8, and 3 cassette tapes. She spent a total of $35. Find the price of 1 cassette tape if each cost the same amount.

Estimate the product or quotient.

1. $\frac{4}{5} \times \frac{6}{7}$

2. $1\frac{3}{4} \times 5\frac{1}{5}$

3. $12\frac{1}{2} \div 5\frac{2}{5}$

4. $4\frac{1}{2} \div 8\frac{3}{5}$

Find the product or quotient.

5. $\frac{1}{4} \times \frac{2}{5}$

6. $12 \times 4\frac{1}{3}$

7. $1\frac{3}{4} \times 2\frac{3}{8}$

8. $\frac{12}{9} \times \frac{2}{10}$

9. $\frac{5}{6} \div \frac{3}{7}$

10. $1\frac{2}{3} \div 3\frac{1}{4}$

11. $15\frac{2}{5} \div 3\frac{1}{2}$

12. $3\frac{6}{10} \div 2\frac{1}{4}$

Solve the equation.

13. $t - 1\frac{1}{2} = 2\frac{1}{3}$

14. $s \div \frac{4}{5} = 12$

15. $\frac{c}{4} + \frac{3}{5} = 1\frac{1}{3}$

Write a decimal for the fraction.

16. $\frac{3}{8}$

17. $\frac{4}{5}$

18. $\frac{5}{9}$

Write a fraction in simplest form for the decimal.

19. 0.6

20. 0.05

21. 0.25

Solve.

22. Bob and 7 friends are going to take rides on the Ferris wheel. They decide to go in pairs and ride until each friend rides with each of the other friends exactly once. How many rides will be taken?

23. Each of the 10 members of the Wilson family gave a gift to each of the other members of the family. Find the total number of gifts given.

24. The Print Shop charged $15 for the first 500 copies of a flier and $2 for each additional 100 copies. The total bill was $31. How many copies of the flier were made?

25. Rita and Mike collect stamps. Rita has 15 more than 2 times the number of stamps Mike has. Together they have 156 stamps. How many stamps does Mike have?

PLAN A GARDEN

Your class has been asked to participate in a community project called "Adopt a Lot." Each group participating in the project is to plan a flower garden or a vegetable garden on a vacant lot and then maintain it. The city will pay all expenses, and water will be available.

Suppose you and your team have adopted a lot that is $50\frac{1}{4}$ ft wide and 100 ft long.

DECIDE

As a team, discuss whether your lot will have a flower garden or a vegetable garden. Discuss the types of flowers or vegetables that you will plant.

Discuss the design of your garden. Consider whether there will be walkways, benches, grassy areas, or fences.

DO

As a team, prepare a sketch of the lot, showing all of the planting areas, walkways, and so on that will be included. Be sure to include the dimensions of each part.

Prepare a schedule showing when each member of the team is responsible for planting, watering, and weeding the garden.

SHARE

Compare your sketch of the garden with those of other teams. Tell why you chose your design.

TALK ABOUT IT

a. What is the area of your lot? How much area is used for plants?

b. Suppose you decide to put a fence around the lot. How much fencing will you need?

c. In what other situation might you need to multiply or divide with fractions?

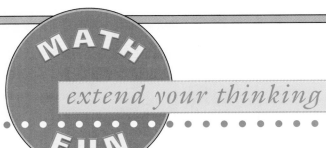

Continued Fractions

An expression such as $2 + \cfrac{1}{3 + \cfrac{1}{2 + \frac{1}{2}}}$ is a continued fraction.

Each of the numerators within a continued fraction is 1.

To simplify a continued fraction, start at the bottom and work up.

$$2 + \cfrac{1}{3 + \cfrac{1}{2 + \frac{1}{2}}} = 2 + \cfrac{1}{3 + \cfrac{1}{\frac{5}{2}}} = 2 + \cfrac{1}{3 + \frac{2}{5}} = 2 + \cfrac{1}{\frac{17}{5}} = 2 + \frac{5}{17} = 2\frac{5}{17}$$

↑

Start here.

Simplify.

1. $3 + \cfrac{1}{3 + \frac{1}{2}}$

2. $\cfrac{1}{3 + \cfrac{1}{2 + \frac{1}{4}}}$

3. $5 + \cfrac{1}{2 + \cfrac{1}{1 + \frac{1}{3}}}$

4. $4 + \cfrac{1}{1 + \cfrac{1}{2 + \frac{1}{3}}}$

CHALLENGE

Number Sense

A number has the factors 1, 2, 3, 4, 5, 6, 7, and 8. What is the smallest such number?

Patterns

Find the next two fractions.

$\dfrac{1}{6}, \dfrac{1}{3}, \dfrac{1}{2}, \blacksquare, \blacksquare$

$\dfrac{2}{9}, \dfrac{1}{3}, \dfrac{5}{9}, \blacksquare, \blacksquare$

CUMULATIVE REVIEW

Write the letter of the correct answer.

1. Which is the best estimate for $6\frac{1}{4} \div 1\frac{2}{3}$?

   A. $\frac{1}{3}$ **B.** 3

   C. 6   **D.** 12

2. Which whole number or numbers make $3n > 21$ true?

   A. 0, 1, 2, ... 6   **B.** 7

   C. 7, 8, 9, ...   **D.** 8, 9, 10, ...

3. $1\frac{1}{2} \times 2\frac{3}{4}$

   A. $1\frac{5}{6}$ **B.** $2\frac{3}{8}$

   C. $4\frac{1}{8}$ **D.** not here

4. Which is the reciprocal of $\frac{5}{3}$?

   A. $\frac{3}{5}$ **B.** $\frac{2}{3}$

   C. 1.3   **D.** $1\frac{2}{3}$

5. Solve. $0.5b = 12$

   A. $b = 0.24$ **B.** $b = 2.4$

   C. $b = 6$ **D.** $b = 24$

6. Which is the value of 8^3?

   A. 24   **B.** 64

   C. 512   **D.** 6,561

7. Which is the closest estimate?
$$245 \times 62$$

   A. 1,200   **B.** 1,800

   C. 2,100   **D.** 15,000

8. A number n is rounded to 3,400. Which is the greatest number n can be?

   A. 3,350   **B.** 3,449

   C. 3,549   **D.** not here

9. Which is a composite number?

   A. 11   **B.** 29

   C. 36   **D.** 37

10. $2\frac{1}{2} + 5\frac{3}{5}$

   A. $3\frac{1}{10}$ **B.** $7\frac{1}{10}$

   C. $7\frac{4}{7}$ **D.** $8\frac{1}{10}$

11. Mimi wants to hang a poster in the center of a wall that is 84 in. wide. The poster is 22 in. wide. How much wall space should she leave on each side of the poster?

   A. $15\frac{1}{2}$ in.   **B.** 20 in.

   C. 31 in.   **D.** 62 in.

12. The Skyway roller coaster has 12 cars. Each car holds 6 people. The roller coaster completes 6 rides per hour, 10 hours per day. How many people can ride the Skyway in a day?

   A. 34 people   **B.** 720 people

   C. 1,080 people   **D.** 4,320 people

Chapter 4 • 129

5

GEOMETRIC
RELATIONSHIPS
AND CONSTRUCTIONS

Did you know ...

... that the most popular shapes in architecture through the years have been the square, the rectangle, and the sphere?

Talk About It

Look at the pictures of the ancient Greek Parthenon and the modern office building. What geometric shapes do both buildings have? What shapes are in one building but not in the other?

THEME: Construction ● 131

WARM
U P . . .

Name some objects in your classroom
that represent geometric figures.

BASIC IDEAS
IN GEOMETRY

This view of a picnic table provides several
examples of basic geometric figures. For
example, the table legs can represent
intersecting line segments *EG* and *FH*. There
are many other examples that you can find by
studying the picture carefully.

Talk About It

▶ What geometric figure does *I* represent?

▶ What geometric figure does one leg of the
table represent?

▶ What geometric figure does the top of the
table represent?

▶ What would have to be true of the edge of the
tabletop in order for it to represent a line?

▶ If the legs of the table continued down from the top of the table
to an indefinite length, what figure would be formed by rays *IH*
and *IG*?

Check for Understanding

Tell what parts in each figure represent points, lines, line segments,
intersecting lines, angles, or planes.

1.

2.

3.

Draw the following geometric figures.

4. a line

5. a ray

6. two intersecting lines

7. an angle

8. a line segment

9. a point

Practice

Match one or more names from the list with each figure in
Exercises 10–13.

10.

11.

a. $\angle TRS$
b. $\overline{AB}$
c. $\overleftrightarrow{XY}$
d. $\overrightarrow{CD}$
e. $\angle SRT$
f. $\overline{BA}$
g. $\overrightarrow{CE}$
h. $\overleftrightarrow{YX}$
i. $\angle R$

12.

13.

Use this line for Exercises 14–17.

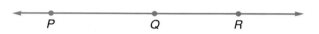

14. Use the point P to name the line in three different ways.

15. Name two rays that have Q as an endpoint.

16. Name three line segments.

17. Name $\overleftrightarrow{PR}$ in a different way.

Write *true* or *false* for each statement. Use lines *AB* and *CD*, which intersect at *M*.

18. Point M is between points A and D.

19. Point M is on $\overleftrightarrow{AB}$.

20. Point M is on $\overleftrightarrow{CD}$.

21. Another name for $\overrightarrow{MD}$ is $\overrightarrow{DM}$.

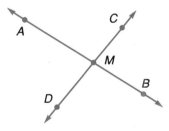

Mixed Applications

22. Ray PT contains points R and W. Draw $\overrightarrow{PT}$. Can the ray be renamed $\overrightarrow{PR}$? Why or why not?

23. Draw $\overleftrightarrow{XY}$ and $\overleftrightarrow{ST}$, which intersect at B. Name the angles that are formed by the intersection.

24. Three towns, Tilton, Arway, and Sewall, lie along a highway, although not necessarily in that order. It is 16 km from Tilton to Arway and 25 km from Arway to Sewall. What are the two possible distances from Tilton to Sewall?

25. Look at Exercise 24. Suppose the distance from Tilton to Sewall is 9 km. Which town is between the other two?

In your own words, describe the difference between a line and a line segment.

WRAP
UP...

UP...

How do acute angles and obtuse
angles compare with right angles?

ANGLES
and Angle Pairs

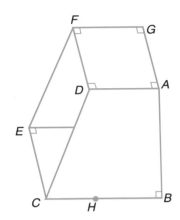

Tim's soccer team built a goal for their practice
field. This view of the goal shows examples of
some of the different types of angles.

- Name a right angle in the figure.

- Name an obtuse angle in the figure.

- Name an acute angle in the figure.

- What type of angle is $\angle CHB$?

Recall that you can use a protractor to measure
and draw angles. The measure of $\angle DCB$ is 60°.
Write: m $\angle DCB = 60°$.

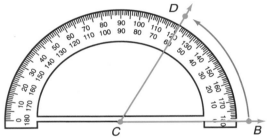

- Use a protractor to draw a 130° angle.

Angle pairs that appear often in geometry
have special names.

If the sum of the measures of two angles is
90°, the angles are **complementary.** If the
sum of the measures of two angles is 180°,
the angles are **supplementary.**

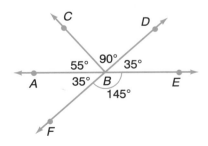

Examples

A. Which angles are complements of $\angle ABC$?

 Think: 90° − 55° = 35°. Which angles have a
 measure of 35°?

So, $\angle ABF$ and $\angle DBE$ are complements of $\angle ABC$.

B. Which angles are supplements of $\angle CBD$?

 Think: 180° − 90° = 90°. Which angles have a
 measure of 90°?

So, $\angle CBF$ is a supplement of $\angle CBD$.

 Idea Bank, page 490, Exercise 7

Look at these pairs of angles.

∠1 and ∠2 are adjacent angles.

∠3 and ∠4, and ∠5 and ∠6 are *not* adjacent angles.

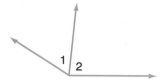

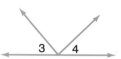

- Do the adjacent angles have a common vertex? Do any of the angles that are not adjacent have a common vertex?

- Do the adjacent angles have a common side? Do the angles that are not adjacent have a common side?

- How can you define *adjacent angles*?

_____

Now use a straightedge to trace intersecting lines *ST* and *PQ*.

Turn your tracing and put it over the figure on the page so that your *S* is over the *T*, your *P* is over the *Q*, and your *O* is over the *O*.

- Does your tracing fit exactly on the figure on the page?

- What is true about the size of ∠*POS* and the size of ∠*QOT*?

- What is true about the size of ∠*POT* and the size of ∠*SOQ*?

Angles that have the same measure are congruent. **Vertical angles** are nonadjacent congruent angles formed by intersecting lines. ∠*POS* and ∠*QOT* are vertical angles.

Talk About It

▶ Is it possible for adjacent angles to be complementary or supplementary? Explain.

▶ Draw two vertical angles that are complementary. What is the measure of each angle? Draw two vertical angles that are supplementary. What is the measure of each angle?

When all four vertical angles formed by two intersecting lines are right angles, the intersecting lines are called **perpendicular lines.**

$$\overleftrightarrow{AB} \perp \overleftrightarrow{CD}$$

Read: Line AB is perpendicular to line CD.

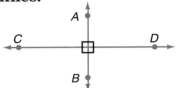

- What is the measure of each of the angles formed by the intersection of $\overleftrightarrow{AB}$ and $\overleftrightarrow{CD}$? Explain.

Check for Understanding

Use a protractor to measure the angle. Tell whether the angle is *acute, right,* or *obtuse.*

1.   2.   3.   4.

Name a pair of angles as described.

5. adjacent

6. complementary

7. supplementary

8. vertical

Find the measure of the angle.

9. m $\angle ABF$ 10. m $\angle EBC$ 11. m $\angle FBC$

12. m $\angle ABE$ 13. m $\angle ABC$ 14. m $\angle ABD$

15. Suppose $\overleftrightarrow{EB} \perp \overleftrightarrow{AC}$. What is the measure of $\angle EBC$? Explain.

Practice

Measure the angle. Write *acute, right,* or *obtuse.*

16.   17.   18.   19.

Find the missing measures.

20.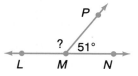

21.

22.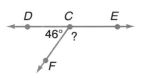

23.

24.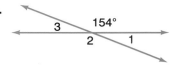

25.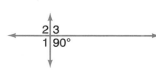

Draw the angle that is the complement and the angle that is the supplement of the angle with the given measure.

26. 35°   **27.** 80°   **28.** 45°   **29.** 72°

30. Does an angle with a measure of 120° have a complement? Why or why not?

Mixed Applications

The braces for some bleachers form the given angles. Use the figure for Exercises 31–33.

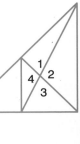

31. The measure of ∠ 2 is 110°. What are the measures of ∠ 1, ∠ 3, and ∠ 4?

32. Name a pair of adjacent angles, a pair of vertical angles, and a pair of supplementary angles.

33. **Mental Math**   There are 4 bleachers at a football field. Each has 25 rows. Each row can hold 76 spectators. How many spectators in all can sit in the bleachers?

VISUAL THINKING

34. These five short pieces of chain must be linked to form one long chain. Explain how the pieces can be linked by cutting only three of the rings.

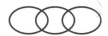 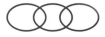 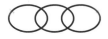 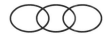 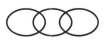

What is the measure of each of two vertical angles that are complementary? supplementary?

WRAP
UP...

What do you know about two line segments that are congruent?

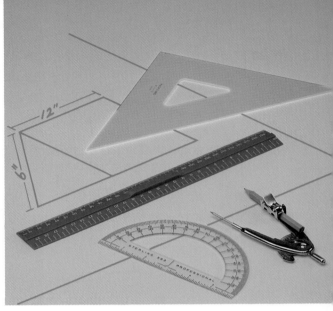

You can use a ruler and a protractor to draw congruent segments and angles. However, to construct congruent figures, you use only a compass and a straightedge.

WORK TOGETHER

Use a straightedge to draw line segment $\overline{AB}$. Then draw line segment CD longer than $\overline{AB}$.

- If you put the point of your compass on point A, how can you use the compass to measure the length of $\overline{AB}$?

- Explain how you can use this same compass opening to indicate a segment on $\overline{CD}$ that is congruent to $\overline{AB}$.

- Explain the steps you can use to construct a line segment that is congruent to a given line segment.

You can use these steps to construct an angle congruent to $\angle S$.

Step 1	**Step 2**	**Step 3**
Use a straightedge to draw $\overrightarrow{LM}$.	Draw an arc through $\angle S$ as shown.	Use the same compass opening to draw an arc through $\overrightarrow{LM}$ as shown.

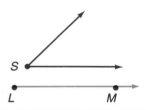
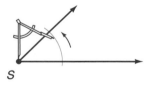
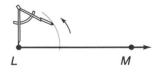

Step 4	**Step 5**	**Step 6**
Change the compass opening to measure the opening of the angle as shown.	Use the same compass opening to locate point G as shown.	Draw $\overrightarrow{LG}$. $\angle GLM \cong \angle S$

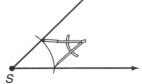
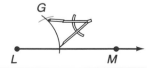
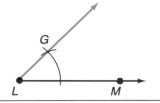

Check for Understanding

Trace the figure. Then use your tracing to construct a congruent figure.

1.

2.

3.

Practice

Trace the figure. Then use your tracing to construct a congruent figure.

4.

5.
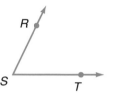

6.
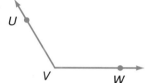

Draw the figure, using a ruler and a protractor. Then use the figure to construct a congruent figure, using a compass and a straightedge.

7. a 5-cm line segment   **8.** a 30-mm line segment   **9.** an 80-mm line segment

10. a 90° angle   **11.** a 40° angle   **12.** a 150° angle

Use the given figures to construct the figures described in Exercises 13–15.

13. a line segment that has a length equal to the length of $\overline{AB}$ + the length of $\overline{CD}$

14. an angle with a measure equal to m $\angle HIJ$ − m $\angle PQR$

15. an angle with a measure equal to m $\angle HIJ$ + m $\angle PQR$

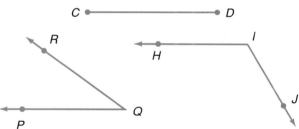

Mixed Applications

16. Construct quadrilateral $ABDC$ by constructing line segments congruent to the line segments shown.

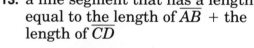
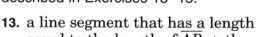

17. The measure of an angle is 30° more than the measure of its complement. Find the measure of the angle and its complement.

Explain how you can check that a line segment you have constructed is congruent to the given line segment.

EXPLORING
Parallel Lines and Transversals

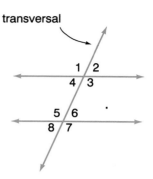
transversal

Recall that two lines in the same plane that do not intersect are parallel.

When two parallel lines are cut by a third line, a **transversal,** four pairs of **corresponding angles** are formed.

WORK TOGETHER

Building Understanding

On lined paper or graph paper, draw a pair of parallel lines. Then draw a transversal that intersects the parallel lines. Label the angles as shown.

Copy the table, and complete the "Measure" columns as you answer these questions.

Angle	Measure	Angle	Measure
1	▪	5	▪
2	▪	6	▪
3	▪	7	▪
4	▪	8	▪

Talk About It

▶ Use a protractor to find the measure of ∠ 1. How is ∠ 2 related to ∠ 1? Without measuring, find the measure of ∠ 2.

▶ How is ∠ 3 related to ∠ 1? Without measuring, find the measure of ∠ 3.

▶ How is ∠ 4 related to ∠ 1? Without measuring, find the measure of ∠ 4.

▶ Use a protractor to find the measure of ∠ 6. How are ∠ 5, ∠ 7, and ∠ 8 related to ∠ 6? Without measuring, find the measure of each angle.

The pairs of corresponding angles in the figure are ∠ 1 and ∠ 5, ∠ 2 and ∠ 6, ∠ 3 and ∠ 7, and ∠ 4 and ∠ 8.

● What pattern do you see in the measures of corresponding angles?

● When a transversal intersects two parallel lines, are the angles that look congruent actually congruent? Explain.

Making the Connection

You have found that congruent pairs of corresponding angles are formed by a transversal that intersects parallel lines. Other angle pairs formed are interior and exterior angles.

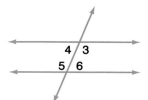

Interior angles   Exterior angles

You can use what you know about corresponding angles, supplementary angles, and vertical angles to find the measures of interior and exterior angles.

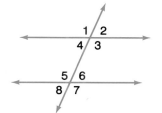

1. Copy and complete the table.

Angle	Measure	Angle	Measure
1	120°	7	▦
2	▦	8	▦
3	▦	5	▦
4	▦	6	▦

2. Angles 3 and 5 and angles 4 and 6 are **alternate interior angles.** Looking at your completed table, what do you know about the measure of alternate interior angles?

3. Angles 1 and 7 and angles 2 and 8 are **alternate exterior angles.** Looking at your completed table, what do you know about the measure of alternate exterior angles?

Remember that two angles that have a sum of 180° are supplementary angles.

Checking Understanding

Use the figure to find the measure of the given angle.

4. m ∠ 1   **5.** m ∠ 2   **6.** m ∠ 3

7. m ∠ 4   **8.** m ∠ 5   **9.** m ∠ 6

10. m ∠ 7   **11.** m ∠ 8

12. Explain how you found m ∠ 2.

13. Explain how you found m ∠ 5.

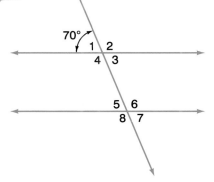

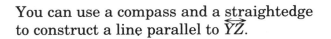

CONSTRUCTING
Parallel and Perpendicular Lines

If two intersecting lines form
four right angles, what do you
know about the lines?

You can use a compass and a straightedge to construct a line parallel to $\overleftrightarrow{YZ}$.

Step 1	**Step 2**	**Step 3**
Choose any point P above $\overleftrightarrow{YZ}$. Draw any line through point P that intersects $\overleftrightarrow{YZ}$. Label the point of intersection W.	Construct an angle congruent to $\angle PWZ$ at point P. Label the point Q.	Draw $\overleftrightarrow{PQ}$. $\overleftrightarrow{PQ}$ is a line parallel to $\overleftrightarrow{YZ}$. $\overleftrightarrow{PQ} \parallel \overleftrightarrow{YZ}$
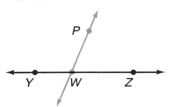	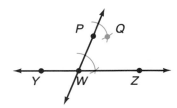	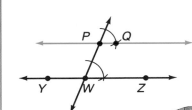

Construct a line perpendicular to $\overleftrightarrow{AB}$ through point P.

Step 1	**Step 2**	**Step 3**
Place the compass point on point P. Draw an arc that intersects $\overleftrightarrow{AB}$ as shown. Label C and D.	Using the same compass opening, draw intersecting arcs from points C and D. Label the point of intersection E.	Draw $\overleftrightarrow{PE}$. $\overleftrightarrow{PE}$ is a perpendicular line from P to $\overleftrightarrow{AB}$. $\overleftrightarrow{PE} \perp \overleftrightarrow{AB}$
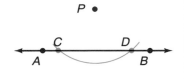	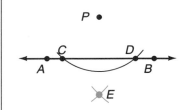	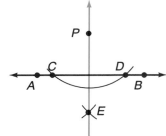

Talk About It

▶ In the first construction, how are $\angle PWZ$ and the angle you constructed related?

▶ How can you construct a line perpendicular to this line through point R? (HINT: First, place the compass point on point R and draw two arcs that intersect the line.)

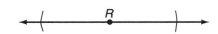

Check for Understanding

Draw a line *RS* and a point *Q* as shown for each.

1. Construct a line through point *Q* parallel to $\overleftrightarrow{RS}$.

2. Construct a perpendicular line from point *Q* to $\overleftrightarrow{RS}$.

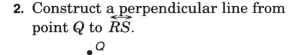

Practice

3. Draw a line *CD* and a point *S* as shown. Then construct a line through point *S* parallel to $\overleftrightarrow{CD}$.

4. Draw a line *AB* and a point *P* as shown. Then construct a line through point *P* perpendicular to $\overleftrightarrow{AB}$.

5. In Exercise 3, how many lines through point *S* can be parallel to $\overleftrightarrow{CD}$?

6. In Exercise 4, how many lines through point *P* can be perpendicular to $\overleftrightarrow{AB}$?

Mixed Applications

7. Trace $\overleftrightarrow{AB}$, point *C*, and point *R*. Construct $\overleftrightarrow{CD} \perp \overleftrightarrow{AB}$. Then construct $\overleftrightarrow{RT} \perp \overleftrightarrow{CD}$. What is the relationship between $\overleftrightarrow{AB}$ and $\overleftrightarrow{RT}$?

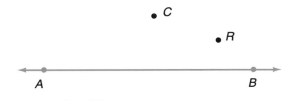

8. Trace $\overleftrightarrow{XY}$ and $\angle B$. Construct an angle congruent to $\angle B$ at point *T*. Label the angle *STY*. If m $\angle B$ is 90°, what is the relationship between $\overleftrightarrow{XY}$ and $\overleftrightarrow{TS}$?

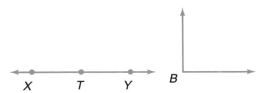

MIXED REVIEW

Write as a fraction in simplest form.

1. $\frac{40}{25}$ **2.** $4\frac{1}{2}$ **3.** $\frac{9}{3}$ **4.** $\frac{15}{60}$ **5.** $9\frac{2}{4}$ **6.** $\frac{18}{45}$

7. 0.6   **8.** $0.\overline{3}$ **9.** 0.35   **10.** $0.\overline{18}$ **11.** 0.125   **12.** 0.24

Explain how you can check that the lines you constructed in Exercise 4 are perpendicular.

WRAP UP...

BISECTING
Segments and Angles

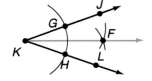

Architects use computer-aided design techniques to develop and modify their design drawings. Frequently, they must bisect line segments and angles. You can also bisect line segments and angles by using a compass and a straightedge.

To **bisect** means to divide into two congruent parts.

Construct the perpendicular bisector of $\overline{AB}$.

Step 1	**Step 2**	**Step 3**
Open the compass more than half the distance from *A* to *B*. Place the compass point on *A*. Draw a large arc.	Using the same compass opening, place the compass point on *B* and draw a large arc. Label *C* and *D*.	Draw $\overleftrightarrow{CD}$. Label *M*, the point of intersection of $\overline{AB}$ and $\overleftrightarrow{CD}$. $\overline{AM} \cong \overline{MB}$, and $\overleftrightarrow{CD} \perp \overline{AB}$.
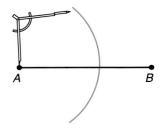	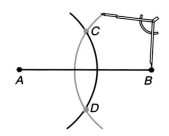	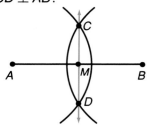

Talk About It

▶ How does the length of $\overline{AM}$ compare with the length of $\overline{MB}$?

▶ What are the measures of $\angle CMB$, $\angle CMA$, $\angle DMA$, and $\angle DMB$?

You can use these steps to bisect $\angle JKL$.

Step 1	**Step 2**	**Step 3**
Draw an arc through $\angle JKL$ intersecting its sides at *G* and *H*.	Use the same compass opening to draw intersecting arcs from *G* and *H*. Label the point *F*.	Draw $\overrightarrow{KF}$. $\overrightarrow{KF}$ is the bisector of $\angle JKL$. $\angle LKF \cong \angle FKJ$
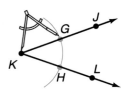	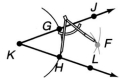	

Check for Understanding

Trace the figures. Then bisect them.

1.

2.

3.

4.

Practice

Trace the figures. Then bisect them.

5.

6.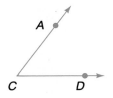

7.

8.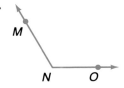

Draw the figures, using a ruler and a protractor. Construct bisectors, using a compass and a straightedge.

9. a 7-cm line segment

10. a 45-mm line segment

11. a 55° angle

12. a 125° angle

13. a 12-cm line segment

14. a 95° angle

Mixed Applications

15. Trace △*RST*. Construct the bisector of each angle in the triangle. What do you observe about the bisectors?

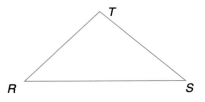

16. Trace △*DEF*. Construct the bisector of each side of the triangle. What do you observe about the bisectors?

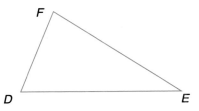

17. A window is 2 m wide. The builder wants the window to be centered in a wall that is 10 m wide. How much wall space will be left on each side of the window?

18. Logical Reasoning Draw any line segment. Then use a compass and a straightedge to divide the segment into four congruent parts.

Explain the difference between constructing a line perpendicular to a line segment and constructing a perpendicular bisector.

PROBLEM Solving

Strategy • Find a Pattern

Beth is putting a tile border around her room. The design of the tiles repeats after every four tiles. The first three tiles are shown. What is the design of the fourth tile?

Frequently, problems can be solved by identifying a pattern.

▶ **UNDERSTAND**

What are you asked to find?

What information is given?

▶ **PLAN**

What strategy can you use?

You can *find a pattern* in the design of the tiles. Then use the pattern to find the design of the fourth tile.

▶ **SOLVE**

How does the design change from tile to tile?

The second tile is turned 90° to the left. The third tile is turned an additional 90° to the left.

By using this pattern, you can see that the fourth tile will be turned an additional 90° to the left. The design of the fourth tile is shown.

▶ **LOOK BACK**

How can you check your answer?

WHAT IF... . . . Beth increases the pattern to five tiles? What will be the design of the fifth tile?

146

Apply

Choose the figure that completes the pattern.

   a. b. c.

   a. b. c.

   a. b. c.

Mixed Applications ▸ **STRATEGIES** • Draw a Picture • Find a Pattern • Solve a Simpler Problem • Write an Equation • Work Backward • Guess and Check

Choose a strategy and solve.

(4) In a footrace Mark is 18 yd behind Jake and 8 yd behind Ellen. Nancy is 4 yd ahead of Ellen. How far behind Jake is Nancy?

(5) Draw the figure that completes the pattern.

(6) In how many ways can eleven $1 bills be divided among 3 people if each person receives at least two $1 bills?

(7) Jason paid $2.50 more for a gallon of paint than for some wallpaper. He paid $19.72 for the paint. How much did he pay for the wallpaper?

(8) Ellen has a 12-ft board that she is going to cut into 12 equal pieces. How many cuts will she have to make?

(9) Jim has $3 more than Ali. Ali has $8 more than Tom. Jim has twice as much money as Tasha. Ali has $10. How much does Tasha have?

WRITER'S CORNER

(10) Write a problem similar to the problem on page 146. Draw the first three tiles of the pattern. Exchange with a classmate and solve.

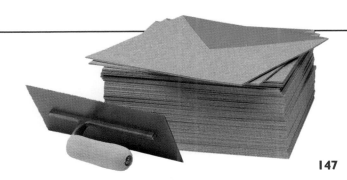

WARM UP...

What names are given to 3-sided, 4-sided, and 5-sided polygons?

POLYGONS

The Pentagon, in Arlington, Virginia, is one of the largest office buildings in the world. The building has the shape of a 5-sided polygon.

WORK TOGETHER

- Draw and name four different polygons.

- How are the polygons the same? How are they different?

- Draw four different figures that are not polygons. Explain why each figure is not a polygon.

The sum of the measures of the angles of a polygon can be found by drawing diagonals. Remember that a diagonal is a line segment that connects two nonadjacent vertices in a polygon.

- Trace rectangle *ABCD*. What is the measure of each angle in the rectangle? What is the sum of the measures of the angles?

- Draw a diagonal from vertex *A* to vertex *C* to form two triangles. What is the sum of the measures of the angles in each triangle?

- Trace the pentagon and the hexagon. Draw diagonals from one vertex to each of the other vertices in each polygon. How many triangles are formed in each polygon? What is the sum of the measures of the angles in the pentagon? the hexagon?

- What pattern do you see between the number of sides in a polygon and the number of triangles formed by diagonals?

- Explain how you can find the sum of the measures of the angles for any polygon.

- What is the sum of the measures of the angles in a 10-sided polygon? a 15-sided polygon?

You can also use a pattern to find the total number of diagonals a polygon can have.

- Look at the table. What pattern can you find in the way the number of diagonals increases?

- How many diagonals can a hexagon have?

- Predict how many diagonals an octagon can have.

Number of Sides of Polygon	Number of Diagonals
3	0
4	2
5	5
6	9
7	14

To find the total number of diagonals a polygon can have, you may use the expression $\frac{n(n-3)}{2}$, where n is the number of sides of the polygon.

- Use the given expression to find the total number of diagonals an octagon can have. How does this answer compare with the prediction you made earlier?

_____

A quadrilateral is one type of polygon. Recall that there are many types of quadrilaterals.

parallelogram
opposite sides
parallel and
congruent

rectangle
parallelogram
with four
right angles

square
rectangle with
four congruent
sides

rhombus
parallelogram
with four
congruent sides

trapezoid
only one pair
of parallel
sides

When you classify quadrilaterals, consider characteristics such as lengths of sides, angle measures, and parallel lines.

Talk About It

▶ How are the square and the rectangle the same? How are they different?

▶ How are the square and the rhombus the same? How are they different?

▶ How are the parallelogram and the rectangle the same? How are they different?

Another way to classify quadrilaterals is to determine the lines of symmetry and the points of rotation.

A square has four lines of symmetry. If you fold the square along any of the lines of symmetry, the two parts formed will match exactly.

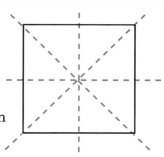

- Make a paper model of a parallelogram similar to the one on page 149. Can you fold it along a line so that the two parts formed match exactly? How many lines of symmetry does the parallelogram have?

A square also has a point of rotation. If you rotate the square 90° or 180° on the point where the diagonals of the square intersect, the square will look the same after each turn as it did before each turn.

45°

- Draw the diagonals on the paper model of the parallelogram. Place a pin on the point where the diagonals intersect. Turn the parallelogram 90° and then 180°.

- Does the parallelogram look the same after each turn as it did before each turn? Does the parallelogram have a point of rotation?

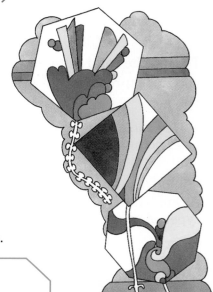

Check for Understanding

Find the sum of the measures of the angles for each polygon.

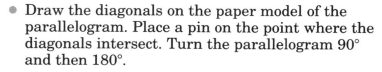

1.   2.   3.   4.

Tell the total number of diagonals each polygon can have.

5. square   6. pentagon   7. decagon   8. 12-sided polygon

Tell the number of lines of symmetry each quadrilateral has.

9.   10.    11.    12.

Practice

Find the sum of the measures of the angles for each polygon.

13. pentagon   **14.** octagon   **15.** 20-sided polygon   **16.** 12-sided polygon

Tell the total number of diagonals each polygon can have.

17. triangle   **18.** octagon   **19.** 10-sided polygon   **20.** 20-sided polygon

The sequence of drawings shows a quadrilateral as it is pulled out of a box. In each step, a–c, tell the possible quadrilaterals that the figure can be.

21. a. 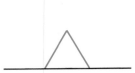   **b.**    **c.**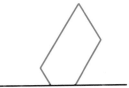

22. a.    **b.**    **c.**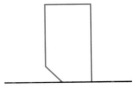

Draw the quadrilateral. Then draw all the lines of symmetry.

23. rectangle   **24.** rhombus   **25.** trapezoid   **26.** parallelogram

27. Look back at Exercises 23–26. Which quadrilaterals have a point of rotation for a rotation of 90°? for a rotation of 180°?

Mixed Applications

Draw quadrilateral *ABCD* as described in Exercises 28–29. Then identify the quadrilateral.

28. $\overline{AB}$ is parallel to $\overline{DC}$, and $\overline{BC}$ is parallel to $\overline{AD}$. $\overline{AB}$, $\overline{BC}$, $\overline{DC}$, and $\overline{AD}$ are congruent. $\angle ABC$ is a right angle.

29. $\overline{AB}$ is parallel to $\overline{DC}$. $\overline{BC}$ is not parallel to $\overline{AD}$. $\angle ADC$ is a right angle. $\overline{AD}$ is not congruent to $\overline{DC}$, and $\overline{AD}$ is not congruent to $\overline{BC}$.

30. The measure of one angle in a parallelogram is 73°. Find the measures of the other three angles.

31. In rectangle *RSTV*, the length of $\overline{RS}$ is 25 cm. Find the length of $\overline{TV}$.

Are squares and rectangles also parallelograms? Explain.

EXPLORING Triangles

You know that the sum of the measures of the angles in a triangle is 180°. You also know that supplementary angles have a sum of 180°. You can use these facts to discover relationships among the interior and exterior angles of triangles.

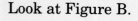
WORK TOGETHER

Building Understanding

In Figure A, $\angle 1$, $\angle 2$, and $\angle 3$ are interior angles of the triangle. $\angle 4$ and $\angle 5$ are exterior angles of the triangle. Trace the figure.

- Use a protractor to find m $\angle 1$ and m $\angle 2$.

- Without measuring, find m $\angle 3$. Explain the procedure you used.

- Without measuring, find m $\angle 4$. Explain the procedure you used.

- How does m $\angle 4$ compare with m $\angle 1$ + m $\angle 2$?

- Find m $\angle 5$.

- How does m $\angle 5$ compare with m $\angle 1$ + m $\angle 3$?

Look at Figure B.

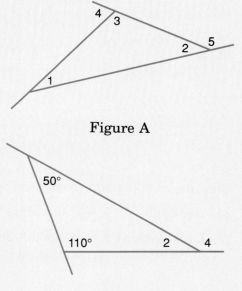

Figure A

Figure B

Talk About It

▶ Without using a protractor, how can you find m $\angle 4$? Can you use this measure to find the measure of any other angles? Explain.

▶ What generalization can you make about the measures of the interior angles and the exterior angles of triangles?

Making the Connection

You have found that the measure of an exterior angle of a triangle is equal to the sum of the measures of the two nonadjacent interior angles. You can find the measure of any interior or exterior angle of a triangle if you know the measure of at least two angles.

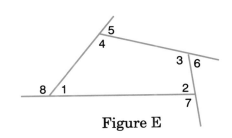

Example m ∠ 4 = 110°, and m ∠ 1 = 50°.
Find m ∠ 3.

Since m ∠ 1 + m ∠ 3 = m ∠ 4,
50° + m ∠ 3 = 110°.

So, m ∠ 3 = 110° − 50° = 60°.

1. How can you find the measure of ∠ 2?

2. Find m ∠ 5.

3. Find m ∠ 6.

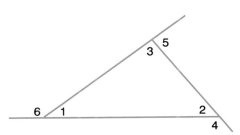

Figure C

Checking Understanding

Use Figure D for Exercises 4–6. Tell which two angle measures have a sum equal to the measure of the given angle.

4. ∠ 4   **5.** ∠ 5   **6.** ∠ 6

Use Figure D for Exercises 7–12. Find the indicated angle measure.

7. m ∠ 2 = 45°, and m ∠ 3 = 35°. Find m ∠ 1.

8. m ∠ 3 = 60°, and m ∠ 2 = 40°. Find m ∠ 5.

9. m ∠ 1 = 50°, and m ∠ 3 = 75°. Find m ∠ 6.

10. m ∠ 1 = 100°, and m ∠ 2 = 32°. Find m ∠ 4.

11. m ∠ 6 = 130°, and m ∠ 3 = 75°. Find m ∠ 1.

12. In the triangle, m ∠ 1 = 60°, m ∠ 2 = 70°, and m ∠ 3 = 50°.
Find m ∠ 4 + m ∠ 5 + m ∠ 6.

13. In Figure E, m ∠ 1 = 60°, m ∠ 2 = 80°, m ∠ 3 = 100°, and m ∠ 4 = 120°.
Find m ∠ 5 + m ∠ 6 + m ∠ 7 + m ∠ 8.

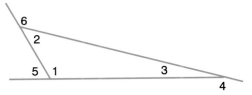

Figure D

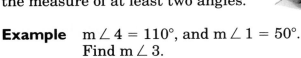

Figure E

More Practice, Lesson 5.9, page H48

REVIEW AND MAINTENANCE

1. Steven receives an allowance of $2.20 each week. This week he was paid with nickels, dimes, and quarters. If he was given 13 coins in all, how many of each was he given?

2. To frame a door, a carpenter needs a piece of wood $37\frac{1}{2}$ in. long and two pieces of wood each $76\frac{2}{3}$ in. long. How much wood does he need in all?

3. Jenny needs $12\frac{2}{3}$ square yards of carpet for a hallway and $9\frac{3}{4}$ square yards of the same carpet for a bedroom. If she buys 22 square yards of carpet, will she have enough for both areas?

4. Draw the figure that completes the pattern.

Find the value.

5. 2^3 6. 4^2 7. 7^1 8. 12^4 9. 25^0

Write an algebraic expression for the word expression.

10. 3 more than the number of hats, h 11. 2.4 m less than the distance, d

12. 4 times the cost, c 13. the number of days, d, divided by 7

Write the prime factorization, using exponents.

14. 12   15. 44   16. 25   17. 100   18. 36

Write as a fraction.

19. $3\frac{1}{2}$ 20. $1\frac{3}{4}$ 21. $7\frac{1}{5}$ 22. $2\frac{5}{6}$ 23. $8\frac{1}{2}$

Find the product or quotient.

24. $\frac{1}{2} \times \frac{2}{5}$ 25. $1\frac{1}{4} \times 5\frac{2}{3}$ 26. $\frac{8}{7} \div \frac{4}{5}$ 27. $3\frac{1}{2} \div 1\frac{1}{4}$

28. $\frac{3}{8} \times 2\frac{1}{2}$ 29. $9 \times \frac{3}{5}$ 30. $\frac{9}{5} \div \frac{4}{3}$ 31. $2\frac{1}{3} \div 4\frac{1}{2}$

Measure the angle. Write *acute*, *right*, or *obtuse*.

32.   33.   34.    35.

Spotlight ON PROBLEM SOLVING

Understand
Plan
Solve
Look Back

VISUALIZE THE RESULTS

Often the solution to a problem can be seen or visualized. Study the following problem.

Fifty square tables, each with sides 4 ft long, are placed side by side in a row. One person can sit at each open side of a table. How many people can be seated at the row of 50 tables?

TALK ABOUT IT

a. Is it practical to draw a picture of all 50 tables? Explain.

b. Draw a row of 5 square tables. How many people can sit at each end table? How many can sit at each table that is not an end table?

c. Imagine adding more tables to the row. How many more people can be seated for each table added?

d. Explain how you can find how many people can be seated at a row of 50 tables. Then tell how many people can be seated at the 50 tables.

e. How many people can be seated at a row of 75 tables?

Apply

Solve each problem by visualizing the result.

1. Twenty equilateral triangles, each with sides that are 1 in. long, are placed in a row as shown. What is the distance around the row of triangles?

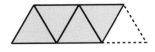

2. A row is made with 100 hexagons. Each side of each hexagon is 2 in. long. What is the distance around the row of hexagons?

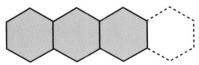

CONGRUENT POLYGONS

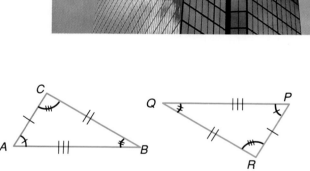

In the building shown, all the windows have the same size and shape. Polygons that have the same size and shape are **congruent polygons.**

In congruent polygons, corresponding angles are congruent and corresponding sides are congruent.

Use dot paper to draw a quadrilateral congruent to *RSTV*. Label your quadrilateral *ABCD*.

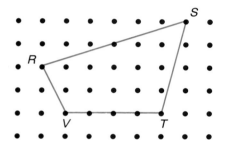

- In your quadrilateral, which angle corresponds to ∠*R*?

- In your quadrilateral, which side corresponds to $\overline{ST}$?

Triangles *ABC* and *PQR* are congruent. NOTE: The same mark on two angles or on two sides indicates congruence.

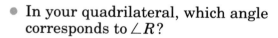

- Which angle corresponds to ∠*A*? ∠*B*? ∠*C*?

- Which side corresponds to $\overline{AB}$? $\overline{BC}$? $\overline{CA}$?

When you name congruent polygons, list the vertices in the order of the corresponding parts.

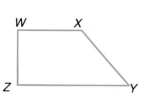

Example   Quadrilateral *WXYZ* ≅ quadrilateral *DEFG*.
Name the corresponding congruent parts.

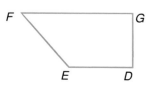

Corresponding Sides	Corresponding Angles
$\overline{WX} \cong \overline{DE}$	∠*W* ≅ ∠*D*
$\overline{XY} \cong \overline{EF}$	∠*X* ≅ ∠*E*
$\overline{YZ} \cong \overline{FG}$	∠*Y* ≅ ∠*F*
$\overline{ZW} \cong \overline{GD}$	∠*Z* ≅ ∠*G*

Check for Understanding

△*UVW* ≅ △*XYZ*. Complete.

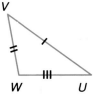
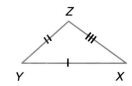

1. $\overline{XY}$ ≅ ■   2. ∠*V* ≅ ■
3. $\overline{WU}$ ≅ ■   4. ∠*Z* ≅ ■
5. m∠*X* = 38°. Find m∠*U*.
6. The length of $\overline{ZX}$ is 4 cm. Find the length of $\overline{UW}$.

Practice

7. Quadrilateral *ABCD* ≅ quadrilateral *PQRS*. Name the corresponding congruent sides and angles.

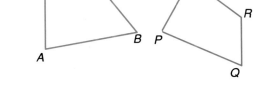

The polygons in each of Exercises 8–11 are congruent. Find *a*, *b*, and *c*.

8.
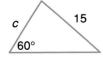
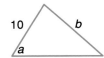

9.

10.
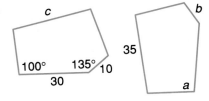

11.
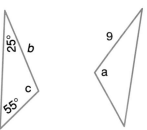

Mixed Applications

12. A carpenter uses a pattern to cut two congruent polygons. How can the carpenter be sure that the polygons are congruent?

13. Quadrilateral *ABCD* can be divided into two congruent triangles by each of its diagonals. Is *ABCD* a parallelogram? Explain.

14. **Visual Thinking** Make four copies of this trapezoid. Then show how you can use the four congruent trapezoids to make a larger trapezoid that has the same shape.

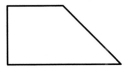

In your own words, explain what must be true of two congruent figures.

WRAP
UP...

CONSTRUCTING
Congruent Triangles

The city of Bedford is building a
recreation center. The architect wants
to make sure that the triangular roof
trusses being used for the building are
exactly the same. Does the architect
need to measure all six corresponding
parts of each truss?

To show that triangles are congruent,
you need at least three corresponding
congruent parts. These rules can be
used to determine whether two
triangles are congruent.

Side-Side-Side (SSS)   If three sides of
one triangle are congruent to three sides
of another triangle, then the triangles
are congruent.

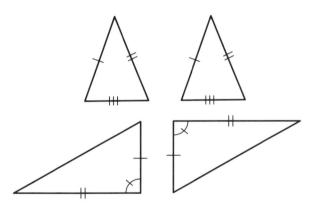

Side-Angle-Side (SAS)   If two sides
and the included angle of one triangle
are congruent to two sides and the
included angle of another triangle, then
the triangles are congruent.

Angle-Side-Angle (ASA)   If two angles
and the included side of one triangle
are congruent to two angles and the
included side of another triangle, then
the triangles are congruent.

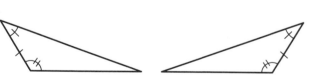

So, the architect needs to measure only
three corresponding parts.

Talk About It

▶ If two triangles are congruent by the SSS rule, are the
corresponding angles of the triangles also congruent? Explain.

▶ If three angles of one triangle are congruent to three angles of
another triangle, must the triangles be congruent? In other
words, do you think there is an Angle-Angle-Angle rule? Why
or why not?

You can use the rules for showing the congruence of two triangles to construct congruent triangles.

Examples

A. Using the SSS rule, construct a triangle congruent to △*JKL*.

Think: The corresponding sides must have the same length.

Step 1 Draw $\overrightarrow{MN}$. Construct $\overline{MO} \cong \overline{JK}$. 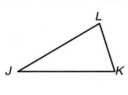	**Step 2** Use the compass to measure $\overline{JL}$. Place the compass point on *M,* and draw an arc as shown.	**Step 3** Use the compass to measure $\overline{KL}$. Place the compass point on *O,* and draw an arc that intersects the arc drawn in Step 2. Label the point *P.*	**Step 4** Draw $\overline{MP}$ and $\overline{OP}$. △*MOP* ≅ △*JKL*
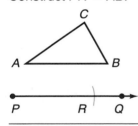	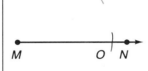	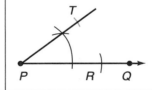	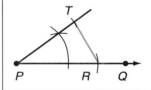

B. Using the SAS rule, construct a triangle congruent to △*ABC*.

Think: Use these parts: $\overline{AB}$, ∠*A*, and $\overline{AC}$.

Step 1 Construct $\overline{PR} \cong \overline{AB}$. 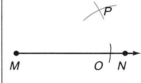	**Step 2** Construct ∠*P* ≅ ∠*A*.	**Step 3** Construct $\overline{PT} \cong \overline{AC}$.	**Step 4** Draw $\overline{TR}$. △*PRT* ≅ △*ABC*
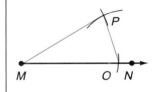	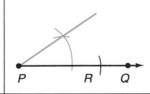	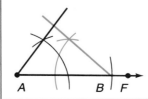	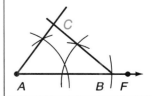

C. Using the ASA rule, construct a triangle congruent to △*DEF*.

Think: Use these parts: $\overline{DE}$, ∠*D*, and ∠*E*.

Step 1 Construct $\overline{AB} \cong \overline{DE}$. 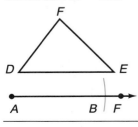	**Step 2** Construct ∠*A* ≅ ∠*D*.	**Step 3** Construct ∠*B* ≅ ∠*E*.	**Step 4** Label *C.* △*ABC* ≅ △*DEF*
	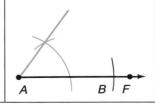		

Talk About It

▶ Suppose ∠3 ≅ ∠6 and ∠2 ≅ ∠5. What else do you need to know in order to show that △ABC ≅ △DEF? Which rule does this illustrate, SSS, SAS, or ASA?

▶ Suppose ∠1 ≅ ∠4 and $\overline{AB}$ ≅ $\overline{DE}$. What else do you need to know in order to show that △ABC ≅ △DEF? Which rule does this illustrate, SSS, SAS, or ASA?

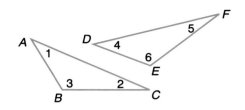

Check for Understanding

Determine whether the triangles are congruent by SSS, SAS, or ASA.

1.

2.

3.

Determine whether there are enough marks to show that the two figures are congruent. Answer *yes* or *no*.

4.

5.

6.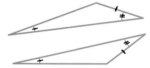

Practice

Determine whether the triangles are congruent by SSS, SAS, or ASA.

7.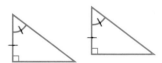

8.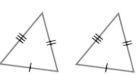

9.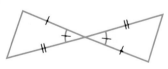

Trace the triangle. Use the indicated rule to construct a congruent triangle.

10. SSS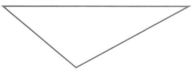

11. ASA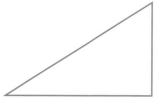

12. SAS

Each pair of triangles is congruent. Find the missing measures.

13.

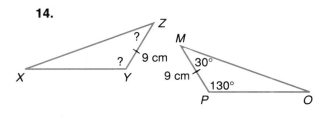

14.

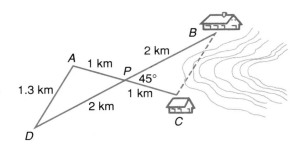

Mixed Applications

In the figure, two houses are located at points B and C on either side of a lake. Road distances PB, PA, PC, PD, and AD are measured. Angle BPC is measured.

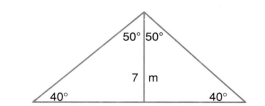

15. What is the measure of $\angle APD$? Give a reason for your answer.

16. Find BC, the distance between the houses. Give a reason for your answer.

17. The triangles shown have two angles and one side congruent, but the side is not the included side. Are the other two angles congruent? Explain. Are the triangles congruent? Explain.

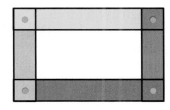

EVERYDAY CONNECTION

The triangle is a useful shape to use in construction because it is a rigid figure. You can show this property by completing Exercises 18–20.

18. Use paper strips and brass fasteners to make a quadrilateral. Try to push in at one of the vertices of the figure. Does the quadrilateral change shape?

19. Use paper strips and brass fasteners to make a triangle. Try to push in at one of the vertices of the figure. Does the triangle change shape?

20. Use paper strips and brass fasteners to make other polygons. Are any other polygons rigid figures?

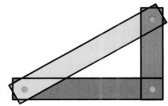

Explain the rules that you use to decide whether two triangles are congruent.

WRAP UP...

CIRCLES

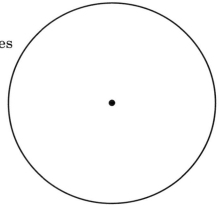

You can use a circle to form many different regular polygons. Recall that in a regular polygon, all the sides are congruent and all the angles are congruent.

WORK TOGETHER

Trace this circle several times, and then cut out your circles. Be sure to include the point that represents the center of the circle.

- Take one of the circles and fold it in half. The crease formed represents what part of the circle?

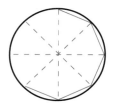

- Fold the circle in half again to form right angles. Open the circle, and draw line segments from the endpoints of adjacent creases. What polygon is formed inside the circle?

- Take another circle and fold it in half twice as before. Then fold it in half one more time. Into how many parts have you divided the circle? What polygon will you form if you draw line segments from the endpoints of the adjacent creases?

You can also use a compass to make some polygons.

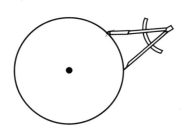

Use a compass to draw a circle. Using the same compass opening, place the point on the circle, and draw an arc that intersects the circle. Move the point to the intersection of the arc and the circle, and draw another arc. Continue this procedure until you are back at your original position.

- How many arcs did you make? What polygon will you form if you draw line segments from each arc to the adjacent arc?

- How can you use this circle to draw a triangle?

- What is the relationship between the distance from one arc to the next and the length of the radius of the circle?

Check for Understanding

Name the polygon formed when a line segment is drawn between the endpoints of each diameter.

1.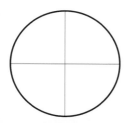

2.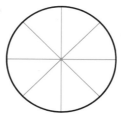

3.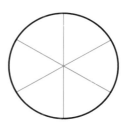

Practice

Name the polygon formed when a line segment is drawn from each arc to the adjacent arc.

4.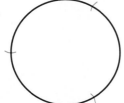

5.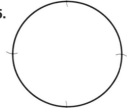

6.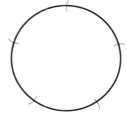

Mixed Applications

Use the figure for Exercises 7–9. $\overleftrightarrow{AB} \parallel \overleftrightarrow{RS}$

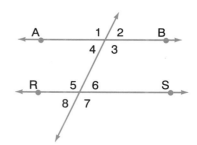

7. Name two pairs of vertical angles, adjacent angles, and supplementary angles.

8. Suppose m ∠ 1 = 110°. What is m ∠ 6? Explain how you found the measure.

9. Suppose the transversal is perpendicular to $\overleftrightarrow{AB}$. Would the transversal be perpendicular to $\overleftrightarrow{RS}$? Why or why not?

MIXED REVIEW

Write a fraction in simplest form for the decimal.

1. 0.5   **2.** 0.35   **3.** 0.3   **4.** 0.625   **5.** 0.08

Compare. Write $<$, $>$, or $=$.

6. $1\frac{1}{2}$ ● 1.32   **7.** 2.655 ● 2.566   **8.** $9\frac{2}{3}$ ● $9\frac{4}{5}$ **9.** 7.589 ● $7\frac{3}{5}$

What polygon could you draw if you folded a circle in half four times?

The Bennetts have decided to add a room onto their house. The table shows the estimates and the terms of payment provided by three different builders. Which builder should the Bennetts choose?

Builder	Estimate	Terms of Payment
Elgin Builders	$19,000	$19,000 when work is completed
Taylor Construction	$21,000	36 monthly payments of $690
Best Construction	$20,000	60 monthly payments of $430

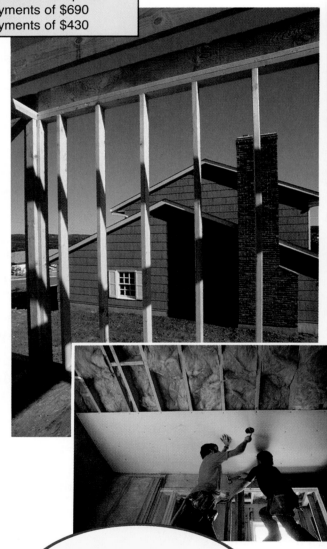

▶ UNDERSTAND

What are you asked to find?

What facts are given?

▶ PLAN

How will you solve the problem?

You can find each builder's total cost for the new room. Then consider the advantages and disadvantages of each.

▶ SOLVE

What questions should you ask to consider the advantages and disadvantages of each builder?

- What is the total cost of the room for each builder?

- With which builder will the Bennetts spend the least amount of money?

- Are monthly payments more convenient even though the total cost would be greater?

Which builder would you choose?

▶ LOOK BACK

What reasons did you use for making your choice?

WHAT IF... . . . the Bennetts do not have $19,000 available? Would this affect your choice? Why or why not?

Apply

Suppose the Bennetts decide to get a loan for $19,000 from a bank and have Elgin Builders build the room.

① If the payments on the loan are $700 per month for 36 months, how much will the Bennetts pay back to the bank in all?

② How does the total amount the Bennetts will pay the bank compare with the cost of having Taylor Construction build the room?

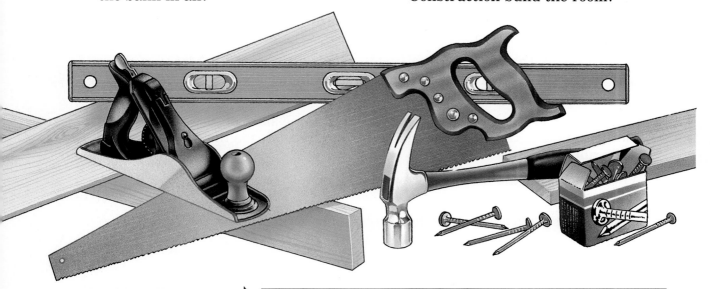

Mixed Applications ➤	STRATEGIES	• Work Backward • Guess and Check • Write an Equation • Use a Formula

Choose a strategy and solve.

③ The Bennetts bought some furniture for the new room. The sofa cost $240 more than the recliner. Together the sofa and the recliner cost $810. What was the cost of the sofa? What was the cost of the recliner?

④ The Bennetts bought 2 paintings on sale for $27.98 each. The regular price of the paintings was $35.45 each. How much did the Bennetts save by buying the paintings on sale?

⑤ A plumber charged the Bennetts $155 to install some pipes for the new room. To determine the amount of the bill, the plumber doubled the cost of the pipes for his markup. Then he added $112 for labor. What was the plumber's cost?

⑥ Before buying carpeting for the new room, Michael Bennett used the formula $A = lw$ to find the area of the floor. If the room is 27 ft long and 15 ft wide, what is the area of the floor in square feet?

⑦ Michael Bennett paid $537.75 for carpeting for the new room. The cost of the carpeting was $11.95 per square yard. How many square yards did he buy?

⑧ After the room was built, Mrs. Bennett found 135 nails and screws in the yard. There were twice as many nails as screws. How many nails did she find?

More Practice, Lesson 5.13, page H49

Vocabulary Check

Choose a word from the box to complete each sentence.

bisect
complementary
SAS
SSS
supplementary
transversal
vertical

1. When you divide a line segment into two congruent parts, you __?__ the line segment. *(page 144)*

2. When the sum of the measures of two angles equals 90°, the angles are __?__. *(page 134)*

3. When two parallel lines are cut by a __?__, four pairs of corresponding angles are formed. *(page 140)*

4. If three sides of one triangle are congruent to three sides of another triangle, then the triangles are congruent. This is the __?__ rule. *(page 158)*

5. When the sum of the measure of two angles equals 180°, the angles are __?__. *(page 134)*

6. Nonadjacent congruent angles formed by intersecting lines are called __?__ angles. *(page 135)*

7. If two sides and the included angle of one triangle are congruent to two sides and the included angle of another triangle, then the triangles are congruent. This is the __?__ rule. *(page 158)*

Concept Check

Draw the following geometric figures. *(page 132)*

8. a line   9. a line segment   10. a ray   11. an angle

Use the figure for Exercises 12–14. *(page 134)*

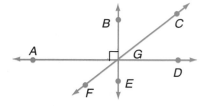

12. Name two adjacent angles.

13. Name two vertical angles.

14. Name two complementary angles.

Identify each polygon described. *(page 148)*

15. a quadrilateral with only one pair of parallel sides

16. a parallelogram with four right angles

17. a polygon whose interior angles have a sum of 540°

18. a 6-sided polygon

Skill Check

Use the figure to find the measure of the given angle.
$\overleftrightarrow{AB} \parallel \overleftrightarrow{CD}$ *(pages 134, 140)*

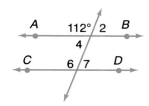

19. m ∠ 2

20. m ∠ 4

21. m ∠ 6

22. m ∠ 7

Draw the figures for Exercises 23–25, using a ruler and a protractor. Then construct congruent figures, using a compass and a straightedge. *(pages 138, 158)*

23. 7-cm line segment

24. 70° angle

25. triangle

26. Draw $\overleftrightarrow{AB}$ and point P above $\overleftrightarrow{AB}$. Construct a line through point P parallel to $\overleftrightarrow{AB}$. *(page 142)*

27. Draw $\overline{CD}$. Construct the perpendicular bisector of $\overline{CD}$. *(page 144)*

Tell the number of diagonals each polygon can have. *(page 148)*

28. quadrilateral

29. hexagon

30. 15-sided polygon

31. Does a rectangle have a point of rotation for a rotation of 180°? *(page 150)*

32. Draw a square and all its lines of symmetry. *(page 150)*

33. Use the figure to find m ∠ 6 when m ∠ 2 = 75° and m ∠ 3 = 45°. *(page 152)*

34. Quadrilateral $ABCD \cong$ quadrilateral $PRST$. Draw the quadrilaterals and name the corresponding congruent angles and sides. *(page 156)*

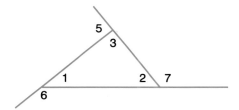

Problem-Solving Check

Draw the figure that completes the pattern. *(page 146)*

35.

36.

37. Mike can open a regular checking account at a bank and pay a service charge of $3.50 per month plus $0.20 for each check written. What will be the service charge if he writes 10 checks in one month? *(page 164)*

38. Mike can open a Plus account at the bank and pay no service charge as long he maintains a minimum balance of $500. Give one advantage and one disadvantage of this choice. *(page 164)*

CHAPTER TEST

Use the figure for Exercises 1–8. $\overleftrightarrow{AB} \parallel \overleftrightarrow{CD}$, and $\overleftrightarrow{EF}$ is a transversal.

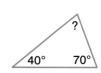

1. Name a line that intersects $\overleftrightarrow{CD}$.

2. Name an acute angle with side $\overrightarrow{PE}$.

3. Name a pair of supplementary angles.

4. $\angle EPB$ is adjacent to what angle?

5. If m $\angle PTD = 36°$, what is m $\angle PTC$?

6. If m $\angle EPA = 115°$, what is m $\angle DTF$?

7. Suppose $\overleftrightarrow{EF}$ bisects $\overline{CD}$ and the length of $\overline{CD}$ is 5 cm. What is the length of $\overline{CT}$?

8. Suppose m $\angle APT = 90°$. What is the relationship between $\overleftrightarrow{EF}$ and $\overleftrightarrow{AB}$?

9. How many lines of symmetry can a parallelogram have?

10. What is the sum of the measures of the interior angles of a hexagon?

11. What is m $\angle 6$?

12. $\triangle ABC \cong \triangle XYZ$. Name the corresponding sides.

Find the missing measures.

13.

14.

15.

16.

Draw the figure that completes the pattern.

17.

18.

19. Julie can buy 2 lb of nails at one store for $1.50 or 3 lb of the same size nails at another store for $2.16. Which choice will cost her the least per pound?

20. The Mitchells are buying a new VCR. They can pay $345.00 in cash, or they can make 24 payments of $16.75 each. How much more will they pay for the VCR if they choose the 24 payments?

Teamwork P-R-O-J-E-C-T

 Find Geometry in Architecture

Whether you live in a small town or in a large metropolitan area, there are probably some nearby houses or buildings that have interesting or unique designs.

Work with your classmates to draw a picture of an interesting building in your area.

 **DECIDE**

As a team, discuss buildings in your area that you can use for this project. Choose one building. Decide which will be better to use as a reference: a photograph of the building, or rough sketches and notes.

Decide how large the final picture will be.

 DO

As a team, visit the building you have chosen. Find out whether any information about the building is available, such as when it was built, the name of the builder, and the name of the owner.

Draw a picture of the building. Include with the picture any information about the building.

SHARE

Compare your picture with those of other teams. Tell why you chose your building.

Talk About It

• What ornamentation or other details make the building special?

• What geometric shapes are shown in the design of the building?

Tessellations

Designs on tile floors are often made with congruent squares, equilateral triangles, or regular hexagons. Such patterns that fill a plane are called tessellations. You can use any triangle or quadrilateral as a basic unit for a tessellation.

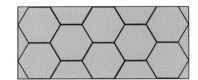

Examples

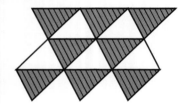 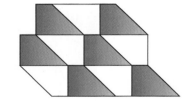 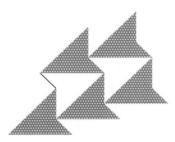

Copy the following tessellation on a sheet of graph paper. Then extend the tessellation to show at least 40 congruent quadrilaterals.

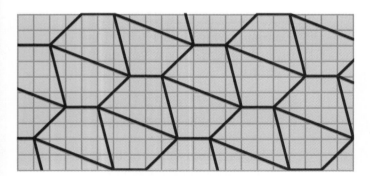

On another sheet of graph paper, draw your own quadrilateral, and use it to complete a tessellation.

Challenge

Number Sense

Jill paid for a $1.00 ticket with 25 coins. What coins did she use?

Logical Reasoning

With 5 fives, write an expression equal to 1. Use any operation signs you need.

Write the letter of the correct answer.

1. Which fraction is greater than $\frac{3}{8}$?

   A. $\frac{1}{4}$

   B. $\frac{3}{10}$

   C. $\frac{1}{3}$

   D. $\frac{1}{2}$

2. $\frac{1}{2} \times \frac{1}{3} \div \frac{1}{4}$

   A. $\frac{1}{12}$

   B. $\frac{1}{6}$

   C. $\frac{2}{3}$

   D. not here

3. $9 + n = 86$

   A. $n = 9.5$

   B. $n = 77$

   C. $n = 95$

   D. $n = 774$

4. $4\frac{1}{12} - 3\frac{2}{9}$

   A. $\frac{11}{12}$

   B. $\frac{31}{36}$

   C. $1\frac{1}{3}$

   D. $7\frac{11}{36}$

5. $\frac{15}{20} = \frac{n}{4}$

   A. $n = 2$

   B. $n = 3$

   C. $n = 5$

   D. $n = 75$

6. Which is the best estimate for $8,493 \times 4,986$?

   A. 4,500

   B. 45,000

   C. 450,000

   D. 45,000,000

7. Which line always divides another line into two equal parts?

   A. parallel

   B. perpendicular

   C. bisector

   D. intersecting

8. Which angles have a combined measure of 180°?

   A. complementary

   B. supplementary

   C. obtuse

   D. acute

9. $2\frac{2}{5} + 3\frac{3}{7}$

   A. $5\frac{5}{12}$

   B. $5\frac{29}{35}$

   C. $5\frac{6}{7}$

   D. $6\frac{6}{35}$

10. Which is the best estimate for $5\frac{1}{3} \times 6\frac{1}{4}$?

    A. 20

    B. 30

    C. 40

    D. 100

11. $0.984 \div 0.3$

    A. 0.328

    B. 3.28

    C. 32.8

    D. 328

12. $648 = 8t$

    A. $t = 81$

    B. $t = 640$

    C. $t = 5,184$

    D. not here

13. Lisa wants to hang a 20-in.-wide poster in the center of a wall that is 88 in. wide. How much wall space should she leave on each side of the poster?

    A. 17 in.

    B. 24 in.

    C. 34 in.

    D. 68 in.

14. Jason has a total of 24 dimes and quarters. The value of the coins is $4.05. He has 2 more dimes than quarters. How many dimes does Jason have?

    A. 10 dimes

    B. 11 dimes

    C. 13 dimes

    D. 15 dimes

6

RATIO, PROPORTION, AND PERCENT

Did you know . . .

. . . that a fast-food meal consisting of a cheeseburger, corn on the cob, and a vanilla milk shake provides a total of 803 calories?

Talk About It

What information will you need in order to find what percent of your total daily intake of calories this meal provides?

corn ON THE cob

eseburgers

RATIOS AND RATES

Andrea is making lemonade from 2 cans of frozen concentrate and 6 cans of water. What is the ratio of the number of cans of concentrate to the number of cans of water?

Recall that a **ratio** is a comparison of two numbers.

Cans of concentrate $\longrightarrow$ 2 $\longleftarrow$ first term
Cans of water $\longrightarrow$ 6 $\longleftarrow$ second term

This comparison is read as "the ratio of 2 to 6." It can also be written as 2:6 or 2 to 6. The order of the terms in a ratio is important. The ratio 2:6 is not the same as the ratio 6:2.

Ratios, like fractions, can be written in simplest form.

$$\frac{2}{6} = \frac{1}{3} \longleftarrow \text{simplest form}$$

The ratios $\frac{2}{6}$ and $\frac{1}{3}$ are equivalent.

Table of Equivalent Ratios				
Cans of concentrate	1	2	3	4
Cans of water	3	6	9	12

You can use cross multiplication to determine whether two ratios are equivalent. If cross products are equal, the ratios are equivalent.

Examples

A. $\frac{3}{4} \underset{60}{\overset{60}{\times}} \frac{15}{20}$ Since 60 = 60, the ratios are equivalent.

B. $\frac{5}{6} \underset{250}{\overset{252}{\times}} \frac{42}{50}$ Since 250 ≠ 252, the ratios are *not* equivalent.

Talk About It

▶ How can you use division to determine whether $\frac{3}{4}$ and $\frac{15}{20}$ are equivalent ratios?

A **rate** is a ratio that compares quantities of different units.

A **unit rate** is a rate that has 1 as the second term.

Mary Beth drank 24 oz of milk yesterday. Her calorie intake from the milk was 480 calories. What was the unit rate of calories per ounce?

calories $\longrightarrow$ $\frac{480}{24} = \frac{480 \div 24}{24 \div 24} = \frac{20}{1}$ So, the unit rate was 20 calories per ounce.
ounces $\longrightarrow$

Check for Understanding

Write the ratio in the form $\frac{a}{b}$.

1. triangles to circles
2. circles to triangles
3. circles to all shapes
4. triangles to all shapes
5. 8 to 15
6. 7:9

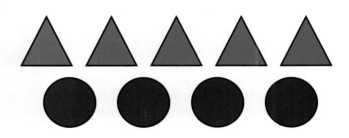

Practice

Write the ratio in the form $\frac{a}{b}$.

7. 5:7
8. 10 to 11
9. 6 out of 7
10. 47:100

Write the ratio in simplest form.

11. $\frac{16}{24}$
12. $\frac{14}{18}$
13. $\frac{24}{30}$
14. $\frac{42}{56}$

Tell whether the ratio is equivalent to $\frac{2}{3}$. Write *yes* or *no*.

15. 8:12
16. 4:9
17. 10 to 15
18. 30 to 20

Write = or ≠.

19. $\frac{5}{4}$ ● $\frac{10}{8}$
20. $\frac{7}{8}$ ● $\frac{15}{16}$
21. $\frac{30}{40}$ ● $\frac{3}{4}$
22. $\frac{10}{12}$ ● $\frac{20}{32}$

Write the unit rate.

23. $\dfrac{\$1.00}{4\ \text{oranges}}$
24. $\dfrac{\$1.80}{10\ \text{lb of potatoes}}$
25. $\dfrac{120\ \text{calories}}{8\ \text{oz}}$
26. $\dfrac{\$21}{5\ \text{dinners}}$

Mixed Applications

27. Andrea plans to serve lemonade at the family picnic. She combines the concentrate and the water in a 1:3 ratio. How many cans of water does she combine with 11 cans of concentrate?

28. David is preparing hamburgers for the picnic. He can make 4 hamburgers from 1 lb of ground beef, so the ratio is 4:1. How many hamburgers can he make from 4 lb of ground beef?

29. LaShonda is making potato salad. Her recipe calls for 3 lb of potatoes, 6 eggs, and 4 cups of celery. LaShonda wants to triple the recipe. What quantities of potatoes, eggs, and celery are needed?

30. Last year 45 people attended the picnic. This year 60 people attended. What is the ratio of last year's attendance to this year's attendance? Write the ratio in simplest form.

Two numbers are in the ratio of 1:4. If 12 is the smaller number, what is the larger number?

WARM UP...

What do you know about the cross products of two equivalent ratios?

PROPORTIONS

On Friday, 12 of the 30 students in Mrs. DePalma's class brought their lunch. The ratio of the number of students who brought their lunch to the total number of students was the same in Mr. Howard's class. Mr. Howard had 35 students in his class. How many of them brought their lunch?

A **proportion** is an equation stating that two ratios are equivalent.

You can use a proportion to solve this problem.

Step 1

Write a proportion.

Let a = the number of Mr. Howard's students who brought their lunch.

proportion ⟶ $\dfrac{12}{30} = \dfrac{a}{35}$ ⟵ number of students who brought their lunch
⟵ total number of students

Step 2

Solve the proportion. You can solve a proportion by using cross multiplication.

$30a = 12 \times 35$ Find the cross products.

$30a = 420$

$\dfrac{30a}{30} = \dfrac{420}{30}$ Divide each side by 30 to solve the equation.

$a = 14$

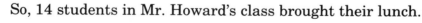

So, 14 students in Mr. Howard's class brought their lunch.

Other Methods

A calculator may be used to solve a proportion.

$\dfrac{n}{0.8} = \dfrac{3.5}{5.6}$

$5.6n = 0.8 \times 3.5$

$n = \dfrac{0.8 \times 3.5}{5.6}$ 0.8 ⊗ 3.5 ÷ 5.6 ◻

$n = 0.5$ | 0.5 |

Mental math may be used to solve a proportion.

$\dfrac{1}{2} = \dfrac{b}{8}$ **Think:** $\dfrac{1 \times 4}{2 \times 4} = \dfrac{4}{8}$

$\dfrac{1}{2} = \dfrac{4}{8}$

So, $b = 4$.

or   **Think:** $2b = 8$

$b = 4$

Talk About It

▶ Name two different ways to find the missing term for $\dfrac{2}{9} = \dfrac{6}{n}$. Which do you prefer? Why?

Check for Understanding

Solve the proportion.

1. $\dfrac{80}{d} = \dfrac{8}{16}$ **2.** $\dfrac{16}{48} = \dfrac{n}{240}$ **3.** $\dfrac{b}{10} = \dfrac{27}{90}$ **4.** $\dfrac{2}{\$5.00} = \dfrac{9}{y}$

Write a proportion. Use n to represent the missing term. Then solve.

5. $0.70 for 2 pounds. How much for 8 pounds?

6. 900 calories in 18 ounces. How many in 1 ounce?

Complete these ratio tables.

7.

Pounds of sliced turkey	1	2	3	4	9
Servings	4	■	■	■	■

8.

Pints of orange juice	3	6	9	12	15
Pints of cranberry juice	2	■	■	■	■

Practice

Write a proportion using two of the ratios.

9. $\dfrac{45}{63}, \dfrac{30}{35}, \dfrac{5}{7}$ **10.** $\dfrac{75}{80}, \dfrac{15}{16}, \dfrac{5}{8}$ **11.** $\dfrac{9}{10}, \dfrac{108}{120}, \dfrac{135}{140}$ **12.** $9:11, \dfrac{90}{111}, 99 \text{ to } 121$

Write the equation that results when you cross multiply.

13. $\dfrac{1}{9} = \dfrac{40}{n}$ **14.** $\dfrac{7}{12} = \dfrac{n}{48}$ **15.** $\dfrac{n}{600} = \dfrac{1}{100}$

Solve the proportion.

16. $\dfrac{1}{10} = \dfrac{19}{n}$ **17.** $\dfrac{3}{4} = \dfrac{n}{28}$ **18.** $\dfrac{5}{7} = \dfrac{n}{98}$

19. $\dfrac{52}{n} = \dfrac{4}{11}$ **20.** $\dfrac{n}{5} = \dfrac{42}{35}$ **21.** $\dfrac{2}{n} = \dfrac{80}{120}$

22. $\dfrac{n}{57.6} = \dfrac{1}{8}$ **23.** $\dfrac{4}{5} = \dfrac{n}{1.25}$ **24.** $\dfrac{4}{1} = \dfrac{0.56}{n}$

Mixed Applications

25. Mr. Howard told the class that the ratio of the number of students who bought lunch today to the number of students who bought lunch yesterday was $5:6$. Yesterday 12 students bought lunch. How many students bought lunch today?

26. Natasha is baking bread. Her recipe requires $2\frac{1}{2}$ cups of flour for each loaf. Natasha wants to increase the recipe so that she can bake 4 loaves of bread. What quantity of flour does she need for 4 loaves of bread?

How can you prove that two ratios form a proportion?

WRAP UP...

On a map, what does the scale
1 in. = 60 mi tell you?

SCALE DRAWINGS

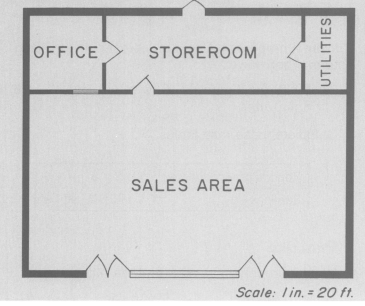

OFFICE   STOREROOM   UTILITIES

SALES AREA

Scale: 1 in. = 20 ft.

Paul is a commercial architect.
The scale drawing shows his
plan for a new health food
store. The scale is 1 in. : 20 ft.
The scale tells you that in the
drawing 1 in. represents 20 ft.
In a scale drawing, the actual
size of an object is reduced
or enlarged. Maps, blueprints,
and mechanical drawings are
examples of scale drawings.
The **scale** is a ratio between
the dimensions of the drawing
and the actual dimensions of
the object. The scale may be
expressed in many ways.

1 in. : 20 ft   1 in. = 20 ft $\dfrac{1 \text{ in.}}{20 \text{ ft}}$ $\dfrac{1 \text{ in.}}{240 \text{ in.}}$ To express the scale in the same unit, change 20 ft to 240 in.

Example   In Paul's scale drawing, the length of the health food store
is 3 in. What will be the actual length of the store?

Step 1	**Step 2**
Use the scale and the given measure to write a proportion.	Solve the proportion.
drawing width → $\dfrac{1}{20} = \dfrac{3}{n}$ ← actual width	$1n = 3 \times 20$ $n = 60$

So, the actual length of the store will be 60 ft.

Paul wants to make a scale drawing of the rectangular
kitchen that will be located at the rear of the store. The
actual kitchen will be 9 ft by 12 ft. Paul will use the
scale of 1 in. : 3 ft to reduce the kitchen's dimensions in
the scale drawing.

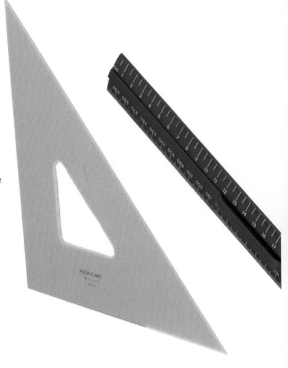

- Will Paul's scale drawing be larger or smaller than
  the actual kitchen?

- What actual distance in the kitchen will be
  represented by 1 in. in the scale drawing?

- What will be the dimensions of the scale drawing?

This year the 2.5 cm-long Rocky Mountain grasshoppers have been destructive to crops. Mary is completing a scale drawing of this grasshopper. Her scale is 12 cm:1 cm. On her drawing, 12 cm represents 1 cm.

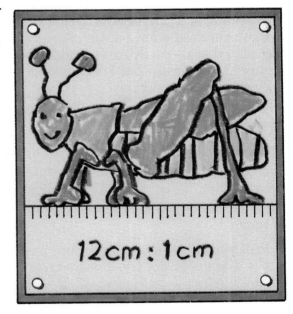

- Will Mary's drawing be larger or smaller than the actual grasshopper? Explain.

The actual length of the grasshopper's head is 0.4 cm. What will be the length of the grasshopper's head in Mary's drawing?

Think: Write and solve a proportion using the scale 12 cm:1 cm.

drawing length $\longrightarrow$
actual length $\longrightarrow$
$$\frac{12}{1} = \frac{n}{0.4}$$
$$1n = 12 \times 0.4$$
$$n = 4.8$$

So, the length of the grasshopper's head in Mary's drawing will be 4.8 cm.

Mary draws the grasshopper's legs. The length of each of the grasshopper's back legs in the drawing is 28 cm. What is the actual length of each of the grasshopper's back legs?

$$\frac{12}{1} = \frac{28}{n}$$
$$12n = 28$$
$$n = 2\frac{1}{3}$$

So, the actual length of each of the grasshopper's back legs is $2\frac{1}{3}$ cm.

Mary goes shopping for some drawing supplies. On the way home she buys some whole-wheat crackers at the health-food store. She snacks on these crackers while she works on her drawing. Mary measures one of these crackers and finds its dimensions to be 3 cm by 6 cm.

Suppose Mary makes a scale drawing of the cracker using the scale of 3:1 to enlarge the dimensions.

- Is the drawing larger or smaller than the actual cracker?

- A measurement of 3 cm in the drawing represents what actual measurement of the cracker?

- What are the dimensions of the scale drawing?

A scale drawing may either reduce or enlarge the dimensions of the object it represents. It is important to choose an appropriate scale for a scale drawing. A completed scale drawing should be large enough to be useful but small enough to fit on your paper.

Scale: $\frac{1}{4}$ in. = 15 ft.

ELEVATION

1st

2nd

FLOOR PLAN

WORK TOGETHER

Measure the length and the width of your classroom. Round the measurements to the nearest foot. Next, make a scale drawing of your classroom on an $8\frac{1}{2}$-in. by 11-in. sheet of paper.

- Will your scale drawing reduce or enlarge the dimensions of the classroom?

- Choose an appropriate scale for the drawing. Is 1 in.:20 ft an appropriate scale? Explain.

- Is 1 in.:1 ft an appropriate scale? Explain.

Suppose your scale is 1 in.:5 ft. What will be the scale-drawing dimensions of your classroom? Will this scale drawing fit on an $8\frac{1}{2}$-in. by 11-in. sheet of paper?

Check for Understanding

Find the missing dimension.

1. scale: 1 in.:3 mi
   drawing length:3 in.
   actual length:■ mi

2. scale: 1,000 mm:1 mm
   drawing length:■ mm
   actual length:5 mm

Write *enlarge* or *reduce* to describe whether the scale will enlarge or reduce the dimensions of the object it represents.

3. 1 cm:10 cm

4. 1 in.:500 mi

5. 1 cm:1 mm

6. 100 mm:1 mm

7. 1 in.:3 ft

8. 1 mm:0.001 mm

Write an appropriate scale for a scale drawing of each item. Each scale drawing should fit on an $8\frac{1}{2}$-in. by 11-in. sheet of paper.

9. truck: 21 ft long

10. ant: 0.63 cm long

11. Empire State Building: 1,250 ft

12. distance from the earth to the moon: 250,000 mi

Practice

Use the scale of 1 cm : 12 cm to find the missing dimension.

13. drawing: 3 cm
actual: ■ cm

14. drawing: 10 cm
actual: ■ cm

15. drawing: ■ cm
actual: 60 cm

16. drawing: ■ cm
actual: 72 cm

17. drawing: ■ cm
actual: 15.6 cm

18. drawing: 18.9 cm
actual: ■ cm

Use the scale of 12 cm : 1 cm to find the missing dimension.

19. drawing: 30 cm
actual: ■ cm

20. drawing: ■ cm
actual: 8 cm

21. drawing: 18 cm
actual: ■ cm

22. drawing: ■ cm
actual: 7 cm

23. drawing: 144 cm
actual: ■ cm

24. drawing: ■ cm
actual: 0.5 cm

Paul completed a scale drawing of a warehouse. His scale is 1 in. : 50 ft.

Measure the drawing. Then use the drawing dimensions and the scale to find the actual dimensions. Write the drawing dimensions and the actual dimensions.

25. workshop

26. office

27. utility room

| | Workshop |
| Utility Room | Office |

Mixed Applications

28. Suppose the dimensions of a scale drawing of a store are 6 in. by 11 in. The scale is 1 in.:20 ft. What are the actual dimensions of the store?

29. Tyrone ordered catalog items which cost $157.89. Sales tax was $9.47. The handling charge was $3.00. Postage cost $2.50. What was the total cost?

Use the given scale to make a scale drawing of each. Use a ruler and a compass.

30. a square with a 20-in. side — scale: 1 in. : 10 in.

31. a rectangle 9.8 m by 7 m — scale: 1 cm : 1 m

32. a rectangle 6 mm by 8 mm — scale: 1 cm : 1 mm

33. a circle with a 100-ft radius — scale: 1 in. : 50 ft

34. a circle with a 15-ft radius — scale: 1 in.:10 ft

The scale for a drawing is 15 : 1. How do you represent a 6-cm length in the drawing? Explain.

WRAP
UP...

What is the actual distance between Sunnyvale and Santa Clara?

Sometimes you can solve a problem by using a map.

▶ **UNDERSTAND**

What are you asked to find?

What facts are given?

▶ **PLAN**

How will you solve the problem? You can use a map and follow these steps:

1. Read the scale of the map.
2. Find the map locations given in the question.
3. Connect these map locations with a ruler, and measure the straight-line distance between them.
4. Write and solve a proportion comparing the map distance with the actual distance.

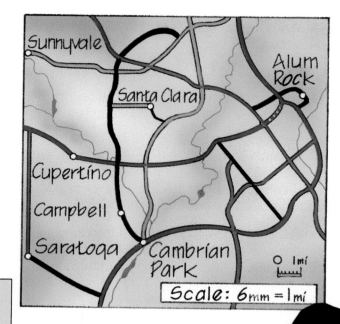

Scale: 6 mm = 1 mi

Every 6 mm of map distance represents 1 mi of actual distance.

▶ **SOLVE**

How will you carry out your plan?

The map scale is 6 mm : 1 mi. It can be written as $\frac{6 \text{ mm}}{1 \text{ mi}}$, or $\frac{6}{1}$.

The straight-line map distance between Sunnyvale and Santa Clara is 36 mm. You can write a proportion using the map-scale ratio and the ratio of the map distance to the actual distance.

Let n = the actual distance in miles between Sunnyvale and Santa Clara.

map-scale ratio ⟶ $\frac{6}{1} = \frac{36}{n}$ ⟵ ratio of the map distance to the actual distance

$$6n = 36$$
$$n = 6$$

So, the actual distance between Sunnyvale and Santa Clara is 6 mi.

▶ **LOOK BACK**

How can you check your answer?

WHAT IF... ... you travel from Sunnyvale to Alum Rock and the road distance is $14\frac{1}{2}$ mi? How much more is this distance than the straight-line distance?

Apply

Find the straight-line distance in miles between the two locations.
Use the map on page 182.

(1) Saratoga and Cupertino

(2) Sunnyvale and Cambrian Park

(3) Campbell and Saratoga

(4) Cambrian Park and Alum Rock

Mixed Applications **STRATEGIES**
- Guess and Check • Find a Pattern
- Solve a Simpler Problem • Write an Equation

Choose a strategy and solve. Use the map on page 182 if necessary.

(5) Susan and Jeremy bought their lunches at a new restaurant. Jeremy's lunch cost twice as much as Susan's lunch. The total for the two lunches was $7.20. What was the cost of Susan's lunch?

(6) Mrs. Hynes asked her son Todd to purchase 6 items at the supermarket. He purchased bread, milk, and a carton of eggs. The total bill was $7.95. How many loaves of bread and how many gallons of milk did he purchase?

Bread	$1.00/loaf
Milk	$2.10/gal
Eggs	$0.75/carton

(7) What is the ones digit of the number represented by 2^{32}?

(8) During four weeks, Abdul has earned $100.00, $125.00, $156.25, and $195.31. If his earnings continue to increase at this rate, what will he earn this week?

WRITER'S CORNER

(9) Write a problem similar to Exercise 5. Use a total of $540 in your problem. Exchange with a classmate and solve.

(10) Write a problem similar to Exercise 8. Use at least four numbers for the pattern. Exchange with a classmate and solve.

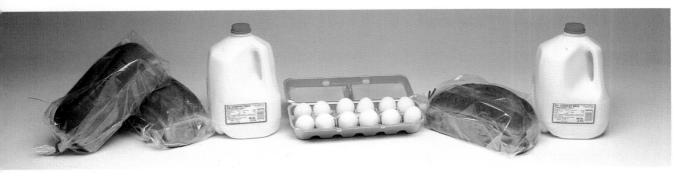

UNDERSTANDING PERCENT

Mario's Pizzeria sold 100 pizzas yesterday. Of these, 35 were cheese pizzas. What percent of the pizzas were cheese pizzas?

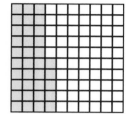

The 100 squares represent the pizzas sold. The 35 shaded squares represent the cheese pizzas sold. The ratio of 35 to 100 can be written as $\frac{35}{100}$.

Recall that **percent** means "per hundred." The ratio $\frac{35}{100}$ can be written as 35%. So, 35% of the pizzas were cheese pizzas.

To write a ratio as a percent, you can write an equivalent ratio that has 100 as the second term.

$$\frac{1}{4} = \frac{1 \times 25}{4 \times 25} = \frac{25}{100} = 25\%$$

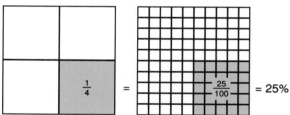

More Examples Write each ratio as a percent.

A. 90 out of 100

$\frac{90}{100} = 90\%$

B. $\frac{4}{25}$

$\frac{4}{25} = \frac{16}{100} = 16\%$

C. 15:10

$\frac{15}{10} = \frac{150}{100} = 150\%$

Another Method

Since it is not always possible to write an equivalent ratio that has 100 as the second term, you can use a proportion to write a ratio as a percent.

A. Write the ratio 11:88 as a percent.

$\frac{11}{88} = \frac{n}{100}$

$88n = 11 \times 100$

$88n = 1,100$

$n = 12.5$

So, 11:88 is equal to 12.5%.

B. Write the ratio 4 out of 500 as a percent.

$\frac{4}{500} = \frac{n}{100}$

$500n = 4 \times 100$

$500n = 400$

$n = 0.8$

So, 4 out of 500 is equal to 0.8%.

Check for Understanding

Write as a percent.

1. $\frac{3}{5}$ 2. $\frac{1}{4}$ 3. $\frac{7}{20}$ 4. $\frac{12}{10}$ 5. $\frac{2}{1}$

6. $\frac{9}{10}$ 7. $\frac{2}{50}$ 8. $\frac{6}{25}$ 9. $\frac{13}{50}$ 10. $\frac{1}{100}$

Practice

Write as a percent.

11. 17 per 100   12. $\frac{27}{100}$ 13. $\frac{6}{1}$ 14. 7:50   15. 52 out of 100

16. $\frac{19}{20}$ 17. $\frac{97}{100}$ 18. $\frac{21}{20}$ 19. $\frac{1}{1}$ 20. $\frac{5}{4}$

21. $\frac{6}{5}$ 22. $\frac{29}{50}$ 23. $\frac{17}{25}$ 24. $\frac{78}{80}$ 25. $\frac{7}{16}$

Mixed Applications

26. Mario's Pizzeria sold 126 pizzas today. Mario calculated that $\frac{1}{2}$ of these pizzas were large. What percent of the pizzas were large?

27. According to his records, Mario makes $\frac{4}{5}$ of his pizza sales in the evening. What percent of the pizza sales does he make in the evening?

28. Mario sold 179 pizzas in five days. He sold twice as many in the next two days. How many pizzas did Mario sell?

29. **Write a Question** Mario is planning to hire another clerk. Of the 10 applicants, 8 are teenagers. Write a question for this situation.

EVERYDAY MATH CONNECTION

A baseball batting average is a ratio of the number of hits to the number of times at bat. The batting average is written as a decimal rounded to the thousandths place.

Example What is Joe's batting average? The ratio of the number of Joe's hits to the number of his times at bat is $\frac{80}{260}$. Divide to change $\frac{80}{260}$ to 0.308. Joe's batting average is 0.308, read as "308."

Batting Record		
Player	Number of Hits	Number of Times at Bat
Joe	80	260
Tandy	110	267
Bobby	64	265
Chris	93	265
Eric	72	255

30. Compute the batting average for Tandy, Bobby, Chris, and Eric.

Why can 1:25 be written as 4%?

WRAP UP...

PERCENTS, DECIMALS, AND RATIOS

The concession stand sold burritos during the basketball game. Of the 100 burritos sold, 42 were bean burritos. The comparison of the number of bean burritos to the total number of burritos can be written as a ratio, a decimal, and a percent. The shaded area of the figure can be represented by $\frac{42}{100}$, 0.42, or 42%.

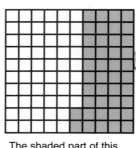

The shaded part of this figure represents the bean burritos.

$$\frac{42}{100} = 0.42 = 42\%$$

You can use several methods to write equivalent percents, decimals, and ratios.

Examples

Write as a decimal.

A. $81\% = \frac{81}{100} = 0.81$

B. $25\frac{1}{2}\% = 25.5 \div 100$
$= 0.255$

C. $\frac{1}{4} = 4\overline{)1.00}$ (quotient 0.25)
$\frac{1}{4} = 0.25$

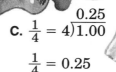

Write as a percent.

A. $0.34 = \frac{34}{100}$
$= 34\%$

B. $\frac{1}{3} = 1 \div 3 = \boxed{0.3333333}$
$\frac{1}{3} = 0.333\overline{3}$
$= 33.\overline{3}\%$, or $33\frac{1}{3}\%$

C. $\frac{3}{4} = \frac{n}{100}$
$4n = 300$
$n = 75$
$\frac{3}{4} = 75\%$

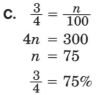

Write as a ratio.

A. $40\% = \frac{40}{100} = \frac{2}{5}$

B. $33\frac{1}{3}\% = 33\frac{1}{3} \div 100$
$= \frac{100}{3} \times \frac{1}{100}$
$= \frac{1}{3}$

C. $150\% = \frac{150}{100}$
$= \frac{3}{2}$

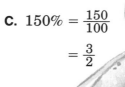

Talk About It

▶ To write a percent as a decimal, you can divide the percent by 100. What is a shortcut for doing this?

▶ You know that $0.42 = 42\%$ and that $0.255 = 25.5\%$. What rule can you use to change any decimal to a percent?

Check for Understanding

Copy and complete this table.

	1.	2.	3.	4.	5.	6.
Ratio	$\frac{45}{100}$	31 per 100	$\frac{1}{1}$	■	■	$\frac{5}{1}$
Decimal	■	■	1.00	0.73	■	■
Percent	■	■	■	■	9%	■

Practice

Write as a decimal. Use mental math to solve.

7. 28%   **8.** 17%   **9.** 10%   **10.** 58%

11. 89%   **12.** 175%   **13.** 1%   **14.** 650%

Write as a percent. Use mental math to solve.

15. 0.81   **16.** 0.06   **17.** 0.53   **18.** 0.8

19. 0.72   **20.** 0.098   **21.** 0.01   **22.** 4.7

Write as a ratio in simplest form.

23. 50%   **24.** 79%   **25.** 90%   **26.** 4%

27. 45%   **28.** 500%   **29.** 225%   **30.** 9%

Write as a percent. Use mental math, pencil and paper, or a calculator to solve.

31. $\frac{4}{5}$ **32.** $\frac{2}{3}$ **33.** $\frac{7}{8}$ **34.** $\frac{1}{20}$

35. $\frac{5}{8}$ **36.** $\frac{1}{25}$ **37.** $\frac{6}{1}$ **38.** $\frac{10}{1}$

Mixed Applications

39. Of the 100 burritos sold by the concession stand, 17 were beef burritos. Write a decimal for the ratio that compares the number of beef burritos sold with the total number of burritos sold.

40. **Visual Thinking**   Write a decimal that represents the part of the figure that is shaded. How many more parts would have to be shaded to represent 50% of the figure?

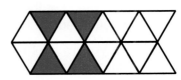

41. In one day Marci consumed foods containing 2,500 calories. Fruits and vegetables represented 20% of the total calories. Write this percent as a decimal.

Explain how $\frac{1}{5}$ can be written as a decimal and as a percent.

WRAP UP...

EXPLORING
Percent Problems

In this lesson you will explore the three different kinds of percent problems.

WORK TOGETHER

Building Understanding

Use two-color counters to model each percent problem. Place 10 yellow counters in a row on your desk. How many counters can you turn over so that 20% of the counters are red?

Talk About It

► Recall that $20\% = \frac{20}{100}$. What proportion can you write to show how this ratio is related to the number of red counters out of 10 counters?

► Solve the proportion. How many counters can you turn over so that 20% are red? What is 20% of 10?

Place 25 yellow counters on your desk. Then turn over 10 of the counters.

Talk About It

► What ratio can you write to compare the number of red counters with the total number of counters?

► Using this ratio, what proportion can you write to find how many red counters you would have if you had a total of 100 counters?

► Solve the proportion. How many of the 100 counters would be red? What percent of the counters would be red?

► What percent of 25 is 10?

Place 3 counters on your desk. Let the 3 counters represent 30%. How many counters do you need to show a total of 100%?

● What proportion can you write to show that 3 out of some number equals 30 out of 100?

● Solve the proportion. How many counters do you need to show 100%?

● 30% of what number is 3?

188

Making the Connection

You can use the procedures for the activities on page 188 to solve percent word problems.

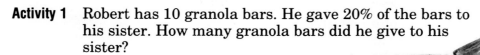

Activity 1 Robert has 10 granola bars. He gave 20% of the bars to his sister. How many granola bars did he give to his sister?

Think: 20% of 10 = ▨

$\frac{20}{100} = \frac{2}{10}$ So, he gave his sister 2 granola bars.

Activity 2 April had 25 pounds of flour. She used 10 pounds of the flour to bake muffins for a school carnival. What percent of the flour did she use?

Think: ▨% of 25 = 10

$\frac{10}{25} = \frac{40}{100}$ So, she used 40% of the flour.

Activity 3 Richard has made 3 pizzas for a party. This is 30% of the total number of pizzas he plans to have. How many pizzas does he plan to have?

Think: 30% of ▨ = 3

$\frac{30}{100} = \frac{3}{10}$ So, he plans to have 10 pizzas.

Checking Understanding

Choose the correct percent problem for each word problem. Write **a, b,** or **c.**

1. Ted had 40 peaches. He gave 30% of the peaches to his neighbor. How many peaches did he give to his neighbor?

    a. 30% of 40 = ▨   **b.** 30% of ▨ = 40   **c.** ▨% of 30 = 40

2. Beth spent $12 on ingredients for a recipe. This was 40% of her money. How much money did she have before buying the ingredients?

    a. 40% of 12 = ▨   **b.** ▨% of 40 = 12   **c.** 40% of ▨ = 12

3. There are 25 people in a cooking class. Of these, 10 are male. What percent of the people in the cooking class are male?

    a. 10% of ▨ = 25   **b.** ▨% of 25 = 10   **c.** 10% of 25 = ▨

4. Write a word problem for each of the three kinds of percent problems.

WARM UP...

Explain why $\frac{1}{4} \times 36$ and 0.25×36 are equivalent.

Finding a Percent of a Number

Jim surveyed all 32 members of his math class about their favorite foods. His survey showed that 25% of the students chose hamburgers. How many students chose hamburgers?

You can use an equation to solve this problem.

Think: *What number* is 25% of 32?

$$\blacksquare = 25\% \times 32$$

Step 1 Write an equation. Let n = the number of students who chose hamburgers. $n = 0.25 \times 32 \longleftarrow$ 25% = 0.25	**Step 2** Multiply to solve the equation. $n = 0.25 \times 32$ $n = 8$

You can also use a ratio in the equation.

$$25\% = \frac{25}{100} = \frac{1}{4} \qquad \qquad n = \frac{1}{4} \times 32$$
$$n = 8$$

So, 8 students chose hamburgers.

Another Method

You can also use a proportion to find a percent of a number.

Jim's math class is planning a class picnic. A total of $96 was spent for food and supplies. A 6% sales tax was charged on these items. What was the amount of the sales tax?

Think: 6 out of 100 is what amount out of 96?

$$\frac{6}{100} = \frac{n}{96} \qquad \begin{array}{l} \longleftarrow \text{ amount of sales tax} \\ \longleftarrow \text{ cost of items} \end{array}$$
$$100n = 576$$
$$n = 5.76 \quad \text{So, the sales tax was \$5.76.}$$

More Examples

A. Find 60% of 180.

$$\frac{3}{5} = \frac{n}{180} \longleftarrow \frac{60}{100} = \frac{3}{5}$$
$$5n = 540$$
$$n = 108$$

B. Find 110% of 482.

$$1.10 \times 482 = n$$
$$530.2 = n$$

C. Find $33\frac{1}{3}\%$ of 126.

$$\frac{1}{3} \times \frac{126}{1} = n \longleftarrow 33\frac{1}{3}\% = \frac{1}{3}$$
$$42 = n$$

Idea Bank, page 490, Exercise 8

Check for Understanding

Write an equation for the problem.

1. Find 10% of 290.　　　**2.** Find 20% of 160.　　　**3.** Find 50% of 4,800.

Write a proportion for the problem.

4. Find 3% of 210.　　　**5.** Find 86% of 90.　　　**6.** Find 125% of 40.

Practice

Find the percent of the number.

7. 25% of 180　　　**8.** 62% of 95　　　**9.** 75% of 48　　　**10.** 6% of 38

11. 140% of 116　　**12.** 32% of 982　　**13.** 5% of 200　　**14.** 12.5% of 164

15. 12% of 142　　**16.** 110% of 970　　**17.** 0.9% of 4.8　　**18.** 250% of 4.8

Solve.

19. Find 18% of $322.　　**20.** What number is 48% of 420?　　**21.** Find 2% of 900.

22. Find 200% of 256.　　**23.** 0.5% of 100 is what number?　　**24.** Find 10% of 14.

Complete. Write <, >, or =.

25. (20% of 50) + (80% of 50) ● 100% of 50

26. (50% of 100) + (50% of 80) ● 100% of 180

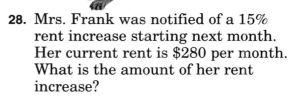

Mixed Applications

27. Jim surveyed all 30 members of his English class about their favorite foods. In the survey 60% of the students chose pizza. How many students chose pizza?

28. Mrs. Frank was notified of a 15% rent increase starting next month. Her current rent is $280 per month. What is the amount of her rent increase?

29. Organize and Analyze Data Survey your classmates about their favorite foods, sports, or pets. Record and organize the data. Then calculate the percent of the students making each choice. Determine the three most popular choices. Then graph your results and share them with the class.

MIXED REVIEW

Write as a percent.

1. 5 per 100　　　**2.** 0.79　　　**3.** 0.3　　　**4.** 1.5

5. $\frac{7}{100}$　　　**6.** 6:18　　　**7.** 0.003　　　**8.** 4.0

Is 14.7 a reasonable answer for 150% of 98? Explain.

WRAP UP...

1. There are 7 people on a school committee. Each person shakes hands with every other person one time. Find the total number of handshakes.

2. Sandy and Lisa are shopping at a shoe store. There is a 20% discount on all purchases. Lisa purchased shoes with a regular price of $26. How much did Lisa save?

3. Kim scored 70 out of 100 points on a science test. Van correctly answered the same ratio of questions on his 20-question history test. How many questions did Van answer correctly?

4. Luna is paid every 10 days. Diego is paid every 14 days. How many days will pass before Luna and Diego are paid on the same day?

Write in standard form.

5. 6.05 million

6. 74.89 thousand

7. 4.35 billion

Name the property shown.

8. $57 + 0 = 57$

9. $2.9 + 6.8 = 6.8 + 2.9$

10. $(9 \times 4) + (9 \times 6) = 9 \times (4 + 6)$

Add or subtract. Write the answer in simplest form.

11. $\frac{5}{9} + \frac{5}{9}$

12. $4\frac{5}{7} + 2\frac{2}{3}$

13. $12 - 1\frac{3}{8}$

14. $33\frac{3}{4} - 1\frac{1}{3}$

Multiply or divide. Write the answer in simplest form.

15. $\frac{3}{4} \times \frac{4}{5}$

16. $2\frac{1}{2} \times \frac{3}{7}$

17. $\frac{5}{7} \div 6$

18. $1\frac{2}{3} \div \frac{2}{3}$

Solve the equation.

19. $n - \frac{1}{3} = 7\frac{2}{3}$

20. $6 = r + 3\frac{1}{2}$

21. $3k + \frac{1}{2} = 2$

22. $\frac{c}{4} - \frac{1}{6} = 5\frac{5}{6}$

Write as a decimal.

23. $\frac{3}{25}$

24. $\frac{7}{20}$

25. $2\frac{3}{4}$

26. $\frac{2}{9}$

27. $4\frac{1}{3}$

Write as a percent.

28. $\frac{9}{25}$

29. $24:4$

30. 3 out of 50

31. $\frac{6}{5}$

Use the triangle for Exercises 32–33.

32. Is triangle ABC scalene, right, or equilateral?

33. What is the measure of $\angle CAB$?

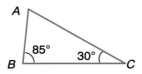

192

Spotlight ON
PROBLEM SOLVING

Decide When to Estimate

There are times when only an estimate is needed to solve a problem. At other times an exact answer is needed. Study this problem.

Lu Ann is a chef specializing in the preparation of pastries. Of approximately 9,600 students enrolled in cooking school, Lu Ann was among about 2,300 students who had completed three years of on-the-job training before beginning cooking school. About what fraction of all the students had completed three years of on-the-job training?

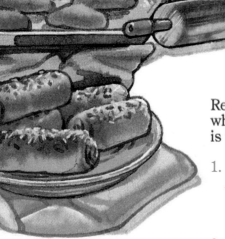

Apply

Read and solve each problem. Tell whether an exact answer or an estimate is needed.

1. Ingrid ran for president of the Chefs' Association. She received 429 votes out of 955 votes cast. Did Ingrid receive more than or less than 40% of the votes cast?

2. Theo sold 3 pumpkin pies for $4.95 each. The sales tax was $0.89. Mrs. Kuhn gave Theo a $20.00 bill. How much change should Theo return to Mrs. Kuhn?

3. Of the 19,234 graduates of the cooking school, 8,784 are still residents of this state. Are more than half of the school's graduates residents of the state?

4. Lu Ann's taxable income is $9,528. She will pay 15% tax on her income. How much tax will she pay?

Talk About It

Work with a classmate. Read and discuss these questions.

a. Does the problem call for an estimate or an exact answer?

b. How can you solve the problem? Solve it.

c. Discuss with the class how you solved the problem.

Finding the Percent One Number Is of Another

The Robinsons budget $110 per week for food. Last week they spent $22 on beef, chicken, and fish. What percent of their food budget was spent on beef, chicken, and fish?

Think: *What percent of $110 is $22?*

$$n \times \$110 = \$22$$

Step 1 Write an equation.	**Step 2** Solve using division.
$n \times 110 = 22$	$110n = 22$ $\dfrac{110n}{110} = \dfrac{22}{110}$ $n = 0.20$, or 20%

A proportion can be used to solve this problem.

Think: $22 out of $110 is *how much* out of $100?

$$\frac{22}{110} = \frac{n}{100}$$
$$110n = 22 \times 100$$
$$110n = 2{,}200$$
$$n = 20 \leftarrow \tfrac{20}{100} = 20\%$$

So, 20% of the food budget was spent on beef, chicken, and fish.

16 is *what percent* of 40?

Use an equation.

$$16 = n \times 40$$
$$16 = 40n$$
$$\frac{16}{40} = \frac{40n}{40}$$
$$0.4 = n, \text{ or } n = 40\%$$

So, 16 is 40% of 40.

Use a proportion.

$$\frac{16}{40} = \frac{n}{100} \quad \leftarrow \text{Think: 16 out of 40 is how many out of 100?}$$
$$40n = 16 \times 100$$
$$40n = 1{,}600$$
$$n = 40$$
$$\frac{40}{100} = 40\%$$

▶ For what everyday situations would you need to find the percent one number is of another?

Check for Understanding

Write an equation. Then solve.

1. 9 is what percent of 45?

2. What percent of 24 is 8?

3. 25 is what percent of 50?

4. What percent of 45 is 90?

Write a proportion. Then solve.

5. What percent of 96 is 24?

6. 180 is what percent of 36?

7. What percent of 5 is 8?

8. What percent of 70 is 14?

Practice

Find the percent.

9. 3 is what percent of 5?

10. What percent of 48 is 18?

11. 1 is what percent of 5?

12. What percent of 36 is 12?

13. What percent of 60 is 50?

14. 350 is what percent of 200?

15. What percent of 90 is 72?

16. 2 is what percent of 5?

17. 20 is what percent of 20?

18. What percent of 1,200 is 6?

19. What percent of 50 is 5?

20. 25 is what percent of 125?

21. 20 is what percent of 16?

22. What percent of 52 is 13?

23. 63 is what percent of 120?

24. What percent of 180 is 9?

25. What percent of 60 is 0.6?

26. 620 is what percent of 500?

27. 68 is what percent of 17?

28. What percent of 123 is 82?

29. What percent of 290 is 58?

30. 0.45 is what percent of 9?

31. 160 is what percent of 16?

32. What percent of 0.16 is 0.02?

Mixed Applications

33. Tandy was named the most valuable baseball player. She earned 24 of the possible 32 votes. What percent of the votes did Tandy receive?

34. Mrs. Robinson spent $13.75 of her $110.00 food budget for refreshments and decorations for Thuy's birthday party. What percent of her food budget did she spend?

35. The face of a clock is in the shape of a circle. What are the measures of the two angles formed by the hour hand and the minute hand at 9:25 A.M.?

36. **Make Up a Problem**   Write a word problem that can be solved using the ratio $\frac{126}{180}$. Exchange with a classmate and solve.

Ken has $35 of the $80 he needs. Does he have 50% of what he needs? Explain.

Lee ate 4 slices, or 50%, of a pizza.
How many slices were in the *whole* pizza?

This week Mrs. Madeira spent $14.40 for fruits and vegetables. This represents 15% of her weekly food budget. What is her weekly food budget?

Think: 15% of *what amount* is $14.40?

15% of n = $14.40

Step 1 Write an equation. $0.15 \times n = 14.40$ $0.15n = 14.40$	**Step 2** Solve. $\frac{0.15n}{0.15} = \frac{14.40}{0.15}$ $n = 96$

So, Mrs. Madeira's weekly food budget is $96.00.

Other Methods

Sometimes it is helpful to write the equation using a ratio for the percent.

75% of what number is 120?

Since $75\% = \frac{3}{4}$, write 75% as $\frac{3}{4}$.

$\frac{3}{4} \times n = 120$

$\frac{3}{4}n = 120$

$\frac{3}{4}n \times \frac{4}{3} = 120 \times \frac{4}{3}$ ← Multiply by the reciprocal of $\frac{3}{4}$.

$n = 160$

So, 75% of 160 is 120.

A proportion can be used to solve this problem.

Mrs. Madeira spent $9 for milk this week. This was 60% of the total amount she paid for dairy products. What did she pay for dairy products?

Think: 60 out of 100 is $9 out of *what amount*?

$\frac{60}{100} = \frac{9}{n}$

$60n = 900$

$\frac{60n}{60} = \frac{900}{60}$

$n = 15$

So, Mrs. Madeira paid $15 for dairy products.

Talk About It

▶ What equation can you write to solve "128 is 160% of what number"?

▶ To solve "0.5% of what number is 12," do you prefer to use an equation or a proportion? Why?

Check for Understanding

Write an equation. Then solve.

1. 25% of what number is 41?

2. 51 is 3% of what number?

Write a proportion. Then solve.

3. 180% of what number is 9?

4. 89 is $33\frac{1}{3}$% of what number?

Practice

Find the number.

5. 10% of what number is 30?

6. 40 is 20% of what number?

7. 34 is 200% of what number?

8. 25% of what number is 77?

9. 46.2 is 84% of what number?

10. 1% of what number is 15?

11. 75% of what number is 66?

12. 372 is 93% of what number?

13. 58 is 20% of what number?

14. 16% of what number is 0.32?

15. 190% of what number is 760?

16. 30.8 is 35% of what number?

17. 4,500 is 1% of what number?

18. 250% of what number is 10?

19. 12.75 is 15% of what number?

20. 100% of what number is 121?

21. 0.4% of what number is 1.44?

22. 3 is 1,000% of what number?

Mixed Applications

23. Mrs. Madeira spent $7.54 for school supplies. This was 12.5% of what she spent altogether. How much did she spend in all?

24. Chee worked 9.75 hr on Monday, 8.75 hr on Tuesday, 8.75 hr on Wednesday, 8 hr on Thursday, and 8.25 hr on Friday. What is the total number of hours that Chee worked?

25. **Analyze Data** Debbie played basketball for six days. The table shows her free-throw performance for each day. Copy and complete the table. On which day was Debbie most successful?

Debbie's Free Throws						
Day	1	2	3	4	5	6
Completed free throws	15	10	20	17	20	11
Attempted free throws	20	15	25	20	21	12
Percent completed	75	■	■	■	■	■

20% of what number is 100? Use mental math and explain.

More Practice, Lesson 6.10, page H52

ESTIMATING PERCENTS

Mrs. Melrose has collected $55.50 for the field trip to the Ridgeway Foods factory. She must collect a total of $184.00. About what percent of the total has she collected?

Estimate what percent $55.50 is of $184.00. Use compatible numbers.

$\frac{\$55.50}{\$184.00}$ is about $\frac{60}{180}$. $\frac{60}{180} = \frac{1}{3} = 33\frac{1}{3}\%$ or

$\frac{\$55.50}{\$184.00}$ is about $\frac{50}{200}$. $\frac{50}{200} = \frac{1}{4} = 25\%$

So, two possible estimates of the amount of money that she has collected are $33\frac{1}{3}\%$ and 25%.

Recall the common percents and their equivalent ratios. Make your own chart showing these common percents and ratios.

Common Percents and Ratios	
$10\% = \frac{1}{10}$	$66\frac{2}{3}\% = \frac{2}{3}$
$20\% = \frac{1}{5}$	$50\% = \frac{1}{2}$
$25\% = \frac{1}{4}$	$75\% = \frac{3}{4}$
$12.5\% = \frac{1}{8}$	$33\frac{1}{3}\% = \frac{1}{3}$
$40\% = \frac{2}{5}$	$16\frac{2}{3}\% = \frac{1}{6}$

- Which simple ratios are nearly equivalent to these percents: 48%, 19%, 77%, and 42%?

- Natasha chose the ratio $\frac{3}{5}$ as an estimate of 65%. Which ratio would you choose?

Use compatible numbers and common percents and ratios to estimate solutions.

Examples

A. Estimate 76% of 781.
76% is about 75%.
$75\% = \frac{3}{4}$
781 is about 800.
$\frac{3}{4} \times 800 = 600$
So, 76% of 781 is about 600.

B. 42 out of 445 is about what percent?
42 is about 40.
445 is about 400.
$\frac{40}{400} = \frac{1}{10} = 10\%$
So, 42 is about 10% of 445.

C. 95 is 18% of about what number?
95 is about 100.
18% is about 20%.
$20\% = \frac{1}{5}$
$\frac{1}{5} = \frac{100}{n}$
$n = 500$
So, 95 is 18% of about 500.

Check for Understanding

Estimate the percent for each ratio. Choose 1%, 10%, or 100%.

1. 19 out of 22

2. 59 out of 613

3. 4 : 387

4. 37 out of 4,135

5. 77 out of 802

6. 714 : 699

Practice

Choose the best estimate. Write **a, b,** or **c.**

7. 10% of 29
  a. 10% of 20
  b. 10% of 15
  c. 10% of 30

8. 50% of $91.30
  a. 50% of $90
  b. 50% of $95
  c. 50% of $100

9. 21% of 150
  a. 30% of 150
  b. 25% of 150
  c. 20% of 150

10. 37.5% of $800
  a. $240
  b. $320
  c. $400

11. 40% of 179
  a. 60
  b. 90
  c. 70

12. 75% of $101.79
  a. $75
  b. $90
  c. $60

13. 10.5% of $1,200
  a. $60
  b. $120
  c. $240

14. 110% of $87.50
  a. $80
  b. $35
  c. $90

15. 280% of 31
  a. 90
  b. 60
  c. 6

Write the common ratio that is nearly equivalent to the percent.

16. 34%   **17.** 26%   **18.** 52%   **19.** 9%

Estimate the percent.

20. $\frac{56}{118}$ **21.** 31:42   **22.** 9 out of 40   **23.** $\frac{110}{532}$

24. 181 of 192 is about what percent?   **25.** 66 is about what percent of 98?

Estimate the number.

26. 48 is 20% of what number?   **27.** 10% of what number is 81?

28. 73 is 26% of what number?   **29.** 25% of what number is 29?

30. 208 is 52% of what number?   **31.** $33\frac{1}{3}$% of what number is 97?

32. 94 is 20% of what number?   **33.** 2% of what number is 71?

Mixed Applications

34. Mrs. Melrose reports that 298 of the 409 students have paid for the field trip. Estimate what percent of the students have paid.

35. Ridgeway Foods has canned 598 cases of corn. This is only 42% of the expected daily total. About what is the expected daily total?

36. Shani's age this year is a multiple of 6. Last year her age was a multiple of 5. She is between 7 and 60 years old. How old is Shani now?

37. **Number Sense**   Using the signs + and −, complete the expression so that it has a value of 103.5.

20% of 650 ■ 45% of 90 ■ 100% of 14

Explain how you can estimate 1% of 7,062.

WRAP UP...

EXPLORING
Percent of Increase and Decrease

When the price of an item is increased, the price goes up. When the price is decreased, the price goes down. You can write the increase or decrease as a percent of the original price.

WORK TOGETHER

Building Understanding

Use counters to model each problem.

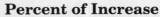

Percent of Increase
Place 10 red counters in a row on your desk.

Talk About It

▶ Add 1 yellow counter. What is the ratio of the number of yellow counters to the number of red counters? Write the ratio as a percent.

▶ By what percent did you increase the original number of counters? This is the percent of increase.

▶ Now add enough yellow counters until you have a total of 18 counters. What is the ratio of the number of yellow counters to the number of red counters? Write the ratio as a percent.

▶ Adding the 8 yellow counters to the original 10 red counters represents what percent of increase?

Percent of Decrease
Place 20 counters in a row on your desk.

Talk About It

▶ Remove 1 counter. What is the ratio of the number of counters removed to the original number of counters? Write this ratio as a percent.

▶ What percent does 1 counter represent? **Think:** $\frac{1}{20} = \frac{n}{100}$

▶ By what percent did you decrease the original number of counters? This is the percent of decrease.

▶ Continue removing counters until only 10 remain. What is the ratio of the total number of counters removed to the original number of counters? What is the percent of decrease?

Making the Connection

You can use ratios to solve problems about percent of increase and decrease.

Percent of Increase

Roberto is a cook at Carol's Restaurant. For one year he has earned an hourly rate of $10. This week his hourly rate was increased by $1. What is the percent of increase?

Think: $\dfrac{\text{amount of increase}}{\text{original rate}} = \dfrac{1}{10} = \dfrac{10}{100} = 10\%$ ← percent of increase

So, the percent of increase is 10%.

Sally is an apprentice baker at the restaurant. Last week she prepared 50 loaves of whole-wheat bread. This week she prepared 90 loaves of whole-wheat bread. What is the percent of increase?

Think: Find the amount of increase.

amount of increase = 90 − 50 = 40

$\dfrac{\text{amount of increase}}{\text{original amount}} = \dfrac{40}{50} = \dfrac{80}{100} = 80\%$ ← percent of increase

So, the percent of increase is 80%.

Percent of Decrease

Babs is planning a birthday party. Last week she bought cans of fruit punch. Each can cost $1.20. This week the fruit punch is on sale for $0.60 a can. What is the percent of decrease?

Think: Find the amount of decrease.

amount of decrease = 120 − 60 = 60

$\dfrac{\text{amount of decrease}}{\text{original price}} = \dfrac{60}{120} = \dfrac{1}{2} = \dfrac{50}{100} = 50\%$ ← percent of decrease

So, the percent of decrease is 50%.

Checking Understanding

1. Find the percent of increase.
   amount of increase: 25
   original amount: 200

2. Find the percent of decrease.
   amount of decrease: 5
   original amount: 125

3. Find the percent of increase.
   amount of increase: $148.50
   original price: $165

4. Find the percent of decrease.
   amount of decrease: $4,000
   original salary: $25,000

5. Last month 50 pieces of fruit were served during the lunch hour. This month 168 pieces of fruit were served. What is the percent of increase?

More Practice, Lesson 6.12, page H53

UP...

Percent of Increase and Decrease

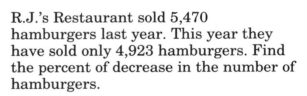

The cost of lunch goes from $0.95 to $1.10. What is the increase?

Last year R.J.'s Restaurant had a total of 15 employees. This year the restaurant has 18 employees. What is the percent of increase in the number of employees?

Step 1
Subtract to find the amount of increase. $18 - 15 = 3$

Step 2
Write the ratio of the amount of increase to the original amount. Rewrite the ratio as a percent.

amount of increase → $\frac{3}{15} = \frac{1}{5} = 20\%$ ← percent of
original amount → increase

So, the percent of increase in the number of employees is 20%.

At R.J.'s Restaurant a roast beef dinner costs $6.50. If the cost is increased by 30%, what is the amount of increase?

Think: 30% of $6.50 is the amount of increase. $0.30 \times 6.50 = n$

You can use a calculator.

6.5 ⨯ 30 % [1.95]

You can use mental math.

Think:
10% of $6.50 = $0.65
30% of $6.50 = $1.95 ← 3 × $0.65

So, the amount of increase is $1.95.

R.J.'s Restaurant sold 5,470 hamburgers last year. This year they have sold only 4,923 hamburgers. Find the percent of decrease in the number of hamburgers.

Think: What is the amount of decrease? $5,470 - 4,923 = 547$

You can use an equation.

Think:
What percent of 5,470 is 547?
$n \times 5,470 = 547$
$5,470n = 547$
$\frac{5,470n}{5,470} = \frac{547}{5,470}$
$n = 0.10$ ← 0.10 = 10%

So, the percent of decrease is 10%.

Talk About It

▶ How can you use percent to find the new cost of a roast beef dinner? HINT: Represent the original cost as 100%.

▶ How can you use percent to represent a new cost that is 2.5 times the original cost?

202

Check for Understanding

Write **I** if there is an increase. Then write the amount of the increase.
Write **D** if there is a decrease. Then write the amount of the decrease.

1. 20 to 25   **2.** 75 to 50   **3.** 242 to 484

Find the percent of increase or decrease.

4. 50 to 30   **5.** 80 to 160   **6.** 48 to 36

Practice

Find the percent of increase or decrease.

7. 1980 cost: $80
1990 cost: $100

8. 1990 sales: $690
1991 sales: $460

9. 1970 sales: 50
1990 sales: 57

10. 1985 earnings: $20,000
1990 earnings: $30,000

11. 1990 cost: $600
1991 cost: $450

12. 1980 amount: 550
1990 amount: 1,100

13. 1980 earnings: $25,500
1990 earnings: $23,970

14. 1990 amount: 1,800
1991 amount: 2,400

15. 1990 cost: $13,800
1991 cost: $4,600

16. 1989 savings: $10,500
1990 savings: $11,550

17. 1980 sales: 1,490
1990 sales: 745

18. 1989 amount: 880
1991 amount: 704

Mixed Applications

19. R.J. placed the restaurant's seafood order and was notified of a price increase. The original cost of his order was $148.00. The new cost is $177.60. What is the percent of increase?

20. Logical Reasoning During a sale the price of a radio was decreased by 25%. By what percent must the sale price be increased to restore the original price?

HEALTH CONNECTION

To promote good health, some nutrition experts recommend limiting fat intake to 30% or less of total calorie intake.

Example Is Julie's fat intake within the 30% guideline?

$$\frac{800}{2,400} = 33\tfrac{1}{3}\%$$

The percent of Julie's fat intake is $33\tfrac{1}{3}\%$. So, she is not within the 30% guideline.

21. Is Jason's or Vicki's fat intake within the 30% guideline?

Fat Intake		
Name	**Fat Intake** (in calories)	**Total Number of Calories**
Julie	800	2,400
Jason	770	2,800
Vicki	960	2,900

Use mental math to find the percent of increase from $0.80 to $1.00.

WRAP
UP...

Find 10% of $3,000. Which is the
best answer choice: $3, $30, or $300?

SIMPLE INTEREST

Interest is the fee paid for using someone else's
money. Interest is the amount you pay a bank
when you borrow money. Interest is the amount a
bank pays you when you deposit money.

Mr. and Mrs. White want to buy a small grocery
store. They plan to borrow $100,000 to use toward
this purchase. A bank has agreed to lend them the
money for 5 yr at a yearly interest rate of 9%. How
much interest will they pay?

You can find the simple interest, I, to be paid by
using the formula $I = prt$.

Principal (p): amount of money borrowed or saved

Rate (r): percent

Time (t): time the money is borrowed or saved

$I = prt$
$I = p \times r \times t$ Think: p = $100,000,
$I = 100,000 \times 0.09 \times 5$ r = 9% per year, t = 5 years
$I = 45,000$

So, Mr. and Mrs. White will pay $45,000 in interest.

Find the total amount (principal + interest) that
Mr. and Mrs. White will pay in loan payments.

You can find the total amount, A, by using the formula $A = p + I$.

$A = p + I$ Think: p = $100,000, I = $45,000
$A = 100,000 + 45,000$
$A = 145,000$

So, the total amount that Mr. and Mrs. White will pay is $145,000.

Jay White earned $1,600 from his summer job at a local potato
farm. He deposited $1,200 and earned a yearly interest rate of
6.5% on his savings. His $1,200 has been in the bank for 6 mo. How
much interest has he earned?

Think: 6 mo is what part of a year? $\frac{6 \text{ mo}}{12 \text{ mo}} = 0.5$ year

$I = prt$
$I = 1,200 \times 0.065 \times 0.5$ $1,200 \;\boxed{\times}\; 0.065 \;\boxed{\times}\; 0.5 \;\boxed{=}\; \boxed{\qquad 39.}$
$I = 39$

So, Jay has earned $39 in interest.

Check for Understanding

Find the interest and the total amount for each situation.

1. $p = \$4{,}500$
$r = 12\%$ per year
$t = 4$ yr

2. $p = \$5{,}000$
$r = 9.5\%$ per year
$t = 3$ mo

3. $p = \$35{,}000$
$r = 10\%$ per year
$t = 25$ yr

Practice

Find the interest.

4. $p = \$196$
$r = 4\%$ per year
$t = 2$ yr

5. $p = \$900$
$r = 8\%$ per year
$t = 1$ yr

6. $p = \$1{,}276$
$r = 9\%$ per year
$t = 1\frac{1}{2}$ yr

7. $p = \$290$
$r = 4\%$ per year
$t = 6$ mo

8. $p = \$725$
$r = 12\%$ per year
$t = 3$ mo

9. $p = \$1{,}300$
$r = 11\%$ per year
$t = 1$ yr

10. $p = \$950$
$r = 1.2\%$ per month
$t = 6$ mo

11. $p = \$8{,}500$
$r = 1\%$ per month
$t = 7$ mo

12. $p = \$940$
$r = 1.5\%$ per month
$t = 1$ yr

Mixed Applications

13. Cindy is borrowing $1,200 for 18 mo. The bank charges an interest rate of 1.5% per month. How much interest must she pay? Find the total amount that she must pay.

14. Mr. and Mrs. White kept $400 in a savings account for 3 yr and earned a total of $60 in interest. What yearly interest rate did the bank pay?

15. Visual Thinking Josh created this 4-section pattern with hexagons, trapezoids, and triangles. How many hexagons, trapezoids, and triangles will he need in order to extend the pattern to 24 sections?

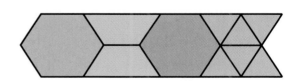

MIXED REVIEW

Estimate the value of n.

1. 26% of 196 = n

2. 41% of 59 = n

3. 61 is 5% of n.

4. 9 is 21% of n.

Estimate the percent.

5. $\frac{269}{273}$

6. 247 out of 495

7. 5 per 511

8. 19:202

Explain which loan you would choose: $2,000 at 8% for 3 yr or $2,000 at 9.5% for 2 yr.

WRAP
UP...

Strategy ● Use Estimation

Nikki eats lunch at a restaurant. Her bill totals $7.85. She wants to leave the waiter a tip that is about 15% of the bill. About how much money should she leave the waiter?

In everyday life there are many situations in which you may want to use estimation.

▶ **UNDERSTAND**

What are you asked to find?

What facts are given?

▶ **PLAN**

What strategy will you use?
You can *use estimation* to solve the problem. Change the amount of the bill to an amount that is easy to compute mentally. Then, think of 15% as 10% + 5%.

▶ **SOLVE**

How will you solve the problem?

Change $7.85 to an amount that is easy to compute mentally.

You can use $8.00.

Since you know that 15% = 10% + 5%, first find 10% of $8.00.

10% of $8.00 = $0.80

You know that 5% is $\frac{1}{2}$ of 10%, so 5% of $8.00 = $\frac{1}{2}$ of $0.80, or $0.40.

Find the total amount of the tip. $0.80 + $0.40 = $1.20

So, Nikki should leave the waiter about $1.20.

▶ **LOOK BACK**

What method can you use to check your solution?

WHAT IF... . . . Nikki decides to leave a 20% tip? About how much should she leave?

Apply

Estimate a 15% tip for each bill.

1. $42.97
2. $11.36
3. $29.42
4. $8.81
5. $5.30
6. $17.65
7. $9.67
8. $32.09

Use estimation to solve.

9. The barber gives Martin and his 3 brothers haircuts. The total bill is $22. Martin wants to give the barber a tip that is about 15% of the bill. Estimate the amount of the tip.

10. As Connie left the restaurant last night, she noticed a $20 tip on a table. If $20 was 15% of the total bill, what was the amount of the total bill?

Mixed Applications → **STRATEGIES**
- Guess and Check
- Use a Formula
- Use Estimation
- Draw a Picture

Choose a strategy and solve.

11. Stephanie made these deposits in her savings account: $102, $57, $41, and $29. What is her approximate savings account balance?

12. Bob's age is 3 times Nathan's age. Nathan's age is 2 times Rachel's age. The sum of their ages is 18. Find the age of Bob, Nathan, and Rachel.

13. Gordon deposited $5,600 for 3 yrs at an interest rate of 7.5% per year. How much interest will he receive?

14. Rodney's dinner bill totals $28.57. He wants to leave a tip that is about 15% of the bill. Estimate the amount of the tip.

15. Jennifer has a total of 11 coins, all quarters and dimes. The total value of the coins is $1.85. How many of each coin does she have?

16. Natalie is borrowing $5,000 for 4 yr at an interest rate of 9% per year. How much will she pay in interest? What total amount will she pay?

17. Al is mowing Ms. Green's yard. The rectangular lot measures 100 ft by 50 ft. The mower cuts a 2-ft-wide path. Al has mowed a 2-ft-wide path along the perimeter. What percent of the total area has he mowed? Round to the nearest percent.

18. You enter a hotel elevator. You go up 5 floors, down 6 floors, and up 13 floors. You are now on the top floor. Then you go down 10 floors, up 2 floors, and down 6 floors. You are now on the first floor. On what floor did you enter the elevator?

CHAPTER REVIEW

Vocabulary Check

Choose a word from the box to complete each sentence.

divide
interest
left
proportion
rate
ratio
right

1. A comparison of two numbers is a __?__. *(page 174)*

2. A ratio that compares quantities of different units is a __?__. *(page 174)*

3. An equation stating that two ratios are equivalent is a __?__. *(page 176)*

4. To write a decimal as a percent, move the decimal point two places to the __?__. Then write a percent sign. *(page 186)*

5. To write a ratio as a decimal, __?__ the first term by the second term. *(page 186)*

6. The fee paid for using someone else's money is __?__. *(page 204)*

Concept Check

Write the ratio in the form $\frac{a}{b}$. *(page 174)*

7. stars to squares
8. squares to all shapes
9. squares to stars

Write as a ratio in simplest form. *(pages 174, 186)*

10. 6:12

11. 35 to 15

12. $\frac{\$21}{3}$ T-shirts

13. 184 mi per 4 hr

14. 75%

15. $33\frac{1}{3}\%$

16. 24%

17. 208%

Write = or ≠. *(page 174)*

18. $\frac{3}{5} \bullet \frac{9}{15}$

19. $\frac{5}{9} \bullet \frac{20}{27}$

20. $\frac{5}{73} \bullet \frac{10}{143}$

21. $\frac{3}{8} \bullet \frac{15}{40}$

Write *enlarge* or *reduce* to describe whether the scale will enlarge or reduce the dimensions of the object it represents. *(page 178)*

22. 1 in.:10 ft

23. 5:1

24. 2:7

25. 100 mm:1 mm

Write as a percent. *(pages 184, 186)*

26. 0.91

27. 3.84

28. 0.006

29. $\frac{13}{25}$

30. $\frac{5}{4}$

Write as a decimal. *(page 186)*

31. 12%

32. 6%

33. 150%

34. $2\frac{1}{2}$

35. $\frac{3}{8}$

Write **I** if there is an increase. Write **D** if there is a decrease. *(page 200)*

36. 99 to 107

37. 48 to 31

38. 300 to 3,000

Skill Check

Solve the proportion. *(page 176)*

39. $\frac{1}{7} = \frac{n}{28}$ **40.** $\frac{2}{9} = \frac{12}{n}$ **41.** $\frac{3}{1} = \frac{n}{5.1}$ **42.** $\frac{3}{5} = \frac{4.2}{n}$

Write a proportion. Use *n* to represent the missing term. *(page 176)*

43. Alex earned $245 for 45 hours of work. If his hourly rate remains the same, what will be his earnings for 40 hours of work?

Solve. *(pages 190, 194, 196)*

44. What number is 15% of 200?

45. 36 is what percent of 18?

46. What percent of 55 is 11?

47. $33\frac{1}{3}$% of what number is 27?

Estimate. *(pages 198, 206)*

48. $\frac{89}{102}$ is about what percent?

49. 59 is about what percent of 122?

50. 162 is 25% of about what number?

51. 9.5% of 51 is about what number?

Find the percent of increase or decrease. *(page 202)*

52. original amount: $98.00
new amount: $117.60

53. first-year earnings: $15,000
second-year earnings: $8,700

Find the interest. *(page 204)*

54. $p = \$1,500$
$r = 12\%$ per year
$t = 2$ yr

55. $p = \$390$
$r = 8\%$ per year
$t = 4$ mo

56. $p = \$800$
$r = 1.5\%$ per month
$t = 1$ yr

Problem-Solving Check

Solve. Use the scale drawing for Exercises 57–58. *(pages 178, 182, 194)*

57. The scale drawing shows the recent addition to the Steele house. The scale of the drawing is $\frac{1}{2}$ in.: 6 ft. Find the actual length and width of the addition.

58. The actual length of the bathroom is 9 ft. What should be the length of the bathroom in the scale drawing?

59. Jerry Lee is reading a road map with the scale of 1 in.: 50 mi. The map distance between two cities is $4\frac{1}{2}$ in. What is the actual distance?

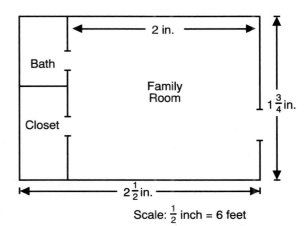

Scale: $\frac{1}{2}$ inch = 6 feet

60. Lily has saved $3,800 of the $5,000 required as a down payment on a house. What percent of the down payment has she saved?

Write as a ratio in simplest form.

1. 45 to 60 **2.** 30:20 **3.** 50% **4.** $\dfrac{180 \text{ calories}}{9 \text{ oz}}$

Solve the proportion.

5. $\dfrac{7}{a} = \dfrac{28}{44}$ **6.** $\dfrac{3}{5} = \dfrac{c}{30}$ **7.** $\dfrac{n}{9} = \dfrac{2}{3}$

Use the scale of 1 in.:12 ft to find the missing dimension.

8. drawing: 9 in.
actual: ■ ft

9. drawing: ■ in.
actual: 144 ft

Write as a percent.

10. 0.83 **11.** 3.097 **12.** $\dfrac{29}{50}$ **13.** $3\dfrac{4}{5}$

Write as a decimal.

14. 32% **15.** 620% **16.** $\dfrac{2}{5}$ **17.** $3\dfrac{1}{10}$

Solve.

18. Find 26% of 480. **19.** Find 200% of 325.

20. 987 is what percent of 282? **21.** 338 is what percent of 845?

22. 0.5 is what percent of 200? **23.** 160 is 25% of what number?

24. 180.9 is 22.5% of what number? **25.** 1,050 is 140% of what number?

Find the percent of increase or decrease.

26. 1990 sales: 260
1991 sales: 338

27. 1990 cost: $46.00
1991 cost: $43.47

Estimate.

28. $\dfrac{41}{158}$ is about what percent? **29.** 32 is 76% of about what number?

Solve.

30. Dan's car used 5 gal of gasoline on a 190-mi trip. How many gallons of gasoline will his car use on a 456-mi trip?

31. Eli is reading a map with the scale of 1 cm:1,000 km. If the map distance is 5.8 cm, what is the actual distance?

32. Vivian used a credit card to buy a television for $350. She paid an interest rate of $1\frac{1}{2}\%$ per month for 3 mo. How much interest did Vivian pay?

33. The Acunto family's lunch bill is $20.56. The family wants to leave a tip of about 15% of the bill. Estimate the amount of the tip.

eamwork P-R-O-J-E-C-T

Make a Table

What nutrition does your favorite snack food provide? Work with your classmates, and select five or six kinds of snack foods to evaluate for nutritional value. If the snack food does not have nutrition information on its packaging, obtain the information from a nutrition book.

DECIDE

As a team, discuss your favorite snack foods. Make five or six selections from the list.

Discuss the kind of table you will make so that you can compare the nutrients of the snacks.

Discuss the headings you will need for the table.

SHARE

Compare all your snack-food information with that of other teams. Identify the least nutritious snack food and the most nutritious snack food. Give the reasons for your choices.

DO

Assign an equal number of snack foods to each team member. Record the name of each snack food and the amount of each of its nutrients. Compare the cost of the snack food with the weight of the snack food. Include this ratio in the table.

Talk About It

- What did you learn about snack foods?

- Which snack food provides the most nutrition for the least amount of money?

- What is the number of calories in 1 ounce of your favorite snack?

- Does any snack food have as many as 4 times the number of calories as another? Explain.

- What percent of your snack food's total calories is provided by fat?

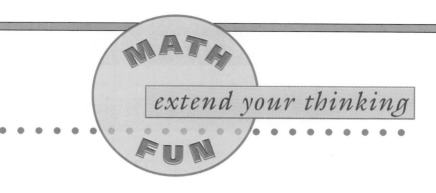

Who's the Greek Mathematician?

The diagonal, *d*, and the side, *s*, of any square have lengths that cannot be compared exactly as a ratio of two whole numbers. Such quantities are called **incommensurable.**

A Greek mathematician who lived about 370 B.C. developed a theory of proportions that included such incommensurable quantities.

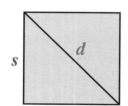

To find the name of this mathematician, write the letter that matches the number missing from each exercise.

40 E
50 D
60 O
70 S
80 X
90 U

1. 20% of 60 is __?__ percent of 30. __?__
2. 25% of 36 is 10% of __?__. __?__
3. 50% of 18 is 18% of __?__. __?__
4. 300% of 15 is $\frac{3}{4}$ of __?__. __?__
5. If $\frac{3}{4} = \frac{2}{n}$, $30n =$ __?__. __?__
6. If $\frac{1+2}{2} = \frac{n+180}{180}$, $n =$ __?__. __?__
7. At the Belle Boutique, a $70 coat was discounted by 20%. Later the discounted price was increased by 25%. The price of the coat was then $__?__. __?__

Challenge

Logical Reasoning

Three sisters, Etta, Kara, and Lona, are 18, 19, and 20 years old, but not in the order given. When a stranger asked them their ages, the sisters replied as follows:

Etta — I am the oldest.
Kara — I am not the youngest.
Lona — I am younger than Kara.

None of the sisters told the truth. What is the age of each sister?

Challenge

Number Sense

Using this target, how can you score exactly 100 points?

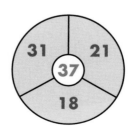

CUMULATIVE REVIEW

Write the letter of the correct answer.

1. 12% of 162 is which number?

    A. 14.86   **B.** 17.39

    C. 19.44   **D.** 1,350

2. Which triangle has no congruent sides?

    A. equilateral   **B.** parallel

    C. scalene   **D.** isosceles

3. $5{,}414.85 \div 94.5$

    A. 5.57   **B.** 57.3

    C. 573   **D.** not here

4. Which decimal equals $\frac{16}{5}$?

    A. 0.31   **B.** 3.1

    C. 3.2   **D.** 80

5. Which is an equivalent ratio for $3:6$?

    A. $0:2$ **B.** $1:2$

    C. $6:3$ **D.** $\frac{3}{1}$

6. Which is the decimal for $\frac{7}{8}$?

    A. 0.817   **B.** 0.873

    C. 0.875   **D.** 8.75

7. Which fraction is equal to $\frac{8}{96}$?

    A. $\frac{1}{16}$ **B.** $\frac{2}{24}$

    C. $\frac{4}{42}$ **D.** $\frac{1}{12}$

8. $70 - 3 \cdot (15 - 2)$

    A. 31   **B.** 41

    C. 109   **D.** 871

9. Which angles are always congruent?

    A. vertical   **B.** complementary

    C. adjacent   **D.** supplementary

10. $8 \div 2\frac{1}{2}$

    A. $3\frac{1}{5}$ **B.** $3\frac{1}{2}$

    C. $4\frac{1}{4}$ **D.** $4\frac{1}{2}$

11. Gene drove 280 mi on 8 gal of gasoline. How many miles could Gene drive on 13.8 gal of gasoline?

    A. 400 mi   **B.** 427 mi

    C. 438 mi   **D.** 483 mi

12. Carol wants to buy 15 rosebushes. The price of the rosebushes is 2 for $5.98. What will Carol pay for 15 rosebushes?

    A. $38.50   **B.** $41.86

    C. $42.60   **D.** $44.85

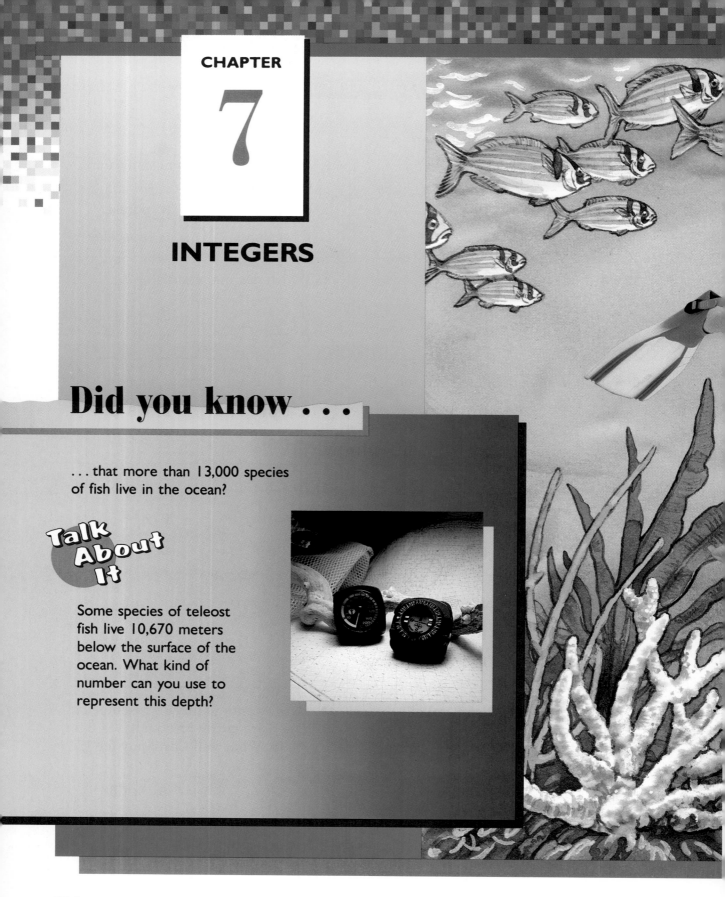

Did you know . . .

. . . that more than 13,000 species of fish live in the ocean?

Talk About It

Some species of teleost fish live 10,670 meters below the surface of the ocean. What kind of number can you use to represent this depth?

UNDERSTANDING INTEGERS

A marine biologist enters the water from a platform that is 3 m above the surface of the water. The biologist then descends in the water to a depth of 8 m. After taking specimens, the biologist ascends back to the surface of the water.

The path of the biologist is represented on the vertical number line. The numbers on the number line are integers.

The positive integer 3 represents the height *above* the surface. The negative integer ⁻8 represents the depth *below* the surface. The integer 0 represents the surface of the water. Zero is neither positive nor negative.

The **absolute value** of an integer is its distance from 0 on the number line. Since distance always has a positive value, the absolute value of any number except 0 is always positive.

| $|4| = 4$ | Read: The absolute value of positive four is four. | $|^-4| = 4$ | Read: The absolute value of negative four is four. |

Since the integers 4 and ⁻4 are the same distance from 0 and are on opposite sides of 0, they are called **opposites.**

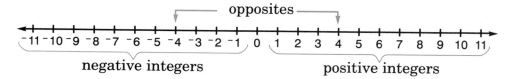

You can use a number line to compare and order integers. Remember that on a number line, an integer to the right is greater than an integer to the left.

Examples

A. Which is greater, 9 or ⁻10?

   Think: 9 is to the right of ⁻10 on the number line.

$$9 > {}^-10$$

B. Order 7, ⁻6, 4, 0, and ⁻3 from least to greatest.

   Think: 0, 4, and 7 are to the right of ⁻6 and ⁻3 on the number line.

$${}^-6, {}^-3, 0, 4, 7$$

Check for Understanding

Write an integer for each point on the number line.

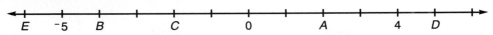

1. point A 2. point B 3. point C 4. point D 5. point E

Practice

Write an integer for each description.

6. 18° above zero   7. 23° below zero   8. a loss of 3 lb

9. 112 m below   10. a gain of 6 yd   11. a deposit of $150

Write the absolute value.

12. $|^-9|$ 13. $|^-18|$ 14. $|0|$ 15. $|^-1|$ 16. $|18|$ 17. $|253|$

18. $|^-3|$ 19. $|^-196|$ 20. $|^-72|$ 21. $|^-12|$ 22. $|15|$ 23. $|^-115|$

Write the opposite.

24. rising 10°C   25. walking south 2 km   26. earning 15 dollars

27. $^-4$ 28. 40   29. $^-116$ 30. 19   31. 34   32. $^-19$

Compare. Write $<$, $>$, or $=$.

33. $^-7$ ● $^-10$ 34. 30 ● 20   35. 11 ● $^-15$ 36. $^-8$ ● 4

37. $^-12$ ● $^-3$ 38. $^-8$ ● 8   39. $|2|$ ● $|^-4|$ 40. $|9|$ ● $|^-9|$

Order the integers from least to greatest.

41. 4, $^-4$, $^-7$, $^-9$ 42. 42, 0, $^-41$, $^-1$ 43. 6, 7, 9, $^-7$, $^-6$

44. 1, $^-2$, $^-6$, 0, $^-4$ 45. 20, $^-21$, 10, $^-19$ 46. 0, $^-5$, 6, 9, $^-10$

Mixed Applications

47. Ships A and B are using sonar to search for a sunken treasure ship. Ship A searches north at a rate of 19 km per day. This rate is shown by 19. Ship B searches south at a rate of 21 km per day. This rate is shown by $^-21$. Which ship searches farther each day?

48. A diving barge extends 3 m above and 3 m below the ocean's surface. This extension can be expressed by the equation $|n| = 3$. What two integers represent the barge's extensions above and below the surface?

49. The measure of an angle is 40° more than the measure of its supplement. Find the measure of the angle and its supplement.

Why do any integer and its opposite have the same absolute value?

ADDING INTEGERS

The elevation of Mount McKinley in Alaska is about 7 km higher than the elevation of Pensacola Seamount, an underwater mountain in the Pacific Ocean. The elevation of Pensacola Seamount is about ⁻1 km. What is the approximate elevation of Mount McKinley?

You can use a number line to find the sum, 7 + ⁻1. Start at zero. Remember that adding a positive number is shown by moving right and that adding a negative number is shown by moving left.

So, the elevation of Mount McKinley is about 6 km.

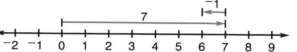

● Use a number line to find these sums.

   a. 6 + 2   **b.** ⁻8 + ⁻3   **c.** 10 + ⁻6   **d.** 7 + ⁻15

Talk About It

▶ Look at the sums you got for **a** and **b.** Without using a number line, how can you find the sum of two integers with the same sign? How can you determine whether the sum is positive or negative?

▶ Look at the sums you got for **c** and **d.** Without using a number line, how can you determine the sum of two integers with different signs? How can you determine whether the sum is positive or negative?

Another Method   To find the sum of two integers with different signs, you can subtract the absolute values of the integers. The sum has the same sign as the addend with the greater absolute value.

Examples

A. 12 + ⁻8

|12| − |8| = 12 − 8 = 4

Since 12 has the greater absolute value,
12 + ⁻8 = 4.

B. 19 + ⁻32

|32| − |19| = 32 − 19 = 13

Since ⁻32 has the greater absolute value,
19 + ⁻32 = ⁻13.

Check for Understanding

Tell whether the sum will be *positive* or *negative.* Then find the sum.

1. 3 + 2   **2.** ⁻4 + ⁻3   **3.** ⁻5 + 2   **4.** 3 + ⁻1   **5.** ⁻16 + 8

Practice

Find the sum.

6. 9 + ⁻8   **7.** 14 + ⁻19   **8.** 19 + ⁻6   **9.** 20 + 9

10. ⁻15 + 20   **11.** ⁻18 + 8   **12.** ⁻10 + 10   **13.** 29 + ⁻31

14. ⁻15 + ⁻8   **15.** 21 + ⁻21   **16.** 19 + 4   **17.** ⁻18 + 4

18. ⁻9 + 50   **19.** ⁻31 + ⁻36   **20.** 6 + ⁻24   **21.** 52 + ⁻38

22. ⁻63 + 104   **23.** 82 + ⁻19   **24.** ⁻113 + 92   **25.** ⁻162 + 204

26. 5 + ⁻2 + ⁻8   **27.** 12 + ⁻6 + 7   **28.** ⁻15 + 12 + ⁻10

29. (8 + ⁻14) + 22   **30.** (⁻61 + 19) + 32   **31.** ⁻6 + (3 + ⁻9)

Mixed Applications

32. About 18,000 years ago, sea level was 100 m below the present sea level, or ⁻100 m. It then rose 65 meters in 9,000 years. What was the sea level 9,000 years ago?

33. A research submarine is cruising at ⁻40 m. The submarine then descends 15 m and rises 18 m. What is the submarine's new location?

34. Look at Exercise 19. Explain how the procedure for finding the sum would change if ⁻31 is changed to 31. What would be the sum?

35. Each term in a number sequence is 3 more than the term before. The first term is ⁻10. Write the next five terms in the sequence.

MATH CONNECTION

To add integers with a calculator, use the change of sign key, , after a negative number.

Examples   18 + ⁻6   18 (+) 6 (+/−) (=)   [12.]

            ⁻52 + 45   52 (+/−) (+) 45 (=)   [⁻   7.]

Use a calculator to find the sum.

36. ⁻13 + 28   **37.** 56 + ⁻78   **38.** ⁻112 + ⁻155   **39.** ⁻43 + 22 + 96

Explain how you find the sum of a negative integer and a positive integer.

WRAP UP...

SUBTRACTING INTEGERS

In 1934 William Beebe, an American naturalist, descended 2,640 ft into the ocean near Bermuda in a bathysphere. In 1960 explorer Jacques Piccard and Lieutenant Don Walsh descended 35,800 ft into the Mariana Trench in the Pacific Ocean in the bathyscaphe *Trieste*. What is the difference in the depths?

The depths can be represented by ⁻2,640 and ⁻35,800.

$$^-35{,}800 - {}^-2{,}640 = {}^-35{,}800 + 2{,}640$$
$$= {}^-33{,}160$$

So, the difference in the depths is ⁻33,160 ft.

Compare the subtraction problem with the addition problem.

$8 - 5 = 3$	$^-8 - 5 = {}^-13$
$8 + {}^-5 = 3$	$^-8 + {}^-5 = {}^-13$

In each subtraction problem, you subtract 5. In each addition problem, you add the opposite of 5 and get the same answer as in the subtraction problem.

> To subtract an integer, add the opposite of the integer.

$10 - {}^-4 = ?$

Examples

A. $9 - 6 = 9 + {}^-6 = 3$ Add ⁻6, the opposite of 6.

B. $10 - {}^-4 = 10 + 4 = 14$ Add 4, the opposite of ⁻4.

C. $^-5 - 7 = {}^-5 + {}^-7 = {}^-12$ Add ⁻7, the opposite of 7.

D. $^-8 - {}^-2 = {}^-8 + 2 = {}^-6$ Add 2, the opposite of ⁻2.

Check for Understanding

Write an addition problem for each subtraction problem.

1. $10 - {}^-3$ **2.** $8 - {}^-9$ **3.** $11 - 3$ **4.** $2 - 12$

5. $^-1 - 5$ **6.** $^-14 - 7$ **7.** $^-6 - {}^-12$ **8.** $^-10 - {}^-3$

Practice

Find the difference.

9. $6 - {}^-15$ **10.** ${}^-5 - {}^-11$ **11.** ${}^-15 - {}^-12$ **12.** ${}^-6 - {}^-3$

13. ${}^-42 - {}^-83$ **14.** ${}^-20 - 32$ **15.** $20 - 8$ **16.** ${}^-4 - {}^-10$

17. ${}^-17 - {}^-20$ **18.** ${}^-21 - {}^-32$ **19.** $21 - {}^-14$ **20.** $6 - 4$

21. $19 - 28$ **22.** $110 - {}^-14$ **23.** ${}^-19 - 4$ **24.** ${}^-8 - 5$

25. $13 - {}^-24$ **26.** ${}^-84 - 66$ **27.** $116 - 124$ **28.** ${}^-49 - {}^-50$

29. ${}^-25 - {}^-21$ **30.** $9 - 21$ **31.** $52 - 52$ **32.** ${}^-32 - {}^-30$

33. ${}^-54 - 82$ **34.** ${}^-304 - 50$ **35.** ${}^-25 - {}^-56$ **36.** ${}^-180 - 232$

Compute.

37. ${}^-6 - {}^-3 - 5$ **38.** $7 - {}^-3 + 4$ **39.** ${}^-9 + 7 - 3$

40. $({}^-3 + 5) - {}^-6$ **41.** ${}^-9 - (4 - 7)$ **42.** $({}^-10 - 3) + {}^-13$

43. $({}^-8 + 6) - (3 - 13)$ **44.** ${}^-9 - {}^-5 - {}^-6$ **45.** $({}^-11 - 4) - ({}^-8 - 5)$

Mixed Applications

46. Special sonars are used to map the ocean floor. While being towed at ${}^-140$ ft, one of these sonars indicated that the ocean floor was at ${}^-6,000$ ft. What was the distance between the sonar and the ocean floor?

47. A mapping sonar locates a volcano that rises 4,200 ft above the ocean floor. The ocean floor is at ${}^-7,350$ ft. What is the location of the top of the volcano?

48. **Making Choices** Write a calculator key sequence that you can use to find ${}^-4 - {}^-6$. Then write a different key sequence for the problem. Which key sequence is easier to use? Explain.

49. **Number Sense** The sum of two integers is ${}^-13$. When the smaller integer is subtracted from the larger integer, the difference is 3. What are the integers?

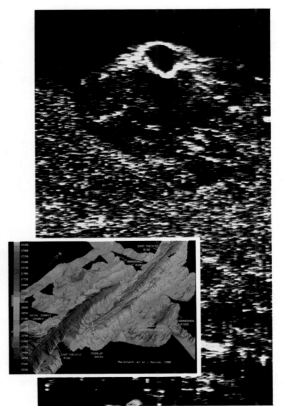

Explain the result when you subtract a negative integer from itself.

Is this sum positive or negative?
⁻3 + ⁻3 + ⁻3 + ⁻3 + ⁻3

Evita made a series of exploratory dives along the Great Barrier Reef off the coast of Australia. She dove to ⁻3 m on her first dive. Each dive that she made thereafter was 3 m deeper than the one before. How far did Evita dive on her fifth dive?

You can find the product 5 · ⁻3 by completing this pattern.

1 · ⁻3 = ⁻3
2 · ⁻3 = ⁻3 + ⁻3 = ⁻6
3 · ⁻3 = ⁻3 + ⁻3 + ⁻3 = ⁻9
4 · ⁻3 = ⁻3 + ⁻3 + ⁻3 + ⁻3 = ▪
5 · ⁻3 = ⁻3 + ⁻3 + ⁻3 + ⁻3 + ⁻3 = ▪

So, Evita dove to ⁻15 m on her fifth dive.

- Is the product of two integers with different signs a positive integer or a negative integer?

You know that the product of two positive integers is positive. Now look at the pattern below. If the pattern continues, what are the missing products?

⁻5 · 2 = ⁻10   ⁻5 · ⁻1 = 5

⁻5 · 1 = ⁻5   ⁻5 · ⁻2 = ▪

⁻5 · 0 = 0   ⁻5 · ⁻3 = ▪

Using the pattern, you find that the missing products are 10 and 15.

- Is the product of two integers with the same sign a positive integer or a negative integer?

More Examples

A. ⁻8 · ⁻7 = 56   **B.** 12 · ⁻5 = ⁻60 ← 12 5 ⊜ | ⁻   60. |

Talk About It

▶ What is the sign of the product of three negative integers? of four negative integers? of five negative integers?

▶ What rule can you write about the product of any number of negative integers?

Idea Bank, page 491, Exercise 11

Check for Understanding

Tell whether the product will be *positive* or *negative*.
Then find the product.

1. $7 \cdot 5$

2. $12 \cdot 3$

3. $8 \cdot {}^-5$

4. $7 \cdot {}^-10$

5. ${}^-9 \cdot 4$

6. ${}^-6 \cdot 11$

7. ${}^-5 \cdot {}^-12$

8. ${}^-13 \cdot {}^-6$

Practice

Find the product.

9. ${}^-6 \cdot {}^-3$

10. ${}^-8 \cdot 2$

11. $2 \cdot 1$

12. ${}^-3 \cdot {}^-2$

13. $9 \cdot {}^-1$

14. ${}^-8 \cdot 1$

15. $6 \cdot {}^-7$

16. $5 \cdot 1,000$

17. ${}^-11 \cdot {}^-8$

18. ${}^-5 \cdot 10$

19. ${}^-9 \cdot 10$

20. ${}^-5 \cdot {}^-8$

21. $15 \cdot 3$

22. ${}^-11 \cdot 0$

23. ${}^-1 \cdot {}^-16$

24. ${}^-8 \cdot {}^-1$

25. ${}^-13 \cdot {}^-2$

26. $12 \cdot 3$

27. ${}^-7 \cdot {}^-11$

28. ${}^-11 \cdot 6$

29. ${}^-3 \cdot {}^-2 \cdot 6$

30. ${}^-2 \cdot 6 \cdot {}^-1$

31. $5 \cdot {}^-6 \cdot {}^-2$

32. ${}^-4 \cdot 8 \cdot {}^-1$

33. ${}^-3 \cdot {}^-5 \cdot {}^-2$

34. ${}^-6 \cdot {}^-4 \cdot {}^-5$

Compute.

35. $({}^-3 \cdot {}^-2) + 6$

36. $6 \cdot ({}^-3 - {}^-5)$

37. ${}^-4 + ({}^-2 \cdot 5)$

38. ${}^-8 \cdot {}^-3 + 5$

39. ${}^-6 + 9 \cdot {}^-4$

40. $4^2 + {}^-3 \cdot 6$

Mixed Applications

41. Evita descended from the surface of the ocean at the rate of 3 m per minute. At what depth was she at the end of 6 minutes?

42. An oceanographer is taking water samples by using bottles attached to a long cable. The first bottle is at ${}^-100$ m. The other bottles are at intervals of 200 m. What is the location of the ninth bottle?

43. Last month Evita made 4 more than twice the number of dives she has made this month. She made 22 dives last month. How many dives has she made this month?

Explain how multiplying integers is different from multiplying whole numbers.

Strategy ● Make a Table

Launch vehicles provide the thrust necessary to launch and orbit space probes, satellites, and other spacecraft. The United States has used a variety of launch vehicles in its space program. The thrusts of some of these vehicles (in pounds) are as follows: Vanguard, 28,000; Atlas Agena, 400,000; Titan 34D, 2,600,000; Atlas H, 439,000; and the space shuttle system, 6,925,000. Which two of the vehicles are the closest in thrust?

Sometimes you can *make a table* to organize data.

▶ **UNDERSTAND**

What are you asked to find?
What facts are given?

▶ **PLAN**

What strategy will you use?
You can *make a table* listing the names of the vehicles, the thrusts, and the differences in the thrusts.

▶ **SOLVE**

In what order will you list the vehicles in the table? List the vehicles in order from the least amount of thrust to the greatest amount of thrust.

Vehicle	Thrust (in lb)	Difference (in lb)
Vanguard	28,000	
		372,000
Atlas Agena	400,000	
		39,000
Atlas H	439,000	
		2,161,000
Titan 34D	2,600,000	
		4,325,000
Space Shuttle System	6,925,000	

So, the Atlas Agena and the Atlas H are the closest in thrust.

▶ **LOOK BACK**

What other strategy can you use to solve the problem?

WHAT IF... . . . you want to know the difference in thrust of the vehicle with the greatest thrust and the vehicle with the least thrust? Which two vehicles?

Apply

The heights of some of the U.S. launch vehicles are as follows:
Scout, 72 ft; Delta, 116 ft; Atlas Centaur, 109 ft; Saturn V, 363 ft;
Titan IIIC, 135 ft; and the space shuttle system, 184 ft.

Use this information for Exercises 1–2.

1. Make a table that shows the heights of the launch vehicles in order from greatest to least. Which has the second-greatest height?

2. Which of the launch vehicles has a height that is about 5 times greater than the height of one of the other vehicles?

Mixed Applications | STRATEGIES | • Make a Table • Write a Number Sentence • Find a Pattern • Use Estimation

Choose a strategy and solve. Use this information for Exercises 3–8.

After visiting the Kennedy Space Center, Bart and his family took an airboat tour on the Banana River. The tours cost $8.75 for a 1-hour trip, $11.25 for a 2-hour trip, $13.75 for a 3-hour trip, and so on.

3. Make a table that shows the costs of the airboat tours for 1 hour, for 2 hours, and for 3 hours.

4. By how much does the cost of the tours increase per hour?

5. Extend the table you made in Exercise 3 to include the costs of boat tours for 4 hours, for 5 hours, and for 6 hours.

6. How much more would a 6-hour tour cost than a 4-hour tour?

7. Bart bought 3 tickets for the 3-hour airboat tour. He gave the boat operator $50 to pay for the tickets. How much change did Bart receive?

8. On Monday 75 persons took the 4-hour tour, and 45 persons took the 2-hour tour. Find the total amount of money collected by the airboat company for both tours.

9. On Saturday 48% of the airboat riders took the 2-hour tour. There were 282 riders in all. Estimate the number of riders that took the 2-hour boat tour.

10. The airboat operator earns $1.70 per rider for each hour of the tour. Estimate how many riders he would have to carry on a 1-hour tour in order to earn $100.00.

WRITER'S CORNER

11. Use an almanac or an encyclopedia to find additional information about some U.S. launch vehicles. Write a problem using the information. Then exchange the information and problem with a classmate and solve.

DIVIDING INTEGERS

Sean and Gwen made an exploratory flight in a hot-air balloon. Their speed as they came down can be expressed as $^-2.5$ ft per second. At that speed, how long did it take them to descend the last 20 ft before touching ground?

Divide. $^-20 \div ^-2.5$

You know how to divide 20 by 2.5. However, when you divide with integers, you also must know how to determine the sign of the quotient. Look at these related multiplication and division sentences.

Multiplication	Division
$2.5 \cdot 8 = 20$	$20 \div 2.5 = 8$
$2.5 \cdot ^-8 = ^-20$	$^-20 \div 2.5 = ^-8$
$^-2.5 \cdot ^-8 = 20$	$20 \div ^-2.5 = ^-8$
$^-2.5 \cdot 8 = ^-20$	$^-20 \div ^-2.5 = 8$

So, it took them 8 seconds to descend the last 20 ft.

Talk About It

▶ Look at the division sentences. What rule can you write about the quotient of two integers with the same sign?

▶ What rule can you write about the quotient of a negative and a positive integer?

NOTE: Zero divided by any integer except zero is zero.

Check for Understanding

Write *positive, negative,* or *zero* for each quotient.

1. $^-24 \div 3$ **2.** $^-30 \div ^-10$ **3.** $32 \div ^-8$ **4.** $^-54 \div 9$

5. $18 \div 6$ **6.** $64 \div ^-8$ **7.** $0 \div 9$ **8.** $^-49 \div ^-7$

Find the quotient.

9. $^-15 \div 3$ **10.** $27 \div 9$ **11.** $^-25 \div ^-5$ **12.** $45 \div ^-9$

Practice

Find the quotient.

13. $^-81 \div ^-9$ **14.** $15 \div ^-5$ **15.** $^-12 \div 4$ **16.** $0 \div ^-8$

17. $^-48 \div ^-12$ **18.** $36 \div 12$ **19.** $^-30 \div 15$ **20.** $^-120 \div 60$

21. $^-100 \div ^-2$ **22.** $50 \div ^-10$ **23.** $35 \div ^-7$ **24.** $^-180 \div ^-20$

25. $\frac{^-28}{2}$ **26.** $\frac{^-36}{^-4}$ **27.** $\frac{800}{^-20}$ **28.** $\frac{75}{^-5}$

29. The quotient of $^-125 \div 25$ is $^-5$. Find two other pairs of numbers that have a quotient of $^-5$.

Compute.

30. $^-9 \cdot 3$ **31.** $^-15 - ^-4$ **32.** $18 + ^-21$ **33.** $25 \div ^-5$

34. $(8 \div ^-2) + 6$ **35.** $(18 \div ^-9) - ^-6$ **36.** $(^-6 \div 3) \cdot ^-2$ **37.** $18 \div (9 + ^-6)$

38. $(^-16 \div ^-8)(^-6 \div 3)$ **39.** $(^-12 \div ^-3) - (15 \div ^-3)$

40. $(^-27 \div 3) - (48 \div 8)^2$ **41.** $(24 \div ^-3) \div (^-52 \div ^-13)$

Mixed Applications

42. A helium-filled balloon has a leaking valve. The change in the amount of gas is $^-15$ cubic ft per minute. At that rate, in how many minutes will the total change be $^-120$ cubic ft?

43. **Write a Question** The position of a hot-air balloon changed $^-24$ ft in 3 min. Write a question for this situation.

Logical Reasoning Let p be any positive number, let n be any negative number, and let z be zero. Write *positive, negative,* or *zero* for the value of each expression.

44. $p + p$ **45.** $n + n$ **46.** $n \cdot n$ **47.** $z \cdot n$

48. $p - n$ **49.** $n \div p$ **50.** $z - p$ **51.** $n \div n$

MIXED REVIEW

Find the product or quotient.

1. 45.6×32.4 **2.** $6\frac{1}{2} \times 2\frac{2}{3}$ **3.** $16 \times ^-12$ **4.** 325×10

5. $2\frac{4}{5} \div \frac{4}{5}$ **6.** $1.404 \div 0.6$ **7.** $145 \div ^-5$ **8.** $^-100 \div ^-20$

Which problem has the greater quotient, $^-16 \div 2$ or $^-16 \div ^-2$? Explain.

1. The amount of Jason's bill at a restaurant is $8.78. Jason is going to leave about 15% for a tip. About how much will he leave for the tip?

2. Nancy has a sheet of poster board 32 cm wide by 36 cm long. How many 10-cm square pieces can she cut from the sheet?

3. Draw the next figure in the pattern.

4. Ric decides to save $6.00 more each week than the amount he spends for entertainment. This week he saved $12.78. How much did he spend on entertainment?

5. An Arctic research team spent a total of 40 days performing three-day and four-day experiments. They performed fewer than 6 three-day experiments. How many four-day experiments did they perform?

6. An explorer walked 300 ft south from his camp. He then walked 112 ft west, 212 ft north, 62 ft east, and 88 ft north. How far was he from camp when he stopped?

Find the value.

7. 3^3
8. 2^5
9. 6^0
10. 10^7
11. 12^2

Solve. Write the whole numbers that make the inequality true.

12. $t + 1 < 4$
13. $b - 4 \geq 3$
14. $4c \leq 12$
15. $2x + 1 > 15$

Write the prime factorization, using exponents.

16. 48
17. 28
18. 75
19. 100
20. 120

Write a decimal for the fraction or mixed number.

21. $\frac{3}{10}$
22. $\frac{2}{3}$
23. $1\frac{1}{4}$
24. $\frac{5}{8}$
25. $\frac{7}{9}$

Use the figure to find each measure. $\overleftrightarrow{MN} \parallel \overleftrightarrow{PQ}$, and $\overleftrightarrow{RS}$ is a transversal.

26. $m \angle 1$
27. $m \angle 3$
28. $m \angle 6$

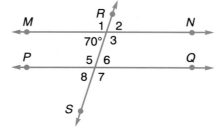

Write as a percent.

29. $1:4$
30. 0.86
31. $\frac{3}{2}$
32. 0.03
33. $\frac{9}{10}$
34. 1.64

Find the percent of the number.

35. 10% of 94
36. 85% of 20
37. 100% of 163
38. 125% of 40

Write *expression*, *equation*, or *inequality* for each.

39. $3a - 11 \leq 19$
40. $5^4 - 3^2 + {}^-8.41$
41. $\frac{n}{19} = 6$
42. $12c - 7$

Spotlight ON PROBLEM SOLVING

Understand
Plan
Solve
Look Back

Collect and Analyze Data

To create or solve problems, you can analyze data that has been collected.

SURVEY RESULTS	
Student	**Difference from Average Height (in inches)**
Eric	−1
Rhonda	2
Steve	5
Enid	−3
Daniel	0
Linda	−2

Talk About It

Work with a classmate. Answer the questions by analyzing the data in the table.

a. Who is the tallest student? the shortest?

b. Suppose the average height of 14-year-olds is 62 inches. Which student is 62 inches tall?

c. How much taller is Steve than Eric?

d. How much shorter is Linda than Rhonda?

e. Which students are above the average height?

Apply

Work with a classmate to record the temperature at each of the following times during a school day. Use your data for Exercises 1–4.

| 10:00 A.M. | 11:00 A.M. | noon |
| 1:00 P.M. | 2:00 P.M. | 3:00 P.M. |

1. At what time did you record the lowest temperature? the highest?

2. Between what hours did the temperature rise? fall?

3. Compare the temperatures you recorded with the average temperatures for your area. Were your temperatures above or below the average temperatures? By how much?

4. Create a problem based on the temperatures that you recorded. Exchange with another pair of classmates and solve.

229

PROPERTIES OF INTEGERS

At 6:00 A.M. the temperature was $^-5°C$ at an Antarctic research station. By 10:00 A.M. the temperature had risen 2°C. What was the temperature at 10:00 A.M.?

You can use either of these numerical equations to solve the problem.

$^-5 + 2 = ^-3$ or $2 + ^-5 = ^-3$

So, the temperature at 10:00 A.M. was $^-3°C$.

The example shows that addition of integers is commutative.

Talk About It

▶ Do the Associative Properties of Addition and Multiplication apply to integers? Give an example for each property to support your answer.

▶ Does the Distributive Property apply to integers? Give an example to support your answer.

▶ Does $^-8 + 0 = ^-8$? What property does this illustrate?
Does $^-24 \cdot 1 = ^-24$? What property does this illustrate?

An additional property applies to integers. When you add a number and its opposite, the sum is zero. This is called the **Additive Inverse Property.**

● Give two examples that show the Additive Inverse Property.

Talk About It

▶ How can the Associative Property be used to compute $(9 + ^-3) + ^-4$ using mental math?

▶ How can the Distributive Property be used to compute $(12 \cdot ^-6) + (12 \cdot 10)$ using mental math?

▶ Which properties can you use to compute $(^-9 + 12) + (8 + ^-11)$ using mental math?

Check for Understanding

Complete.

1. $^-8 + 6 = 6 + $ ■
2. $5 + $ ■ $ = 0$
3. $^-7 \cdot 1 = $ ■
4. $4 \cdot (3 \cdot {}^-6) = (4 \cdot $ ■ $) \cdot {}^-6$
5. $^-5 \cdot 3 = $ ■ $ \cdot {}^-5$
6. $9 \cdot ($ ■ $ + {}^-5) = (9 \cdot 2) + (9 \cdot {}^-5)$
7. ■ $ + 0 = {}^-13$

Practice

Name the property shown.

8. $7 + {}^-11 = {}^-11 + 7$
9. $^-12 + 0 = {}^-12$
10. $^-5 \cdot 1 = {}^-5$
11. $^-8 + 8 = 0$
12. $9 \cdot (6 \cdot {}^-5) = (9 \cdot 6) \cdot {}^-5$
13. $13 \cdot ({}^-18 + 8) = (13 \cdot {}^-18) + (13 \cdot 8)$

Use the properties to find each answer. Use mental math where possible.

14. $({}^-8 + 7) + {}^-2$
15. $5 \cdot ({}^-18 \cdot 2)$
16. $^-20 + 18 + 0$
17. $12 \cdot (20 + 3)$
18. $^-8 + 0 + {}^-12 + 9$
19. $^-16 + 25 + 16 + 10$
20. $(25 \cdot {}^-7) \cdot 4$
21. $75 + 365 + {}^-75$
22. $22 + 19 + {}^-19 + {}^-20$
23. $({}^-7 \cdot 14) + ({}^-7 \cdot 6)$
24. $(19 \cdot 13) + (19 \cdot {}^-13)$
25. $({}^-17 + 4) + (6 + {}^-3) + 12$
26. $(35 + {}^-75) + ({}^-25 + 65) + 100$

Mixed Applications

27. A research submarine was 18 m below ($^-18$ m) the ocean surface. It ascended 3 m, descended 12 m, and then ascended 17 m. What was the submarine's new position?

28. In 1990 a marine biologist earned a salary of $35,000. In 1991 the biologist's salary was $36,750. By what percent did the salary increase from 1990 to 1991?

29. Using his calculator, Tim got the answer 40 for $^-6 + 12 + {}^-8 + 14$. Is the answer correct? If not, what mistake do you think Tim made?

30. **Logical Reasoning**   What is the sum of these 99 integers?

$$1 + {}^-1 + 2 + {}^-2 + \ldots + 50$$

Explain why $5 - 5 = 0$ and $5 + {}^-5 = 0$ are equivalent equations.

WRAP UP...

INTEGERS AS EXPONENTS

Astronomers have discovered micrometeorites in space that are less than 0.0001 inch in diameter.

Numbers like 0.0001 can be written using negative exponents. You can use what you know about positive powers of 10 to see how numbers can be represented by negative exponents.

Since $10 = 10^1$, then $0.1 = \frac{1}{10} = \frac{1}{10^1}$, or 10^{-1}.

Since $100 = 10^2$, then $0.01 = \frac{1}{100} = \frac{1}{10^2}$, or 10^{-2}.

Since $1,000 = 10^3$, then $0.001 = \frac{1}{1,000} = \frac{1}{10^3}$, or 10^{-3}.

● How can you write 0.0001 using a negative exponent?

To find the value of an expression having a negative exponent, first write the expression as a fraction with 1 as the numerator.

Examples

A. $3^{-2} = \frac{1}{3^2} = \frac{1}{9}$ **B.** $5^{-3} = \frac{1}{5^3} = \frac{1}{125}$ **C.** $4^{-1} = \frac{1}{4^1} = \frac{1}{4}$

$\quad\quad\quad = 0.\overline{1}$ $= 0.008$ $= 0.25$

Talk About It

▶ Is the value of an expression having a negative exponent greater than 1 or less than 1?

▶ Explain why the value of 2^{-2} is $\frac{1}{4}$ and not $^-4$.

Check for Understanding

Write as an expression having a negative exponent.

1. $\frac{1}{3^2}$ **2.** $\frac{1}{4^3}$ **3.** $\frac{1}{10^5}$ **4.** $\frac{1}{8^5}$ **5.** $\frac{1}{6^{10}}$

Write as a fraction.

6. 10^{-4} **7.** 7^{-2} **8.** 3^{-1} **9.** 4^{-3} **10.** 2^{-5}

Practice

Write as an expression having a negative exponent.

11. $\frac{1}{10^1}$ **12.** $\frac{1}{10^6}$ **13.** $\frac{1}{4^2}$ **14.** $\frac{1}{3^3}$

15. $\frac{1}{1,000}$ **16.** $\frac{1}{2 \cdot 2 \cdot 2}$ **17.** $\frac{1}{5 \cdot 5}$ **18.** $\frac{1}{7 \cdot 7 \cdot 7 \cdot 7}$

19. $\frac{1}{16}$ **20.** $\frac{1}{81}$ **21.** $\frac{1}{100,000}$ **22.** $\frac{1}{49}$

Write as a fraction.

23. 10^{-2} **24.** 4^{-3} **25.** 10^{-3} **26.** 2^{-2} **27.** 7^{-4}

28. 6^{-3} **29.** 9^{-2} **30.** $(^-8)^{-1}$ **31.** $(^-2)^{-2}$ **32.** $(^-3)^{-4}$

Write as a decimal.

33. 2^{-1} **34.** 10^{-5} **35.** 6^{-1} **36.** 5^{-2}

37. 5^{-3} **38.** $(^-10)^{-3}$ **39.** $(^-10)^{-2}$ **40.** $(^-2)^{-4}$

Mixed Applications

Tell whether you would use an expression with a *positive exponent* or an expression with a *negative exponent* for Exercises 41–43.

41. The diameter of a hydrogen atom is 0.0000000106 cm.

42. The weight of the earth is 6,600,000,000,000,000,000,000 T.

43. The diameter of one influenza virus is about 0.000001 m.

44. Meteorites add about 2,000,000 lb to the earth's weight each day. How much weight do meteorites add to the earth in one year?

MATH CONNECTION

Scientific calculators have a y^x or an x^y key that can be used to evaluate powers.

Example   Evaluate 4^{-3}.   4 $\boxed{y^x}$ 3 $\boxed{+/-}$ $\boxed{=}$ $\boxed{ 0.015625 }$

Use a scientific calculator to evaluate each power.

45. 2^{-5} **46.** 3^7 **47.** 5^{-6} **48.** 13^{-3} **49.** 7^8

Which is greater, 2^{-3} or 2^3? Explain.   **WRAP UP...**

EXPLORING

Products and Quotients of Powers

You know how to evaluate powers such as 2^3 and 3^{-2}. In this lesson you will explore the products and quotients of powers.

WORK TOGETHER

Building Understanding

You know that $2^3 = 2 \cdot 2 \cdot 2$ and that $2^4 = 2 \cdot 2 \cdot 2 \cdot 2$. To find the product of the powers, you can write

$$2^3 \cdot 2^4 = 2 \cdot 2 \cdot 2 \cdot (2 \cdot 2 \cdot 2 \cdot 2).$$

Talk About It

▶ How many twos are used as factors in the product?

▶ What is the product in exponent form?

▶ How is the exponent of the product related to the exponents of 2^3 and 2^4?

▶ Follow the same procedure to find $3^2 \cdot 3^5$. What rule can you use for finding the exponent of the product?

You can use a similar procedure to find the quotient of two powers.

You can write $4^5 \div 4^2$ as $\dfrac{4^5}{4^2}$, or $\dfrac{4 \cdot 4 \cdot 4 \cdot 4 \cdot 4}{4 \cdot 4}$

Talk About It

▶ Write the fraction in simplest form by dividing by the common factors. What power of 4 remains?

$$\dfrac{\overset{1}{\cancel{4}} \cdot \overset{1}{\cancel{4}} \cdot 4 \cdot 4 \cdot 4}{\underset{1}{\cancel{4}} \cdot \underset{1}{\cancel{4}}}$$

▶ How is the exponent of the quotient related to the exponents of 4^5 and 4^2?

▶ Follow the same procedure to find $5^6 \div 5^2$. What rule can you use for finding the exponent of the quotient?

▶ Why will your rule not work for $3^6 \div 2^4$?

Making the Connection

You have discovered that you can find the product of two powers with the same base by adding the exponents, and the quotient of two powers with the same base by subtracting the exponents.

Consider these examples.

A. $5^4 \cdot 5^2 = 5^{4+2}$
$= 5^6$

B. $2^{-3} \cdot 2^7 = 2^{-3+7}$
$= 2^4$

C. $7^6 \div 7^4 = 7^{6-4}$
$= 7^2$

D. $10^{-5} \div 10^{-3} = 10^{-5--3}$
$= 10^{-2}$

Talk About It

▶ If you rewrite the division problem in Example **C** as a multiplication problem, can the divisor be written as an expression having a negative exponent? Explain.

▶ Look at Example **D**. Change the divisor and the dividend to equivalent decimals. Then use a calculator to find the quotient. Is the quotient equivalent to 10^{-2}? Why or why not?

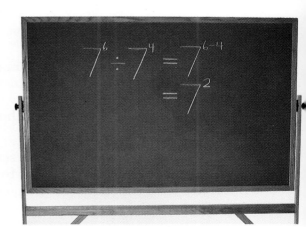

Checking Understanding

Write the addition or subtraction expression that will give you the exponent of the answer.

1. $2^4 \cdot 2^1$ **2.** $8^3 \cdot 8^8$ **3.** $4^4 \cdot 4^{-2}$ **4.** $5^{-3} \div 5^{-2}$

5. $10^4 \div 10^2$ **6.** $10^3 \cdot 10^{-8}$ **7.** $4^5 \div 4^2$ **8.** $5^{-3} \div 5^{-3}$

Write the product as one power.

9. $2^3 \cdot 2^5$ **10.** $4^3 \cdot 4^1$ **11.** $9^4 \cdot 9^{12}$ **12.** $13^{-7} \cdot 13^{-5}$

13. $10^5 \cdot 10^4$ **14.** $3^{-2} \cdot 3^{-4}$ **15.** $12^{-4} \cdot 12^9$ **16.** $4^3 \cdot 4^9$

17. $(^-1)^3 \cdot (^-1)^5$ **18.** $(^-3)^6 \cdot (^-3)^{-2}$ **19.** $(2.4)^2 \cdot (2.4)^{-8}$

Write the quotient as one power.

20. $3^4 \div 3^2$ **21.** $2^5 \div 2^1$ **22.** $5^6 \div 5^3$ **23.** $12^8 \div 12^2$

24. $4^6 \div 4^8$ **25.** $10^2 \div 10^{-1}$ **26.** $9^{-6} \div 9^3$ **27.** $7^3 \div 7^7$

28. $(^-1)^3 \div (^-1)^5$ **29.** $(^-6)^0 \div (^-6)^4$ **30.** $(3.6)^{-3} \div (3.6)^{-7}$

WARM
U P . . .

Explain the steps you would follow
to evaluate 4.5×10^3.

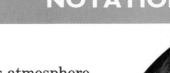

SCIENTIFIC NOTATION

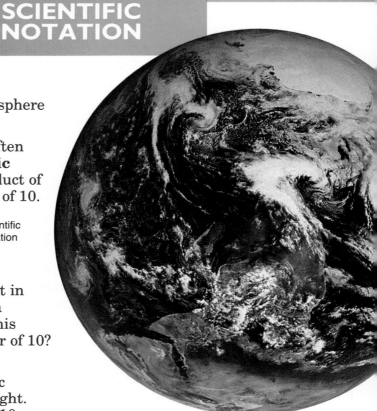

The estimated weight of the earth's atmosphere
is about 5,700,000,000,000,000 tons.

Very large and very small numbers are often
expressed in scientific notation. **Scientific
notation** expresses a number as the product of
a number between 1 and 10, and a power of 10.

$$5{,}700{,}000{,}000{,}000{,}000 = 5.7 \times 10^{15} \leftarrow \text{scientific notation}$$

number between ——
1 and 10

power
of ten

● How many places was the decimal point in
5,700,000,000,000,000 moved to write a
number between 1 and 10? How does this
compare with the exponent of the power of 10?

To write a number less than 1 in scientific
notation, move the decimal point to the right.
Use a negative exponent for the power of 10.

$$0.00043 = 4.3 \times 10^{-4}$$

More Examples   Write in scientific notation.

A. $18{,}144{,}000 = 1.8144 \times 10^{7}$ **B.** $0.000045 = 4.5 \times 10^{-5}$

To change a number from scientific notation to standard form, multiply.

Examples   **A.** $7.528 \times 10^{5} = 7.528 \times 100{,}000 = 752{,}800$

B. $3.215 \times 10^{-4} = 3.215 \times 0.0001 = 0.0003215$

Talk About It

▶ When a number you are writing in scientific notation is greater
than 1, will the exponent of the power of 10 be positive or
negative?

▶ When a number you are writing in scientific notation is less than
1, will the exponent of the power of 10 be positive or negative?

▶ What shortcut can you use to multiply by a power of 10 when
changing from scientific notation to standard form?

Check for Understanding

Complete.

1. $4{,}600 = 4.6 \times 10^{\blacksquare}$
2. $87{,}000{,}000 = \blacksquare \times 10^{7}$
3. $0.0031 = \blacksquare \times 10^{-3}$
4. $0.00000716 = 7.16 \times \blacksquare$
5. $9 \times 10^{4} = 9 \times \blacksquare$
6. $4.6 \times 10^{-3} = 4.6 \times \blacksquare$

Practice

Write in scientific notation.

7. 164,000
8. 1,240,000
9. 95,000
10. 0.008
11. 0.0016
12. 0.0000074
13. 0.0000052
14. 76,320,000
15. 5,200,000,000

Write in standard form.

16. 6×10^{5}
17. 8.3×10^{4}
18. 9.1×10^{8}
19. 4.1×10^{-5}
20. 8.1×10^{-9}
21. 6.31×10^{-8}
22. 7.03×10^{5}
23. 2.15×10^{6}
24. 7.04×10^{-4}

Mixed Applications

25. At one point in its orbit, the earth is 151,288,000 km from the sun. Express this distance in scientific notation.

26. The diameter of a hydrogen atom is 0.000000000106 m. Write the diameter in scientific notation.

27. **Number Sense** Input $450{,}000 \times 370{,}000$ on a calculator. What does your calculator display as the product? Now write each of the factors in scientific notation and use your calculator to multiply the two factors that are between 1 and 10. What does your calculator display as the product? By what power of 10 can you multiply this product to find $450{,}000 \times 370{,}000$?

MIXED REVIEW

Compute.

1. $12 \cdot {}^-8$
2. $^-16 + 34$
3. $^-22 - 17$
4. $100 - {}^-132$
5. $120 \div {}^-6$
6. $^-52 \cdot {}^-4$
7. $^-25 + {}^-39$
8. $^-23 - {}^-154$
9. $^-81 \cdot {}^-4$
10. $^-136 \div 17$
11. $^-9 \cdot 14 - {}^-6$
12. $23 \cdot {}^-4 \div {}^-2$

How can you tell whether a number written in scientific notation is greater than 1 or less than 1?

PROBLEM *Solving*

Strategy • Write an Equation

Flying a glider along the side of a mountain range, Beth hit a strong downdraft. This caused her to drop from an altitude of 10,000 ft to 7,200 ft in 5 min. What was the average change in altitude per minute?

Writing a word problem in the form of an equation often makes the problem simpler to solve.

▶ **UNDERSTAND**

What are you asked to find?

What facts are given?

▶ **PLAN**

What strategy will you choose?
You can *write an equation* for the problem.
Then you can solve the equation.

▶ **SOLVE**

What equation can you write?
Let c = the average change in altitude per minute.
Then $5c$ = the altitude change in 5 min.

The original altitude plus the change in altitude equals the new altitude.

$$10,000 + 5c = 7,200$$
$$10,000 - 10,000 + 5c = 7,200 - 10,000$$
$$5c = {}^-2,800$$
$$\frac{5c}{5} = \frac{{}^-2800}{5}$$
$$c = {}^-560$$

So, the average change in altitude was ⁻560 ft per minute.

▶ **LOOK BACK**

How can you check your solution?

WHAT IF... . . .Beth's altitude had dropped to 6,800 ft? What would have been the average change in altitude per minute?

238

Apply

Write an equation to solve the problem.

1 Over a 2-min period, Beth changed the altitude of her glider by ⁻934 ft. What was the average change in altitude per minute?

2 The cost of Beth's glider plus the cost of 3 flying lessons was $7,305. The cost of the glider was $7,200. What was the cost of each flying lesson?

3 The low temperature in March was 35°F. This was 45° higher than the low temperature in January. What was the low in January?

4 The temperature in Syracuse, New York, is ⁻11°F. It is 38° warmer in Tuscaloosa, Alabama. What is the temperature in Tuscaloosa, Alabama?

Mixed Applications → **STRATEGIES**

- Write an Equation • Use Estimation
- Draw a Picture • Guess and Check

Choose a strategy and solve.

5 After practicing turns, Beth practiced climbs and descents. Starting at an altitude of 4,000 ft, she climbed 625 ft, descended 450 ft, climbed 275 ft, and descended 95 ft. At what altitude was she after her last descent?

6 In planning her landing, Beth decided to descend at a rate of 200 ft per minute. At the start of her descent, she was at an altitude of 2,500 ft. If Beth started her descent at 11:00 A.M., at what time did she land?

7 An airplane used 825 gal of fuel on two flights. The number of gallons used on the first flight was twice the number used on the second flight. How many gallons were used on the second flight?

8 The flight school lowered the regular price for a flying lesson by 9%. The regular price of a lesson was $48. Estimate how much the regular price of a lesson was lowered.

9 Beth wants to hang a photo of her glider on a wall that is 48 in. wide. The photo is 18 in. wide. If she centers the photo on the wall, how much wall space will be on each side of the photo?

10 A glider's forward airspeed is 45 mph. How far can the glider travel in 25 min?

CHAPTER REVIEW

Vocabulary Check

Choose a word or words from the box to complete each sentence.

| negative |
| opposite |
| positive |
| scientific notation |

1. On a number line, the numbers to the left of the zero are the __?__ integers. *(page 216)*

2. The absolute value of a number is always __?__. *(page 216)*

3. To subtract an integer, add the __?__ of the integer. *(page 220)*

4. The number 86,500 is written as 8.65×10^4 in __?__. *(page 236)*

5. The product of two integers with unlike signs is a __?__ integer. *(page 222)*

6. The quotient of two negative integers is a __?__ integer. *(page 226)*

Concept Check

Write an integer for each description. *(page 216)*

7. a loss of 5 yd
8. a deposit of $98
9. 14° below zero

Write the absolute value. *(page 216)*

10. $|4|$
11. $|^-16|$
12. $|0|$
13. $|^-37|$

Compare. Write $<$, $>$, or $=$. *(page 216)*

14. $^-7 \bullet ^-13$
15. $^-9 \bullet 1$
16. $15 \bullet ^-6$
17. $|12| \bullet |^-12|$

Tell whether the answer will be *positive* or *negative*. *(pages 218, 220, 222, 226)*

18. $7 + ^-2$
19. $^-7 + ^-4$
20. $^-18 + 13$
21. $8 + 9$

22. $7 - 9$
23. $15 - ^-3$
24. $^-4 - 6$
25. $^-6 - ^-5$

26. $4 \cdot ^-6$
27. $^-8 \cdot ^-5$
28. $12 \div ^-3$
29. $^-45 \div ^-5$

Complete. *(page 230)*

30. $^-12 + 7 = 7 + \blacksquare$
31. $8 + \blacksquare = 0$
32. $^-14 \times 1 = \blacksquare$

Tell whether the value of the expression is *greater than 1* or *less than 1*. *(pages 232, 234)*

33. 3^{-2}
34. 5^3
35. 8^{-6}
36. $\frac{1}{2^4}$

37. 1.2×10^3
38. 4.5×10^{-3}
39. 2.56×10^{-5}
40. 4.8×10^7

Skill Check

Find the sum or difference. *(pages 218, 220)*

41. $13 + 20$ **42.** $^-5 + {}^-8$ **43.** $8 + {}^-8$ **44.** $^-3 + 21 + 17$

45. $^-7 - {}^-3$ **46.** $^-5 - 16$ **47.** $63 - 46$ **48.** $55 - {}^-30$

Find the product or quotient. *(pages 222, 226)*

49. $^-8 \cdot {}^-11$ **50.** $9 \cdot {}^-1$ **51.** $^-12 \cdot 18$ **52.** $^-12 \cdot {}^-9$

53. $^-16 \div 4$ **54.** $^-153 \div {}^-3$ **55.** $\frac{20}{5}$ **56.** $\frac{^-270}{3}$

Use the properties to find each answer. *(page 230)*

57. $(^-12 + 17) + {}^-8$ **58.** $(34 \cdot 2) \cdot {}^-5$ **59.** $433 + 576 + {}^-433$

Write as an expression having a negative exponent. *(page 232)*

60. 0.00001 **61.** $\frac{1}{36}$ **62.** $\frac{1}{1,000}$ **63.** $\frac{1}{4^6}$

Write the product or quotient as one power. *(page 234)*

64. $12^5 \cdot 12^{-2}$ **65.** $5^{-6} \cdot 5^{-4}$ **66.** $14^2 \div 14^5$ **67.** $7^{-2} \div 7^3$

Write in scientific notation. *(page 236)*

68. 0.0000000000543 **69.** $237,000,000,000$ **70.** 0.00004

Write in standard form. *(page 236)*

71. 6.59×10^{-4} **72.** 9.82×10^7 **73.** 4.37×10^{-8}

Problem-Solving Check

To join the Explorer's Video Club, you must pay a basic membership fee. With the payment of the membership fee, rental of 3 tapes is free. The total cost for membership with 4 rentals is $20.00; with 5 rentals, $22.50; with 6 rentals, $25.00.

Use this information for Exercises 74–77. *(page 224)*

74. Make a table to show the total cost for 4, 5, and 6 rentals.

75. What is the rental cost for each additional tape?

76. What is the cost of the basic membership fee in the video club?

77. Extend the table to show the cost for membership and the rental of 7, 8, and 9 tapes.

78. The number of tapes Susan has is 4 fewer than twice the number of tapes Janice has. If Susan has 8 tapes, how many does Janice have? *(page 238)*

79. John's age is 2 more than 5 times the age of his nephew, Billy. If John is 22 years old, how old is Billy? *(page 238)*

CHAPTER TEST

Compare. Write $<$, $>$, or $=$.

1. $34 \bullet {}^-21$ **2.** ${}^-12 \bullet {}^-22$ **3.** $|8| \bullet |{}^-9|$

Find the sum or difference.

4. $22 + {}^-8$ **5.** ${}^-7 + {}^-9$ **6.** ${}^-16 - {}^-9$ **7.** ${}^-8 - 3$

8. ${}^-5 - 6$ **9.** ${}^-23 + {}^-6$ **10.** ${}^-8 - {}^-17$ **11.** ${}^-11 + 5$

Find the product or quotient.

12. $5 \cdot {}^-7$ **13.** ${}^-3 \cdot {}^-11$ **14.** ${}^-27 \div {}^-9$ **15.** ${}^-40 \div 8$

16. ${}^-4 \cdot 3$ **17.** $18 \div {}^-6$ **18.** $8 \cdot {}^-7$ **19.** ${}^-36 \div {}^-4$

Write as an expression having a negative exponent.

20. $\frac{1}{100}$ **21.** $\frac{1}{4^5}$ **22.** $\frac{1}{49}$

Find the product or quotient.

23. $5^6 \cdot 5^4$ **24.** $6^2 \cdot 6^5$ **25.** $4^{-3} \div 4^1$ **26.** $12^9 \div 12^{-5}$

Write in scientific notation.

27. $340,000,000,000$ **28.** 0.00021 **29.** 0.00000000542

Solve.

30. Julia has a new job that pays $21,000 per year. She was told that she will receive a 5% raise at the end of each year. How much will Julia be earning at the end of 3 years?

31. The low temperature in February was ${}^-10°F$. This was 16° lower than twice the low temperature in January. What was the low in January?

32. Admission to Sea Park costs $26.95 for a 1-day pass, $33.55 for a 1-week pass, and $49.95 for an annual pass. Make a table that shows the costs of a 1-day pass, a 1-week pass, and an annual pass for a family of 4.

33. The world's lowest temperature, ${}^-128.6°F$, was recorded at Vostok Station, Antarctica, in 1983. Antarctica's average high temperature is 160.6° warmer than this. What is Antarctica's average high temperature?

Teamwork P-R-O-J-E-C-T

MAKE A SCALE DRAWING

The science department is organizing a Space and Underwater Exploration Festival. Your class has been asked to make posters for the exhibit area. The posters can be as large as 5 ft by 10 ft but no smaller than 4 ft by 6 ft. Each poster should include pictures, important information, and challenging questions.

Work with your classmates to plan a poster for the festival.

Decide

As a team, discuss topics for posters about space and underwater exploration. Choose one topic for your poster.

Decide on resources for information about your topic.

Discuss the size you want your poster to be.

Do

As a team, collect information on your topic. Decide what information will be used on the poster and what questions will be asked.

Prepare a scale drawing of your poster. Draw sketches of the pictures you will use and the placement of the information and questions.

Share

Compare your team's scale drawing with those of other teams. Tell why you chose your topic. Then ask members of the other teams to answer the questions on your topic.

Talk About It

• Are any integers used in the information for your poster? Are any other types of numbers used?

• What scale did you use for your scale drawing? How did you determine what scale to use?

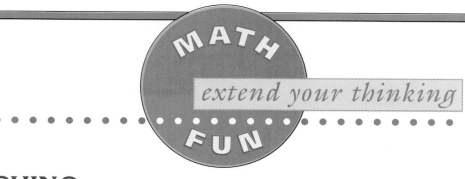

extend your thinking

MATCHING INTEGERS: A Game for Two

Materials: pencil and paper
Object of the game: to use the numbers in the box and any operation or grouping symbols to compute the target integers

Box numbers									
⁻1	⁻3	⁻5	⁻7	⁻9	2	4	6	8	10

The expressions used to compute the target numbers will vary.

Target integers
⁻10, ⁻9, ⁻8, ⁻7, ⁻6, ⁻5, ⁻4, ⁻3, ⁻2, ⁻1, 0, 1, 2, 3,
4, 5, 6, 7, 8, 9, 10

On the first turn, Player 1 uses three box numbers to compute any target integer. Then both Player 1 and Player 2 try to match the target integer by using four box numbers. The first player to match the target wins a point. (As an alternative, Player 1 can start with four box numbers. Then both players can use three box numbers to match the target integer.)

Using three box numbers

$$\frac{^-1 + ^-9}{2} = \frac{^-10}{2} = ^-5$$

Using four box numbers

$$\frac{2 \times 10}{^-7 - ^-3} = \frac{20}{^-4} = ^-5$$

The player takes turns at selecting the target integers, until all 21 integers have been used. The player with more points wins.

Challenge

Logical Reasoning

Alma had half as many sports cards as Rick. Then she lost 6 cards. Now she has only one third as many cards as Rick. How many cards does Rick have?

Number Sense

Each letter represents a different digit. Find the digit each letter represents.

$$AB + AB + AB = BC$$

This problem has three solutions. Try to find all three.

Write the letter of the correct answer.

1. $15 + {}^-4$

   A. $^-19$ **B.** $^-11$

   C. 11   **D.** 19

2. 166 is 83% of which number?

   A. 137.78   **B.** 190

   C. 200   **D.** 210

3. Which polygon has 5 sides?

   A. octagon   **B.** hexagon

   C. pentagon   **D.** triangle

4. $^-8 + {}^-6$

   A. $^-14$ **B.** $^-2$

   C. 2   **D.** 14

5. $\frac{3}{4} \times \frac{8}{9}$

   A. $\frac{1}{3}$ **B.** $\frac{2}{3}$

   C. $\frac{27}{32}$ **D.** not here

6. Which kind of angle is formed by perpendicular lines?

   A. acute   **B.** obtuse

   C. right   **D.** straight

7. Which number is 150% of 60?

   A. 40   **B.** 90

   C. 250   **D.** 900

8. Which is $\frac{2}{5}$ written as a percent?

   A. 40%   **B.** 80%

   C. 100%   **D.** 250%

9. Which number represents the absolute value of $^-24$?

   A. $^-24$ **B.** $\frac{-1}{24}$

   C. $\frac{1}{24}$ **D.** 24

10. Which expression means "8 more than a number, p"?

   A. $8p$ **B.** $p + 8$

   C. $8 - p$ **D.** $\frac{p}{8}$

11. Juan drove 21 mi out of his way on a trip. He drove a total of 624 mi. What would have been the total miles if he had not made the error?

   A. 29.7 mi   **B.** 603 mi

   C. 645 mi   **D.** 13,104 mi

12. Almena wants to buy a new outfit. She has $20 in cash and a $36 blouse she is returning. How much more does she need if the outfit costs $96?

   A. $40   **B.** $56

   C. $60   **D.** $76

CHAPTER

8

REAL NUMBERS

Did you know . . .

. . . that one of the first computers built, ENIAC, was finished in 1945, weighed 30 tons, and was so large that it filled a basement?

Talk About It

ENIAC could multiply two 10-digit numbers in 0.002 second. How can you compare ENIAC's speed to your own speed when multiplying two 10-digit numbers?

RATIONAL NUMBERS

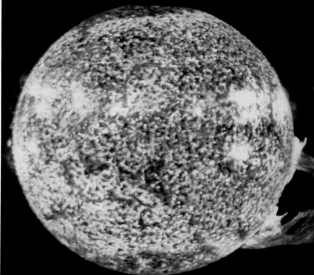

As scientists have studied temperature, they have found a lower limit, called absolute zero, which has a value of ⁻459.67°F. There does not seem to be an upper limit to temperature, however. Scientists believe that the center of the sun may have a temperature of 27,000,000°F.

The numbers ⁻459.67 and 27,000,000 are rational numbers. A **rational number** is any number that can be written in the form $\frac{a}{b}$, where a and b are integers and b is not equal to zero.

$$^-459.67 = \frac{^-45967}{100} \qquad 27,000,000 = \frac{27,000,000}{1}$$

Rational numbers can be located on a number line. Recall that the number to the right on a number line is greater than the number to the left.

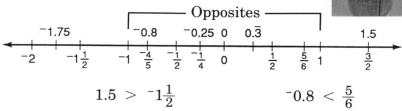

$$1.5 > {^-1\tfrac{1}{2}} \qquad\qquad {^-0.8} < \tfrac{5}{6}$$

Between any two rational numbers is at least one other rational number. This is called the **Property of Density.**

Example Find a rational number between 0.4 and $\frac{1}{2}$.

$0.4 = \frac{4}{10} \qquad \frac{1}{2} = \frac{5}{10}$ Write 0.4 and $\frac{1}{2}$ as fractions with a common denominator.

$\frac{4}{10} = \frac{8}{20} \qquad \frac{5}{10} = \frac{10}{20}$ Write equivalent fractions using a larger common denominator.

$\frac{9}{20}$ is between $\frac{8}{20}$ and $\frac{10}{20}$. So, $\frac{9}{20}$ is between 0.4 and $\frac{1}{2}$.

Talk About It

▶ Explain how you can find a rational number between $\frac{9}{20}$ and $\frac{1}{2}$.

Check for Understanding

Write each rational number in the form $\frac{a}{b}$.

1. 0.4   **2.** $^-1\frac{1}{3}$ **3.** $^-5$ **4.** 3.5   **5.** 0.6

Find a rational number between each pair of numbers.

6. $\frac{1}{3}$ and $\frac{3}{3}$ **7.** $\frac{3}{10}$ and $\frac{4}{10}$ **8.** 3.20 and 3.22   **9.** 0.45 and 0.47

Practice

Write each rational number in the form $\frac{a}{b}$.

10. $^-2$ **11.** $3\frac{1}{5}$ **12.** 0.3   **13.** $^-5\frac{3}{4}$ **14.** 2.5

Compare. Write $<$, $>$, or $=$.

15. $\frac{1}{6}$ ● $^-\frac{1}{6}$ **16.** $^-0.8$ ● 0.8 **17.** $^-\frac{4}{5}$ ● $^-\frac{2}{3}$ **18.** 3 ● $\frac{3}{1}$

19. $^-1.5$ ● $^-\frac{2}{5}$ **20.** $^-\frac{3}{5}$ ● $\frac{1}{5}$ **21.** $8\frac{1}{4}$ ● 8.25 **22.** $^-\frac{5}{4}$ ● $^-1.6$

Write in order from least to greatest.

23. $^-1\frac{1}{2}, 2\frac{1}{2}, \frac{1}{2}$ **24.** $^-\frac{3}{4}, ^-\frac{4}{3}, 1, \frac{3}{4}, 0$ **25.** $^-1.2, 3.5, ^-\frac{4}{5}, \frac{1}{2}, ^-\frac{6}{3}$

Find a rational number between each pair of numbers.

26. 0.6 and 0.7   **27.** $^-2.5$ and $^-2.6$ **28.** 0 and $^-\frac{1}{2}$ **29.** $\frac{2}{5}$ and 0.6

Mixed Applications

30. At 6:00 P.M. the temperature was $^-15°F$. At 9:00 P.M. the temperature was $^-15.3°F$. Was the temperature higher at 6:00 P.M. or at 9:00 P.M.?

31. On a certain day the temperature is between 10.0°F and 10.1°F. Give three possible temperatures that meet this condition.

Write *true* or *false* for each statement. Give an example to explain your answer.

32. Every integer is a rational number.

33. Some rational numbers are negative integers.

34. No whole numbers are rational numbers.

In your own words, explain what is meant by the Property of Density.

WRAP UP...

SQUARES AND SQUARE ROOTS

Sometimes volcanic eruptions occur along cracks in the ocean bottom. If these eruptions recur, mountains build up and, in time, become islands. The island of Surtsey, off the south coast of Iceland, is an example of this. The island began forming in 1963, and after the last eruption in 1967, the island covered more than 1 square mile.

This square represents the area of the island. What is the length, s, of each side of the square?

$A = s^2$
$1 = s \cdot s$
$1 = 1 \cdot 1$
So, $s = 1$ mile.

Think: What number times itself is 1?

s

Recall that when you **square** a number, you multiply the number by itself. The inverse of squaring a number is taking its **square root.** The example shows that 1 is the square root of 1.

● Draw a square with an area of 36 units. What is the length of each side of the square? What is the square root of 36?

Every positive rational number has two square roots, one negative and one positive. The radical symbol, $\sqrt{}$, is used to represent the positive square root. A negative square root is represented by $^-\sqrt{}$.

$\sqrt{36} = 6$ **Read:** The positive square root of 36 is 6.

$^-\sqrt{64} = ^-8$ **Read:** The negative square root of 64 is $^-8$.

More Examples

A. Find $\sqrt{16}$.

Think: $4^2 = 16$

So, $\sqrt{16} = 4$.

B. Find $^-\sqrt{49}$.

Think: $7^2 = 49$

So, $^-\sqrt{49} = ^-7$.

C. Find $\sqrt{0.81}$.

Think: $(0.9)^2 = 0.81$

So, $\sqrt{0.81} = 0.9$.

The numbers 1, 16, 36, 49, and 64 are examples of perfect squares. **Perfect squares** are numbers that have integers as their square roots.

Talk About It

▶ How can you find $^-\sqrt{100}$?

Check for Understanding

Find the length of each side of the square.

1. $A = 16$ m²
2. $A = 625$ m²
3. $A = 49$ cm²
4. $A = 144$ in.²

Write *SR* if the first number is the square root of the second number, write *S* if it is the square, or write *N* if it is neither.

5. 8, 64
6. 15, 125
7. 144, ⁻12
8. 25, 5
9. 8, 16

Practice

Find the square.

10. 4^2
11. 13^2
12. $(^-6)^2$
13. $(^-12)^2$
14. 15^2

15. $(0.5)^2$
16. $\left(\frac{2}{5}\right)^2$
17. $(1.2)^2$
18. $\left(\frac{1}{4}\right)^2$
19. $\left(\frac{3}{7}\right)^2$

Find the two square roots of the number.

20. 81
21. 100
22. 49
23. 64
24. 121

Find the square root.

25. $^-\sqrt{81}$
26. $^-\sqrt{49}$
27. $\sqrt{36}$
28. $\sqrt{121}$
29. $^-\sqrt{144}$

30. $\sqrt{\frac{9}{25}}$
31. $\sqrt{0.64}$
32. $\sqrt{\frac{1}{36}}$
33. $\sqrt{0.16}$
34. $^-\sqrt{\frac{25}{49}}$

35. $^-\sqrt{0.01}$
36. $\sqrt{\frac{4}{9}}$
37. $\sqrt{0.04}$
38. $^-\sqrt{\frac{1}{100}}$
39. $\sqrt{\frac{64}{81}}$

Mixed Applications

40. The area of a square is 225 square meters. What is the length of each side of the square?

41. The area of a square garden is 400 square feet. How much fencing is needed to enclose the garden?

42. The formula $d = 4.9t^2$ gives the approximate distance in meters traveled in t seconds by an object falling from rest. How long will an object take to fall 122.5 meters from rest?

43. Number Sense Gary said that he was thinking of a number between 1 and 11 that when squared and added to 19 equals the square of the next number between it and 11. What was Gary's number?

Explain why $(^-4)^2$ equals 16 and not ⁻16.

WRAP UP...

More Practice, Lesson 8.2, page H58

WARM UP...

Is $\sqrt{35}$ greater than or less than 5? greater than or less than 6?

An integrated circuit is a small device that controls electric signals in electronic equipment such as computers and calculators. The square integrated circuit shown has an area of 20 square millimeters (20 mm²). About what length is each side?

$s^2 = 20$
$s = \sqrt{20}$ **Think:** Since 20 is not a perfect square, $\sqrt{20}$ is not an integer.

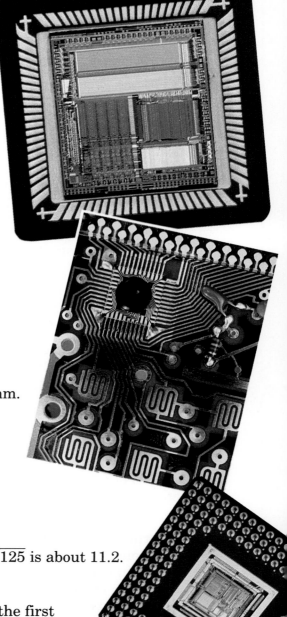

You can estimate $\sqrt{20}$ by using the perfect squares that are close to 20.

Step 1	**Step 2**
Locate 20 between two perfect squares.	Locate $\sqrt{20}$ between two integers.
$16 < 20 < 25$	$\sqrt{16} < \sqrt{20} < \sqrt{25}$
$4^2 < 20 < 5^2$	$4 < \sqrt{20} < 5$
Step 3	**Step 4**
Try squaring numbers between 4 and 5.	Choose the number whose square is closer to 20.
$(4.5)^2 = 20.25$	$\sqrt{20}$ is about 4.5.
$(4.4)^2 = 19.36$	

So, the length of each side of the circuit is about 4.5 mm.

Another Example   Estimate $\sqrt{125}$.

$121 < 125 < 144$
$11 < \sqrt{125} < 12$ **Think:** Is $\sqrt{125}$ closer to 11 or to 12?

$(11.1)^2 = 123.21$
$(11.2)^2 = 125.44$ 11.2 ⊗ 11.2 ⊜ [125.44]
$(11.3)^2 = 127.69$

Since 125.44 is closer to 125 than 123.21 or 127.69, $\sqrt{125}$ is about 11.2.

Talk About It

▶ Explain why 4.4 and 4.5 were chosen as guesses in the first example instead of 4.1 or 4.9.

▶ Explain why 11.1, 11.2, and 11.3 were chosen as guesses in the second example instead of 11.7, 11.8, and 11.9.

You can use the Table of Squares and Square Roots on page H103 to find the square root of a perfect square or the approximate square root of a number that is not a perfect square.

Example Use the table on page H103 to find $\sqrt{55}$. Round the answer to the nearest tenth.

Find 55 in the Number column in the table. Look directly right and read the square root of 55 in the Square Root column.

Number	Square	Square Root
53	2,809	7.280
54	2,916	7.348
55	3,025	7.416

So, $\sqrt{55}$ is about 7.416. Rounded to the nearest tenth, it is 7.4.

Another Method

One of the fastest ways to find the square root of a number is to use a calculator with a $\boxed{\sqrt{}}$ key.

The area of a square is 47 square meters (47 m²). What is the length of each side of the square to the nearest hundredth of a meter?

Use a calculator.   47 $\boxed{\sqrt{}}$ ☐ 6.8556546

Round to the nearest hundredth. $6.8556546 \approx 6.86$

So, the length of each side of the square is approximately 6.86 m.

More Examples

A. $\sqrt{12}$
12 $\boxed{\sqrt{}}$ ☐ 3.4641016
$\sqrt{12} \approx 3.5$

B. $\sqrt{345}$
345 $\boxed{\sqrt{}}$ ☐ 18.574175
$\sqrt{345} \approx 18.6$

C. $^-\sqrt{2,124}$
2124 $\boxed{\sqrt{}}$ ☐ 46.086874
$^-\sqrt{2,124} \approx {}^-46.1$

Talk About It

▶ Explain how you can use a calculator to check whether 3.5 is a close approximation of $\sqrt{12}$.

▶ Explain what happens when you use this key sequence to find $^-\sqrt{15}$.

15 $\boxed{+/-}$ $\boxed{\sqrt{}}$

▶ Do you use the $\boxed{+/-}$ key on a calculator to show a negative square root before or after the calculation?

▶ How can you use a calculator without a $\boxed{\sqrt{}}$ key to find $\sqrt{74}$?

253

You can also use a calculator to find the approximate
square roots of decimals and fractions.

Examples

A. Find $\sqrt{12.5}$.

12.5 $\boxed{\sqrt{}}$ $\boxed{3.5355339}$

$\sqrt{12.5} \approx 3.5$

B. Find $\sqrt{\dfrac{3}{4}}$.

3 $\boxed{\div}$ 4 $\boxed{=}$ $\boxed{\sqrt{}}$ $\boxed{0.8660254}$

$\sqrt{\dfrac{3}{4}} \approx 0.9$

● Explain why the first step in Example **B** is to divide 3 by 4.

Check for Understanding

Determine the perfect squares x and y between which each number lies.

1. $x < 12 < y$ **2.** $x < 47 < y$ **3.** $x < 101 < y$

4. $x < 14 < y$ **5.** $x < 56 < y$ **6.** $x < 150 < y$

Estimate the square root to the nearest tenth.

7. $\sqrt{75}$ **8.** $\sqrt{108}$ **9.** $\sqrt{227}$ **10.** $^-\sqrt{130}$ **11.** $\sqrt{198}$

Find the square root to the nearest hundredth. Use the Table of Squares
and Square Roots on page H103 or a calculator.

12. $\sqrt{24}$ **13.** $\sqrt{48}$ **14.** $\sqrt{76}$ **15.** $\sqrt{72}$ **16.** $^-\sqrt{15}$

17. $\sqrt{21}$ **18.** $^-\sqrt{13}$ **19.** $\sqrt{2.49}$ **20.** $\sqrt{\dfrac{1}{2}}$ **21.** $^-\sqrt{0.8}$

Practice

Estimate the square root to the nearest tenth.

22. $\sqrt{57}$ **23.** $\sqrt{78}$ **24.** $\sqrt{131}$ **25.** $^-\sqrt{66}$ **26.** $\sqrt{29}$

27. $^-\sqrt{56}$ **28.** $\sqrt{405}$ **29.** $\sqrt{184}$ **30.** $\sqrt{980}$ **31.** $\sqrt{145}$

Find the square root to the nearest hundredth. Use the Table of Squares
and Square Roots on page H103 or a calculator.

32. $\sqrt{2}$ **33.** $\sqrt{19}$ **34.** $^-\sqrt{43}$ **35.** $\sqrt{94}$ **36.** $^-\sqrt{102}$

37. $\sqrt{117}$ **38.** $\sqrt{52}$ **39.** $\sqrt{88}$ **40.** $^-\sqrt{111}$ **41.** $\sqrt{107}$

42. $\sqrt{0.08}$ **43.** $\sqrt{0.15}$ **44.** $^-\sqrt{\dfrac{4}{5}}$ **45.** $\sqrt{\dfrac{2}{3}}$ **46.** $\sqrt{2.44}$

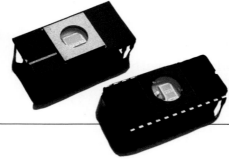
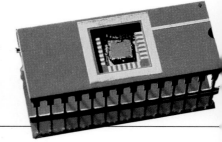

Find the square root to the nearest tenth when $a = 5$, and $b = 3$.

47. $\sqrt{a + b}$ **48.** $\sqrt{ab}$ **49.** $\sqrt{a^2}$ **50.** $\sqrt{b^2}$ **51.** $\sqrt{a^2 - b}$

Approximations for $\sqrt{2}$, $\sqrt{3}$, and $\sqrt{5}$ are given.

$$\sqrt{2} \approx 1.414 \qquad \sqrt{3} \approx 1.732 \qquad \sqrt{5} \approx 2.236$$

Using these approximations, you can find the square root of many numbers without using a calculator or the Table of Squares and Square Roots. First, find a perfect square factor of the number.

Example $\sqrt{200}$ ⟶ $200 = 100 \cdot 2$ So, $\sqrt{200} = \sqrt{100} \cdot \sqrt{2}$
$$= 10\sqrt{2} \approx 10\,(1.414) \approx 14.14$$

Find the square root to the nearest hundredth.

52. $\sqrt{8}$ **53.** $\sqrt{12}$ **54.** $\sqrt{20}$ **55.** $\sqrt{27}$ **56.** $\sqrt{80}$

Mixed Applications

The graph shows the positive square roots of the numbers from 1 to 50. Use the graph for Exercises 57–59.

57. What is the square root of 25?

58. What is the approximate square root of 40?

59. Copy and extend the graph to show the square roots of the numbers from 1 to 100.

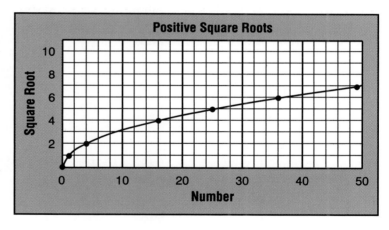

60. Mental Math   Of the first 50 whole numbers, 7 are perfect squares. What percent are perfect squares?

SCIENCE CONNECTION

Many formulas involve finding the square root. For example, the formula $s = \sqrt{12d}$ can be used to estimate the speed, s, in miles per hour that a car was traveling when it skidded d feet on a wet concrete road after the brakes were applied.

Use the formula $s = \sqrt{12d}$ to find the speed for each given distance. Round the answer to the nearest tenth.

61. 10 ft   **62.** 50 ft   **63.** 100 ft   **64.** 200 ft

How can you approximate the square root of a number that is not a perfect square?

WRAP UP...

More Practice, Lesson 8.3, page H58

Recall that rational numbers can be written in the form $\frac{a}{b}$, and as terminating or repeating decimals.

$$4\frac{1}{2} = \frac{9}{2} = 4.5 \qquad \frac{1}{3} = 0.33333 = 0.\overline{3} \qquad \sqrt{4} = 2 = \frac{2}{1}$$

Are there some numbers that are not rational numbers?

WORK TOGETHER

Building Understanding

Use a calculator with a $\boxed{\sqrt{}}$ key to find square roots.

● What is $\sqrt{1.44}$?

Talk About It

▶ How can you check your result? Is the square root you found the exact square root of 1.44? Why or why not?

▶ Is the square root of 1.44 a repeating decimal or a terminating decimal?

▶ Is $\sqrt{1.44}$ a rational number? Explain.

● What is $\sqrt{2}$? Write the result on a sheet of paper.

● Check your result by multiplying it by itself. Is the product 2? If not, what is it?

The number that your calculator showed for $\sqrt{2}$ is an approximation. $\sqrt{2}$ is not a rational number because it is not a terminating decimal and it is not a repeating decimal.

● Repeat the activity with $\sqrt{5}$, $\sqrt{12}$, and $\sqrt{20}$. Tell whether any of the numbers are rational numbers.

Making the Connection

You have discovered that the numbers $\sqrt{2}$, $\sqrt{5}$, $\sqrt{12}$, and $\sqrt{20}$ are not rational numbers. They can be written as decimals that are nonterminating and nonrepeating.

$$\sqrt{2} = 1.4142135\ldots \qquad \sqrt{5} = 2.2360679\ldots$$

$$\sqrt{12} = 3.4641016\ldots \qquad \sqrt{20} = 4.4721359\ldots$$

Numbers that are not rational numbers are called **irrational numbers.** The set of **real numbers** contains all the rational numbers and all the irrational numbers.

The table shows numbers classified as real numbers, rational numbers, whole numbers, integers, and irrational numbers. Notice that rational numbers can have more than one name.

	Real Number	Rational Number	Whole Number	Integer	Irrational Number
8	X	X	X	X	
12.5	X	X			
⁻15	X	X		X	
$\sqrt{5}$	X				X
2.8284271 . . .	X				X
1.3333 . . .	X	X			

Make a table like the one shown. Then classify the number by placing an X in each appropriate column.

1. 18
2. ⁻6.2
3. $\frac{3}{4}$
4. 182
5. 8.1240384 . . .

6. $\sqrt{25}$
7. ⁻$\sqrt{3}$
8. $(1.2)^2$
9. $2\frac{1}{2}$
10. 2.6457513 . . .

11. Order the numbers in Exercises 1–10 from least to greatest.

Checking Understanding

Find the square root. Then classify it as a *rational number,* a *whole number,* an *integer,* or an *irrational number.*

12. $\sqrt{36}$
13. $\sqrt{14}$
14. $\sqrt{0.90}$
15. $\sqrt{0.09}$
16. $\sqrt{81}$

17. $\sqrt{1}$
18. $\sqrt{5.17}$
19. ⁻$\sqrt{144}$
20. $\sqrt{\frac{1}{9}}$
21. ⁻$\sqrt{\frac{25}{49}}$

Explain how you can find
this difference: $12 - {}^-8$.

ADDING AND SUBTRACTING

Satellite information confirms that the water temperature varies greatly in and around the Gulf Stream. Suppose the temperature is 64.6°F at the center of the Gulf Stream and changes by ⁻9.8°F at the western edge. What is the temperature at the western edge?

Find the sum. $64.6 + {}^-9.8$

To add rational numbers, follow the rules for adding integers.

Think: Since $|64.6| > |{}^-9.8|$, the sum will be positive.

$64.6 + {}^-9.8 = 54.8$ Subtract the absolute values.

So, the temperature at the western edge is 54.8°F.

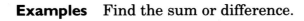

To subtract a rational number, add its opposite.

Examples Find the sum or difference.

A. $-2\frac{1}{2} - 6\frac{3}{4} = {}^-2\frac{2}{4} + {}^-6\frac{3}{4}$
$= {}^-8\frac{5}{4} = {}^-9\frac{1}{4}$

B. $-10.7 - {}^-12.4 = {}^-10.7 + 12.4$
$= 1.7$

Talk About It

▶ Is $-4.5 + {}^-3.45$ positive or negative? Explain.

▶ Explain how to find $-3\frac{2}{3} - 4.5$.

▶ Explain how you would estimate the difference in Example **A.**

Check for Understanding

Tell whether the sum or difference will be *positive* or *negative*.
Then find the sum or difference.

1. $12.7 - {}^-9.2$ **2.** $9.4 - 10.3$ **3.** $-5.9 + {}^-2.8$ **4.** $-0.7 + 7$

5. $\frac{-1}{6} + \frac{-4}{6}$ **6.** $\frac{-3}{5} - \frac{4}{5}$ **7.** $\frac{-1}{4} - \frac{-1}{3}$ **8.** $-2 + \frac{7}{8}$

Practice

Find the sum or difference.

9. $\frac{1}{4} + {}^-\frac{3}{4}$

10. ${}^-\frac{4}{7} + \frac{4}{7}$

11. $2 + {}^-\frac{2}{11}$

12. $\frac{4}{5} + {}^-\frac{5}{10}$

13. ${}^-\frac{7}{9} + {}^-\frac{8}{18}$

14. ${}^-3 + {}^-\frac{3}{16}$

15. $0.2 + {}^-0.9$

16. ${}^-1.9 + {}^-5.2$

17. ${}^-4.13 + {}^-7.25$

18. ${}^-6.35 + {}^-1.07$

19. ${}^-12.31 + {}^-4.98$

20. ${}^-2.21 + {}^-0.79$

21. $\frac{2}{3} - {}^-\frac{3}{4}$

22. ${}^-\frac{4}{5} - {}^-\frac{1}{2}$

23. ${}^-\frac{7}{11} - {}^-\frac{3}{22}$

24. ${}^-\frac{7}{12} - {}^-\frac{2}{6}$

25. ${}^-\frac{6}{15} - {}^-\frac{7}{30}$

26. ${}^-2\frac{2}{3} - {}^-5\frac{1}{6}$

27. $2.4 - {}^-0.6$

28. ${}^-4.7 - {}^-1.9$

29. ${}^-6.89 - {}^-0.97$

30. ${}^-7.32 - {}^-9.10$

31. ${}^-0.94 - {}^-2.7$

32. ${}^-0.043 - {}^-9.6$

33. ${}^-6.39 - {}^-4.8$

34. $0.057 + {}^-6.5$

35. ${}^-4.2 + 8.3 + {}^-9.07$

36. ${}^-6.4 + {}^-3.1 + 5.2$

37. ${}^-\frac{2}{3} + \frac{1}{3} + {}^-\frac{5}{6}$

38. ${}^-5.8 - {}^-6.1 + 3.2$

Mixed Applications

39. Suppose that the western edge of the Gulf Stream, with a temperature of 12°C, collided with the southern edge of the cold Labrador Current. After the collision of these two currents, there was a ⁻14.6°C change in temperature at the western edge of the Gulf Stream. What was the new temperature?

40. Find Data Use an encyclopedia or an almanac to find information on the oceans. Include the area and average depth of each ocean. List the oceans in order from the least area to the greatest area. Write the average depths as negative numbers.

MIXED REVIEW

Find the product or quotient.

1. $\frac{1}{2} \times \frac{5}{6}$

2. $1\frac{1}{4} \times 3\frac{2}{3}$

3. ${}^-8 \cdot {}^-15$

4. ${}^-22 \cdot 16$

5. $\frac{7}{8} \div \frac{1}{4}$

6. $5\frac{1}{2} \div 2\frac{2}{5}$

7. $192 \div {}^-8$

8. ${}^-378 \div {}^-21$

9. $7\frac{4}{5} \times 2\frac{1}{3}$

10. $6\frac{1}{9} \div 1\frac{2}{3}$

11. ${}^-49 \times {}^-23$

12. ${}^-837 \div 31$

When a negative rational number is subtracted from a positive rational number, is the difference positive or negative? Explain.

WRAP UP...

PROBLEM Solving

Strategy • Make a Table

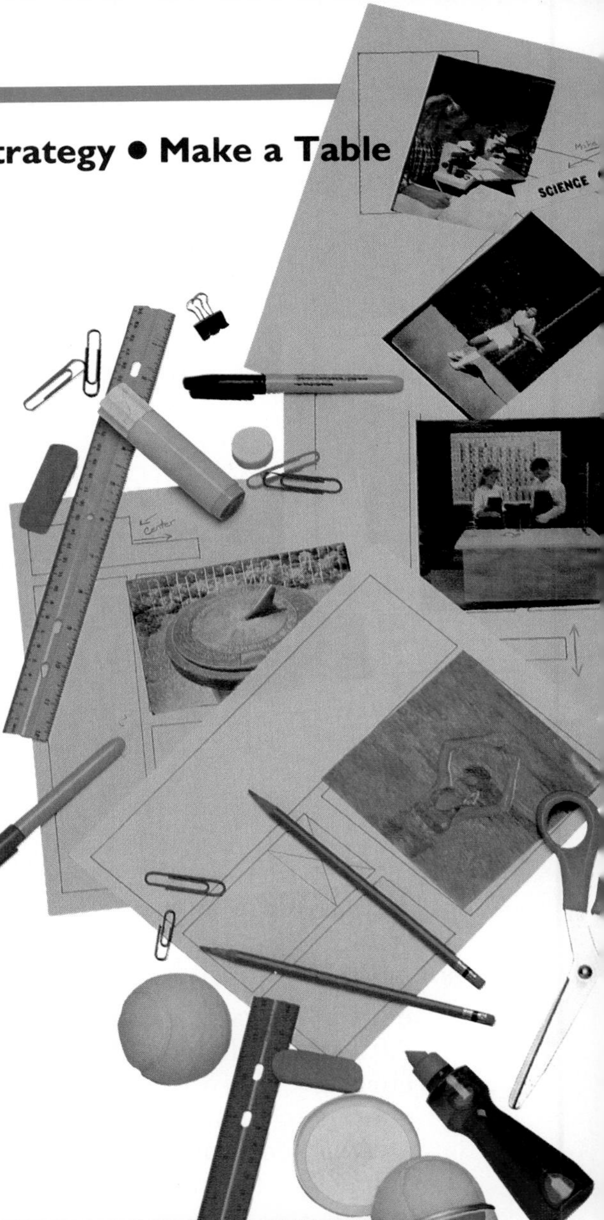

Jess, Kathy, and Linda work on the newspaper for the science club. One is the editor, one is a reporter, and one is a word processor. Linda's only exercise is swimming. Jess and the editor play tennis together. Linda and the reporter are cousins. Find each person's job.

▶ UNDERSTAND

What are you asked to find?
What facts are given?

▶ PLAN

What strategy can you use to solve the problem? You can *make a table* to organize the data. Then you can use the information in the problem and logical reasoning to complete the table.

▶ SOLVE

How can you carry out your plan?

Make a table to show all the possibilities. Use an X to show that a possibility cannot be true. Use a ✔ when you are certain a possibility is true.

Complete the table as you answer these questions.

- Is Jess the editor? Why or why not?
- Is Linda the editor? Why or why not?
- Who is the editor?
- Is Linda the reporter? Why or why not? Who is the reporter?
- Who is the word processor?

	Editor	Reporter	Word Processor
Jess	X	✔	X
Kathy	✔	X	X
Linda	X	X	✔

So, Jess is a reporter, Kathy is the editor, and Linda is a word processor.

▶ LOOK BACK

How can you check your answer?

WHAT IF... the problem did not state that Linda and the reporter were cousins? Could you still solve the problem? Explain.

Apply

① Sue, Alan, Don, and Mark are athletes. One is on the soccer team, one is on the baseball team, one is on the track team, and one is on the golf team. Sue is taller than the soccer player, Alan and Don do not know how to play golf, neither Sue nor Alan has time to play baseball, and Mark's sport does not use a ball. Who plays on the soccer team?

② Charles, Lucy, Dennis, and Bess have different hobbies. The hobbies are baseball-card collecting, painting, photography, and making model cars. Charles and Dennis are older than the baseball-card collector, Dennis and Bess do not paint or take photographs, and Charles and the photographer are cousins. What is Lucy's hobby?

Mixed Applications	STRATEGIES	• Make a Table • Use Estimation • Write an Equation • Guess and Check

Choose a strategy and solve.

③ Julie was selling tickets for the science fair. Adult tickets cost $7 each, and student tickets cost $3 each. Julie sold 12 tickets for $52. How many student tickets did she sell?

④ The science fair earned $900. This included $350 from ticket sales and the $5 entry fee paid by each of the exhibitors. How many exhibitors paid the entry fee?

⑤ Roger has to plan the seating for the four speakers at the science club banquet. Mr. Smith, Ms. Baker, Ms. Thomas, and Mr. Kubach will be sitting in a row at the front of the room. Roger knows that Ms. Baker wants to sit by Mr. Smith and does not want to sit by Ms. Thomas. Ms. Thomas does not want to sit by Mr. Kubach. What seating arrangement should Roger use for the four speakers?

⑥ The science club wants to earn at least $200.00 from the sale of solar calculators. The club makes a profit of $1.95 on each calculator. The members have sold 135 calculators. Have they sold enough calculators to earn $200.00?

WRITER'S CORNER

⑦ Write a problem similar to Exercise 1 or Exercise 2. Make a table that can be used to solve the problem. Exchange with a classmate and solve. (HINT: You may want to make and complete a table before writing the problem.)

More Practice, Lesson 8.6, page H59

MULTIPLYING AND DIVIDING

Although it is not always obvious to the eye, the earth's mountains are being eroded by the forces of wind, water, and ice. For the high mountains of the Himalayas, the erosion is particularly severe. These mountains lose more than 7,500 tons of soil and rock from each square mile every year. At that rate, how many tons of soil and rock are lost in a 10.5-square-mile area during a year?

$10.5 \times {}^-7{,}500$

$10.5 \boxed{\times} 7500 \boxed{+/_-} \boxed{=} \boxed{-\qquad 78750.}$

So, 78,750 tons of soil and rock are lost during a year.

More Examples Find the product or quotient.

A. $\dfrac{^-4}{7} \cdot \dfrac{^-1}{3} = \dfrac{^-4 \cdot {}^-1}{7 \cdot 3}$

$\qquad = \dfrac{4}{21}$

B. $^-24 \div 3\dfrac{1}{2} = \dfrac{^-24}{1} \div \dfrac{7}{2}$

$\qquad = \dfrac{^-24}{1} \cdot \dfrac{2}{7}$

$\qquad = \dfrac{^-48}{7}, \text{ or } {}^-6\dfrac{6}{7}$

C. $9.6 \div {}^-1.6 = {}^-6$

Talk About It

▶ What is the sign of the product of two negative rational numbers? a negative and a positive rational number?

▶ What do the rules for finding the products and the quotients of rational numbers have in common?

▶ What is the sign of the product of five negative rational numbers?

▶ How are the rules for multiplying and dividing rational numbers the same as the rules for multiplying and dividing integers?

Check for Understanding

Find the product or quotient.

1. $^-3.1 \cdot 5.9$

2. $^-8.7 \cdot {}^-1.3$

3. $6.4 \div {}^-0.8$

4. $^-1.05 \div {}^-2.1$

5. $\dfrac{5}{9} \cdot \dfrac{^-6}{7}$

6. $^-15 \cdot \dfrac{^-3}{5}$

7. $^-3\dfrac{1}{8} \div \dfrac{5}{6}$

8. $\dfrac{^-3}{4} \div \dfrac{^-3}{8}$

Practice

Find the product or quotient.

9. $\dfrac{^-5}{6} \cdot \dfrac{1}{8}$
10. $\dfrac{1}{4} \cdot \dfrac{^-7}{12}$
11. $\dfrac{^-2}{3} \cdot \dfrac{^-3}{8}$
12. $\dfrac{^-5}{9} \cdot \dfrac{^-9}{10}$

13. $1\dfrac{1}{2} \cdot \dfrac{^-1}{6}$
14. $\dfrac{^-3}{8} \cdot {}^-4\dfrac{4}{6}$
15. $^-1\dfrac{1}{3} \cdot 6$
16. $^-2\dfrac{1}{8} \cdot 3\dfrac{7}{9}$

17. $\dfrac{4}{5} \div \dfrac{^-8}{10}$
18. $\dfrac{^-7}{16} \div \dfrac{^-1}{2}$
19. $\dfrac{^-3}{8} \div \dfrac{4}{3}$
20. $\dfrac{^-5}{16} \div \dfrac{^-8}{12}$

21. $\dfrac{2}{9} \div {}^-2$
22. $^-3\dfrac{1}{8} \div \dfrac{^-5}{16}$
23. $\dfrac{^-2}{9} \div 4$
24. $^-7 \div \dfrac{^-5}{5}$

25. $0.9 \cdot {}^-4.5$
26. $^-13.02 \cdot 2.1$
27. $0.82 \cdot {}^-4$

28. $8.4 \div {}^-0.21$
29. $^-6.6 \div 1.5$
30. $^-21.28 \div {}^-3.04$

31. $\dfrac{1}{4} \cdot \left(8 \cdot \dfrac{^-1}{3}\right)$
32. $^-2.4 \cdot {}^-0.4 \cdot {}^-1.8$
33. $\left(\dfrac{1}{3} + \dfrac{^-1}{2}\right) \div \dfrac{^-5}{3}$

Evaluate the expression for $n = {}^-1.5$ and $t = \dfrac{2}{3}$.

34. $^-6 \cdot t$
35. $n \cdot 3.2$
36. $n \div 0.3$
37. $^-9 \div n$

38. $1\dfrac{1}{2} \cdot t$
39. $t \cdot \dfrac{3}{4}$
40. $\dfrac{^-3}{8} \div t$
41. $n \cdot t$

Find the value of *x* that makes each statement true.

42. $480 \div x = {}^-8$
43. $^-3.6 \div x = {}^-4$
44. $2\dfrac{1}{3} \cdot x = 1\dfrac{3}{4}$

Mixed Applications

45. The lava and ash from a volcano increase the size of an island at the rate of 32.5 square meters per year. How many years will it take to increase the size of the island by 390 square meters?

46. A beach is eroding at the rate of $1\dfrac{1}{4}$ inches per year. At that rate, how many inches of beach will be eroded in 50 years?

47. **Analyze Data** A city's low temperatures for one week are shown in the table. Find the mean low temperature for the week to the nearest tenth.

Low Temperatures for One Week							
Day	Sun.	Mon.	Tues.	Wed.	Thurs.	Fri.	Sat.
Temperature	$^-2.5$°C	$^-3.8$°C	4.2°C	2.9°C	$^-2.8$°C	$^-1.4$°C	$^-3.2$°C

When does the product of two rational numbers having the same sign have the opposite sign?

1. Sid had $12.00. He bought a pen for $1.89, 2 pencils for $0.20 each, and 3 packs of paper for $0.98 each. How much money does Sid have left?

2. There are 12 students in a chess club. If each student plays a game with every other student in the club, how many games will be played?

3. This year a research project has $320,340,000 in its budget. This is $65,000 more than the amount in the budget for last year. How much did the research project have in its budget last year?

4. A lab technician used 56 mL of a chemical solution to perform 2 experiments. She used 12 mL more for the first experiment than for the second. How many milliliters of solution did she use for the second experiment?

5. What is the total cost for an 8-minute telephone call if the cost for the first minute is $0.55 and the cost for each additional minute is $0.38?

6. The local newspaper charges $3.45 for a 1-line ad, $4.05 for a 2-line ad, $4.65 for a 3-line ad, and so on. How much will Mark pay for a 7-line ad?

Compute.

7. $6 + 9 - 3$

8. $12 + 6 \times 3$

9. $\frac{12 + 8}{4} - 1$

10. $35 - 3^2$

Evaluate the expression for the given value of the variable.

11. $n + 4$ for $n = 2.5$

12. $5t$ for $t = 22$

13. $\frac{45}{a}$ for $a = 1.5$

14. $100 - p$ for $p = 16$

15. $3y + 2$ for $y = \frac{1}{3}$

16. $a + a$ for $a = 2.65$

Write the fraction in simplest form.

17. $\frac{12}{8}$

18. $\frac{15}{35}$

19. $\frac{7}{56}$

20. $\frac{20}{6}$

21. $\frac{81}{90}$

22. $\frac{6}{21}$

Solve the proportion.

23. $\frac{x}{32} = \frac{3}{4}$

24. $\frac{t}{9} = \frac{49}{63}$

25. $\frac{54}{x} = \frac{6}{9}$

26. $\frac{5}{4} = \frac{15}{y}$

27. $\frac{8}{5} = \frac{r}{15}$

28. $\frac{3}{x} = \frac{5}{8}$

Write as a percent.

29. $\frac{3}{5}$

30. $\frac{1}{2}$

31. $\frac{2}{3}$

32. 0.56

33. 0.007

34. 1.4

Spotlight ON PROBLEM SOLVING

Understand
Plan
Solve
Look Back

DETERMINE REASONABLE SOLUTIONS

When a problem is solved, the answer must be reasonable. Always check to see that your solution to a problem is reasonable. Read the following problem.

The product of Mark's and Robin's ages is 50. The difference in their ages is 5. Mark is older than Robin. What are their ages?

Talk About It

a. What are the possible solutions to the problem?(HINT: Use positive and negative numbers.)

b. What is the more reasonable solution to the problem? Why?

Apply

Read and study each problem. Decide which solution is reasonable. Be prepared to tell why the other solution is unreasonable.

1. The product of the length and width of a rectangle is 40 in. The length is 3 in. more than the width. Find the length.
   Solutions: 8 in.; ⁻5 in.

2. The product of two numbers is 8. Their difference is 2. What are the numbers?
   Solutions: 2 and 4; ⁻2 and ⁻4

3. A band has 120 members. They march in a rectangular formation. The number of rows is 7 more than the number of columns. How many rows and columns are there?
   Solutions: 15 rows and 8 columns; ⁻8 rows and ⁻15 columns

4. The quotient of Albert's and Tina's ages is 2. Albert's age is 9 less than Tina's age. What are their ages?
   Solutions: Albert is ⁻18 years old, and Tina is ⁻9 years old; Albert is 9 years old, and Tina is 18 years old.

SOLVING ONE-STEP EQUATIONS

Ted is spending a week in the mountains helping his older brother, who is a park service ranger. One of Ted's chores is to record the temperature, pressure, and humidity readings.

While making his readings on a foggy morning, Ted notices that there has been a 3.4°C rise in the air temperature since he last recorded it. The temperature reading is $^-5.8°$C. What was the earlier temperature reading?

Recall the methods that you used to write and solve equations with whole numbers, decimals, and fractions. You can use these same methods to write and solve equations involving integers and rational numbers.

Let t = the earlier temperature reading.

Then $t + 3.4$ = the present temperature reading.

$$t + 3.4 = {}^-5.8$$
$$t + 3.4 - 3.4 = {}^-5.8 - 3.4 \quad \longleftarrow \text{Subtract 3.4}$$
$$t = {}^-5.8 + {}^-3.4 \quad \text{from each side.}$$
$$t = {}^-9.2$$

Check:
$$t + 3.4 = {}^-5.8$$
$${}^-9.2 + 3.4 = {}^-5.8$$
$${}^-5.8 = {}^-5.8$$

So, the earlier temperature reading was $^-9.2°$C.

Another Example

$$d - \frac{1}{2} = \frac{^-3}{4}$$
$$d - \frac{1}{2} + \frac{1}{2} = \frac{^-3}{4} + \frac{1}{2}$$
$$d = \frac{^-3}{4} + \frac{2}{4}$$
$$d = \frac{^-1}{4}$$

Check:
$$d - \frac{1}{2} = \frac{^-3}{4}$$
$$\frac{^-1}{4} - \frac{2}{4} = \frac{^-3}{4}$$
$$\frac{^-1}{4} + \frac{^-2}{4} = \frac{^-3}{4}$$
$$\frac{^-3}{4} = \frac{^-3}{4}$$

Remember to find the LCD of the fractions.

Talk About It

▶ In the first example, can you add the opposite of 3.4 to each side instead of subtracting 3.4 from each side? Explain.

▶ What is the first decision you make before you begin solving an equation?

▶ What do you think is the most difficult part of solving one-step equations that use rational numbers?

Check for Understanding

Tell the step you would use to solve the equation.

1. $n + {}^-3.2 = 18$

2. $t - \frac{1}{2} = {}^-\frac{5}{8}$

3. $s + 9.2 = {}^-7.4$

4. $1.5x = {}^-60$

5. $\frac{{}^-5x}{6} = 4.5$

6. $\frac{b}{{}^-9} = 21$

Practice

Solve the equation. Check your solution.

7. $a + 7 = {}^-3$

8. ${}^-0.3y = 2.1$

9. ${}^-5.4 + x = 2.8$

10. $c + 4 = {}^-10$

11. $d - 12 = {}^-9$

12. $f + 3.9 = {}^-4.7$

13. $2a = {}^-30$

14. ${}^-7b = 35$

15. $4.8y = {}^-28.8$

16. $\frac{x}{15} = {}^-30$

17. $\frac{m}{{}^-3} = {}^-15$

18. $\frac{5}{6}b = {}^-10$

19. ${}^-8 + p = 9$

20. $m + 3.6 = {}^-9$

21. $q - 20 = {}^-7$

22. $20 = {}^-15 - n$

23. $12 = {}^-8 - n$

24. $6 - n = {}^-14$

Write an equation for the word sentence.

25. A number decreased by 12.4 is ${}^-6.5$.

26. The sum of a number and ${}^-2.3$ is 5.6.

Mixed Applications

Write an equation for the problem. Then solve.

27. There were 420 people in the park the first day it opened in the spring. This was $\frac{2}{3}$ of the number of people who came the second day. How many people were in the park on the second day?

28. The high temperature on Thursday was 4.5°C lower than the high temperature on Tuesday. The high temperature on Thursday was 6°C. What was the high temperature on Tuesday?

MIXED REVIEW

Solve.

1. 14% of 21 is what number?

2. What percent of 2,500 is 500?

3. 24 is 40% of what number?

4. What is 15% of 220?

Write a word problem that can be solved by using the equation $c + 8 = {}^-22$.

WRAP UP...

SOLVING TWO-STEP EQUATIONS

Recall that when you solve a two-step equation, you do addition or subtraction first and then do multiplication or division. Sometimes it is easier to add the opposite of a number instead of subtracting a number.

Example   Solve and check. $6n + 7 = {}^-17$

$$6n + 7 = {}^-17$$
$$6n + 7 + {}^-7 = {}^-17 + {}^-7 \quad \text{Add the opposite of 7.}$$
$$6n = {}^-24$$
$$\frac{6n}{6} = \frac{{}^-24}{6} \quad \text{Divide by 6.}$$
$$n = {}^-4$$

Check:
$$6n + 7 = {}^-17$$
$$6 \cdot {}^-4 + 7 = {}^-17$$
$${}^-24 + 7 = {}^-17$$
$${}^-17 = {}^-17$$

Another Example

$$\frac{t}{4.6} - 1.6 = {}^-2.8$$
$$\frac{t}{4.6} - 1.6 + 1.6 = {}^-2.8 + 1.6$$
$$\frac{t}{4.6} = {}^-2.8 + 1.6$$
$$\frac{t}{4.6} = {}^-1.2$$
$$\frac{t}{4.6} \cdot 4.6 = {}^-1.2 \cdot 4.6$$
$$t = {}^-5.52$$

Check:
$$\frac{t}{4.6} - 1.6 = {}^-2.8$$
$$\frac{{}^-5.52}{4.6} - 1.6 = {}^-2.8$$
$${}^-1.2 - 1.6 = {}^-2.8$$
$${}^-1.2 + {}^-1.6 = {}^-2.8$$
$${}^-2.8 = {}^-2.8$$

Talk About It

▶ In the first example, why was $^-7$ added to each side of the equation? What other way can this step be written?

▶ In the second example, how will the solution change if $\frac{t}{4.6}$ is changed to $\frac{t}{{}^-4.6}$?

Check for Understanding

Solve the equation. Check your solution.

1. $2n - 4 = {}^-10$ **2.** ${}^-\frac{1}{2}a + 1 = 14$ **3.** $\frac{m}{{}^-3} - {}^-5 = {}^-2$

4. ${}^-8n + 3 = 51$ **5.** $\frac{h}{{}^-9} + {}^-2 = 3$ **6.** ${}^-\frac{7}{8}b - 4 = {}^-11$

Idea Bank, page 491, Exercise 12

Practice

Solve the equation. Check your solution.

7. $3n + 10 = 1$

8. $^-7m - 2 = 54$

9. $0.9n + 1.5 = 1.8$

10. $\frac{b}{3} + 5 = 9$

11. $\frac{3}{4}n - 3 = 12$

12. $\frac{m}{2} - \frac{1}{2} = 3$

13. $^-25c - 17 = 183$

14. $15a - {}^-4 = 64$

15. $5b + {}^-4 = {}^-24$

16. $\frac{2}{3}m = {}^-4\frac{1}{3}$

17. $\frac{5}{6}h + 6 = {}^-9$

18. $\frac{n}{3} + 2 = 0$

19. $\frac{1}{2}s + 4 = {}^-2$

20. $^-5m = {}^-4\frac{2}{5}$

21. $\frac{1}{8}u - 1 = 1$

22. $4p - p = {}^-18$

23. $6m - 8m - 3 = {}^-9$

24. $7n - 9 = 3n + 7$

Write the calculator key sequence you can use to solve the equation.

25. $3(7 + 11) = 5n$

26. $8(10 - 2) = 8t$

27. $6y = 2(9 + 6)$

Write an equation for the word sentence. Then solve the equation.

28. Six more than $^-8$ times a number is 30. What is the number?

29. Five less than a number divided by 4 is $^-2$. What is the number?

30. Four subtracted from the product of $^-12$ and a number is 56. What is the number?

31. The sum of 10 and a number divided by 3 is $^-17$. What is the number?

Mixed Applications

Write an equation for Exercise 32. Then solve.

32. This year a team of petroleum geologists drilled 41 test wells. This is 5 fewer than twice the number of test wells they drilled last year. How many wells did the team drill last year?

33. Rob bought 3 notebooks at $1.98 each, 6 pens at $0.79 each, and 2 textbooks. He spent $42.48. How much did he spend for the textbooks?

HEALTH CONNECTION

A person who is moderately active can multiply his or her weight by 15 to determine how many calories he or she can eat each day to maintain a constant weight.

34. Mark weighs 145 pounds. He wants to lose 5 pounds in 4 weeks. To lose 1 pound in 4 weeks, Mark must reduce his daily caloric intake by 125 calories. How many calories should he eat each day while he diets?

Name the steps you can use to find the value of n in $4n - 2\frac{1}{2} = {}^-3\frac{4}{5}$.

WRAP
UP...

SOLVING INEQUALITIES

The Grand Coulee Dam, in Washington, is the greatest single source of hydroelectric power in the United States. Suppose the dam's power plants are generating 4,635 megawatts of power when a decision is made to increase the power by no more than 1,365 megawatts. The increase in power will be equally distributed to five regional centers. How much additional power will each regional center receive?

An inequality can be used to solve the problem. Solving an inequality is similar to solving an equation.

Let $p =$ the power that each center will receive.
Then $5p \le 1,365$.

$$5p \le 1,365$$
$$\frac{5p}{5} \le \frac{1,365}{5}$$ Divide each side of the inequality by 5.
$$p \le 273$$

So, each regional center will receive an additional 273 megawatts of power or less.

You can graph the solution of an inequality on a number line.

Examples

A. Solve and graph. $x + 8 < 6$

$$x + 8 < 6$$
$$x + 8 + {}^-8 < 6 + {}^-8$$
$$x < {}^-2$$

Solution: all real numbers less than ${}^-2$

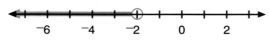

The open circle means that ${}^-2$ is not a solution.

B. Solve and graph. $\frac{x}{-2} \le \frac{{}^-3}{4}$

$$\frac{x}{-2} \le \frac{{}^-3}{4}$$
$$\frac{x}{-2} \cdot {}^-2 \ge \frac{{}^-3}{4} \cdot {}^-2$$ When you multiply or divide by a negative number, reverse the inequality symbol.
$$x \ge \frac{3}{2}$$

Solution: all real numbers greater than or equal to $\frac{3}{2}$

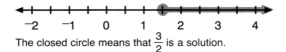

The closed circle means that $\frac{3}{2}$ is a solution.

Talk About It

▶ In which direction on the number line do you draw the graph of an inequality where the solution uses the symbol $>$?

▶ Does the graph of $b < 6$ include the 6? Why or why not?

Check for Understanding

Solve and graph the inequality.

1. $x + 4 > 2$ **2.** $a - 3 < {}^-2$ **3.** $2n \leq {}^-10$

4. $\frac{t}{4} \geq {}^-1$ **5.** $c + {}^-3 > 2$ **6.** ${}^-3b < 12$

Practice

Solve and graph the inequality.

7. $3n > 6$ **8.** ${}^-4s < {}^-12$ **9.** $6 + n < 8$

10. $\frac{r}{2} \geq \frac{{}^-1}{2}$ **11.** $\frac{a}{3} > 3$ **12.** $\frac{m}{0.5} > {}^-7$

13. $6 + c \leq 1$ **14.** $d - {}^-5 < 3$ **15.** $s + \frac{{}^-1}{3} \geq \frac{8}{3}$

16. $\frac{x}{{}^-5} - 4 > {}^-1$ **17.** $6n + 3 \geq 21$ **18.** $\frac{2}{3}n - 1 < 3$

Match the inequality with the graph.

19. $4n < 8$

a.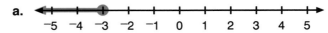

20. $t + 5 > 6$

b.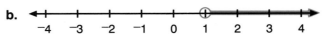

21. $\frac{n}{2} \geq 1$

c.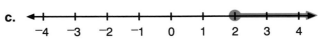

22. ${}^-3c + 1 \geq 10$

d.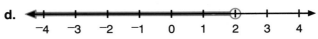

Mixed Applications

Write an inequality for Exercise 23. Then solve.

23. Last week the first group of 5 electricians was hired for the electrical department. The total number of personnel in the department will be fewer than 29. How many more persons can be hired for the department?

24. The freezing point of a mixture of antifreeze and water is 2°C greater than 3 times the freezing point of the antifreeze. The freezing point of the mixture is ${}^-37$°C. What is the freezing point of the antifreeze?

25. Visual Thinking Describe the solution shown by the graph. What numbers are not part of the solution?

Explain why the graph of $t \leq 2$ is different from the graph of $t < 2$.

PROBLEM *Solving*

Jerry and Gwen are working with a team of archaeologists. They spend a total of 3.5 hr each day traveling to and from work. Going to work early in the morning, they drive at a speed of 45 mph. Returning home in the afternoon, they drive only 30 mph. How many hours do they drive each morning and each afternoon?

Many problems are quickly solved by *using a formula*.

▶ **UNDERSTAND**

What are you asked to find?

What facts are given?

▶ **PLAN**

What strategy will you use to solve the problem?

You can *use a formula*. Use the distance formula $d = rt$, where d = distance, r = rate, and t = time.

▶ **SOLVE**

How can you use the formula to solve the problem?

Let t = the driving time in the morning.
Then $3.5 - t$ = the driving time in the afternoon.

Using $d = rt$, you can write the distance in the morning as $d = 45t$ and the distance in the evening as $d = 30(3.5 - t)$. Since the distances to and from work are the same, you can write $45t = 30(3.5 - t)$. Solve the equation for t.

$$45t = 30(3.5 - t)$$
$$45t = 105 - 30t$$
$$45t + 30t = 105 - 30t + 30t$$
$$75t = 105$$
$$t = 1.4 \text{ hr}$$
$$3.5 - t = 2.1 \text{ hr}$$

So, Jerry and Gwen drive 1.4 hr each morning and 2.1 hr each afternoon.

▶ **LOOK BACK**

How can you check your solution?

WHAT IF...

... you also want to know the number of miles Jerry and Gwen drive to work? How can you use the formula to find this information?

Apply

Jerry and Gwen found a second route to work. Taking this route, they drive in town at an average speed of 15 mph and on the freeway at an average speed of 60 mph.

Use this information for Exercises 1–4.

1 Jerry and Gwen spend 65 min on the freeway. How far do they drive on the freeway?
(HINT: 65 min = ■ hr)

2 Jerry and Gwen drive 3 miles in town. How long do they drive in town?

3 One day Jerry and Gwen were delayed by an accident on the freeway, and drove for 1 hour and 12 minutes. Use your answer for Exercise 1 to find their average speed on the freeway.

4 On Friday morning the traffic in town was light, so Jerry and Gwen were able to drive at an average speed of 25 mph. How much time did they save on Friday?

Mixed Applications ▶ **STRATEGIES**
- Guess and Check • Use a Formula
- Draw a Picture • Work Backward

Choose a strategy and solve.

5 The archaeologists at the excavation site found a total of 123 pots and statues. They found twice as many pots as statues. How many pots did the archaeologists find?

6 Joey bought a shovel, a trowel, and a pair of work gloves. He lost his receipt, but knows that he paid $8.95 for the shovel, $3.50 for the trowel, and $16.30 in all. How much did he pay for the gloves?

7 One of the archaeologists found a drawing of a fish on a wall. The body of the fish is 3 times as long as the head. The tail of the fish is as long as the head and the body combined. The total length of the fish is 64 in. How long is the head of the fish?

8 A truck drove from the excavation site to the museum in $2\frac{1}{2}$ hr. The truck traveled a total of 130 mi. What was the average speed of the truck in miles per hour?

9 Toni is asked to carry 4 quarts of water in one container to the work site. She has a container that holds 3 quarts and a container that holds 5 quarts. How can she use these containers to get exactly 4 quarts of water?

10 David and Anne have to fence in an area that is 20 m long and 12 m wide. They want to put fence posts every 4 m. How many fence posts do they need?

Vocabulary Check

Choose a word or words from the box to complete each sentence.

Density
irrational
perfect squares
rational
solution
square
square root

1. Any number that can be written in the form $\frac{a}{b}$ where a and b are integers and b is not equal to zero is a(n) __?__ number. *(page 248)*

2. All the numbers that make an inequality a true statement are the __?__ of the inequality. *(page 270)*

3. The product of a number multiplied by itself is the __?__ of a number. *(page 250)*

4. Between any two rational numbers is at least one other rational number. This is called the Property of __?__ . *(page 248)*

5. Numbers that have integers as their square roots are called __?__ . *(page 250)*

6. Numbers that are not rational numbers are __?__ numbers. *(page 257)*

7. The inverse of squaring a number is taking its __?__ . *(page 250)*

Concept Check

Write each rational number in the form $\frac{a}{b}$. *(page 248)*

8. $^-3$
9. 2.5
10. $1\frac{2}{3}$
11. $^-8.5$
12. 1.05

Write *SR* if the first number is the square root of the second number, or write *S* if it is the square. *(page 250)*

13. $9, 81$
14. $144, 12$
15. $36, 6$
16. $1.2, 1.44$
17. $400, ^-20$

Tell whether each number is *rational* or *irrational*. *(page 256)*

18. 32.5
19. $2.6457513\ldots$
20. $\sqrt{36}$
21. $\sqrt{17}$

Tell whether the answer will be *positive* or *negative*. *(pages 258, 262)*

22. $\frac{^-3}{4} + \frac{^-2}{3}$
23. $1.42 - {}^-3.56$
24. $^-1.5 \cdot 4.1$
25. $\frac{^-4}{7} \div \frac{^-5}{6}$

Tell the step you would use to solve the equation. *(page 266)*

26. $x + {}^-1.2 = 4.4$
27. $4n = \frac{5}{6}$
28. $b - \frac{2}{3} = {}^-1\frac{1}{8}$
29. $\frac{c}{^-5} = 1.34$

Skill Check

Compare. Write < or > . *(page 248)*

30. $^-3.7 \bullet \ ^-4.8$ **31.** $\frac{1}{2} \bullet \frac{^-14}{9}$ **32.** $^-1.4 \bullet \frac{^-3}{5}$ **33.** $1\frac{1}{5} \bullet 1.3$

Find a rational number between each pair of numbers. *(page 248)*

34. 0.89 and 0.9 **35.** $\frac{^-3}{5}$ and $\frac{^-7}{10}$ **36.** 0 and 0.4 **37.** $\frac{4}{6}$ and $\frac{5}{6}$

Find the square or square root. *(pages 250, 252)*

38. 13^2 **39.** 17^2 **40.** $(^-8)^2$ **41.** $\sqrt{144}$ **42.** $\sqrt{\frac{1}{9}}$ **43.** $^-\sqrt{36}$

Find the square root to the nearest tenth. *(page 252)*

44. $\sqrt{32}$ **45.** $\sqrt{15}$ **46.** $\sqrt{86}$ **47.** $^-\sqrt{70}$ **48.** $\sqrt{63}$ **49.** $\sqrt{105}$

Find the sum, difference, product, or quotient. *(pages 258, 262)*

50. $9.2 + \ ^-5.6$ **51.** $5\frac{1}{2} + \ ^-9\frac{1}{2}$ **52.** $^-3.12 - \ ^-2.63$ **53.** $\frac{^-2}{3} - \frac{3}{4}$

54. $^-3.1 \cdot \ ^-34$ **55.** $3\frac{1}{3} \cdot \frac{3}{5}$ **56.** $^-24 \div \frac{^-8}{5}$ **57.** $^-27.2 \div 8.5$

Solve the equation. Check your solution. *(pages 266, 268)*

58. $\frac{n}{4} = \ ^-18$ **59.** $\frac{3}{4} + n = \frac{1}{4}$ **60.** $3.6n = \ ^-14.4$ **61.** $2n + \ ^-7 = \ ^-21$

Solve and graph the inequality. *(page 270)*

62. $n - 3 > \ ^-7$ **63.** $n + 4 \le 10$ **64.** $^-5n \ge 30$ **65.** $\frac{n}{^-3} < 3$

Problem-Solving Check

66. Aaron, Nancy, and Mitch play in the school band. One plays the drum, one plays the saxophone, and one plays the flute. Aaron is a senior. Aaron and the saxophone player practice together after school. Nancy and the flute player are sophomores. Who plays each instrument? *(page 260)*

67. An elephant runs at a rate of 31 feet per second. At this rate, how many seconds will it take the elephant to run 248 ft? *(page 272)*

68. The fastest passenger train in France can travel 690 mi in 3 hr. Find the average speed in miles per hour. *(page 272)*

Compare. Write $<$ or $>$.

1. $^-1.3 \bullet ^-2.4$ **2.** $1\frac{1}{3} \bullet ^-1\frac{1}{3}$

Find a rational number between the pair of numbers.

3. $^-1.3$ and $^-1.4$ **4.** $\frac{1}{8}$ and $\frac{1}{4}$

Find the squares or square roots.

5. 19^2 **6.** 23^2 **7.** $(^-9)^2$ **8.** $^-\sqrt{49}$ **9.** $\sqrt{64}$ **10.** $\sqrt{\frac{1}{16}}$

Find the square root to the nearest tenth.

11. $\sqrt{19}$ **12.** $\sqrt{75}$ **13.** $\sqrt{23}$ **14.** $\sqrt{84}$

Find the sum, difference, product, or quotient.

15. $^-6\frac{1}{3} + 2\frac{2}{3}$ **16.** $^-7\frac{1}{8} - ^-1\frac{1}{4}$ **17.** $^-16.2 + ^-3.2$ **18.** $^-11.6 - 4.5$

19. $^-0.6 \cdot 8.4$ **20.** $\frac{3}{4} \cdot 2\frac{2}{3}$ **21.** $^-63 \div \frac{^-7}{8}$ **22.** $^-4.48 \div ^-3.2$

Solve the equation.

23. $\frac{n}{3} = ^-9$ **24.** $n - 6 = ^-7$ **25.** $\frac{1}{8}n + 3 = ^-2$ **26.** $5n - 3 = ^-28$

Solve and graph the inequality.

27. $n - 2 \geq 2$ **28.** $5 + n < 8$ **29.** $3n \leq ^-12$

Solve.

30. Ann, Beth, and Carol each have a different piece of fruit for lunch. The fruits are an apple, an orange, and a banana. Carol does not like bananas, and Beth does not have to peel her fruit. Who has each fruit?

31. Darin, Kyle, and Rita each get to school in a different way. One rides the bus, one drives a car, and one walks. Kyle is too young to drive. Darin does not walk or drive. How does each get to school?

32. The speed of sound is about 343 m per second. How many meters will sound travel in 6 sec?

33. The Concorde SST can fly about 4,650 mi in 3 hr. What is the speed of the Concorde in miles per hour?

Write an Article

Every Thursday the local newspaper has a special 12-page insert designed for teenagers. The editor has asked your class to write an article for an upcoming insert. The article should deal with some topic in science and should contain about 500 words.

Work with your classmates to write an article for the insert.

DECIDE

As a team, discuss the science topics that might make an interesting article. Choose one topic.

Discuss where you will find information on the topic you have chosen.

Decide whether you will include pictures or photographs with the article.

SHARE

Display your article on the wall or bulletin board. Compare your article with those of other teams. Tell why you chose your topic.

DO

As a team, do the research that is needed for your article. Then write your article. Be sure to include any pictures and photographs that were discussed.

Talk About It

- Did you learn anything that you did not know about a topic in science?

- Did your article include any numbers? If so, were the numbers rational numbers or irrational numbers?

- How can you estimate the number of words in your article?

TWIN SOLUTIONS

Complete each pair of equations, using only two numbers from the box.
Use the same two numbers in each equation.

$\underline{?} \cdot \underline{?} = {}^-2.25$ 3 [+/-] [×] 0.75 [=] [⁻ 2.25]

$\underline{?} + \underline{?} = {}^-2.25$ 3 [+/-] [+] 0.75 [=] [⁻ 2.25]

1. $\underline{?} \cdot \underline{?} = 7.2$
    $\underline{?} + \underline{?} = 7.2$

2. $\underline{?} \cdot \underline{?} = {}^-3.2$
    $\underline{?} + \underline{?} = {}^-3.2$

3. $\underline{?} \cdot \underline{?} = {}^-0.9$
    $\underline{?} + \underline{?} = {}^-0.9$

4. $\underline{?} \cdot \underline{?} = {}^-0.5$
    $\underline{?} + \underline{?} = {}^-0.5$

5. $2(\underline{?} + \underline{?}) = {}^-10$
    $(\underline{?} - \underline{?}) = {}^-10$

6. $2(\underline{?} \cdot \underline{?}) = {}^-0.25$
    $(\underline{?} + \underline{?}) = {}^-0.25$

0.25	0.5
0.6	0.75
0.8	1.2
2.5	6
⁻0.5	⁻1
⁻1.5	⁻3
⁻4	⁻7.5

Now, write your own pair of equations, using the same numbers but different operations.

CHALLENGE

Number Sense

If 1, $AA5$ is divisible by 45, what digit does A represent?

Logical Reasoning

If five days ago was the day after Saturday, what was the day before yesterday?

Write the letter of the correct answer.

1. Which is the opposite of the rational number 0.76?

    A. $^-76$ B. $^-0.76$

    C. $\frac{1}{76}$ D. 0.76

2. Which numbers are ordered from greatest to least?

    A. $1\frac{1}{8}$, $^-0.6$, 1.3   B. 1.3, $^-0.6$, $1\frac{1}{8}$

    C. 1.3, $1\frac{1}{8}$, $^-0.6$ D. not here

3. Which angle has a measure that is less than 90°?

    A. straight   B. obtuse

    C. acute   D. right

4. Which whole numbers make the inequality $n + 8 < 13$ true?

    A. 0, 1, 2, 3, 4   B. 1, 2, 3, 4, 5

    C. 5, 6, 7, . . .   D. 6, 7, 8, . . .

5. $^-46 + ^-1$

    A. $^-47$ B. $^-45$

    C. 45   D. 47

6. $97 + ^-14 - ^-3$

    A. $^-86$ B. 86

    C. 89   D. 108

7. $n + \frac{1}{3} = \frac{2}{5}$

    A. $n = \frac{1}{15}$ B. $n = \frac{2}{15}$

    C. $n = \frac{3}{8}$ D. $n = \frac{1}{2}$

8. Which decimal equals $\frac{3}{8}$?

    A. 0.3   B. 0.375

    C. 0.38   D. 2.66

9. Which number equals $|^-10|$?

    A. $^-10$ B. $^-1$

    C. 1   D. 10

10. Which decimal equals $2\frac{3}{4}$?

    A. 0.63   B. 2.3

    C. 2.34   D. not here

11. Karen deposited $200 in a bank paying 6.4% interest per year. About how much simple interest will Karen earn in one year?

    A. $1.20   B. $12

    C. $20   D. $120

12. The parking charge at Lot A is $3 for the first hour and $1 for each additional hour. The charge at Lot B is $2 for each hour. How much more does it cost for 5 hours in Lot B than in Lot A?

    A. $3   B. $7

    C. $10   D. $17

CHAPTER

9

ALGEBRA
GRAPHING RELATIONS AND FUNCTIONS

Did you know . . .

. . . that the Rose Bowl in Pasadena, California, has a seating capacity of 104,000?

Talk About It

All the seats in a stadium must be labeled so that spectators can easily find their places. What system could you use to identify each seat in a stadium as large as the Rose Bowl?

GRAPHING ORDERED PAIRS

WARM UP...

To go from 0 to ⁻3 on a number line, in which direction do you move?

For designs like the one shown, each seat in the stadium can be named by an ordered pair (row letter, seat number). A seat, such as (B,6), can then be located and assigned the card needed for the design.

To locate or graph a point on a coordinate plane, you use an **ordered pair** of numbers (x, y). The horizontal axis of the coordinate plane is the x-axis, and the vertical axis is the y-axis. The axes intersect at a point called the **origin** and divide the coordinate plane into four parts called **quadrants.**

The first number of an ordered pair, the **x-coordinate,** tells the direction and the number of spaces to move horizontally. The second number, the **y-coordinate,** tells the direction and the number of spaces to move vertically.

The coordinates of point B are $(⁻3,4)$.

● What are the coordinates of point C?

● In which quadrant would you graph point $T(5, ⁻3)$?

Talk About It

▶ How would you graph the point $T(5, ⁻3)$?

▶ Do the coordinates $(3,4)$ and $(4,3)$ name the same point? Explain.

Check for Understanding

Name the quadrant in which the point is located.

1. $(4, 3)$
2. $(2, ⁻1)$
3. $\left(⁻\frac{3}{4}, 6\right)$
4. $(3, ⁻1)$
5. $(⁻3.1, 2)$
6. $(⁻2, ⁻4)$

Write the coordinates of the point.

7. A
8. B
9. C
10. D

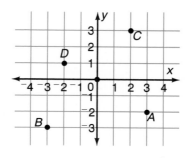

Idea Bank, page 490, Exercise 3

Practice

Write the coordinates of the point.

11. A **12.** C **13.** D

14. H **15.** G **16.** M

17. L **18.** B **19.** I

20. E **21.** F **22.** N

Name the point given by the coordinates.

23. $(0, {}^-5)$ **24.** $(5,4)$ **25.** $(3, {}^-3)$

26. $(2,1)$ **27.** $({}^-5, {}^-2)$ **28.** $(1, {}^-2)$

29. $({}^-3, {}^-4)$ **30.** $({}^-3.5, {}^-7)$ **31.** $({}^-4.5, 2.5)$

Name the quadrant in which the point is located.

32. $(4, {}^-2)$ **33.** $({}^-8,3)$

34. $({}^-9, {}^-2)$ **35.** $(4,6)$

Draw a coordinate plane. Graph and label these points.

36. $A({}^-4,5)$ **37.** $B(5, {}^-2)$ **38.** $C({}^-3, {}^-2)$ **39.** $D({}^-2,1)$

40. $E(4,4)$ **41.** $F({}^-5, {}^-4)$ **42.** $G\left({}^-5,1\frac{1}{2}\right)$ **43.** $H\left({}^-\frac{1}{2}, {}^-4\frac{1}{2}\right)$

Mixed Applications

44. A spectator at a football game is sitting in row W, seat 12. Write coordinates that could be used to identify the spectator's location.

45. Three vertices of a square are $({}^-4,3)$, $(4,3)$, and $(4, {}^-5)$. Graph the ordered pairs. Give the coordinates of the fourth vertex of the square.

46. Robbie walked 6 blocks north, 3 blocks east, 9 blocks south, and 12 blocks west. How many blocks north does he need to walk in order to be directly west of where he started?

47. Sixty hikers set out on a 25-km hike. One fourth of the group stopped at 8 km. One third of the remainder stopped at 16 km. The rest finished the hike. What percent of the original group finished the hike?

Explain how to graph the point $(6, {}^-2)$ on a coordinate plane.

WRAP UP...

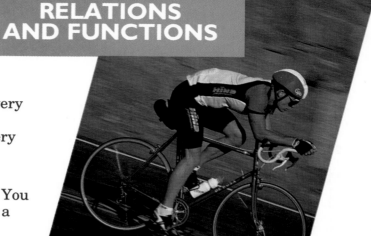

RELATIONS AND FUNCTIONS

On a trip, how is the distance you travel related to your travel time?

Chad is a bicycle racer. He trains every day by riding at least 30 miles. On Monday he recorded his mileage every 15 minutes. How is the distance he rode related to the time he rode?

A **relation** is a set of ordered pairs. You can describe a relation in a table, in a graph, or by writing a word rule.

Time, x	0	15	30	45	60	75	90
Distance, y	0	5	10	15	20	25	30

- What are the ordered pairs of the relation?

- Which word rule shows the relationship between the distance and the time?
  a. Multiply each time value by 3.
  b. Divide each time value by 3.

A **function** is a relation in which no two ordered pairs have the same x-value.

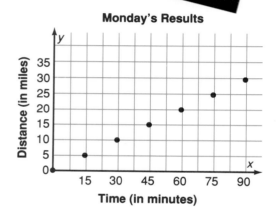

Monday's Results

Examples

A. This relation is a function.

(0,1), (1,2), (2,3)

Each of the ordered pairs has a different x-value.

B. This relation is not a function.

(1,1), (1,2), (2,3)

(1,1) and (1,2) have the same x-value.

Talk About It

▶ Is the relation that shows Chad's time and distance a function? Explain.

▶ What word rule can you use to describe this relation?

Original price, x	$12	$16	$18	$23	$30
Sale price, y	$ 8	$12	$14	$19	$26

Is every function a relation?

Check for Understanding

Write the ordered pairs for each relation.

1.

Ages of Brother and Sister				
Tom's age, x	5	8	10	15
Ann's age, y	2	5	7	12

2.

Wages of Part-Time Employee					
Hours, x	1	2	3	4	5
Wages, y	$4	$8	$12	$16	$20

Tell whether the relation is a function. Write *yes* or *no*.

3. (1,2), (2,3), (3,4), (3,1) **4.** (0,2), (2,4), (3,6), (4,8) **5.** (1,4), (⁻1,4), (2,8), (⁻2,8)

Practice

Write the ordered pairs for each relation. Write *yes* if the relation is a function and *no* if it is not.

6. 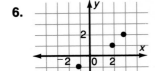 **7.** 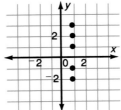 **8.** 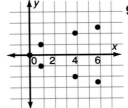 **9.**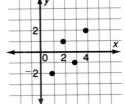

Write a word rule for each relation.

10.

Miles Traveled on Trip				
Hours, x	1	2	3	4
Distance, y	50	100	150	200

11.

Average Quiz Scores				
Total score, x	95	90	85	80
Average score, y	19	18	17	16

Mixed Applications

12. Stan paid $9,450 for a new truck. He knows that the value of the truck will decrease $800 each year. He plans to keep the truck for 5 years. Make a table to show the relation between the value and the number of years. (HINT: Use $9,450 and 0 as the first x and y values.)

13. Write a Problem The word rule for a relation is "decrease the x-value by 4." Write a problem in which two items or situations show this relation.

14. Estimation Chad spends 15% of his riding time going uphill. If he rode for 10.5 hr last week, about how much time did he ride uphill?

Explain the difference between a relation and a function.

EQUATIONS WITH TWO VARIABLES

Jeanette jogs 2 miles every day. The equation $y = 2x$ shows the relation between the total number of miles she jogs, y, and the number of days that she jogs, x.

The equation $y = 2x$ is an equation with two variables. To solve an equation with two variables, choose a replacement value for one variable and then find the value of the other variable. An equation with two variables usually has many solutions.

Examples Find the solutions of the equations $y = 2x$ and $y = 3x + 2$ for $x = {}^-1, 0, 1$, and 2. Make a table of values for each equation.

A. $y = 2x$

x	$2x$	y
$^-1$	$2 \cdot {}^-1$	$^-2$
0	$2 \cdot 0$	0
1	$2 \cdot 1$	2
2	$2 \cdot 2$	4

The ordered pairs $({}^-1, {}^-2)$, $(0,0)$, $(1,2)$, and $(2,4)$ are solutions of the equation. Other solutions are possible.

B. $y = 3x + 2$

x	$3x + 2$	y
$^-1$	$3 \cdot {}^-1 + 2$	$^-1$
0	$3 \cdot 0 + 2$	2
1	$3 \cdot 1 + 2$	5
2	$3 \cdot 2 + 2$	8

The ordered pairs $({}^-1, {}^-1)$, $(0,2)$, $(1,5)$, and $(2,8)$ are solutions of the equation. Other solutions are possible.

You can test an ordered pair to determine whether it is a solution of a given equation.

Example Is $({}^-2, {}^-4)$ a solution of $y = 3x + 2$?

Replace x with $^-2$ and y with $^-4$.

$$y = 3x + 2$$
$$^-4 = 3({}^-2) + 2$$
$$^-4 = {}^-6 + 2$$
$$^-4 = {}^-4 \qquad \text{So, } ({}^-2, {}^-4) \text{ is a solution.}$$

- Is $(6,5)$ a solution of $y = 3x + 2$? Why or why not?

Check for Understanding

Solve the equation, using 4 as the replacement value for x.
Write the solution as an ordered pair.

1. $y = x + 3$ **2.** $y = x - 1$ **3.** $y = 3x$

Practice

Make a table of values for each equation. Then write the ordered pairs
that are solutions of each equation.

4. $y = x + 6$ **5.** $y = 4x$ **6.** $y = x - 4$

7. $y = x + {}^-3$ **8.** $y = 2x - 5$ **9.** $y = 3x + 6$

10. $y = 4(x + 2)$ **11.** $y = \frac{1}{2}x$ **12.** $y = {}^-\frac{1}{3}x + 2$

Determine whether the ordered pair is a solution of $y = {}^-3x + 4$.
Write *yes* or *no*.

13. $(1,2)$ **14.** $(2,{}^-2)$ **15.** $({}^-1,7)$ **16.** $(0,7)$ **17.** $\left(\frac{1}{3},3\right)$

Rewrite the equation to express *y* in terms of *x*. Then make a table of
values for the equation. Let $x = {}^-2, {}^-1, 0, 1,$ and 2.

18. $x - y = 3$ **19.** $2x + y = 6$ **20.** $8x + 2y = 20$

Mixed Applications

21. The number of hours Tim practices
soccer each week, *y*, is 2 hr more
than the number of hours he runs, *x*.
Write an equation to show the
relationship of the two activities.
Show three solutions of the
equation.

22. Margo earns four times as much
babysitting for the Perez family as
she does for the Lynn family. If she
earns $22.50 babysitting for both
families, how much does she earn
babysitting for each?

MATH CONNECTION

In a relation the *x*-coordinates of the ordered pairs are the **domain.**
The *y*-coordinates are the **range.** Give the domain and the range for
each relation.

23. $(0,0), (1,4), (2,{}^-4)$ **24.** $(1,1), (2,2), (3,3), (4,4)$ **25.** $(0,{}^-2), ({}^-1,{}^-3), ({}^-2,{}^-4)$

26. $({}^-5, {}^-5), ({}^-2,{}^-4), (3,{}^-5)$ **27.** $({}^-3,{}^-3), (0,4), ({}^-2,8)$ **28.** $(1,3), (3,5), (4,9), (7,{}^-6)$

Explain how you can find ordered pairs that are
solutions of an equation with two variables.

GRAPHING EQUATIONS

Jackson has decided that he will spend 2 more hours each week practicing lay-up shots than practicing other basketball skills.

You can write and graph an equation that shows the relation between the time he will practice other skills and the time he will practice lay-up shots.

Let x = the time for other skills, and let y = the time for lay-up shots.

$y = x + 2$ ⬅ 2 more hours

To graph $y = x + 2$, make a table of values. Then graph the ordered pairs and join them with a line.

x	$x + 2$	y	Solutions
0	$0 + 2$	2	(0,2)
1	$1 + 2$	3	(1,3)
2	$2 + 2$	4	(2,4)
3	$3 + 2$	5	(3,5)

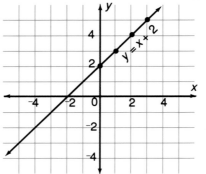

Notice that the ordered pairs lie on a straight line. An equation whose graph is a straight line is a **linear equation.** Other solutions of the equation can also be found on the line.

Talk About It

▶ What does the ordered pair (1,3) tell you about Jackson's practice times?

▶ Is the ordered pair ($^-4, ^-2$) a solution of the equation? Would you include this point on a graph that just showed Jackson's practice times? Why or why not?

Check for Understanding

Copy and complete each table of values. Then graph each equation.

1.

x	$y = x - 5$	y
0	$y = 0 - 5$	◼
1	$y = 1 - 5$	◼
2	$y = 2 - 5$	◼

2.

x	$y = 2x + 1$	y
0	$y = 2 \cdot 0 + 1$	◼
1	$y = 2 \cdot 1 + 1$	◼
2	$y = 2 \cdot 2 + 1$	◼

Connection, pages 482–483

Practice

Graph the equation. Let $x = {}^-1, 0, 1,$ and 2.

3. $y = x - 1$ **4.** $y = 2x + 2$ **5.** $y = {}^-x + 3$

Use the graph of $y = 2x + 4$ for Exercises 6–10.

6. What is the solution of the equation at point A?

7. What is the solution of the equation at point B?

8. What is the value of x when the value of y is 0?

9. What is another solution of $y = 2x + 4$?

10. Since the graph of $y = 2x + 4$ is a straight line, how many solutions of the equation do you think there are?

Graph the equations. Use at least three ordered pairs.

11. $y = x + 4$ **12.** $y = 2x - 2$ **13.** $y = 4x + 2$ **14.** $y = 4x$

15. $y = 9x - 3$ **16.** $y = x - 2$ **17.** $x + 2y = 2$ **18.** $y = x^2 + 1$

Mixed Applications

19. Jackson practices twice as long as Martin. Write an equation to find the number of hours, y, Jackson practices when Martin practices x hours. Graph the equation.

20. Use the graph in Exercise 19 to find how many hours Jackson practices when Martin practices $2\frac{1}{2}$ hr. How can you check your answer?

MIXED REVIEW

Evaluate the expression for $b = 3$ and $s = {}^-2$.

1. $b - 6$ **2.** $2s + 8$ **3.** $4b - s$ **4.** $\frac{2b}{3} + 3s$

Solve the equation.

5. $2x + 2 = 12$ **6.** $\frac{a}{2} = 4$ **7.** $y - 15 = 36$ **8.** $\frac{4}{9}n - 2 = 2$

9. $7x = 4.9$ **10.** $c + {}^-2 = 9$ **11.** $3t + 1 = {}^-2$ **12.** $\frac{d}{3} + 5 = {}^-2$

Describe the graph of the equation $y = {}^-5.$

WRAP UP...

PROBLEM *Solving*

Use a Graph to Estimate

Lucy is watching a thunderstorm approach. She counts 7 seconds between the time she sees lightning and the time she hears thunder. What is the approximate distance between Lucy and the lightning?

The graph shows the relation of the time between a flash of lightning and the resulting sound of thunder. Often a graph can be used to solve a problem when an approximate answer is needed.

▶ **UNDERSTAND**

What are you asked to find?

What facts are given?

▶ **PLAN**

How will you solve the problem?

You can use the graph to estimate the distance in miles. Find the point that shows the distance at 7 seconds, and read that distance from the graph.

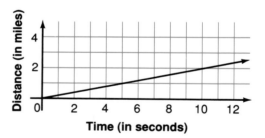

▶ **SOLVE**

On the graph, what distance corresponds to a time of 7 seconds?

Find 7 seconds on the horizontal axis. Then move straight up, and find the point where 7 intersects the graph. Look at the vertical axis to find the corresponding distance.

The distance between Lucy and the lightning is about 1.5 miles.

▶ **LOOK BACK**

How can you check your answer?

WHAT IF... . . . Lucy is 2 miles away from the lightning? How much time will pass from when she sees the lightning to when she hears the thunder?

Apply

The graph shows the rate at which sound travels in water. Use the graph for Exercises 1–4.

1. What is the approximate distance that sound travels in water in 2 sec?

2. A fisherman using sonar finds that sound waves take 0.5 sec to reach the bottom of the ocean. Estimate the depth of the ocean at this point.

3. About how many seconds does it take sound to travel 5 km in water?

4. Predict the approximate distance sound travels in water in 8 sec.

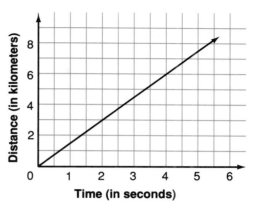

Distance (in kilometers) / **Time (in seconds)**

Mixed Applications ▶ **STRATEGIES** • Work Backward • Find a Pattern • Write an Equation • Use a Formula

Choose a strategy and solve.

5. Jess needs to catch a flight that leaves at 5:00 P.M.. It takes 1 hr to get to the airport, and he wants to be there 1 hr 15 min early. At what time should Jess leave home?

6. If the cost to rent a car is $25.00 per day and $0.08 for each mile traveled, how much will it cost to rent the car for 2 days and drive 210 mi?

7. The formula $d = 4.9t^2$ relates the distance, d, in meters to the number of seconds, t, that an object falls. Use the formula to find how far a baseball falls in 3.5 sec.

8. Draw the next figure in the pattern.

WRITER'S CORNER

9. Write a problem that can be solved by using the graph for the speed of sound in water. Exchange with a classmate and solve.

10. Write a problem that can be solved with the strategy *find a pattern*. Exchange with a classmate and solve.

EXPLORING
Slope of a Line

The measure of the steepness of a line is called the **slope** of the line. You can use graph paper to explore the slope of a line.

WORK TOGETHER

Building Understanding

In a coordinate plane, graph $A(2,1)$. Then graph $B(6,3)$. Draw a line through the points.

Talk About It

▶ From point A, move right until you are directly below point B. This is the horizontal change from point A to point B. How many units did you move?

▶ From point A, move up until you are directly across from B. This is the vertical change. How many units did you move?

▶ What is the ratio, in simplest form, of the vertical change to the horizontal change?

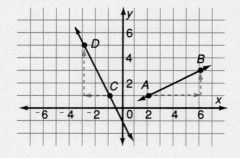

The ratio you found is the slope of the line that contains points A and B.

In the same coordinate plane, graph $C(^-1,1)$ and $D(^-3,5)$. Draw a line through the points.

Talk About It

▶ What is the horizontal change from C to D? Since you moved left in the coordinate plane, write this as a negative number.

▶ What is the vertical change from C to D?

▶ What is the ratio of the vertical change to the horizontal change? What is the slope of the line that contains points C and D?

Making the Connection

You can find the slope of a line as long as you know at least two points on the line. You can graph the points, or you can subtract the y-coordinates and the x-coordinates of the points.

Example Find the slope of the line containing the points $(3,1)$ and $(^-2,2)$.

Subtract the y-coordinates. $1 - 2 = {}^-1$ ← vertical change

Subtract the x-coordinates. $3 - {}^-2 = 5$ ← horizontal change

$$\frac{\text{vertical change}}{\text{horizontal change}} = \frac{^-1}{5} \leftarrow \text{slope}$$

Find the slope of the line containing the given points.

1. $(3,2), (^-2,^-1)$ **2.** $(4,^-4), (^-2,1)$ **3.** $(6,2), (1,^-3)$

Talk About It

▸ For Exercise 1, will you get the same slope if you use $2 - {}^-1$ for the vertical change and $^-2 - 3$ for the horizontal change? (HINT: Remember that the quotient of two negative numbers is positive.)

▸ Is the slope of a line that rises from left to right positive or negative?

▸ Is the slope of a line that falls from left to right positive or negative?

Checking Understanding

Find the slope of the line containing the given points.

4. $(4,2), (6,5)$ **5.** $(^-1,3), (4,6)$ **6.** $(2,2), (0,0)$

7. $(^-1,4), (5,2)$ **8.** $(2,^-3), (4,7)$ **9.** $(^-2,^-3), (^-4,^-1)$

Tell whether the slope is *positive* or *negative*.

10.
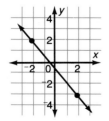

11.
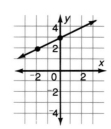

12.
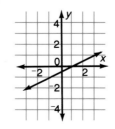

13.
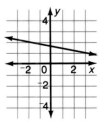

REVIEW AND MAINTENANCE

1. Tyrone bought a total of 9 audio cassettes and CD's for $61.00. The cassettes cost $6.20 each, and the CD's cost $7.50 each. How many of each item did Tyrone buy?

2. Paula borrowed $175 at a yearly interest rate of 11%. She paid her loan off in 18 months. About how much did Paula pay in interest?

3. A pet-store owner wanted to separate his fish so that the same number of fish were in each tank. When he separated the fish by twos, threes, fours, fives, or sixes, there was always one fish left over. What is the least number of fish the store owner could have had?

4. A building has six stories that are each the same height. It takes an elevator 6 sec to rise to the third floor. How many additional seconds will it take the elevator to rise from the third floor to the sixth floor?

5. Draw the figure that completes the pattern.

6. Richie has $15 more than Anne. Anne has $10 more than Jack. Together they have a total of $56. How much does Richie have?

Write in standard form.

7. 3.34 billion
8. 94 thousandths
9. 99.4 million
10. 0.38 thousand

Find the sum or difference.

11. $^-5 + ^-9$
12. $^-13 + 34$
13. $7 - ^-12$
14. $^-24 - 15$
15. $0.9 + ^-0.121$
16. $^-\frac{1}{2} + ^-1\frac{1}{6}$
17. $^-12.31 - 2.65$
18. $1\frac{1}{3} - 5$

Write in order from least to greatest.

19. $^-\frac{4}{5}, \frac{5}{4}, 1.3, ^-\frac{6}{4}$
20. $^-3.7, 3, ^-\frac{6}{8}, 3.1$
21. $1\frac{1}{8}, 1.4, 0.14, ^-1\frac{3}{4}$

Use the figure to find the measure of the given angle. $\overleftrightarrow{AB} \parallel \overleftrightarrow{CD}$ and $m\angle 1 = 125°$.

22. $m\angle 2$
23. $m\angle 4$
24. $m\angle 5$
25. $m\angle 7$
26. $m\angle 8$
27. $m\angle 3$

Write as a percent.

28. 0.65
29. $\frac{3}{4}$
30. 1.4
31. 0.04

Solve.

32. What number is 35% of 52?
33. What percent of 180 is 36?

294

Spotlight ON
PROBLEM SOLVING

Recognize Multiple Solutions

Sometimes, there is more than one solution to the same problem. Read and study this problem.

The school store is selling pencils for $0.10 each or 3 for a quarter. If Stacey buys 2 pencils and Ralph buys 10, what is the total amount they will pay for a dozen pencils? How is this different from what Ms. Sedlock will pay for a dozen pencils?

Talk About It

Work with a classmate to answer these questions. Be prepared to share your responses with the class.

a. How much will Stacey pay for her pencils?
b. How much will Ralph pay for his pencils?
c. How much will Stacey and Ralph pay together?
d. How much will Ms. Sedlock pay for her pencils?
e. How much more will Stacey and Ralph pay for a dozen pencils than Ms. Sedlock?

Apply

Read and solve. Make sure you answer all parts of each problem.

1. A one-way subway ticket costs $1.40. A round-trip ticket costs $2.60. A ten-pack has 10 round-trip tickets and costs $24.00. If you were going to take one trip on the subway and then return home, how much would you pay for your ticket? If you were going to use the subway every day for a full week, how much would you pay for your tickets? What would you pay for 30 days' worth of round-trip tickets on the subway?

2. A round-trip flight between Orlando and Baltimore costs $430 during the week. If the round-trip includes staying over on Saturday night, the cost is reduced to $300. Children under 12 can fly for half price during the week. If a family stays over on Saturday night, children can fly for $100 each. How much would it cost for a family of 4, with 2 children under 12, to fly during the week? How much less would the same family pay if they stayed over on Saturday night?

295

SYSTEMS OF EQUATIONS

Julia bought a baseball and a cap for $10. The baseball cost $2 more than the cap. What was the price of each item?

You can write two equations for the problem.

Let x = the price of the cap.
Let y = the price of the baseball.

$x + y = 10$, or $y = 10 - x$ ⟵ The cap and the baseball cost $10.

$y = x + 2$ ⟵ The baseball costs $2 more than the cap.

Two or more equations such as $y = 10 - x$ and $y = x + 2$ form a **system of equations.** To solve the system, you can graph both equations on the same coordinate plane. If the lines intersect at a point, the coordinates of that point are the **solution of the system.**

Step 1
Make a table of values for each equation.

x	$10 - x$	y	(x,y)
6	$10 - 6$	4	(6,4)
5	$10 - 5$	5	(5,5)
4	$10 - 4$	6	(4,6)
3	$10 - 3$	7	(3,7)

x	$x + 2$	y	(x,y)
0	$0 + 2$	2	(0,2)
1	$1 + 2$	3	(1,3)
2	$2 + 2$	4	(2,4)
3	$3 + 2$	5	(3,5)

Step 2
Graph both equations on the same coordinate plane.

Step 3
Label the point where the graphs of the equations intersect.

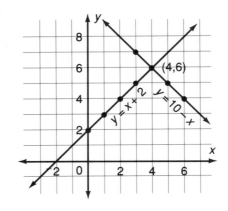

The ordered pair (4,6) is the solution of the system of equations. You can check the solution by substituting (4,6) in each equation.

So, the price of the baseball was $6 and the price of the cap was $4.

Check for Understanding

Solve the system by graphing.

1. $y = x - 2$
$y = 4x + 1$

2. $y = {}^-x + 2$
$y = 2x - 1$

3. $y = {}^-3x + 2$
$y = {}^-x + 4$

Practice

Solve the system by graphing.

4. $y = x + 5$
$y = 3 - x$

5. $y = x - 2$
$y = {}^-x + 6$

6. $y = 2x$
$y = 3x - 3$

7. $y = x + 4$
$y = 2x + 5$

8. $y = 2x$
$y = 3x + 1$

9. $y = {}^-2x$
$y = x + 3$

10. $y = 2x + 1$
$y = x - 1$

11. $y = 2x + 4$
$y = x + 5$

12. $x + y = 7$
$x - y = 1$

Mixed Applications

Write a system of equations for each of Exercises 13–14.
Solve the system by graphing.

13. Jane and Eric delivered a total of 20 newspapers. Jane delivered 4 more than Eric. How many newspapers did each deliver?

14. Alana spent a total of 12 hr last week on her math and science homework. She spent twice as much time on math as on science. How long did she spend on each?

15. Visual Thinking How many triangles are in this figure?

16. Logical Reasoning The sum of two numbers is 16. The first number is 3 times the second. What are the two numbers?

GEOGRAPHY CONNECTION

You can give the location of a point on a map as an ordered pair by using the longitude (a vertical line) and the latitude (a horizontal line). The location of Lusaka, for example, is (30° E, 15° S).

Give the location (longitude, latitude) of each city.

17. Cairo

18. Folgares

19. St. Louis

20. Mogadishu

21. El Obeid

22. Durban

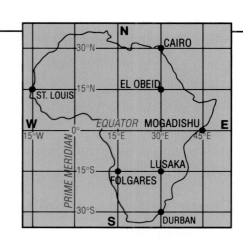

What are you finding when you find the solution of a system of equations?

WRAP UP...

GRAPHING INEQUALITIES

Wynn is on the school volleyball team. She found that the number of points she makes in each game is always greater than 3 times the number of times she serves.

You can find all the possible combinations of points and serves by writing and solving an inequality in two variables.

Let x = the number of times Wynn serves.
Let y = the number of points Wynn makes.

Then $y > 3x$. ⟵ inequality

Follow these steps to graph $y > 3x$.

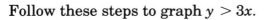

Step 1
Graph the line $y = 3x$. Use a dashed line to show that the line $y = 3x$ is not included in the solution of the inequality.

Step 2
Pick any point that is not on the line. ($^-4$,1) is not on the line. Replace x with $^-4$ and y with 1 in $y > 3x$.

$$1 > 3 \cdot {}^-4$$
$$1 > {}^-12$$

Since $1 > {}^-12$ is true, shade the graph on the side of the line containing ($^-4$,1).

Talk About It

▶ If the inequality in Step 2 had not been true, which side of the line would you have shaded?

▶ Is it possible for Wynn to serve 2 times and score 4 points in a game? Explain.

▶ Is it possible for Wynn to serve 2 times and score 7 points in a game? Explain.

▶ How would the graph of $y \geq 3x$ be different from the graph of $y > 3x$?

Check for Understanding

Graph each inequality.

1. $y > x + 3$ **2.** $y \leq 2x - 2$ **3.** $y \geq {}^-x + 4$

Practice

Graph each inequality.

4. $y > 2x$

5. $x < 1$

6. $x \le {}^-2$

7. $y \le 3x + 3$

8. $y > 2x - 1$

9. $y \le x$

10. $y < x - 1$

11. $y \ge 2x + 4$

12. $x + y \le 5$

Use the graph of $y < x - 2$ for Exercises 13–17.

13. Is $(0,0)$ a solution of $y < x - 2$?

14. Name an ordered pair that is a solution of the inequality.

15. Name an ordered pair that is not a solution of the inequality.

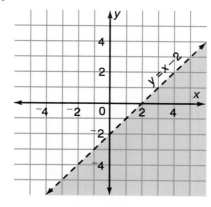

16. Is $(4,2)$ a solution of $y < x - 2$?

17. Name an ordered pair that is a solution of $y \le x - 2$.

Mixed Applications

Tracy keeps the statistics for the volleyball team. Her graph shows how she can spend up to $1.80 on pencils at $0.20 each and on pads of paper at $0.30 each. In the graph, $(4,3)$ means a purchase of 4 pencils and 3 pads of paper.

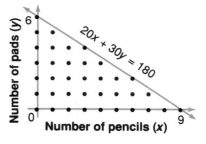

Use the graph for Exercises 18–22.

18. Since x pencils cost $0.20x$, what do y pads of paper cost?

19. Can Tracy buy 6 pencils and 4 pads of paper? Is $(6,4)$ on the graph?

20. Suppose Tracy does not buy any pencils. How many pads of paper can she buy?

21. Which four ways can Tracy spend exactly $1.80? Write the answers as ordered pairs.

22. In how many ways can Tracy spend $1.80 or less?

23. Making Choices The volleyball coach can buy knee pads at 6 for $25.50 or 4 pair for $32.40. Which choice gives the coach the lower price per knee pad?

24. Logical Reasoning A building has 6 doors. Find the number of ways a person can enter the building by one door and leave by another door.

How do you know whether to make the line solid or broken when you graph an inequality?

How can you move the letter N to make it look like a Z?

TRANSFORMATIONS

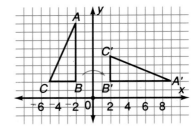

In each of the following graphs, the original figure, △ *ABC,* has been moved to a new location. △ *A'B'C'* is the image of the original figure. (Read: triangle *A* prime, *B* prime, *C* prime.)

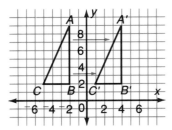

△ *ABC* was moved 6 units to the right. △ *A'B'C'* is a **translation,** or slide image, of △ *ABC.*

△ *ABC* was flipped over the *y*-axis, the **line of symmetry.** △ *A'B'C'* is a **reflection,** or mirror image, of △ *ABC.*

△ *ABC* was turned around (0,0), the **point of rotation.** △ *A'B'C'* is a **rotation,** or turn image, of △ *ABC.*

Translations, reflections, and rotations are types of transformations. A **transformation** is the movement of a geometric figure. Translations, reflections, and rotations are transformations that do not change the shape or size of the figure.

Example Translate △ *RST* down 6 units. Write the coordinates of the vertices of the figure and its translation.

Mark *R'* 6 units down from *R.*
Mark *S'* 6 units down from *S.*
Mark *T'* 6 units down from *T.*

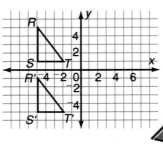

Figure	Translation
$R(^-5,5)$	$R'(^-5,^-1)$
$S(^-5,1)$	$S'(^-5,^-5)$
$T(^-2,1)$	$T'(^-2,^-5)$

Talk About It

▶ In the translation of △ *RST,* why did the *y*-coordinates of the vertices change and the *x*-coordinates remain the same?

▶ How would △ *RST* have to be translated if you wanted the *x*-coordinates of the vertices to change?

▶ Is △ *R'S'T'* the same size and shape as △ *RST*?

More Examples

A. Reflect rectangle *WXZY* over the *x*-axis. Write the coordinates of the figure and its reflection.

Figure	Reflection
$W(^-2,4)$	$W'(^-2,^-4)$
$X(3,4)$	$X'(3,^-4)$
$Z(3,2)$	$Z'(3,^-2)$
$Y(^-2,2)$	$Y'(^-2,^-2)$

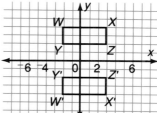

B. Rotate $\triangle DEF$ 180° counterclockwise, using (0,0) as the point of rotation. Write the coordinates of the figure and its rotation.

Step 1 Trace $\triangle DEF$. Draw a ray as shown from (0,0).

Step 2 Hold down the tracing paper with your pencil point on (0,0). Turn the paper counterclockwise until the ray has moved 180°.

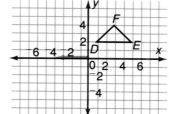

Step 3 Press through the tracing paper to mark the vertices of the rotation. Remove the paper and draw the rotation, $\triangle D'E'F'$, on the coordinate plane.

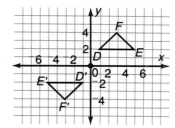

Figure	Rotation
$D(1,2)$	$D'(^-1,^-2)$
$E(5,2)$	$E'(^-5,^-2)$
$F(3,4)$	$F'(^-3,^-4)$

Talk About It

▶ In Example **A,** the *y*-coordinates changed from *y* in the figure to ^-y in the reflection. What would the line of symmetry have to be in order for the *x*-coordinates to change from *x* to ^-x?

▶ In Example **B,** would the rotation be in a different position if the figure had been turned 180° clockwise? Explain.

▶ Does the position of the point of rotation affect the position of the rotation? Give an example to support your answer.

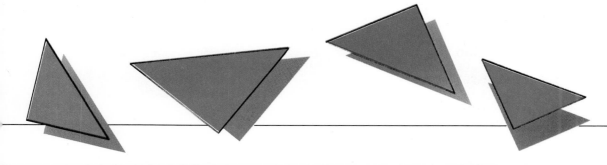

301

Check for Understanding

Identify the type of transformation. Write *translation, reflection,* or *rotation.*

1.

2.

3.

4.

5.

6.

Copy △ *ABC* on a coordinate plane. Perform the given transformation. Give the coordinates of the vertices of the transformation.

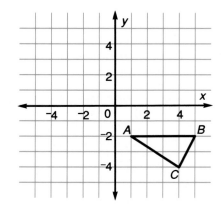

7. Reflect △ *ABC* over the x-axis.

8. Rotate △ *ABC* 90° clockwise, using (0,0) as the point of rotation.

9. Translate △ *ABC* left 4 units.

Practice

Graph the figure and its image. Then tell whether the transformation is a *translation,* a *reflection,* or a *rotation.*

	Figure	Image
10.	$A(^-5,^-2)$	$A'(2,^-2)$
	$B(^-5,^-6)$	$B'(2,^-6)$
	$C(^-2,^-6)$	$C'(5,^-6)$

	Figure	Image
11.	$A(1,3)$	$A'(^-1,3)$
	$B(5,5)$	$B'(^-5,5)$
	$C(5,3)$	$C'(^-5,3)$

	Figure	Image
12.	$A(3,^-3)$	$A'(3,3)$
	$B(5,^-3)$	$B'(3,5)$
	$C(3,^-6)$	$C'(6,3)$
	$D(5,^-6)$	$D'(6,5)$

	Figure	Image
13.	$A(1,1)$	$A'(^-5,^-6)$
	$B(2,5)$	$B'(^-4,^-2)$
	$C(6,6)$	$C'(0,^-1)$

	Figure	Image
14.	$A(^-2,^-1)$	$A'(2,^-1)$
	$B(^-1,^-2)$	$B'(1,^-2)$
	$C(^-4,^-5)$	$C'(4,^-5)$
	$D(^-5,^-4)$	$D'(5,^-4)$

	Figure	Image
15.	$A(^-1,^-2)$	$A'(1,2)$
	$B(^-4,^-3)$	$B'(4,3)$
	$C(^-4,^-8)$	$C'(4,8)$

Give the coordinates of the point that is a translation of the given point.

16. Move (5,9) 6 units left.

17. Move ($^-2,^-4$) 5 units up.

18. Move (0,3) 4 units down and 3 units left.

19. Move ($^-4$,3) 2 units up and 5 units right.

Using the x-axis as the line of symmetry, give the coordinates of the point that is the reflection of the given point.

20. $(6,1)$ **21.** $(^-2,3)$ **22.** $(0,^-4)$ **23.** $(^-4,^-5)$

Using the y-axis as the line of symmetry, give the coordinates of the point that is the reflection of the given point.

24. $(4,2)$ **25.** $(2,^-7)$ **26.** $(^-1,^-5)$ **27.** $(^-4,0)$

Copy quadrilateral *ABCD* on a coordinate plane. Then draw the rotation. Use (0,0) as the point of rotation.

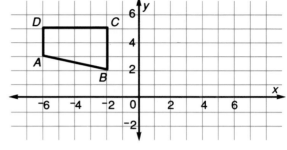

28. Rotate 180° clockwise.

29. Rotate 90° clockwise.

30. Rotate 90° counterclockwise.

31. Rotate 270° counterclockwise.

32. Rotate quadrilateral *ABCD* 90° clockwise, using $(^-2,2)$ as the point of rotation. What are the coordinates of the vertices of the rotation? How is this image different from the image you found in Exercise 29?

Mixed Applications

33. An artist created a border design by reflecting this figure over the y-axis, translating the reflection 5 units to the right, and rotating the translation 180° clockwise. The point of rotation was a point 1 unit to the right of the point inside the translation. Use a piece of graph paper to show the design.

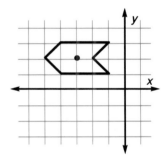

34. Ted and Will live 3 mi apart. At 9:00 A.M. each leaves his house and walks toward the other's house. Ted walks at a rate of 5 mph. Will walks at a rate of 4 mph. At what time do they meet?

MIXED REVIEW

Compare. Write $<$, $>$, or $=$.

1. $|^-8|$ ● $|^-10|$ **2.** 0 ● $|^-7|$ **3.** 23^{-2} ● 23^2

4. 5.6×10^4 ● $5,600$ **5.** 5.685 ● $5\frac{3}{4}$ **6.** 0.00034 ● 3.4×10^{-4}

Explain how you can find a translation, a reflection, and a rotation of a figure.

WRAP UP...

Martha has $0.95 in nickels and quarters. She has fewer than 5 of each type of coin. Find the number of each type of coin she has.

Word problems that seem to have less information than needed to solve them can often be solved using a *guess-and-check* strategy.

► **UNDERSTAND**

What are you asked to find?

What facts are given?

► **PLAN**

What strategy will you use?

You can *write an equation* with two variables and use the *guess-and-check* strategy to find the solution.

► **SOLVE**

How can you represent the number of nickels and the number of quarters?

Let x = the number of nickels, with a value of $0.05 each.
Let y = the number of quarters, with a value of $0.25 each.

$$\underbrace{\text{value of nickels}}_{0.05x} + \underbrace{\text{value of quarters}}_{0.25y} = \$0.95$$

$$0.05x + 0.25y = 0.95$$

Think: x and y must be whole numbers less than 5, and y cannot be 4 because the value of the coins would exceed the total amount.

Guess 1: Let $x = 2$ and $y = 2$.
Check 1: $0.05(2) + 0.25(2) = 0.60$ ← too small; use greater values

Guess 2: Let $x = 4$ and $y = 3$.
Check 2: $0.05(4) + 0.25(3) = 0.95$ ← correct: 4 nickels, 3 quarters

► **LOOK BACK**

What other strategy can you use to solve the problem?

WHAT IF... . . . the total value of Martha's coins were $0.65? How many of each type of coin would Martha have?

Apply

(1) Max sold some baseball cards for $0.55 each and some football cards for $0.15 each. He sold fewer than 7 of each type and made $3.10 in all. How many of each type of card did Max sell?

(2) Carol earned $19.75 working part-time at two stores. She made $3.75 an hour at one store and $4.25 at another. She worked fewer than 5 hr at each store. How many hours did Carol work at each store?

(3) Tickets for the soccer game cost $5.00 for adults and $2.50 for students. Connie paid $17.50 for fewer than 5 tickets. How many adult tickets and how many student tickets did Connie buy?

(4) Sid bought some stamps for $0.29 each and some for $0.19 each. He has fewer than 6 stamps of each type. How many of each type did Sid buy for $1.83?

Mixed Applications	STRATEGIES	• Draw a Picture • Guess and Check • Make a Table • Write an Equation

Choose a strategy and solve.

(5) At the Athletic Club bake sale, Julia sold slices of apple pie for $0.50 each and slices of carrot cake for $0.75 each. How many of each did Julia sell if she made $5.75? Give all possible combinations.

(6) An assistant coach divided all the football uniforms into 2 equal piles. After the coach gave each of 10 players a uniform from one pile, there were 12 uniforms left in that pile. How many uniforms were there in the beginning?

(7) The Athletic Club is mailing 10,000 newsletters to area families. On Monday the club mailed 30% of the newsletters. Each day after Monday, the club mailed 30% of the remaining newsletters. How many newsletters were left to mail after Thursday?

(8) Mr. Hedron earns $24,000 per year and receives an 8% raise each year. Mr. Stiles earns $27,300 per year and receives a 5% raise each year. About how many years will it be before Mr. Hedron and Mr. Stiles earn about the same amount of money per year?

WRITER'S CORNER

(9) Write a problem similar to Exercise 1. Exchange with a classmate and solve.

(10) Write a problem similar to Exercise 7. Exchange with a classmate and solve.

Vocabulary Check

Choose a word from the box to complete each sentence.

function
origin
quadrants
relation
slope
transformation

1. The x-axis and the y-axis of the coordinate plane intersect at a point called the __?__. *(page 282)*

2. The coordinate plane is divided into four parts called __?__. *(page 282)*

3. The measure of the steepness of a line is called the __?__ of the line. *(page 292)*

4. A set of ordered pairs is a __?__. *(page 284)*

5. A movement of a geometric figure that does not change the size or shape of the figure is a __?__. *(page 300)*

6. A relation in which no two ordered pairs have the same x-value is a __?__. *(page 284)*

Concept Check

Give the coordinates of each point, and identify the quadrant in which each point is found. *(page 282)*

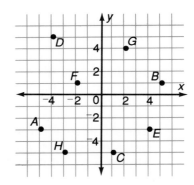

7. A 8. B 9. C 10. D

11. E 12. F 13. G 14. H

For Exercises 15–16, tell whether the relation is a function. Write *yes* or *no*. *(page 284)*

15. (3,5), (4,7), (5,9), (6,10)   16. ($^-$1,4), ($^-$2,0), ($^-$1,4)

17. When you find the slope of a line, which coordinates do you subtract to find the horizontal change? *(page 292)*

18. How can you find the solution of a system of equations? *(page 296)*

19. Does the graph of the inequality $y < x - 4$ include the graph of $y = x - 4$? *(page 298)*

20. Is this transformation of the letter B a translation, a reflection, or a rotation? *(page 300)*

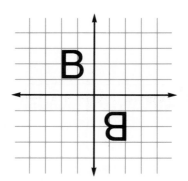

Skill Check

Graph the equation. Let $x = {}^-1$, 0, 1, and 2. *(pages 286, 288)*

21. $y = x + 6$ **22.** $y = 4x - 5$ **23.** $y = 12 - 3x$

Find the slope of the line containing the given points. *(page 292)*

24. $(1,1), ({}^-3,{}^-3)$ **25.** $(2,4), ({}^-2,2)$ **26.** $({}^-3,3), (1,1)$

Solve the system by graphing. Write the ordered pair of the solution.
(page 296)

27. $y = 4 - x$ **28.** $y = {}^-2x$ **29.** $y = x + 2$
     $y = x - 2$ $y = x + 3$ $y = 4 - x$

Graph each inequality. *(page 298)*

30. $y \geq x - 1$ **31.** $y > x$ **32.** $y < x + 1$

Graph △ ABC on a coordinate plane. Graph the transformation of △ ABC. Write the coordinates of the vertices of the transformation. *(page 300)*

33. Translate △ ABC 6 units to the right.

34. Rotate △ ABC 180° clockwise, using (0,0) as the point of rotation.

35. Reflect △ ABC over the x-axis.

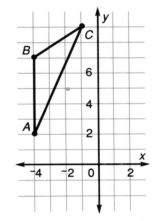

Problem-Solving Check

The graph shows reaction distance—the distance a car travels between the time the driver decides to stop and the time the driver applies the brakes. Use the graph for Exercises 36–37.
(page 290)

36. Estimate the reaction distance for a car traveling 30 mph.

37. Estimate the reaction distance for a car traveling 50 mph.

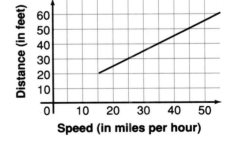

Solve. *(page 304)*

38. Joyce paid $25.32 for 36 T-shirts. Packages of 8 cost $5.25 each, and packages of 4 cost $3.19 each. If Joyce bought fewer than 5 packages of each size, how many of each size did she buy?

39. Bobby has $1.25 in dimes and quarters. He has fewer than 6 of each type of coin. How many of each type of coin does he have?

CHAPTER TEST

Write the coordinates of the point.

1. D **2.** B **3.** J

4. F **5.** G

Name the point given by the coordinates.

6. $(1,3)$ **7.** $(2,^-2)$

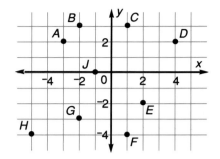

Copy the figure for Exercises 8–10.

8. Translate the figure 5 units down.

9. Reflect the figure over the y-axis.

10. Rotate the figure 180°, using $(0,0)$ as the point of rotation.

Graph the equation.

11. $y = 2x + 3$ **12.** $y = x - 4$ **13.** $y = x$

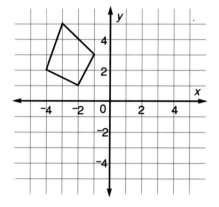

Find the slope of the line containing the given points.

14. $(4,5), (^-1,^-1)$ **15.** $(^-2,^-2), (4,6)$

Solve the system of equations by graphing.

16. $y = x - 3$
    $y = ^-x + 3$

17. $y = 2x + 1$
    $y = ^-x + 4$

18. $y = 3 - x$
    $y = x - 5$

Graph the inequality.

19. $y < x + 3$ **20.** $y \geq 2x - 5$ **21.** $y > ^-x + 1$

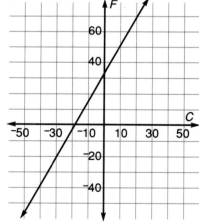

The graph shows the relation between degrees Fahrenheit, °F, and degrees Celsius, °C. Use the graph for Exercises 22–23.

22. Estimate the Celsius temperature for a Fahrenheit temperature of 60°.

23. Estimate the Fahrenheit temperature for a Celsius temperature of $^-10°$.

24. Sue bought some pens for $0.80 each and some pencils for $0.25 each. She bought fewer than 5 of each and paid $3.95. How many pens did Sue buy?

25. Rob has $3.45 in dimes and quarters. He has fewer than 13 of each type of coin. Find the number of each type of coin he has.

Teamwork PROJECT

EXERCISE AND THE HEART

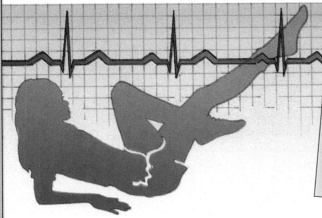

Your body needs more oxygen when you exercise than when you are sitting still. To get more oxygen to your body, your heart pumps blood faster. Your heartbeat rate increases.

Work with your teammates to show the relationship between a person's heartbeat rate and the elapsed time from the start of exercising to the finish.

DECIDE

As a team, discuss the exercises you can perform that will increase heartbeat rate. You may want to consider walking, running in place, or climbing stairs. Choose one exercise.

Choose one teammate to perform the exercise.

DO

Have the teammate sit quietly for a few minutes. Then measure the heartbeat rate by taking the pulse. Use the ordered pair (0, rate) to record the results.

Have the teammate perform the exercise for $\frac{1}{2}$ min, 1 min, and $1\frac{1}{2}$ min, with rest periods between the exercise periods. Measure the heartbeat rate at the end of each exercise period. Record the ordered pairs (minutes, rate).

Graph your results on a coordinate plane.

SHARE

Compare your team's results with those of other teams.

Talk About It

- Did your teammate's heartbeat rate increase as the exercise time increased? Predict rates for longer times.

- Is the relation you graphed also a function? Explain.

- Do all of the graphs look the same? Explain.

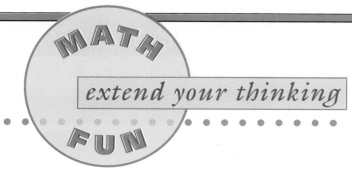

EQUATIONS FOR IMAGE POINTS

You can map points in the coordinate plane onto image points with equations that relate (x,y) to (x',y'). Below is the equation and graph for a transformation of $\triangle ABC$ with vertices $A(1,2)$, $B(1,4)$, and $C(5,4)$.

$x' = x + 3$ and $y' = y - 1$

A(1,2)	A'(4,1)
B(1,4)	B'(4,3)
C(5,4)	C'(8,3)

$\triangle ABC$ is translated 3 units to the right and 1 unit down.

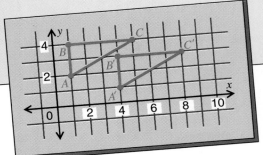

Graph $\triangle ABC$ on a coordinate plane. Then graph the image of $\triangle ABC$, using the equations. Describe each transformation.

1. $x' = x - 6$, and $y' = y$
2. $x' = x$, and $y' = {}^-y$

On a new coordinate plane, graph trapezoid $ABCD$ with vertices $A(1,3)$, $B(1,1)$, $C(5,3)$, and $D(3,4)$. Then graph the three images of trapezoid $ABCD$, using the equations in Exercises 3–5.

3. $x' = {}^-x$, and $y' = {}^-y$
4. $x' = y$, and $y' = {}^-x$
5. $x' = {}^-y$, and $y' = x$

 CHALLENGE

Logical Reasoning

If $\frac{1}{3}$ of 12 pears cost $0.36, what does $\frac{1}{4}$ of 12 pears cost?

Number Sense

What digit does each letter represent?

$$\begin{array}{r} AAA \\ -BB \\ \hline AC \end{array}$$

Write the letter of the correct answer.

1. Which is the opposite of $\frac{1}{17}$?

   A. $^-17$
   B. $^-\frac{1}{17}$
   C. $\frac{17}{17}$
   D. 17

2. Which is the LCD of $\frac{1}{3}$ and $\frac{5}{12}$?

   A. 3
   B. 4
   C. 12
   D. 36

3. Which is greater than 0.00586?

   A. 0.00565
   B. 0.0058
   C. 0.00587
   D. not here

4. $11 + {}^-21$

   A. $^-32$
   B. $^-10$
   C. 10
   D. 32

5. Which ordered pair is a solution of the equation $y = 2x - 1$?

   A. (2,3)
   B. ($^-$2,3)
   C. (3,3)
   D. (3,2)

6. Which rational number is between 0.56 and 0.57?

   A. 0.55
   B. 0.563
   C. 0.5701
   D. 0.575

7. Which is the average of 17, 3.6, 0.24, and 3.86?

   A. 3.73
   B. 6.175
   C. 24.7
   D. 61.75

8. Which is the name of the point (0,0) in the coordinate plane?

   A. quadrant
   B. origin
   C. axis
   D. slope

9. Which is the reciprocal of $\frac{15}{3}$?

   A. $\frac{3}{15}$
   B. $\frac{1}{3}$
   C. 5
   D. 15

10. Which angle has a degree measure that is less than 90°?

    A. obtuse
    B. acute
    C. right
    D. straight

11. Garth's bill at the restaurant totals $6.85. Garth leaves a tip that is about 15% of the bill. Estimate the amount of the tip.

    A. about $0.15
    B. about $1.05
    C. about $7.00
    D. about $10.50

12. Monica has 7 more books than Sue has. Monica has 29 books. Which equation can you use to find the number of books Sue has?

    A. $x - 29 = 7$
    B. $x + 7 = 29$
    C. $7x = 29$
    D. $\frac{x}{7} = 29$

10

STATISTICS AND GRAPHING

Did you know . . .

. . . that the three most popular school sports are football, basketball, and track and field?

Talk About It

What information will you need to determine the three most popular sports at your school?

What number describes the age of most of the students in your class?

ANALYZING DATA
Mean, Median, and Mode

Amanda scored the following points in the first 12 basketball games of the season. How can she analyze her scores to determine how well she is doing?

11   13   25   16   12   14   12   23   10   19   22   12

The mean, the median, and the mode are **measures of central tendency.** They can describe her scores.

The **mean,** or average, is the sum of a set of data divided by the number of items in the set.

The **median** of a set of data is the middle number, or the average of the two middle numbers, when the numbers are arranged in order.

The **mode** is the number or numbers that occur most frequently in a set of data. There is no mode when all of the numbers occur an equal number of times.

This table summarizes the measures of central tendency for Amanda's basketball scores.

Amanda's Basketball Scores		
Mean	Median	Mode
15.75	13.5	12

- How were the mean, median, and mode determined?

- Which measure of central tendency most accurately describes her scores?

- Is arranging the set of data in order helpful? For which measures of central tendency?

- What if Amanda's two lowest scores had not been included? How would the mean, median, and mode of the scores be affected?

- Suppose the score of 14 is replaced with a score of 15. How would the median of Amanda's scores change?

Talk About It

▶ Which measure of central tendency gives the best description of these salaries? $1,050; $570; $460; $430; $410; $390; $390

▶ Which measure of central tendency is the fairest representation of these test scores? 95, 95, 90, 67, 66, 60, 55

▶ Give an example of data that would best be described by the mode.

Check for Understanding

Tell which measure of central tendency was used. Write *mean, median,* or *mode.*

1. Blue is the students' favorite color.

2. The average American household contains 2.66 people.

3. The age of half the students is 13 yr 4 mo or greater.

Find the mean, the median, and the mode of each set of data.

4. 0, 1, 3, 5, 0, 5, 6, 2

5. 2.3, 6.2, 5.1, 4.7, 3.8

6. $4, 2\frac{3}{4}, 4, 3, 5\frac{1}{2}, 4\frac{3}{4}$

Practice

Find the mean, the median, and the mode for each set of data. Round the answers for Exercises 7–8 to the nearest hundredth.

7. 75, 88, 90, 56, 75, 77, 90

8. 2.63, 9.61, 3.057, 8.39, 5.12

9. 8 ft 7 in., 7 ft 10 in., 5 ft 4 in., 5 ft 4 in., 10 ft 5 in.

10. 4 lb, 6 lb 8 oz, 2 lb, 4 lb, 3 lb, 1 lb 8 oz

Use the set of data in Exercise 7. Write the number or numbers that you should remove from the set of data to make each statement correct.

11. There is no mode.

12. The mode is 90.

13. The median is 82.5.

Write *true* or *false* for each.

14. Some sets of data have no mode.

15. Every set of data has a median.

16. The mean is included as an item in every set of data.

17. The median may be the average of the two middle numbers in the data.

Mixed Applications

Robert did lawn work for his neighbors 8 times last summer. The numbers of hours he worked were 2, 4, 2, 3, $3\frac{1}{2}$, 4, $5\frac{1}{2}$, and 4.

18. Find the mean, the median, and the mode of the number of hours Robert worked.

19. Robert charged his neighbors $20 each time he worked for them last summer. How much did he earn?

EVERYDAY CONNECTION

20. Make a list of your test and quiz scores in each of three of your classes. Find the mean, median, and mode for each set of data. Which measure of central tendency best represents each set of scores? Explain. Which measure of central tendency would you use as your average test score? Explain.

When can a mean be a misleading measure of central tendency? Give an example.

WRAP UP...

How can you find the range of heights of the students in your math class?

The height of each student in Mrs. Rheem's class was measured in centimeters. How can the class organize and display the data?

The class uses a **side-by-side frequency table** and a **side-by-side histogram** to organize and display this data.

Students' Heights				
Boys		Interval	Girls	
Tally	Frequency	Height in cm	Frequency	Tally
II	2	170–179		
I	1	160–169	2	II
III	3	150–159	1	I
II	2	140–149	2	II
I	1	130–139	3	III
		120–129	2	II

Students' Heights				
Boys		Interval	Girls	
		Height in cm		
		170–179		
		160–169		
		150–159		
		140–149		
		130–139		
		120–129		

4 3 2 1   **Frequency**   1 2 3 4

Both the frequency table and the histogram show the frequency within intervals of height. The data is grouped into six equal intervals. The first interval is 120–129 cm.

- Which interval represents $33\frac{1}{3}\%$ of the boys' heights?

- How many students have a height between 130 and 139 cm?

> The mode is the midpoint of the interval that contains the greatest number of items of data.

You can calculate the midpoint of an interval. For example, the midpoint of the interval 170–179 cm is 174.5 cm.   **Think:** $\frac{170 + 179}{2} = 174.5$

- What is the midpoint of the interval 140–149 cm?

The definitions of range and mode must be adapted to apply to intervals. The range is the difference between the midpoint of the highest interval and the midpoint of the lowest interval.

How do you calculate the boys' range of heights?

Think: $174.5 - 134.5 = 40$ So, the range is 40 cm.

midpoint of highest interval └── midpoint of lowest interval

- How can you find the mode for the girls heights?

Check for Understanding

Use the frequency table for Exercises 1–3.

1. What is the midpoint of the 71–80% interval?

2. What is the range of the girls' test scores?

3. What is the mode of the boys' test scores?

Use the histogram for Exercises 4–6.

4. What is the mode for the students' heights?

5. What is the range of heights for all students?

6. Which height interval represents the least number of girls?

Math Test Scores				
Boys		Interval	Girls	
Tally	Frequency	Score (%)	Frequency	Tally
IIII	4	91–100	3	III
IIII	4	81–90	4	IIII
HH	5	71–80	5	HH
III	3	61–70	2	II
I	1	51–60	1	I
I	1	41–50	1	I

Practice

7. Make a side-by-side frequency table and a side-by-side histogram for the science test scores. Use intervals of 20–29, 30–39, 40–49, . . .

Students' Heights		
Boys	Height (cm)	Girls
	165–169	
	160–164	
	155–159	
	150–154	
	145–149	

6 5 4 3 2 1   Frequency   1 2 3 4 5 6

Use your side-by-side frequency table and side-by-side histogram for Exercises 8–11.

8. What is the range of scores for the boys? for the girls?

9. What is the mode of scores for all students?

10. How many students have scores in the 70–79% interval or greater?

11. How many girls scored in the 60–69% interval or less?

Science Test Scores (in percent)									
Boys					Girls				
90	84	97	59	80	68	83	95	78	22
52	75	80	66	76	74	31	77	82	85
95	77	54	80	49	83	28	99	62	76

Mixed Applications

12. **Organize and Analyze Data** Look at Exercises 1–6. Calculate the frequency with which each vowel appears. Display the data in a frequency table. Which vowel appears most frequently? Which vowel appears least frequently?

13. A pound of turkey costs $5.99. Estimate the cost per ounce and the cost for $\frac{3}{4}$ lb.

What are the advantages and disadvantages of displaying data in a histogram?

WRAP
UP...

More Practice, Lesson 10.2, page H66

317

LINE GRAPHS

Yvette recorded the average high and low temperatures every month in Atlanta. How can she display this data for her science project?

Yvette used **line graphs** because they show changes that occur over a period of time.

This line graph shows average high temperatures in Atlanta each month.

This double-line graph shows Atlanta's average monthly high and low temperatures.

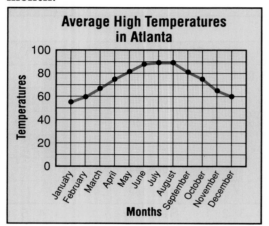

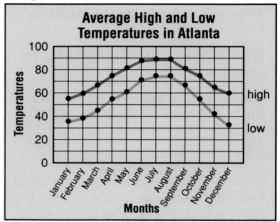

- Which months have the same high temperature and the same low temperature?

- If you want to visit Atlanta when the daily temperatures range between 55° and 80°F, which months should you choose?

These line graphs show a car's speed over time.

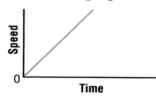

A car starting from a stop and increasing in speed

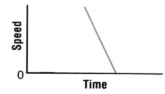

A car decreasing in speed and coming to a stop

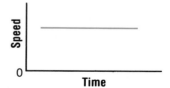

A car moving at a constant speed

Talk About It

▶ How can you describe the car-speed situation that the line graph represents?

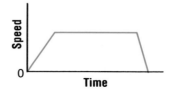

318

Check for Understanding

Use the graph for Exercises 1–4.

1. What interval does the vertical scale use?

2. How many bicycle club members were there in May 1991?

3. During which time period did the greatest growth in club membership occur?

4. How can you tell that the bicycle club membership was greater in 1991 than in 1990?

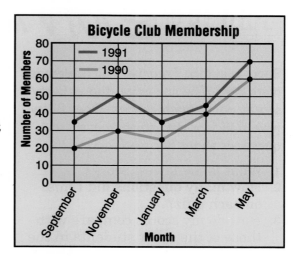

Practice

For Exercise 5, identify the graph that represents the situation. Write **a**, **b**, or **c**.

5. You are driving at the speed limit. You slow down and stop the car to have lunch. Then you start, accelerate to the speed limit, and drive at this speed.

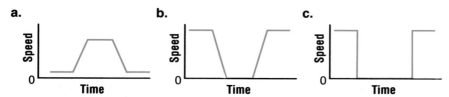

6. Construct a double-line graph for the data in the following table.

Average Monthly Precipitation (in inches)											
Month	Jan.	Feb.	Mar.	Apr.	May	June	July	Aug.	Sept.	Oct.	Nov.	Dec.
Anchorage	0.8	0.9	0.7	0.7	0.6	1.1	2.0	2.1	2.5	1.7	1.1	1.1
Honolulu	3.8	2.7	3.5	1.5	1.2	0.5	0.5	0.6	0.6	1.9	3.2	3.4

Mixed Applications

7. You are building a set of shelves. You need two 28-in. boards to complete the project. You have a $3\frac{1}{2}$-ft board. Do you have enough lumber? Why or why not?

8. **Logical Reasoning** Make a graph to represent an estimate of the speed of the roller coaster as it travels along the track.

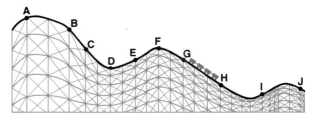

When is it appropriate to use a double-line graph?

Betty is in Mrs. Freeman's eighth-grade math class. The line graph shows Betty's scores on 12 math quizzes. Does Betty have sufficient data to answer these questions about her math quizzes?

1. What is my lowest score?
2. How many questions did I miss on each quiz?
3. How do my scores compare with those of the other students in the class?
4. What is my average score?

Sometimes, you may find that you do not have sufficient data to solve a problem.

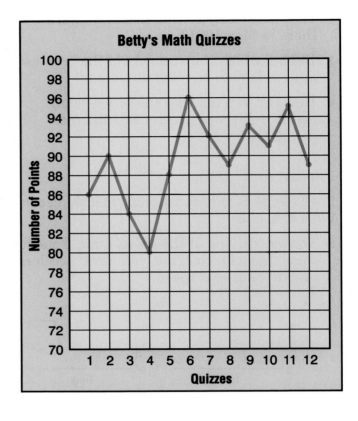

▶ **UNDERSTAND**

What are you asked to find?

What information are you given?

▶ **PLAN**

How can you solve the problem?

You can analyze the data to see whether it is sufficient or insufficient to solve the problem.

▶ **SOLVE**

Is there sufficient information to answer the questions?

1. The information needed is Betty's scores on the 12 quizzes. The data is sufficient.

2. The information needed is the number of questions Betty missed on each quiz. The data is insufficient.

3. The information needed is a comparison of Betty's scores with those of other students. The data is insufficient.

4. The information needed is Betty's scores on the 12 quizzes. The data is sufficient.

▶ **LOOK BACK**

How can you check your answers?

WHAT IF... . . . you are given the number of points for each question on the quizzes? Which question can you answer?

320

Apply

The map shows the national weather forecast for February 21. Decide whether the map gives you sufficient data to answer Exercises 1–5. Write *sufficient* or *insufficient* for each question. Then answer those for which the data is sufficient.

(1) What is the symbol for a cold front?

(2) When will it stop snowing in Chicago?

(3) What is the range of temperatures in Miami?

(4) What range of temperatures is shown?

(5) How much warmer will it be in Denver than in Boise?

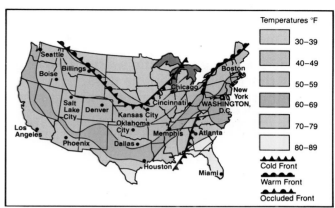

Mixed Applications | **STRATEGIES** | • Guess and Check • Work Backward • Find a Pattern • Use a Formula

Choose a strategy and solve.

(6) Find the ages of 4 college students who have a mean age of 27 yr. The median and mode of their ages is 25 yr. The range of their ages is 16 yr.

(7) Mr. and Mrs. Martin borrow $6,800 for 3 yr. The interest rate is 14% per year. How much interest will they pay? Find the total amount they will pay.

(8) The original price of a stereo was $150.00. The stereo is marked down every week until it is sold. So far, the sale prices have been $135.00, $121.50, and $109.35. What is the pattern?
HINT: Find the discount rate.

(9) The Ames family's porch is 8 ft by 10 ft. They plan to enlarge the width to 16 ft and the length to 20 ft. How many times greater is the area of the new porch than the area of the old porch?

(10) Jovita bought one share of stock in the ABC Toy Company. The price of the stock increased $0.30. Then, the price went down $1.20. Next, the price decreased $0.38. Soon, the price fell another $1.38. When it fell another $0.15, Jovita sold the stock for $17.08. What was the original price of the share of stock?

(11) Mr. Russo has a circular flower bed with a radius of 14 ft. He plans to spread peat moss, using one bag to cover each 50 sq ft. How many bags of peat moss will Mr. Russo need? He also plans to spread fertilizer at the rate of one bag per 60 sq ft. How many bags of fertilizer are required?
HINT: area of a circle = πr^2

BAR GRAPHS

Tyler is writing a newspaper article on school clubs. He wants to
compare the membership totals and the distribution of male and
female membership. How can Tyler organize and display this data?

Tyler uses a **bar graph** and a **double-bar graph** to organize and
display this club membership data.

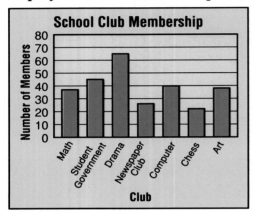

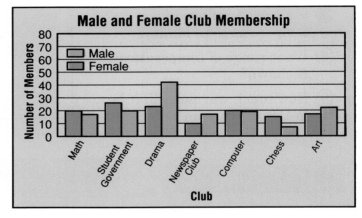

WORK TOGETHER

● What do the vertical scale and the horizontal scale show?

● What is the interval of the vertical scale?

● How will the graph change when the interval is 20 members?
2 members?

● Which club has the greatest number of members? Which bar
graph is the better source of this information?

● Which club has the greatest range between the numbers of male
and female members? smallest range? Which bar graph is the
better source of this information?

Check for Understanding

Use the graph for Exercises 1–3.

1. What do the vertical and horizontal
scales show?

2. What is the interval of the vertical
scale?

3. How does the graph change when
the interval is 1 point? 6 points?

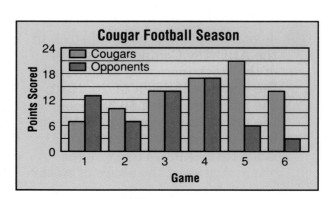

Connection, pages 480–481

Practice

Construct a double-bar graph that compares average daily temperatures for January and July. Use your graph for Exercises 4–8.

Average Daily Temperature (°F)		
City	**January**	**July**
Chicago	21	73
Denver	30	73
Houston	51	83
San Francisco	49	62
Tampa	60	82

4. Which cities have an average July temperature above 80°F?

5. Which city has the greatest range of temperatures between January and July? What is the range?

6. Which cities have a higher average January temperature than San Francisco?

7. Which city has the smallest range of temperatures between January and July? What is the range?

8. For which two cities is the average January temperature about the same?

Mixed Applications

Use your bar graph for Exercise 10.

9. Tyler once lived in Tampa, Florida. Which city's summer temperature is only slightly higher than Tampa's winter temperature?

10. Suppose you are paid $0.05 for your first day of work. Each day your wage is twice the wage of the day before. How much will you earn on the tenth day of work?

11. **Find, Organize, and Analyze Data** Survey a minimum of thirty classmates to find the number of male and female students who were born in each of the 12 months. Graph the data in a double-bar graph. Which is the most common birth month for girls? for boys?

12. **Visual Thinking** The cube is painted on all sides. The cube is cut into 64 small cubes. How many small cubes have no painted faces? one painted face?

MIXED REVIEW

Solve for d.

1. $3d = 51.9$

2. $\frac{d}{5} = 210$

3. $d - \frac{3}{4} = \frac{9}{10}$

4. $\frac{3}{4} = \frac{d}{152}$

5. $114.1 - 0.7 = d$

6. $15 - 13\frac{5}{9} = d$

What are the advantages and disadvantages of using a bar graph?

WRAP UP...

1. Jake has a 10-ft-square garden. He plans an enlarged garden that has four times as much area. What will be the length of the larger garden?

2. Lori borrows $4,500 for 3 years. The bank charges 18% interest per year. How much interest must she pay?

3. Julie purchases a compact disc player on sale at a 15% discount. The sale price is $254.15. What is the regular price of the compact disc player?

4. Tyrone's weekly salary is $520. His taxes and other withholdings total about 20% of his total salary. Estimate his take-home pay.

Name the quadrilateral.

5.   6.  7.   8.

Name each polygon and find the sum of the measures of the angles.

9.  10.   11.   12.

In the diagram, $\triangle ABC \cong \triangle FED$. Complete the statements.

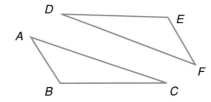

13. $\angle D \cong$ ■

14. $\overline{AB} \cong$ ■

15. $m\angle C = 20°$, $m\angle D =$ ■

16. $\overline{DE} = 5$ cm, $\overline{CB} =$ ■

Write equivalent ratios in simplest form.

17. $\frac{6}{8}$ 18. 5 to 15 19. $\frac{18}{20}$ 20. $\frac{12}{30}$

Write the absolute values.

21. $|^-9|$ 22. $|18|$ 23. $|0|$ 24. $|^-194|$

Write <, >, or =.

25. $^-30 \bullet 20$ 26. $11 \bullet ^-5$ 27. $^-7 \bullet 10$ 28. $^-12 \bullet ^-3$

Find the sum or difference.

29. $^-6 + ^-12$ 30. $^-9 - 15$ 31. $4.3 - ^-1.8$ 32. $^-6.5 + 2.1$

33. $^-\frac{1}{3} + \frac{1}{2}$ 34. $^-2\frac{1}{4} + 1\frac{3}{8}$ 35. $\frac{4}{5} - ^-\frac{1}{4}$ 36. $4\frac{1}{6} - 2\frac{1}{2}$

Spotlight ON PROBLEM SOLVING

Understand
Plan
Solve
Look Back

ANALYZE MISLEADING GRAPHS

Graphs can be useful for displaying information. We often use graphs to help in solving problems. Graphs can be misleading, however. The three graphs depict the same information. Review each of the graphs.

Moton
Middle School
Enrollment 1992

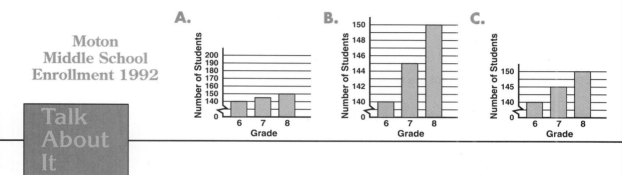

Talk About It

Work with a classmate. Read and discuss these questions.

a. Are there about the same number of students at each of the grade levels?

b. Which of the three graphs most accurately depicts the enrollment patterns?

c. Why are Graphs A and B misleading?

Apply

Study each of the graphs below and then solve the problems.

Lunch Costs at Moton Middle School

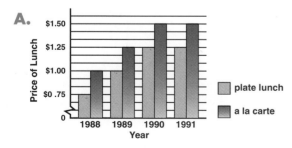

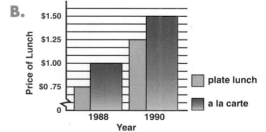

1. Has the price of plate lunches risen each year?

2. What was the amount of each plate lunch increase?

3. Did the a la carte lunch prices increase at the same rate as the plate lunch prices?

4. Which of the graphs is misleading? Explain how it is misleading.

325

CIRCLE GRAPHS

Carmen records how she usually spends her time on weekdays. Next, she wants to compare and display her data. What method can Carmen choose?

Carmen chooses to compare and display her data in a circle graph. A **circle graph** compares the parts of a whole.

Carmen follows these steps to construct her circle graph.

Carmen's Day	
Activity	**Number of Hours**
Attending school	6
Doing homework	3
Sleeping	8
Eating	1.5
Playing	2
Other	3.5

Step 1 Find the percent of the total hours for each activity.

Step 2 Find the measure of the central angle represented by each percent.

Step 3 Use a compass to draw a circle. Draw a radius.

Step 4 Use a protractor to draw a central angle for each percent.

Step 5 Label each section of the graph. Then write a title for the graph.

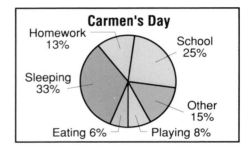

Round percents and degrees to the nearest whole number.

Activity	Number of Hours	Percent of Total Hours	Measure of Central Angle in Graph
Attending school	6	$\frac{6}{24}$ = 25%	25% of 360° = 90°
Doing homework	3	$\frac{3}{24}$ ≈ 13%	13% of 360° ≈ 47°
Sleeping	8	$\frac{8}{24}$ ≈ 33%	33% of 360° ≈ 119°
Eating	1.5	$\frac{1.5}{24}$ ≈ 6%	6% of 360° ≈ 21°
Playing	2	$\frac{2}{24}$ ≈ 8%	8% of 360° ≈ 29°
Other	3.5	$\frac{3.5}{24}$ ≈ 15%	15% of 360° = 54°
TOTALS	24	≈ 100%	≈ 360°

You can use a calculator to find the central angle measure.

13% of 360° = 360 ⨯ 13 % ⬚ 46.8 ≈ 47. So, 13% of 360° ≈ 47°.

- What percent of the circle is equal to 24 hours?

- How many degrees of the circle represent 24 hours?

Check for Understanding

Use the Ridgefield Raiders Football data for Exercises 1–9.

Ridgefield Raiders Football (number of games)		
Won	Lost	Tied
6	4	2

1. How many games did the Ridgefield Raiders play?

Find the percent of the total number of games represented by each.

2. games won   3. games lost   4. games tied

5. How many degrees of a circle represent the total number of football games?

Find the central angle measure to represent each. Round to the nearest degree.

6. games won   7. games lost   8. games tied

9. Construct a circle graph to represent the Raiders' football record.

Practice

Use the Drama Club Membership data for Exercises 10–16.

Find the percent of the total drama club membership.

10. Grade 6   11. Grade 7   12. Grade 8

Drama Club Membership	
Grade 6	15
Grade 7	25
Grade 8	35

Find the central angle measure to represent each. Round to the nearest degree.

13. Grade 6   14. Grade 7   15. Grade 8

16. Construct a circle graph to represent the drama club membership.

17. Construct a circle graph to display the career choices of the 840 Wilson Middle School students.

Mixed Applications

Use the circle graph in Exercise 17 for Exercises 18–20.

18. What percent of the students chose medicine?

19. Which career did about $\frac{1}{3}$ of the students choose?

20. Which careers did fewer than 5% of the students choose?

21. **Make Up a Problem** Use the information in the table to write a problem that can be solved by adding.

Wilson Middle School Career Choices	
Career	Number of Votes
Agriculture	17
Business	272
Computer Programming	238
Education	77
Engineering	102
Entertainment	51
Law	34
Medicine	42
Military	7

How can rounding complicate the construction of a circle graph?

WRAP
UP...

What numeral represents 9 tens and 4 ones?

Mr. Lee has finished grading the class's science tests. How can Mr. Lee organize and group the boys' science test scores?

Boys' Science Test Scores
80 98 85 57 87 95 49 86 79 66 78 89

Mr. Lee has organized the boys' science test scores in a stem-and-leaf plot.
A **stem-and-leaf plot** is a way of organizing and grouping data.

The stem values are the tens digits of the numbers in this set of data. The stems are displayed vertically, from top to bottom, in increasing order.

A vertical line separates the stems from the leaves.

The leaves are the ones digits of the numbers in the set of data. The leaves are displayed horizontally, in order from least to greatest, moving outward from the stem. All scores are listed, even though they may be duplicated.

Boys' Science Test Scores

Stems	Leaves
4	9
5	7
6	6
7	8 9
8	0 5 6 7 9
9	5 8

How can Mr. Lee compare the boys' and the girls' science test scores?

Girls' Science Test Scores
78 82 89 99 80 76 90 52 81 97 76

Mr. Lee organized the girls' science test scores and the boys' science test scores in a back-to-back stem-and-leaf plot.

A **back-to-back stem-and-leaf plot** organizes and displays two sets of data.

Girls' Science Test Scores Leaves	Stems	Boys' Science Test Scores Leaves
	4	9
2	5	7
	6	6
8 6 6	7	8 9
9 2 1 0	8	0 5 6 7 9
9 7 0	9	5 8

Talk About It

▶ What are the highest and lowest science test scores for the girls? for the boys?

▶ What is the mode of science test scores for the girls?

▶ What is the median of science test scores for the boys?

▶ How can you find the ten-point range that includes the largest quantity of test scores?

Check for Understanding

This stem-and-leaf plot shows the prices of admission to a movie in 20 cities. Use the stem-and-leaf plot for Exercises 1–6.

1. List the prices as they appear from top to bottom in the stem-and-leaf plot.

2. What part of the price is the stem?

3. What part of the price is the leaf?

4. Do the leaves *increase* or *decrease* in value as they go farther from the stem?

5. In which dollar range is the most common price of admission to a movie?

Prices of Movie Admission

$1	.50
$2	.25 .50 .75
$3	.00 .00 .00 .50 .50
$4	.00 .50 .80 .90
$5	.00 .00 .50
$6	.00 .50
$7	.00 .50

6. What is the median price? Is it included in the set of data?

Practice

Make a back-to-back stem-and-leaf plot for each set of data. Find the median, the mode, and the range for each set of data.

7. November 14 Temperatures (°F)

Highs	55	47	64	81	58	62	72	81	61	51	78
Lows	39	27	44	51	41	39	55	65	40	38	49

8. Super Bowl Scores

Winner	42	39	46	38	38	27	26	24	14	24
Loser	10	20	10	16	9	17	21	7	7	3

Mixed Applications

The back-to-back stem-and-leaf plot displays average annual snowfall data. One plot is for cities throughout the United States; the other plot is for cities south of 40°N latitude.

9. What is the range of snowfall for Plot A? for Plot B?

10. What is the median amount of snowfall for Plot A? for Plot B?

11. Which plot do you think represents the cities south of 40°N latitude? Explain.

12. **Logical Reasoning** What is the next term in the sequence 1, 8, 27, 64, . . . ?

Average Annual Snowfall (inches)

Plot A		Plot B
9 8 3 2 1 1	0	2 2 3 9
8 7 5	1	3 7
2 0	2	0 0 2 3 6
	3	5
	4	0 0 5 9
	5	7 9
0	6	0

What are the advantages and disadvantages of using a back-to-back stem-and-leaf plot for two sets of data? Explain.

WRAP UP...

QUARTILES AND EXTREMES

Mr. Howard is the basketball coach at Eastmount Middle School. He is reviewing the attendance records for the seven basketball games this season. He wants to organize and compare this data.

First, he arranges the data in increasing order.
280   350   424   487   500   535   580

- What is the median of these attendance records?

- How many attendance records are greater than the median?

- How many attendance records are less than the median?

The median divides the set of data into two parts.

Quartiles divide the set of data into four parts.

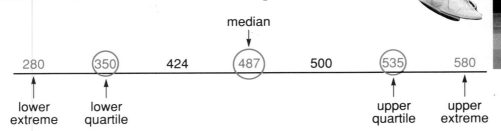

The **upper quartile** is the median of the numbers greater than the median.

The **lower quartile** is the median of the numbers less than the median.

The **upper extreme** is the greatest number in the set of data.

The **lower extreme** is the least number in the set of data.

You can calculate the **range** by finding the difference between the upper extreme and the lower extreme.

Think: $580 - 280 = 300$ So, the range of this set of data is 300.

Check for Understanding

Use this set of data for Exercises 1–4.

Vocabulary Test Scores
59   67   70   73   76   84   85   88   93

1. Find the median of the set of data.

2. Find the range of the set of data.

3. Identify the lower extreme and the upper extreme of the set of data.

4. Find the lower quartile and the upper quartile of the set of data.

Practice

Find the median, the lower extreme, the upper extreme, the lower quartile, and the upper quartile for each set of data.

5.

Basketball Scores			
28	36	49	27
62	43	54	31
27	69	40	31

6.

History Test Scores				
80	52	65	76	75
97	69	86	99	80
46	82	79	81	68

Number of Absentees Reported

7.

May 8				
8	5	4	3	9
2	6	4	1	2

8.

May 9				
1	4	2	1	2
9	7	3	4	8

Mrs. Wong promises a picnic for the math class that earns the highest median test average. Use the Average Test Scores for Exercises 9–11.

Average Test Scores	
Class 1	80 84 78 85 82 81 88 79
Class 2	75 82 76 79 78 83 85 75
Class 3	74 85 83 82 76 79 82 76

9. Which class has the widest range of test scores?

10. Which class has the widest range between the lower and upper quartiles?

11. Which class has the lowest lower quartile test score?

Mixed Applications

Use the Average Test Scores data for Exercises 12–13.

12. Suppose you can decide the winning class today. Which class has the greatest median test average?

13. Is the upper extreme a fairer description of overall math test performance? Why?

14. Visual Thinking How many blocks are used to build this model?

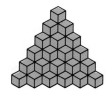

15. Make Up a Problem Write a word problem that can be solved using the proportion $\frac{3}{5} = \frac{n}{100}$. Exchange with a classmate and solve.

MIXED REVIEW

Write in scientific notation.

1. 9,200

2. 3,963,000

3. 0.037

4. 0.000765

5. $\frac{1}{10^2}$

6. 0.6639

7. 6,853,332,000,000

8. $\frac{8}{200}$

9. $\frac{1}{10^5}$

10. 5^4

How do you determine the lower quartile or upper quartile when there is an even number of data?

WRAP UP...

BOX-AND-WHISKER GRAPHS

What is the median of a set of data?

The Millbrook Middle School students collected canned food. Mr. Ruiz, the assistant principal, recorded the daily collection totals. How can he compare the collection data for the three grades?

Daily Canned-Food Collection Totals									
Grade 6	45	80	69	42	71	32	69	75	102
Grade 7	22	99	57	65	83	24	61	82	103
Grade 8	64	111	79	88	112	48	82	99	139

Mr. Ruiz chooses **box-and-whisker graphs** to organize and group his data. He uses one number line so that comparisons can be made.

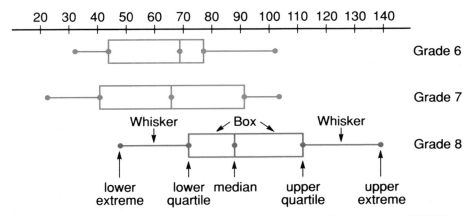

- Which grade level has the highest median collection total? Which grade level has the lowest median collection total?

- What parts of the graph represent the highest and the lowest daily collection total?

- Which grade level has the highest daily collection total? Which grade level has the lowest daily collection total?

- What are the lower and upper extremes, lower and upper quartiles, and the median for Grade 6?

- Which grade level's graph has the longest whiskers? What do the long whiskers indicate about the data?

- Which grade level has the widest range of collection totals in the middle quartiles? What part of the box-and-whisker graph represents this range?

Talk About It

▶ Is the upper extreme a reasonable measure of overall performance?

▶ Is the median a reasonable measure of overall performance?

▶ How will you rank the performance of the three grade levels in the collection? How do the box-and-whisker graphs help you decide?

Check for Understanding

The box-and-whisker graph represents math-club attendance data. Use the graph for Exercises 1–6.

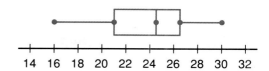

1. What is the median attendance?

2. What is the lower extreme and the upper extreme?

3. What is the lower quartile and the upper quartile?

4. How is the length of the box determined?

5. What percent of the data items is represented by each quartile?

6. Why is one whisker longer than the other?

Practice

Make a box-and-whisker graph for each set of data.

7.

8	12	16	19	9	6	10
7	5	8	13	4	7	11

8.

$2.00	$3.50	$3.10	$7.00	$12.00
$2.50	$4.50	$4.75	$3.50	$10.00

Make a box-and-whisker graph for each set of data. Use one number line for Exercises 9–10. Use one number line for Exercises 11–12.

9.

Kim's Weekly Earnings			
$4.50	$3.00	$8.00	$ 5.60
$9.40	$6.00	$2.00	$12.00

10.

John's Weekly Earnings			
$ 3.00	$5.00	$9.00	$2.50
$10.60	$8.40	$1.00	$4.50

All-Star Baseball Game Scores												
11. National League	2	7	1	4	3	4	1	4	5	1	3	7
12. American League	4	9	4	3	8	1	3	0	7	3	5	1

Mixed Applications

Use the graphs in Exercises 11–12 for Exercises 13–16.

13. What is the median score for each league? How do the scores compare?

14. What is the range of scores for each league?

15. How many runs did each league score? How many more runs did the leader score?

16. Is the median a fair measure of the overall performance of both leagues? Explain.

How does the box-and-whisker graph divide the data into four parts?

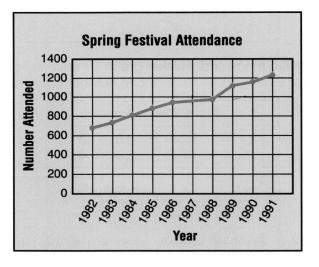

MAKING INFERENCES

How can the PTA estimate the Spring Festival attendance for 1992?

An **extrapolation** is an estimate or a prediction of an unknown value based on known values.

To estimate the attendance for 1992, study the line connecting the last few data points in the graph. Determine the trend established by this line. Then, extend the graph along this line.

So, 1,300 is the estimated attendance for 1992.

You can also extrapolate this value by looking at nearby data points. Calculate the differences between their values. Try to detect a pattern. Then, base your estimate on extending this pattern.

- What is the increase in attendance for each of the last three years? What is the average of those increases?

- What increase in attendance do you estimate for 1992?

There is no attendance total for 1987. You can use interpolation to estimate this number from the known data. An **interpolation** is an estimated value between two known values.

- Read the value where the line graph crosses the 1987 position. Is the graph reading of 960 people part of the known data or an interpolation based on known data? Is this value exact?

Check for Understanding

Graph the enrollment data in a line graph. Use the data to estimate the enrollment each year.

1. 1995   2. 2000   3. 2005

4. 1972   5. 1983   6. 1967

Spring Festival Attendance	
Year	Attendance
1982	685
1983	747
1984	807
1985	898
1986	948
1988	998
1989	1,131
1990	1,173
1991	1,218

Henry County School Enrollment	
Year	Number of Students
1965	15,491
1970	19,648
1975	25,357
1980	28,402
1985	31,573
1990	36,050

Practice

Display Tony's weight data in a line graph. Then use the table and the graph for Exercises 7–10.

Tony's Weight						
Age (years)	7	9	11	13	14	15
Weight (pounds)	47	60	78	94	110	125

7. What trend summarizes the weight data?

8. What is the interpolation of Tony's weight at 8 yr and at 12 yr?

9. Predict Tony's weight at 16 yr.

10. Can you accurately extrapolate Tony's weight for age 35? Why?

Use the United States Farm Population data for Exercises 11–13.

11. What is the farm population trend?

12. Interpolate the percent of farm population in 1950 and in 1910.

13. If the trend continues, what percent of the population will live on farms in 2000?

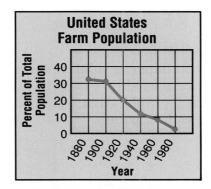

Mixed Applications

Use the United States Population data for Exercises 14–17.

14. Display the data in a line graph.

15. What might have been the United States population in 1870? in 1910?

16. If the trend continues, what is the predicted population for 2000?

17. What was the increase in United States population between 1840 and 1980?

United States Population	
Year	**Population (millions)**
1840	17.1
1860	31.4
1880	50.2
1900	76.2
1920	106.0
1940	132.2
1960	179.3
1980	226.5

SOCIAL STUDIES CONNECTION

The United States Constitution requires the United States government to conduct a population census every ten years.

A *census* is a government survey that gathers a variety of data. The United States Bureau of the Census gathers, processes, organizes, analyzes, and publishes the data.

18. What trend describes the changes in the median age?

19. Why is this trend occurring?

United States Population	
Year	**Median Age (years)**
1860	19.4
1900	22.9
1940	29.0
1980	30.0

How can extrapolation or interpolation be misleading?

EXPLORING

Scattergrams

A **scattergram** is a graph of two sets of data.

In this lesson you will explore the three possible relationships between the two sets of data graphed in a scattergram.

WORK TOGETHER

Building Understanding

Use large grid paper, a ruler, and counters to graph each relationship. First, draw and label the scales for each graph. Then, place the counters to represent the data points.

Height (cm)	176	171	195	151	200	163	190
Weight (kg)	79	61	91	44	97	53	85

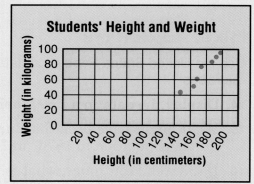

Talk About It

▶ Do the counters form a pattern?

▶ Do the counters appear to be almost in a straight line? If so, describe the line.

▶ As height increases, what happens to weight? What happens when height decreases?

Age of Car (yr)	1	2	3	4	5	6
Value (dollars)	6,825	5,500	4,475	3,625	2,700	2,375

Talk About It

▶ Do the counters form a pattern?

▶ Do the counters appear to be almost in a straight line? If so, describe the line.

▶ What is the relationship between the age of the car and its value?

Making the Connection

You can use scattergrams to show the correlation, or relationship, between two sets of data.

A scattergram's **line of best fit** is the straight line that is drawn through as much data as possible. The line of best fit helps you to interpret the correlation, or relationship, between two sets of data.

When the values of both sets of data increase or decrease at the same time, there is a **positive correlation.** The line of best fit slants upward.

When the value of one set of data increases and the other decreases, there is a **negative correlation.** The line of best fit slants downward.

When the data points are scattered and no line of best fit can be drawn, there is **no correlation.**

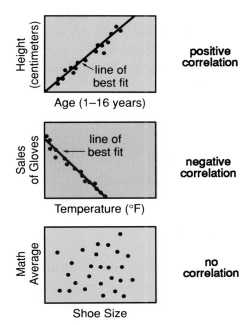

positive correlation

negative correlation

no correlation

Checking Understanding

Draw a scattergram to represent each set of data. Draw the line of best fit. Write *positive, negative,* or *no correlation* to describe the relationship.

1.

400-Meter Relay	
Year	Time (seconds)
1928	48.4
1936	46.9
1952	45.9
1960	44.5
1968	42.8
1976	42.55
1984	41.65

2.

Tree Age and Diameter	
Age (years)	Diameter (inches)
5	1.0
8	2.1
10	2.7
16	4.3
23	4.8
30	6.0
35	7.2
40	7.6

3.

Phone Number and Weight	
Phone Number's Last Digit	Weight (pounds)
0	85
5	180
2	90
1	198
8	93
4	78
7	110

Write *positive, negative,* or *no correlation* to describe the relationship between the two sets of data.

4. amount of traffic and number of traffic lights

5. number on uniform and batting average

6. speed and time for a 200-mi trip

7. outside temperature and use of heating oil

More Practice, Lesson 10.11, page H69

PROBLEM *Solving*

Choose an Appropriate Graph

Charlotte is president of the school's Teen Center. The club's annual membership is as follows: 1987, 20 members; 1988, 42 members; 1989, 75 members; 1990, 125 members; and 1991, 198 members. Which type of graph will best show the Teen Center's change in annual membership?

When you want to display data in a graph, you must decide which type of graph will present the data most clearly.

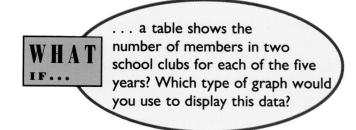

TEEN CENTER
1987   20
1988   42
1989   75
1990   125
1991   198

▶ **UNDERSTAND**

What are you asked to find?

What information are you given?

▶ **PLAN**

What are the strengths and weaknesses of each type of graph?

Type of Graph	Strengths	Weaknesses
Bar graph	Compares data	Is often difficult to get exact readings
Line graph	Shows relation between two changing quantities	Is often accurate only at data points
Circle graph	Compares parts to whole and is easy to read	Cannot show trends over time; cannot show increases or decreases
Stem-and-leaf plot	Displays all data; sorts data quickly	Is difficult to display a large quantity of data
Box-and-whisker graph	Shows distribution of data around median	Shows five summary numbers instead of entire set of data

▶ **SOLVE**

Which type of graph is appropriate for showing this data?

A line graph is appropriate for showing the change in the club's membership over a period of time.

▶ **LOOK BACK**

How can you check your answer?

WHAT IF... . . . a table shows the number of members in two school clubs for each of the five years? Which type of graph would you use to display this data?

338

Apply

Identify the type of graph that will best display each set of data.

(1)

Gases in the Earth's Atmosphere	
Gas	**Percent**
Nitrogen	78
Oxygen	21
Other	1

(2)

Scores on Quizzes

98	97	78	79
87	93	96	82
19	85	95	68
83	77	96	80

(3)

Average High Temperatures	
Month	**Temperature(°F)**
January	44
February	46
March	54
April	66
May	76
June	83

Mixed Applications ▷ **STRATEGIES**
- Work Backward • Guess and Check
- Write an Equation • Draw a Diagram

Choose a strategy and solve.

(4) Mary and Linda get the same allowance. Their brother Jorge receives an allowance of $3.00. The three allowances total $14.00. What is Mary's allowance?

(5) What is the area of the largest circle that can be cut from a square piece of poster board that is 28 in. on a side? ($\pi = 3.1416$)

(6) Today's high temperature was recorded at noon. By 3 P.M. the temperature had fallen 20°F. By 6 P.M. it had dropped another 26°F. At 11 P.M. it had fallen 14°F to a low of 24°F. What was today's high temperature?

(7) In 1991 there is a total of 198 Teen Center members. There are more girls than boys. If 8 more boys join, the number of boys and girls will be equal. How many boys are Teen Center members? How many girls?

(8) Hank's age is 12 times Tina's age. Marie's age is the reciprocal of Tina's age. Hank's age is 48 times Marie's age. The sum of their ages is $26\frac{1}{2}$ yr. What are the ages of Hank, Marie, and Tina?

(9) Mr. Dean is fencing his 150-ft by 300-ft lot. He places a fence post at each corner and then every 15 ft. How many fence posts are needed to enclose the entire lot?

WRITER'S CORNER

(10) Write a problem similar to Exercise 6. Use temperature, yards lost or gained on a football field, or gallons of oil in a tank. Exchange with a classmate and solve.

(11) Write a problem similar to Exercise 9. Use different dimensions and a different interval for the fence posts. Exchange with a classmate and solve.

Vocabulary Check

Choose a word from the box to complete each sentence.

| extrapolation |
| interpolation |
| mean |
| median |
| mode |
| negative |
| positive |
| quartile |
| range |

1. The middle number in a set of data when the numbers are arranged in order is the __?__. *(page 314)*

2. The difference between the upper extreme and the lower extreme is the __?__. *(page 330)*

3. A set of data can be divided into four parts. Each part is a __?__. *(page 330)*

4. An estimated value between two known values is a(n) __?__. *(page 334)*

5. If a number occurs more often than any other number in a set of data, it is called the __?__. *(page 314)*

6. When the values of one set of data increase and the values of the other set of data decrease, a __?__ correlation exists. *(page 337)*

7. The sum of a set of data divided by the number of items in a set is the __?__, or average. *(page 314)*

Concept Check

Use Graph A for Exercises 8–10.

8. How does the graph change when the vertical scale interval is 25? is 100? *(page 322)*

9. Interpolate the total on day 6. *(page 334)*

10. Extrapolate the total on day 10. *(page 334)*

Write *positive correlation, negative correlation,* or *no correlation* to describe the relationship between the two sets of data. *(page 337)*

A
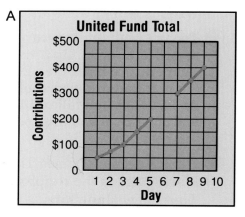

11.
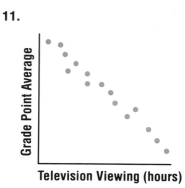

12.
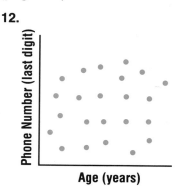

13.
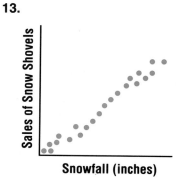

Skill Check

For each set of data, find the mean, the median, the mode, and the range. *(pages 314, 330)*

14. 39, 53, 97, 61, 42, 83, 26, 91, 88, 76

15. 11, 23, 58, 66, 2, 14, 19, 3, 11

16. For the data in Exercise 14, make a frequency table and a histogram using intervals of 20–29, 30–39, . . . *(page 316)*

17. Identify the upper extreme, the lower extreme, the upper quartile, and the lower quartile for the data in Exercise 15. *(page 330)*

18. For the data in Exercise 15, make a stem-and-leaf plot and a box-and-whisker graph. *(pages 328, 332)*

Use Graph B for Exercises 19–20, Graph C for Exercises 21–22, and Graph D for Exercise 23.

19. Find the mode of the physical fitness scores. *(page 316)*

20. Find the number of students scoring above 19. *(page 316)*

21. Describe the trend in popcorn sales. *(page 318)*

22. Find the range of popcorn sales. *(pages 318, 330)*

23. Find the most popular television choice. *(page 322)*

Problem-Solving Check *(pages 320–338)*

24. Is there sufficient data in Graph B to determine the number of girls who scored above 15?

25. In Graph C, can you find the number of popcorn containers sold? Why or why not?

26. Using the data in Graph D, what kind of graph can you make to compare the percent of each part to the whole group?

27. What kind of graph can describe 480 history scores using the lower extreme, the lower quartile, the median, the upper quartile, and the upper extreme?

B

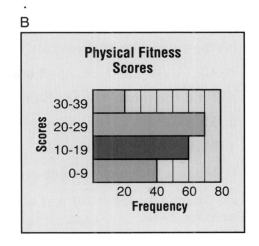

C

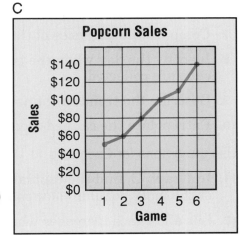

D

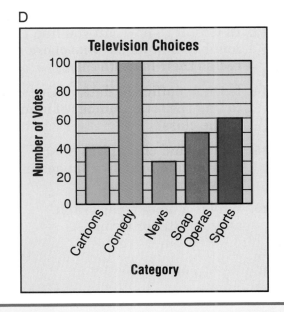

Use the set of data for Exercises 1–4.

43, 11, 61, 92, 5, 88, 46, 39, 29, 88

1. Find the mean, the median, the mode, and the range.

2. Make a histogram using intervals of 0–9, 10–19, . . .

3. Make a stem-and-leaf plot.

4. Make a box-and-whisker graph.

Use Graph A for Exercises 5–7 and Graph B for Exercises 8–10.

5. Find the total number of absences during Week 4.

6. Find the range of absences for the girls.

7. Compare the absences of the boys and the girls.

8. Identify the day when the greatest number of cans are collected.

9. Describe the trend in canned-food totals.

10. Extrapolate the canned-food total for day 8.

Use the graphs for Exercises 11, 13, 14 and 16.

11. In Graph C, find the central angle measure of the most popular color choice.

12. Li's allowance increases when her number of chores increases. Describe the correlation between her allowance and her number of chores.

13. In Graph C, how can you find the number of students who chose red as their favorite color?

14. Is there sufficient data in Graph A to find the total number of students in the class?

15. Which kind of graph is most appropriate to show changes in your allowance over time?

16. Why is a double-bar graph appropriate for Graph A?

A
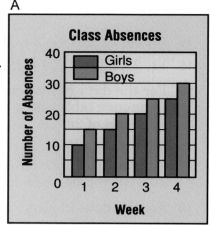

B
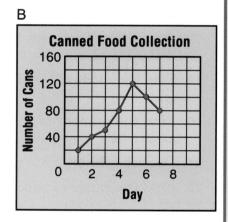

C
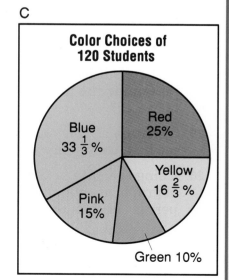

Teamwork P-R-O-J-E-C-T

Choose a Field-Trip Destination

What should be the destination for the eighth-grade field trip?

The Wilson Middle School is planning a field trip on May 8. The students must be transported by bus and return on the same day. The cost for each student cannot be greater than $10. The eighth-grade students can offer suggestions and vote on the field-trip choice. Each math class has been asked to suggest a destination to Mr. Ruiz, the assistant principal.

Decide

As a team, brainstorm all possible field-trip ideas. Choose the best field-trip destination that meets all the requirements.

Do

As a team, research the costs, scheduling, and transportation for your field-trip destination. Estimate the cost for each student.

Share

Each team will present its research data to the class. Statistics, graphs, or pictures should be used in an effort to "sell" the destination to the other teams. The teams will compare all the destinations. The class will discuss all the choices and then vote on the field-trip destination.

Talk About It

- How many destinations were discussed?

- What is the total amount that can be spent on the field trip?

- Were any destinations omitted because of cost or transportation problems?

- How do the transportation bids compare?

- Are there any group discounts?

- What is the schedule?

- How many chaperones are needed? Who will pay their expenses?

- What factors, other than cost, did you consider?

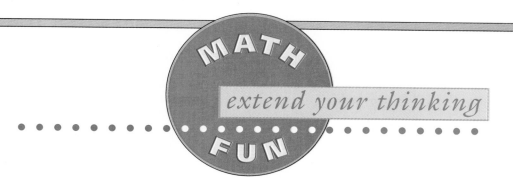

Use a Stem-and-Leaf Plot to Find the Mean

The weights in pounds of 16 dogs at the Kingston Dog Show are shown at the right. Find the mean weight.

Weights of Dogs			
60	50	56	71
64	42	45	50
86	64	72	58
70	75	79	66

To find the mean weight, you can use the stem-and-leaf plot below. Multiply the stem value by its frequency, and add the values of the leaves. Then divide the total by the number of leaves.

Stem	Leaves				
4	2	5			
5	0	0	6	8	
6	0	4	4	6	
7	0	1	2	5	9
8	6				

Stem Frequency	Totals
$(40 \times 2) + 7 =$	87
$(50 \times 4) + 14 =$	214
$(60 \times 4) + 14 =$	254
$(70 \times 5) + 17 =$	367
$(80 \times 1) + 6 =$	86
	$\overline{1,008}$

So, the mean weight is $1,008 \div 16$ pounds, or 63 pounds.

1. Use this stem-and-leaf plot to find the mean of the data. HINT: $(0 \times 5) + 20 = 20$

Stem	Leaves				
0	1	4	5	5	5
1	0	5	6		
2	1	1	2	2	6
3	0	3	3	5	8

2. The data below shows the numbers of absences for 20 students at a day-care center last year. Use a stem-and-leaf plot to find the mean of the data.

7	3	31	35	16	0	22
33	24	14	29	21	25	8
18	20	43	25	31	15	

Challenge

Number Sense

1. What nonzero number equals twice the number added to its square?

2. $\frac{4}{5}$ of what number is equal to 1?

Number Sense

Arrange the digits 1, 5, 6, and 8 in the boxes to make a true statement.

■■% × ■.■ = 1.29

CUMULATIVE REVIEW
CHAPTERS 1–10

Write the letter of the correct answer.

1. Which is the mode of the set of data?
   66, 84, 95, 84, 80

   A. 66   B. 82

   C. 84   D. 85

2. Which is the median of the set of data?   25, 18, 32, 21, 39

   A. 21   B. 25

   C. 27   D. 32

3. Which angles have a combined measure of 180°?

   A. acute   B. complementary

   C. obtuse   D. supplementary

4. Which is 8.35 written as a mixed number?

   A. $8\frac{1}{3}$ B. $8\frac{35}{100}$

   C. $8\frac{5}{7}$ D. not here

5. $10^3 \div 10^{-2}$

   A. 10^{-6} B. 10^{-1}

   C. 10^1 D. 10^5

6. Solve. $3n - 2 = 16$

   A. $n = 5$ B. $n = 6$

   C. $n = 7$ D. $n = 10$

7. $^-15 + 15$

   A. $^-225$ B. $^-30$

   C. 0   D. 30

8. $\frac{^-1}{5} + \frac{2}{5} + \frac{^-6}{5}$

   A. $^-1$ B. $\frac{1}{5}$

   C. 1   D. $1\frac{3}{5}$

9. Which is the opposite of 2.798?

   A. $^-2.798$ B. 0

   C. $\frac{1}{2.798}$ D. 3

10. Which is 17.3% of $577?

    A. $9.99   B. $99.82

    C. $99.83   D. $594.3

11. Which is the ratio $\frac{82}{12}$ written in simplest form?

    A. $\frac{6}{41}$ B. $\frac{41}{24}$

    C. $\frac{6}{1}$ D. $\frac{41}{6}$

12. Which is a solution of $y = x + 3$?

    A. (3,2)   B. (0,0)

    C. (4,1)   D. (1,4)

13. What is the fifth score if the mean of the scores is 80.6 and four of the scores are 68, 91, 77, and 82?

    A. 78.5   B. 82

    C. 85   D. 91

14. Sam spends $333 of his $2,000 monthly salary to repay a loan. Estimate the part of his salary that this represents.

    A. about $\frac{1}{10}$ B. about $\frac{1}{6}$

    C. about $\frac{1}{4}$ D. about $\frac{1}{3}$

CHAPTER

11

PROBABILITY

Did you know . . .

. . . that when you shuffle a deck of 52 playing cards, there are over 8×10^{67} ways that the cards can be arranged?

Talk About It

Suppose you are playing a game with 8 cards numbered 1–8. How can you determine the number of two-digit numbers that are possible using pairs of cards?

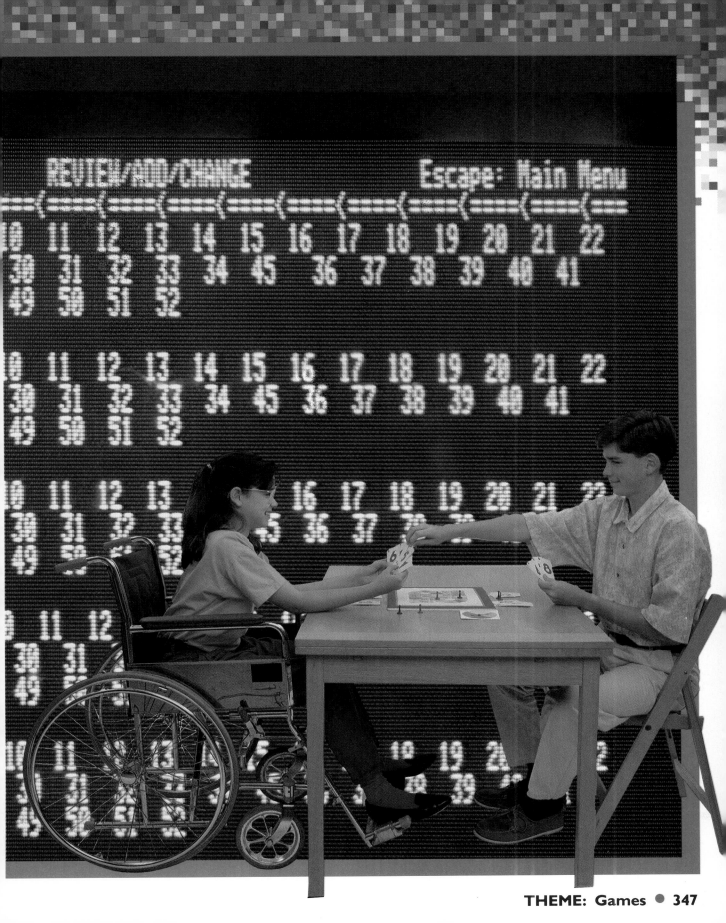

How many outfits could you make using 1 red and 1 white shirt and 1 red and 1 white pair of pants?

FUNDAMENTAL COUNTING PRINCIPLE

Ben Wilson schedules the games and activities for summer camp. In his schedule for this week, campers can choose checkers, cards, or chess in the morning. In the afternoon they can choose video games or word games. How many choices does each camper have for a daily game schedule?

You can use a tree diagram to find the number of choices.

Morning	checkers		cards		chess	
Afternoon	video games	word games	video games	word games	video games	word games

So, each camper has 6 choices for a daily game schedule.

Talk About It

▶ How can you find the number of choices that include chess in the morning?

▶ How many games are in the morning? in the afternoon? What relationship can you find between the number of games in the morning and afternoon and the total number of choices for a daily schedule?

Another Method

You can also use multiplication to find the number of choices.

At dinner the campers can choose from 3 salads, 4 entrees, and 3 desserts. How many different three-course choices are there?

Number of salads		Number of entrees		Number of desserts	
3	×	4	×	3	= 36

So, there are 36 different three-course choices.

> **Fundamental Counting Principle** If there are p choices for the way one thing can be done and q choices for the way another thing can be done, then together they can be done in $p \times q$ different ways.

Check for Understanding

Find the total number of choices.

1. socks: red, blue, green
   shoes: brown, black

2. breads: whole-wheat, white, rye
   fillings: cheese, meat, tuna

3. trips: ski, swim
   dates: December, March, June

4. colors: red, blue, white, green
   sizes: small, medium, large

Practice

Find the total number of choices.

5. 5 music groups, record or tape

6. 3 movies, 4 showings of each

7. 2 hats, 4 shirts, 2 sweaters

8. 4 flavors, 6 toppings

Mr. Stone is going to buy a new vehicle. The table shows his choices.
Use the table for Exercises 9–12.

9. How many choices does Mr. Stone
   have if he chooses 1 type, 1 color,
   and 1 option?

10. Suppose Mr. Stone does not want
    any options. How many choices does
    he have?

11. Suppose that a car can be a hard top
    or a convertible. How many choices
    will this give Mr. Stone?

12. Mr. Stone decides he wants a blue
    car with one option. How many
    choices does he have?

Type	Color
Car	Blue
Van	Red
Truck	White
	Green

Options
Radio
Air Conditioning
Tinted Windows

Mixed Applications

13. A dinner menu offers
    5 appetizers, 7 entrees,
    4 salads, and 6 desserts. In
    how many different ways can a
    dinner include an appetizer, an
    entree, a salad, and a dessert?

14. **Logical Reasoning** If $4x = 12$, what does $4x - 3$ equal?

15. A certain state uses 3 numbers and
    3 letters on license plates. How
    many choices for license plates are
    there if any letter and any digit 0–9
    can be used?

16. **Mental Math** Four golf balls cost
    $3.00. What is the cost of 3 dozen
    golf balls?

In your own words, explain the
Fundamental Counting Principle.

W R A P
U P . . .

WARM UP...

PERMUTATIONS

Two people are standing in line. In how many ways can they be arranged?

Dave, Ted, and Jose are members of the first-place tennis team. In how many different ways can they line up for a picture?

You can make a list of all the possible ways.

Dave, Ted, Jose   Dave, Jose, Ted
Ted, Dave, Jose   Ted, Jose, Dave
Jose, Dave, Ted   Jose, Ted, Dave

A faster way to solve the problem is to use the Fundamental Counting Principle.

● How many choices are there for the first position? If one team member is in the first position, how many choices are left for the second position?

Choices for position 1		Choices for position 2		Choices for position 3	
3	×	2	×	1	= 6

So, the members can line up in 6 different ways.

Another Example In how many ways can the tennis coach choose a captain and a co-captain from the 8 members of the team?

Choices for captain		Choices for co-captain	
8	×	7	= 56

So, there are 56 ways.

An arrangement of the members of a group in a definite order is called a **permutation.** In the first example, there are 6 permutations. In the second example, there are 56 permutations.

Talk About It

▶ In the first example, how is the permutation Dave, Ted, Jose the same as the permutation Dave, Jose, Ted? How is it different?

▶ Suppose Dave was first in every permutation for the team picture. How would this affect the total number of permutations?

A short way to write the product $4 \cdot 3 \cdot 2 \cdot 1$ is to use the **factorial** symbol.

$4 \cdot 3 \cdot 2 \cdot 1$ can be written as 4!.　Read 4! as 4 factorial.

You can use factorial expressions to find the number of permutations.

Examples

A. How many five-digit numbers can be formed from the digits 1, 2, 3, 4, and 5 if the digits cannot be repeated?

$5! = 5 \cdot 4 \cdot 3 \cdot 2 \cdot 1 = 120$ ← 120 five-digit numbers

B. How many three-digit numbers can be formed from the digits 1, 2, 3, 4, and 5 if the digits cannot be repeated?

$$\frac{5!}{(5-3)!} = \frac{5!}{2!}$$

$$= \frac{5 \cdot 4 \cdot 3 \cdot \overset{1}{\cancel{2}} \cdot \overset{1}{\cancel{1}}}{\underset{1}{\cancel{2}} \cdot \underset{1}{\cancel{1}}}$$

$$= 5 \cdot 4 \cdot 3 = 60$$ ← 60 three-digit numbers

● What factorial would you use as the denominator if you were forming two-digit numbers?

You can use symbols to represent permutations. The symbol $_6P_6$, for example, can represent the permutations for 6 people sitting in a row of 6 chairs.

$$_6P_6 = \underbrace{6 \cdot 5 \cdot 4 \cdot 3 \cdot 2 \cdot 1}_{6 \text{ factors}} = 720$$ ← Use a calculator.

number of people ↱
number of chairs ↱

To represent the permutations for 2 out of 6 people sitting in a row of 2 chairs, you can use the symbol $_6P_2$.

$$_6P_2 = \underbrace{6 \cdot 5}_{2 \text{ factors}} = 30$$

number of people ↱
number of chairs ↱

● $_6P_2$ and $\frac{6!}{4!}$ represent the same number of permutations. What factorial expression represents the same number of permutations as $_8P_3$?

● What permutation symbol can you use to represent Example **A**? Example **B**?

Check for Understanding

Find the value.

1. $3!$ **2.** $5!$ **3.** $8!$ **4.** $\frac{4!}{2!}$ **5.** $\frac{8!}{3!}$

Find the number of permutations.

6. $_2P_2$ **7.** $_5P_5$ **8.** $_4P_3$ **9.** $_5P_2$ **10.** $_7P_5$

Solve.

11. In how many ways can the letters A, B, and C be arranged if the letters cannot be repeated?

12. In how many ways can 6 books be arranged on a shelf?

13. In how many ways can a coach arrange 10 players on a team with 5 positions?

14. In how many ways can 6 out of 10 people sit in a row of 6 chairs?

Practice

Find the value. You may use a calculator.

15. $6!$ **16.** $4!$ **17.** $10!$ **18.** $\frac{6!}{3!}$ **19.** $\frac{8!}{6!}$

20. $\frac{9!}{5!}$ **21.** $\frac{12!}{(12-8)!}$ **22.** $5!-3!$ **23.** $4!+4!$ **24.** $3! \cdot 2!$

Write the number of permutations as a factorial expression.

25. $_4P_4$ **26.** $_5P_3$ **27.** $_{10}P_2$ **28.** $_{14}P_5$ **29.** $_{20}P_3$

Find the number of permutations. You may use a calculator.

30. $_3P_3$ **31.** $_5P_4$ **32.** $_7P_3$ **33.** $_{20}P_2$ **34.** $_{15}P_3$

35. $_8P_6$ **36.** $_{100}P_3$ **37.** $_7P_7$ **38.** $_{12}P_8$ **39.** $_{200}P_3$

Find the number of permutations.

40. Four people sit in a row of 4 chairs.

41. Three-digit numbers are formed from the digits 5, 6, 7, and 8, with no digits repeated.

42. Two students are chosen for president and vice-president from a class of 24 students.

43. A baseball coach chooses the first, second, and third batters for a team of 9 players.

Copy and complete the table.

	Kind of Number	Digits Used	Number of Permutations (without repeating digits)
44.	two-digit	2, 4, 6, 8	▨
45.	three-digit	1, 2, 3, 4, 5	▨
46.	four-digit	9, 8, 7, 6	▨
47.	five-digit	5, 7, 1, 3, 9, 2	▨

Solve.

48. In how many ways can 9 different books be arranged on a shelf?

49. In how many ways can a secretary and a treasurer be chosen from a club with 15 members?

50. In how many ways can you choose 2 frozen-yogurt flavors out of 26 possible flavors?

51. How many three-digit numbers with 4 as the first digit can be formed from the digits 1, 2, 3, and 4?

Mixed Applications

52. There are 6 swimmers who can swim either the lead or anchor leg in the 440-yd freestyle relay. In how many different ways can the lead and anchor positions on the relay team be filled?

53. There are 16 members in the 4-H Club. In how many different ways can a president, a vice-president, and a secretary be chosen from the club members?

54. The basketball team had 5% more field goals in their second game than in their first. The team had 21 field goals in the second game. How many field goals did the team have in the first game?

55. What are the next two terms in this sequence?

$$1, 4, 10, 19, 31, \ldots$$

MIXED REVIEW

Write the fraction in simplest form.

1. $\frac{12}{15}$ **2.** $\frac{8}{16}$ **3.** $\frac{24}{15}$ **4.** $\frac{6}{18}$ **5.** $\frac{35}{50}$

Compute.

6. $\frac{4 \times 6}{3 \times 2}$ **7.** $\frac{5 \times 6 \times 7}{1 \times 2 \times 3}$ **8.** $\frac{12 \times 10 \times 9}{60}$ **9.** $\frac{2 \times 3 \times 4 \times 5}{5 \times 4}$

Explain why the number of permutations found by using $_6P_6$ and $_6P_5$ are the same.

WRAP
UP...

WARM

UP...

How is the arrangement ABCD
similar to the arrangement BCDA?

COMBINATIONS

Rachel, Ted, Steve, and Jason are softball
umpires. Two of them will be selected to
serve at the softball championships. How
many combinations of 2 umpires are there?

You can make a list of all the permutations.

Rachel, Ted	Rachel, Steve	Rachel, Jason
Ted, Rachel	Ted, Steve	Ted, Jason
Steve, Rachel	Steve, Ted	Steve, Jason
Jason, Rachel	Jason, Ted	Jason, Steve

The same items can appear in different
orders in two or more permutations.

A **combination,** however, is a selection in
which the order of items does not matter.
The pairs Rachel, Ted and Ted, Rachel, for
example, are the same combination. So,
there are only 6 possible combinations.

Another Method   The combinations of
2 umpires is represented by $_4C_2$. You can use
permutations and factorials to evaluate $_4C_2$.

number at championship
number of umpires

$$_4C_2 = \frac{_4P_2}{2!} \longleftarrow \text{number of permutations}$$
$$\longleftarrow \text{number of ways items can be arranged}$$

$$= \frac{4 \cdot 3}{2 \cdot 1}$$

$$= \frac{12}{2} = 6$$

Example   How many teams of 6 players can be formed from a
group of 10 players?

$$_{10}C_6 = \frac{_{10}P_6}{6!} = \frac{10 \cdot 9 \cdot 8 \cdot 7 \cdot \overset{1}{\cancel{6}} \cdot \overset{1}{\cancel{5}}}{\underset{1}{\cancel{6}} \cdot \underset{1}{\cancel{5}} \cdot 4 \cdot 3 \cdot 2 \cdot 1} = \frac{5,040}{24} = 210 \text{ teams}$$

Talk About It

▶ Which is greater for a set of items, the number of permutations
or the number of combinations? Why?

▶ If teams of 5 players instead of teams of 6 players were formed
from a group of 10 players, would there be more teams or fewer
teams? Explain.

Check for Understanding

Find the number of combinations.

1. There are 5 players. How many teams of 3 can be formed?

2. There are 8 students. How many committees of 3 can be formed?

3. There are 6 pizza toppings. How many pizzas with 3 different toppings can be made?

4. There are 8 boys in a gym class. How many teams of 5 boys can be formed?

Practice

Find the number of combinations. You may use a calculator.

5. $_4C_2$ 6. $_6C_3$ 7. $_8C_6$ 8. $_8C_2$ 9. $_{10}C_5$

10. $_3C_2$ 11. $_6C_5$ 12. $_{12}C_{10}$ 13. $_{15}C_{12}$ 14. $_{20}C_{15}$

Determine whether the solution represents a *permutation* or a *combination.* Then solve.

15. There are 5 finalists in a tennis competition. In how many ways can the first, second, and third prizes be awarded?

16. Kelly must select 5 out of 7 students to help pick up trash. How many different selections can she make?

17. Martin can choose 2 toppings for a taco. He selects from onions, lettuce, cheese, and tomatoes. In how many ways can he make a taco?

18. Eight students will go hiking in pairs. How many different pairs of students are possible?

Mixed Applications

19. The student council is planning a dance. A decoration committee of 8 students is to be chosen from a total of 15 students. How many different committees can be formed?

20. A history test has 2 parts. Each part has 5 questions. Every student must choose 3 questions to answer from each part. In how many ways can a student choose the 6 questions? (HINT: Multiply the combinations.)

21. A dinner menu offers 3 soups, 4 entrees, and 2 desserts. In how many different ways can a dinner include a soup, an entree, and a dessert?

22. **Logical Reasoning** Would it be cheaper for you to take one friend to the movies twice or to take two friends at the same time? Explain.

What is the difference between a combination and a permutation?

WRAP
UP...

PROBABILITY

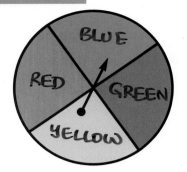

Juanita is playing a game that involves
spinning the spinner shown. What is
the probability that the spinner will
land on red when Juanita spins?

The **probability** of an event is the
chance that the event will occur.

Since each of the sections of the spinner
is the same size, all the outcomes are
equally likely. The set of all possible
outcomes is the **sample space.** The
sample space for the spinner is red,
blue, green, and yellow.

To find the mathematical probability,
P, of an event, you can use this ratio.

$$P = \frac{\text{number of favorable outcomes}}{\text{number of possible outcomes}}$$

The probability ratio for the problem is

number of favorable outcomes (number of red sections) → $\frac{1}{4}$.
number of possible outcomes (total number of sections) →

So, the probability that the spinner will
land on red is $\frac{1}{4}$.

An event may consist of 0, 1, or more outcomes.

Examples One card is picked without looking. Find the
probability.

A. P(A)   **B.** P(B or C)   **C.** P(Z)

$\frac{3}{6} = \frac{1}{2}$ $\frac{2}{6} = \frac{1}{3}$ $\frac{0}{6} = 0$

Talk About It

▶ Suppose each of the six cards has an A. What is P(A)?

▶ Can a probability ever be greater than 1? Explain.

▶ Explain why P(Z) = 0 in Example **C.**

Check for Understanding

A bag contains 3 blue marbles, 1 green marble, 2 red marbles, and 2 black marbles. You pick one marble without looking.

1. What is the sample space?
2. How many outcomes are there?

3. Find P(blue).
4. Find P(red or green).
5. Find P(white).

Practice

You spin the spinner. Find each probability.

6. P(1)
7. P(not 3)

8. P(4 or 6)
9. P(1, 3, or 6)

10. P(4 and pink)
11. P(4 or pink)

You roll a number cube numbered from 1 to 6. Find each probability.

12. P(3)
13. P(5 or 6)
14. P(not 2)
15. P(number > 3)

16. P(odd number)
17. P(number < 5)
18. P(number < 0)
19. P(multiple of 3)

20. What is the sample space when you flip 1 coin? 2 coins?

Mixed Applications

21. There are six cards numbered 1 to 6. Jerry needs to pick an even number to win a game. He picks a card without looking. What is the probability that it is an even number?

22. Tasha bought 8 tickets in a raffle for a bicycle. If 300 tickets were sold, what is Tasha's probability of winning the bicycle?

MATH CONNECTION

The odds in favor of an event can be found by using this ratio.

$$\text{odds in favor} = \frac{\text{number of favorable outcomes}}{\text{number of unfavorable outcomes}}$$

Example On a number cube, what are the odds in favor of rolling a 2? $\frac{1}{5}$, or 1 to 5

You roll a number cube numbered from 1 to 6. Find the odds in favor of each event.

23. rolling a 3
24. rolling a 2 or a 3
25. rolling an even number

Explain how to find the probability of a given event.

WRAP
UP...

EXPLORING

Pascal's Triangle

This array shows the first rows of Pascal's triangle. The patterns in the triangle can be used to solve many problems in mathematics. You will learn how to use the triangle to solve probability problems.

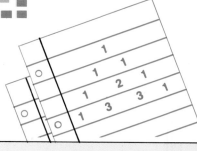

WORK TOGETHER

Building Understanding

Extend the triangle by finding a pattern in the numbers.

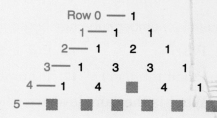

Talk About It

▶ Look at Row 3. How is each 3 in Row 3 related to the two numbers above it?

▶ Look at Row 4. How is the 4 related to the two numbers above it? What pattern do you see?

▶ Copy the triangle. Use the pattern to complete Row 4.

▶ What are the first and last numbers in each row? What should be the first and last numbers in Row 5?

▶ Complete Row 5. Then extend the triangle through Row 7.

You can also find a pattern in the sums for the rows of the triangle.

Talk About It

▶ Find the sum of the numbers in each of Rows 0–7. What pattern do you see?

▶ Use the pattern in the sums to find the sums for Rows 8–10.

Making the Connection

You can use the numbers in each row of Pascal's triangle and the sum of the numbers when solving probability problems.

The table shows the outcomes for flipping 1–3 coins.

Number of Coins	Sample Space (outcomes)	Number of Outcomes for Getting Each Number of Heads				
		0 heads	1 head	2 heads	3 heads	Total Outcomes
1	H, T	1	1			2
2	HH, HT, TH, TT	1	2	1		4
3	HHH, HHT, HTH, HTT, THH, THT, TTH, TTT	■	■	■	■	■

1. What relationship do you see between the numbers of outcomes in the table and Rows 1 and 2 of Pascal's triangle?

2. Using Pascal's triangle, complete the table for 3 coins. Which row of the triangle did you use?

You have used Pascal's triangle to find the number of outcomes for an event and to find the total number of outcomes. So, you can also use it to find the probability of an event.

Example

For 2 coins, the probability of getting 1 head is $\frac{2}{4}$, or $\frac{1}{2}$.

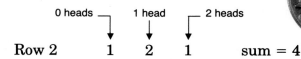

Row 2   1   2   1   sum = 4

Checking Understanding

You toss 4 coins. Find the probability. Use the numbers and their sum from Row 4 of Pascal's triangle.

3. P(2 heads)   **4.** P(3 heads)   **5.** P(5 heads)

You toss 5 coins. Find the probability.

6. P(1 head)   **7.** P(3 heads)   **8.** P(5 heads)

PROBLEM *Solving*

A bowling team has 9 members. The team wants to choose a committee of 4 from its members. How many combinations of 4 members can be made from the team of 9 members?

A diagram, chart, or graph, such as Pascal's triangle, can be used to solve problems involving combinations.

► **UNDERSTAND**

What are you asked to find?

What facts are given?

► **PLAN**

How can you solve the problem?

You can use a diagram such as Pascal's triangle to find the number of possible combinations.

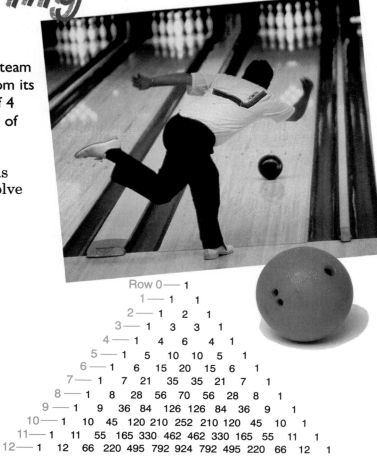

```
Row 0 — 1
     1 — 1   1
     2 — 1   2   1
     3 — 1   3   3   1
     4 — 1   4   6   4   1
     5 — 1   5   10  10  5   1
     6 — 1   6   15  20  15  6   1
     7 — 1   7   21  35  35  21  7   1
     8 — 1   8   28  56  70  56  28  8   1
     9 — 1   9   36  84  126 126 84  36  9   1
    10 — 1  10  45 120 210 252 210 120 45  10  1
    11 — 1  11  55 165 330 462 462 330 165 55  11  1
    12 — 1  12  66 220 495 792 924 792 495 220 66  12  1
```

Pascal's Triangle

► **SOLVE**

Which row of the triangle should you use?

Since the team has 9 members, use Row 9.

Row 9 ⟶ 1　9　36　84　126　126　84　36　9　1
　　　　　 |　|　 |　 |　　|
Start with 1 in ⟶ 0　1　2　3　4
Row 9, and count
4 additional places.

So, there are 126 combinations of 4 members from the team of 9 members.

► **LOOK BACK**

How can you check your answer?

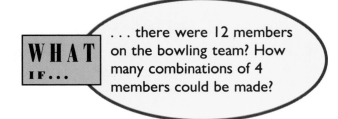

WHAT IF... . . . there were 12 members on the bowling team? How many combinations of 4 members could be made?

Apply

Use Pascal's triangle to solve.

1 A table-tennis club with 11 members wants to elect 3 officers. How many combinations of 3 officers can be elected from the 11 members?

2 A travel club with 10 members won a contest. The prize was a trip for 2 of the members. In how many ways can 2 members be chosen from the 10 members?

3 There are 7 runners on the schedule for a race. Only 3 of them can be selected to meet the mayor before the race. How many groups of 3 runners can be formed from the 7 runners?

4 At a bus stop, 9 people want to get on the bus, but only 4 seats are available. How many combinations of 4 people from 9 people can there be?

Mixed Applications | **STRATEGIES** | • Make a Drawing • Find a Pattern
| | • Use a Formula • Work Backward

Choose a strategy and solve.

5 Tess is making a design with decorative blocks. She has used 4 blocks in the first row, 7 in the second row, 11 in the third row, and 16 in the fourth row. If Tess continues this pattern, how many blocks will she use in the sixth row?

6 Benjamin put a fence around a rectangular garden that is 20 ft long and 12 ft wide. He used a fence post every 4 ft. How many fence posts did Benjamin use?

7 A tour bus traveled 182 mi in $3\frac{1}{2}$ hr. What was the average speed of the bus in miles per hour?

8 A bicyclist rode for $2\frac{2}{3}$ hr at 23 mph. How far did the bicyclist ride?

9 Meg spent $\frac{1}{4}$ of the quarters she had saved. She gave her brother $\frac{3}{4}$ of the rest. Then she had 3 quarters left. How many quarters had she saved?

WRITER'S CORNER

10 Write a problem similar to Exercise 1. Be sure that your problem can be solved by using Pascal's triangle.

If you roll a number cube six times, will each of the numbers 1 to 6 show up?

The Crispilight Cracker Company is having a contest. To win a prize, you have to collect six different puzzle pieces. One puzzle piece is placed in each box of crackers produced, and the six different puzzle pieces are divided equally among the boxes. How many boxes will you have to buy to get all six puzzle pieces?

You can predict the answer to this problem by doing an experiment that simulates the situation.

WORK TOGETHER

Work with a partner. Use a number cube numbered from 1 to 6 to generate random numbers. Each of the numbers 1 to 6 will represent one of the puzzle pieces. Roll the number cube and record the number you get. Continue to roll the number cube until you have rolled all of the numbers.

● How many rolls did it take until you rolled all of the numbers?

Repeat the experiment four times.

● For the five times you performed the experiment, what is the average number of rolls it took to get all six numbers?

● How many boxes of crackers will you have to buy?

Talk About It

▶ How do your results compare with those of your classmates?

▶ What is the mathematical probability of rolling a 3? How do your results compare to this probability?

▶ Suppose you perform the experiment one more time. Will the results change your average? Explain.

▶ Why are the numbers in your results called random numbers?

Idea Bank, page 490, Exercise 2

Check for Understanding

Use your results from the experiment on page 362.

1. Find the number of times each of the numbers 1, 2, 3, 4, 5, and 6 was rolled. For each number, write a ratio comparing the number of times the number was rolled to the total number of rolls.

2. How do your ratios in Exercise 1 compare with the mathematical probability of rolling a 1, 2, 3, 4, 5, or 6 on a number cube?

Practice

The random numbers 0–9 in the table were generated by a computer. Use the table for Exercises 3–6. Select any row and column as a starting point.

3. You are playing a game using the spinner shown. Use the table to simulate 100 spins. How many spins will it take before you get all the numbers 0 to 9?

4. Using the mathematical probability, predict how many times the spinner will stop on 7 if you spin 30 times. How does your prediction compare with the results shown in the table for 30 spins?

Mixed Applications

5. Robert put ten cards numbered 0–9 in a bag. Susan takes out a card and puts it back. Predict the number of times Susan will pick the 5 card if she picks 40 times. How does your prediction compare with the results of the simulation?

6. Let the table be a simulation of tossing a coin 100 times. Let 0 and the even numbers equal heads and the odd numbers equal tails. Predict the number of heads in 100 tosses. How does your prediction compare with the results of the simulation?

7. Mr. Thomas expects to drive his new car 45,000 mi. The tires on the car and the tires he will buy will last a maximum of 30,000 mi. Find the least number of new tires he will have to buy to travel 45,000 mi.

8. For Exercise 5, suppose you begin with the second row of numbers in the table. Will this change the number of times the 5 card is picked in the simulation? Explain.

100 Random Numbers									
6	1	5	0	8	7	9	4	0	4
8	3	6	0	9	2	0	1	4	4
8	1	8	3	4	0	7	0	9	7
4	9	8	8	1	6	4	7	6	6
7	6	5	8	5	5	7	6	2	6
4	1	1	3	7	8	4	2	4	0
5	8	1	0	4	9	3	1	2	4
2	8	2	9	3	7	2	1	4	1
3	4	5	3	5	0	3	8	4	3
6	2	0	1	2	7	0	5	6	0

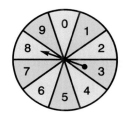

Give an advantage of using computer-generated random numbers for simulating an experiment.

WRAP
UP . . .

More Practice, Lesson 11.7, page H72

PREDICTIONS

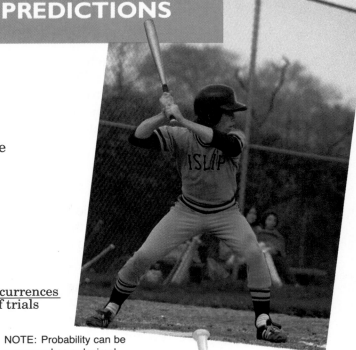

Robbie hit the ball 45 times out of his last 150 times at bat. What is Robbie's probability of getting a hit his next time at bat?

When an experiment is repeated many times, the results can be used to find the probability of an event. These probabilities are called **experimental probabilities.**

$$\text{experimental probability} = \frac{\text{number of occurrences}}{\text{number of trials}}$$

$$P(\text{hit}) = \frac{45}{150} = \frac{3}{10}, \text{ or } 0.3$$

NOTE: Probability can be expressed as a decimal.

So, the probability of Robbie getting a hit his next time at bat is $\frac{3}{10}$, or 0.3.

You can use the experimental probability to determine how many hits Robbie can expect to get during his next 50 times at bat.

$$\text{hits expected} = \text{times at bat} \times \text{probability}$$
$$= 50 \times \frac{3}{10}$$
$$= 15$$

Robbie can expect to get 15 hits during his next 50 times at bat.

● How many hits can Robbie expect to get during his next 120 times at bat?

Talk About It

▶ If getting a hit and not getting a hit are equally likely events, what is the mathematical probability of getting a hit?

▶ How does this mathematical probability compare with the experimental probability of Robbie getting a hit?

▶ If you use the mathematical probability to find the number of hits Robbie can expect to get during his next 50 times at bat, what is the result?

Check for Understanding

In an experiment, a thumbtack lands point up 40 out of 100 times.
Use this information for Exercises 1–2.

1. What is the experimental probability that the thumbtack will land point up on the next throw?

2. How many times can you expect the thumbtack to land point up on the next 30 throws?

Practice

A football quarterback completes 8 out of 10 passes. Use this information for Exercises 3–6.

3. What is the experimental probability of the quarterback completing the next pass?

4. What is the experimental probability of the quarterback not completing the next pass?

5. How many completed passes can the quarterback expect during the next 15 tries?

6. How many incompleted passes can the quarterback expect during the next 15 tries?

Mixed Applications

The table shows the sports preferences of 300 middle school students.
Use the table for Exercises 7–10.

7. What is the experimental probability that a sixth grader prefers baseball?

8. What is the experimental probability that an eighth grader prefers football?

Sports Preference			
	Football	Baseball	Soccer
Sixth graders	32	45	23
Seventh graders	40	35	25
Eighth graders	36	32	32

9. Out of 250 eighth graders, how many can be expected to prefer football?

10. What percent of the seventh graders prefer baseball? soccer?

MIXED REVIEW

Find the product.

1. $\frac{1}{4} \times \frac{1}{2}$

2. $\frac{2}{3} \times \frac{1}{5}$

3. $\frac{3}{4} \times \frac{1}{3}$

4. $\frac{2}{5} \times \frac{3}{8}$

Find the mean and the median of each set of data.

5. 73, 64, 92, 73, 83, 79, 96

6. 5.1, 5.4, 6.0, 5.6, 5.9, 5.4, 5.8

How is an experimental probability different from a mathematical probability?

WRAP UP...

1. Last week, 10 students held a checkers marathon to raise money for charity. They played checkers for 33 hr. Each student had a sponsor who paid $1.25 for each hour of the marathon. How much money was raised?

2. Andy is having dinner at a local restaurant. His bill totals $8.85. He wants to leave a tip that is about 15% of the total bill. How much should Andy leave for a tip?

3. Jake is trying to remember how far he moved on each of his turns in the game. He knows that in 3 turns he moved a total of 26 spaces. His second move was 1 space more than his first move, and his third move was 3 spaces more than his second move. How many spaces did he move on each turn?

4. Jenny is playing a word game. The first word she used had 3 letters. The second word had 5 letters, the third word had 8 letters, and the fourth word had 12 letters. If Jenny continues to use this pattern, how many letters will the fifth word have?

5. Timothy earns $5.60 per hour for a 40-hr week. He earns $1\frac{1}{2}$ times his pay for any hours that he works over 40. Last week he worked 45 hr. Find the total amount he earned.

6. There were 30 people at a ball game when the game started. Every 20 min about 25 people joined the crowd. How many people were at the game after 1 hr?

Find the sum or difference.

7. $\frac{2}{3} + \frac{3}{5}$

8. $1\frac{3}{4} + 2\frac{5}{6}$

9. $12 - 3\frac{3}{8}$

10. $6\frac{1}{3} - 2\frac{3}{4}$

Estimate the product or quotient.

11. $1\frac{3}{4} \times 5\frac{1}{3}$

12. $8\frac{1}{4} \times 3\frac{5}{6}$

13. $5\frac{2}{3} \times 5\frac{2}{3}$

14. $10 \times 3\frac{3}{8}$

15. $9\frac{2}{3} \div 1\frac{7}{8}$

16. $4\frac{1}{4} \div 3\frac{5}{6}$

17. $12\frac{1}{5} \div 5\frac{3}{4}$

18. $4\frac{1}{3} \div 8\frac{1}{4}$

Find the quotient.

19. $2\frac{1}{2} \div \frac{1}{3}$

20. $3\frac{1}{4} \div 1\frac{1}{8}$

21. $6\frac{3}{5} \div 8\frac{1}{4}$

22. $1\frac{1}{2} \div 7$

Use the scale of 1 cm : 8 m to find the missing dimension.

23. drawing: 3 cm
    actual: ■ m

24. drawing: 8 cm
    actual: ■ m

25. drawing: ■ cm
    actual: 96 m

Write the product or quotient as one power.

26. $10^3 \cdot 10^2$

27. $6^4 \cdot 6^2$

28. $5^{-4} \cdot 5^8$

29. $8^4 \div 8^2$

30. $7^3 \div 7^6$

31. $9^{-5} \div 9^3$

Spotlight ON PROBLEM SOLVING

Understand
Plan
Solve
Look Back

Understand the Question

Some problems that you are asked to solve involve tricky wording or twists that require interpretation. Be aware that some problems may be easier than you think!

Read the problem.

If it takes 3 min to boil 1 egg on a stove, how many minutes will it take to boil 3 eggs?

Talk About It

a. Do you think that it will take 9 min to boil 3 eggs? Explain your answer.

b. Can all 3 eggs be boiled in the same pan?

c. Is there any difference in the amount of time required to boil 1 egg in a pan and the time required to boil 3 eggs in a pan?

d. How many minutes will it take to boil 3 eggs?

Apply

Solve. Watch out for the obvious.

1. Amy has 2 United States coins that have a total value of $0.55. One of the coins is not a nickel. What are the coins?

2. Robin had 12 marbles. She lost all but 3 of the marbles. How many marbles did she have left?

3. You have only 1 match. You enter a dark room where there is a candle, a kerosene lamp, and a fireplace. Which would you light first?

4. If 5 persons can pack 5 boxes of flowers in 5 min, how many persons are needed to pack 50 boxes in 50 minutes?

367

INDEPENDENT EVENTS

In a game, Jenny has to spin two different spinners. What is the probability that she will spin red on the first spinner and 4 on the second spinner?

The two events are **independent events** because the outcome of spinning the first spinner has no effect on the outcome of spinning the second spinner. You can find the probability of independent events by finding the product of their probabilities.

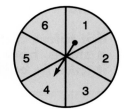
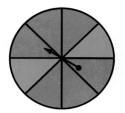

First spinner: $P(\text{red}) = \frac{4}{8}$, or $\frac{1}{2}$

Second spinner: $P(4) = \frac{1}{6}$

$P(\text{red}, 4) = P(\text{red}) \times P(4) = \frac{1}{2} \times \frac{1}{6} = \frac{1}{12}$

So, the probability that Jenny will spin red on the first spinner and 4 on the second spinner is $\frac{1}{12}$.

Another Example   Jenny spins both spinners. What is $P(\text{green}, 4 \text{ or } 6)$?

First spinner: $P(\text{green}) = \frac{2}{8}$, or $\frac{1}{4}$

Second spinner: $P(4 \text{ or } 6) = \frac{2}{6}$, or $\frac{1}{3}$

$P(\text{green}, 4 \text{ or } 6) = \frac{1}{4} \times \frac{1}{3} = \frac{1}{12}$

So, $P(\text{green}, 4 \text{ or } 6)$ is $\frac{1}{12}$.

If 2 events, A and B, are independent, then $P(A, B) = P(A) \times P(B)$.

Talk About It

▶ Suppose Jenny had to spin just one of the spinners two times. Are the events independent? Why or why not?

▶ Using the first spinner for two spins, what is $P(\text{red}, \text{red})$? $P(\text{red}, \text{blue})$?

Check for Understanding

You toss the coin and then spin the spinner. Find the probability.

1. $P(\text{heads, blue})$

2. $P(\text{tails, blue})$

3. $P(\text{heads, red})$

4. $P(\text{heads, green})$

5. $P(\text{tails, red or blue})$

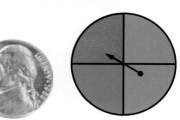

Practice

A dime is tossed and a number cube is rolled. Find the probability.

6. P(heads, 5) **7.** P(tails, even number) **8.** P(heads, odd number)

9. P(heads, not 1) **10.** P(tails, 8) **11.** P(tails, 1 or 2)

You spin the spinners. Find the probability.

12. P(red, 2) **13.** P(blue, 2)

14. P(green, 3) **15.** P(red, 1)

16. P(red, even number) **17.** P(red, odd number)

18. P(blue, even number) **19.** P(red, 8)

20. P(blue, 1, 2, 3, or 4)

One cube is drawn from the bag and replaced. Another cube is drawn. Find the probability.

21. P(blue, white) **22.** P(blue, blue)

23. P(blue, yellow) **24.** P(red, yellow)

25. P(red, blue) **26.** P(blue, red)

27. P(blue, blue, blue) **28.** P(white, red, yellow)

Mixed Applications

29. Toshi tosses a coin and rolls a number cube. What is the probability of heads and an even number?

30. In Exercise 29, what is the probability that Toshi will get heads and a multiple of 3?

31. **Mental Math** Steven correctly answered 78% of the questions on a test. There were 100 questions. How many questions did Steven answer correctly?

32. **Number Sense** There are red and white marbles in a bag. The probability of picking a red marble is $\frac{3}{8}$. What is the probability of picking a white marble?

Explain why tossing a coin and spinning a spinner are independent events.

WRAP
U P . . .

If you take 2 socks out of your drawer, what happens to the total number of socks in the drawer?

DEPENDENT EVENTS

In the game Simon is playing, he must pick a card, keep it, and then pick another card. He can win the game if he picks the 3 card and then the 5 card. What is the probability that Simon will win the game?

The chance of picking the 5 card depends on the card that was picked first. These events are **dependent.** You can find the probability of dependent events by finding the product of the probabilities.

$P(3) = \frac{1}{8}$ $P(5) = \frac{2}{7}$ ← One card was removed, so there are only 7 cards left.

$P(3, \text{then } 5) = \frac{1}{8} \times \frac{2}{7} = \frac{1}{28}$

So, the probability that Simon will win the game is $\frac{1}{28}$.

| 1 | 2 | 3 | 4 |

| 5 | 5 | 6 |

| 7 |

● What is $P(5, \text{then } 5)$?

Talk About It

▶ What is $P(5, \text{then } 3)$? Does the order of the events matter?

▶ Suppose each card is replaced after it is drawn. What is $P(3, \text{then } 5)$ and why is it different from the probability when the card is not replaced?

Check for Understanding

Ten cards numbered 0–9 are in a box. You select one card at random. Without replacing the card, you select a second card. Find the probabilities.

1. $P(1, \text{then } 4)$ **2.** $P(3, \text{then } 8)$ **3.** $P(1, \text{then even})$ **4.** $P(6, \text{then odd})$

5. $P(\text{multiple of 5, then even})$ **6.** $P(4, \text{then } 10)$

Tell whether the events are *independent* or *dependent.*

7. A cube is drawn from a bag and not replaced. Then a second cube is drawn.

8. A number cube is rolled twice.

 Idea Bank, page 490, Exercise 4

Practice

A jar contains these tickets. You select one ticket at random.
Without replacing the ticket, you select a second ticket.
Find the probabilities.

9. P(yellow, then yellow) 10. P(yellow, then green)

11. P(green, then yellow) 12. P(green, then green)

Without replacing the tickets, you select a third ticket.
Find the probabilities.

13. P(yellow, then yellow, then yellow)

14. P(yellow, then green, then green)

A box contains 5 red marbles, 3 blue marbles, and 7 white marbles. The
marbles are selected at random, one at a time, and not replaced. Find
the probabilities.

15. P(red, then blue)   16. P(white, then red)

17. P(red, then white, then blue)   18. P(red, then red, then white)

19. P(blue, then not blue)   20. P(white, then blue, then blue)

Mixed Applications

21. **Logical Reasoning** Two shirts and
one jacket cost the same amount as
two sweaters. One sweater and two
shirts cost the same amount as one
jacket. Which costs least—a shirt, a
jacket, or a sweater?

22. A box contains 3 mystery books, 5
science books, and 2 history books.
Marla randomly picks 3 books. What
is the probability that she picks one
of each type of book?

SCIENCE CONNECTION

According to the laws of genetics, if two red flowers each carry a
gene for white flowers, then the probability that a flower resulting
from cross-pollination will be white is $\frac{1}{4}$.

23. How many white flowers could you
expect in 100 flowers that resulted
from this cross-pollination?

24. How many nonwhite flowers could
you expect in 160 flowers that
resulted from this cross-pollination?

Explain the difference between two dependent
events and two independent events.

WRAP
UP...

VENN DIAGRAMS

Jan surveyed her classmates to find how many are in the science club and how many are in the computer club. The results of her survey are shown in the diagram. How many of Jan's classmates are in the science club?

The diagram is called a **Venn diagram.** Venn diagrams can be used to show relationships between groups.

The parts in the Venn diagram can be described as follows.

blue part: students in science club only
yellow part: students in computer club
            only
green part: students in both science and
            computer clubs

To find the number of students in the science club, you can find the sum 4 + 6. So, 10 of Jan's classmates are in the science club.

● How many of Jan's classmates are in the computer club?

WORK TOGETHER

● Draw a Venn diagram that shows the relationships described in this problem.

   In a group of 40 people, 25 like only rock music, 10 like only country and western music, and 5 like both.

● How many people like rock music?

Talk About It

▶ What do you know about the two groups represented by this Venn diagram?

▶ Name two groups of items that could be described by this Venn diagram.

▶ Could one circle of a Venn diagram ever be completely inside another circle in the diagram? Explain.

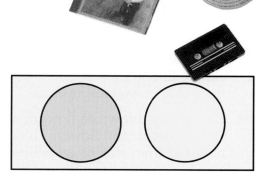

Check for Understanding

Use the Venn diagrams. Write *true* or *false*.

1.

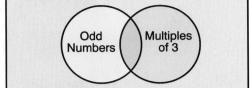

a. All multiples of 3 are odd numbers.

b. Some multiples of 3 are odd numbers.

c. No multiples of 3 are odd numbers.

2.

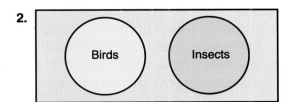

a. Some birds are insects.

b. No birds are insects.

c. All birds are insects.

Practice

Draw Venn diagrams for these statements.

3. Some students play both soccer and baseball.

4. Some multiples of 5 are even numbers.

5. No prime numbers are composite numbers.

6. All squares are rectangles.

Use the Venn diagram for Exercises 7–11.

7. How many students play piano? guitar?

8. How many students play both piano and guitar?

9. How many students play piano but not guitar?

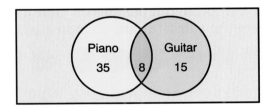

10. How many students play guitar but not piano?

11. How many students play piano or guitar but not both?

Mixed Applications

12. In a class of 30 students, 16 take French only, 8 take Spanish only, and 4 take French and Spanish. How many students take neither French nor Spanish?

13. Make Up a Question Robbie has 300 baseball and football cards. Of these, 35% are more than 10 years old.

14. Draw a Venn diagram to show the relationships among squares, rectangles, and parallelograms.

Name an advantage of representing information with a Venn diagram.

PROBLEM *Solving*

Strategy ● Act It Out

Erika places ten pennies in a row on top of her desk. She then replaces every other coin with a dime. Then she replaces every third coin with a nickel. What is the value of the ten coins on her desk?

Sometimes, you can solve a problem by acting out the situation.

► **UNDERSTAND**

What are you asked to find?
What facts are given?

► **PLAN**

What strategy will you use?

You can use the strategy *act it out*. Work through the problem exactly as it is described.

► **SOLVE**

How will you solve the problem?

You can place ten pennies on your desk. Then make the substitutions as indicated.

Replace every other coin with a dime.

Replace every third coin with a nickel.

So, the value of the coins is $0.58.

► **LOOK BACK**

What other strategy can you use to solve the problem?

WHAT IF . . . . . . every third coin is replaced with a quarter instead of a nickel? What is the value of the ten coins?

Apply

Solve.

① Tomas arranged 4 pennies, 4 dimes, 4 nickels, and 4 quarters into 4 rows of 4 coins each. Each of the rows, columns, and diagonals had exactly 1 penny, 1 nickel, 1 dime, and 1 quarter. Show how Tomas could have arranged the coins.

② Four friends, Luise, Maria, Carol, and Glenn, are sitting in a row. Neither Maria nor Carol is sitting next to Glenn. Carol is sitting just to the right of Maria. Write the seating arrangement from left to right.

Mixed Applications → **STRATEGIES**

- Make a Table • Act It Out
- Work Backward • Write an Equation
- Guess and Check • Draw a Picture

Choose a strategy and solve.

③ A store owner is trying to sell a $450 stereo. First, the owner raises the price by 20%. Then, the owner advertises a 20%-off sale on the new price. What is the final price of the stereo?

④ Albert had $1.19 in coins. Tammy asked him for change for a dollar, but he did not have the correct change. What coins did Albert have?

⑤ Amy paid $64 for a computer game and a joystick. The joystick cost 1.5 times as much as the game. How much did the game cost?

⑥ Louisa is $\frac{3}{4}$ as tall as Carla. The difference between their heights is 0.4 m. How tall is each girl?

⑦ Lisa, Diane, and David attend the same school. One is a basketball player, one is a band member, and one is a glee club member. Lisa and the glee club member have the same lunch period. David and the basketball player's brother are not related. Lisa plays no sports. Who is the glee club member?

⑧ In a shop class of 10 students, exactly 2 students are given the responsibility of cleaning the shop after class. A schedule pairs each student with every other student in the class exactly once. How many pairs of students are listed on the schedule?

Vocabulary Check

Choose a word or words from the box to complete each sentence.

| combination |
| dependent |
| experimental |
| independent |
| mathematical |
| permutation |
| sample space |

1. An arrangement of the members of a group in a definite order is called a __?__. *(page 350)*

2. The ratio of the number of favorable outcomes for an event to the number of possible outcomes is the __?__ probability of the event. *(page 356)*

3. The set of all possible outcomes is the __?__. *(page 356)*

4. The events of tossing a quarter and tossing a dime are examples of __?__ events. *(page 368)*

5. A selection of items in which the order does not matter is called a __?__. *(page 354)*

6. Probabilities based on the results of an experiment are called __?__ probabilities. *(page 364)*

7. Drawing a marble from a bag and not replacing it before a second marble is drawn is an example of __?__ events. *(page 370)*

Concept Check

8. **Complete:** If there are p choices for the way one thing can be done and q choices for the way another thing can be done, then together they can be done in __?__ ways. *(page 348)*

9. The pairs AB, BA, AC, CA, BC, and CB are permutations of the letters in the word CAB. How many of the pairs are combinations? *(pages 350, 354)*

Find the value of each factorial expression. You may use a calculator. *(page 351)*

10. $3!$ 11. $5!$ 12. $\frac{6!}{3!}$ 13. $\frac{8!}{5!}$ 14. $\frac{10!}{2!}$

You spin the spinner. Find the probability. *(page 356)*

15. $P(4)$ 16. $P(\text{pink})$ 17. $P(4 \text{ or pink})$

18. $P(\text{blue or green})$ 19. $P(1, 2, \text{ or } 3)$

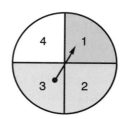

Skill Check

Find the number of permutations or combinations. You may use a calculator. *(pages 350, 354)*

20. $_4P_4$ **21.** $_8P_3$ **22.** $_5C_3$ **23.** $_8C_4$

24. There are 4 pizza toppings. How many pizzas with 3 different toppings can be made?

25. In how many ways can 4 out of 6 people sit in a row of 4 chairs?

In an experiment a number cube is rolled 100 times. The number 6 shows up 20 times. *(page 364)*

26. What is the experimental probability that the 6 will show up on the next roll?

27. How many times can you expect the number cube to show a 6 on the next 25 rolls?

A bag contains 4 green, 1 red, 3 yellow, and 4 black marbles. One marble is drawn and replaced. Then another marble is drawn. Find the probability. *(page 368)*

28. P(green, not black)   **29.** P(yellow, red)   **30.** P(yellow, green)

The first marble drawn from the bag used for Exercises 28–30 is not replaced. Then another marble is drawn. Find the probability. *(page 370)*

31. P(black, then green)   **32.** P(green, then red)   **33.** P(red, then red)

Use the Venn diagram for Exercises 34–35. *(page 372)*

34. How many students write for the newspaper? for the yearbook?

35. How many students write for both the newspaper and the yearbook?

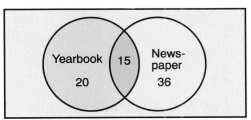

Problem-Solving Check

Solve. Use Pascal's triangle on page 360 for Exercises 36–37.
(pages 360, 374)

36. For his report Robert can choose 3 books from a list of 12 books. How many combinations of 3 books can he choose?

37. How many combinations of 4 students are possible from a group of 10?

38. Rhonda tells her test score to 3 persons, each of whom tells 2 more persons. Each of these tells 1 more person. How many persons have been told Rhonda's test score?

39. In how many ways can you make change for $0.50 using exactly 6 coins that are nickels and dimes?

CHAPTER TEST

Find the number of permutations or combinations.

1. In how many ways can 6 students sit in a row of 6 chairs?

2. There are 8 girls in a gym class. How many teams of 4 girls can be formed?

You spin the spinner. Find the probability.

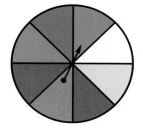

3. P(red)

4. P(yellow)

5. P(yellow or blue)

6. P(not green)

You toss a coin and spin the spinner shown. Find the probability.

7. P(tails, blue)   8. P(heads, yellow)   9. P(heads, purple)   10. (heads, red or blue)

A bag contains 8 cards numbered 1–8. You draw a card and do not replace it. Then you draw a second card. Find the probability.

11. P(8, then 4)   12. P(2, then 6)   13. P(even, then odd)

A basketball player made 24 out of 40 shots. Use this information for Exercises 14–15.

14. What is the experimental probability that the basketball player will make a shot on the next try?

15. How many times can the basketball player expect to make a shot during the next 10 tries?

16. Draw a Venn diagram for this statement: Some people play both chess and checkers.

Solve.

17. A chess club with 10 members wants to elect 4 officers. How many combinations of 4 officers can be elected from the 10 members?

18. In a classroom 8 students want to sit in a row, but only 6 seats are available. How many combinations of 6 students from 8 can there be?

19. Trish has 8 dimes in a row on her desk. She replaces every third coin with a nickel. Then she replaces every fourth coin with a quarter. What is the value of the coins on her desk?

20. John, Robert, Lisa, and Steve are sitting in a row. Neither Robert nor Lisa is sitting next to Steve. Lisa is sitting just to the left of John. Write the seating arrangement from left to right.

Teamwork P-R-O-J-E-C-T

Batting Averages

Statistics are used in many sports to judge how well a player plays. In baseball a player's batting average is an experimental probability written as a decimal.

Work with your teammates to simulate part of a season for a baseball team and to determine the batting averages of the players.

DECIDE

Determine the number of players you want on your baseball team. You should have at least 10 players. Give your players names or numbers so they can be identified. Decide on a name for your team.

SHARE

Compare your results with those of other students.

DO

Use a coin to determine whether or not a player gets a hit. Each player should be up to bat at least 10 times. Record your results.

After each player has been at bat 10 times, determine each player's batting average as a decimal. Display your data in a table.

Talk About It

• How can you use the batting averages you found to predict the number of hits each player on your team will get out of the next 30 tries?

• Compare your batting averages to those of players on real baseball teams. What do you notice? Explain.

Number Patterns

```
        Row 0 — 1
       Row 1 — 1      1
      Row 2 — 1    2    1
     Row 3 — 1   3    3    1
    Row 4 — 1  4    6    4    1
```

In Pascal's triangle the outer diagonals are 1's. Between the 1's each number is the sum of the two numbers diagonally above it.

Copy Pascal's triangle, extending it through row 9.

1. How many diagonals of counting numbers do you find?

2. Add pairs of numbers in the third diagonals, $(1 + 3)$, $(3 + 6)$, and so on. What pattern do you find?

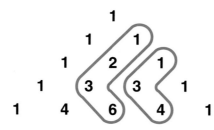

3. In your triangle, draw some "stockings" like those shown. What do you notice about the "toe"?

4. Use a "stocking" to find the sum of $1 + 3 + 6 + 10 + 15 + 21$.

Challenge

Patterns and Relations

Use Pascal's triangle to write the first 8 triangular numbers. For the first 3, count the dots.

Challenge

The Fibonacci Sequence

$1, 1, 2, 3, 5, 8, 13, 21, 34, 55, 89, \ldots$

The sequence starts with two 1's. Each number that follows is the sum of the two preceding numbers. This sequence has many patterns and applications. Look at these partial sequences.

```
3   5   8   13
3 × 13 = 39,  5 × 8 = 40
```

```
3   5   8   13   21
8² = 64,  5 × 13 = 65,  3 × 21 = 63
```

Write other sequences of 4 and 5 successive numbers. Multiply the numbers as shown. What pattern do you find in the products?

CUMULATIVE REVIEW

CHAPTERS I–II

Write the letter of the correct answer.

1. Which is the value of 4^3?

   A. 7   B. 12

   C. 48   D. 64

2. $45 - (18 \div 3) \times 2$

   A. 18   B. 33

   C. 42   D. 78

3. $13\frac{1}{4} - 5\frac{2}{3}$

   A. $7\frac{1}{2}$ B. $7\frac{7}{12}$

   C. $8\frac{7}{12}$ D. not here

4. $^-6 + 3$

   A. $^-9$ B. $^-3$

   C. 3   D. 9

5. $10^4 \cdot 10^7$

   A. 10^{-11} B. 10^{-3}

   C. 10^3 D. 10^{11}

6. Solve. $x - {}^-8 = {}^-5$

   A. $x = {}^-13$ B. $x = {}^-3$

   C. $x = 3$ D. $x = 13$

7. Which is the value of $2n + 3$ for $n = 5$?

   A. 5   B. 10

   C. 13   D. 28

8. Which ratio is equivalent to 2 to 5?

   A. 1 to 2   B. 4 to 10

   C. 5 to 2   D. 4 to 25

9. What is the radius of the circle?

   A. 3.14 cm

   B. 5 cm

   C. 10 cm

   D. 20 cm

   (10 cm)

10. What is P(3)?

    A. $\frac{1}{4}$

    B. $\frac{1}{3}$

    C. $\frac{1}{2}$

    D. $\frac{3}{4}$

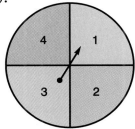

11. Neal spent $22.50 at the carnival. He spent $5.00 on admission, $6.25 on food, and the rest on ride tickets. If the tickets cost $0.75 each, how many tickets did Neal buy?

    A. 15 tickets   B. 21 tickets

    C. 30 tickets   D. 45 tickets

12. Rose surveyed the 243 eighth graders at her school. She found that the number of students that ride a bus is twice the number that do not ride a bus. How many students ride a bus?

    A. 27 students   B. 81 students

    C. 162 students   D. 486 students

CHAPTER

12

PLANE GEOMETRY AND MEASUREMENT

Did you know . . .

. . . that *Tyrannosaurus rex* was about 14 m long and 6 m tall?

What information would you need to determine whether *Tyrannosaurus rex* could fit into your gym?

SELECTING AN APPROPRIATE UNIT

Maria plans to decorate her room with a
wallpaper border all around the room,
at the edge of the ceiling. The wallpaper
border is sold in 15-ft lengths or 10-m
lengths. Each package costs $9.99.
Which is the better buy?

Maria measures her room in feet
and in meters.

	Customary System	Metric System
Room dimensions	10 ft by 12 ft	3.0 m by 3.6 m
Perimeter	10 + 10 + 12 + 12 = 44 ft	2(3.0 + 3.6) = 13.2 m
Required number of packages	44 ÷ 15 = 2.93 ≈ 3	13.2 ÷ 10 = 1.32 ≈ 2
Total cost	3 × $9.99 = $29.97	2 × $9.99 = $19.98

So, the 10-m package is the better buy.

● Suppose Maria measures her room, using the centimeter as
  the unit of length. What are the room dimensions?

● Is it easier to use centimeters or meters for measuring the
  dimensions of your room? Explain.

The unit selected to measure a length depends on the length to be
measured and the way the measurement is to be used.

Length to Be Measured	Thickness of a Nickel	Teacher's Desk	Football Pass
Customary unit	inch	foot	yard
Metric unit	millimeter	decimeter	meter

Talk About It

▶ How does the size of the unit compare to the number of units required?

▶ Which customary unit of length is appropriate for measuring the
  length of the Mississippi River? the length of your foot?

▶ How do you decide whether a unit of length is appropriate?

Check for Understanding

Measure each line segment, using the most appropriate customary unit of length. Include both the number and the unit in your answer.

1. _____   **2.** _____

Choose the most appropriate customary unit of length for measuring each length. Write *in., ft, yd,* or *mi.*

3. pencil   **4.** football field   **5.** your height

Choose the most appropriate metric unit for measuring each length. Write *mm, cm, m,* or *km.*

6. moving van   **7.** distance from Boston   **8.** paper clip
                                      to New York City

Practice

Measure each line segment, using the most appropriate metric unit of length. Include both the number and the unit in your answer.

9. __   **10.** _____

Choose the most appropriate customary unit of length for each situation. Write *in., ft, yd,* or *mi.*

11. distance from your   **12.** thickness of   **13.** height of school
       home to school   your math book   flagpole

Choose the most appropriate metric unit of length for each situation. Write *mm, cm, m,* or *km.*

14. height of a house   **15.** width of a sheet   **16.** length of an ant
                                        of notebook paper

Mixed Applications

17. Hector is purchasing some items for his mother. His shopping list says 35- ____ film. The metric unit is missing. What metric film size should he request?

18. John wants to mark the size and location of a new porch. Which measuring device is most appropriate: a 6-in. ruler, a 12-in. ruler, or a yardstick?

19. **Making Decisions**   Jill ran 100 m in 14 sec and Amy ran 880 m in 133 sec. Which runner had the faster speed?

20. **Making Choices**   Which is the better buy: 4 yd of ribbon for $1.86 or 10 ft for $1.69? Explain.

How should the size of the measurement unit relate to the size of the object?

ESTIMATING MEASURES

Mary Ann will go to Greensboro, North Carolina, this summer to visit her grandmother. She will travel on Route 85 from Atlanta, Georgia, to Greensboro. Suppose the car averages 50 mph. What is a reasonable estimate of her travel time?

Mary Ann uses the map scale, the map, and a piece of string to estimate her travel time from Atlanta to Greensboro.

Step 1
She uses a string to measure the interstate-highway route between the two cities.

Step 2
Mary Ann compares the string length to the map scale length. She estimates that the string length is about $3\frac{1}{2}$ times the map scale length.

Step 3
She converts the string length to miles.
Think: $3\frac{1}{2} \times 100$ mi $= 350$ mi

Step 4
She estimates the travel time by dividing by the speed: $350 \div 50 = 7$.

So, her travel time will be about 7 hr.

Sometimes it is more appropriate to estimate. Estimation is used in everyday life in activities such as cooking, sewing, travel, drawing, carpentry, and sports.

● Use a string and the map above to estimate the distance between Atlanta, Georgia, and Columbia, South Carolina.

● Measure your hand span in centimeters. Then use your hand span to estimate the length of your desk.

Talk About It

▶ How can you estimate the height of the XYZ building in stories? in feet?

Check for Understanding

Measure the item, using the given unit for Exercises 1–4.

1. length of desk, thumbnail width
2. width of classroom, book length
3. length of a shoe, paper-clip length
4. height of door, your shoe length
5. Which is the smallest unit?
6. Which is the largest unit?
7. Name something about 1 m wide.
8. Name something about 1 mm thick.

Practice

Tell whether an estimate is appropriate for each measurement.
Write *yes* or *no*.

9. room dimensions for a carpet order
10. height of a stack of 10 nickels
11. Which is the most reasonable estimate of Mr. Santini's height?

    a. 2 km   **b.** 2 m   **c.** 2 cm   **d.** 2 mm

Estimate the highway distances between the two cities. Use the map on page 386 for Exercises 12–15.

12. Atlanta to Charlotte
13. Atlanta to Macon
14. Charlotte to Savannah
15. Columbia to Charleston
16. Newbury to Burton
17. Claridon to Windsor
18. Huntsburg to Wick

Mixed Applications

19. A stack of 3 quarters is 5 mm high. What is the value of a stack of quarters 25 mm high?

20. The ship in the photograph is 5 m tall. Estimate the height of the iceberg.

21. **Logical Reasoning** Wilbur and Orville Wright's first flight was 120 ft long and lasted 12 sec. Their plane cost $1,000. What was the cost of the flight in dollars per second? dollars per foot?

What is the meaning of the carpenter's motto: "Measure twice, cut once"?

PRECISION
Greatest Possible Error

Jason and Tawana each measure the diameter of a
sand dollar during a science lab. Jason's measurement
is 5 cm. Tawana's measurement is 50 mm. Which
measurement is more precise?

Tawana's unit of measure is smaller than Jason's
unit of measure. Tawana's measurement is more
precise than Jason's measurement. The smaller the
unit of measure, the greater the **precision** of the
measurement.

Work Together

- Use a metric ruler to measure each line segment.

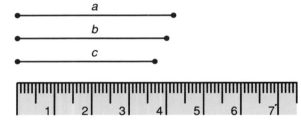

To the nearest centimeter, what is the
measure of line segment a, line segment
b, and line segment c?

- If you had no drawings of line segments a, b, and c but were told
  the measure of each line segment to the nearest whole centimeter,
  would you know which of the lines is actually longest?

- To the nearest millimeter, what is the measure of each line
  segment?

- If you had no drawings of line segments a, b, and c but were told
  the measure of each to the nearest tenth of a centimeter (mm),
  would you now know which of the line segments is longest?

Think of the bar at the right as a ruler,
marked in whole units.

- How could you tell more precisely the
  measure of line segments p and q?

- If you divided the 1-unit measure into
  $\frac{1}{2}$-unit measures and $\frac{1}{4}$-unit measures,
  what would be the measure of line
  segments p and q to the nearest $\frac{1}{2}$ unit?
  nearest $\frac{1}{4}$ unit? Which measurement of
  line segment p is more precise?

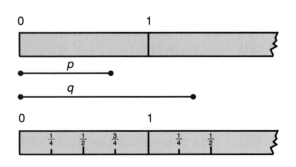

 Idea Bank, page 490, Exercise 5

Talk About It

▶ Why is 24 in. a more precise measurement than 2 ft?

▶ Which measurement is more precise, 1.3 km or 1,300 m? Explain.

▶ As the unit of measure gets smaller, what happens to the precision of the measurement?

▶ As the unit of measure gets larger, what happens to the precision of the measurement?

The precision of a measurement depends on the unit of measure used. A measurement tool, such as a ruler, is only as precise as its smallest unit.

● What is the most precise unit on your metric ruler?

● What is the most precise unit on your customary ruler?

_____

You can keep measuring in smaller and smaller units until your instruments (or your eyes) are no longer capable of distinguishing the difference between two measuring units. Since there is a limit to how precise any measurement is, there is a certain amount of possible error in any measurement.

The **greatest possible error** (GPE) of any measurement is $\frac{1}{2}$, or 0.5, of the precision of the units used in the measurement. The actual measurement can be at most 0.5 unit greater or 0.5 unit less than the reported measurement. This is written as ± 0.5 unit and is read as "plus or minus 0.5 unit."

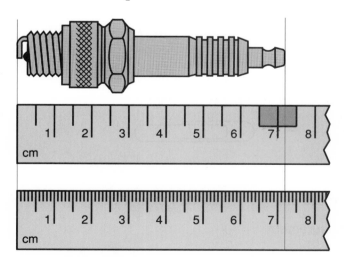

When the spark plug is measured to a precision of the nearest centimeter, it is 7 cm long. The greatest possible error in this measurement is 0.5 cm. The actual length of the spark plug is between 6.5 cm and 7.5 cm. When the spark plug is measured to a precision of the nearest tenth of a centimeter, it is 7.2 cm long. The greatest possible error in the measurement is 0.5 of 0.1 cm, or 0.05 cm.

● With a reported measurement of 7.2 cm, what are the least and greatest possible actual measurements of the spark plug?

More Examples

Measurement	Precision Unit of Measurement	GPE	Actual Measurement
3 cm	1 cm	0.5 cm	2.5 cm to 3.5 cm
25.9 mm	0.1 mm	0.05 mm	25.85 mm to 25.95 mm
38 km	1 km	0.5 km	37.5-km to 38.5 km
86 in.	1 in.	$\frac{1}{2}$ in.	$85\frac{1}{2}$ in. to $86\frac{1}{2}$ in.
16 ft	1 ft	$\frac{1}{2}$ ft	$15\frac{1}{2}$ ft to $16\frac{1}{2}$ ft
$4\frac{1}{2}$ mi	$\frac{1}{2}$ mi	$\frac{1}{4}$ mi	$4\frac{1}{4}$ mi to $4\frac{3}{4}$ mi
$7\frac{3}{4}$ yd	$\frac{1}{4}$ yd	$\frac{1}{8}$ yd	$7\frac{5}{8}$ yd to $7\frac{7}{8}$ yd

Work Together

Measure $\overline{GH}$ to the nearest tenth of a centimeter.

- What is the greatest possible error of the measurement of $\overline{GH}$?

- The actual length of $\overline{GH}$ can be between what two measurements?

Measure $\overline{JP}$ to the nearest $\frac{1}{4}$ inch.

- What is the greatest possible error of the measurement of $\overline{JP}$?

- The actual length of $\overline{JP}$ can be between what two measurements?

Check for Understanding

Measure the length to the nearest centimeter and to the nearest millimeter.

1.

2.

Tell which measurement is more precise.

3. 4 ft or 48 in.   **4.** 19 mm or 1.9 cm   **5.** 12.0 m or 12 m

Find the greatest possible error of each measurement.

6. 8 ft   **7.** 56 mi   **8.** 0.3 cm   **9.** 3.21 km

10. For a measurement of $5\frac{1}{2}$ in., how small could the actual length be? How large?

Practice

Give the precision of each measurement.

11. 7 m

12. $4\frac{1}{2}$ ft

13. $9\frac{1}{8}$ in.

14. 3.2 km

Find the greatest possible error of each measurement.

15. 9 cm

16. 62 mm

17. 20 yd

18. 14 in.

19. $4\frac{1}{3}$ mi

20. 0.51 cm

21. 8.67 km

22. $168\frac{1}{4}$ ft

For the given measurement, tell how small and how large the actual length can be.

23. 55 mi

24. 64 mm

25. 82.7 km

26. $11\frac{1}{4}$ yd

Measure to the nearest centimeter and the nearest millimeter. Give the least and greatest possible actual measurement.

27.

28. ▭

Mixed Applications

29. A sea horse is a fish that swims upright. A sea horse with a $5\frac{1}{2}$-in. length was found last summer. What is the greatest possible error of this measurement?

30. A starfish collected in 1969 had a total arm span of 63 cm. Allow for the greatest possible error, and find the two values between which the actual arm span can be.

31. The Mariana Trench is the deepest part of all the oceans. It lies 36,198 ft below the surface of the Pacific Ocean. Find the largest and smallest values for the actual depth.

32. Write a Question There are more than 13,000 kinds of fish in the oceans. The smallest fish is the 13-mm goby. The largest fish is the 12-m whale shark. Write a question using this information.

MIXED REVIEW

Write the reciprocal.

1. 4

2. $\frac{1}{7}$

3. $\frac{4}{5}$

4. $5\frac{1}{2}$

5. $3\frac{2}{9}$

Find the sum or difference.

6. $^-8 + {}^-3$

7. $9 + {}^-5$

8. $0 - 8$

9. $^-6 - 5$

10. $^-2 - {}^-9$

How is the greatest possible error of a measurement determined?

More Practice, Lesson 12.3, page H74

Which is probably a more careful measurement, 3 m or 3.25 m?

Robert and Chris are constructing birdhouses as a woodworking class project. They measure the width of their birdhouses and report different measurements: 19 cm and 19.0 cm. Are these measurements equally accurate? If not, which is more accurate?

The **accuracy** of a measurement is determined by the number of significant digits it contains. **Significant digits** indicate the number of measured units.

Robert's measurement of 19 cm has two significant digits. He measures to the nearest centimeter. Chris's measurement of 19.0 cm has three significant digits. She measures to the nearest tenth of a centimeter.

So, the two measurements are not equally accurate. The measurement 19.0 cm has more significant digits, so it is more accurate.

Measurement	Unit	Number of Units	Significant Digits	Number of Significant Digits
120.1 m	0.1 m	1,201	1, 2, 0, 1	4
120 m	1 m	120	1, 2, 0	3
1.2 m	0.1 m	12	1, 2	2
0.048 cm	0.001 cm	48	4, 8	2
3.06 cm	0.01 cm	306	3, 0, 6	3

In general, when computing with measurements, express the answer to the same number of digits as in the measurement that has the fewest significant digits.

Example Write the product, using the appropriate number of significant digits.

$125 \text{ m} \times 6.093 \text{ m} = 761.625 \text{ m}^2$
$\approx 762 \text{ m}^2$

Since 125 has 3 significant digits, the product is rounded to 3 significant digits.

Check for Understanding

Find the number of significant digits in each measurement.

1. 6 m   **2.** 6.42 m   **3.** 6.429 m   **4.** 6.4 m

5. Which of the measurements in Exercises 1–4 is most accurate? Explain.

Tell which of the two measurements is more accurate.

6. 34 mm or 34.1 mm   **7.** 9 m or 9.3 m   **8.** 172.75 km or 172.7 km

Practice

Find the number of significant digits for each statistic about ostriches.

9. height: 8 ft   **10.** weight: 345 lb   **11.** stride: 15 ft   **12.** speed: 40 mph

Find the appropriate number of significant digits for each answer.

13. 7.3 m + 6.09 m   **14.** 17.89 m − 16.3 m   **15.** 9.1 cm × 8.6 cm   **16.** 18.06 m ÷ 2 m

Find each sum or difference. Use rounding to express the answer with the correct number of significant digits.

17. 14.87 m + 15 m   **18.** 1.017 m + 2.95 m   **19.** 176.88 m − 98 m   **20.** 6.243 m − 4 m

Find each product. Use rounding to express the answer with the correct number of significant digits.

21. 2.1 m × 1.5 m   **22.** 3.2 m × 4.55 m   **23.** 3.88 mm × 2 mm   **24.** 8.7 m × 3.61 m

Mixed Applications

25. The established nest of a bald eagle may be 10 ft wide and 20 ft deep. How many significant digits does each measure have?

26. The 4-ft-tall emperor penguin is the largest penguin. How many significant digits does this height contain?

27. The blackpoll warbler flies 2,500 mi nonstop from its North American home to spend the winter in South America. The trip takes 90 hours. What is the speed in miles per hour?

28. Number Sense An ostrich egg weighs 1.2 kg. A hummingbird egg weighs 0.6 g. How many times heavier is the ostrich egg than the hummingbird egg?

How is the accuracy of a measurement related to the number of significant digits?

WRAP UP...

PROBLEM Solving

Teresa uses triangular tiles to form a mosaic design, a regular hexagon whose sides measure 4 in. The tiles are equilateral triangles whose sides measure 2 in. All tiles must tessellate. There can be no gaps or overlapping. How many triangular tiles does Teresa need?

▶ **UNDERSTAND**

What are you asked to find?
What facts are given?

▶ **PLAN**

What strategy will you use?

You can *make a model* to solve the problem. Make at least 6 paper models of the 2-in. equilateral-triangle tiles.

▶ **SOLVE**

How can you solve this problem?

You can draw a hexagon and use diagonals to divide it into 6 large congruent triangles.

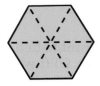

Use the paper triangle to create a tessellation pattern that forms one of the large triangles.

Then calculate the total number of triangles needed to form the hexagon.

Think:

number of tiles in each large triangle	×	number of large triangles	=	total number of tiles
4	×	6	=	24

So, Teresa needs 24 triangular tiles to form the hexagon.

▶ **LOOK BACK**

What method can you use to check your solution?

WHAT IF... . . . the hexagon's sides measure 8 in.? How many triangular tiles are needed?

Apply

The art club is creating mosaic tile projects in a variety of geometric shapes. Find the required number of mosaic tiles for each of the four projects. HINT for Exercises 3–4: Use diagonals to divide the figures into triangular sections.

1 How many 2-in.-square tiles are required for an 8-in. by 10-in. rectangular project?

2 How many 1-in.-square tiles are needed for a 14-in. by 14-in.-square project?

3 How many 1-in. equilateral triangle tiles are required for a regular hexagon whose sides each measure 1 in.?

4 How many 1-in. equilateral triangle tiles are needed to complete a regular hexagon whose sides each measure 3 in.?

Mixed Applications ➤ **STRATEGIES** • Draw a Picture • Make a Model • Write an Equation • Solve a Simpler Problem • Work Backward

Choose a strategy and solve.

5 Mrs. Cassidy uses 6 lb of beans for her chili recipe, which makes 20 servings. How many pounds of beans does she need to provide 75 servings of chili?

6 Fencing is sold in 10-ft sections at $12 a section. Fence posts cost $17 a post and are placed between sections and at each end of the fence. What is the cost of a 110-ft straight fence?

7 Stacey traveled many miles on business for her new job. Her employer paid her 27.5¢ for each mile, for a total of $1,204.50. How many miles did she travel?

8 Cheniqua has 18 links in her 20-cm bracelet. Suppose she removes one link. What is the new length of the bracelet?

9 Mr. Hansen wants to complete his ceramic tile jobs quickly and use the least number of tiles. Should he choose triangular, square, or hexagonal tiles that are 1 in. on each side?

10 Derek's starting salary doubled. Then, it decreased by $100. Next, it decreased by another $50. Then, it increased by $30. Today, his salary is $650. What was his starting salary?

PERIMETER OF POLYGONS

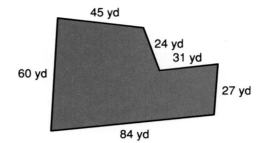

45 yd

24 yd

31 yd

60 yd

27 yd

84 yd

Mr. Curry's agriculture students plan to fence a small, irregularly shaped pasture. The pasture must be completely enclosed before their two goats can be put there. How much fencing is needed?

The length of the fencing is equal to the perimeter of the pasture.

The perimeter, P, of the pasture can be calculated by adding the measures of all the sides.

> The **perimeter** is the distance around a figure.

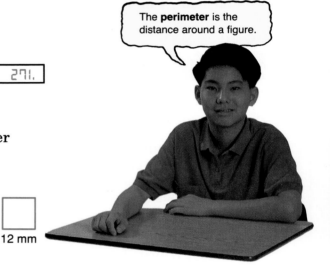

$60 \boxed{+} 84 \boxed{+} 27 \boxed{+} 31 \boxed{+} 24 \boxed{+} 45 \boxed{=}$ $\boxed{271.}$

So, 271 yd of fencing are needed.

Formulas can be used to calculate the perimeter of regular polygons. Recall that in a regular polygon, all the sides are the same length.

Examples

A. What is the perimeter of this square?

12 mm

Think: $P = s + s + s + s$, or $P = 4s$.
$P = 4s$
$P = 4 \times 12$
$P = 48$ So, the perimeter is 48 mm.

B. What is the perimeter of this rectangle?

65 mm

20 mm

Think: $P = l + l + w + w$, or $P = 2(l + w)$
$P = 2(l + w)$
$P = 2(65 + 20)$ $65 \boxed{+} 20 \boxed{\times} 2 \boxed{=}$ $\boxed{170.}$
$P = 170$ So, the perimeter of the rectangle is 170 mm.

- What must you do before you find the perimeter of this rectangle?

7.3 mm

29.2 cm

Talk About It

▶ What happens to the perimeter of the square in Example **A** when the length of each side is doubled?

▶ How can you find the perimeter of an equilateral triangle?

▶ How can you find the perimeter of a regular octagon?

Check for Understanding

Find the perimeter.

1.

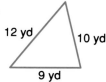

12 yd 10 yd 9 yd

2.

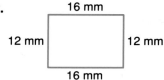

16 mm 12 mm 12 mm 16 mm

3.

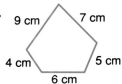

9 cm 7 cm 4 cm 5 cm 6 cm

4. Explain how you can use multiplication to find the perimeter of a square.

Practice

Find the perimeter.

5.

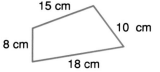

15 cm 10 cm 8 cm 18 cm

6.

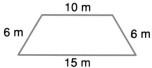

10 m 6 m 6 m 15 m

7.

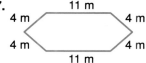

11 m 4 m 4 m 4 m 4 m 11 m

Find the perimeter of each regular polygon.

8.

14 in.

9.

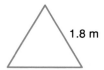

1.8 m

10.

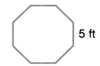

5 ft

The perimeter of each polygon is given. Find the missing length.

11. $P = 51.6$ cm

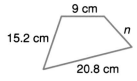

9 cm 15.2 cm n 20.8 cm

12. $P = 88$ in.

w 32 in.

Mixed Applications

13. Andrea is installing an electric fence around the pasture of her angora-goat farm. Will 1,000 ft of wire be adequate to enclose the 208-ft-wide by 290-ft-long rectangular pasture? Explain.

14. Ace is a 16-hand quarter horse. A horse is measured in hands from the hoof to the shoulders. A hand is equal to 4 in. What is Ace's height in inches? in feet?

15. Bill uses 500 ft of fencing to enclose a 75-ft-wide rectangular corral. What is the length of this corral?

16. There are about 3 million domestic goats in the United States. Write this number in scientific notation.

How can you use multiplication to find the perimeter of a regular polygon?

WRAP UP...

1. Alex scored 76 points on the science exam. Alex's score was about 150% of Ben's score. Estimate Ben's score.

2. Use the map scale to find the straight-line distance between Dallas and Oklahoma City.

3. Angelo's Restaurant has special prices for children under 9. What is the price for a 7-yr-old? for an 8-yr-old? Use the table below.

Age in years	1	2	3	4	5	6
Price in dollars	0	0	0	0.5	1.5	2.5

Compute.

4. $8 \times {}^-6$

5. $5 - {}^-3$

6. $116 \div {}^-2$

7. ${}^-9 + 3$

Write as a fraction with a positive exponent.

8. 10^{-2}

9. 10^{-8}

10. 2^{-6}

11. 4^{-3}

Write as an expression with a negative exponent.

12. $\frac{1}{10}$

13. $\frac{1}{10,000}$

14. $\frac{1}{49}$

15. $\frac{1}{8}$

Write the product as one power.

16. $6^2 \times 6^3$

17. $2^{-1} \times 2^5$

18. $8^6 \times 8^{-4}$

19. $5^{-6} \times 5^{-3}$

Write in scientific notation.

20. 0.008

21. 0.00044

22. 0.09

23. 0.0000074

Find the square root.

24. $\sqrt{4}$

25. $\sqrt{16}$

26. $\sqrt{64}$

27. ${}^-\sqrt{121}$

Order the rational numbers from least to greatest.

28. ${}^-4, \frac{1}{3}, {}^-\frac{1}{6}$

29. $8, \frac{3}{4}, {}^-\frac{1}{2}$

30. $\frac{5}{16}, {}^-\frac{5}{16}, 1\frac{1}{8}$

Solve the equation.

31. $n + \frac{1}{2} = 7\frac{3}{4}$

32. $\frac{2}{3}n = 24$

33. $n - {}^-3 = 15$

Solve the inequality.

34. $3n < {}^-6$

35. $\frac{1}{2}n > 9$

36. $n + {}^-8 < {}^-10$

Check the Reasonableness of the Solution

In solving problems, your work is not complete until you check your solution. Review the following problem and solution.

Jason took 25 seconds to run a 200-m race. What was his speed in kilometers per second?

Solution: $\frac{200}{25} = 8$. Jason's speed was 8 km/second.

Talk About It

Work with a classmate. Complete the following.

a. Is this solution reasonable?

b. How could you solve the problem correctly?

c. Mark is in charge of the school art contest. He has a total of 2 km of wall space for displaying the artwork. There are 400 art projects submitted. If each project is hung on the wall, can each project have at least 3 m of wall space, with 1 m of blank space on each side? Explain.

APPLY

Read each problem. Decide whether the solution is reasonable. Correct any unreasonable solutions.

1. Steve took 40 minutes to run a 10,000-m race. What was his speed in kilometers per minute? Solution: Steve's speed was 250 km/min.

2. Three brothers have heights of 120 cm, 165 cm, and 171 cm. What is their average height in meters? Solution: Their average height is 4.56 m.

3. A board is 0.396 m long and 0.016 m wide. How many meters greater is the length than the width? Solution: The length is 380 m greater.

4. Two models of the Aristo car have lengths of 4.496 m and 4.385 m. How many centimeters longer is the first model than the second model? Solution: The first model is 111 cm longer than the second model.

CIRCUMFERENCE OF CIRCLES

Li and Mary Carmen are decorating circular hats as a home economics project. They attach lace all around the brim and crown of each hat. The diameter of the brim is 15 in. The radius of the crown is $3\frac{1}{2}$ in. How much lace is required for each hat?

The **circumference** of a circle is the distance around the circle.

To find the amount of lace, find the sum of the circumference of the brim and the circumference of the crown.

Recall the formula for the circumference of a circle.

$$C = \pi d \quad \text{or} \quad C = 2\pi r \qquad \pi \approx 3.14, \text{ or } \tfrac{22}{7}$$

Circumference of the brim

$C = \pi d$

$C \approx 3.14 \times 15$

$C \approx 47.1$

Circumference of the crown

$C = 2\pi r$

$C \approx \frac{2}{1} \times \frac{22}{7} \times \frac{7}{2} \quad \leftarrow 3\frac{1}{2} = \frac{7}{2}$

$C \approx 22$

Find the sum of the circumferences. $47.1 + 22 = 69.1$

So, approximately 69.1 in. of lace are required for the hat. The sum rounded to 2 significant digits is 69 in.

Talk About It

▶ How can you write 69.1 in. as a mixed number?

▶ Why is the formula $C = 2\pi r$ used instead of $C = \pi d$ to find the circumference of the crown?

▶ Suppose a circumference is 34.54 m. How can you find the diameter?

Check for Understanding

1. When the diameter of a circle is 24 m, what is the radius?

2. Find the circumference of the circle in Exercise 1. Use 3.14 for π.

3. When the radius of a circle is 7 in., what is the diameter?

4. Find the circumference of the circle in Exercise 3. Use $\frac{22}{7}$ for π.

Practice

Find the circumference to the nearest hundredth. Use 3.14 for π.

5. $d = 8.11$ cm   **6.** $d = 0.06$ cm   **7.** $r = 0.24$ m   **8.** $r = 11.8$ m

9. $d = 0.08$ mm   **10.** $r = 6.42$ mm   **11.** $d = 81.8$ cm   **12.** $r = 0.46$ km

Find the circumference. Use $\frac{22}{7}$ for π.

13. $d = 7$ in.   **14.** $d = 42$ yd   **15.** $r = 21$ ft   **16.** $r = 28$ ft

17. $d = 35$ yd   **18.** $r = 140$ in.   **19.** $r = 70$ in.   **20.** $d = 70$ ft

Find the diameter of each circle. The circumference is given. Use 3.14 for π.

21. 25.12 km   **22.** 72.22 m   **23.** 628 m   **24.** 47.1 mm

25. A circle has a circumference of 200.96 cm. What is the radius of the circle?

26. Which is greater, the perimeter of the square or the circumference of the circle?

27. A circle has a diameter of 10 cm. Its circumference is approximately the same as the perimeter of a square. How long is a side of the square?

15 m (square)   15 m (circle)

Mixed Applications

28. Leta is purchasing lace to decorate the brim and the crown of an 18-in. straw hat with a crown diameter of 8 in. How much lace is required?

29. **Logical Reasoning** How many revolutions does a 26-in. bicycle wheel make during a 10-mi race? HINT: A 26-in. bicycle wheel has a diameter of 26 in.

30. Archie runs a circular track in 5 min. Tonya completes the track in 6 min. After starting together, how many minutes will elapse before the runners meet?

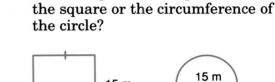

How do you decide whether to use $C = \pi d$ or $C = 2\pi r$?

WRAP UP...

AREA OF RECTANGLES AND PARALLELOGRAMS

The math club volunteered to help pave the 30-ft-wide and 37-ft-long rectangular patio next to the cafeteria. The students will pave this patio with 1-ft-square paving tiles. How many tiles will they need?

Area is the number of square units needed to cover a surface. Area can be measured in square inches (in^2), square feet (ft^2), square centimeters (cm^2), and so on.

The formula for the area of a rectangle is $A = lw$.

$A = lw$ ← Multiply the length times the width.
$A = 37 \times 30$ ← $l = 37$, $w = 30$
$A = 1,110$ ← The area is 1,110 ft^2.

So, the students will need 1,110 tiles for the patio.

Recall that a **parallelogram** is a quadrilateral with opposite sides parallel and congruent.

The formula for the area of a parallelogram is $A = bh$. ← Multiply the base times the height.

Example

Find the area of this parallelogram.

$A = bh$
$A = 6.7 \times 3.8$ 6.7 ⊗ 3.8 ⊟ [25.46]
$A = 25.46$ cm^2 ← The area rounded to two significant digits is 25 cm^2.

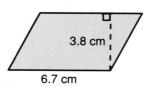

3.8 cm

6.7 cm

Talk About It

▶ Find the area of a rectangle that is 6.7 cm long and 3.8 cm wide. How do the area of the parallelogram in the example and the area of the rectangle compare? Explain.

▶ Draw a parallelogram with a height of 6 cm and a base of 10 cm. Cut a triangular section from one end of the parallelogram as shown. Move this triangular section to the opposite end of the parallelogram. What kind of polygon is formed?

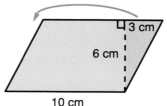

3 cm

6 cm

10 cm

▶ How does the area of a parallelogram compare to the area of a rectangle with an equal base and an equal height?

Check for Understanding

Find the area of each polygon.

1.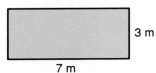
3 m
7 m

2.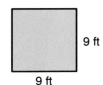
9 ft
9 ft

3.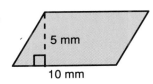
5 mm
10 mm

Practice

Find the area of each rectangle.

4. $l = 6$ in., $w = 2$ in.   **5.** $l = 13$ ft, $w = 8$ ft   **6.** $l = 9.4$ m, $w = 6.7$ m

Find the area of each parallelogram.

7. $b = 16$ ft, $h = 21$ ft   **8.** $b = 4.8$ m, $h = 6.2$ m   **9.** $b = 3.1$ cm, $h = 9.2$ cm

Find the area of the shaded region of each figure.

10.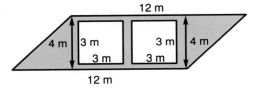
12 m
4 m 3 m 3 m 4 m
3 m 3 m
12 m

11.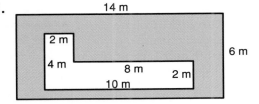
14 m
2 m
4 m
8 m 2 m
10 m
6 m

Consider the possible dimensions of each rectangle.
Use a whole number of units for the length and the width.

12. When the area of a rectangle is 150 ft², what is its maximum perimeter? minimum perimeter?

13. When the perimeter of a rectangle is 24 m, what is its maximum area? minimum area?

Mixed Applications

14. The world's largest omelet used 45,000 eggs and was cooked in a rectangular pan 10 ft wide and 43 ft long. What was the area of the omelet?

15. Willie increases the size of his parallelogram-shaped mosaic design from 30 cm high and 40 cm long to 45 cm high and 60 cm long. How does the area change? How does the perimeter change?

16. Housing codes require a house to be at least 25 ft long or 25 ft wide. Ola's rectangular house contains 1,800 ft². The width exceeds the minimum by 5 ft. What are the dimensions of Ola's house?

17. Visual Thinking
Move four toothpicks. Place them to form a total of 12 squares.

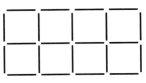

How are the area formulas for a rectangle and a parallelogram similar?

WRAP
UP...

Show how two equilateral triangles can form a parallelogram.

AREA OF TRIANGLES AND TRAPEZOIDS

The art club is preparing its entries for the community arts-and-crafts show. John completed a triangular stained-glass design with a height of 54 cm and a base of 38 cm. John is concerned about one of the rules on the entry form: "The area of an entry may not exceed 2,500 cm². " Is the area of John's stained-glass design acceptable?

The formula for the area of a parallelogram can help you determine the formula for the area of a triangle.

The diagonal separates the parallelogram into two congruent

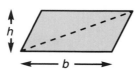

triangles. Each triangle's area is $\frac{1}{2}$ that of the parallelogram. So, the formula for the area of a triangle is $A = \frac{1}{2}bh$ or $A = \frac{bh}{2}$.

Find the area of the triangular stained-glass design.

$A = \frac{1}{2}bh$

$A = \frac{1}{2} \times 38 \times 54$ ← $b = 38, h = 54$

$A = 1,026$ ← The area of the stained-glass design is 1,026 cm².

Since 1,026 cm² is less than 2,500 cm², the area of John's stained-glass design is acceptable.

You can apply the formula for triangles to trapezoids.

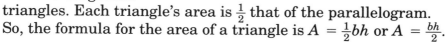

- A diagonal separates the trapezoid into two triangles. What is the height of the two triangles?

- What is the formula for the area of each triangle?

- What is the sum of the areas of the two triangles?

The Distributive Property of Multiplication over Addition allows us to simplify $A = \frac{1}{2}b_1h + \frac{1}{2}b_2h$ into $A = \frac{1}{2}h(b_1 + b_2)$.

Talk About It

▶ How can you find the area of this trapezoid?

▶ How can you find the area of any trapezoid? Explain the formula in your own words.

Check for Understanding

Find the area.

1.
5 m
6 m

2.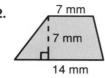
7 mm
7 mm
14 mm

3.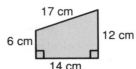
17 cm
6 cm
12 cm
14 cm

4.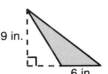
9 in.
6 in.

Practice

Find the area of each triangle.

5. $b = 4$ cm, $h = 5$ cm   **6.** $b = 9$ ft, $h = 7$ ft   **7.** $b = 3.6$ m, $h = 2.9$ m

Find the area of each trapezoid.

8. $h = 5$ in., $b_1 = 2$ in., $b_2 = 4$ in.   **9.** $h = 9.2$ m, $b_1 = 10.3$ m, $b_2 = 9.4$ m

Find the area of each shaded region.

10.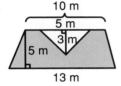
10 m
5 m
3 m
5 m
13 m

11.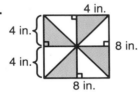
4 in.
4 in.
4 in.
4 in.
8 in.
8 in.

12.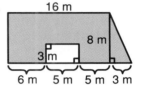
16 m
8 m
3 m
6 m 5 m 5 m 3 m

Mixed Applications

13. The front and back sides of an A-frame house are triangular, with a 55-ft base and a 35-ft height. What is the combined area of the two sides?

14. Peter's stained-glass entry is trapezoidal, with a 40-cm height and 62-cm and 80-cm bases. Is his entry within the 2,500 cm^2 limit? Explain.

15. A 30-ft sailboat has two triangular sails. The mainsail has an 18-ft base and a 40-ft height. The jib has a 12-ft base and a 28-ft height. What is the total area of the two sails?

16. Number Sense Arrange the digits 1, 2, 3, 4, and 5 to get the greatest possible quotient.

■■)■■■

MIXED REVIEW

Evaluate the expression for $n = 10$.

1. $7n$ **2.** $n + 11$ **3.** $\frac{n}{5}$ **4.** $2n + 4$ **5.** $6(n - 8)$

Write a decimal for the fraction.

6. $\frac{3}{20}$ **7.** $\frac{4}{25}$ **8.** $\frac{3}{50}$ **9.** $\frac{1}{6}$ **10.** $\frac{2}{9}$

How are the area formulas for a triangle and a trapezoid similar?

WRAP UP...

AREA
OF CIRCLES

The Greenfield Middle School students are completing a park beautification project. This weekend they will lay sod on the 81-foot-long by 42-ft-wide rectangular area surrounding the center garden. The circular center garden is 28 ft in diameter and will not be sodded. How much sod is needed?

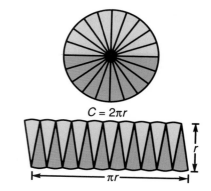

To solve this problem, you can use the formula for the area of a rectangle and the formula for the area of a circle.

You can determine the formula for the area of a circle by cutting a circle into wedges. You can then fit the wedges together to form a shape that looks like a parallelogram.

Work Together

- What part of the original circle is now the height of the parallelogram?

- How can you express the base of the parallelogram in terms of the parts of the original circle?

The area of this parallelogram can be written as $A = \pi r \times r$ or $A = \pi r^2$.

So, the formula for the area of a circle is $A = \pi r^2$.

To find the amount of sod needed, subtract the area of the circle from the area of the rectangle.

Area of rectangle

Think: $l = 81, w = 42$
$A = lw$
$A = 81 \times 42$
$A = 3{,}402$

Area of circle

Think: $d = 28, r = 14$
$A = \pi r^2$
$A \approx \frac{22}{7} \times 14^2$
$A \approx 616$

Subtract to find the amount of sod.

$3{,}402 - 616 = 2{,}786$

So, approximately 2,786 ft² of sod are needed.

Talk About It

- How can you find the area of the shaded region?

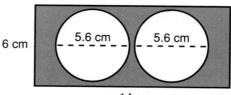

Check for Understanding

Find each quantity.

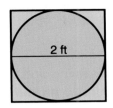

1. radius of circle
2. area of circle
3. area of square
4. area of blue region

Practice

Find the area to the nearest hundredth. Use 3.14 for π.

5.

9 cm

6.

22 m

7.

14.8 m

8. $r = 16$ mm   9. $r = 20$ in.   10. $r = 1.7$ m   11. $r = 8.1$ m

Find the area of the shaded region.

12.
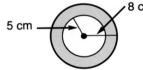
5 cm   8 cm

13.
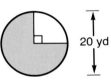
20 yd

14.

14 in.

Mixed Applications

15. A sundial sits in the center of a garden. The sundial has a diameter of 6 m. What is its area?

16. A city's circular fountain has an area of 379.94 ft². What is the circumference of the fountain?

17. The world's largest pizza had an area of 6,079.04 ft². If its diameter had been increased by 1 ft, what would have been the new radius?

18. The United States Mint produced 1,223,028,064 quarters in 1984. What is the total value of those coins?

| SOCIAL STUDIES CONNECTION |

A nautical mile, a unit of length at sea, is related to the measure of latitude and longitude. The circumference of the earth is divided into 360°. Each degree is divided into 60 minutes. One nautical mile is equivalent to one minute, or $\frac{1}{21,600}$ of the circumference of the earth. One nautical mile equals about 6,076 ft at the equator.

19. A ship travels 7 nautical miles at the equator. What is the distance, to the nearest thousand feet?

20. 73° of longitude at the equator is what distance in nautical miles?

How can you use the diameter of a circle to find its area?

WRAP UP...

# PROBLEM Solving

Strategy • Use a Formula

Mrs. Roberts and the members of her math club promise to measure the teachers' workroom and then hang wallpaper. How many rolls of wallpaper are needed?

▶ **UNDERSTAND**

What are you asked to find?

What facts are given?

▶ **PLAN**

What strategy will you use?

You can *use a formula* to solve the problem.

$$R = \frac{Ph}{3} - w$$
R = number of rolls of paper
P = perimeter of room (m)
h = height of room (m)
w = reduction for doors and windows

Use the door-and-window reduction rule. Subtract one roll of paper for every door and one roll of paper for every two windows.

▶ **SOLVE**

How will you solve the problem?

Measure the teachers' workroom, and count the doors and windows.

Find the amount of paper needed.

Teachers' Workroom				
Length	Width	Height	Number of Doors	Number of Windows
7 m	6 m	3 m	1	2

$R = \frac{Ph}{3} - w$ ← $P = 2(7 + 6)$, $h = 3$, $w = 2$

$R = \frac{2(7 + 6)(3)}{3} - 2$ 7 6 2 3 ÷ 3 − 2 = [24.]

$R = 24$

So, 24 rolls of wallpaper are needed.

▶ **LOOK BACK**

What method can you use to check your solution?

WHAT IF... *. . . the wallpaper costs $12.99 a roll? How much would the wallpaper cost?*

Apply

Use the formula $R = \dfrac{Ph}{3} - w$ for Exercises 1–4.

1 A kitchen is 3 m wide and 5 m long with a 2.5-m ceiling. There are 3 doors and 2 windows. How many rolls of wallpaper are needed?

2 A restaurant is 9 m wide and 13 m long with a 3-m ceiling. There are 6 doors and 10 windows. How many rolls of wallpaper are needed?

3 A principal's office is 4 m wide and 5 m long, with a 3-m ceiling. There are 2 windows and 1 door. One roll of wallpaper costs $8.99. What is the total cost for the wallpaper?

4 A doctor's waiting room measures 5 m wide and 8 m long with a 2.5-m ceiling. There are 4 windows and 3 doors. How many rolls of wallpaper are needed?

> **Mixed Applications** | **STRATEGIES** | • Use a Formula • Make a Drawing • Work Backward • Solve a Simpler Problem

Choose a strategy and solve.

5 A pony's 16-ft lead rope is tied to a hitching post in the center of a grassy field. How much grazing area does the pony have?

6 The Besser Warehouse has a 12-ft ceiling. How many 18-in. cartons can be piled on top of one another in one stack in the warehouse?

7 Ken pays a total of $8.45 to mail a 6-lb package. He pays $2.35 for insurance and $2.50 for guaranteed two-day delivery. What is the delivery cost per pound?

8 Mr. Fried is installing drainage pipes near the school playground. Which provides more drainage, one 10-in. pipe or two 5-in. pipes? Explain.

9 Al, Jack, and Steve are bus drivers who leave the bus depot at 6:30 A.M. to begin their round-trip routes. Al's round-trip route takes 40 min, Jack's takes 60 min, and Steve's takes 30 min. What is the next time that all three drivers will be in the depot?

10 Mr. Rose is calculating the area of his property so that he can determine the quantity of sod to purchase. Each of three rectangular sections will be sodded: 70 ft by 75 ft, 20 ft by 52 ft, and 70 ft by 110 ft. How much sod does Mr. Rose need?

WRITER'S CORNER

11 Write a problem similar to Exercise 7. Use money spent or money earned. Exchange with a classmate and solve.

12 Write a problem similar to Exercise 10. Use several polygons with different dimensions. Exchange with a classmate and solve.

CHAPTER REVIEW

Vocabulary Check

Choose a word or words from the box to complete each sentence.

accuracy
area
circumference
greatest possible error
perimeter
precision
significant digits

1. The number of __?__ in a measurement indicates the number of measured units. *(page 392)*

2. The distance around a figure is the __?__ . *(page 396)*

3. As the size of the unit of measure decreases, the __?__ of a measurement increases. *(page 388)*

4. $\frac{1}{2}$, or 0.5, of the precision of the unit used in the measurement is the __?__ of any measurement. *(page 389)*

5. The number of significant digits a measurement contains determines its __?__ . *(page 392)*

6. The distance around a circle is the __?__ of the circle. *(page 400)*

7. The number of square units needed to cover a surface is the __?__ . *(page 402)*

Concept Check

Choose the most appropriate metric unit of length for each situation. Write *km, m, cm,* or *mm.* *(page 384)*

8. length of classroom   9. thickness of two dimes   10. distance to the moon

Estimate the highway distances between the two cities. *(page 386)*

11. Freeport to Rockford

12. Elizabeth to Hanover

13. Woodbine to Elroy

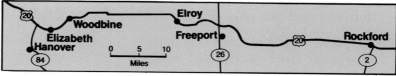

Tell which measurement is more precise. Give the precision of the more precise measurement. *(page 388)*

14. 4.2 cm or 42 mm   15. 18 in. or $1\frac{1}{2}$ yd   16. 600 cm or 6 m

Give the greatest possible error (GPE) of each measurement. *(page 389)*

17. 2 yd   18. 43 m   19. 3.9 cm   20. $7\frac{1}{2}$ in.

For the given measurement, tell how small and how large the actual length can be. *(page 389)*

21. 6 cm   22. 9.6 km   23. $8\frac{1}{4}$ ft   24. 3.21 m

Skill Check

Find each product. Use rounding to express the answer with the appropriate number of significant digits. *(page 392)*

25. $5.3 \text{ m} \times 1.2 \text{ m}$

26. $2.971 \text{ cm} \times 3 \text{ cm}$

27. $4.983 \text{ km} \times 0.7 \text{ km}$

Find the perimeter and the area of each figure. *(pages 396, 402, 404)*

28.

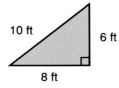

29.

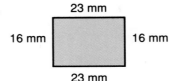

30.

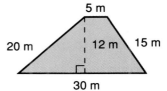

Find the circumference. Use $\frac{22}{7}$ for π. *(page 400)*

31. $d = 14 \text{ yd}$

32. $r = 35 \text{ ft}$

33. $d = 84 \text{ in.}$

34. $r = 3 \text{ mi}$

Find the area of the shaded region. *(pages 402, 404, 406)*

35.

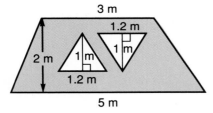

36.

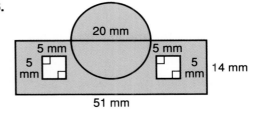

Find the area to the nearest hundredth. Use 3.14 for π. *(page 406)*

37. $r = 6 \text{ cm}$

38. $d = 10.5 \text{ m}$

39. $d = 30 \text{ in.}$

40. $r = 25 \text{ ft}$

Problem-Solving Check

41. Aunt Helen is making a 90-in.-wide by 105-in.-long bedspread. She wants to add fringe to the two long sides and one short side of the bedspread. How many yards of fringe should she purchase? *(page 394)*

42. David wants to fence an 80-ft-wide area behind his house. The fence will connect to the back corners of his 80-ft-long house. He has 400 ft of fencing. How long can the fenced area be? *(page 394)*

43. Mr. Luis wants to carpet his circular restaurant and its 3-yd-wide and 6-yd-long rectangular hall. The restaurant's diameter is 40 yd. How many square yards of carpet should Mr. Luis order? *(page 408)*

44. Jesse is calculating the cost of covering a 5-m-wide and 7-m-long rectangular office with ceramic tile. What is the cost of using 10-cm-square tiles at 39¢ each? What is the cost of using 20-cm-square tiles at 89¢ each? *(page 408)*

CHAPTER TEST

Choose the most appropriate customary unit of length for each situation.
Write *in., ft, yd,* or *mi.*

1. length of Hudson River   2. length of pencil   3. height of school

Estimate the highway distances between the two towns.

4. Huey to Salem

5. Centralia to Carlyle

6. Carlyle to Shattuc

For the given measure, tell how small and how large the actual length can be.

7. 27 yd   8. $8\frac{1}{2}$ mi   9. 5.9 cm   10. 4.38 m

Find each sum or difference. Use rounding to express the answer with
the appropriate number of significant digits.

11. 4 m + 2.39 m   12. 3.6 m + 2.1 m   13. 173.4 cm − 69.1 cm

Find the perimeter and the area of each figure.

14.
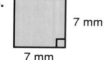
7 mm
7 mm

15.
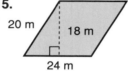
20 m
18 m
24 m

16.
3.4 mm   3.4 mm
3 mm
3.4 mm

17.
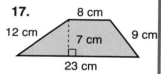
8 cm
12 cm
7 cm
9 cm
23 cm

Find the circumference and the area of each circle. Use 3.14 for π.
Round the answer to the nearest hundredth.

18. $r = 15$ mm   19. $r = 6.7$ m   20. $d = 28$ m   21. $d = 7.8$ cm

Solve.

22. A baseball diamond is actually a
square with 90-ft sides. After hitting
a home run, how far does a player
run from home plate, around the
bases, and back to home plate?

23. The baseball pitcher is confined to
the pitcher's mound while he is
throwing a pitch. The pitcher's
mound has an 18-ft diameter. What
is the area of the pitcher's mound?

24. Julie is painting the four walls of
her 13-ft-wide, 20-ft-long, and
7-ft-high living room. One gallon
of paint covers 800 ft². How many
gallons of paint are needed to paint
her living room with 2 coats of
paint?

25. Mr. Russo is planning to install
hexagonal paving stones. Each
regular hexagonal stone has an area
of 0.8 ft². How many hexagonal
stones does he need to cover a
30-ft-wide by 50-ft-long rectangular
patio?

Teamwork PROJECT

Just the Facts
Brainteasers

This is Fact-Finding Week in the library. All classes are finding facts through reading. Each class is asked to contribute three "Just the Facts" brainteasers, in which two different facts are used in a question. These should be serious facts, but you can present them in an interesting or humorous way. Each week the best brainteasers will be displayed on the library's Just the Facts bulletin board.

Would an adult giraffe be able to stand up in our gym?

Decide
As a team, brainstorm possible sources that you can use to find facts. Brainstorm possible topics for the facts.

Do
As a team, create and write five Just the Facts brainteasers. Draw or cut out pictures to add interest or humor.

Share
Present one of your brainteasers to the class. Display all of them in your classroom. Students should try to solve one another's brainteasers. Then the whole class should select the three most interesting brainteasers to display on the library bulletin board.

Talk About It

a. What topics can you use for brainteasers?

b. How are measurements reported in reference sources?

c. Why should you check more than one source to verify a fact?

d. Can knowing about measurement help you solve brainteasers? Explain.

e. What makes a brainteaser difficult to solve?

f. How can you use a variety of types of illustrations?

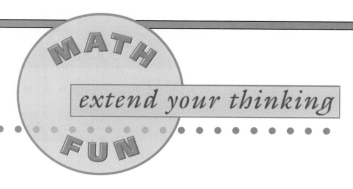

Conversion Factors

To change measurements from one unit to another, you can use conversion factors such as the fraction $\frac{1\,ft}{12\,in.}$, since 1 ft = 12 in.

Example

150 in. = $\underline{?}$ ft

Change inches to feet.

$$\frac{150\,in.}{1} \times \frac{1\,ft}{12\,in.} = \frac{150\,ft}{12}, \text{ or } 12\frac{1}{2}\,ft$$

Another Example

4,500 sec = $\underline{?}$ hr

Change seconds to minutes.

$$\frac{4,500\,sec}{1} \times \frac{1\,min}{60\,sec} = \frac{4,500\,min}{60}, \text{ or } 75\,min$$

Change minutes to hours.

$$\frac{75\,min}{1} \times \frac{1\,hr}{60\,min} = \frac{75\,hr}{60}, \text{ or } 1\frac{1}{4}\,hr$$

Use conversion factors to solve.

1. 5,500 pounds = $\underline{?}$ tons.

2. 40 in. = $\underline{?}$ yd

3. 11,700 sec = $\underline{?}$ hr

4. An airplane is descending at a speed of 450 mph. What is its speed in feet per second? HINT: You can multiply

$$\frac{450\,mi}{1\,hr} \times \frac{5,280\,ft}{1\,mi} \times \frac{1\,hr}{60\,min} \times \frac{1\,min}{60\,sec}$$

    in one step.

5. If 1 rod = 5.5 yd and 1 link = 0.66 ft, then 1 rod = $\underline{?}$ links.

Challenge

Number Sense

The product of two numbers is ⁻90. When the first number is multiplied by 1 more than the second number, the product is ⁻75. What are the two numbers?

Patterns

What are the next three numbers in the sequence? 3, 5, 8, 13, 21, . . .

CUMULATIVE REVIEW

Write the letter of the correct answer.

1. $3.2 \text{ km} = \blacksquare \text{ m}$

   A. 32   **B.** 3,200

   C. 32,000   **D.** not here

2. $2\frac{2}{3} \text{ yd} = \blacksquare \text{ ft}$

   A. $6\frac{2}{3}$ **B.** 8

   C. 12   **D.** 16

3. Which decimal is equivalent to $\frac{5}{8}$?

   A. 0.58   **B.** 0.6

   C. 0.62   **D.** 0.625

4. $\frac{4}{7} + \frac{1}{6}$

   A. $\frac{5}{13}$ **B.** $\frac{3}{4}$

   C. $\frac{33}{42}$ **D.** not here

5. Which has all prime numbers?

   A. 1, 2, 3, 5   **B.** 0, 1, 2, 3

   C. 2, 3, 5, 7   **D.** 2, 4, 6, 8

6. Which is a solution of $y = 2x + 1$?

   A. (2,4)   **B.** (1,3)

   C. (3,6)   **D.** (3,1)

7. $27 + n < 30$

   A. $n < 3$ **B.** $n > 3$

   C. $n < 57$ **D.** $n > 57$

8. Which is 20% of 182?

   A. 36.4   **B.** 162

   C. 202   **D.** 910

9. Which is 4.1583 rounded to the nearest hundredth?

   A. 44.158   **B.** 4.16

   C. 4.2   **D.** 4.24

10. Which is greater than $\frac{1}{2}$?

   A. $\frac{1}{4}$ **B.** $\frac{1}{3}$

   C. $\frac{2}{5}$ **D.** $\frac{2}{3}$

11. Which is the median of 3, 7, 2, 6, 5, 4, and 9?

   A. 4   **B.** 4.6

   C. 5   **D.** 6

12. Which is the greatest common factor of 8 and 12?

   A. 2   **B.** 4

   C. 24   **D.** 96

13. Julie worked 38 hr during the week. From her week's earnings, she spent $20.00 for groceries and put the balance of $189.00 in the bank. How much did she earn per hour?

   A. $4.45   **B.** $4.97

   C. $5.50   **D.** $209.00

14. Card tables are set together in two long rows to seat dinner guests. Each card table can seat only 1 person on a side. How many card tables are needed to seat 60 guests?

   A. 14 tables   **B.** 15 tables

   C. 28 tables   **D.** 30 tables

CHAPTER
13

SOLID GEOMETRY AND MEASUREMENT

Did you know . . .

. . . that recycling a $3\frac{1}{2}$-ft stack of newspapers saves one 20-ft tree?

What information will you need to find how many trees can be saved by recycling enough newspapers to fill the World Trade Center?

416

SOLID FIGURES
(POLYHEDRA)

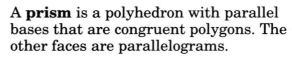

Jose is building models for his "math in
architecture" project. How are the shapes of the
Great Pyramid and the World Trade Center
similar? How are they different?

These models are three-dimensional figures.
Each is a polyhedron.

A **polyhedron** is a three-dimensional figure
whose faces are polygons. The plural of
polyhedron is polyhedra or polyhedrons.

The models of the Great Pyramid and the World
Trade Center represent two different classes of
polyhedra—pyramids and prisms.

A **pyramid** is a polyhedron with one
base that is a polygon. The other faces
are triangles.

A **prism** is a polyhedron with parallel
bases that are congruent polygons. The
other faces are parallelograms.

The Great Pyramid is a pyramid
with a square base. So, it is
a **square pyramid.**

The World Trade Center is a prism with
rectangular bases. So, it is a
rectangular prism.

WORK TOGETHER

Use your patterns to make polyhedra. Fold and fasten the tabs.

square pyramid

rectangular prism

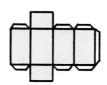

triangular prism

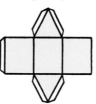

Talk About It

▶ How are polyhedra named?

▶ How are the pentagonal pyramid
and the pentagonal prism different?

▶ How does a polyhedron's base
determine the number of faces?

▶ What kind of polyhedron
does this pattern form?

pentagonal pyramid

pentagonal prism

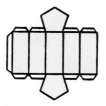

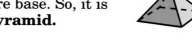

Check for Understanding

Write *yes* or *no* to tell whether each figure is a polyhedron.

1. rectangle
2. triangle
3. triangular prism
4. square pyramid

Write the name of each polyhedron.

5.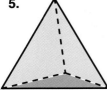

6.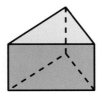

7.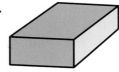

8.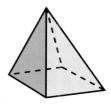

Practice

Write *pyramid* or *prism* to describe each polyhedron. Then write the specific name for each.

9. two congruent, parallel triangular bases; other faces, parallelograms

10. one square base; other faces, triangles

11. one octagonal base; other faces, triangles

12. two congruent, parallel octagonal bases; other faces, parallelograms

Describe each polyhedron. Include the shape of the base or bases and the shape of the other faces.

13. square pyramid
14. triangular prism
15. pentagonal prism
16. hexagonal pyramid
17. triangular pyramid
18. octagonal prism

Mixed Applications

19. Jessica wants to cut a piece of wood into the shape of a pyramid. She wants to have the fewest faces possible. What kind of pyramid should she make?

20. **Logical Reasoning** Jack is designing an aquarium. Which would be a better shape for his aquarium, a hexagonal pyramid or a hexagonal prism? Explain.

21. Nan's house is built in the shape of an octagonal prism. Each side is 25 ft long. What is the perimeter of her house?

22. The United States uses 14 million barrels of oil each day. Write this number in scientific notation.

23. Mt. Vesuvius is an active volcano shaped like a cone. It erupted in A.D. 79 and destroyed Pompeii. How many years ago did this occur?

24. **Estimation** A skating rink is circular, with a 25-ft radius. Estimate the circumference of the skating rink.

How are prisms and pyramids alike?
How are they different?

CYLINDERS, CONES, AND SPHERES

Sims Signs makes signs in a variety of shapes. Three of Sims' business customers have chosen unusual signs. One sign is cylindrical. Another is conical. The newest is spherical. How are the shapes of these three signs similar, and how are they different?

Each of these signs is a three-dimensional figure, but they are not polyhedra, because some of their surfaces are not polygons. Some of their surfaces are curved, and some are flat. All are related to the circle.

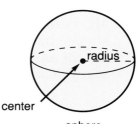

WORK TOGETHER

Trace your patterns for the cylinder and the cone. Notice the parts from which each figure is made. Construct models by folding and fastening the edges.

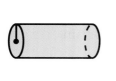 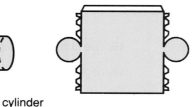    

cylinder   cone

- How many curved surfaces does the cylinder have?

- How many flat, parallel surfaces does the cylinder have?

- The cylinder is composed of what geometric shapes?

- What flat surface does the cone have? What is its shape?

- Does the cone have any parallel surfaces?

Use a basketball or a globe as a model of a sphere.

- What is the appearance of the sphere? Are there any flat surfaces? parallel surfaces?

- Suppose you could slice through the center of the sphere. What geometric shape would the cut be?

- A **sphere** is a solid with all points at an equal distance from the center. What is the name for this distance?

- View the sphere from any side. What is its geometric shape?

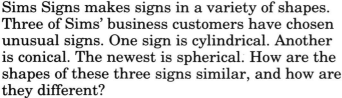

radius

center

sphere

Check for Understanding

Write *cylinder, cone,* or *sphere* to identify the shape of each object.

1. orange **2.** can of soup **3.** anthill **4.** piece of chalk

Practice

Write *cylinder, cone,* or *sphere* to identify the geometric figure that casts the shadow. Two shadows are shown for each figure.

5.

Side   Bottom

6. Top   Side

7. Side   Top

Write *cylinder, cone,* or *sphere* for each description.

8. two parallel surfaces

9. no flat surfaces

10. one flat surface, one curved surface

11. two flat surfaces, one curved surface

Write *cylinder, cone,* or *sphere* to identify the described geometric figure or figures. Explain.

12. ideal shape for a ball

13. ideal shape for cans of food

14. shape generally not used for food containers

15. same appearance from any view

Mixed Applications

16. A museum has a cylindrical tower topped by a conical roof. The circumference of the base of the roof is 37.68 m. What is the radius of the base of the roof?

17. Visual Thinking Carol's Yarn Shop ordered a spherical sign, a giant ball of yarn with a 9-ft diameter. What is the circumference of the equator of the sign?

18. Number Sense A dripping faucet loses 20 drops (2 mL) a minute. How many liters of water are lost in 12 hours?

19. Write a Question A small frozen yogurt cone costs $1.29. A medium cone costs $1.79. Liz purchased 3 small cones and 4 medium cones with a $20 bill. Write a question for this situation.

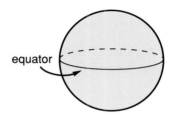

equator

How are the cylinder, the cone, and the sphere related to the circle?

WRAP
UP...

What are the three dimensions in a three-dimensional figure?

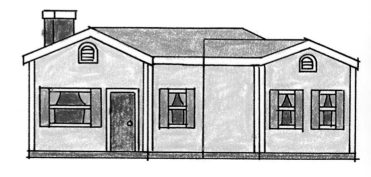

Kristen is completing her art assignment, a three-dimensional drawing of her home. Kristen's three-dimensional drawing does not look quite right. What is missing?

Kristen's drawing does not appear to have depth and distance. She did not use perspective in her three-dimensional drawing.

You can use **perspective** to make three-dimensional figures appear to have depth and distance in drawings.

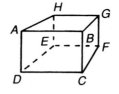

- Use one-point perspective (one vanishing point) to draw a left view of a prism.

Step 1
Draw the front face. For the left view, mark a vanishing point, *V,* to the left of the face. Join the corners of the face to *V.* Then choose a point *G* on $\overline{BV}$ and draw horizontal segment $\overline{GH}$.

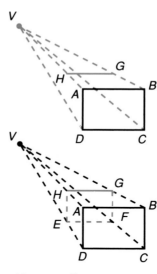

Step 2
Draw vertical segments $\overline{HE}$ and $\overline{GF}$. Then draw $\overline{EF}$. Darken the visible edges of the prism, including $\overline{AH}$, $\overline{HG}$, $\overline{GB}$, $\overline{ED}$, and $\overline{HE}$. Show dashed segments for the hidden edges, $\overline{FE}$, $\overline{FG}$, and $\overline{FC}$.

Step 3
Erase the vanishing point and all segments that join it to the prism.

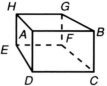

Talk About It
▶ Where do you place the vanishing point to draw a left view?

▶ Where do you place the vanishing point to draw a right view?

▶ How does the use of a vanishing point change the appearance of a drawing?

Check for Understanding

Start with the front triangular face and draw each view, using one-point perspective.

1. Draw a right view of the prism.

2. Draw a left view of the prism.

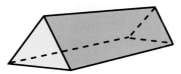

Practice

Use one-point perspective to draw each view. Do not show the hidden lines.

3. Draw a left view.

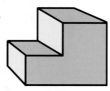

4. Draw a right view.

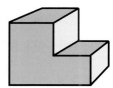

5. Draw a right view.

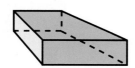

6. Draw a left view.

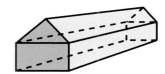

Mixed Applications

7. **Make Up a Problem** Write a word problem whose solution is the name of an object. Exchange with a classmate, solve, and then draw the object.

9. Matt is an architect who earns $22 an hour. He works 40 hr each week and 50 weeks a year. What are his earnings for one year?

8. **Visual Thinking** How many blocks are needed to build this tower?

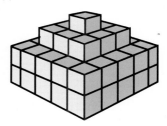

Write all the factors of each number.

1. 7
2. 12
3. 24
4. 45
5. 63

Write in simplest form.

6. $\frac{8}{10}$
7. $\frac{27}{36}$
8. $\frac{15}{40}$
9. $\frac{60}{100}$
10. $\frac{7}{497}$

Why does the use of perspective make a drawing look realistic?

W R A P
U P . . .

Jake constructs models of polyhedra out of straws and clay. He shows only the skeleton of each polyhedron—the edges and the vertices. How many straws and pieces of clay will he need for an octagonal prism and an octagonal pyramid?

▶ **UNDERSTAND**

What are you asked to find?

What facts are given?

▶ **PLAN**

How will you solve the problem?

You can *make a table* of data for some known prisms and pyramids. Identify patterns in the number of sides in each base and in the numbers of faces, vertices, and edges. Use the patterns to make predictions.

▶ **SOLVE**

How will you carry out your plan?

Name of Figure	Number of Sides in Each Base (n)	Number of Faces (F)	Number of Vertices (V)	Number of Edges (E)
Triangular prism	3	5	6	9
Rectangular prism	4	6	8	12
Pentagonal prism	5	7	10	15
Triangular pyramid	3	4	4	6
Square pyramid	4	5	5	8
Pentagonal pyramid	5	6	6	10

Patterns for Prisms
$V = 2n$, and $E = 3n$.
Let $n = 8$ for an octagonal prism.
$V = 16$, and $E = 24$.

Patterns for Pyramids
$V = n + 1$, and $E = 2n$.
Let $n = 8$ for an octagonal pyramid.
$V = 9$, and $E = 16$.

So, Jake needs 16 pieces of clay and 24 straws for the octagonal prism. He needs 9 pieces of clay and 16 straws for the octagonal pyramid.

▶ **LOOK BACK**

How can you check your answer?

 WHAT IF... . . . you have a hexagonal prism? How many edges does it have?

 Connection, pages 486–487

Apply

Use the patterns in the table on page 424 to solve Exercises 1–4.

1 Shani is cleaning her glass paperweight, which is shaped like a hexagonal pyramid. How many surfaces does she have to clean?

2 Gordon's hexagonal aquarium leaks. So, Gordon is sealing all the edges that connect two pieces of glass. How many edges should he seal?

3 Kasa is decorating a parade float built in the shape of a nonagonal prism. The bases have nine sides. Kasa needs to place a huge red bow at each vertex. How many bows are needed?

4 A park's monument is built in the shape of a decagonal pyramid. The base has ten sides. On Veterans Day each 30-ft vertical edge will be decorated with bunting. How much bunting will be needed?

Mixed Applications   **STRATEGIES**   • Make a Table • Use a Formula • Use an Equation • Guess and Check • Work Backward

Choose a strategy and solve.

5 Birmingham received 5.05 in. of rain in the last five days. On day 1, there was 0.5 in. of rain. On day 2, there was 1.2 in.; on day 3, 0.8 in.; and on day 4, 1.15 in. How much rain fell on day 5?

6 Together the seventh and eighth graders planted a total of 157 seedlings this week. Each grade planted a minimum of 75 seedlings. What are the possible numbers of seedlings planted by each grade?

7 Eli and Rachel help care for injured birds. They started the month with 27 birds. Then, 3 were added. Next, 5 were released. Later, 2 more were added. This week, 6 were released. How many birds remain?

8 Cheniqua's rectangular room has a 54-ft perimeter. The area of her room is 180 ft². The length is 125% of the width. What are the length and the width of her room?

9 Mrs. Pearce makes leaded-glass jewelry boxes in an octagonal-prism shape. Each face of a box is made with a single piece of glass. How many pieces of glass does she need to make 5 jewelry boxes?

10 The ecology club collected 58 bags of roadside litter during this month's community cleanup campaign. This was 8% of the total number of bags. What was the total?

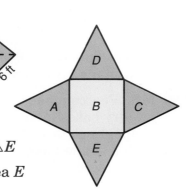

Clearview Window Cleaning, Inc., specializes in high-rise buildings. Clearview cleans Corbett Tower, a glass office building measuring 60 ft wide, 70 ft long, and 96 ft high. The cleaning rate is $0.20 per square foot. What is the total cost of window cleaning at Corbett Tower?

Corbett Tower is built in the shape of a rectangular prism. This pattern shows all the faces of the prism.

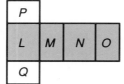

- Which are glass faces and must be cleaned?

Find the surface area of the four glass faces.

Think: The opposite faces of a rectangular prism are congruent parallelograms.

area L = area N = 70×96 = 6,720
area M = area O = 60×96 = 5,760
glass area = area L + area M + area N + area O
   = 6,720 + 5,760 + 6,720 + 5,760
   = 24,960 ← Glass area is 24,960 ft².

cost = $0.20 \times 24,960$ = $4,992
So, the cost of window cleaning at Corbett Tower is $4,992.

Chuck and Dexter want to spray their tent with water repellent. One can of water repellent covers 100 ft². The tent has a 6-ft by 6-ft floor and a 5-ft slant height. Is one can of water repellent enough for the tent?

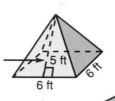

The **surface area** is the sum of the areas of all the surfaces of a solid.

Think: The tent is a square pyramid. $\triangle A \cong \triangle C \cong \triangle D \cong \triangle E$

surface area = area B + area A + area C + area D + area E
area A = area C = area D = area E = $\frac{1}{2} \times 6 \times 5$ = 15
surface area = 36 + 4(15) = 96 ← Surface area of tent is 96 ft².
So, one can of water repellent is enough for the tent.

Idea Bank, page 491, Exercise 13

Check for Understanding

Find the surface area of each prism or pyramid.

1.
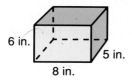
6 in.
5 in.
8 in.

2.
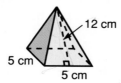
12 cm
5 cm
5 cm

3.
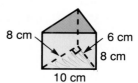
8 cm
6 cm
8 cm
10 cm

Practice

Find the surface area of each prism or pyramid.

4.
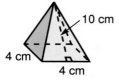
10 cm
4 cm
4 cm

5.
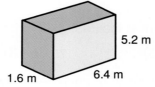
5.2 m
1.6 m
6.4 m

6.
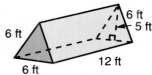
6 ft
5 ft
6 ft
6 ft
12 ft

Find the surface area. Round to the nearest tenth.

7. cube
side = 15.2 cm

8. square pyramid
side = 8 m, slant height = 6.5 m

Mixed Applications

9. Morgan Center is a glass office building that is 40 m tall, 30 m wide, and 33 m long. Glass surfaces will be covered with energy-efficient shades. How much shade material is needed?

10. Kele is wrapping a $1\frac{1}{2}$-ft-wide, $2\frac{1}{2}$-ft-long, and 3-ft-high box. Each package of wrapping paper contains 12 ft^2. How many packages of wrapping paper does Kele need?

11. Bo and Chen are experimenting with a pentagonal-pyramid-shaped greenhouse. Each side of the base is 22 ft long. The slant height of each triangular face is 20 ft. What is the area of the glass surface?

12. Logical Reasoning Each year 2.4×10^8 tires are discarded. One tire can produce enough energy for one home for one day. For how many 30-day months can 2.4×10^8 tires provide energy for one home?

MIXED REVIEW

Find the quotient.

1. $15 \div 0.3$ **2.** $645 \div 0.05$ **3.** $1,088 \div 6.4$ **4.** $2.7 \div 3$ **5.** $38.4 \div 9.6$

6. $\frac{3}{4} \div \frac{1}{8}$ **7.** $8 \div \frac{2}{5}$ **8.** $\frac{3}{10} \div \frac{6}{7}$ **9.** $5 \div \frac{11}{20}$ **10.** $\frac{1}{4} \div 9$

How can you use multiplication to calculate quickly the surface area of a prism or a pyramid?

WRAP
U P . . .

REVIEW AND MAINTENANCE

1. Lucita bought T-shirts for $10 each and sweatshirts for $22 each. She spent $84. How many of each did she buy?

2. Shawn borrows $7,000 for 4 yr. The bank charges 10% interest per year. How much interest must he pay?

3. Ned has a collection of Kennedy half dollars and Susan B. Anthony dollars. He has 6 more half dollars than dollars. How many half dollars are in his collection, which is worth $10.50?

4. Natasha has an herb garden that is 12 ft wide and 20 ft long. She plans to double the length and the width of the garden. How will the area change?

Name the quadrant in which the point is located.

5. $(5, {}^-8)$

6. $({}^-11, {}^-3)$

7. $(9, 13)$

8. $({}^-7, 10)$

Find the mean, the median, and the mode of each set of data.

9. 8, 9, 11, 20, 5, 3, 11

10. 54, 97, 66, 80, 78, 91

The Williams family spends $2,400 yearly for medical expenses. Use the circle graph to find the amount spent on each kind of expense.

11. eye

12. dental

13. insurance premiums

14. noncovered medical

Yearly Medical Expenses

Insurance Premiums 33%

Eye 21%

Noncovered Medical 32%

Dental 14%

Find the total number of choices.

15. 6 shirts, 7 skirts, 2 hats

16. 5 entrees, 6 beverages, 4 desserts

Find the number of permutations.

17. $_8P_2$

18. $_5P_4$

19. $_7P_5$

20. $_9P_3$

Find the greatest possible error of each measurement.

21. 4 in.

22. 2.5 cm

23. 12 yd

24. $8\frac{1}{2}$ ft

Find the circumference of each circle. Use $\pi = \frac{22}{7}$.

25. $d = 7$ in.

26. $r = 28$ ft

27. $d = 35$ ft

28. $r = 140$ in.

Spotlight ON
PROBLEM SOLVING

CHOOSE A METHOD FOR SOLUTION

In solving problems you will discover a variety of methods you can use. What is the area of the figure below?

Talk About It

a. Find the area by counting. Each square represents 1 cm².
b. You can also find the area by dividing the figure into smaller polygons. What smaller polygons can you use?
c. What formulas can you use to find the areas of the smaller polygons?
d. Find the area of the figure by using the formulas. Is it the same as you found by counting?

APPLY

Divide each of the figures below into smaller polygons or plane figures. Each square represents 1 cm². Then find the area in square centimeters by counting or by using your calculator and the appropriate formulas. Describe your solution method.

1.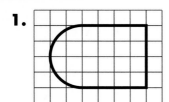

2.

3.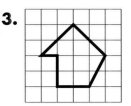

4.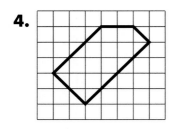

5.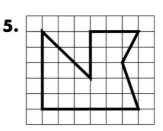

6.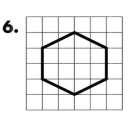

429

EXPLORING
Surface Area of Cylinders and Cones

You can find the surface area of a cylinder or a cone by adding the areas of the parts.

WORK TOGETHER

Building Understanding

Use your cylinder pattern to construct a cylinder.

- Take your cylinder apart. What shape are the bases? How can you find the area of the bases?

- Flatten the curved surface. What is the shape?

- The height of the cylinder represents the length of this rectangle. This rectangle's width is the same as what part of the circular base?

- How can you find the area of this rectangle?

- How can you find the surface area of a cylinder?

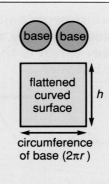

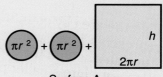

Surface Area

Use your cone pattern to construct a cone.

- Take your cone apart. What is the shape of the base? How can you find its area?

- Flatten the curved surface. What is its shape?

- The length of the curved side of the triangular part is the same as what part of the base? What is the formula for this part of a circle?

- The slant height (l) is the distance from the base of the cone to its vertex. How many straight sides of the triangular part have this length? Label these sides l.

- Fold these two l sides together and cut along the fold. Place these two pieces together to form a parallelogram. The length of each curved side is half of what part of the base of the cone?

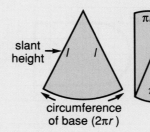

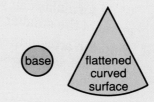

Talk About It

▶ How can you find the area of this parallelogram?

▶ How can you find the surface area of a cone?

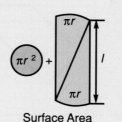

Surface Area

Making the Connection

You can use formulas to find the surface area
of a cylinder or a cone.

Surface Area of a Cylinder

To find the surface area, S, of a cylinder,
add the areas of the two bases (circles) and
the area of the curved surface (rectangle).

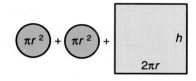

$S = 2(\text{area of circle}) + \text{area of rectangle}$
$S = 2(\pi r^2) + (2\pi r \times h)$

Find the surface area of a cylinder with a 10-cm height
and a 4-cm radius.

Think: $h = 10$ cm, $r = 4$ cm, and $\pi = 3.14$.

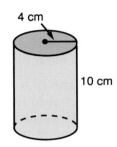

$S = 2(\pi r^2) + (2\pi r \times h)$
$S \approx 2(3.14 \times 4^2) + (2 \times 3.14 \times 4 \times 10)$
$S \approx 100.48 + 251.2$
$S \approx 351.68$ ← The surface area is about 351.68 cm^2.

Surface Area of a Cone

To find the surface area, S, of a cone, add
the area of the base (circle) and the area
of the curved surface (parallelogram).

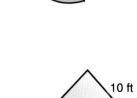

$S = \text{area of circle} + \text{area of parallelogram}$
$S = \pi r^2 + \pi r l$

Find the surface area of a cone with a 10-ft slant height
and a 7-ft radius.

Think: $l = 10$ ft, $r = 7$ ft, and $\pi \approx \frac{22}{7}$.

$S = \pi r^2 + \pi r l$
$S \approx \frac{22}{7} \times 7^2 + \frac{22}{7} \times 7 \times 10$
$S \approx 154 + 220$
$S \approx 374$ ← The surface area of the cone is about 374 ft^2.

Checking Understanding

Find the surface area. Use $\pi = 3.14$.

1. 6 cm
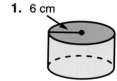
10 cm

2.
5 m
4 m
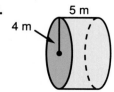

3. 4 cm
5 cm

4.
5 cm
16 cm

How many building blocks are needed to build a tower that is 2 blocks wide, 1 block deep, and 5 blocks tall?

VOLUME OF PRISMS AND PYRAMIDS

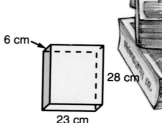

The town of Bloomfield is recycling used phone books instead of dumping them in a landfill. So far, 360 phone books have been collected. What volume of landfill space has been saved?

A phone book is a rectangular prism. To find the landfill space that has been saved, first find the volume of each phone book.

The **volume** of a prism is the number of cubic units needed to fill it. Volume is measured in cubic centimeters (cm^3), cubic meters (m^3), cubic feet (ft^3), cubic inches ($in.^3$), and so on.

To find the volume, V, of any prism, multiply the area of the base, B, times the height, h.

$$V = Bh$$

Find the volume of a phone book.
Think: $V = Bh$, or $V = lwh$ ← The base is a rectangle, so $B = lw$.
$$V = 28 \times 23 \times 6$$
$$V = 3{,}864 \leftarrow \text{The volume is 3,864 } cm^3.$$

Find the volume of 360 phone books.
The volume of 360 phone books is $360 \times 3{,}864$, or $1{,}391{,}040 \ cm^3$.
So, $1{,}391{,}040 \ cm^3$ of landfill space have been saved.

To find the volume, V, of a pyramid, multiply $\frac{1}{3}$ times the area of the base times the height.

$$V = \frac{1}{3} Bh$$

Find the volume of this pyramid.
Think: The base is a triangle. So, $B = \frac{1}{2} \times 4 \times 6 = 12$.

$$V = \frac{1}{3} Bh \leftarrow \frac{1}{3} \times 12 \times 10$$

$$V = 40 \leftarrow \text{The volume is 40 } ft^3.$$

Talk About It

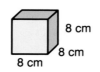

▶ How can you find the volume of a cube whose sides measure 8 cm?

▶ How can you find the volume of a pyramid with the same base and height?

▶ How many cubic centimeters are in $1 \ m^3$?

Check for Understanding

Find each volume.

1.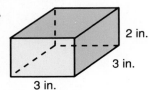
2 in.
3 in.
3 in.

2.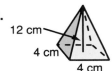
12 cm
4 cm
4 cm

3.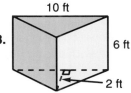
10 ft
6 ft
2 ft

Practice

Find each volume.

4.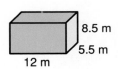
4 m
6 m
9 m

5.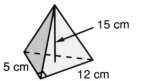
3 cm
6 cm
20 cm

6.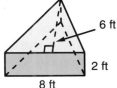
6 ft
2 ft
8 ft

7.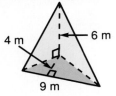
8.5 m
5.5 m
12 m

8.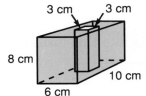
15 cm
5 cm
12 cm

9.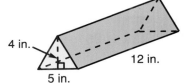
4 in.
5 in.
12 in.

Find the volume of the shaded portion.

10.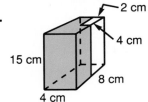
2 cm
4 cm
15 cm
8 cm
4 cm

11.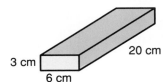
3 cm   3 cm
8 cm
6 cm
10 cm

12.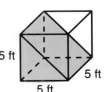
5 ft
5 ft
5 ft

Mixed Applications

13. The Great Pyramid of Egypt has a square base. Each side of the base is 230 m long. The height is 147 m. What is the volume?

14. Make Up a Question There are 420 names on each page of a 560-page phone book. Write a question for this situation.

15. Yoki and Tyee built a mesh framework for a compost pile. The framework encloses a 12-ft-long and 8-ft-wide area. The maximum volume of their compost pile is 576 ft². What is its height?

16. The base of each of the Twin Towers in New York City's World Trade Center is a square. The side of each square is 63 m long. The height of one tower is 408 m. The height of the second tower is 415 m. What is the total volume?

How are the volume formulas for a prism and a pyramid similar?

WRAP
UP...

There is a large cylindrical natural gas storage tank near the highway. The tank is 52 ft in diameter and 46 ft high. What volume of natural gas, to the nearest cubic foot, can this tank hold?

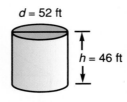

$d = 52$ ft

$h = 46$ ft

To find the volume of a cylinder, multiply the area of the base, B, times the height, h. $V = Bh$

Find the volume of the gas storage tank.

Think: The diameter is 52 ft, so the radius is 26 ft.

$V = \pi r^2 \times h$ ← The base is a circle, so $B = \pi r^2$.

$V \approx 3.14 \times 26^2 \times 46$ ← Use 3.14 for π.

$V \approx 97{,}641.44$

So, the tank can hold about 97,641 ft^3 of natural gas.

- A new tank is 26 ft in diameter and 46 ft high. How does the volume of the tank compare to the volume of the tank in the example?

- What other formula for volume is like this formula for a cylinder?

The volume of a cone is $\frac{1}{3}$ the volume of a cylinder with the same base and the same height.

To find the volume of a cone, V, multiply $\frac{1}{3}$ times the area of the base, B, times the height, h.

$V = \frac{1}{3} Bh$ ← Use the height, not the slant height.

$V = \frac{1}{3} \pi r^2 h$ ← The base is a circle, so $B = \pi r^2$.

$V = \frac{1}{3} Bh$

Find the volume of this cone. Use 3.14 for π.

$1 \; \boxed{\div} \; 3 \; \boxed{\times} \; 3.14 \; \boxed{\times} \; 6 \; \boxed{\times} \; 6 \; \boxed{\times} \; 16 \; \boxed{=} \; \boxed{\quad 602.88 \quad}$

$V \approx 602.88$ ← The volume is about 602.88 cm³.

16 cm

6 cm

Talk About It

▶ For what other solid figure can you use this formula for volume?

▶ Suppose you are given the volume of a cone. How can you find the volume of a cylinder with the same radius and height?

Check for Understanding

Find the volume. Use π = 3.14, and round to the nearest whole number.

1.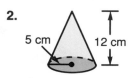
6 cm
10 cm

2.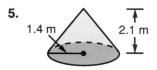
5 cm 12 cm

3.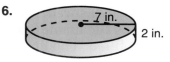
8 m
4 m

Practice

Find the volume. Use π = 3.14, and round to the nearest whole number.

4.
1.8 m
2.4 m

5.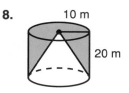
1.4 m 2.1 m

6.
7 in.
2 in.

Find the volume of the shaded portion. Round to the nearest whole number.

7.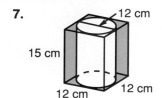
12 cm
15 cm
12 cm
12 cm

8.
10 m
20 m

9.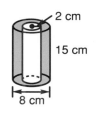
2 cm
15 cm
8 cm

Mixed Applications

10. A paper drinking cup shaped like a cone has a 10-cm height and an 8-cm diameter. What is the volume of the cup?

11. An oil-storage tank shaped like a cylinder has a 157,000-m³ volume. The area of the base is 7,850 m². What is the height of the tank?

Natural gas is stored underground and is moved through 1,000,000 mi of pipeline.

12. Estimate the total volume of natural gas produced by the three leading states.

13. What volume of natural gas can a 1,000-ft length of a 10-ft-diameter pipeline hold?

Leading Producers of Natural Gas	
State	**Annual Production**
Texas	6.185×10^{12} ft³
Louisiana	5.825×10^{12} ft³
Oklahoma	1.986×10^{12} ft³

How are the formulas for the volume of a cylinder and the volume of a cone alike? How are they different?

WRAP UP...

CAPACITY

What units of measure can you use
to describe the amount of lemonade
in a container?

Jeff received a hexagonally shaped
aquarium for his birthday. The area of the
base is 360 cm², and the height is 30 cm.
How much water can the aquarium hold?
What is the mass of the water?

Liquids are measured in units of capacity.
Capacity is the amount a container will
hold when filled. The liter and the milliliter
are metric units of capacity. The gram and
the kilogram are metric units of mass.

The Metric System		
Volume	**Mass**	**Capacity**
1 cm³	1 g	1 mL
1,000 cm³	1 kg	1 L

To find the amount of water and the mass of the water the
aquarium can hold, first find the volume of the aquarium.

To find the volume of the aquarium, a hexagonal prism,
multiply the area of the base times the height.

$V = Bh$ ← $B = 360$ cm², $h = 30$ cm
$V = 360 \times 30$
$V = 10,800$ ← The volume is 10,800 cm³.

$h = 30$ cm →

$B = 360$ cm²

Find the capacity of the aquarium.
Think: 1 cm³ has a capacity of 1 mL.
So, 10,800 cm³ have a capacity of 10,800 mL, or 10.8 L.

Find the mass of the water in the aquarium.
Think: 1 mL of water has a mass of 1 g.
So, 10,800 mL have a mass of 10,800 g, or 10.8 kg.

So, the aquarium can hold 10.8 L of water, and the water's
mass is 10.8 kg.

The metric system
relates mass of
water to volume
and capacity.

Talk About It

▶ The capacity of a rectangular prism is 60 mL. How can
you find the mass of the water that fills the prism?

▶ The volume of a cylinder is 28 cm³. How can you find the
mass of the water that fills the cylinder?

Check for Understanding

1. What are the dimensions of a cube that can hold 1 mL of water?

2. What are the dimensions of a cube that can hold 1 L of water?

3. What is the mass of 1 cm^3 of water?

4. What is the mass of 1,000 cm^3 of water?

Practice

Each statement is about water. Complete.

5. ■ cm^3 = 4.5 mL

6. 8 L have a mass of ■ kg.

Find the capacity of each container and the mass of the water it can hold.

7.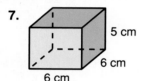
5 cm
6 cm
6 cm

8.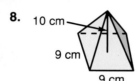
10 cm
9 cm
9 cm

9.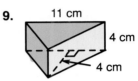
11 cm
4 cm
4 cm

10.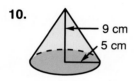
9 cm
5 cm

11.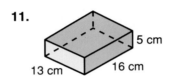
5 cm
13 cm
16 cm

12.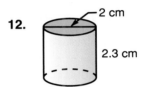
2 cm
2.3 cm

Mixed Applications

13. A barrel with a 40-cm diameter collected rainwater to a depth of 44 cm. How many milliliters of water were collected? liters?

14. United States consumers use 2,500,000 plastic bottles every hour. At that rate of use, how many are used in one week?

15. The horses' rectangular watering trough is 1 m wide, 0.8 m deep, and 3 m long. When it is filled, what is the mass of the water in grams? HINT: 1 m^3 = 1,000,000 cm^3

16. A cone-shaped paper cup has a 9-cm diameter and an 11-cm height. What is the capacity of the cup? When it is filled with water, what is the mass of the water?

EVERYDAY MATH CONNECTION

An average American uses about 260 L of water in the home each day.

17. How much water does an average American use in 4 weeks?

18. What is the mass of 260 L of water? What volume does it fill?

What is the advantage of relating mass to volume and capacity measures?

WRAP UP...

PROBLEM Solving

The town of Greenfield built a new water tower. The water tank is spherical, with a radius of 10 m. What is the volume of the water tank?

▶ **UNDERSTAND**

What are you asked to find?

What facts are you given?

▶ **PLAN**

How will you solve the problem?

You can *use a formula.*
The formula for the volume of a sphere is

$V = \frac{4}{3}\pi r^3$. ◀── r = radius of sphere

In the formula, substitute 10 m for the radius of the sphere. Use 3.14 for π.

▶ **SOLVE**

How will you carry out your plan?

You can make all the substitutions in the formula and then find the volume of the tank to the nearest whole number.

$V = \frac{4}{3}\pi r^3$ ◀── r^3 means $r \times r \times r$.

$V \approx \frac{4}{3} \times 3.14 \times 10^3$

$V \approx 4 \;\boxed{\times}\; 3.14 \;\boxed{\times}\; 10 \;\boxed{\times}\; 10 \;\boxed{\times}\; 10 \;\boxed{\div}\; 3 \;\boxed{=}\; \boxed{4186.6666}$

$V \approx 4,186.6666$

So, the volume of the water tank is about 4,187 m³.

▶ **LOOK BACK**

How can you check your answer?

WHAT IF... . . . the radius of the water tank is 5 m? What is the volume of the water tank?

438

Apply

Use the formula $V = \frac{4}{3}\pi r^3$ for Exercises 1–4.

(1) Toby's helium-filled spherical balloon has a 20-cm diameter. How many cubic centimeters of helium are needed to fill his balloon?

(2) Evansville's new spherical water tank has a 32-ft radius. What volume of water can it hold?

(3) A soccer ball has a 22-cm diameter. A basketball has a 29-cm diameter. How much greater is the volume of the basketball?

(4) One of the world's largest globes was made in France in 1824. It has a 128-ft diameter. What is its volume?

Mixed Applications	**STRATEGIES**	• Use a Formula • Use an Equation • Make a Table • Draw a Picture

Choose a strategy and solve.

(5) Tony and Ruth Ann spent a total of $10 on food at the park concession stand. They bought at least 5 slices of pizza at $1.00 a slice and at least 5 drinks at $0.60 each. What quantities did they buy?

(6) The Johnsons have decreased their water consumption by 30% since last month. This month they used 5,880 gal. How many gallons of water did they use last month?

(7) How many 5-cm-long, 4-cm-wide, and 8-cm-high boxes can you put in a cardboard box that is 60 cm long, 28 cm wide, and 24 cm deep?

(8) Greg has twice as many quarters as dimes. He has a total of 24 coins in all. How much money does Greg have?

(9) Kevin can mow a square lawn that is 30 m on a side in 45 min. If he works at the same rate, how long will it take him to mow a square lawn that is 60 m on a side?

(10) Consuela buys an apple pie that costs $3.60. The diameter of the pie is 10 in. If the pie is cut into 8 slices, what is the area of 3 slices?

WRITER'S CORNER

(11) Write a problem similar to Exercise 8. Use coins, paper money, or sale items. Exchange with a classmate and solve.

(12) Write a problem similar to Exercise 9. Use lawns, carpeting, screening, or fabric. Exchange with a classmate and solve.

Vocabulary Check

Choose a word or words from the box to complete each sentence.

| capacity |
| polyhedron |
| prism |
| pyramid |
| sphere |
| surface area |
| volume |

1. A three-dimensional figure whose faces are polygons is a ___?___. *(page 418)*

2. A polyhedron whose base is a polygon and whose other faces are triangles is a ___?___. *(page 418)*

3. A polyhedron whose bases are parallel congruent polygons and whose other faces are parallelograms is a ___?___. *(page 418)*

4. A solid that is the set of all points at an equal distance from the center is a ___?___. *(page 420)*

5. The sum of the areas of all the surfaces of a solid is ___?___. *(page 426)*

6. The number of cubic units needed to fill a solid figure is the ___?___. *(page 432)*

7. The amount a container will hold when filled is the ___?___. *(page 436)*

Concept Check

Write the name of each solid figure. *(pages 418, 420)*

8.

9.
8 cm
8 cm

10.

11.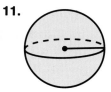

12.

Write *prism, pyramid, cylinder, cone,* or *sphere* for each description.
(pages 418, 420)

13. one flat surface, one curved surface

14. two congruent, parallel bases; other faces, parallelograms

15. one polygonal base; other faces, triangles

16. two flat, parallel surfaces; one curved surface

17. two circular bases; flattened curved surface is rectangular

18. no flat surfaces

Skill Check

Use one-point perspective to draw each view. *(page 422)*

19. Draw a right view.

20. Draw a left view.

Find the surface area. Round to the nearest whole number.
(pages 426, 431)

21.
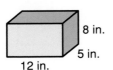

22.

23.

24.
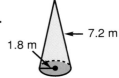

Find the volume. Round to the nearest whole number. *(pages 432, 434)*

25.
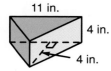

26.
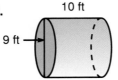

27.
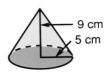

28.
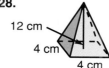

Find the capacity of each container and the mass of the water it holds.
Round to the nearest whole number. *(page 436)*

29.
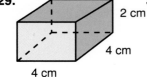

30.
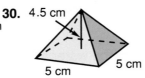

31.
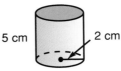

32.

Problem-Solving Check

Solve. *(pages 424, 438)*

33. Sims Signs is installing neon strip lights along each edge of the KMP building. The building is a pentagonal-prism shape. How many edges will be lighted?

34. Maria has a cylindrical container with a diameter of 9 cm. Water is stored in the container to a height of 20 cm. What is the mass of the water?

35. Jerome is wrapping a large cylindrical can that is 3 ft high and has a diameter of 2 ft. How much wrapping paper does Jerome need?

36. Jan and Jamie mowed a total of 47 lawns and earned $446. Jan's rate was $9 per lawn; Jamie's rate was $10 per lawn. Each mowed a minimum of 22 lawns. How many lawns did each mow?

CHAPTER TEST

Write the name of each solid figure.

1.   **2.**   **3.**   **4.**   **5.**

Use one-point perspective to draw each view.

6. Draw a left view.

7. Draw a right view.

Find the surface area. Round to the nearest whole number.

8.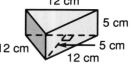
12 cm 5 cm 5 cm 12 cm 12 cm 12 cm

9.
16 ft 10 ft 10 ft 10 ft

10.
20 mm 23mm

11.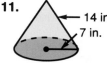
14 in. 7 in.

Find the volume. Round to the nearest whole number.

12.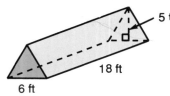
5 ft 18 ft 6 ft

13.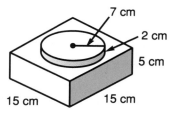
7 cm 2 cm 5 cm 15 cm 15 cm

Find the capacity of each container and the mass of the water it can hold.

14.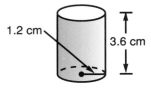
1.2 cm 3.6 cm

15.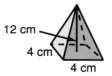
12 cm 4 cm 4 cm

16.
5 cm 20 cm

Solve.

17. Mrs. Allen bought a freezer shaped like a rectangular prism. The freezer is 4 ft long, 3 ft deep, and 2 ft wide. What is its volume?

18. Willie is modeling the skeleton of a pentagonal prism with straws and pieces of clay. How many straws and pieces of clay does he need?

19. Matt purchased a tent shaped like a square pyramid. The tent's floor is 8 ft on a side, and the slant height is 10 ft. What is the surface area of the tent?

20. The Nguyen family bought 8 pairs of shoes for a total of $120. Each pair cost either $12 or $20. They bought at least 3 pairs at each price. How many $20 pairs did they buy?

Teamwork
P-R-O-J-E-C-T

Recycle Containers

Many communities collect and recycle aluminum cans, glass bottles, and plastic jugs. Do you recycle these containers? What kinds of containers are thrown away at your house? How many containers do you discard each day?

Work with your teammates to create a data sheet for keeping track of every container discarded from the home during 5 days. Include categories such as the kind of container (glass, cardboard, metal, plastic), general size (cup, quart, gallon, milliliter, liter), and the type of contents (food, clothing, household item).

DECIDE	Brainstorm to identify the common sizes of containers. Brainstorm ideas for a system for collecting and tallying every container before it is thrown away.
DO	Find the totals on the individual data sheets. Compile the data onto a team summary sheet. Then prepare a graph, table, or other display for your data.
SHARE	Present your findings to the class. Compare the teams' findings. Find the class total for each kind of container. Then find the total volume of containers for the class.

Talk About It

a. In order to compare volumes of containers, what part of the volume measures should be the same?

b. Were any results surprising? Explain.

c. Suppose you build a class storeroom for unbroken and uncrushed containers. How large would it need to be?

d. Does your school have a room large enough to hold the containers you tallied?

e. What can you do to reduce the volume of individual containers to be recycled?

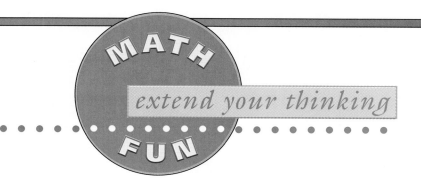

Spheres, Cylinders, and Cones

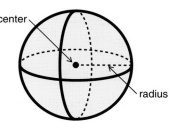

center

radius

Archimedes (c. 287–212 B.C.) discovered these formulas for a sphere.

volume of a sphere $= \frac{4}{3}\pi r^3$

surface area of a sphere $= 4\pi r^2$

In the three solids below, the radii are the same, the heights are the same, and $h = 2r$.
Archimedes found that the volumes are in the ratio 1:2:3.
If $r = 3$, show that the volumes are 18π, 36π, and 54π cubic units.
Do these volumes have the ratio 1:2:3?

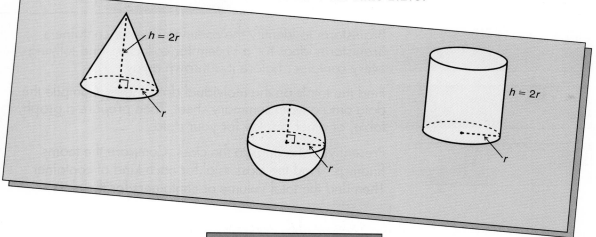

$h = 2r$

r

r

$h = 2r$

r

Challenge

Visual Thinking

This figure consists of congruent squares. If its area is 80 cm², what is its perimeter?

Number Sense

A painting is now worth $6,400. Its value has doubled each year for the past 8 years. How long ago was it worth $3,200?

Write the letter of the correct answer.

1. Which is the perimeter of a room that is 4 m wide and 6 m long?

   A. 10 m   **B.** 20 m

   C. 24 m   **D.** not here

2. Which is the area of a circle that has a radius of 5 m?

   A. 15.7 m^2 **B.** 25 m^2

   C. 31.4 m^2 **D.** 78.5 m^2

3. Which is $\frac{3}{5}$ written as a percent?

   A. 30%   **B.** 60%

   C. 75%   **D.** $166\frac{2}{3}\%$

4. $7\frac{1}{8} \div 2\frac{1}{4}$

   A. $3\frac{1}{4}$ **B.** $15\frac{1}{32}$

   C. $16\frac{1}{32}$ **D.** not here

5. What percent of 24 is 8?

   A. 25%   **B.** 30%

   C. $33\frac{1}{3}\%$ **D.** 300%

6. Which rational number is between ⁻1.5 and ⁻2.0?

   A. ⁻1.90   **B.** ⁻1.45

   C. ⁻1.06   **D.** ⁻1.05

7. Which is the best estimate for the product? 322×19

   A. 60   **B.** 600

   C. 6,000   **D.** 60,000

8. What is the probability that the spinner will land on 4?

   A. $\frac{1}{8}$ **B.** $\frac{1}{6}$

   C. $\frac{4}{6}$ **D.** 4

9. Which is $\frac{18}{24}$ written in simplest form?

   A. $\frac{1}{6}$ **B.** $\frac{2}{3}$

   C. $\frac{9}{12}$ **D.** $\frac{3}{4}$

10. Which equation means 6 times a number is 93?

    A. $6n = 93$ **B.** $n + 6 = 93$

    C. $n - 6 = 93$ **D.** $\frac{n}{6} = 93$

11. Julio is designing a swimming pool that is 18 ft wide, 20 ft long, and 8 ft deep. He changes the plans and makes the pool 16 ft wide. How much less is the volume of the pool in the new plans than in the old plans?

    A. 8 ft^3 **B.** 320 ft^3

    C. 2,560 ft^3 **D.** 2,880 ft^3

12. The Farulli family wants to buy an encyclopedia set on the installment plan. They must make a down payment of $150 and 24 monthly payments of $30. How much will the family pay for the set?

    A. $570   **B.** $720

    C. $870   **D.** $3,630

Did you know . . .

. . . that you can find the approximate height of a tall object without measuring the object directly?

Suppose you need to find the height of the goalposts on a football field. Think of ways you can find the height without having to climb to the top to measure.

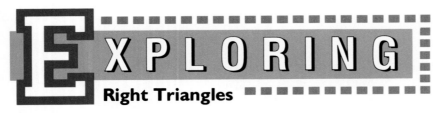

EXPLORING
Right Triangles

There is a special relationship among the lengths of the sides of a
right triangle. Use graph paper and a straightedge to explore this
relationship.

WORK TOGETHER

Building Understanding

On a piece of graph paper, draw the figure shown. Study it.

- What is the length of each side of the larger square?
- What is the area of the larger square?
- What is the area of any one of the four triangles?

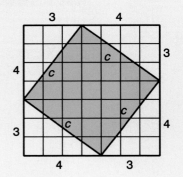

Suppose the four triangles are cut off.

- What remains?
- What is its area?
- What is the length of each of its sides?

Now, square the known lengths of the sides of any of the triangles.

$$3^2 = \blacksquare \text{ and } 4^2 = \blacksquare.$$

Talk About It

▶ What is the sum of the squared
lengths of these sides?

▶ How does this sum compare with
the area of the smaller square?

▶ What is c^2?

▶ In this triangle, is the sum of the
squares of a and b equal to the
square of c?

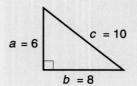

Making the Connection

The relationship among the sides of a right triangle is known as the **Pythagorean Property.** The name honors Pythagoras, the Greek mathematician who proved the relationship.

In a right triangle, the sides adjacent to the right angle are called **legs.** The side opposite the right angle is called the **hypotenuse.**

The Pythagorean Property states that if a and b are the lengths of the legs of a right triangle and c is the length of the hypotenuse, then $a^2 + b^2 = c^2$.

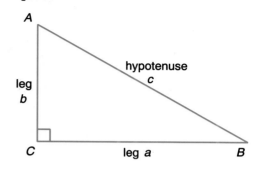

Examples Determine whether the triangles are right triangles.

A.

Does $5^2 + 12^2 \stackrel{?}{=} 13^2$?
$$25 + 144 \stackrel{?}{=} 169$$
$$169 = 169$$

This is a right triangle.

B.

Does $6^2 + 7^2 \stackrel{?}{=} 10^2$?
$$36 + 49 \stackrel{?}{=} 100$$
$$85 \neq 100$$

This is not a right triangle.

Talk About It

▶ Look at the triangle in Example **A.** How does the length of the hypotenuse compare with the length of either leg?

▶ How does the length of the hypotenuse compare to the sum of the lengths of the legs?

Checking Understanding

Name the hypotenuse and the legs of each right triangle.

1.

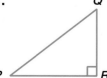

2.

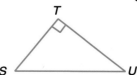

3.

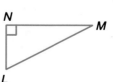

4.

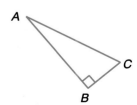

Decide whether the three sides form a right triangle. Write *yes* or *no*.

5. 17 cm, 20 cm, 25 cm

6. 16 m, 30 m, 34 m

7. 11 cm, 60 cm, 61 cm

8. 8 cm, 11 cm, 15 cm

WARM UP...

Tell two ways that you can determine which side of a right triangle is the hypotenuse.

USING THE PYTHAGOREAN PROPERTY

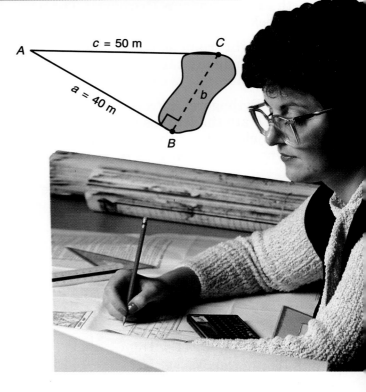

A bridge designer wants to find the distance across a lake. The diagram shows the distance from point A to point B, and from point A to point C. What is the distance across the lake?

You can use the Pythagorean Property to find the distance across the lake. From the diagram, you know that $a = 40$ m and $c = 50$ m.

$a^2 + b^2 = c^2$ ← Replace a with 40 and c with 50.

$40^2 + b^2 = 50^2$

$1{,}600 + b^2 = 2{,}500$

$b^2 = 2{,}500 - 1{,}600$

$b^2 = 900$

$b = \sqrt{900}$ ← Find the square root.

$b = 30$

So, the distance across the lake is 30 m.

More Examples   Find the unknown length to the nearest tenth.

A.
$a^2 + b^2 = c^2$
$7^2 + 9^2 = c^2$
$49 + 81 = c^2$
$130 = c^2$
$\sqrt{130} = c$
$11.4 \approx c$
$c \approx 11.4$ m

$130 \boxed{\sqrt{}}$ 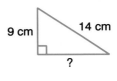 `11.4017154`

B.
$a^2 + b^2 = c^2$
$9^2 + b^2 = 14^2$
$81 + b^2 = 196$
$b^2 = 196 - 81$
$b^2 = 115$
$b = \sqrt{115}$
$b \approx 10.7$ cm

Talk About It

▶ In Example **B,** could you have used 9 cm as the value for b instead of as the value for a? Explain.

▶ In problems involving right triangles, how do you decide whether you need to find the length of a leg or the length of the hypotenuse?

▶ A **Pythagorean triple** is an ordered triple of positive integers (a,b,c) such that $a^2 + b^2 = c^2$. Two such triples are $(3,4,5)$ and $(5,12,13)$. Find two more triples and show how you know they are triples.

Check for Understanding

Find the unknown length.

1.
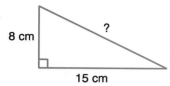
8 cm
?
15 cm

2.
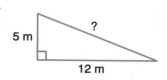
5 m
?
12 m

3.

6 cm
10 cm
?

Practice

Find the unknown length to the nearest tenth.

4.
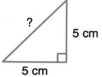
?
5 cm
5 cm

5.

19 mm
?
15 mm

6.

16 cm
?
10 cm

Solve. Round the solution to the nearest tenth.

7.
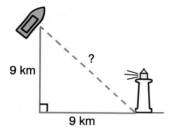
9 km
?
9 km

How far is the ship
from the lighthouse?

8.
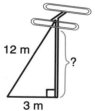
12 m
?
3 m

How high is the
antenna?

9.
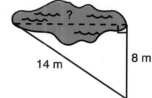
?
14 m
8 m

What is the distance
across the pond?

Mixed Applications

10. Tina walked 90 m up Elm Street, turned 90° left, and then walked another 50 m. Wanda left from the same place as Tina but took a diagonal path across a park to meet Tina. To the nearest meter, how far did Wanda walk?

11. Doug's kite is 30 m above the ground. A tree is directly under the kite. Doug is standing 16 m away from the tree. How long is the kite string?

12. Two 12-m diameters of a circle intersect to form right angles. The ends of the diameters are connected to form four right triangles. Find the difference between the area of the circle and the sum of the areas of the triangles.

13. Logical Reasoning Sam is 5 years older than Linda, who is twice as old as Mark. If Sam is 25, how old is Mark?

Can the Pythagorean Property be used
with an isosceles triangle? Explain.

WRAP
UP...

SPECIAL RIGHT TRIANGLES

Triangles *ABC* and *DEF* are isosceles right triangles. You can use these relationships to find the lengths of the sides of isosceles right triangles.

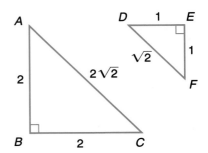

1. The length of the hypotenuse is $\sqrt{2}$ times the length of a leg.

2. The length of a leg is $\frac{\sqrt{2}}{2}$ times the length of the hypotenuse.

Examples Find the unknown length.

A. c = length of leg $\times \sqrt{2}$

$c = 3 \times \sqrt{2}$

$c = 3\sqrt{2}$ cm

B. a = length of hypotenuse $\times \frac{\sqrt{2}}{2}$

$a = 8 \times \frac{\sqrt{2}}{2}$

$a = 4\sqrt{2}$ m

Talk About It

▶ How can you find the length of the hypotenuse in Example **A** to the nearest tenth of a centimeter?

▶ Why do you think an isosceles right triangle is also called a 45–45 right triangle?

$\triangle$ *RST* is a 30–60 right triangle. You can use these relationships to find the lengths of the sides of 30–60 right triangles.

1. The length of the hypotenuse is 2 times the length of the shorter leg.

2. The length of the shorter leg is $\frac{1}{2}$ the length of the hypotenuse.

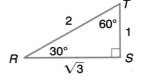

3. The length of the longer leg is $\frac{\sqrt{3}}{2}$ times the length of the hypotenuse.

Example Find the unknown lengths.

$a = \frac{1}{2} \times$ length of hypotenuse

$a = \frac{1}{2} \times 10$

$a = 5$ cm

$b = \frac{\sqrt{3}}{2} \times$ length of hypotenuse

$b = \frac{\sqrt{3}}{2} \times 10$

$b = \sqrt{3} \times 5$, or $5\sqrt{3}$ cm

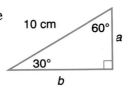

Check for Understanding

Find the unknown length.

1.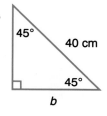

2.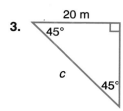

3.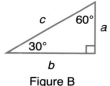

Practice

Use Figure A to find the unknown length.

4. $a = 6, c =$ ▓

5. $a = 4, c =$ ▓

6. $c = 8, a =$ ▓

7. $c = 12, a =$ ▓

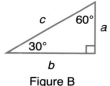

Figure A

Use Figure B to find the unknown length.

8. $c = 4, a =$ ▓

9. $c = 8, b =$ ▓

10. $c = 12, a =$ ▓ $, b =$ ▓

11. $a = 7, c =$ ▓

Figure B

Mixed Applications

12. A flagpole is 32 ft tall. A guy wire attached to the top of the pole makes a 45° angle with the ground. Find the length of the guy wire.

13. James earned $14.50 the first week he worked, $22.20 the second week, and $27.80 the third week. What is the average amount he earned per week?

14. About how high is the kite?

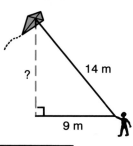

15. **Mental Math** Lawanna bought 20 tickets to the fair for $50. Jack bought 100 tickets to the fair. How much did Jack pay?

VISUAL THINKING

16. Trace the rectangle on a sheet of paper. Then cut the rectangle into two pieces that will fit together to form the square.

What other method can you use to find the length of the hypotenuse in Example **A** on page 452?

WRAP UP . . .

Raphael and his family are going to Washington, D.C. They want to keep their costs down, but they want to be able to get from place to place easily while in Washington. They are considering these options. Which option should they choose?

Car: The trip takes 2 days each way. The costs will include about $320 for meals and lodging and about $130 for gasoline.

Train: The trip takes 14 hr one way. They can take their car on the train. The cost for the family and the car is $850. Meals are included in the cost.

Plane: The trip takes about 3 hr one way. The total cost of the tickets is $475. It will cost about $228 to rent a car in Washington.

▶ UNDERSTAND

What are you asked to find?
What facts are given?

▶ PLAN

How will you solve the problem?
You can consider the advantages and disadvantages of each option.

▶ SOLVE

What questions should you ask in order to consider the advantages and disadvantages of each option?

- With which option will they spend the least money?

- How important is the amount of time spent traveling?

▶ LOOK BACK

What reasons did you use for making your choice?

WHAT IF . . .

. . . the airline company offers the family a good rate on a hotel room in Washington? Would this affect your choice? Why or why not?

Apply

Raphael and his family have three choices for places to stay in Washington, D.C. Use the choices for Exercises 1–4.

Choice 1: The cost is $60 per night.
Choice 2: The cost is $75 per night, and breakfast is free.
Choice 3: The cost is $58 per night plus $4 per night for parking.

1 Which choice will have the lowest cost for 6 nights?

2 What is the difference between the costs of Choice 1 and Choice 2?

3 Suppose Raphael and his family decide on Choice 3. How much will they pay for parking if they stay 8 nights?

4 Which choice do you think Raphael and his family should make? Give reasons for your answer.

Mixed Applications > **STRATEGIES**
- Make a Table • Work Backward
- Write an Equation • Use a Formula

Choose a strategy and solve.

5 Dora wants to determine how many $8–$10 presents she can buy for her friends. She also needs to pay $28 for a ticket to the J. F. Kennedy Performing Arts Center. She wants to have $10 for transportation and to keep a reserve of $8. She has $75. How many presents can she buy?

6 A passenger train leaves Marston for Pickfair, 1,650 mi away. At the same time, a freight train on a parallel track leaves Pickfair for Marston. The passenger train travels 65 mph, and the freight train travels 45 mph. How far from Marston will the freight train be when it meets the passenger train?

7 Jill deposited $150.00 in a savings account. She made no additional deposits, and 1 yr later she had a balance of $161.25 in the account. What annual rate of interest did she earn on the account?

8 A number is doubled and then divided by 6. Then 8 is subtracted from the quotient, and the difference is multiplied by 7. The result is 896. What is the number?

WRITER'S CORNER

9 Describe a situation that involves at least three options or choices. Write two questions for the situation. Then exchange with a classmate and solve.

SIMILAR FIGURES

Mitchell designed the tile shown. Now
he wants to design a tile that has the
same shape but has 4 in. as the length
of its longest side. What will be the
lengths of the other three sides?

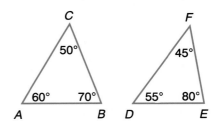

Geometric figures that have the same
shape are **similar figures.** Corresponding
angles are congruent, and corresponding
sides have the same ratio.

Step 1 Find the ratio of the corresponding sides.

longest side of large tile → $\frac{8}{4} = \frac{2}{1}$
longest side of small tile →

Step 2 Use the ratio to write a
proportion for each of
the other three sides.
Solve the proportions.

$$\frac{2}{1} = \frac{5}{c}$$
$$2c = 5$$
$$c = 2\frac{1}{2}$$

$$\frac{2}{1} = \frac{4}{b}$$
$$2b = 4$$
$$b = 2$$

$$\frac{2}{1} = \frac{3}{a}$$
$$2a = 3$$
$$a = 1\frac{1}{2}$$

So, the lengths of the other three sides are $2\frac{1}{2}$ in., 2 in., and $1\frac{1}{2}$ in.

Talk About It

▶ Can the ratio for the corresponding sides in
the example be $\frac{1}{2}$? Explain.

▶ Are congruent figures also similar figures?
Why or why not?

▶ Are $\triangle ABC$ and $\triangle DEF$ similar? Explain.

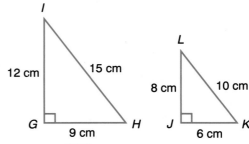

Check for Understanding

The triangles in each pair are similar. Find the ratio of the
corresponding sides.

1.

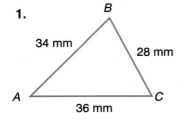

2.

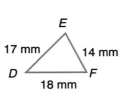

Idea Bank, page 490, Exercise 6

Practice

Tell whether the figures in each pair are similar. Write *yes* or *no*.

3.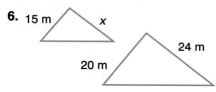

4.
8 cm [tall rectangle] 3 cm 4 cm [shorter rectangle] 3 cm

5.
4 m, 5 m, 3 m [larger triangle] 2 m, 2.5 m, 1.5 m [smaller triangle]

The triangles in each pair are similar. Find *x*.

6. 15 m, *x*, 20 m, 24 m

7. 10 mm, 28 mm, 25 mm, *x*

Write *true* or *false* for each statement.

8. All congruent triangles are similar.

9. All similar triangles are congruent.

Mixed Applications

10. Juan is building a model of a ship. The actual ship is 100 m long and 30 m high. His model is 3 m long and 1 m high. Is Juan's model in proportion?

11. A box has 4 red cards, 5 blue cards, and 7 green cards. A card is picked without looking. What is the probability that the card picked is blue?

12. Norman is 1.8 m tall. On a sunny day, Patty measured Norman's shadow and the shadow of the school at the same time. Use the similar triangles shown to find the height of the school to the nearest tenth.

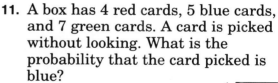

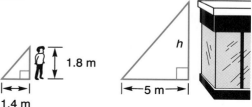

MIXED REVIEW

Solve the proportion.

1. $\frac{2}{3} = \frac{n}{9}$ **2.** $\frac{5}{7} = \frac{25}{n}$ **3.** $\frac{6}{n} = \frac{8}{5}$ **4.** $\frac{n}{8} = \frac{9}{12}$

Write the fraction as a decimal. Round to the nearest hundredth.

5. $\frac{3}{5}$ **6.** $\frac{1}{3}$ **7.** $\frac{8}{15}$ **8.** $\frac{33}{40}$ **9.** $\frac{6}{25}$ **10.** $\frac{5}{6}$

Are all right triangles similar? Why or why not?

WRAP UP...

REVIEW AND MAINTENANCE

1. Bud has to drive through Vineland to get from Moorestown to Taft. There are 4 roads from Moorestown to Vineland and 5 roads from Vineland to Taft. How many ways can Bud drive from Moorestown to Taft?

2. Charles had four 1-cm squares. He arranged them so that each square had at least one side in common with another square. What were the possible perimeters of the arrangement?

3. Stacey earns $8.50 an hour for a 40-hr week. She earns $1\frac{1}{2}$ times her hourly wage for any hours she works over 40 hr. Last week she worked 46 hr. How much did Stacey earn last week?

4. The wheels of April's bicycle have a diameter of 26 in. Yesterday, April rode her bicycle 2 mi. How many revolutions did each wheel of the bicycle make? Use 3.14 for π.

Tell whether the relation is a function. Write *yes* or *no*.

5. (3,4), (4,5), (5,6), (6,7)

6. (1,2), (1,3), (1,4), (1,5)

7. (3,8), (⁻2,5), (2,⁻2), (6,0)

8. (⁻4,4), (⁻3,5), (5,2), (3,6)

Find the volume. Use $\pi = 3.14$.

9. 6 m, 10 m

10. 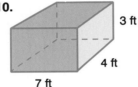 3 ft, 4 ft, 7 ft

11. 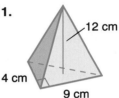 12 cm, 4 cm, 9 cm

A dime is tossed, and a number cube is rolled. Find the probability.

12. P(tails, 5)

13. P(heads, 3)

14. P(tails, 4 or 5)

15. P(heads or tails, 6)

16. P(tails, odd number)

17. P(heads, 8)

Draw the figure, using a ruler and a protractor. Then use the figure to construct a congruent figure, using a compass and a straightedge.

18. a 6-cm line segment

19. a 45° angle

20. a 120° angle

Write a decimal for the fraction.

21. $\frac{3}{5}$

22. $\frac{1}{4}$

23. $\frac{2}{3}$

24. $\frac{3}{20}$

25. $\frac{3}{8}$

26. $\frac{4}{9}$

Solve the equation. Check your answer.

27. $x + 32 = 78$

28. $b - 3.45 = 7.8$

29. $2c + 5 = 10$

30. $7y = 1,554$

31. $d + 8 = {}^-10$

32. $\frac{a}{5} = 3\frac{2}{3}$

Spotlight ON
PROBLEM SOLVING

Understand
Plan
Solve
Look Back

VISUALIZE THE RESULTS

When you are solving problems involving shapes and spatial relationships, you can sometimes visualize the results. Consider this problem.

A ladder is leaning against a wall in the school. The ladder's legs are 5 ft from the bottom of the wall, and its top rung touches the wall 12 ft from the floor. How long is the ladder?

Talk About It
Read, discuss, and solve.
a. Make a drawing of the ladder described above.
b. What shape is formed by the ladder, the floor, and the wall?
c. What facts were used to solve the problem?
d. What relationship helped you determine the length of the ladder?
e. Create a drawing of a ladder that could be used to reach a cat in a tree. If the cat is 8 ft from the ground and the bottom of the ladder is 6 ft from the tree, how tall is the ladder?

APPLY
Create drawings to help you solve the problems. Use your calculator for the computation.
1. A building 10 ft tall is 25 ft away from a building that is 5 ft taller than the first building. How far is it from the top of the first building to the top of the second building?
2. A baseball field is a square with 90-ft sides. What is the distance from home plate to second base?
3. A college radio station put up a 24-ft antenna. A 26-ft cable is connected to the top of the antenna and secured to the ground. How far from the base of the antenna is the cable secured?
4. A door has a square panel with a diagonal brace for security. Each side of the panel is 4 ft long. Is the brace longer than each side? How long is the brace?

In a 30–60 right triangle, which side is opposite the 30° angle?

TRIGONOMETRIC RATIOS

Jason designs skateboard ramps. To be sure that the incline of a ramp is the degree measure he wants, he uses a ratio to compare the height of the ramp to the length of the ramp. For an incline of about 30°, for example, Jason uses the ratio $\frac{5}{9}$.

The ratios Jason uses for the ramps are **trigonometric ratios.** Trigonometric ratios may be defined by using the lengths of the sides of a right triangle.

$$\tan A \text{ (tangent of } \angle A) = \frac{\text{length of opposite side}}{\text{length of adjacent side}} = \frac{BC}{AC}$$

$$\sin A \text{ (sine of } \angle A) = \frac{\text{length of opposite side}}{\text{length of hypotenuse}} = \frac{BC}{AB}$$

$$\cos A \text{ (cosine of } \angle A) = \frac{\text{length of adjacent side}}{\text{length of hypotenuse}} = \frac{AC}{AB}$$

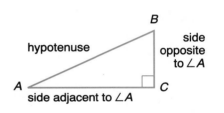

Example In $\triangle ABC$, what are the trigonometric ratios for $\angle B$?

Think: hypotenuse: AB, opposite side: AC, adjacent side: BC

$$\tan B = \frac{AC}{BC} \qquad \sin B = \frac{AC}{AB} \qquad \cos B = \frac{BC}{AB}$$

Talk About It

▶ Suppose the length of $\overline{AC}$ in the example is 8 cm and the length of $\overline{BC}$ is 3 cm. How can you find tan B to the nearest tenth of a centimeter?

> The sine and cosine ratios use the length of the hypotenuse as the second term.

Check for Understanding

Copy and complete.

1. $\tan F = \dfrac{GE}{\blacksquare}$

2. $\sin F = \dfrac{\blacksquare}{GF}$

3. $\cos F = \dfrac{\blacksquare}{\blacksquare}$

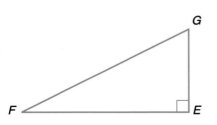

Practice

Copy and complete.

4. $\tan A = \dfrac{BC}{\blacksquare}$

5. $\tan B = \dfrac{AC}{\blacksquare}$

6. $\sin A = \dfrac{\blacksquare}{AB}$

7. $\cos A = \dfrac{\blacksquare}{AB}$

8. $\sin F = \dfrac{\blacksquare}{\blacksquare}$

9. $\tan F = \dfrac{\blacksquare}{\blacksquare}$

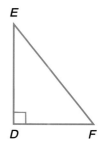

Find the trigonometric ratio to the nearest hundredth.
You may use a calculator.

10. $\tan 25° = \dfrac{2.66}{\blacksquare} = \blacksquare$

11. $\sin 25° = \dfrac{\blacksquare}{6.3} = \blacksquare$

12. $\cos 25° = \dfrac{\blacksquare}{\blacksquare} = \blacksquare$

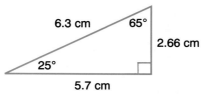

13. $\tan 65° = \dfrac{\blacksquare}{\blacksquare} = \blacksquare$

14. $\sin 65° = \dfrac{\blacksquare}{\blacksquare} = \blacksquare$

15. $\cos 65° = \dfrac{\blacksquare}{\blacksquare} = \blacksquare$

Mixed Applications

16. In $\triangle ABC$, the length of the side opposite $\angle A$ is 6 ft. The length of the hypotenuse is 13 ft. What is the sine of $\angle A$?

17. In $\triangle RST$, the tangent of $\angle R$ equals 1. What do you know about the length of the side opposite $\angle R$ and of the side adjacent to $\angle R$?

18. **Logical Reasoning**   There are three empty glasses and three full glasses in a row. The arrangement of the glasses is empty, empty, empty, full, full, full. By moving one glass, change the arrangement to empty, full, empty, full, empty, full.

EVERYDAY MATH CONNECTION

19. Trigonometry is used by many people to measure distances indirectly. Use an encyclopedia or other research material to find two occupations that involve the use of trigonometry. Tell how trigonometry is used in each.

Look back at Exercise 10. Will tan 25° change if the length of each side of the triangle is doubled?

USING THE TANGENT RATIO

An architect is designing a sloping roof. He wants the pitch of the roof to be 25° and the length to the center to be 20 ft. What length will he have to use for h in the diagram?

You can use the tangent ratio to solve the problem.

$$\tan 25° = \frac{\text{length of opposite side}}{\text{length of adjacent side}} = \frac{h}{20}$$

If you know the value of tan 25°, you can solve for h. The Table of Trigonometric Ratios on page H104 gives the values of the trigonometric ratios for acute angles.

Step 1	**Step 2**

Step 1
Use the table to find tan 25°.

tan 25° = 0.466

Angle	Sin	Cos	Tan
24°	0.407	0.914	0.445
25°	0.423	0.906	0.466

Step 2
Solve for h.

$\tan 25° = \frac{h}{20}$ ← Replace tan 25° with 0.466.

$\frac{0.466}{1} = \frac{h}{20}$ ← Solve the proportion.

$h = 9.32$

So, the architect will have to make h about $9\frac{1}{3}$ ft.

● What information can you find by using the table on page H104?

● What is tan 55°? What angle measure has a tangent of 1.732?

Talk About It

▶ In Step 2, why was 0.466 written as $\frac{0.466}{1}$?

▶ Look at the table on page H104. What happens to the value of the tangent as the angle measure increases?

Check for Understanding

Use the table on page H104 to find the ratio.

1. tan 37°   **2.** tan 12°   **3.** tan 85°   **4.** tan 50°

Practice

Use the table on page H104 to find the ratio.

5. tan 53° **6.** tan 75° **7.** tan 30° **8.** tan 40°

9. tan 89° **10.** sin 30° **11.** cos 82° **12.** sin 45°

Use the table on page H104 to find *a*.

13. tan $a = 0.364$ **14.** tan $a = 2.050$ **15.** tan $a = 1.00$

16. sin $a = 0.985$ **17.** cos $a = 0.883$ **18.** tan $a = 1.327$

Find *x* to the nearest tenth.

19.

20.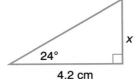

21.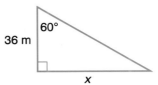

22.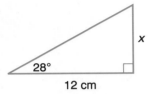

23.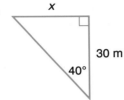

24.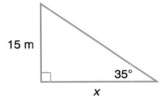

Mixed Applications

25. Find the height of the tower in the figure to the nearest meter.

26. A tree casts a shadow that is 20 m long when the sun's rays make a 42° angle with the ground. Find the height of the tree to the nearest meter.

27. Write a Problem Write a word problem that can be solved by using the tangent ratio.

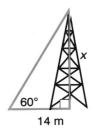

CALCULATOR CONNECTION

You can use a scientific calculator to find tangent values.

Example Find tan 52°. 52 [tan] [1.2799416]

Use a scientific calculator to find each ratio.

28. tan 5° **29.** tan 18° **30.** tan 28° **31.** tan 81°

Compare the product tan 45° · cos 45° with sin 45°. Is this true for any angle? Explain.

WRAP UP . . .

In △ ABC, sin A equals the cosine of which angle?

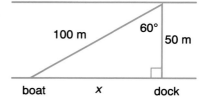

A boat heads for a dock 50 m straight across a river. A strong current makes the boat travel twice the expected distance, on a course 60° to the right of that intended. How far downstream from the dock is the boat?

The diagram shows that the distance you want to find is the side opposite the 60° angle. You know the length of the hypotenuse, so you can use the sine ratio to solve the problem.

$$\sin 60° = \frac{\text{length of opposite side}}{\text{length of hypotenuse}} = \frac{x}{100}$$ Use the table on page H104.

$$\frac{0.866}{1} = \frac{x}{100}$$

$x = 86.6$ So, the boat is 86.6 m downstream from the dock.

Another Example Find the length of $\overline{DF}$ to the nearest tenth.

Use the cosine ratio.

$$\cos 50° = \frac{x}{5.4}$$

$$\frac{0.643}{1} = \frac{x}{5.4}$$ $0.643 \boxed{\times} 5.4 \boxed{=} \boxed{3.4722}$

$x \approx 3.5$ cm

Talk About It

▶ Since you know the lengths of $\overline{DE}$ and $\overline{DF}$, how can you find the length of $\overline{EF}$?

Check for Understanding

Find x to the nearest tenth. Use the table on page H104.

1.

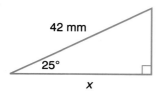

2.

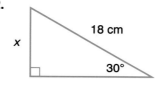

3.

Practice

Find x to the nearest tenth. Use the table on page H104.

4.
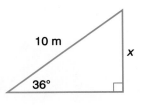
10 m

x

36°

5.
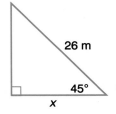
26 m

45°

x

6.
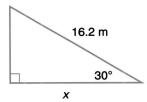
16.2 m

30°

x

7.
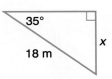
35°

18 m

x

8.
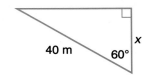
40 m

60°

x

9.
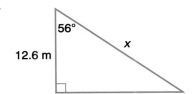
56°

12.6 m

x

Solve.

10. How high is the kite?

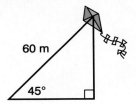
60 m

45°

11. How tall is the tree?

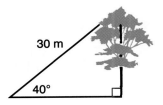
30 m

40°

Mixed Applications

12. A ladder leaning against a building makes an angle of 50° with the ground. The top of the ladder reaches a window 7 m above the ground. To the nearest tenth, how long is the ladder?

13. Company K's sales for this year were 118% of last year's sales. Last year's sales amounted to $1.38 million. Estimate the sales for this year.

MIXED REVIEW

Find the square or the square root. Round the square root to the nearest tenth.

1. 6^2

2. 15^2

3. $(9.2)^2$

4. $\left(\frac{1}{2}\right)^2$

5. 200^2

6. $\sqrt{130}$

7. $\sqrt{27}$

8. $\sqrt{62}$

9. $\sqrt{86}$

10. $\sqrt{155}$

How do the sine and cosine ratios compare in an isosceles right triangle?

WRAP UP...

Marcy designed a 3-row beaded bracelet. There are 7 beads in each row. The pattern in the top and bottom rows is white, blue, white, blue. . . . All the beads in the center row are blue. Horizontally and vertically there is a gold bead between each pair of colored beads. How many blue beads, white beads, and gold beads are in the bracelet?

▶ **UNDERSTAND**

What are you asked to find?

What facts are given?

▶ **PLAN**

What strategy will you use?

You can use the strategy *draw a picture*. Then count the number of each type of bead.

▶ **SOLVE**

How will you solve the problem?

Draw a picture.

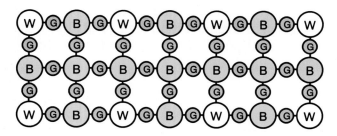

So, there are 13 blue beads, 8 white beads, and 32 gold beads.

▶ **LOOK BACK**

What other strategy can you use to solve the problem?

WHAT IF . . . . . . the pattern white, blue, white, blue . . . is used for all three rows? How many blue beads will there be?

466

Apply

(1) Marcy designed a two-row beaded bracelet. There are 10 beads in each row. The pattern in the top row is red, white, red . . . . The pattern in the bottom row is blue, white, red, blue, white, red . . . . How many red beads, white beads, and blue beads are in the bracelet?

(2) David put a shelf 6 ft long on a wall 18 ft long. The distance from the left end of the shelf to the left end of the wall is 2 times the distance from the right end of the shelf to the right end of the wall. How far is the left end of the shelf from the left end of the wall?

(3) A square-shaped park has an area of 1,600 m². Doug took a diagonal path through the park. To the nearest meter, how far did Doug walk?

(4) Jessica and her father stand next to each other. Jessica is 120 cm tall. Her father is 180 cm tall. Jessica's shadow is 90 m long. How long is her father's shadow?

Mixed Applications	STRATEGIES	• Write an Equation • Draw a Picture • Find a Pattern • Use Estimation • Guess and Check • Work Backward

Choose a strategy and solve.

(5) Carmen spent $26.50 on camera batteries and rolls of film. Batteries cost $2.75 for a set of 3, and film costs $4.75 a roll. How many batteries and rolls of film did Carmen buy?

(6) Wesley tells Tom that he is thinking of two integers that are each less than 10. The square of the first number equals the cube of the second. What are the numbers?

(7) Wanda sold or gave away all but 3 of her tapes. This was $\frac{1}{5}$ of the number that she gave away. She sold 2 fewer than 3 times the number she gave away. How many tapes did Wanda have originally?

(8) Sam bought some oranges and some tangerines for $1.72. The cost of the tangerines was 15% more than the cost of the oranges. How much did Sam pay for the tangerines?

Vocabulary Check

Choose a word from the box to complete each sentence.

> cosine
> hypotenuse
> isosceles
> legs
> right
> similar
> tangent

1. A 45–45 right triangle is also called a(n) __?__ right triangle. *(page 452)*

2. Geometric figures that have the same shape are __?__ figures. *(page 456)*

3. In a right triangle, the ratio of the length of the side adjacent to an angle to the length of the hypotenuse is the __?__ ratio. *(page 460)*

4. In a right triangle, the side opposite the right angle is called the __?__. *(page 449)*

5. If three sides of a triangle satisfy the Pythagorean Property, the triangle is a(n) __?__ triangle. *(page 449)*

6. In a right triangle, the sides adjacent to the right angle are called the __?__. *(page 449)*

7. In a right triangle, the ratio of the length of the side opposite an angle to the length of the side adjacent to the angle is the __?__ ratio. *(page 460)*

Concept Check

Tell whether the three sides form a right triangle. Write *yes* or *no*.
(page 449)

8. 11 cm, 50 cm, 54 cm   9. 16 m, 30 m, 33 m   10. 15 in., 20 in., 25 in.

The lengths of the sides of a right triangle are given. Tell whether the triangle is a *45–45 right* triangle or a *30–60 right* triangle. *(page 452)*

11. 2 cm, 2 cm, $2\sqrt{2}$ cm   12. 4 m, $4\sqrt{3}$ m, 8 m   13. 7 ft, 7 ft, $7\sqrt{2}$ ft

Tell whether the figures in each pair are similar. Write *yes* or *no*.
(page 456)

14.

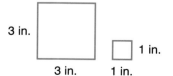

15.

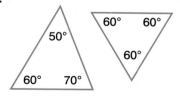

16.

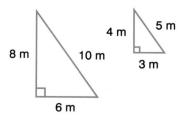

Skill Check

Find the unknown length. Round the answers for Exercises 17–18 to the nearest tenth. *(pages 450, 452)*

17.

8 cm   10 cm

?

18.

?

8 mm

21 mm

19.

60°   ?

5 in.

30°

5 √3 in.

Each pair of triangles is similar. Find *x*. *(page 456)*

20.

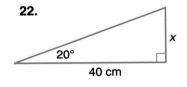

28 m

x

2 m   4 m

21.

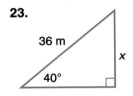

55 cm

25 cm

5 cm   *x*

Find *x* to the nearest tenth. Use the table on page H104. *(pages 462, 464)*

22.

x

20°

40 cm

23.

36 m

x

40°

24.

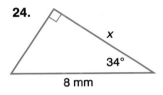

x

34°

8 mm

Problem-Solving Check

Paula is considering these job options for the summer. Use the options for Exercises 25–26. *(page 454)*

Option 1: Work at the bank 40 hr per week and earn $8 per hour.
Option 2: Sell cosmetics 35 hr per week and earn 60% of the price of each cosmetic article as commission.

25. Most of the cosmetic articles Paula would sell cost about $5 each. How many cosmetic articles would Paula need to sell per week to equal or exceed her weekly pay at the bank?

26. Which job do you think Paula should take? Give the reasons for your decision.

27. An airplane leaves its base and flies east for 90 mi. Then it turns south and flies for 120 mi. Finally it turns northwest and flies directly back to its base. How many miles does the airplane fly northwest? *(page 466)*

28. How can you find the measure of the angle between the plane's path south and its flight back to its base? *(page 466)*

CHAPTER TEST

For the right triangle, find the unknown length to the nearest tenth.

1. $a = 4$ m
   $b = 9$ m
   $c = $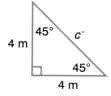

2. $a = $
   $b = 12$ cm
   $c = 15$ cm

3. $a = 12$ m
   $b = $
   $c = 14$ m

4. $a = 6$ cm
   $b = 6$ cm
   $c = $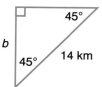

Find the unknown length.

5.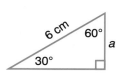

6.

7.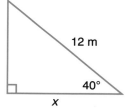

Each pair of triangles is similar. Find x.

8.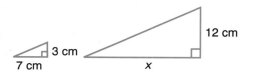

9.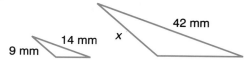

Find x to the nearest tenth. Use the table on page H104.

10.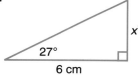

11.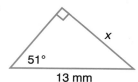

12.

Solve.

13. Jeremy can do 3 chores and earn $7.50, or he can do 4 chores and earn $9.50. With which choice will Jeremy earn more per chore?

14. Michelle can take a job paying $350 each week, or she can take a different job paying $1,500 each month. Which job will pay her more per year?

15. The area of a square field is 900 m^2. A path runs diagonally across the field. To the nearest tenth, what is the length of the path?

16. Jill is 1.8 m tall. On a sunny day, her shadow is 2 m long at the same time that the shadow of a water tower is 40 m long. Find the height of the tower.

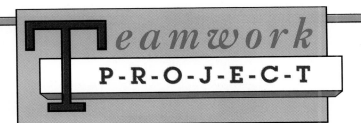

Teamwork PROJECT

DESIGN A YOUTH CENTER

The town council recently approved the construction of a new youth center. The council wants ideas from teenagers before the project is turned over to an architect.

Work with your teammates to design a youth center and to make a scale drawing of it. The design should be for a one-story building with a maximum floor area of 2,100 ft².

DECIDE

As a team, discuss the types of activities you would like to have available at the center. Decide how large the rooms should be for each of these activities. Make a list of the activity areas that you will include in your design.

SHARE

Compare your team's scale drawing with those of other teams. Tell why you chose each activity.

DO

Make a sketch of your youth center. Make any revisions necessary to keep the floor area to a maximum of 2,100 ft². Then make a scale drawing of your youth center.

Talk About It

- What activities did other teams choose that were different from your activities?
- What is the total floor area of your youth center? Did any team go over the maximum of 2,100 ft²? Did any team have a floor area less than 2,100 ft²?
- What shape did you use for your youth center? Did other teams use the same shape?

MATH FUN

extend your thinking

Enlargements from Unit Figures

You know that you can draw larger squares by using a unit square 4, 9, 16, 25, 36, . . . times.

You can draw enlargements of other unit figures in the same way, as shown by these similar triangles.

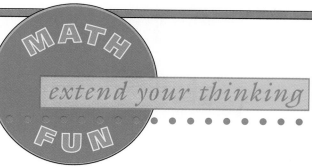

Using graph paper, try to draw similar figures as indicated.

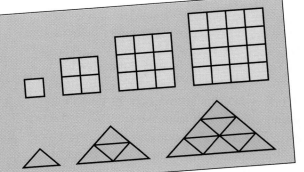

1. Enlarge the figure by using it **4 times.**

2. Enlarge the figure by using it **4 times.**

3. Enlarge the figure in Exercise 2 by using it 9 times.

4. Enlarge the figure by using it **16 times.**

Challenge

Logical Reasoning

An enlargement is made using 169 unit figures. How many times longer is a side or line segment in the enlargement than the corresponding length in the unit figure?

Visual Thinking

Draw this figure. Then try to separate it into four smaller figures of the same shape.

4 cm

60°   60°

CUMULATIVE REVIEW

CHAPTERS 1–14

Write the letter of the correct answer.

1. What is 62% of 125?

   A. 38   **B.** 49.6

   C. 77.5   **D.** 201

2. What is 0.0000067 in scientific notation?

   A. 6.7×10^{-6} **B.** 6.7×10^{5}

   C. 6.7×10^{6} **D.** 67×10^{7}

3. Which ordered pair is a solution of $y = 3x - 8$?

   A. $(3, {}^-2)$ **B.** $(3, 1)$

   C. $(1, 3)$ **D.** $(2, {}^-3)$

4. What is the area?

   A. 21 ft²   **B.** 42 ft²

   C. 45 ft²   **D.** 90 ft²

5. $3.4\overline{)3.672}$

   A. 0.108   **B.** 1.08

   C. 1.8   **D.** 180

6. What is $\sqrt{89}$ to the nearest tenth?

   A. 9.3   **B.** 9.4

   C. 9.5   **D.** not here

7. What is the solution of this system of equations?

$$y = 4 - x$$
$$y = x + 6$$

   A. $({}^-1, 5)$ **B.** $({}^-1, {}^-5)$

   C. $(1, 5)$ **D.** $(1, {}^-5)$

8. The triangles are similar. Find x.

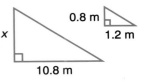

   A. 8.5 m   **B.** 16.2 m

   C. 72 m   **D.** not here

9. What is the value of $x + 6$ for $x = {}^-8$?

   A. $^-14$ **B.** $^-2$

   C. 2   **D.** 14

10. $5\frac{1}{3} - 2\frac{2}{5}$

   A. $2\frac{1}{15}$ **B.** $2\frac{14}{15}$

   C. $3\frac{1}{2}$ **D.** $3\frac{14}{15}$

11. Lisa bought 3 greeting cards for $1.25 each, 1 notebook for $3.44, and 4 pens for $0.89 each. She had a coupon for 20% off. How much did she pay?

   A. $2.15   **B.** $5.58

   C. $8.60   **D.** $10.75

12. Rob, James, Alice, and Steve are running in a race. Steve is 25 m ahead of James and 10 m ahead of Alice. Alice is 23 m ahead of Rob. Who is farthest behind?

   A. Steve   **B.** James

   C. Alice   **D.** Rob

COMPUTER
Connection

Computers are powerful tools for doing many kinds of tasks quickly and accurately. They are used by programmers, graphic artists, word processors, accountants, doctors, and other professionals. Students often apply computer programs to mathematics.

In this section you will explore LOGO, use a word processing program, make a spreadsheet, and build a data base. You will be using the same types of software that many people use at home and at work.

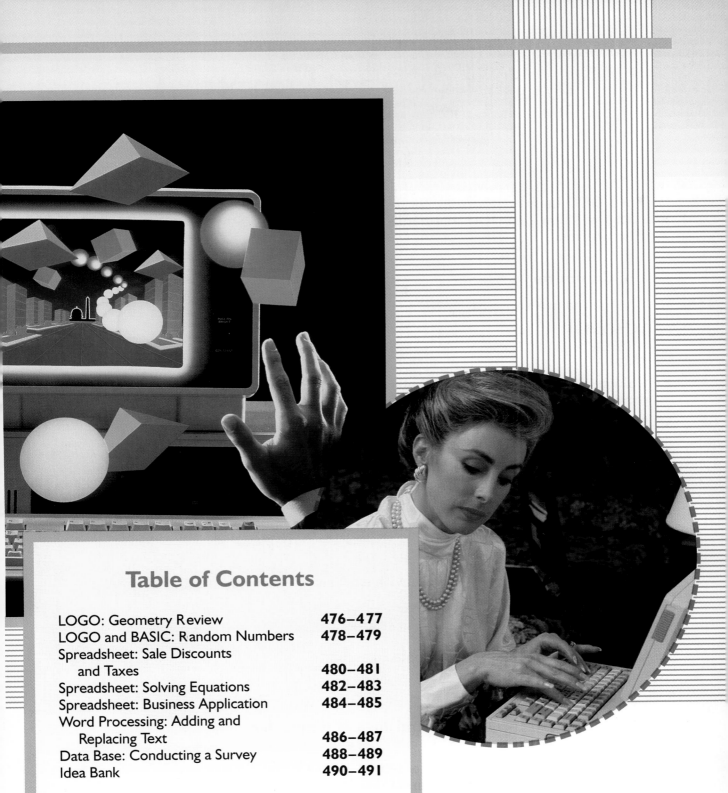

Table of Contents

LOGO: Geometry Review   **476–477**
LOGO and BASIC: Random Numbers   **478–479**
Spreadsheet: Sale Discounts
    and Taxes   **480–481**
Spreadsheet: Solving Equations   **482–483**
Spreadsheet: Business Application   **484–485**
Word Processing: Adding and
    Replacing Text   **486–487**
Data Base: Conducting a Survey   **488–489**
Idea Bank   **490–491**

LOGO and Geometry
Review

The **LOGO** language is useful for drawing geometric figures. Practice the following LOGO commands with some of these geometry terms.

At the Computer

1. Change the procedure SQUARE so that each side is twice as long.

   TO SQUARE
     REPEAT 4 [RT 90 FD 50]
   END

2. Change the procedure SQUARE above so that the computer draws a square of any size. HINT: Use the variable :SIDE.

3. Type a procedure that will draw each regular polygon of any size.

   a. pentagon   **b.** hexagon   **c.** octagon   **d.** decagon

4. Type a procedure to draw a figure with each set of characteristics.

   a. an obtuse angle
   b. an acute angle
   c. an equilateral triangle
   d. a triangle whose perimeter equals 30 steps

Talk About It

▶ What is the measure of each central angle of the regular polygons in Exercise 3?

▶ How are the measurements of the central angles of the regular polygons related to the LOGO commands?

▶ How do variables used in LOGO procedures work?

At the Computer

5. In the nineteenth century, scientists began to discover the Fibonacci sequence (1, 1, 2, 3, 5, 8, 13, . . .) in spirals of sunflower heads and snail shells, pine cones, and even in animal horns. Type the procedure FIBONACCI and explain what the steps in the procedure are doing.

```
TO FIBONACCI :NUM1 :NUM2 :COUNTER :ANGLE
  IF :COUNTER = 0 THEN STOP
  PRINT :NUM1 + :NUM2
  FD :NUM1 + :NUM2
  RT :ANGLE
  FIBONACCI :NUM2 :NUM1 + :NUM2 :COUNTER −1 :ANGLE
END
```

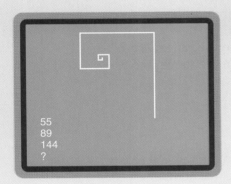

FIBONACCI 0 1 11 90
will draw this spiral

6. Use recursion to write a procedure to draw a figure like the one below.

7. Imagine the coordinate plane below. SETXY −40 60 puts the turtle in the upper left corner of the screen. Use the SETXY function to draw a quadrilateral with a length of 40 and width of 20. Start the figure at coordinate point (⁻30, 50).

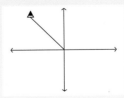

LOGO and BASIC

Random Numbers

Using a random number function, you can write programs to print a range of decimals or integers with the same probability of being selected. The statement PRINT RND(1) prints a decimal number *between* 0 and 1 in **BASIC**. The statement PRINT RANDOM 2 prints the integers 0 or 1 in Terrapin™ Logo.

At the Computer

1. Experiment with the following BASIC examples.

   a. PRINT RND(1)*10   prints a decimal number between 0 and 10

   b. PRINT INT(RND(1)*10)   prints an integer from the range 0 to 9

   c. 10 FOR I = 1 to 5   prints 5 integers from the range 0 to 9
        20 PRINT INT(RND(1)*10)
        30 NEXT I
        40 END

2. Experiment with the following LOGO examples.

   a. PRINT RANDOM 7   prints an integer from the range 0 to 6

   b. PRINT (RANDOM 100)/100   prints a two-digit decimal number between 0 and 1

   c. REPEAT 5 [PRINT RANDOM 7]   prints 5 integers from the range 0 to 6

3. Type or write BASIC commands to print:

   a. 50 random integers from the range 1 to 4.
   b. 100 random decimal numbers.
   c. 20 random integers from the range 0 to 20.
   d. 10 random decimal numbers between 0 and 50.

4. Type or write in LOGO the commands in Exercise 3a, b, and c.

Talk About It

▶ How can you use a random function to *simulate* the flip of a coin, the roll of a pair of number cubes, or the spinning of a spinner?

Look at a computer program in BASIC that simulates the spin of this spinner.

```
]LIST
  20  LET R = INT (RND  (1) *  4) + 1
  30  IF R = 1 THEN PRINT "RED"
  40  IF R = 2 THEN PRINT "BLUE"
  50  IF R = 3 THEN PRINT "YELLOW"
  60  IF R = 4 THEN PRINT "GREEN"
  70  PRINT "DO YOU WANT TO SPIN AGAIN?"
  80  PRINT "TYPE I FOR YES OR 0 FOR NO"
  90  INPUT A
 100  IF A = 1 THEN GOTO 20
 110  END

]RUN
YELLOW
DO YOU WANT TO SPIN AGAIN?
TYPE I FOR YES OR 0 FOR NO
?
```

At the Computer

5. Change the example above so that the program simulates a spinner with six colors.

6. Finish this computer simulation, in BASIC, to roll a pair of number cubes.

   10 LET D1 = INT (RND (1) * ■) + ■
   20 LET D2 = INT (RND (1) * ■) + ■
   30 PRINT "YOUR ROLL IS ";D1", ";D2
   40 END

7. Type or write a program in LOGO that simulates the toss of a coin.

8. Type or write a procedure in LOGO that will generate and print any number of random integers from 1 to any range.
   HINT: TO NUMBERS :ANYNUM :ANYRANGE

Talk About It

▶ What will happen if you run or type the commands again?

▶ How do BASIC and LOGO functions differ?

▶ Why are computer simulations useful?

Spreadsheet

Sale Discounts and Taxes

Jane and a group of friends found some items marked down in a sale at the Buckhead Mall. They put the information in a **spreadsheet** like this one to calculate the savings, the new prices, and the taxes.

```
File:SHOPPING                  REVIEW/ADD/CHANGE                Escape: Main Menu
========== A ======== B ========== C ======== D ======== E ======= F ====== G === H
  1 | BUCKHEAD MALL SALE
  2 | $$$$$$$$$$$$$$$$$$$$$$$
  3 |
  4 | ITEM           REGULAR    MARK-      SAVINGS      SALE      TAX     TOTAL
  5 |                PRICE      DOWN                    PRICE     6%      COST
  6 | ----------     --------   --------   --------     --------  -----   --------
  7 | JEANS          $30.95     10%        $3.10        $27.86    $1.67   $29.53
  8 | COMPACT DISK   $15.75     20%        $3.15        $12.60    $.76    $13.36
  9 | SUNGLASSES     $10.00     15%        $1.50        $8.50     $.51    $9.01
 10 | HIGH TOPS      $55.99     50%        $28.00       $28.00    $1.68   $29.67
 11 | T-SHIRT        $21.50     30%        $6.45        $15.05    $.90    $15.95

------------------------------------------------------------------------------------
F9: (Value, Layout-D2) (E9*F5)
Type entry or use ⌘ commands                                        ⌘-? for Help
```

Answer the questions about the spreadsheet.

1. What formula could go in cell D7?

2. How could you copy the formula in cell D7 to cells D8 through D11?

3. Write formulas for cells E7, F7, and G7.

Jane decided to present on a **bar graph** the information calculated by the spreadsheet. Bar graphs can be easily drawn by hand, or they can be generated by some computer programs.

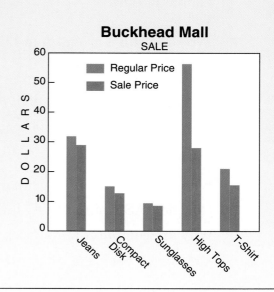

Buckhead Mall
SALE

- Regular Price
- Sale Price

DOLLARS: 0, 10, 20, 30, 40, 50, 60

Jeans, Compact Disk, Sunglasses, High Tops, T-Shirt

At the Computer

4. Type the example spreadsheet on your computer. Type formulas that will calculate the values for columns D, E, F, and G from columns B and C and cell F5. Think about:

a. adding ***, $$$, or --- symbols to highlight titles.
b. using the layout tools to align the numbers and titles on your spreadsheet.
c. using the format tools to change the number values to dollar or percent values.
d. using the copy tools to repeat formulas or formats.
c. deciding which cell references are **relative** and which are **absolute**.

5. Computer project: Collect sales information from a newspaper. Design a spreadsheet like Jane's. Use your state's tax rate, and add sales tax to the total cost of each item.

6. The stacked bar graph shows the total cost of each item, including a 6% sales tax. Use your sales and tax data from Exercise 5, and make a stacked bar graph on a sheet of paper or on a computer.

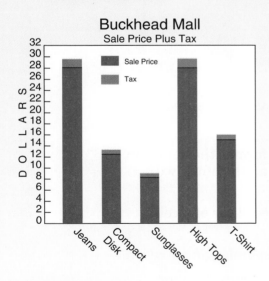

Talk About It

▶ Explain why cell F5 in the spreadsheet in Exercise 4 might be an absolute cell.

▶ What happens when a title does not fit in one cell? What can you do to a cell to fit more text?

Tammy and Rodney studied how to solve algebraic equations in their mathematics class. They developed a spreadsheet to check their work. They set up three types of equations and typed **formulas** in three **cells** to calculate solutions.

At the Computer

```
File: EQUATIONS                REVIEW/ADD/CHANGE                Escape: Main Menu
======== A ======== B ====C===D===E===F===G===H=======I=========J========K====
 1| SOLVING EQUATIONS
 2|
 3|
 4| FORMAT 1              2   Y+  2     =    12
 5|                                Y =     5
 6|
 7| FORMAT 2                       7     =    B   -8
 8|                                B =    15
 9|                                        .
10| FORMAT 3                      3H=    270
11|                               H=     90
   -----------------------------------------------------------------------------
   A11
   Type entry or use ⌂ commands                                    ⌂-? for Help
```

1. Follow these guidelines to format the equations in the spreadsheet.

   a. Type each number in its own cell.

   b. Type +, = ,–, and variables as characters to format the equation. This is done on most spreadsheets by starting the entry with a quotation mark (").

   c. Align labels to the right, to the left, or in the center of a cell so that the equations are in a neat format.

   d. Narrow columns so that the information resembles an equation.

   e. Write the formulas so that they will solve the equations for different number values.

Talk About It

▶ What formula is contained in cell G5?

▶ Why do the 3 and the H appear to be in the same cell?

At the Computer

Follow similar guidelines to create a list of ordered pairs that represent a **function**, a relationship in which each value of x has one value of y.

2. Finish the spreadsheet and answer the questions.

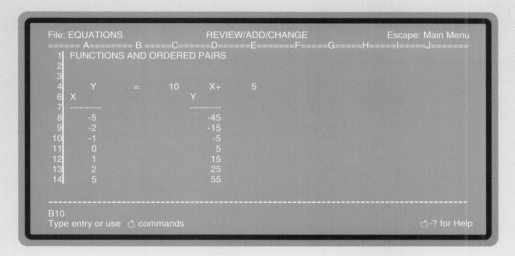

```
File: EQUATIONS                      REVIEW/ADD/CHANGE              Escape: Main Menu
====== A======= B =====C======D======E=======F=====G=====H=====I=====J=======
 1| FUNCTIONS AND ORDERED PAIRS
 2|
 3|
 4|     Y        =    10     X+    5
 6| X                     Y
 7| ----------            ----------
 8|     -5                   -45
 9|     -2                   -15
10|     -1                   -5
11|      0                    5
12|      1                   15
13|      2                   25
14|      5                   55


------------------------------------------------------------------------------
B10
Type entry or use  ⌂ commands                               ⌂-? for Help
```

a. What formula belongs in cell D8?

b. How does the formula change for cells D9 to D14?

c. If you copy the formula in cell D8 to the other cells, which cell references should be relative and which absolute?

3. Change the number values of the equation, and pick new values for x. What are the new y values? Is the equation still a function?

4. Using paper or a computer graphing program, graph the ordered pairs you found in Exercise 3. This is a computer-generated graph of $y = 10x + 5$.

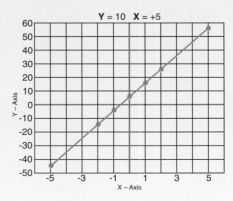

5. Use the equation $y = 3x - 2$ to create a list of ordered pairs in a spreadsheet.

Spreadsheet

Business Application

New Bottlers, Inc., a new fruit juice distributer, used this spreadsheet to project income and expenses for five years. The company wants to know how long it will take to make a profit.

```
File: INCOME                    REVIEW/ADD/CHANGE                  Escape: Main Menu
========== A =========== B ====== C ====== D ======== E ======= F ======= G =====
 1| PROJECTIONS FOR NEW BOTTLERS
 2|
 3|                  YEAR 1    YEAR 2    YEAR 3    YEAR 4    YEAR 5
 4|
 5| SALES INCOME    $100,000  $135,000  $182,250  $246,038  $332,151
 6|
 7| EXPENSES
 8| SUPPLIES        $40,000   $44,000   $48,400   $53,240   $58,564
 9| RENT            $12,000   $12,600   $13,230   $13,892   $14,586
10| ADVERTISING     $20,000   $27,000   $36,450   $49,208   $66,430
11| SALARY          $60,000   $63,000   $66,150   $69,458   $72,930
12| TAXES           $20,000   $24,000   $28,000   $32,000   $36,000
13| TOTAL EXPENSES
14|
15| NET INCOME
----------------------------------------------------------------------------
A1:    (Label) PROJECTIONS FOR
Type entry or use ⌂ commands                              ⌂-? for Help
```

At the Computer

1. Type the spreadsheet on your computer. Use formatting tools to align titles and to add dollar signs.

2. Add formulas to calculate the amounts for cells B13 and B15. HINT: NET INCOME = SALES INCOME – TOTAL EXPENSES

3. Copy the formulas to the corresponding cells in columns C through F.

4. What formula, in cell C5, can calculate the amount of sales for year 2?

5. Calculate the percent of increase for cells D5, C11, and F10 from the previous year.

6. What formulas can calculate the amounts for cells D5, C11, and F10?

7. In which years will the company make a profit?

At the Computer

8. Change the spreadsheet so that the formulas in columns C, D, E, and F calculate the following yearly increases.

Item	Increase
Sales	30%
Supplies	10%
Rent	5%
Advertising	20%
Salaries	5%

9. Change the projected sales figure for year 1 to $200,000. Does your spreadsheet match the one below?

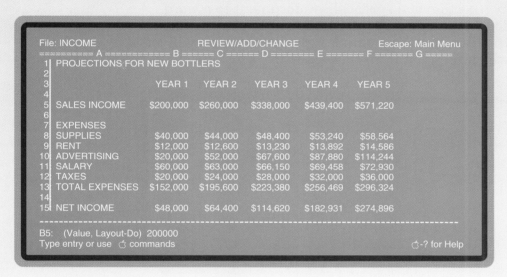

```
File: INCOME                    REVIEW/ADD/CHANGE                Escape: Main Menu
=========== A ============= B ====== C ====== D ======== E ======= F ======= G =====
  1| PROJECTIONS FOR NEW BOTTLERS
  2|
  3|                 YEAR 1    YEAR 2    YEAR 3    YEAR 4    YEAR 5
  4|
  5| SALES INCOME   $200,000  $260,000  $338,000  $439,400  $571,220
  6|
  7| EXPENSES
  8| SUPPLIES        $40,000   $44,000   $48,400   $53,240   $58,564
  9| RENT            $12,000   $12,600   $13,230   $13,892   $14,586
 10| ADVERTISING     $20,000   $52,000   $67,600   $87,880  $114,244
 11| SALARY          $60,000   $63,000   $66,150   $69,458   $72,930
 12| TAXES           $20,000   $24,000   $28,000   $32,000   $36,000
 13| TOTAL EXPENSES $152,000  $195,600  $223,380  $256,469  $296,324
 14|
 15| NET INCOME      $48,000   $64,400  $114,620  $182,931  $274,896
-------------------------------------------------------------------------
B5:  (Value, Layout-Do)  200000
Type entry or use  ⌂ commands                                    ⌂-? for Help
```

10. From a library, get financial information about a company from a yearly report. Use some of the numbers to make a spreadsheet. Use formulas and the copy command whenever possible.

Talk About It

▶ Why do you think companies try to project their income and expenses?

▶ How is a spreadsheet useful for experimenting with projections?

▶ How does your spreadsheet show negative values?

▶ What can you do to the spreadsheet to fit larger numbers like 7,456,000,000 or long titles like YEAR ELEVEN?

Word processors have features that allow you to add or replace text in a document. AppleWorks® has a feature that moves text within the same document or to other word processing, spreadsheet, or data base documents. It uses a **clipboard,** which stores text to be moved from one document to another.

At the Computer

1. Learn to copy a section of a spreadsheet document to a word processing document. To move information from one document to another, the files must be created. A **desktop index** will let you choose which files you want to work with.

Desktop Screen

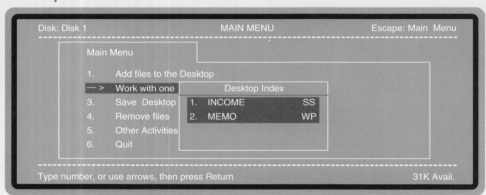

Spreadsheet Screen

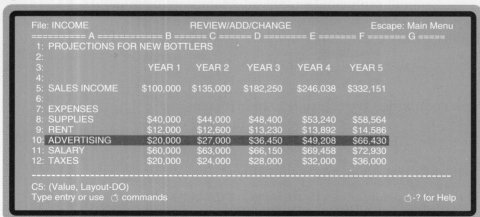

The employees of New Bottlers, Inc., copied the highlighted row from the spreadsheet file INCOME to the word processing file MEMO to avoid retyping.

At the Computer

2. The following word processing file contains information directly from the spreadsheet file.

Word Processing Screen

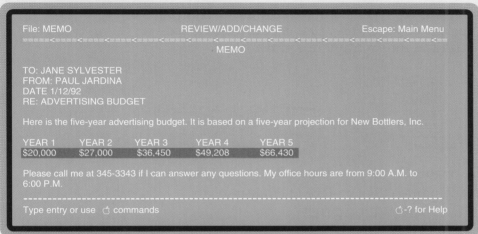

```
File: MEMO                 REVIEW/ADD/CHANGE              Escape: Main Menu
====<====<====<====<====<====<====<====<====<====<====<====<====<====<==
                              MEMO

TO: JANE SYLVESTER
FROM: PAUL JARDINA
DATE 1/12/92
RE: ADVERTISING BUDGET

Here is the five-year advertising budget. It is based on a five-year projection for New Bottlers, Inc.

YEAR 1     YEAR 2     YEAR 3     YEAR 4     YEAR 5
$20,000    $27,000    $36,450    $49,208    $66,430

Please call me at 345-3343 if I can answer any questions. My office hours are from 9:00 A.M. to
6:00 P.M.
------------------------------------------------------------------------
Type entry or use ⌘ commands                                    ⌘-? for Help
```

Suppose that Paul wants to send memos to other people in the company, but with a few changes. Most word processors have a function that will find and replace characters or numbers. Type the MEMO file on your word processor. Then use the find and replace function to insert new information in the place of old information.

Old Information	New Information
a. 9:00	8:00
b. 1/12/92	4/20/92
c. 345-3343	222-3376
d. JANE	ALICE
e. SYLVESTER	GARCIA

Talk About It

▶ What is the difference between moving information and copying it?

▶ What happens if the word or number you need to find and replace occurs more than once in the file?

▶ If you use a long word, like *mathematics* many times in a document, how can the code *mmm* and the find and replace functions help?

Data Base

Conducting a Survey

Nicole conducted a survey to investigate how different groups of people recognized computer hardware. She used a specific code for each result to organize the information in a **data base**.

Figure 1   **Figure 2**   **Figure 3**   **Figure 4**

What is the name of each piece of equipment?

ANSWER CODES

LP - lap top, PC - personal computer, PR - printer,
DD - disk drive, O - other (name unknown or wrong answer)

Nicole also used codes to collect information about the students she interviewed.

INTERVIEWEE CODES

Age Group	Gender	Computer Ed*
12	M - male	Y - yes
13	F - female	N - no
14		

*Computer Ed is the category for students who have had some computer education in school.

The following data base shows how Nicole organized the results of the computer survey.

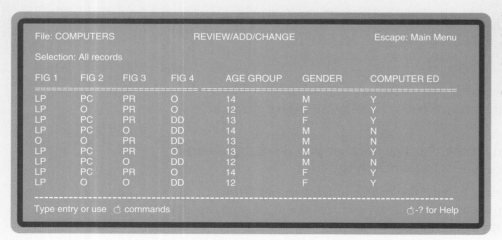

File: COMPUTERS   REVIEW/ADD/CHANGE   Escape: Main Menu

Selection: All records

FIG 1	FIG 2	FIG 3	FIG 4	AGE GROUP	GENDER	COMPUTER ED
LP	PC	PR	O	14	M	Y
LP	O	PR	O	12	F	Y
LP	PC	PR	DD	13	F	Y
LP	PC	O	DD	14	M	N
O	O	PR	DD	13	M	N
LP	PC	PR	O	13	M	Y
LP	PC	O	DD	12	M	N
LP	PC	PR	O	14	F	Y
LP	O	O	DD	12	F	Y

Type entry or use ⌂ commands   ⌂-? for Help

Talk About It

▶ Use the code descriptions and data base on page 488 to answer the questions.

   a. How many females that have had computer education recognized Figure 1 to be a lap top?

   b. How many 14-year-olds recognized that Figure 2 is a personal computer, that Figure 3 is a printer, or that Figure 4 is a disk drive?

   c. How many students who have not had computer education recognized Figure 1 and Figure 3?

▶ Why is using a data base program better than just reading for answering these questions?

▶ What does the following computer screen show?

```
File: COMPUTERS              REVIEW/ADD/CHANGE              Escape: Main Menu

Selection:    FIG 1 equals LP
and           FIG 2 equals PC
and           COMPUTER ED equals Y
FIG 1     FIG 2     FIG 3     FIG 4      AGE GROUP     GENDER      COMPUTER ED
============================================  ===============================
LP        PC        PR        O          14            M           Y
LP        PC        PR        DD         13            F           Y
LP        PC        PR        O          13            M           Y
LP        PC        PR        O          14            M           Y

------------------------------------------------------------------------------
Type entry or use ⌂ commands                                     ⌂-? for Help
```

At the Computer

1. With a partner, draw or collect three or four other computer pictures, such as monitors, disks, or graphic designs. Conduct a survey like the example, and put your results in a data base.

2. Create your own format and layout. Decide which categories give you valuable information. Determine the widths of the fields.

3. Sort each of the fields to see whether there are any interesting results.

4. Print a list of the selections that have patterns.

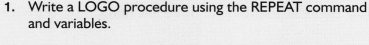

IDEA BANK

1. Write a LOGO procedure using the REPEAT command and variables.

2. Write a LOGO procedure using the RANDOM function.

3. Write a LOGO procedure using the SETXY function.

WORD PROCESSING IDEAS

4. Write directions explaining how to use the functions for random numbers in BASIC and LOGO. Type example problems.

5. Use the find and replace function to change the example problems in Exercise 4.

6. Write directions for copying text from one document to another on your word processor.

SPREADSHEET IDEAS

7. Collect statistics about your favorite athlete from an almanac or a newspaper. Put the information on a spreadsheet. Type a one page report about the person on your word processor.

8. Collect information about new and used cars of a specific make. Put the information for at least ten prices on a spreadsheet, and calculate how much the tax would be for each vehicle. Type a report on your word processor to explain how you calculated the tax amount on the speadsheet.

DATA BASE IDEAS

9. Make a data base about a hobby. Gather and organize information that would be useful.

10. Sort the information in Exercise 9 in different ways, such as alphabetically or numerically. Print copies of the different lists.

PROJECTS

11. On your word processor, write a plan for a survey about sports. Make a list of the questions you will ask and the people you will interview. Conduct the survey, and organize your results in a data base.

12. Use the spreadsheet to calculate algebraic equations discussed in your math class. Set up the equations so that number values can be changed.

13. From the library, gather statistical information about a company. Put the data in a spreadsheet. Copy part of that spreadsheet into a word processing file. Write a memo on the word processor that uses numbers from the spreadsheet.

14. On your word processor, write a plan for a survey of your choice. Think about what questions will give you valuable information. Conduct the survey by questioning enough people to make the results meaningful. Using codes, organize the information in a data base.

Student Handbook

1. Bridge Lessons H2–H21
2. School-Home Connection H22–H28
3. More Practice H30–H85
4. Learning Resources H86–H100
5. Tables H101–H104
6. Glossary H105–H114
7. Selected Answers H115–H126
8. Index H127–H137

Bridge Lessons

CHAPTER 1
Place Value

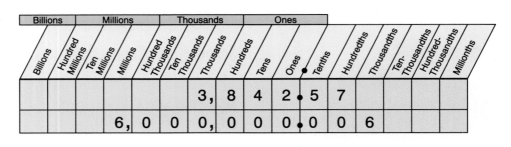

				Thousands			Ones								

Numbers to the left of the decimal point are separated into periods by commas.

Read "and" for the decimal point.

Numbers to the right of the decimal point are named by the place value of the last digit.

Write the numbers in the place-value chart in words.

3,842.57 → three thousand, eight hundred forty-two and fifty-seven hundredths
6,000,000.006 → six million and six thousandths

You can use these symbols when you compare and order numbers.

| = means "is equal to." |
| ≠ means "is not equal to." |
| < means "is less than." |
| > means "is greater than." |

8 = 8.0 ← Annex a zero.
8 is equal to 8.0.

16.5 < 18.9
16.5 is less than 18.9.

16.3 ≠ 16.03
16.3 is not equal to 16.03.

4.39 > 4.3 ← 4.3 is equivalent to 4.30.
4.39 is greater than 4.3.

Write these numbers in order from least to greatest. Use <.

679.14, 678.99, 678.9

Think: 678.9 < 678.99, and 678.99 < 679.14 → 678.9 < 678.99 < 679.14

Talk About It

▶ How would you write the numbers in the last example in order from greatest to least, using >?

▶ How can you use equivalent decimals to write these numbers in order from least to greatest? 4.695, 4.6, 4.58

Practice

Write each number in words.

1. 3,467
2. 78,592
3. 6,000,849
4. 530.76
5. 4,945.007
6. 954.351

Name the place of the underlined digit.

7. 1,2̲54.7
8. 34̲,987.2
9. 1,983.5̲6
10. 85.602̲3̲
11. 579.2̲7̲
12. 37.697̲5

Compare. Write $=$ or $\neq$.

13. 0.54 ● 5.4
14. 67.8 ● 678
15. 0.53 ● 0.530

Compare. Write $<$, $>$, or $=$.

16. 19,876 ● 19,678
17. 654.80 ● 654.8
18. 14.6 ● 16.4
19. 789.54 ● 789.544
20. 4.9863 ● 4.986
21. 295.6573 ● 295.65
22. 3,423 ● 3.423
23. 0.645 ● 6.45
24. 49.02 ● 49.2
25. 64,125 ● 64,125.1
26. 800.4 ● 804
27. 3,975 ● 3,957

Write in order from least to greatest. Use $<$.

28. 6,371; 6,137; 6,173
29. 0.9; 0.2; 0.6
30. 8.9; 9.8; 0.89
31. 4.67; 4.76; 4.7
32. 9.9; 9.09; 0.99
33. 5.098; 5.089; 5.89

Write in order from greatest to least. Use $>$.

34. 0.78; 0.87; 0.8
35. 5,788.812; 5,789.812; 5,789.821
36. 576.23; 576.32; 576.233
37. 83.129; 83.21; 83.219
38. 5.114; 51.14; 51.144
39. 19.473; 19.0473; 19.743

Solve.

40. What is the most popular program type?

41. What is the least popular program type?

42. Compare the viewing times for general drama, mystery, and adventure. Order the viewing times from least to greatest, using $<$.

Television Program Preferences	
Program Type	Average Audience Viewing Time in Minutes
General drama	19,130,000
Mystery	18,500,000
Situation comedy	25,350,000
Adventure	17,270,000
Feature films	22,020,000

CHAPTER I

Rounding Whole Numbers and Decimals

Last year 19,330,375 color televisions were sold.
Use rounding to estimate the sales to the nearest million.

You can use a number line.

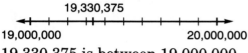

19,330,375 is between 19,000,000
and 20,000,000.

19,330,375 is closer to 19,000,000.
19,330,375 rounds to 19,000,000.

You can use the rounding rules.

a. Find the digit in the place to be rounded.
b. Now look at the digit to its right.
c. If the digit to the right is less than 5, the digit being rounded remains the same.
d. If the digit to the right is 5 or more, the digit being rounded is increased by 1.

19,330,375 ← Look at the 3.
3 < 5   The 9 remains the same.
19,330,375 rounds to 19,000,000.

So, about 19,000,000 color televisions were sold last year.

Round the following numbers to the nearest ten thousand.

45,782
5 = 5   Increase the 4.
45,782 → 50,000

214,978
4 < 5   Remains the same.
214,978 → 210,000

7,853
7 > 5   Increase the 0.
7,853 → 10,000

- What happens to the digits to the right of the whole number to be rounded?

_____

Olga Bryzguina ran the 400-m dash in 48.65 sec.
Use rounding to estimate her time to the nearest second.

You can use a number line.

48.65 is between 48 and 49.
48.65 is closer to 49.
48.65 rounds to 49.
So, Olga Bryzguina ran the 400-m dash in about 49 sec.

You can use the rounding rules.

48.65 ← Look at the 6.
6 > 5   Increase the 8.
48.65 rounds to 49.

Round the following numbers to the nearest hundredth.

27.346
6 > 5   Increase the 4.
27.346 → 27.35

4.674
4 < 5   Remains the same.
4.674 → 4.67

$1.299
9 > 5   Increase the 9.
$1.299 → $1.30

Talk About It

▶ What happens to the digits to the right of the decimal number to be rounded?

▶ In your own words, state the rule for rounding decimals.

Practice

Round to the nearest hundred.

1. 739   2. 4,624   3. 47,873

Round to the nearest thousand.

4. 45,482   5. 600,987   6. 555,683

Round to the nearest million.

7. 8,915,027   8. 8,185,679   9. 987,631

Round to the nearest ten dollars.

10. $43.86   11. $58.72   12. $385.03

Round to the nearest whole number.

13. 17.6   14. 143.09   15. 67.53   16. 8.471

Round to the nearest tenth.

17. 0.671   18. 5.081   19. 87.032   20. 30.946

21. 3.752   22. 12.049   23. 45.191   24. 0.055

Round to the nearest hundredth.

25. 0.987   26. 5.081   27. 87.034   28. 30.946

29. 17.546   30. 72.901   31. 3.0347   32. 475.098

Round to the nearest thousandth.

33. 0.5391   34. 6.0008   35. 34.0069   36. 86.5536

37. 145.9999   38. 0.0049   39. 9.9999   40. 4.4446

Round to the nearest ten-thousandth.

41. 5.067328   42. 8.65473   43. 2.09843   44. 86.37018

45. 0.43216   46. 104.85972   47. 0.00045   48. 9.004163

Solve.

49. To the nearest million, how many homes have color TV sets?

50. To the nearest hundred thousand, how many homes have one TV set?

51. To the nearest ten million, how many homes have 2 or more TV sets?

52. To the nearest thousand, how many homes have cable TV?

TV Sets in United States Homes	
TV Category	**Number of Homes**
Color sets	87,300,000
Black-and-white only	3,070,000
2 or more sets	56,600,000
One set	33,810,000
Cable	50,241,840

CHAPTER I

Adding and Subtracting Decimals

Calvin and Monroe are buying two pieces of stereo equipment costing $169.99 and $99.98. How much change will they receive from three $100 bills?

Step 1
Find the total cost of the purchases.

$169.99
+   99.98   ← Line up the decimal points.
$269.97   ← Write the decimal point in the answer.

Step 2
Find the total amount paid.

Think: $3 \times \$100 = \$300$

Step 3
Find the amount of change.

$300.00   ← Annex two zeros.
− 269.97   ← Line up the decimal points.
$ 30.03   ← Write the decimal point in the answer.

So, Calvin and Monroe will receive $30.03 in change.

More Examples

Find the sum. $36 + 15.4 + 9$

Think: Annex zeros to 36 and 9 so that all the numbers have the same number of decimal places.

36.0   ← equivalent to 36
15.4
+ 9.0   ← equivalent to 9
60.4   ← The sum is 60.4.

Find the difference. $8 - 0.05$

Think: Annex zeros to 8 so that it has the same number of decimal places as 0.05.

8.00   ← equivalent to 8
−0.05
7.95

So, the difference is 7.95.

Talk About It

▶ How do you find the correct number of decimal places for each number in $4.87 + 7 + 9.0087$?

▶ Suppose you subtract 0.000008 from 9.3. How can you find the correct number of decimal places in the answer?

▶ Why can you annex zeros to decimal numbers?

Practice

Find the sum.

1. 7.9
   +2.4

2. 5.88
   +3.42

3. 46.3
   + 9.82

4. 76.856
   +31.9

5. 95.46
   +37.5

6. 3.65
   +0.912

7. 51.7
   +38.004

8. 8.974
   +21.8

9. 4.15
   8.6
   +9.283

10. 10.4213
    3.5
    + 2.96

11. 115.402
    803.1
    + 27.86

12. 9,116
    2,127.8
    + 114.23

13. 46 + 9.65 + 0.832

14. 0.073 + 52 + 8.91

15. 47.5 + 384 + 6.199

16. 82 + 7.2 + 0.61

17. 19.2 + 61 + 452.821

18. 31 + 7 + 41.86 + 387

Find the difference.

19. 9.3
    −2.6

20. 12.05
    − 9.37

21. 80
    −14.89

22. 11
    − 4.12

23. 36.752
    − 8.491

24. 72.1
    −49.3

25. 5.026
    −2.3

26. 6.789
    −6.24

27. 29.8
    − 8.765

28. 56
    − 0.43

29. 37.1
    − 6.99

30. 3
    −2.006

31. 25 − 6.93

32. 97.1 − 0.87

33. 9.662 − 7.8

34. 126 − 0.79

35. 45.6 − 9.38

36. 8.327 − 5.6

37. 6.1 − 3.92

38. 13.2 − 7.623

39. 5 − 4.325

Solve.

40. A 19-in. color television at Matt's Television Circus is on sale for $299.00. The regular price is $379.99. If you were going to buy this television, how much could you save by purchasing the television at the sale price?

41. Eric and Terry competed in a 500-m speed-skating race. Eric finished in 38.03 sec and Terry finished in 40.1 sec. How much faster was Eric's time than Terry's time?

42. Greg Louganis received gold medals at the Olympic games in Los Angeles in 1984 and in Seoul in 1988 for his platform diving. He earned 710.91 points in 1984 and 638.61 points in 1988. How many points did he earn in all?

43. Allison's checkbook balance is $1,258.90. What will be her new checkbook balance after writing a $330 check and making a $25 deposit?

CHAPTER I

Multiplying and Dividing Decimals

Joanie bought 3 cassettes.
Each cassette cost $5.98. How
much did she spend in all?

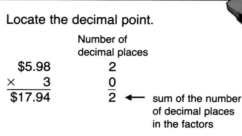

Step 1 Multiply as with whole numbers.	**Step 2** Locate the decimal point.
$5.98 ← factor × 3 ← factor $1794 ← product	Number of decimal places $5.98 2 × 3 0 $17.94 2 ← sum of the number of decimal places in the factors

She spent $17.94 in all.

Sometimes you need to insert zeros in the product.

Find the product of 0.2 and 0.4.

Multiply.

Insert 2 zeros to the left of 8 to make 3 decimal places.

0.02
× 0.4
8   ← 2 + 1, or 3 decimal places

Find the sum of the number of decimal places in the factors.

0.02
× 0.4
0.008

● The product of 0.009 × 0.03 has how many decimal places?

_____

Garrett ran 9 mi in 67.5 min.
What was his average time to run 1 mi?

Think: Divide 67.5 by 9.

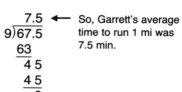

Step 1 Write the decimal point in the quotient directly above the decimal point in the dividend.	**Step 2** Divide as with whole numbers.
9)67.5	7.5 ← So, Garrett's average time to run 1 mi was 7.5 min. 9)67.5 63 45 45 0

● Where do you place the decimal point in the quotient 6)0.036?

● What is the quotient 3.57423 rounded to the nearest hundredth?

● What is the quotient 8)0.00024? How many zeros do you insert?

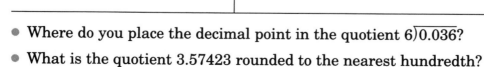

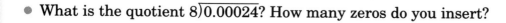

Practice

Use mental math to tell how many decimal places will be in the product.

1. 36.9
× 8

2. 41.2
× 0.7

3. 3.14
× 0.05

4. 0.89
× 0.6

Find the product.

5. 3.3
× 0.05

6. 219
× 4.8

7. 0.36
× 0.19

8. 1.75
× 2.3

9. 14.96
× 0.38

10. 1.36
× 0.25

11. 8.95
× 0.42

12. 2.96
× 0.73

13. 5.75
× 1.29

14. 392
× 5.6

15. 0.94
× 0.653

16. 3.06
× 0.32

17. 0.983
× 100

18. 0.0823
× 10

19. 24.8
× 0.01

20. 3.79
× 0.001

Write the quotient with the decimal point placed correctly.

21. $\dfrac{28}{34)95.2}$

22. $\dfrac{80}{51)408.0}$

23. $\dfrac{16}{23)0.368}$

24. $\dfrac{25}{6)1.50}$

Find the quotient.

25. $4)\overline{3.2}$

26. $8)\overline{0.96}$

27. $5)\overline{2.30}$

28. $42)\overline{15.54}$

29. $62)\overline{7.502}$

30. $98)\overline{4.508}$

31. $93)\overline{37.2}$

32. $18)\overline{9.324}$

33. $9)\overline{0.846}$

34. $16)\overline{0.0416}$

35. $47)\overline{2.4346}$

36. $6)\overline{0.21}$

Find the quotient. Round to the nearest hundredth.

37. $8)\overline{15.23}$

38. $6)\overline{312.8}$

39. $14)\overline{7.614}$

40. $46)\overline{82.163}$

Solve.

41. Joanie bought 4 cassettes and 1 compact disc. Each cassette cost $5.98 and the compact disc cost $15.98. How much did she spend in all?

42. The total restaurant bill was $102.00 for a group of 8 people. What was the average cost per person?

CHAPTER 3

Divisibility

Do you remember these divisibility rules for 2, 3, 5, 9, and 10?

A number is divisible by	Divisible	Not Divisible
2 if the last digit is an even number.	15,792	4,683
3 if the sum of the digits is divisible by 3.	6,291	326
5 if the last digit is 0 or 5.	12,385	860,002
9 if the sum of the digits is divisible by 9.	51,084	4,005,800
10 if the last digit is 0.	206,530	9,325

- Is 425 divisible by 10? by 5?
- Is 804 divisible by 3? by 9?

WORK TOGETHER

You can use a calculator to explore divisibility rules for 4 and 6.

- Use a calculator to divide these numbers by 6.
  Record the quotients.
  132, 140, 128, 125, 216, 152, 210, 378, 438
- Which of the numbers are divisible by 6?
- Which of the numbers that are divisible by 6 are also divisible by 2? by 3?

Talk About It

▶ Why is a number that is divisible by both 2 and 3 also divisible by 6?

▶ How can you state a rule for finding numbers divisible by 6?

- Use a calculator to divide these numbers by 4.
  Record the quotients.
  132, 148, 104, 144, 152, 210, 378, 388
- Which of the numbers are divisible by 4?
- Look at the last two digits of each number that is divisible by 4.
  Is the number formed by these last two digits divisible by 4?

Talk About It

▶ How can you state a rule for finding numbers divisible by 4?

▶ Do the divisibility rules work for decimal numbers? Give two examples.

Practice

Write *yes* or *no* to tell whether the number is divisible by 2.

1. 598   **2.** 6,341   **3.** 43,999

Tell whether the number is divisible by 5 or 10.

4. 460   **5.** 295   **6.** 8,850

Find the sum of the digits for each number.

7. 675   **8.** 348   **9.** 9,207

Tell whether the number is divisible by 3 or 9.

10. 675   **11.** 348   **12.** 9,207

Copy and complete with a digit that makes the number divisible by 3.

13. 1,■61   **14.** 2,1■4   **15.** ■,703   **16.** 6,52■

Copy and complete with a digit that makes the number divisible by 9.

17. 1■,632   **18.** 24,■56   **19.** ■,845   **20.** 821,64■

Tell whether the number is divisible by 2, 3, or 6.

21. 765   **22.** 592   **23.** 4,941   **24.** 93,420

Tell whether the number is divisible by 2 or 4.

25. 882   **26.** 1,416   **27.** 4,624   **28.** 87,138

Copy and complete with a digit that makes the number divisible by 4.

29. 3■4   **30.** 91■   **31.** 50■   **32.** 8■8

Tell whether the number is divisible by 9 or 10.

33. 4,580   **34.** 6,336   **35.** 77,940   **36.** 51,345

37. 3,940   **38.** 495   **39.** 5,949   **40.** 98,910

Solve.

41. All matinee theater tickets cost $3.00. Can the matinee ticket receipts total $610? Why or why not?

42. The Elton Nursery sells orange trees for $9 each. Can a purchase of orange trees cost exactly $144? Why or why not?

43. Jason has 360 apples to divide equally among 15 boxes. Which divisibility rules can you use to determine whether Jason can do this?

44. Stacey has 121 ribbons to divide into groups of 10. Will she have any ribbons left over? Explain.

CHAPTER 3

Greatest Common Factor and Least Common Multiple

The desks in three offices are arranged in rows with the same number of desks in each row. Office A has a total of 24 desks, Office B has 18 desks, and Office C has 12 desks. What is the greatest possible number of desks in each row?

Think: The number of desks in each row is a factor of 24, 18, *and* 12.

You can list the factors.	You can use the prime factorizations.
Factors of 24: 1, 2, 3, 4, 6, 8, 12, 24	$24 = 2 \times 2 \times 2 \times 3$
Factors of 18: 1, 2, 3, 6, 9, 18	$18 = 2 \times 3 \times 3$
Factors of 12: 1, 2, 3, 4, 6, 12	$12 = 2 \times 2 \times 3$
Common factors: 1, 2, 3, and 6	Common prime factors: 2, 3
	Product of prime factors: $2 \times 3 = 6$

The greatest common factor of 24, 18, and 12 is 6.

So, 6 is the greatest possible number of desks in each row.

The **greatest common factor** (GCF) of two or more numbers is the largest number that is a factor of all the numbers.

● How can you use the prime factorization to find the GCF for 40 and 35?

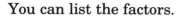

A **multiple** is a number that is the product of a given number and a whole number.	The **least common multiple** (LCM) is the smallest nonzero multiple that two or more numbers have in common.

Multiples of 6: 0, 6, 12, 18, 24, 30, 36, 42, 48, 54, 60, . . .
Multiples of 8: 0, 8, 16, 24, 32, 40, 48, 56, 64, 72, 80, . . .

What is the LCM of 6 and 8?

The smallest nonzero common multiple, 24, is the LCM of 6 and 8.

Find the LCM of 14, 20, and 35.

You can use prime factorizations to find the LCM of two or more numbers.

Prime factorization of 14: 2×7
Prime factorization of 20: $2^2 \times 5$
Prime factorization of 35: 5×7

> The LCM is the product of the highest power of each of the different prime factors.

So, the LCM of 14, 20, and 35 is $2^2 \times 5 \times 7$, or 140.

● How can you find the LCM of 9 and 15?

Practice

List the factors to find the GCF.

1. 10, 25   **2.** 16, 24   **3.** 20, 30

4. 24, 40   **5.** 45, 60   **6.** 25, 75

7. 30, 36   **8.** 42, 56   **9.** 18, 54

Use the prime factorizations to find the GCF.

10. 18, 20   **11.** 30, 45   **12.** 30, 75

13. 48, 60   **14.** 50, 70   **15.** 36, 54

16. 15, 60   **17.** 75, 100   **18.** 24, 27

Find the first five nonzero multiples of each number.

19. 2   **20.** 3   **21.** 5   **22.** 8

23. 6   **24.** 7   **25.** 10   **26.** 20

List multiples to find the LCM.

27. 8, 20   **28.** 6, 12   **29.** 3, 5   **30.** 6, 9

31. 10, 12   **32.** 12, 16   **33.** 15, 30   **34.** 4, 9

35. 2, 11   **36.** 10, 25   **37.** 8, 12   **38.** 50, 75

Use prime factorizations to find the LCM.

39. 4, 6   **40.** 6, 20   **41.** 24, 36   **42.** 20, 50

43. 7, 21   **44.** 16, 36   **45.** 4, 18   **46.** 4, 5, 10

47. 2, 5, 6   **48.** 3, 6, 10   **49.** 2, 3, 11   **50.** 3, 4, 6

Solve.

51. Linda has 56 roses, 63 sprigs of baby's breath, and 49 carnations to use in her floral arrangements. She wants to place the same number of roses, baby's breath, and carnations in each arrangement. What is the greatest number of each kind of flower that she can use in the floral arrangements?

52. Ophelia, Kenny, and Jamie started running on the oval track at 4 P.M. Ophelia can complete the track in 6 min. Kenny's time is 10 min, and Jamie's time is 5 min. Suppose the runners continue at these rates. At what time will all three runners meet at the same track position again?

CHAPTER 5

The Vocabulary of Geometry

There are many examples of geometric figures in the STW building. The corners are examples of points. Each side of the building is part of a plane.

These words and symbols will help you describe geometric figures.

Geometric Figures			
Figure	**Name**	**Symbol**	**Description**
A •	point *A*	no symbol	Shows location. All points are named with capital letters.
•←——•——→• *A* *B*	line *AB*	$\overleftrightarrow{AB}$	Continues forever in opposite directions.
•——————• *A* *B*	line segment *AB*	$\overline{AB}$	Consists of two endpoints and all the points between them.
•——————•→ *A* *B*	ray *AB*	$\overrightarrow{AB}$	Continues forever in one direction from its endpoint. The letter for the endpoint is written first.
A •—————→ •————•→ *B* *C*	angle *ABC*, angle *CBA*, or angle *B*	∠*ABC*, ∠*CBA*, or ∠*B*	A pair of rays that have a common endpoint called the vertex. The vertex is the middle point named.
•*A* *l* •*C* •*B*	plane *l* or plane *ABC*	no symbol	A flat surface that continues forever in all directions. A plane is represented by a four-sided figure.

Talk About It

▶ Look at the drawing of the building. What is the difference between $\overleftrightarrow{CD}$ and $\overline{CD}$?

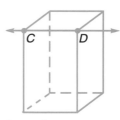

▶ How can you find the vertex of an angle?

▶ Name some objects in nature that suggest line segments and angles.

Practice

Write the letter for the correct figure.

1. $\overleftrightarrow{PQ}$ **2.** $\overrightarrow{PQ}$ **3.** $\angle PQR$ **4.** $\overline{PQ}$ **5.** $\overrightarrow{QP}$

a.
P   Q

b.

Q   R

c.
P   Q

d.
P Q

e.
Q P

6. $\overrightarrow{MN}$ **7.** $\overleftrightarrow{MN}$ **8.** $\overline{MN}$ **9.** $\angle LMN$ **10.** $\overrightarrow{LM}$

a.

M   N

b.
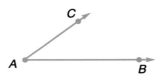

c.

M   N

d.
M   N

e.
M N

Name the figure.

11.
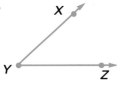

12.
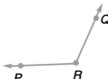

13.
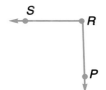

14.
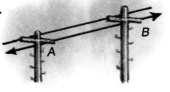

15.

16.
W   X

Name each angle in three ways.

17.

18.

19.

Each object in Exercises 20–23 suggests a geometric figure.
Name the geometric figure.

20.

21.

22.

23.
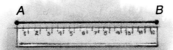

CHAPTER 5

Circles

A **circle** is a closed plane figure made up of all the points in a plane at an equal distance from a point inside the circle called the **center**.

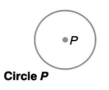

Circle P

Parts of a Circle

Name	Description	Examples
Radius	A line segment joining the center of the circle and a point on the circle.	$\overline{OT}, \overline{OU},$ $\overline{OP}, \overline{OS}$
Chord	A line segment with both endpoints on the circle.	$\overline{RQ}, \overline{SP}$
Diameter	A chord passing through the center of the circle.	$\overline{SP}$
Arc	A part of a circle	$\overset{\frown}{SR}, \overset{\frown}{RQ}$
Central angle	An angle with its vertex at the center of the circle.	$\angle SOT,$ $\angle POU$

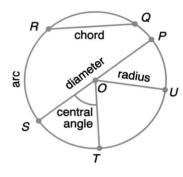

Talk About It

▶ Name two chords in circle H.
  Which is also a diameter?

▶ Name a radius and a diameter in circle H.
  What is the relationship between the length of the radius and the length of the diameter?

▶ How many radii are shown in circle H?
  How many radii can a circle have?

▶ Name two central angles in circle H.
  What is the same about all central angles?

▶ A **semicircle** is an arc formed by a diameter.
  What are two semicircles on circle H?

Circle H

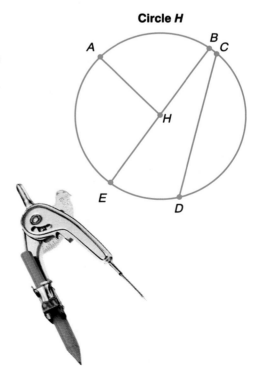

You can use a compass to construct a circle. Open the compass to the radius you desire. Using the point of the compass as the center of the circle, rotate the pencil.

Practice

Use the letters in the figure to name the following.

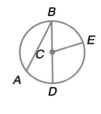

1. the circle
2. the diameter
3. a radius
4. an arc
5. a central angle
6. a chord

Use circle G for Exercises 7–18. Write *center, radius, chord, diameter, arc, central angle,* or *semicircle* to identify each part.

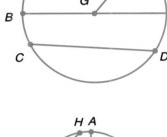

7. $\overline{CD}$
8. $\overline{GB}$
9. $\overarc{AH}$

10. $\angle BGF$
11. G
12. $\overline{BE}$

13. $\overline{EG}$
14. $\overarc{CE}$
15. $\angle EGF$

16. $\overarc{CH}$
17. $\overline{GF}$
18. $\overarc{BE}$

Use circle K for Exercises 19–23.

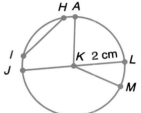

19. How long is radius $\overline{JK}$?

20. How long is radius $\overline{AK}$?

21. How long is diameter $\overline{JL}$?

22. Suppose you draw another diameter. What length will it be?

23. How is the length of diameter $\overline{JL}$ related to the length of radius $\overline{KM}$?

Write *always, sometimes,* or *never.*

24. A radius is a chord.
25. A chord is a diameter.

26. The center is an endpoint for each radius.
27. A diameter is a chord.

Solve.

28. A circular pool has a radius of 5 m. What is the diameter?

29. A Ferris wheel has a diameter of 44 ft. What is the radius?

30. Lisa wants to cut the pizza into 16 parts. Each cut that she makes goes through the center of the pizza. How many cuts will she have to make?

31. The circular building has 6 equally spaced roof beams. Each beam is a diameter of the circular roof. Into how many sections do the beams divide the roof?

CHAPTER 7

Using Counters to Add and Subtract Integers

You can use counters in two colors to model integers. Let ○ represent 1 and ● represent ⁻1. Each ● ○ pair represents ⁻1 + 1, or 0.

WORK TOGETHER

Work with a classmate to model addition of integers by using yellow and red counters.

To model ⁻3 + ⁻2, first model each addend. ●●● ●●

⁻3 + ⁻2

Since all counters are the same color, count the total number of counters.

- What is the sum of ⁻3 + ⁻2?

- What is the sum of 4 + 5? How can you model it using counters?

To model ⁻5 + 3, first model each addend. ●●●●● ○○○

⁻5 + 3

Rearrange the counters to form as many ● ○ pairs as possible.
●●●●●
○○○

- What is the sum of ⁻5 + 3?

- What is the sum of 7 + ⁻2? How can you model it using counters?

Work with a classmate to show how addition and subtraction of integers are related. Compare the subtraction with the addition problem.

Subtraction	Addition
Use counters to model the subtraction equation ⁻1 − ⁻5 = .	Use counters to model the addition equation ⁻1 + 5 = ▦.
To take away 5 red counters from ⁻1, you must start with at least 5 red counters. ●●●●●● ⎫ ○○○○○ ⎬ represents ⁻1 ⎭ Now, to model the subtraction, take away 5 red counters. ●∅∅∅∅∅ ○○○○○ Since 4 unpaired yellow counters remain, ⁻1 − ⁻5 = 4.	● ○○○○○ There are 4 unpaired yellow counters. So, ⁻1 + 5 = 4.
	Comparing Subtraction and Addition
	Compare the subtraction equation with the addition equation. Both equal 4. ⁻1 − ⁻5 = 4 and ⁻1 + 5 = 4 ⁻1 − ⁻5 = ⁻1 + 5 You can subtract an integer by adding its opposite.

- What addition expression can you write that is the same as 3 − 4?

Practice

Tell how many yellow and how many red counters are needed to model
the addition.

1. $5 + 2$

2. $^-3 + ^-5$

3. $^-8 + ^-2$

4. $6 + ^-5$

5. $^-9 + 7$

6. $^-12 + 12$

Model each addition expression by using counters. Solve.

7. $6 + 3$

8. $^-4 + ^-4$

9. $5 + ^-4$

10. $^-9 + 3$

11. $^-5 + 5$

12. $7 + ^-2$

Write *always, sometimes,* or *never* to describe the sum.

13. The sum of two positive integers is a positive integer.

14. The sum of two negative integers is a negative integer.

15. The sum of a positive integer and a negative integer is a positive integer.

16. The sum of a positive integer and a negative integer is a negative integer.

17. The difference between two negative integers is a positive integer.

18. The difference between two positive integers is a positive integer.

Use the model to find the difference. Write the difference as an integer.

19. $6 - 2$

20. $1 - 3$

21. $^-2 - 2$

22. $^-3 - ^-3$

Model each subtraction equation by using counters. Solve.

23. $^-2 - ^-5 = $ ▨

24. $^-2 - 5 = $ ▨

25. $2 - ^-5 = $ ▨

Rewrite each subtraction expression as an addition expression. Solve.

26. $9 - 14$

27. $^-14 - ^-9$

28. $14 - ^-9$

29. $^-6 - 9$

30. $7 - ^-10$

31. $^-9 - 11$

Solve.

32. The sun is 92,900,000 mi from the earth. The moon is 238,857 mi from the earth. Write a subtraction equation to represent the difference in these distances.

33. Amy owed her brother $14 ($^-14$). Then she borrowed another $6 ($^-6$). Write an addition equation to represent the amount that Amy owes her brother now.

CHAPTER 10

Mode, Median, and Mean

Bowling Scores					
Elizabeth	135	150	135	155	190
Hue	140	134	160	148	188

The mode, the median, and the mean are all single numbers that describe data. They are **measures of central tendency.**

Elizabeth's and Hue's scores are shown on this number line.

```
  E
HE   H      H E   E   H                      H E      E ◄──── Elizabeth
◄┼┼┼┼┼┼┼┼┼┼┼┼┼┼┼┼┼┼┼┼┼┼┼┼┼┼┼┼┼┼┼┼┼┼┼┼┼┼┼┼┼►  H ◄──── Hue
 135 140 145 150 155 160 165 170 175 180 185 190
```

The **mode** is the number or numbers occurring most frequently.

● What is the mode for Elizabeth's scores? for Hue's scores?

● Is it possible to have more than one mode for a set of data? Give an example.

The **median** is the middle number, or the average of the middle numbers, when the numbers are arranged in order.

Bowling Scores					
Elizabeth	135	135	150	155	190
Hue	134	140	148	160	188

◄── scores arranged in order from least to greatest

● What is the median for Elizabeth's scores? for Hue's scores?

The **mean,** or average, is the sum for a set of data divided by the number of items of data.

Elizabeth $\quad \dfrac{765}{5}$ ◄── sum of the bowling scores ──► $\dfrac{770}{5}$ Hue
◄── number of bowling scores ──►

● What is the mean for Elizabeth's scores? for Hue's scores?

Talk About It

▶ Is the mean always one of the items of data?

▶ How do you find the median when there is an even number of items?

▶ Which girl seems to have higher scores if the measure you use is the mode? the median? the mean?

Practice

Find the mode, the median, and the mean for each set of data.

1. 8, 12, 6, 2, 12

2. 4, 5, 9, 14, 9, 13, 5

3. 3.5, 6.7, 4.8, 3.2

4. 8.2, 7.6, 4.9, 6.7, 8.8, 7.6

5. 15, 18, 19, 16, 15, 19, 15, 16, 20

6. 8, 9, 7, 9, 10, 8, 5

7. 58, 59, 63, 59, 77, 90, 59, 64, 65, 77, 85

8. 43, 78, 55, 70, 72, 75, 64, 70, 78, 70

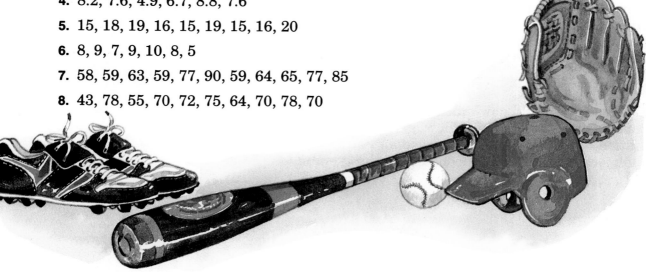

Find the median and the mean for each set of data.

9. 75, 86, 73, 80, 86

10. 17.2, 14.7, 19.8, 16.3

11. 3.5, 6.7, 4.8, 3.2, 5.8

12. 129, 136, 142, 176, 187

13. 64.2, 56.3, 49.7, 38.9, 58.4

14. 1.73, 1.95, 1.86, 1.74

15. 216, 327, 842, 575, 950

16. 48, 75, 47, 83, 49

17. 1.4, 1.8, 1.8, 1.7, 1.5, 1.4

18. 2,108; 3,724; 7,641; 9,275; 5,352

19. 24, 39, 26, 25, 28, 29, 32

20. 8.2, 7.6, 4.9, 6.7, 8.8, 5.4, 7.4

Solve.

21. What is the mean for the Lions' scores?

22. What is the median for the Lions' scores?

23. What is the mode for the visitors' scores?

24. What is the mean for the visitors' scores?

Lakeside Lions Baseball Season							
Team	Game						
	1	2	3	4	5	6	7
Lions	5	3	0	6	10	6	4
Visitors	4	5	3	2	9	5	5

School–Home Connection

CHAPTER 1

Using Whole Numbers and Decimals

Application: Advertising on Television

Advertisers pay a lot of money to television networks to advertise their products. In general, they pay the most to advertise during the programs that have the greatest number of viewers or during times when the most people are watching television.

Now Try This

Do research to find how much advertisers paid for one minute of time during the last Super Bowl game. Then call a local television station to find the amount charged for one minute of advertising in the morning, in the afternoon, and in the evening.

CHAPTER 2

Algebra: Expressions and Equations

Application: Determining Earnings

Some people are paid an hourly rate for the hours that they work. They may be paid at one rate for their normal workweek and at another rate for any overtime.

Suppose your hourly rate is $5.00 per hour for a normal workweek of 40 hours, and the overtime rate is 1.5 times the hourly rate. If you work 48 hours this week, how much will you earn?

$(40 \times 5) + (8 \times 1.5 \times 5) = 200 + 60 = 260$

So, you will earn $260.

Now Try This

Find out the beginning salaries at a fast-food restaurant, a department store, and a grocery store in your area. Determine how much a person will earn for 45 hours of work in one week at each place.

School-Home Connection

CHAPTER 3

Number Theory and Fractions

Application: Time Scheduling

Suppose that you have a summer job with a lawn-service company. This morning you are to mow for $1\frac{1}{2}$ hr, edge flower beds for $\frac{1}{4}$ hr, weed for $\frac{4}{5}$ hr, and rake up cuttings for $\frac{2}{3}$ hr. How long will you work on this assignment?

$$\text{total time} = 1\frac{1}{2} + \frac{1}{4} + \frac{4}{5} + \frac{2}{3} = \frac{3}{2} + \frac{1}{4} + \frac{4}{5} + \frac{2}{3}$$

$$= \frac{90}{60} + \frac{15}{60} + \frac{48}{60} + \frac{40}{60}$$

$$= \frac{193}{60} = 3\frac{13}{60} \text{ hr, or 3 hr 13 min}$$

Now Try This

Record the amount of time it takes you to get dressed, clean up your room, eat breakfast, clear your dishes, and brush your teeth. Write the times as fractional parts of an hour. Then find the difference between the time for the longest activity and the time for the shortest activity.

CHAPTER 4

Using Fractions

Application: Changing a Recipe

Most recipes tell the number of servings the listed ingredients will make. Suppose that you have a recipe for a broccoli casserole. The recipe calls for $2\frac{1}{2}$ cups of broccoli for 6 servings of casserole. However, you want to make 2 times the number of servings, or 12 servings. How much broccoli should you use?

$2 \times 2\frac{1}{2} = \frac{2}{1} \times \frac{5}{2} = 5$ So, you should use 5 cups of broccoli.

Now Try This

Find a recipe with at least 6 ingredients that tells how many servings will be made. Find the amount of each ingredient that you would have to use to make 2 times the recipe, $2\frac{1}{2}$ times the recipe, and $3\frac{1}{2}$ times the recipe. Then tell how many servings you would make in each case.

School-Home Connection

CHAPTER 5

Geometric Relationships and Constructions

Application: Roofing Design and Construction

Climate often determines the design and construction of roofs. In a hot, dry climate, flat roofs are used. Steep, sloping roofs are preferred in climates of heavy rain or snowfall.

Notice the different geometric shapes that form the parts of each roof. What are the geometric shapes in the mansard roof? How many of each geometric shape are present?

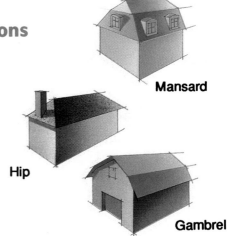

Mansard

Hip

Gambrel

Now Try This

Look at the roofs in your neighborhood. Try to identify at least three different types of roofs. Record the roof type, the geometric shapes in the roof, and the number of each shape.

Gable

CHAPTER 6

Ratio, Proportion, and Percent

Application: Calculating the Percent of Discount

Stores often put items on sale at the end of a season or when they have a surplus of the items. You can calculate the percent of decrease (percent of discount) by dividing the amount of decrease, or discount, by the original price.

Suppose a cassette player that originally sold for $135 is on sale for $90. What is the percent of discount?

amount of discount = $135 − $90 = $45
percent of discount = $\frac{45}{135} = 0.\overline{3}$
So, the percent of discount is $33\frac{1}{3}\%$.

Now Try This

Find five items in the newspaper that are on sale. List the sale price and the original price for each item. Then calculate the percent of discount for each item.

School-Home Connection

School-Home Connection

CHAPTER 7

Integers

Application: Determining Temperature Range

The temperature extremes for five states are listed in the table.

Temperature Extremes for One Year		
State	High	Low
Alaska	90°F	⁻22°F
Hawaii	94°F	53°F
Illinois	104°F	⁻27°F
Ohio	102°F	⁻25°F
Rhode Island	92°F	⁻2°F

Which state had the greatest range in temperature?
Which state had the least range in temperature?

Now Try This

Determine the temperature range in your community for last year.

CHAPTER 8

Real Numbers

Application: Monitoring Stock Performance

Suppose that a company's stock price showed the following changes during a five-day period: $^+\frac{1}{2}$, $^-\frac{3}{8}$, $^-\frac{1}{4}$, $^+1$, and $^-\frac{1}{8}$. If the stock price was $35 per share before these changes, what was it at the end of the five-day period?

$$35 + \left(\frac{1}{2} + {}^-\frac{3}{8} + {}^-\frac{1}{4} + 1 + {}^-\frac{1}{8}\right) = 35 + \frac{6}{8} = 35\frac{3}{4}, \text{ or } \$35.75$$

Now Try This

Select a stock from the listings of the New York Stock Exchange, and record its closing price. Then record the day-to-day changes in price that occur for that stock in the next two weeks. These changes are shown in the newspaper. Calculate the stock price at the end of the two-week period by adding the changes to the original price. Does your answer match the final price in the newspaper?

School–Home Connection

CHAPTER 9

Algebra: Graphing Relations and Functions

Application: World Record for the One-Mile Run

The 4-minute mile world record was broken in 1954. Since then, the record time has been shortened.

These ordered pairs show the year and the record time in minutes and seconds for running the mile.

(1954, 3:59.4), (1958, 3:54.5), (1965, 3:53.6), (1966, 3:51.3), (1975, 3:49.4), (1980, 3:48.8), (1981, 3:47.33), (1985, 3:46.32)

Is this relation a function?

Now Try This

Choose a type of exercise such as bicycling, running, sit-ups, swimming, aerobics, or walking. Record your performance for a two-week period. Graph your performance on the y-axis and the time, in days, on the x-axis. Write the ordered pairs for this relation.

CHAPTER 10

Statistics and Graphing

Application: Cost Prediction and Comparison

Sometimes, you can use what has happened in the past to predict what will happen in the future. This graph shows the amount of electricity used in one year. Based on the data in the graph, in which month of the year 2000 will the greatest number of kilowatt-hours of electricity be used?

Electricity Usage

Now Try This

Look at your family's electricity bills for the past four months. Graph the electricity usage for these four months. Use the graph to predict the amount of electricity your family will use this month.

Then, when this month's electricity bill arrives, check your prediction against the actual usage. Was your prediction close? If not, what factors do you think affected the usage?

School-Home Connection

CHAPTER 11

Probability

Application: Birth Month Probabilities

You can analyze this set of birth month data for 732 students to compare the mathematical and the experimental probabilities for birth month distribution. To determine the mathematical probabilities, consider the number of days in each month and a total of 366 days in one year (leap year). How do the mathematical and the experimental probabilities of a February birthday compare?

mathematical probability: $\frac{29}{366}$

experimental probability: $\frac{68}{732}$, or $\frac{34}{366}$

The experimental probability is greater.

Birth Month Distribution	
Birth Month	**Number of Students**
January	59
February	68
March	47
April	50
May	49
June	65
July	78
August	81
September	65
October	52
November	49
December	69

Now Try This

Record the birth months of at least 24 friends and family members. Determine whether the experimental probabilities of birth month distribution match the mathematical probabilities.

CHAPTER 12

Plane Geometry and Measurement

Application: Mechanical Drawing

In the assembly of large numbers of parts, such as on an assembly line, the parts must fit together. However, absolute accuracy in making the parts cannot be expected, so an allowed variation, or *tolerance*, is set.

Now Try This

Measure the part on the left below. Indicate which of the manufactured parts on the right are within the given tolerance.

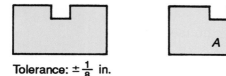

Tolerance: $\pm\frac{1}{8}$ in.

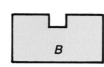

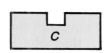

School-Home Connection

CHAPTER 13

Solid Geometry and Measurement

Application: Comparing Volumes

You can use models of solid figures to determine the relationships between the volumes of the figures.

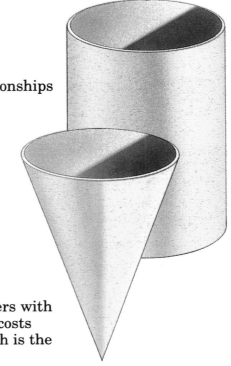

Now Try This

Construct a cone out of cardboard or construction paper. Then construct a cylinder that has the same base and height as the cone.

Fill the cone with rice, beans, or similar material. Pour the material from the cone into the cylinder. Continue until the cylinder is full. How many times do you need to fill the cone in order to fill the cylinder?

Suppose popcorn is sold in conical and cylindrical containers with the same size base and height. A cone filled with popcorn costs $0.89, and a cylinder filled with popcorn costs $2.79. Which is the better buy?

CHAPTER 14

Indirect Measurement

Application: Making Indirect Measurements

When you want to measure the height of something— such as a tree or a flagpole—that would be difficult to measure with a tape measure, you can use a method known as indirect measurement.

Suppose that you want to find the height of a tree that casts a 21-ft shadow at the same time that you cast a 7-ft shadow. You are 5 ft tall. The ratio of your height to your shadow is equivalent to that of the tree's height to its shadow.

$$\frac{5}{7} = \frac{h}{21} \qquad h = 15 \qquad \text{So, the tree is 15 ft tall.}$$

Now Try This

Try using this method to find the height of your house, a tree, or a flagpole.

CHAPTER I

Lesson 1.1 *(pages 2–3)*

Name the place of the underlined digit.

1. 5,497.0<u>2</u>3   **2.** 249,73<u>3</u>.1   **3.** 3.14<u>2</u>7   **4.** 2,<u>5</u>39,413.6

Write the standard form of each number.

5. 100.3 thousand   **6.** 2.59 million   **7.** 3.95 billion   **8.** 65.039 million

Write in shortened form using the word *million*.

9. 25,352,000   **10.** 56,389   **11.** 1,945,000   **12.** 439,876

Compare. Use <, >, or =.

13. 35.2 ● 32.5   **14.** 49.38 ● 49.038   **15.** 57.35 ● 57.3500

16. 168.750 ● 168.705   **17.** 0.0497 ● 0.05   **18.** 93.62 ● 93.620

Lesson 1.2 *(pages 4–5)*

Name the place to which each number appears to be rounded.

1. 2,700   **2.** 580   **3.** 132.9   **4.** 25.38   **5.** 19,700

An exact number has been rounded to the given number. Name the greatest whole number and the least whole number that the exact number can be.

6. 390   **7.** 21,000   **8.** 50   **9.** 9,800   **10.** 149,000

11. 100   **12.** 950   **13.** 9,900   **14.** 750,000   **15.** 5,000,000

Lesson 1.3 *(pages 6–7)*

Choose the overestimate. Write **a** or **b**.

1. $59 \div 3$ **2.** $439 + 168$ **3.** 135×23 **4.** $975 - 264$

   a. $57 \div 3$ **a.** $430 + 160$ **a.** 140×30 **a.** $980 - 260$

   b. $60 \div 3$ **b.** $440 + 170$ **b.** 130×20 **b.** $970 - 260$

Give two estimates for each problem. Tell which is the closer estimate.

5. $23 + 85$ **6.** 19×58 **7.** $236 \div 4$ **8.** $476 - 91$

9. $9,876 - 3,452$ **10.** $2,129 \times 17$ **11.** $846 \div 9$ **12.** $8,356 + 1,999$

Lesson 1.4 *(pages 8–9)*

Name the property shown.

1. $(9 \times 4) + (6 \times 4) = (9 + 6) \times 4$

2. $2.9 \times 5.6 = 5.6 \times 2.9$

3. $13.5 + 42.9 = 42.9 + 13.5$

4. $3 + (29 + 87) = (3 + 29) + 87$

5. $86 = 86 + 0$

6. $5 \times (20 + 69) = (5 \times 20) + (5 \times 69)$

7. $359 \times 1 = 359$

8. $(3 \times 6) \times 9 = 3 \times (6 \times 9)$

Complete.

9. $182 + \blacksquare = 182$

10. $225 \times \blacksquare = 225$

11. $9 \times 32 = 9 \times (30 + 2) = (9 \times \blacksquare) + (9 \times \blacksquare) = \blacksquare + 18 = \blacksquare$

12. $4 \times 47 \times 25 = 4 \times 25 \times \blacksquare = \blacksquare \times 47 = \blacksquare$

13. $15 \times 23 = 15 \times (20 + \blacksquare) = (\blacksquare \times 20) + (15 \times 3) = \blacksquare + \blacksquare = \blacksquare$

Lesson 1.5 *(pages 10–11)*

Solve.

1. Linda bought one compact disc for $9.95 and a cassette for $8.95. What was the total she paid, if the tax was $1.13?

2. Steve ran 3.2 miles before lunch and 4.8 miles before dinner. How many miles did Steve run before breakfast, if he ran 12.2 miles that day?

3. Claire has 195 baseball cards and 258 football cards. How many cards does she have?

4. Juan had $50.00. He spent $12.95 in one store and $25.79 in another store. How much does he have left?

5. Hank Aaron scored 2,174 runs during his baseball career. How close was Aaron to equaling Ty Cobb's lifetime record of 2,245 runs scored?

6. Nikki spent $26.49 for shoes and $21.19 for a shirt. How much change did she receive from a $50 bill?

Lesson 1.6 *(pages 12–13)*

Solve.

1. Yvette burned 1,600 calories last weekend exercising, and 1,250 this weekend. How many more calories does she need to burn this Monday to equal the number burned last weekend?

2. Ed paid $239.56 more for his printer than Margo paid. Margo paid $499.95 plus $22.49 in sales tax for her printer. How much did Ed pay?

3. Todd ran 3.25 miles on Monday and 4.7 miles on Tuesday. How many miles does he need to run on Wednesday to total 10 miles?

4. Candy spent $9.95 for a T-shirt and $12.95 for shorts. If her total was $24.27, how much sales tax did she pay?

Lesson 1.7 *(pages 14–15)*

1. A computer system takes 125 minutes to post 4,750 transactions. How many transactions can it post in one minute?

2. Marc works 35 hours a week and earns $201.25. How much does Marc earn per hour?

3. Martha's car gets 27 miles per gallon. How many gallons will the car burn on a 945-mile trip?

4. Raymond, the pharmacist, can fill 35 prescriptions in one hour. How many prescriptions can he fill in 7.2 hours?

5. Tina paid $1.25 per gallon for gasoline. She paid a total of $20.50. How many gallons of gasoline did she buy?

6. Mike bought 16 floppy disks. Each disk cost $2.23. How much did Mike pay for all of the disks?

Lesson 1.8 *(pages 18–19)*

Find the quotient.

1. $1.1\overline{)1.21}$
2. $0.8\overline{)19.20}$
3. $5.3\overline{)28.09}$
4. $0.04\overline{)1.96}$

5. $0.5\overline{)27.1}$
6. $0.06\overline{)3.6}$
7. $2.5\overline{)11.25}$
8. $1.4\overline{)49.28}$

Find the quotient to the nearest tenth.

9. $0.03\overline{)0.0858}$
10. $0.9\overline{)6.59}$
11. $0.6\overline{)2.55}$
12. $6.8\overline{)1.7}$

13. $2.3\overline{)0.97}$
14. $9.5\overline{)103.8}$
15. $0.38\overline{)766}$
16. $0.009\overline{)0.0273}$

Find the quotient to the nearest hundredth.

17. $0.1\overline{)0.3985}$
18. $3.60\overline{)0.09}$
19. $1.4\overline{)4.927}$
20. $0.24\overline{)0.633}$

Lesson 1.9 *(pages 20–21)*

1. Jack, Bob, and Louise earned $27.50 mowing lawns. Will they be able to divide the money equally among themselves?

2. The Nut Store is selling 1 pound of peanuts for $1.29. How many whole pounds of peanuts can you buy with $9.00?

3. Jeff has 49 plants to put into pots. He will put 3 plants in each pot. How many pots will he use? How many plants will be left over?

4. Allie owns 457 stamps. She wants to put 15 stamps on each page of an album. How many pages will she need in the album?

5. Jim, Mark, and Sue worked together on a job and earned $72. Will they be able to divide the money equally among themselves?

6. Tom paid $4.89 for 5 pounds of plums. Find the cost for 1 lb of plums. Round to the nearest cent.

Lesson 1.10 *(pages 22–23)*

Write in exponent form.

1. $3 \times 3 \times 3$
2. $8 \times 8 \times 8 \times 8$
3. 4.1×4.1
4. $6 \times 6 \times 6 \times 6 \times 6 \times 6 \times 6$
5. $10 \times 10 \times 10 \times 10 \times 10 \times 10$
6. $1.4 \times 1.4 \times 1.4$
7. $2 \times 2 \times 2 \times 2 \times 2 \times 2 \times 2$

Find the value. You may use your calculator.

8. 2^5
9. 5^8
10. 7^3
11. 9^0
12. 8^4
13. $(2.5)^2$
14. $(5.2)^4$
15. $(0.6)^3$
16. $(3.04)^1$
17. $(2.80)^3$
18. $(1.4)^3$
19. $(3.1)^4$
20. 2^7
21. 1^{16}
22. $(0.03)^3$

Lesson 1.11 *(pages 24–25)*

Compute.

1. $4 + 3 \times 2$
2. $9 + 3 \div 3$
3. $14 \div 2 - 2$
4. $11 - 7 + 3$
5. $14 + 4 - 18 \div 3$
6. $14 + 2 \times 5$
7. $8 \times 3 - 7$
8. $82 + 2 \times 10$
9. $6 \times 9 \div 3$
10. $5 + \frac{21}{7}$
11. $\frac{16 + 8}{6}$
12. $4 \times \left(8 - \frac{10}{2}\right)$
13. $9 \times 2 - \frac{30}{15}$
14. $\frac{20 + 12}{8}$
15. $\frac{20}{4} + 19$
16. $50 \times 4 \div 5 + 6 - 6$
17. $18 - (12 - 3)$
18. $10 + (15 \div 5)$
19. $54 \div 9 \times 4 - 7 + 2$
20. $256 \div 2 \div 4 \cdot 3$
21. $\frac{33 - 6}{9} + (5^3 - 4^2)$

Lesson 1.12 *(pages 26–27)*

Write the next two terms in the sequence.

1. 1, 4, 9, 16, 25, . . .
2. 1, 2, 6, 24, 120, . . .
3. 4, 5, 10, 5, 6, . . .
4. 3, 5, 8, 10, 13, . . .
5. 1, 2, 4, 7, 11, . . .
6. 1, 8, 27, 64, 125, . . .

Find the pattern. Then solve the problem.

7. Chloe counted blue, white, and black cars in two parking lots. In Lot A, she counted 200 blue, 140 white, and 84 black. In Lot B, she counted 300 blue and 210 white. If the cars in Lot B follow the same pattern as the cars in Lot A, how many black cars did she count in Lot B?

8. Joe has worked as a stock clerk for 8 months. He earned $4.50 per hour for the first 3 months, $4.75 for the next 3 months, and $5.10 this month. How much per hour will he be earning in 6 months, if the pattern remains the same?

CHAPTER 2

Lesson 2.1 *(pages 36–37)*

Write *expression, equation,* or *inequality* for each.

1. $a + 4 \geq 9$ **2.** $5 + 3$ **3.** $3 - x + 15$ **4.** $24 \neq 5 \times 6$

5. $20 = 5 \times 2y$ **6.** $y - 4.5 \leq 8.2$ **7.** $67 - 8 = 59$ **8.** $3x + 2x = 25$

9. $67 + m + 4$ **10.** $y + 20 = 120$ **11.** $\frac{m}{4} > 6$ **12.** $7 + 21 - 2x$

13. $2^3 + 1^5$ **14.** $3y - 4 = 8$ **15.** $5 + c - m - 2^2$ **16.** $4x \neq 17$

Write an example of each.

17. equation   **18.** inequality   **19.** algebraic expression

Lesson 2.2 *(pages 38–39)*

Write an algebraic expression for each word expression.

1. 7.5 meters less than the width, w

2. the number of hours, h, decreased by 0.25 hour

3. The difference between the number of cars, c, and 15

4. The sum of 59 grams and the total grams, g

Evaluate the expressions for $t = 3$, $m = 0.6$, and $y = 7$.

5. $m + 0.4$ **6.** $4 - t$ **7.** $y + 5$ **8.** $3.95 - m$ **9.** $y + t + m$

10. $22.3 - y$ **11.** $5.2 - m$ **12.** $t + 3.9$ **13.** $t + m$ **14.** $3^3 - y$

15. $t + y - m$ **16.** $y - m$ **17.** $t - 1.2$ **18.** $15 - y$ **19.** $t - m$

20. $y - m - t$ **21.** $37.1 - m$ **22.** $4^3 - t + y$ **23.** $y^2 - t^2$ **24.** $m^2 + t^2$

Lesson 2.3 *(pages 40–41)*

Solve the equation. Check your solution.

1. $n + 5 = 17$ **2.** $25 + b = 26.2$ **3.** $d + 45 = 57$ **4.** $8 + b = 18$

5. $h + 3 = 9$ **6.** $96 + t = 102$ **7.** $x + 2.9 = 3$ **8.** $m + 2 = 105$

9. $y + 2 = 36$ **10.** $m + 25.9 = 34.2$ **11.** $g + 3.5 = 6.75$ **12.** $t + 25.1 = 96.7$

13. $y + 25 = 57$ **14.** $67 + a = 79.4$ **15.** $2.3 + m = 7.9$ **16.** $n + 45.6 = 50$

17. $c + 1.9 = 8.1$ **18.** $97.4 + d + 105.3$ **19.** $0.06 + p = 14.2$ **20.** $x + 3.05 = 7$

Write an addition equation that has the given solution.

21. $b = 6$ **22.** $c = 23$ **23.** $y = 41$ **24.** $x = 9$

Lesson 2.4 *(pages 42–43)*

1. Connie owns a total of 63 books. She has 13 more paperback books than hardcover books. How many hardcover books does she own?

2. Jack has a total of 95 posters and flags. He has 23 more posters than flags. How many flags does he have?

3. Monty bought marbles and paid $4.50 in nickels and quarters. He gave the clerk 24 more nickels than quarters. How many nickels did he give the clerk?

4. Laurie has a total of 60 cassettes and compact discs. She has 14 fewer compact discs than cassettes. How many cassettes does she have?

Lesson 2.5 *(pages 44–45)*

Solve the equation. Check your answer.

1. $y - 38 = 9$
2. $x - 7 = 53$
3. $27 - h = 2$
4. $22 - x = 3.5$

5. $12 - y = 0$
6. $5 - m = 2.3$
7. $x - 3 = 15$
8. $2 - m = 0$

9. $x - 3.5 = 7.9$
10. $x - 33 = 105$
11. $t - 50 = 67$
12. $35 - h = 15$

13. $26 = 42 - y$
14. $59 = h - 61$
15. $x - 42 = 65$
16. $y - 3 = 28$

17. $(5 + 7) = x - 5$
18. $y - 2^2 = 43$
19. $y - 15 = 5^2$
20. $t - (2 \times 6) = 6.8$

21. $(26 + 17) = y - 22$
22. $c - 2^3 = 8^2$

23. $x + (0.3 \times 8) = 7.9$
24. $12^2 - n = 8 + 5^1$

Lesson 2.6 *(pages 48–49)*

Write an algebraic expression for each word expression.

1. three times the weight, w
2. six times the length, l

3. the number of planes, p, divided by 3
4. the difference between the number of gallons, g, and 34

5. twice the sale price, p
6. the product of 8 and the number of cats, c

Evaluate the expression for $a = 5$, $b = 3.9$, and $d = 32$.

7. $21a$
8. $\frac{11.7}{b}$
9. $\frac{d}{16}$
10. ab
11. $2d$

12. $4b$
13. $\frac{50}{a}$
14. $10b$
15. $6d$
16. $\frac{160}{d}$

17. $3a$
18. bd
19. $\frac{d}{4}$
20. ad
21. $\frac{b}{1.3}$

22. $\frac{ad}{4}$
23. $4ab$
24. $\frac{d}{2^3}$
25. $\frac{ab}{50}$
26. abd

Lesson 2.7 *(pages 50–51)*

Solve the equation. Check your answer.

1. $3p = 105$
2. $0.5t = 1$
3. $68 = 100x$
4. $0.04y = 8.6$
5. $4a = 516$
6. $3.5b = 94.5$
7. $12h = 0.24$
8. $3{,}669 = 9{,}172.5x$
9. $0.76x = 0.19$
10. $8b = 632$
11. $6^3 = 24t$
12. $98y = (0.98 \times 4)$
13. $0.08y = 0.24$
14. $14.78c = 162.58$
15. $114b = (38 \times 15)$
16. $9^4 = 27k$

Lesson 2.8 *(pages 52–53)*

Solve the equation. Check your answer.

1. $2.1 = \frac{t}{4}$
2. $\frac{y}{2} = 256$
3. $\frac{x}{16} = 20$
4. $13 = \frac{p}{2}$
5. $\frac{x}{3.3} = 30$
6. $\frac{h}{1.5} = 15$
7. $\frac{a}{6} = 18$
8. $\frac{d}{20} = 0.5$
9. $\frac{c}{2.6} = 41$
10. $59 = \frac{x}{4.7}$
11. $\frac{b}{0.04} = 98$
12. $\frac{y}{9.7} = 6^3$

Write an equation for the word sentence.

13. The quotient of a number, n, and 8 is 12.
14. The number of hours, h, divided by 2.3 equals 6.
15. The number of days, d, divided by 7 equals 5.8.
16. The quotient of the weight, w, and 30 is 17.

Lesson 2.9 *(pages 54–55)*

Solve the equation. Check your answer.

1. $\frac{x}{5} - 2 = 7$
2. $4m - 5 = 27$
3. $2a + 9 = 17$
4. $\frac{h}{8} + 9 = 14$
5. $\frac{a}{6} = 9$
6. $5t + 7 = 32$
7. $\frac{a}{9} - 1 = 6$
8. $9c - 4 = 41$
9. $6 = \frac{2m}{3} - 2$
10. $\frac{x}{7} - 3 = 2$
11. $15 = 3n - 3$
12. $9w + 6 = 24$
13. $17y - 9 = 229$
14. $81 = 6x - 3$
15. $\frac{a}{11} - 8 = 201$
16. $108 = \frac{c}{4} + 5$

Write an equation for the word sentence.

17. Two more than the product of 3 and a number, x, equals 20.
18. Eight less than the quotient of a number, n, and 5 equals 6.
19. The sum of 8.2 and a number, x, equals 17.8.
20. Twelve dollars more than twice the cost, c, equals \$72.
21. The quotient of a number, q, and 6, decreased by 2 equals 28.
22. 19.2 less than the product of 3 and a number, y, equals 7.

Lesson 2.10 *(pages 56–57)*

Solve. Write the whole numbers that make the inequality true.

1. $n + 1 < 12$
2. $5n < 35$
3. $4n + 3 > 27$
4. $9n > 63$
5. $21 > 3n + 6$
6. $5x \leq 25$
7. $4m \leq 12$
8. $2x + 2 < 8$
9. $t - 4 \leq 3$
10. $\frac{c}{5} - 6 \geq 4$
11. $16 < 6x - 2$
12. $\frac{m}{4} + 8 < 15$

Tell whether the given value is a solution of the inequality.
Write *yes* or *no*.

13. $n - 5 > 4, n = 6$
14. $x + 4 < 12, x = 3$
15. $5t \leq 15, t = 7$
16. $3z \neq 21, z = 2$
17. $2s + 4 \geq 9, s = 8$
18. $3r - 4 < 2, r = 4$
19. $\frac{n}{9} > 9, n = 72$
20. $8y + 7 \geq 175, y = 20$
21. $\frac{n}{7} - 3 \leq 6, n = 63$

Lesson 2.11 *(pages 58–59)*

Write an equation for the problem. Then solve.

1. The price of a pair of water skis is 3.5 times the price of a ski vest. The skis cost $139.65. Find the price of the ski vest.

2. The regular price of a ski rope was reduced by $7.00. The sale price was $22.95. Find the regular price of the rope.

3. Corey swam 12 more laps in the pool than Joan. Corey swam 19 laps. Find how many laps Joan swam.

4. The price of a swimming float is 7.25 times the price of earplugs. The float costs $21.75. Find the price of the earplugs.

5. Jake ran a total of 9.1 mi in the last three days. Jake ran 3.9 mi on Day 1. He ran the same distance on both Day 2 and Day 3. What distance did Jake run on both Day 2 and Day 3?

6. Judy owed her brother a total of $39. She made four equal weekly payments. Then, she paid the remaining $15 balance. What was the amount of her equal payments?

CHAPTER 3

Lesson 3.1 *(pages 68–69)*

Write *prime* or *composite* for the number.

1. 29	**2.** 18	**3.** 43	**4.** 49	**5.** 11	**6.** 23
7. 51	**8.** 41	**9.** 79	**10.** 147	**11.** 17	**12.** 207

Write the prime factorization, using exponents.

13. 98	**14.** 176	**15.** 84	**16.** 92	**17.** 3,125	**18.** 6,300
19. 148	**20.** 87	**21.** 768	**22.** 198	**23.** 459	**24.** 10,000

Lesson 3.2 *(pages 70–71)*

1. Louise is making bows. She is cutting from a 200-in. piece of fabric and from a 180-in. piece of fabric. She wants to make all bows the same length and use all of the fabric. To cut all pieces of equal length, what is the length of the longest piece that she can cut?

2. Tanya divided 154 red marbles and 420 blue marbles among her cousins. She gave each of her cousins the same number of marbles. What is the greatest number of cousins that Tanya can give an equal amount of red and blue marbles?

3. Arnold runs every second day and Bob runs every fifth day. They are both running today. How many days will pass before both run again on the same day?

4. George bathes his dog every seventh day, and Marc bathes his dog every fifteenth day. Both dogs are being washed today. How many days will pass before both dogs will again be bathed on the same day?

Lesson 3.3 *(pages 72–73)*

Leslie decides to buy a used car. She is considering these options. Use the options for Exercises 1–4.

Option A: borrow the money from a bank and make payments of $85.10 per month for 36 months, including the interest

Option B: borrow the money from her father and make payments of $112.50 per month for 24 months, with no interest

1. How much will Leslie pay for the car if she chooses Option A?

2. How much will Leslie save in interest charges under Option B?

3. If Leslie chooses Option A, how much will she owe the bank after making her 24th payment?

4. Which option do you think Leslie should choose? Explain.

Lesson 3.4 *(pages 74–76)*

Write three equivalent fractions for each fraction.

1. $\frac{2}{3}$ **2.** $\frac{1}{4}$ **3.** $\frac{5}{6}$ **4.** $\frac{10}{20}$ **5.** $\frac{7}{8}$ **6.** $\frac{8}{6}$

Write the fraction in simplest form.

7. $\frac{35}{50}$ **8.** $\frac{8}{24}$ **9.** $\frac{15}{25}$ **10.** $\frac{20}{30}$ **11.** $\frac{44}{50}$ **12.** $\frac{12}{63}$

13. $\frac{8}{18}$ **14.** $\frac{9}{21}$ **15.** $\frac{14}{36}$ **16.** $\frac{25}{65}$ **17.** $\frac{14}{18}$ **18.** $\frac{48}{18}$

Write as a whole number or a mixed number in simplest form.

19. $\frac{8}{3}$ **20.** $\frac{38}{5}$ **21.** $\frac{27}{4}$ **22.** $\frac{19}{10}$ **23.** $\frac{87}{8}$ **24.** $\frac{83}{17}$

Write as a fraction.

25. $4\frac{1}{4}$ **26.** $3\frac{2}{5}$ **27.** $7\frac{2}{3}$ **28.** $12\frac{4}{5}$ **29.** $9\frac{3}{4}$ **30.** $8\frac{8}{9}$

Lesson 3.5 *(pages 78–79)*

Write the LCD of the fractions.

1. $\frac{1}{2}, \frac{2}{3}$ **2.** $\frac{5}{6}, \frac{1}{4}$ **3.** $\frac{4}{5}, \frac{2}{8}$ **4.** $\frac{1}{8}, \frac{3}{7}$ **5.** $\frac{3}{5}, \frac{4}{15}$

6. $\frac{5}{9}, \frac{2}{3}$ **7.** $\frac{6}{7}, \frac{8}{9}$ **8.** $\frac{3}{4}, \frac{2}{5}$ **9.** $\frac{3}{5}, \frac{4}{25}, \frac{3}{10}$ **10.** $\frac{3}{7}, \frac{1}{4}, \frac{5}{14}$

Compare. Write <, >, or =.

11. $\frac{1}{4} \bullet \frac{2}{5}$ **12.** $\frac{12}{13} \bullet \frac{8}{9}$ **13.** $\frac{25}{4} \bullet \frac{32}{5}$ **14.** $\frac{2}{3} \bullet \frac{3}{4}$ **15.** $\frac{17}{19} \bullet \frac{31}{32}$

16. $\frac{4}{9} \bullet \frac{3}{7}$ **17.** $\frac{4}{21} \bullet \frac{3}{35}$ **18.** $\frac{7}{9} \bullet \frac{8}{3}$ **19.** $\frac{2}{33} \bullet \frac{34}{5}$ **20.** $2\frac{7}{8} \bullet 2\frac{5}{6}$

21. $\frac{29}{30} \bullet \frac{14}{15}$ **22.** $\frac{19}{2} \bullet \frac{45}{4}$ **23.** $\frac{28}{3} \bullet \frac{43}{5}$ **24.** $\frac{154}{112} \bullet 1\frac{3}{8}$ **25.** $6\frac{7}{9} \bullet 6\frac{5}{6}$

Write in order from least to greatest.

26. $\frac{3}{4}, \frac{6}{5}, \frac{2}{3}$ **27.** $\frac{20}{6}, \frac{30}{5}, \frac{14}{3}$ **28.** $\frac{5}{6}, \frac{7}{8}, \frac{3}{12}$ **29.** $\frac{8}{9}, \frac{5}{6}, \frac{7}{9}$

30. $\frac{2}{5}, \frac{1}{2}, \frac{7}{20}$ **31.** $\frac{7}{8}, \frac{4}{5}, \frac{7}{10}$ **32.** $\frac{6}{7}, \frac{2}{3}, \frac{5}{6}$ **33.** $\frac{2}{3}, \frac{5}{6}, \frac{5}{9}$

Lesson 3.6 *(pages 82–83)*

Choose the best estimate. Write **a**, **b**, or **c**.

1. $\frac{3}{4} + \frac{1}{5}$ **a.** 0   **b.** $\frac{1}{2}$ **c.** 1

2. $\frac{8}{9} - \frac{2}{5}$ **a.** 1   **b.** $\frac{1}{2}$ **c.** 0

3. $4\frac{1}{3} + 2\frac{5}{6}$ **a.** 5   **b.** 7   **c.** 10

4. $17\frac{1}{8} - 5\frac{4}{5}$ **a.** 12   **b.** 9   **c.** 11

Estimate the sum or difference.

5. $\frac{1}{3} + \frac{7}{8}$ 6. $5\frac{1}{3} + 2\frac{1}{2}$ 7. $\frac{17}{18} + \frac{1}{6}$ 8. $1\frac{5}{12} - \frac{3}{4}$

9. $\frac{5}{18} + \frac{2}{3}$ 10. $\frac{3}{4} + 4\frac{2}{3}$ 11. $5\frac{5}{6} - 2\frac{3}{4}$ 12. $\frac{5}{6} + \frac{4}{5}$

13. $2\frac{7}{8} + 1\frac{8}{9}$ 14. $\frac{5}{7} + \frac{12}{13}$ 15. $\frac{1}{3} - \frac{1}{4}$ 16. $\frac{5}{6} + \frac{1}{8}$

17. $3\frac{7}{8} - 2\frac{8}{9}$ 18. $8\frac{4}{5} + 3\frac{1}{9} + 2\frac{2}{17}$ 19. $7\frac{1}{10} - 3\frac{1}{5}$ 20. $9 - 5\frac{7}{8}$

Lesson 3.7 *(pages 84–85)*

Find the sum. Write the answer in simplest form.

1. $\frac{1}{5} + \frac{2}{6}$ 2. $\frac{5}{6} + \frac{3}{4}$ 3. $\frac{7}{8} + \frac{6}{8}$ 4. $1\frac{1}{3} + \frac{5}{7}$ 5. $\frac{6}{7} + \frac{1}{3}$ 6. $4\frac{8}{9} + 2\frac{1}{2}$

7. $\frac{10}{11} + \frac{20}{33}$ 8. $\frac{9}{10} + \frac{5}{6}$ 9. $1\frac{3}{8} + \frac{3}{4}$ 10. $\frac{2}{5} + \frac{1}{3}$ 11. $\frac{5}{7} + \frac{3}{4}$ 12. $\frac{3}{5} + \frac{6}{11}$

13. $3\frac{2}{3} + 1\frac{1}{7}$ 14. $2\frac{5}{8} + 1$ 15. $7\frac{1}{5} + \frac{1}{3}$ 16. $3 + 1\frac{1}{6}$ 17. $1\frac{5}{6} + 2\frac{7}{8}$ 18. $2\frac{9}{10} + 3\frac{1}{4}$

19. $\frac{1}{9} + \frac{5}{8}$ 20. $8\frac{3}{4} + 4\frac{1}{2}$ 21. $7\frac{2}{5} + 3\frac{1}{3}$ 22. $6 + 3\frac{9}{11}$ 23. $3\frac{4}{7} + 8 + 5\frac{1}{4}$

Lesson 3.8 *(pages 86–87)*

Tell whether you need to rename in order to subtract.
Write *yes* or *no*.

1. $4\frac{1}{2} - 2\frac{1}{4}$ **2.** $7\frac{3}{5} - 3\frac{5}{6}$ **3.** $15 - 8\frac{2}{3}$ **4.** $9\frac{3}{4} - 5\frac{1}{8}$

Find the difference. Write the answer in simplest form.

5. $\begin{array}{r}\frac{5}{6}\\-\frac{1}{2}\\\hline\end{array}$ **6.** $\begin{array}{r}\frac{24}{25}\\-\frac{14}{25}\\\hline\end{array}$ **7.** $\begin{array}{r}\frac{2}{3}\\-\frac{1}{5}\\\hline\end{array}$ **8.** $\begin{array}{r}\frac{6}{7}\\-\frac{1}{3}\\\hline\end{array}$ **9.** $\begin{array}{r}\frac{8}{9}\\-\frac{1}{6}\\\hline\end{array}$ **10.** $\begin{array}{r}\frac{1}{4}\\-\frac{3}{28}\\\hline\end{array}$

11. $\begin{array}{r}\frac{7}{8}\\-\frac{1}{6}\\\hline\end{array}$ **12.** $\begin{array}{r}\frac{8}{13}\\-\frac{3}{26}\\\hline\end{array}$ **13.** $\begin{array}{r}1\frac{5}{6}\\-\frac{3}{4}\\\hline\end{array}$ **14.** $\begin{array}{r}2\frac{1}{2}\\-1\frac{5}{7}\\\hline\end{array}$ **15.** $\begin{array}{r}5\frac{1}{4}\\-3\frac{1}{2}\\\hline\end{array}$ **16.** $\begin{array}{r}6\frac{1}{7}\\-5\frac{2}{3}\\\hline\end{array}$

17. $\begin{array}{r}2\frac{3}{7}\\-\frac{1}{14}\\\hline\end{array}$ **18.** $\begin{array}{r}3\frac{3}{4}\\-1\frac{7}{8}\\\hline\end{array}$ **19.** $\begin{array}{r}1\frac{7}{10}\\-1\frac{3}{5}\\\hline\end{array}$ **20.** $\begin{array}{r}3\\-2\frac{1}{3}\\\hline\end{array}$ **21.** $\begin{array}{r}1\frac{5}{12}\\-\frac{3}{4}\\\hline\end{array}$ **22.** $\begin{array}{r}3\frac{1}{2}\\-1\frac{5}{12}\\\hline\end{array}$

23. $\begin{array}{r}9\frac{3}{7}\\-4\frac{1}{6}\\\hline\end{array}$ **24.** $\begin{array}{r}8\frac{11}{12}\\-7\frac{3}{4}\\\hline\end{array}$ **25.** $\begin{array}{r}10\frac{1}{4}\\-3\frac{1}{12}\\\hline\end{array}$ **26.** $\begin{array}{r}5\frac{5}{8}\\-1\frac{2}{3}\\\hline\end{array}$ **27.** $\begin{array}{r}9\frac{1}{6}\\-4\frac{4}{9}\\\hline\end{array}$ **28.** $\begin{array}{r}3\frac{4}{5}\\-2\frac{9}{10}\\\hline\end{array}$

29. $\begin{array}{r}6\\-3\frac{5}{8}\\\hline\end{array}$ **30.** $\begin{array}{r}8\frac{2}{3}\\-4\frac{7}{8}\\\hline\end{array}$ **31.** $\begin{array}{r}12\\-8\frac{3}{7}\\\hline\end{array}$ **32.** $\begin{array}{r}5\frac{1}{4}\\-4\frac{5}{6}\\\hline\end{array}$ **33.** $\begin{array}{r}10\frac{1}{3}\\-6\frac{2}{3}\\\hline\end{array}$ **34.** $\begin{array}{r}6\frac{3}{8}\\-3\frac{8}{9}\\\hline\end{array}$

Lesson 3.9 *(pages 88–89)*

Draw a picture to solve the problem.

1. Rick is using square tiles to make a patio. He wants the patio to be 180 in. long and 144 in. wide. The side of each square tile is 9 in. long. How many tiles does Rick need?

2. Diana wants to hang a world map that is 36 in. wide in the center of a wall that is 180 in. wide. How much wall space should she leave on each side of the map?

3. Ralph is putting a fence around his garden. The garden is 12 ft wide and 18 ft long. He will put a fence post every 3 ft. How many fence posts will Ralph need?

4. Susan left her house and walked 14 blocks south, 3 blocks west, 8 blocks north, and 7 blocks east. How many blocks north and how many blocks west does Susan need to walk to be back at her house?

CHAPTER 4

Lesson 4.1 *(pages 98–99)*

Estimate the product.

1. $\frac{2}{5} \times \frac{11}{12}$ 2. $\frac{1}{4} \times \frac{2}{3}$ 3. $\frac{3}{4} \times \frac{7}{8}$ 4. $1\frac{2}{7} \times \frac{1}{3}$

5. $\frac{1}{6} \times \frac{7}{9}$ 6. $2\frac{1}{5} \times 3$ 7. $1\frac{1}{2} \times 2\frac{9}{10}$ 8. $3\frac{1}{4} \times 5\frac{5}{6}$

9. $\frac{15}{16} \times 4\frac{2}{5}$ 10. $1\frac{5}{8} \times 2\frac{1}{6}$ 11. $2\frac{5}{6} \times 2\frac{7}{8}$ 12. $1\frac{2}{7} \times 6\frac{2}{3}$

13. $4\frac{1}{3} \times 3\frac{7}{9}$ 14. $2\frac{1}{9} \times 5\frac{2}{11}$ 15. $\frac{15}{16} \times 7\frac{1}{4}$ 16. $1\frac{9}{10} \times 1\frac{7}{8}$

Lesson 4.2 *(pages 100–101)*

Find the product. Write the product in simplest form.

1. $\frac{1}{3} \times \frac{1}{12}$ 2. $\frac{2}{5} \times \frac{15}{4}$ 3. $\frac{3}{7} \times \frac{21}{45}$ 4. $\frac{1}{2} \times \frac{4}{6}$

5. $\frac{5}{6} \times \frac{12}{25}$ 6. $\frac{7}{8} \times \frac{4}{5}$ 7. $\frac{3}{11} \times \frac{22}{27}$ 8. $\frac{1}{5} \times \frac{1}{8}$

9. $\frac{2}{3} \times \frac{9}{24}$ 10. $\frac{6}{5} \times \frac{10}{3}$ 11. $\frac{3}{8} \times \frac{24}{9}$ 12. $\frac{11}{13} \times \frac{39}{121}$

13. $\frac{14}{13} \times \frac{13}{14}$ 14. $\frac{9}{10} \times \frac{40}{27}$ 15. $\frac{6}{5} \times \frac{8}{7}$ 16. $\frac{2}{3} \times \frac{5}{4}$

17. $\frac{3}{20} \times 9$ 18. $\frac{5}{6} \times \frac{4}{15} \times \frac{2}{3}$ 19. $\frac{4}{9} \times \frac{5}{12} \times \frac{6}{7}$ 20. $\frac{2}{3} \times \frac{5}{8} \times 18$

Lesson 4.3 *(pages 102–103)*

Find the product.

1. $1\frac{5}{6} \times 2\frac{3}{11}$ 2. $\frac{7}{8} \times 2\frac{2}{3}$ 3. $4\frac{1}{4} \times 3\frac{1}{2}$ 4. $1\frac{3}{8} \times 2\frac{4}{11}$

5. $5\frac{5}{6} \times 18$ 6. $1\frac{8}{9} \times 17$ 7. $2\frac{12}{13} \times 1\frac{1}{19}$ 8. $8\frac{1}{8} \times 4\frac{2}{3}$

9. $5\frac{10}{11} \times 1\frac{9}{13}$ 10. $2\frac{1}{8} \times 3\frac{5}{17}$ 11. $5\frac{2}{3} \times 2\frac{7}{10}$ 12. $2\frac{1}{6} \times \frac{9}{13}$

13. $7\frac{1}{2} \times 1\frac{3}{5}$ 14. $3\frac{3}{8} \times 1\frac{1}{3}$ 15. $12 \times 5\frac{7}{8}$ 16. $5\frac{1}{2} \times 6\frac{1}{3} \times \frac{1}{11}$

17. $3\frac{1}{9} \times 2\frac{3}{8}$ 18. $5\frac{1}{6} \times 2\frac{1}{2}$ 19. $\frac{7}{16} \times \frac{4}{21} \times 2\frac{1}{3}$ 20. $\frac{1}{8} \times 6\frac{1}{9} \times 5\frac{3}{5}$

21. $1\frac{1}{4} \times 2 \times \frac{2}{5}$ 22. $1\frac{1}{16} \times 1\frac{1}{3} \times \frac{12}{17}$ 23. $2\frac{3}{8} \times 5\frac{3}{4} \times 1\frac{1}{19}$ 24. $\frac{2}{3} \times 5\frac{1}{4} \times 1\frac{1}{2}$

More Practice

Lesson 4.4 *(pages 104–105)*

Tell whether the quotient is *less than* 1 or *greater than* 1.

1. $\frac{3}{10} \div \frac{1}{5}$ 　　　2. $\frac{1}{2} \div \frac{7}{8}$ 　　　3. $\frac{1}{3} \div \frac{8}{9}$ 　　　4. $\frac{2}{5} \div \frac{5}{8}$

5. $\frac{5}{6} \div \frac{1}{4}$ 　　　6. $3\frac{1}{4} \div 6\frac{1}{8}$ 　　　7. $2\frac{6}{7} \div 1\frac{5}{6}$ 　　　8. $5\frac{2}{3} \div 2\frac{1}{12}$

9. $\frac{1}{10} \div \frac{1}{5}$ 　　　10. $7\frac{2}{3} \div 6\frac{1}{8}$ 　　　11. $\frac{3}{4} \div \frac{2}{3}$ 　　　12. $\frac{5}{6} \div \frac{8}{9}$

Use compatible numbers to estimate the quotient.

13. $35\frac{2}{3} \div 7\frac{1}{2}$ 　　14. $6\frac{1}{3} \div 2\frac{1}{4}$ 　　15. $4\frac{5}{8} \div 2\frac{1}{3}$ 　　16. $7\frac{11}{12} \div 1\frac{3}{4}$

17. $5\frac{5}{6} \div 7\frac{3}{8}$ 　　18. $8\frac{7}{8} \div 3$ 　　19. $2\frac{1}{2} \div 1\frac{3}{10}$ 　　20. $5\frac{2}{3} \div 18\frac{1}{8}$

21. $2\frac{1}{5} \div 12\frac{5}{6}$ 　　22. $4\frac{1}{6} \div 16\frac{1}{3}$ 　　23. $100\frac{1}{8} \div 10\frac{1}{4}$ 　　24. $59\frac{8}{9} \div 15\frac{1}{7}$

25. $56\frac{1}{7} \div 8\frac{2}{11}$ 　　26. $2\frac{9}{10} \div 15\frac{1}{8}$ 　　27. $32\frac{1}{9} \div 15\frac{6}{7}$ 　　28. $7\frac{7}{8} \div 71\frac{5}{6}$

Lesson 4.5 *(pages 108–109)*

Find the quotient. Write the quotient in simplest form.

1. $\frac{5}{6} \div \frac{2}{3}$ 　　2. $\frac{1}{3} \div \frac{1}{12}$ 　　3. $\frac{3}{8} \div \frac{15}{16}$ 　　4. $12 \div \frac{1}{6}$ 　　5. $\frac{4}{5} \div \frac{12}{15}$

6. $\frac{2}{9} \div \frac{1}{6}$ 　　7. $\frac{1}{6} \div 24$ 　　8. $\frac{7}{8} \div \frac{21}{4}$ 　　9. $\frac{7}{9} \div \frac{14}{12}$ 　　10. $20 \div \frac{1}{5}$

11. $\frac{1}{3} \div 12$ 　　12. $\frac{3}{4} \div \frac{8}{9}$ 　　13. $6 \div \frac{1}{3}$ 　　14. $\frac{5}{7} \div \frac{25}{14}$ 　　15. $\frac{3}{7} \div \frac{9}{28}$

16. $4 \div \frac{2}{9}$ 　　17. $\frac{2}{5} \div \frac{8}{25}$ 　　18. $\frac{1}{4} \div 9$ 　　19. $\frac{3}{4} \div 6$

20. $24 \div \frac{5}{6}$ 　　21. $\frac{17}{12} \div \frac{11}{24}$ 　　22. $\frac{7}{8} \div 3$ 　　23. $10 \div \frac{2}{3}$

Lesson 4.6 *(pages 110–111)*

1. There are 20 students working in pairs. Each student is paired with every other student once. How many different pairings are there in all?

2. In how many ways can a group of 8 new players be divided among 3 teams if each team receives at least 1 new player?

3. There are 6 dots on a sheet of paper. No 3 dots are in a straight line. How many line segments are needed to connect each dot to every other dot?

4. There are 10 people at a chess club meeting. Each person shakes hands with every other person in the room once. Find the total number of handshakes.

Lesson 4.7 *(pages 112–113)*

Find the quotient.

1. $8\frac{1}{2} \div 2\frac{1}{6}$ 2. $6\frac{1}{4} \div 2\frac{1}{2}$ 3. $4\frac{2}{3} \div 7$ 4. $15 \div 3\frac{3}{4}$

5. $7\frac{5}{6} \div 3\frac{1}{8}$ 6. $2\frac{1}{2} \div 2\frac{1}{5}$ 7. $1\frac{1}{3} \div 5\frac{3}{4}$ 8. $\frac{1}{18} \div 4\frac{1}{2}$

9. $3\frac{3}{4} \div 1\frac{1}{2}$ 10. $3\frac{1}{6} \div 2\frac{1}{2}$ 11. $8 \div 1\frac{1}{4}$ 12. $3\frac{1}{2} \div 6$

13. $6\frac{1}{4} \div 4\frac{2}{3}$ 14. $30 \div 6\frac{1}{2}$ 15. $12\frac{1}{2} \div 5$ 16. $1\frac{1}{9} \div 2\frac{1}{2}$

17. $6\frac{3}{4} \div 1\frac{7}{8}$ 18. $12 \div 3\frac{3}{4}$ 19. $8 \div 4\frac{1}{3}$ 20. $2\frac{2}{3} \div 5\frac{1}{6}$

Lesson 4.8 *(pages 114–117)*

Solve the equation. Check your answer.

1. $t - \frac{1}{6} = 2\frac{1}{6}$ 2. $m + \frac{1}{4} = 4$ 3. $2 = x + 1\frac{7}{8}$ 4. $d - 8\frac{3}{4} = 6\frac{5}{6}$

5. $\frac{3m}{4} = \frac{1}{8}$ 6. $\frac{4b}{5} = \frac{1}{15}$ 7. $\frac{m}{\frac{1}{2}} = 5$ 8. $\frac{x}{3\frac{1}{3}} = 3$

9. $b - 3 = \frac{1}{6}$ 10. $4a = 2\frac{1}{8}$ 11. $\frac{x}{\frac{1}{3}} = \frac{1}{3}$ 12. $b - 6\frac{1}{3} = 3\frac{1}{3}$

13. $2x + 4\frac{3}{5} = 19\frac{3}{5}$ 14. $10 = 5c + 3\frac{3}{4}$ 15. $\frac{b}{\frac{1}{9}} = 45$ 16. $\frac{n}{\frac{2}{3}} = 12$

Lesson 4.9 *(pages 118–119)*

Write a decimal for the fraction or mixed number.

1. $\frac{1}{5}$ 2. $\frac{1}{6}$ 3. $\frac{1}{3}$ 4. $4\frac{2}{5}$ 5. $3\frac{3}{8}$ 6. $\frac{3}{25}$

7. $\frac{2}{15}$ 8. $\frac{4}{45}$ 9. $1\frac{1}{8}$ 10. $\frac{7}{20}$ 11. $\frac{2}{50}$ 12. $6\frac{1}{9}$

13. $\frac{2}{3}$ 14. $2\frac{5}{8}$ 15. $\frac{19}{25}$ 16. $\frac{6}{11}$ 17. $\frac{5}{6}$ 18. $2\frac{3}{11}$

Compare. Write $<$, $>$, or $=$.

19. $2.2 \bullet 2\frac{1}{3}$ 20. $0.3 \bullet \frac{1}{2}$ 21. $\frac{1}{4} \bullet 0.25$ 22. $0.85 \bullet \frac{4}{5}$

23. $3.4 \bullet 3\frac{2}{5}$ 24. $2\frac{1}{4} \bullet 2.2$ 25. $8.75 \bullet 8\frac{4}{5}$ 26. $5.3 \bullet 5\frac{1}{3}$

27. $3.9 \bullet 3\frac{91}{100}$ 28. $5\frac{2}{3} \bullet 5.6$ 29. $6.4 \bullet 6\frac{4}{9}$ 30. $1.875 \bullet 1\frac{7}{8}$

Lesson 4.10 *(pages 120–121)*

Write a fraction in simplest form or a mixed number for the decimal.

1. 0.42	**2.** 0.25	**3.** 0.5	**4.** 0.06	**5.** 3.25
6. 0.3	**7.** 0.125	**8.** 1.6	**9.** 3.27	**10.** 6.375
11. 1.35	**12.** 1.2	**13.** 0.7	**14.** 0.45	**15.** 0.72
16. $0.\overline{4}$	**17.** $0.\overline{12}$	**18.** $1.\overline{2}$	**19.** $0.3\overline{8}$	**20.** $2.\overline{45}$
21. 0.90	**22.** 1.625	**23.** $0.\overline{6}$	**24.** 8.75	**25.** $9.\overline{5}$

Write in order from least to greatest.

26. $\frac{1}{2}$, 0.4, 1.3, $\frac{3}{4}$

27. 0.7, $\frac{2}{3}$, $\frac{3}{5}$, 1.2

28. $\frac{5}{6}$, 1.2, $\frac{1}{2}$, $2\frac{1}{4}$, 2.4

29. 3.6, $2\frac{9}{10}$, $3\frac{3}{4}$, $3\frac{1}{2}$, $3\frac{4}{5}$

30. 1.09, $\frac{9}{10}$, 0.875, $\frac{8}{9}$, $0.\overline{9}$

31. $\frac{5}{6}$, $\frac{3}{4}$, 0.8, $0.\overline{6}$, $\frac{3}{5}$

Lesson 4.11 *(pages 122–123)*

Solve.

1. Aaron works at the mall 3 days each week. The distance from his house to the mall is 10 miles. How many miles does he travel each week going to and from the mall?

2. Bob spends $10 each week on bus fare and $15 each week for lunch. How much does he spend for bus fare and lunch for 7 weeks?

3. Kathie and Craig each walked for 5 hours on Sunday. Craig walked at a rate of 4 miles per hour, and Kathie walked at a rate of 3 miles per hour. How many miles did they walk in all?

4. Edward and his friends bought 6 concert tickets. The total cost of the tickets was $78. Write an equation to find the cost of one ticket, and solve.

5. Elizabeth works a total of 28 hr each week. She works 4 hr on Mondays, Wednesdays, and Fridays. She works the same number of hours on Thursdays as on Saturdays. Write an equation to find the number of hours worked on Thursday or Saturday and solve.

6. Matt practices his drums 45 min each week day. He practices 30 min on both Saturday and Sunday. How many hours does he practice during one week?

CHAPTER 5

Lesson 5.1 *(pages 132–133)*

Match one or more names from the list with each figure in Exercises 1–4.

1.

2.
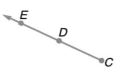

a. $\overrightarrow{CD}$ e. $\angle KLM$
b. $\overleftrightarrow{BA}$ f. $\overrightarrow{CE}$
c. $\angle MLK$ g. $\overline{FG}$
d. $\overrightarrow{GF}$ h. $\overleftrightarrow{AB}$

3.

4.

Lesson 5.2 *(pages 134–137)*

Find the missing measures.

1.
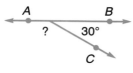

2.

3.
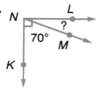

4.

5.

6.
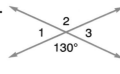

Lesson 5.3 *(pages 138–139)*

Trace the figure. Then use your tracing to construct a congruent figure.

1.
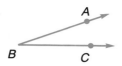

2.

3.
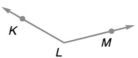

Draw the figure, using a ruler and a protractor. Then use the figure to construct a congruent figure, using a compass and a straightedge.

4. a 70° angle   **5.** a 3-in. line segment   **6.** a 100° angle

7. a 15-mm line segment   **8.** a 30° angle   **9.** a 40-mm line segment

Lesson 5.4 *(pages 140–141)*

Use the figure to find the measure of the given angle. $\overleftrightarrow{AB} \parallel \overleftrightarrow{CD}$

1. m∠1   **2.** m∠2   **3.** m∠3   **4.** m∠4

5. m∠5   **6.** m∠6   **7.** m∠7   **8.** m∠8

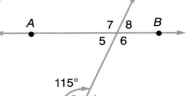
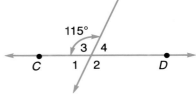

Lesson 5.5 *(pages 142–143)*

Draw the constructions using a straightedge and a ruler.

1. Draw a line AB and a point T as shown. Then construct a line through T parallel to AB.

2. Draw a line KL and a point M as shown. Then construct a line through M perpendicular to KL.

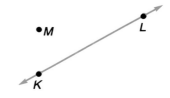

Lesson 5.6 *(pages 144–145)*

Draw the figures using a ruler and a protractor. Construct bisectors using a compass and a straightedge.

1. a 150° angle

2. a 38-mm line segment

3. a 10-cm line segment

4. a 90° angle

5. a 40° angle

6. a 7-cm line segment

Lesson 5.7 *(pages 146–147)*

Choose the figure that completes the pattern.

1.   **a.**   **b.**   **c.**

2.   **a.**   **b.**   **c.**

3.   **a.**   **b.**   **c.**

Lesson 5.8 *(pages 148–151)*

Find the sum of the measures of the angles for each polygon.

1. parallelogram **2.** 7-sided polygon **3.** 9-sided polygon **4.** 30-sided polygon

Tell whether the dashed line is a line of symmetry.
Write *yes* or *no*.

5.   **6.**   **7.** 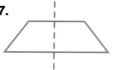   **8.**

Look back at Exercises 5–8. Which quadrilaterals have a point of rotation
for a rotation of 90°? for a rotation of 180°?

Lesson 5.9 *(pages 152–153)*

Use the figure to find the indicated angle measure.

1. m ∠ 2 = 110° and m ∠ 3 = 30°. Find m ∠ 5.

2. m ∠ 4 = 120° and m ∠ 5 = 20°. Find m ∠ 2.

3. m ∠ 1 = 75° and m ∠ 3 = 40°. Find m ∠ 5.

4. m ∠ 6 = 140° and m ∠ 2 = 100°. Find m ∠ 3.

5. m ∠ 2 = 80° and m ∠ 5 = 40°. Find m ∠ 3.

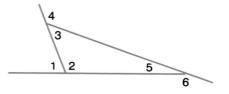

Lesson 5.10 *(pages 156–157)*

The polygons in each of Exercises 1–4 are congruent. Find *a*, *b*, and *c*.

1.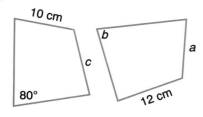

2.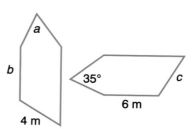

3.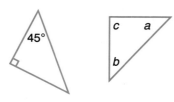

4.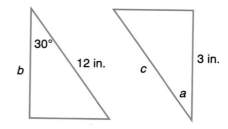

Lesson 5.11 *(pages 158–161)*

Determine whether the triangles are congruent by *SSS*, *SAS*, or *ASA*.

1. 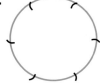   **2.**    **3.**

Trace the triangle. Use the indicated rule to construct a congruent triangle.

4. SAS   **5.** SSS   **6.** ASA

Lesson 5.12 *(pages 162–163)*

Name the polygon formed when a line is drawn from each arc to the adjacent arc.

1. 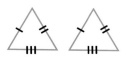   **2.**   **3.**

Lesson 5.13 *(pages 164–165)*

Joan wants to spend 4 days and 3 nights in the Bahamas. She can fly round trip for $150 and stay at a hotel for $100 per night, for 2 people. The cost for her meals should be about $40 per day, per person. She could also take a cruise, instead of flying. The cost of the cruise is $600 per person, all expenses paid.

1. Should Joan fly or take the cruise to the Bahamas?

2. Joan's daughter also wants to go. What would be the less expensive choice if they both went?

3. The hotel rents beach umbrellas. The cost of the umbrella is $4.00 per day or $15.00 for their entire stay at the hotel. Which cost is less?

4. Joan and her daughter rented bicycles to explore the island. The cost of renting one bicycle is $10.00 a day or $3.00 per hour. They estimate they will ride four hours. Which rental cost is greater?

5. Give one reason why they would choose to rent the beach umbrella at $4.00 per day.

CHAPTER 6

Lesson 6.1 *(pages 174–175)*

Write the ratio in the form $\frac{a}{b}$.

1. $2:5$ **2.** 8 to 9   **3.** $23:50$ **4.** 3 out of 7

Write $=$ or $\neq$.

5. $\frac{3}{2} \bullet \frac{4}{6}$ **6.** $\frac{1}{4} \bullet \frac{10}{40}$ **7.** $\frac{2}{5} \bullet \frac{6}{15}$ **8.** $\frac{15}{9} \bullet \frac{5}{2}$

Write the unit rate.

9. $\frac{\$14.95}{5 \text{ hamburgers}}$ **10.** $\frac{\$1.00}{20 \text{ pencils}}$ **11.** $\frac{\$1.75}{7 \text{ calls}}$ **12.** $\frac{120 \text{ calories}}{10 \text{ raisins}}$

Lesson 6.2 *(pages 176–177)*

Solve the proportion.

1. $\frac{2}{3} = \frac{4}{n}$ **2.** $\frac{3}{5} = \frac{n}{15}$ **3.** $\frac{5}{6} = \frac{n}{90}$

4. $\frac{n}{12} = \frac{9}{36}$ **5.** $\frac{33}{n} = \frac{121}{11}$ **6.** $\frac{3}{8} = \frac{24}{n}$

7. $\frac{1}{7} = \frac{n}{10.5}$ **8.** $\frac{7}{8} = \frac{n}{2}$ **9.** $\frac{6}{1} = \frac{6.54}{n}$

10. $\frac{n}{3} = \frac{12}{4}$ **11.** $\frac{44}{n} = \frac{6}{3}$ **12.** $\frac{8}{9} = \frac{18}{x}$

Lesson 6.3 *(pages 178–181)*

Use the scale of 1 in.:9 in. to find the missing dimension.

1. drawing: 6 in.
   actual: ■ in.

2. drawing: 9 in.
   actual: ■ in.

3. drawing: ■ in.
   actual: 27 in.

4. drawing: ■ in.
   actual: 8.1 in.

5. drawing: ■ in.
   actual: 4.5 in.

6. drawing: 20 in.
   actual: ■ in.

Lesson 6.4 *(pages 182–183)*

Find the straight-line distance between the two locations.

1. Tavares and Wilson

2. Clay and Peace

3. Clay and Jovan

4. Peace and Wilson

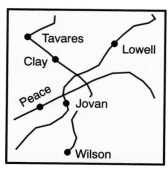

1 cm = 15 km

Lesson 6.5 *(pages 184–185)*

Write as a percent.

1. 15 per 100

2. $\frac{33}{100}$

3. $\frac{3}{25}$

4. 20 out of 100

5. $\frac{24}{20}$

6. $\frac{5}{20}$

7. $\frac{21}{25}$

8. $\frac{120}{100}$

9. $\frac{34}{25}$

10. $\frac{7}{8}$

11. 1 out of 1,000

12. $\frac{20}{32}$

13. $\frac{45}{15}$

14. $\frac{888}{1000}$

15. $\frac{13.5}{150}$

Lesson 6.6 *(pages 186–187)*

Write as a decimal.

1. 2%

2. 76%

3. 25%

4. 44%

5. 225%

6. 95%

Write as a percent.

7. 0.32

8. 0.03

9. $\frac{1}{8}$

10. 0.1

11. 0.57

12. $\frac{3}{1}$

Write as a ratio in simplest form.

13. 25%

14. 200%

15. 2%

16. 35%

17. 33%

18. 575%

Lesson 6.7 *(pages 188–189)*

Choose the correct percent problem for each word problem.
Write **a, b,** or **c.**

1. There are 20 people in an aerobics class. Of these, 15 are female. What percent of the people in the aerobics class are female?

  a. 15% of 20 = ■
  b. 15% of ■ = 20
  c. ■% of 20 = 15

2. Xavier spent $25 on a baseball glove. This was 20% of his money. How much money did he have before buying the glove?

  a. 20% of 25 = ■
  b. 20% of ■ = 25
  c. ■% of 20 = 25

3. Claire had 50 tomatoes. She gave 40% of the tomatoes to her sister. How many tomatoes did she give her sister?

  a. ■% of 40 = 50
  b. 40% of ■ = 50
  c. 40% of 50 = ■

Lesson 6.8 *(pages 190–191)*

Find the percent of each number.

1. 2% of 240

2. 60% of 360

3. 3% of 90

4. 3.75% of 300

5. 150% of 6

6. 43% of 192

7. 0.4% of 164

8. 1.2% of 12

9. 15% of 75

10. 0.8% of 72

11. 95% of 90

12. 400% of 5

13. 300% of 48

14. 106% of 60

15. 1,000% of 5

16. 0.5% of 12

Lesson 6.9 *(pages 194–195)*

Find the percent.

1. 5 is what percent of 50?
2. What percent of 12 is 36?
3. 117 is what percent of 900?
4. 20 is what percent of 20?
5. 14 is what percent of 350?
6. 72 is what percent of 60?
7. 2.7 is what percent of 90?
8. 137.5 is what percent of 220?
9. What percent of 75 is 0.6?
10. 500 is what percent of 1,000?
11. What percent of 56 is 1.4?
12. 148 is what percent of 37?
13. 638.4 is what percent of 760?
14. What percent of 10,000 is 25?

Lesson 6.10 *(pages 196–197)*

Find the number.

1. 10% of what number is 2.5?
2. 13% of what number is 3.51?
3. 44.1 is 63% of what number?
4. 51 is 42.5% of what number?
5. 25% of what number is 22.5?
6. 5% of what number is 11.25?
7. 440 is 55% of what number?
8. 9 is 15% of what number?
9. 400% of what number is 100?
10. 20% of what number is 40?
11. 3.43 is 7% of what number?
12. 28 is 40% of what number?
13. 0.8% of what number is 6?
14. 120% of what number is 120?
15. 6 is $66\frac{2}{3}$% of what number?
16. 100% of what number is 35?

Lesson 6.11 *(pages 198–199)*

Estimate the percent.

1. 12 of 35 is about what percent?
2. 23 of 25 is about what percent?
3. 98 is about what percent of 210?
4. 49 is about what percent of 190?
5. 6 of 594 is about what percent?
6. 147 is about what percent of 50?

Estimate the number.

7. 25 is 11% of what number?
8. 20% of what number is 79?
9. 118 is 66% of what number?
10. 33.3% of what number is 144?
11. 45 is 51% of what number?
12. 5% of what number is 11?
13. 18 is 19% of what number?
14. 75% of what number is 305?

Lesson 6.12 *(pages 200–201)*

1. Find the percent of decrease.
   amount of decrease: 24
   original amount: 60

2. Find the percent of increase.
   amount of increase: 6
   original amount: 30

3. Find the percent of increase.
   amount of increase: 33
   original amount: 120

4. Find the percent of decrease.
   amount of decrease: $3.75
   original amount: $75

Lesson 6.13 *(pages 202–203)*

Find the percent of increase or decrease.

1. 1970 cost: $450
   1990 cost: $640

2. 1990 sales: $200
   1991 sales: $400

3. 1980 sales: 48
   1990 sales: 42

4. 1989 savings: $2,000
   1990 savings: $1,500

5. 1989 sales: $600
   1990 sales: $800

6. 1990 amount: 15
   1991 amount: 18

7. 1988 earnings: $2,000
   1990 earnings: $8,000

8. 1990 cost: $1,750
   1991 cost: $1,925

9. 1980 sales: 400
   1989 sales: 380

10. 1989 earnings: $800
    1990 earnings: $700

11. 1989 cost: $3.20
    1990 cost: $3.80

12. 1989 amount: $15,000
    1990 amount: $21,000

Lesson 6.14 *(pages 204–205)*

Find the interest.

1. $p = \$210$
   $r = 8\%$ per year
   $t = 2$ yr.

2. $p = \$252.00$
   $r = 6\%$ per year
   $t = 6$ months

3. $p = \$468$
   $r = 10\%$ per year
   $t = 3$ months

4. $p = \$1,250$
   $r = 5\%$ per year
   $t = 1\frac{1}{2}$ yr.

5. $p = \$450$
   $r = 9\%$ per year
   $t = 6$ months

6. $p = \$500$
   $r = 12\%$ per year
   $t = 10$ months

7. $p = \$900$
   $r = 1.25\%$ per month
   $t = 3$ months

8. $p = \$12,500$
   $r = 1\%$ per month
   $t = 9$ months

9. $p = \$480$
   $r = 10\%$ per year
   $t = 5$ months

Lesson 6.15 *(pages 206–207)*

Estimate a 15% tip for each bill.

1. $15.49

2. $22.30

3. $12.50

4. $55.00

5. $18.30

6. $14.90

7. $8.75

8. $120.00

Use estimation to solve.

9. Denise noticed her father leave $10 as a tip. If $10 was 15% of the total bill, what was the amount of the total bill?

10. March sells cosmetics for a commission of 25%. She sold $875 worth of cosmetic supplies yesterday. Estimate her commission.

CHAPTER 7

Lesson 7.1 *(pages 216–217)*

Write the absolute value.

1. $\left|^-21\right|$
2. $\left|^-19\right|$
3. $\left|^-23\right|$
4. $\left|^-8\right|$
5. $\left|^-2\right|$
6. $\left|^-42\right|$
7. $\left|15\right|$
8. $\left|^-25\right|$
9. $\left|^-37\right|$
10. $\left|48\right|$
11. $\left|^-32\right|$
12. $\left|^-200\right|$

Write the opposite.

13. going east 3 miles
14. turn left twice
15. giving 5 dollars
16. $^-20$
17. $^-67$
18. 139
19. $^-48$
20. 83
21. $^-5$

Order the integers from greatest to least.

22. $1, 0, \,^-1, 10$
23. $25, \,^-24, \,^-2, 12$
24. $3, \,^-3, 2, \,^-4, \,^-8$
25. $5, \,^-4, 3, \,^-2, \,^-5$
26. $0, 10 \,^-8, 20$
27. $^-9, \,^-8, \,^-3, 4, 6$
28. $0, \,^-3, 5, \,^-6, 13$
29. $^-2, \,^-9, 7, \,^-4, 3$
30. $^-6, 5, \,^-9, \,^-1, 12$
31. $1, \,^-6, \,^-12, \,^-8, 2$
32. $^-4, \,^-9, \,^-10, 10, 0$
33. $^-6, \,^-9, 3, \,^-1, \,^-4$

Lesson 7.2 *(pages 218–219)*

Find the sum.

1. $3 + 10$
2. $21 + \,^-9$
3. $13 + \,^-10$
4. $^-98 + 2$
5. $11 + \,^-15$
6. $^-35 + 42$
7. $100 + \,^-91$
8. $48 + 13$
9. $^-20 + 5$
10. $73 + \,^-102$
11. $41 + \,^-53$
12. $^-19 + 1$
13. $^-69 + 78 + 3$
14. $18 + \,^-12 + 10$
15. $^-13 + \,^-12 + 11$
16. $(5 + 1) + 3$
17. $(^-18 + 12) + 9$
18. $^-6 + \,^-5 + \,^-4$
19. $^-9 + \,^-2 + 5$
20. $^-8 + 14 + \,^-5$
21. $^-4 + \,^-10 + \,^-12$
22. $^-13 + \,^-4 + 7$
23. $^-3 + 7 + \,^-9 + \,^-6$
24. $^-7 + \,^-5 + \,^-15 + \,^-2$

Lesson 7.3 *(pages 220–221)*

Find the difference.

1. $^-10 - \,^-20$
2. $^-8 - 12$
3. $^-61 - \,^-52$
4. $^-8 - \,^-59$
5. $3 - \,^-11$
6. $23 - \,^-40$
7. $^-33 - 42$
8. $12 - \,^-3$
9. $22 - \,^-45$
10. $^-28 - 11$
11. $2 - \,^-3$
12. $38 - \,^-9$
13. $18 - \,^-19$
14. $^-48 - \,^-31$
15. $54 - \,^-29$
16. $99 - \,^-101$
17. $^-25 - \,^-52$
18. $32 - 50$
19. $^-19 - 4$
20. $^-8 - 13$
21. $^-22 - \,^-43$
22. $85 - \,^-56$
23. $^-9 + 7 - 3$
24. $^-2 + 5 - \,^-3$

Lesson 7.4 *(pages 222–223)*

Find the product.

1. $^-4 \cdot 3$
2. $^-4 \cdot 9$
3. $10 \cdot ^-5$
4. $^-2 \cdot ^-2$

5. $5 \cdot ^-2$
6. $^-3 \cdot ^-7$
7. $^-12 \cdot ^-8$
8. $8 \cdot 30$

9. $8 \cdot 7$
10. $^-4 \cdot 0$
11. $^-21 \cdot ^-10$
12. $^-4 \cdot 3$

13. $5 \cdot ^-4 \cdot ^-1$
14. $8 \cdot ^-2 \cdot ^-5$
15. $^-4 \cdot 2 \cdot 3$

16. $^-3 \cdot ^-6 \cdot ^-2$
17. $1 \cdot ^-2 \cdot ^-3$
18. $^-10 \cdot ^-1 \cdot ^-2$

19. $^-8 \cdot ^-3 \cdot 2$
20. $^-4 \cdot ^-1 \cdot ^-9$
21. $^-5 \cdot ^-3 \cdot ^-2$

22. $7 \cdot ^-5 \cdot ^-1$
23. $^-6 \cdot 4 \cdot ^-1$
24. $4 \cdot ^-5 \cdot ^-7 \cdot ^-2$

Lesson 7.5 *(pages 224–225)*

The lengths of time needed to cook some foods in a microwave are as follows: chicken, 35 min; 5-lb ham, 60 min; 2 potatoes, 7 min; soup, 2 min; and 4 bacon slices, 4 min. Use this information for Exercises 1–4.

1. Make a table that shows the length of cooking time in order from least to greatest. Which food has the second-greatest cooking time?

2. Which food takes exactly twice the cooking time as another food?

3. Which food takes exactly 5 times longer than the potatoes?

4. Which two foods, cooked one after the other, take 9 minutes?

Lesson 7.6 *(pages 226–227)*

Find the quotient.

1. $^-16 \div ^-2$
2. $48 \div ^-6$
3. $^-24 \div ^-3$
4. $32 \div ^-8$

5. $42 \div ^-14$
6. $12 \div ^-4$
7. $^-60 \div 5$
8. $0 \div ^-45$

9. $\frac{^-16}{4}$
10. $\frac{200}{50}$
11. $\frac{45}{^-15}$
12. $\frac{^-30}{^-10}$

13. $\frac{^-12}{^-3}$
14. $\frac{^-8}{^-1}$
15. $\frac{^-100}{25}$
16. $\frac{18}{^-6}$

17. $24 \div ^-6$
18. $^-48 \div ^-12$
19. $0 \div ^-6$
20. $^-27 \div ^-9$

21. $\frac{^-300}{^-10}$
22. $\frac{^-75}{5}$
23. $\frac{60}{^-15}$
24. $\frac{^-84}{^-7}$

Compute.

25. $^-6 \cdot 10$
26. $^-8 - ^-8$
27. $13 + ^-30$
28. $42 \div 7$

29. $(4 \cdot ^-5) + ^-12$
30. $(10 \div 2) - (18 \div ^-3)$
31. $(26 \div 13) \cdot ^-8$

32. $62 \div (^-25 - 6)$
33. $(^-3 \div ^-1) \cdot (^-8 \div 2)$
34. $(^-6 \div ^-2) - 5$

35. $^-4 + (^-2 \cdot 5)$
36. $(^-6 \cdot ^-4) \div (48 \div ^-8)$
37. $(^-3 - ^-5) \div (32 \div ^-2)$

Lesson 7.7 *(pages 230–231)*

Use the properties to find each answer. Use mental math where possible.

1. $3 \cdot (^-9 \cdot 4)$
2. $10 \cdot (8 + 4)$
3. $^-3 + 9 + 7 + 4$
4. $^-6 - 0 + ^-13 + 15$
5. $(15 \cdot ^-3) \cdot 10$
6. $34 + 35 + ^-34 + ^-31$
7. $(25 \cdot 25) + (25 \cdot ^-25)$
8. $(^-6 \cdot 5) + (^-8 \cdot 5)$
9. $(28 + ^-17) + (^-17 + 28) + 40$
10. $(^-29 + 12) + (8 + ^-15) + 16$
11. $(^-5 \cdot ^-8) \cdot (^-24 + 6 + ^-2)$
12. $(^-6 \cdot 3) + (^-1 \cdot ^-9 \cdot ^-2)$

Lesson 7.8 *(pages 232–233)*

Write as an expression having a negative exponent.

1. $\frac{1}{10^2}$
2. $\frac{1}{4^3}$
3. $\frac{1}{5^2}$
4. $\frac{1}{10^5}$
5. $\frac{1}{10,000}$
6. $\frac{1}{4 \cdot 4 \cdot 4 \cdot 4}$
7. $\frac{1}{8 \cdot 8 \cdot 8}$
8. $\frac{1}{125}$
9. $\frac{1}{6 \cdot 6}$
10. $\frac{1}{3^4}$
11. $\frac{1}{2 \cdot 2 \cdot 2 \cdot 2 \cdot 2}$
12. $\frac{1}{7 \cdot 7 \cdot 7}$

Write as a fraction or a decimal.

13. 4^{-2}
14. 5^{-1}
15. 10^{-1}
16. 2^{-3}
17. 6^{-2}
18. 5^{-4}
19. 2^{-5}
20. 6^{-4}
21. $(^-3)^{-5}$
22. $(^-6)^{-2}$
23. $(^-7)^{-2}$
24. $(^-10)^{-5}$
25. $(^-2)^{-3}$
26. $(^-12)^{-2}$
27. $(5)^{-4}$
28. $(^-7)^{-3}$

Lesson 7.9 *(pages 234–235)*

Write the product as one power.

1. $7^2 \cdot 7^3$
2. $3^5 \cdot 3^2$
3. $8^8 \cdot 8^7$
4. $21^{-3} \cdot 21^2$
5. $10^2 \cdot 10^8$
6. $4^{-1} \cdot 4^{-5}$
7. $6^{-2} \cdot 6^{12}$
8. $7^{10} \cdot 7^{14}$
9. $(^-2)^2 \cdot (^-2)^6$
10. $(^-6)^3 \cdot (^-6)^{-4}$
11. $(^-5)^2 (^-5)^{-5}$
12. $(^-8)^5 \cdot (^-8)^2$
13. $(^-2)^5 \cdot (^-2)^{-7}$
14. $(^-9)^3 \cdot (^-9)^2 \cdot (^-9)^{-1}$
15. $4^{-3} \cdot 4^7 \cdot 4^5$
16. $(^-10)^{-3} \cdot (^-10)^3$
17. $(^-7)^{10} \cdot (^-7)^{-3} \cdot (^-7)^{-5}$

Write the quotient as one power.

18. $6^6 \div 6^3$
19. $8^{10} \div 8^8$
20. $4^5 \div 4^1$
21. $9^6 \div 9^2$
22. $5^2 \div 5^5$
23. $7^5 \div 7^{-6}$
24. $2^{-3} \div 2^4$
25. $6^{-10} \div 6^4$
26. $(^-3)^4 \div (^-3)^5$
27. $(^-25)^{-5} \div (^-25)^{-10}$
28. $(^-8)^0 \div (^-8)^{-5}$
29. $7^5 \div 7^2$
30. $3^9 \div 3^5$
31. $8^0 \div 8^{-2}$
32. $(^-4)^6 \div (^-4)^3$
33. $(^-10)^{-8} \div (^-10)^5$
34. $(^-9)^1 \div (^-9)^{-3}$

Lesson 7.10 *(pages 236–237)*

Complete.

1. $35{,}000 = 3.5 \times 10^{\blacksquare}$

2. $210{,}000{,}000 = \blacksquare \times 10^{8}$

3. $0.000025 = 2.5 \times 10^{\blacksquare}$

4. $0.00000000000043 = 4.3 \times 10^{\blacksquare}$

5. $58{,}000{,}000{,}000 = 5.8 \times 10^{\blacksquare}$

6. $0.000000000017 = 1.7 \times 10^{\blacksquare}$

Write in scientific notation.

7. 520,000

8. 36,000

9. 33,500,000

10. 0.0012

11. 0.005

12. 0.000033

13. 0.0000049

14. 4,530,000

15. 7,900,000,000

16. 0.000000067

17. 53,800,000

18. 0.000049

Write in standard form.

19. 4×10^{6}

20. 1.5×10^{3}

21. 72.3×10^{3}

22. 6.8×10^{-4}

23. 3.7×10^{-6}

24. 4.89×10^{-5}

25. 2.01×10^{6}

26. 1.6×10^{5}

27. 3.09×10^{-4}

28. 7.94×10^{-9}

29. 1.7×10^{6}

30. 6.03×10^{-8}

Lesson 7.11 *(pages 238–239)*

Write an equation to solve the problem.

1. The high temperature in August was 98°F. This was 120° higher than the low temperature in January. What was the low in January?

2. The cost of Jenny's water skis, plus the cost of 2 skiing lessons, was $329. The cost of one lesson was $40. What was the cost of the skis?

3. Over a 20-second period, Robin changed her driving speed by ⁻30 miles per hour. What was the average change in speed per second?

4. The humidity factor added 8°F to the recorded temperature last Monday. The recorded temperature plus the humidity totaled 84°F. What was the recorded temperature?

5. T.J. opened a savings account with a $35 deposit. Then he made eight equal weekly deposits. His balance is now $259. What was the amount of each weekly deposit?

6. The price of one share of LYZ's stock reached a low of $49.84. This price was $31.92 less than the stock's high price. What was the stock's high for the year?

CHAPTER 8

Lesson 8.1 *(pages 248–249)*

Write each rational number in the form $\frac{a}{b}$.

1. $^-4\frac{1}{8}$ **2.** 4.9   **3.** $^-5$ **4.** $^-0.7$ **5.** $6\frac{1}{4}$

Compare. Write $<$, $>$, or $=$.

6. 0.2 ● $^-0.2$ **7.** $\frac{-1}{3}$ ● $\frac{1}{3}$ **8.** $\frac{-5}{6}$ ● $\frac{7}{8}$ **9.** 4 ● $\frac{1}{4}$

10. 2.75 ● $2\frac{3}{4}$ **11.** $\frac{-1}{6}$ ● $\frac{5}{6}$ **12.** $\frac{2}{3}$ ● 0.62   **13.** 6.5 ● $6\frac{1}{2}$

14. $\frac{9}{10}$ ● $\frac{999}{1000}$ **15.** $^-3.8$ ● $^-3\frac{4}{5}$ **16.** $\frac{2}{3}$ ● $\frac{6}{10}$ **17.** 8.1 ● $8\frac{1}{9}$

Lesson 8.2 *(pages 250–251)*

Find the square.

1. 5^2 **2.** 14^2 **3.** $(^-4)^2$ **4.** $(^-16)^2$ **5.** 20^2

6. $(0.8)^2$ **7.** $\left(\frac{5}{6}\right)^2$ **8.** $(2.1)^2$ **9.** $\left(\frac{-1}{3}\right)^2$ **10.** $\left(\frac{7}{8}\right)^2$

11. $(0.03)^2$ **12.** $\left(\frac{5}{9}\right)^2$ **13.** $(3.2)^2$ **14.** $(^-1.5)^2$

Find the square root.

15. $\sqrt{100}$ **16.** $^-\sqrt{16}$ **17.** $^-\sqrt{625}$ **18.** $\sqrt{64}$ **19.** $\sqrt{169}$

20. $\sqrt{\frac{4}{49}}$ **21.** $\sqrt{0.36}$ **22.** $\sqrt{\frac{1}{9}}$ **23.** $\sqrt{0.01}$ **24.** $^-\sqrt{\frac{36}{81}}$

25. $^-\sqrt{\frac{81}{100}}$ **26.** $\sqrt{1.21}$ **27.** $\sqrt{\frac{25}{144}}$ **28.** $^-\sqrt{196}$ **29.** $\sqrt{0.0049}$

Lesson 8.3 *(pages 252–255)*

Estimate to find the square root to the nearest tenth.

1. $\sqrt{67}$ **2.** $\sqrt{88}$ **3.** $\sqrt{141}$ **4.** $^-\sqrt{76}$ **5.** $\sqrt{39}$

6. $^-\sqrt{96}$ **7.** $\sqrt{445}$ **8.** $\sqrt{205}$ **9.** $\sqrt{879}$ **10.** $\sqrt{165}$

11. $^-\sqrt{29}$ **12.** $^-\sqrt{56}$ **13.** $\sqrt{94}$ **14.** $^-\sqrt{9980}$ **15.** $\sqrt{134}$

Find the square root to the nearest hundredth. Use the table of squares
and square roots on page H103, or use a calculator.

16. $\sqrt{5}$ **17.** $\sqrt{22}$ **18.** $^-\sqrt{53}$ **19.** $\sqrt{85}$ **20.** $^-\sqrt{97}$

21. $\sqrt{0.06}$ **22.** $\sqrt{0.32}$ **23.** $\sqrt{12.56}$ **24.** $^-\sqrt{102}$ **25.** $\sqrt{120}$

26. $\sqrt{6}$ **27.** $^-\sqrt{0.68}$ **28.** $\sqrt{37.59}$ **29.** $^-\sqrt{175}$ **30.** $\sqrt{0.000001}$

Lesson 8.4 *(pages 256–257)*

Copy the table. Then classify the number by placing an **X** in each appropriate column.

		Real Number	Rational Number	Whole Number	Integer	Irrational Number
1.	24					
2.	⁻3.8					
3.	⁻5					
4.	199					
5.	6.345212 . . .					
6.	$\sqrt{47}$					
7.	$\frac{1}{2}$					
8.	0.36					
9.	$3\frac{7}{8}$					
10.	3.786534 . . .					

Lesson 8.5 *(pages 258–259)*

Find the sum or difference.

1. $\frac{1}{8} + \frac{^-5}{8}$

2. $\frac{2}{3} + \frac{^-1}{6}$

3. $4 + \frac{^-1}{12}$

4. $\frac{^-8}{15} - \frac{^-7}{30}$

5. $\frac{^-11}{12} - \frac{^-5}{6}$

6. $^-4\frac{1}{4} - ^-6\frac{1}{3}$

7. $^-8.19 + 5.46$

8. $^-7.13 + ^-1.54$

9. $5.67 + ^-8.97$

10. $^-3 + ^-2.9 + 8.5$

11. $\frac{^-1}{6} + \frac{2}{3} + \frac{^-5}{12}$

12. $^-3.2 - ^-4.2 + 8.2$

13. $6\frac{1}{9} - 4\frac{3}{4} + 3\frac{5}{12}$

14. $^-4\frac{2}{3} + 1\frac{5}{6} - \frac{^-1}{2}$

15. $6.9 - ^-4.3 + ^-7.5$

Lesson 8.6 *(pages 260–261)*

1. Tom, Jane, and Mary belong to their high-school sports program. One plays football. One plays basketball. The other swims. The football team is all male. Jane rides to school with the swimmer. Identify each person's sport.

2. Mike, Rick, Sue, and Marge have different leisure activities. One sings, one runs, one dances, and one swims. Mike and Rick are taller than the swimmer. Sue and Marge do not sing or dance. Mike and the dancer are cousins. Name Rick's leisure activity.

Lesson 8.7 *(pages 262–263)*

Find the product or quotient.

1. $\dfrac{^-2}{3} \cdot \dfrac{9}{10}$

2. $\dfrac{1}{4} \cdot \dfrac{12}{19}$

3. $\dfrac{6}{7} \cdot \dfrac{^-8}{15}$

4. $\dfrac{^-5}{7} \cdot \dfrac{^-6}{25}$

5. $7 \cdot 4\dfrac{1}{8}$

6. $^-3\dfrac{5}{8} \cdot \dfrac{4}{29}$

7. $^-3\dfrac{1}{3} \cdot 6$

8. $^-5\dfrac{1}{6} \cdot {^-4}\dfrac{2}{3}$

9. $^-9 \div \dfrac{5}{6}$

10. $1\dfrac{7}{8} \div {^-5}\dfrac{1}{2}$

11. $\dfrac{^-3}{5} \div 6$

12. $\dfrac{^-2}{3} \div 8$

13. $0.8 \div {^-0.2}$

14. $^-4.2 \cdot {^-3} \cdot \dfrac{1}{4.2}$

15. $^-23.5 \div 5 \div {^-1}$

16. $^-0.9 \cdot {^-0.8}$

17. $6.74 \div {^-0.2}$

18. $^-5.7 \div 3 \cdot 9.7$

19. $^-495 \div {^-0.5} \div {^-25}$

20. $5.9 \cdot {^-6.3} \cdot \dfrac{2}{6.3}$

21. $8.58 \div 0.3 \div 0.2$

Lesson 8.8 *(pages 266–267)*

Solve the equation. Check your answer.

1. $x + 5 = {^-8}$

2. $^-0.2y = 1.8$

3. $^-9.3 + {^-m} = 6.5$

4. $4x = {^-28}$

5. $^-8c = 24$

6. $8.7t = {^-69.6}$

7. $\dfrac{m}{3} = {^-2}$

8. $\dfrac{x}{^-6} = {^-16}$

9. $\dfrac{2}{3}m = {^-6}$

10. $^-13 + t = 45$

11. $x + 4.2 = 12.1$

12. $n - 3 = {^-48}$

13. $^-4d + 3 = 49$

14. $\dfrac{c}{^-9} = {^-15}$

15. $x - {^-5.2} = 12$

16. $^-56 + n = 40.9$

17. $18t - {^-14} = {^-148}$

18. $\dfrac{3}{4}n = {^-9}$

Lesson 8.9 *(pages 268–269)*

Solve the equation. Check your answer.

1. $2n + 3 = 7$

2. $5x - 9 = {^-19}$

3. $3t - 17 = 5$

4. $\dfrac{x}{2} + 11 = 5$

5. $\dfrac{9}{12}b - 2 = 4$

6. $\dfrac{c}{3} - \dfrac{2}{3} = 4$

7. $^-12m - 9 = 63$

8. $12x - {^-12} = 48$

9. $3t + {^-10} = 8$

10. $\dfrac{n}{25} + 10 = 0$

11. $^-7x - {^-11} = {^-17}$

12. $x + {^-7.8} = {^-6.3}$

13. $\dfrac{c}{6} + 3 = 0$

14. $^-6m = 5\dfrac{2}{3}$

15. $\dfrac{3}{13}t - 12 = {^-9}$

16. $12d - 3d = {^-18}$

17. $4x - 12x + 5 = 43$

18. $3n - 9 = 8n - 51$

19. $\dfrac{x}{^-3} - \dfrac{x}{^-7} = 4$

20. $\dfrac{5}{7}c + 25 = {^-10}$

21. $\dfrac{x}{2} - {^-19} = \dfrac{x}{3} + {^-58}$

Lesson 8.10 *(pages 270–271)*

Solve and graph the inequality.

1. $t + 4 > 1$

2. $t + 9 < 16$

3. $y - 5 > 7$

4. $x + 7 > 16$

5. $m + 0.1 < 2.1$

6. $x - 15 > {}^-22$

7. $m - 15 < 3.5$

8. ${}^-5\frac{1}{2} > b + 1\frac{1}{2}$

9. $\frac{t}{3} - 1 < 1\frac{1}{3}t - 1$

10. $n + 3 < 4$

11. $3.5m - 10 \geq 2.5m + 9$

12. $6x + 2 \geq 14 + 5x$

Match the inequality with the graph.

13. $x \leq 6$

a.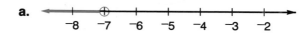

14. $3n \geq 12$

b.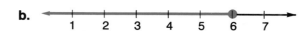

15. $t + 3 < {}^-4$

c.

16. $p - 2 > 0$

d.

Lesson 8.11 *(pages 272–273)*

Jerry and Gwen found a third route to work. Taking this route, they drive
in town at an average speed of 25 mph and on the freeway at an average
speed of 54 mph. Use this information for Exercises 1–4.

1. Jerry and Gwen drive 2.5 miles in town. For how long do they drive in town?

2. Jerry and Gwen spent 90 min on the freeway today. How far did they drive on the freeway?

3. Yesterday Jerry and Gwen caught all green traffic lights and averaged 30 mph. How much time did they save based on Exercise 1?

4. It took Jerry and Gwen 100 min to travel the freeway. Use your answer for Exercise 2 to find their average speed on the freeway.

CHAPTER 9

Lesson 9.1 *(pages 282–283)*

Write the coordinates of the point.

1. A
2. B
3. C
4. D
5. E
6. F
7. N
8. P
9. R

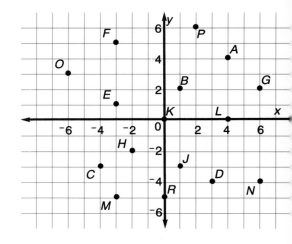

Name the point given by the coordinates.

10. $(0,0)$
11. $(6,2)$
12. $(4,0)$
13. $(^-3,^-5)$
14. $(^-2,^-2)$
15. $(1,^-3)$
16. $(^-6,3)$
17. $(3,^-4)$
18. $(^-4,^-3)$

Lesson 9.2 *(pages 285–286)*

Tell whether the relation is a function. Write *yes* or *no*.

1. $(1,6), (4,2), (3,5), (6,3), (8,^-1)$
2. $(^-1,4), (^-2,5), (^-1,3), (^-3,5), (^-1,^-5)$
3. $(4,3), (3,4), (5,2), (7,3), (^-4,2)$
4. $(6,4), (6,^-1), (6,3), (6,8)$
5. $(5,0), (7,2), (9,3), (5,5), (4,6)$
6. $(^-1,4), (^-2,3), (^-3,2), (^-4,1)$

Write a word rule for each relation.

7. **Cost of Tickets**

Number, x	1	2	3	4	5
Cost, y	$6	$12	$18	$24	$30

8. **Price Increases**

Original price, x	$3	$8	$9	$14	$20
New price, y	$5	$10	$11	$16	$22

Lesson 9.3 *(pages 286–287)*

Make a table of values for each equation. Then write the ordered pairs
that are solutions of each equation.

1. $y = x - 3$
2. $y = x + 5$
3. $y = {}^-3x$
4. $y = 3x - 2$
5. $y = x + {}^-2$
6. $y = x - 6$

Determine whether the ordered pair is a solution of $y = 2x + 2$.
Write *yes* or *no*.

7. $(1,0)$
8. $(^-1,0)$
9. $(3,4)$
10. $(^-3,4)$
11. $(3,8)$
12. $(^-3,^-4)$

Determine whether the ordered pair is a solution of $y = \frac{x}{2} - 3$.
Write *yes* or *no*.

13. $(8,0)$
14. $(6,0)$
15. $(2,^-2)$
16. $(0,3)$
17. $(4,^-1)$
18. $(1,2\frac{1}{2})$

Lesson 9.4 *(pages 288–289)*

Graph the equation. Let $x = {}^-2, {}^-1, 0, 1$, and 2.

1. $y = x + 2$ **2.** $y = x + {}^-3$ **3.** $y = 3x + 1$

4. $y = {}^-2x + 2$ **5.** $y = 4 - x$ **6.** $x + y = 5$

7. $y = x$ **8.** $y = 3x - 2$ **9.** $y - x = {}^-2$

Lesson 9.5 *(pages 290–291)*

The graph shows the distance for a car traveling at 45 mph. Use the graph for Exercises 1–4.

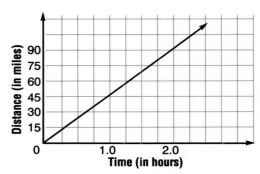

1. What is the approximate distance the car travels in 0.5 hr?

2. What is the approximate distance the car travels in 1.5 hr?

3. About how many hours does it take the car to travel 75 mi?

4. About how many hours does it take the car to travel 15 mi?

Lesson 9.6 *(pages 292–293)*

Find the slope of the line containing the given points.

1. $(3,2), (1,1)$ **2.** $(6,3), ({}^-1,2)$ **3.** $(2,3), ({}^-2,{}^-2)$

4. $({}^-2,2), ({}^-1,{}^-2)$ **5.** $({}^-1,1), (2,{}^-1)$ **6.** $(5,4), (2,1)$

7. $(5,{}^-1), (6,3)$ **8.** $(0,{}^-7), ({}^-3,{}^-8)$ **9.** $(2,{}^-1), (3,{}^-2)$

Tell whether the slope is *positive* or *negative*.

10.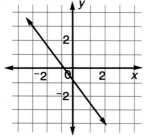

11.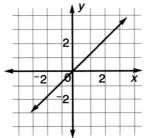

12.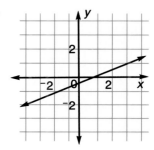

13.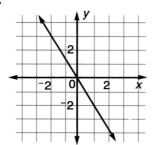

14.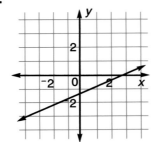

15.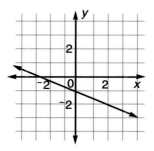

Lesson 9.7 *(pages 296–297)*

Find the solution of the system of equations from its graph.

1. $y = 10 - x$
    $y = x - 4$

2. $y = 2x - 3$
    $y = 7 - 3x$

3. $y = {}^-x + 6$
    $x = 5$

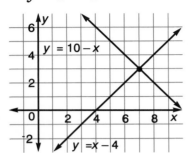 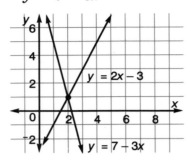 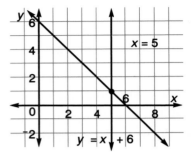

Solve the system by graphing.

4. $y = 10 - x$
    $y = x - 2$

5. $y = x - 5$
    $y = {}^-x + 7$

6. $y = 2x - 1$
    $y = x + 3$

7. $y = x + {}^-4$
    $y = 2 - x$

8. $y = 3x$
    $y = x - 2$

9. $y = 3x - 1$
    $y = x + 1$

Lesson 9.8 *(pages 298–299)*

Graph each inequality.

1. $y > x - 3$

2. $y < x + 3$

3. $y \leq {}^-3x$

4. $y \leq 3x - 2$

5. $y > 2x - 5$

6. $y \geq 4 - x$

7. $y < {}^-5$

8. $x > 3$

9. $y \leq 2 - x$

Determine which of the given points, if any, are solutions of the inequality.

10. $y > x - 2$; $(0,0)$, $({}^-5,{}^-7)$

11. $y < 3x - 2$; $({}^-1,{}^-1)$, $(9,0)$

12. $y < {}^-2x + 1$; $(1,{}^-6)$, $({}^-2,1)$

13. $y > x - 3$; $(4,5)$, $({}^-3,0)$

14. $y \geq x - 4$; $(5,1)$, $(0,{}^-3)$

15. $y \leq 3x + 2$; $(0,3)$, $({}^-2,8)$

Lesson 9.9 *(pages 300–303)*

Copy △*ABC* on a coordinate plane. Perform the given transformation. Give the coordinates of the vertices of the transformation.

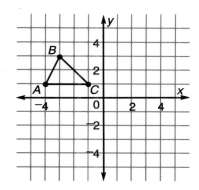

1. Reflect △*ABC* over the *y*-axis.

2. Rotate △*ABC* 180° clockwise, using (0,0) as the point of rotation.

3. Translate △*ABC* 3 units down.

Graph the figure and its image. Then tell whether the transformation is a translation, a reflection, or a rotation.

4. Figure   Image
   $A(1,1)$ $A'(1,^-2)$
   $B(3,2)$ $B'(3,^-1)$
   $C(2,4)$ $C'(2,1)$

5. Figure   Image
   $A(4,^-1)$ $A'(^-1,4)$
   $B(4,^-3)$ $B'(^-3,4)$
   $C(1,^-3)$ $C'(^-3,1)$
   $D(1,^-1)$ $D'(^-1,1)$

Lesson 9.10 *(pages 304–305)*

1. Juan made $21.10 working part-time at two stores. He made $3.80 an hour at one store and $4.50 at another. He worked fewer than 4 hr at each store. For how many hours did Juan work at each store?

2. Celia paid $42 for movie tickets. Tickets cost $6 for adults and $4 for students. If Celia bought fewer than 10 tickets, how many adult tickets did she buy?

3. Allison has $2.30 in dimes and quarters. She has fewer than 10 of each type of coin. Find the number of each type of coin she has.

4. Ted paid $4.35 for pencils and pens. The pencils cost $0.35 each, and the pens cost $0.75 each. He bought fewer than 8 of each. How many pencils did he buy?

CHAPTER 10

Lesson 10.1 *(pages 314–315)*

Find the mean, the median, and the mode of each set of data.

1. 8, 7, 4, 9, 11, 2, 4

2. 33, 29.2, 35.8, 40.1, 25

3. 91, 37, 91, 78, 85, 78

4. 5.9, 6.4, 3.6, 8.7, 9.2

5. 22, 30, 20, 16, 17, 30, 12

6. 2.41, 4.05, 4.05, 3.14, 4.56, 2.25, 5.02

7. 8 ft 2 in., 5 ft 7 in., 5 ft 3 in., 10 ft 4 in., 13 ft 2 in.

8. 2 lb 13 oz, 5 lb, 5 lb 11 oz, 1 lb 10 oz, 4 lb 9 oz, 2 lb 13 oz

Lesson 10.2 *(pages 316–317)*

Make a side-by-side frequency table and a side-by-side histogram for the math test scores. Use intervals of 30–39, 40–49, 50–59, ... Use your frequency table and histogram for Exercises 1–4.

Math Test Scores (in percent)									
Boys					**Girls**				
81	85	90	48	56	75	48	89	62	91
52	36	98	87	74	88	75	62	58	88
76	84	72	64	81	92	45	78	70	60

1. What is the range of scores for the boys? for the girls?

2. What is the mode of scores for all students?

3. How many students have scores in the 80–89% interval or greater?

4. How many boys scored in the 50–59% interval or less?

Lesson 10.3 *(pages 318–319)*

1. Construct a double-line graph for the data in the following table.

Average Monthly Precipitation (in inches)												
Month	Feb.	Mar.	Apr.	May	June	July	Aug.	Sept.	Oct.	Nov.	Dec.	Jan.
Juneau	0.5	1.0	0.6	0.6	0.4	1.2	2.2	2.6	1.9	1.2	1.2	0.9
Oahu	2.5	3.2	1.7	1.1	0.5	0.4	0.6	0.5	1.9	3.3	3.5	3.6

2. A driver is sitting in a car at a stoplight, waiting for the light to turn green. The light turns green and the driver accelerates the car. Which of the graphs fits the situation?

a.
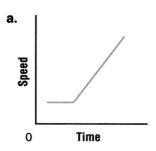

b.
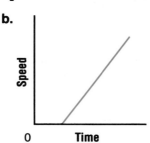

c.
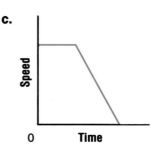

Lesson 10.4 *(pages 320–321)*

Decide whether the graph gives you sufficient data to answer Exercises 1–4. Write *sufficient* or *insufficient*.

1. How much money was made in the first 2 hours?

2. How many items were sold in the first 5 hours?

3. How much money was made between noon and 2 P.M.?

4. Compare money earned in the first hour and the sixth hour.

5. During which hour was the greatest amount of sales made?

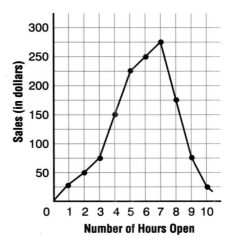

6. How many overtime hours did the employees work?

Lesson 10.5 *(pages 322–323)*

Construct a double-bar graph that compares average daily temperatures for May and December. Use your graph for Exercises 1–5.

1. Which cities have a higher average May temperature than Cores?

2. For which two cities is the average December temperature about the same?

3. Which cities have an average May temperature above 80°F?

4. What city has the smallest range of temperatures between May and December? What is the range?

Average Daily Temperature (°F)		
City	May	December
Ramos	68	25
Cores	75	56
Blate	85	63
Cokey	89	40
Walau	78	21

5. Which city has the greatest range of temperatures between May and December? What is the range?

Lesson 10.6 *(pages 326–327)*

Find the percent of the total park attendance.

1. children   2. women   3. men

Find the central angle measure to represent each. Round to the nearest degree.

4. children   5. women   6. men

Amusement Park Attendance	
Children	300
Women	250
Men	208

7. Construct a circle graph to represent the amusement park attendance.

Lesson 10.7 *(pages 328–329)*

Make a back-to-back stem-and-leaf plot for each set of data.

1. Part-Time Earnings (in dollars)

1991	19	12	15	24	28	37	40	48	15	42	48	20
1992	17	27	19	35	42	56	21	34	17	25	34	22

2. Basketball Scores

Winners	82	98	71	58	99	91	87	90	72	93
Losers	78	95	62	45	97	88	84	86	65	91

3. In Exercise 1, what is the range of earnings for 1991? for 1992?

4. In Exercise 2, what is the median score for winners? for losers?

Lesson 10.8 *(pages 330–331)*

Find the median, the lower extreme, the upper extreme, the lower quartile, and the upper quartile for each set of data.

1.

Football Scores		
35	21	17
42	38	28
15	34	24

2.

Test Scores			
75	84	66	78
88	91	70	84
68	74	85	94

3.

Temperature °F				
84	89	91	75	62
54	65	88	93	78
64	76	80	75	83

Lesson 10.9 *(pages 332–333)*

Make a box-and-whisker graph for each set of data.

1.

Ticket Sales						
8	10	15	16	18	21	14
17	9	14	18	22	20	18

2.

Skateboards Sold							
6	6	12	8	9	14	20	24
	9	10	12	18	17	21	13

3.

Ages of Spectators					
35	32	29	43	67	19
44	47	39	33	30	52

4.

Little League Attendance				
33	29	38	52	64
71	58	66	43	39

5. In Exercise 1, what is the median for the ticket sales?

6. In Exercise 2, what is the lower and upper quartile for skateboard sales?

7. In Exercise 3, what is the upper and lower extreme for the ages?

8. In Exercise 4, what is the median for attendance?

Lesson 10.10 *(pages 334–335)*

Display Kate's weight data in a line
graph. Then use the table and the
graph for Exercises 1–3.

1. What trend summarizes the
   weight data?

2. Can you accurately extrapolate
   Kate's weight for age 25? Why or why
   not?

Kate's Weight							
Age (years)	4	6	8	10	12	14	16
Weight (pounds)	30	40	55	68	90	100	110

3. What is the interpolation of Kate's
   weight at 9 yr and at 13 yr?

Lesson 10.11 *(pages 336–337)*

Draw a scattergram to represent each set of data. Draw the line of best
fit. Write *positive, negative,* or *no correlation* to describe the relationship.

1.

Pages	Hours to Type
10	6
20	8
20	12
30	16
40	18
50	21
60	32
100	46
110	60
120	58

2.

Minutes Between Rest Periods	Pounds Lifted per Minute
0.5	910
2.0	680
2.4	540
3.3	590
4.2	520
4.4	600
5.5	350
7.9	400
9.6	230
13.1	90

Lesson 10.12 *(pages 338–339)*

Identify the type of graph that will best display each set of data.

1.

Family Budget	
Item	Percent
Food	26
Housing	28
Clothing	12
Savings	10
Miscellaneous	24

2.

Profit Record	
Year	Profit
1988	$3.2 million
1989	$1.6 million
1990	$0.4 million
1991	$1.3 million
1992	$2.4 million

3.

Number of Rentals for March
12 15 19 24 18 20 7
8 12 22 14 19 24
18 24 15 13 8 10
9 12 18 24 36 40
8 17 7 6 14 9

CHAPTER 11

Lesson 11.1 *(pages 348–349)*

Find the total number of choices.

1. 3 belts, 5 dresses, 4 scarves
2. 32 flavors, 2 cones
3. 6 curtains, 2 windows
4. 4 drinks, 3 meals
5. 4 songs, 5 arrangements
6. 5 cars, 8 options, 4 colors
7. 3 phones, 4 colors
8. 4 ring styles, 10 stones

Lesson 11.2 *(pages 350–353)*

Find the value. You may use a calculator.

1. $5!$
2. $7!$
3. $8!$
4. $6! - 4!$
5. $4! \cdot 3!$
6. $7! - 5!$
7. $4! + 5!$
8. $\frac{6!}{5!}$
9. $\frac{10!}{(10! - 4!)}$
10. $11!$
11. $6! \cdot 7!$
12. $\frac{9!}{7!}$
13. $5! + 3!$
14. $8! - 6!$
15. $9!$

Find the number of permutations. You may use a calculator.

16. $_4P_3$
17. $_5P_2$
18. $_{14}P_4$
19. $_6P_3$
20. $_8P_5$
21. $_{10}P_2$
22. $_{13}P_4$
23. $_{15}P_5$
24. $_{200}P_2$
25. $_{69}P_3$
26. $_5P_3$
27. $_{21}P_4$
28. $_9P_5$
29. $_{400}P_3$
30. $_{35}P_2$

Solve.

31. In how many ways can a student council representative and an alternate be chosen from a class of 31 students?

32. In how many different ways can 8 high school cheerleaders be arranged in a line?

Lesson 11.3 *(pages 354–355)*

Find the number of combinations.

1. There are 7 players. How many teams of 4 can be formed?

2. There are 10 students. How many groups of 3 can be formed?

3. There are 8 ice cream flavors. How many cones with 3 flavors can be made?

4. There are 9 girls in a debate club. How many teams of 4 girls can be formed?

Find the number of combinations. You may use a calculator.

5. $_5C_2$
6. $_6C_4$
7. $_9C_3$
8. $_{10}C_4$
9. $_8C_5$
10. $_4C_3$
11. $_7C_5$
12. $_{13}C_9$
13. $_{14}C_{10}$
14. $_{16}C_8$
15. $_8C_3$
16. $_{13}C_2$
17. $_{21}C_4$
18. $_{11}C_3$
19. $_{12}C_5$

Lesson 11.4 *(pages 356–357)*

Spin the spinner. Find each probability.

1. P(F)

2. P(A, B, or C)

3. P(G or B)

4. P(A, E, F, or G)

5. P(not A)

6. P(not H and not F)

7. P(not B, not C, and not D)

8. P(A, C, E, or G)

9. P(not E, not F, not G, not H)

10. P(B, C, D, E, or F)

Roll a number cube numbered 7 to 12. Find each probability.

11. P(10)

12. P(7 or 8)

13. P(odd number)

14. P(number < 10)

15. P(not 9)

16. P(number > 9)

17. P(number > 12)

18. P(multiple of 2)

19. P(multiple of 3)

20. P(number < 13)

Lesson 11.5 *(pages 358–359)*

Toss 6 coins. Find the probability. Use the numbers and their sum from row 6 of Pascal's triangle.

1. P(2 heads)

2. P(3 heads)

3. P(6 heads)

Toss 7 coins. Find the probability.

4. P(4 heads)

5. P(5 heads)

6. P(8 heads)

Toss 8 coins. Find the probability.

7. P(2 heads)

8. P(4 heads)

9. P(5 heads)

10. P(3 heads)

11. P(8 heads)

12. P(7 heads)

Lesson 11.6 *(pages 360–361)*

Use Pascal's triangle to solve.

1. A book club with 10 members wants to elect 5 officers. How many combinations of 5 officers can be elected from the 10 members?

2. An ecology club with 8 members wants to elect 2 spokespersons. How many combinations of 2 spokespersons can be elected from the 8 members?

3. At the airport 10 people want to get on Flight 456, but only 4 seats are available. How many combinations of 4 persons can there be from 10 people?

4. How many combinations of 5 people can there be from 9 people?

Lesson 11.7 *(pages 362–363)*

The random numbers 1–6 in the table were generated by a computer.
Use the table for Exercises 1–3.

1. You are playing a game using a
   number cube. Use the table to
   simulate 100 rolls. How many rolls
   will it take before you get all the
   numbers 1–6?

2. Find the number of times the
   number 3 was rolled. Write a ratio
   comparing your answer to the total
   number of rolls.

3. How does your ratio in Exercise 2
   compare with the mathematical
   probability of rolling a 3?

100 Random Numbers

4	5	1	2	3	5	2	2	3	1
5	4	6	2	1	4	1	1	4	5
2	1	1	4	4	1	1	3	3	2
2	6	5	5	2	4	6	6	2	6
2	1	1	6	2	2	2	6	6	5
6	6	5	6	6	1	5	2	3	6
5	3	5	4	5	6	5	3	4	3
1	3	6	1	6	4	6	4	1	3
3	2	1	2	5	6	6	3	5	4
5	1	3	3	3	1	4	5	4	6

Lesson 11.8 *(pages 364–365)*

A baseball player has 72 hits out of 180 pitches. Use this information for
Exercises 1–4.

1. What is the experimental probability
   of the baseball player hitting the
   next pitch?

2. What is the experimental probability
   of the baseball player not hitting the
   next pitch?

3. How many pitches can the baseball
   player expect to hit during the next
   20 tries?

4. How many misses can the baseball
   player expect during the next 20
   tries?

5. How many pitches can the baseball
   player expect to hit during the next
   50 tries?

6. How many misses can the baseball
   player expect during the next
   50 tries?

Lesson 11.9 *(pages 368–369)*

A bag contains 5 green marbles, 1 clear marble, 2 red marbles, and
2 black marbles. One marble is drawn and replaced. Another marble
is drawn.

Find the probability.

1. P(green, clear)

2. P(clear, black)

3. P(green, black)

4. P(red, red, black)

5. P(black, black)

6. P(red, green)

7. P(green, clear, red)

8. P(red, clear)

9. P(red, red, green)

10. P(green, clear, red, black)

11. P(green, green)

12. P(green, green, clear, red, black)

Lesson 11.10 (pages 370–371)

A drawer contains 6 red shirts, 4 blue shirts, and 8 white shirts. The shirts are selected at random, one at a time, and not replaced.

Find the probabilities.

1. P(red, then blue)

2. P(white, then red)

3. P(red, then white, then blue)

4. P(red, then red, then white)

5. P(blue, then not blue)

6. P(white, then blue, then blue)

7. P(blue, then white)

8. P(white, white, white)

Lesson 11.11 (pages 372–373)

Use the Venn diagram for Exercises 1–5.

1. How many students speak French? Spanish?

2. How many students speak both French and Spanish?

3. How many students speak French but not Spanish?

4. How many students speak Spanish but not French?

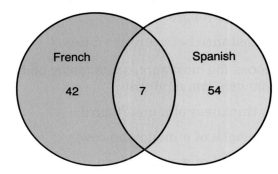

5. How many students speak French or Spanish but not both?

Lesson 11.12 (pages 374–375)

Solve.

1. Coleen has four stuffed animals in a row on a shelf. Neither the duck nor the bear is sitting next to the rabbit. The bear is sitting just to the left of the duck and just to the right of the dog. Write the arrangement from left to right.

2. Phillip places nine nickels in a row on top of his desk. He then replaces every other coin with a penny. Then he replaces every third coin with a dime. What is the value of the nine coins on his desk?

3. Jody has $0.66 in coins. Linda asked her for change for a quarter, but Judy did not have the correct change. What coins did Judy have?

4. Buck tells a joke to four persons, each of whom tells two more persons. Each of these tells one more person. How many persons have been told Buck's joke?

5. Jan, Charles, and Luis are friends. One is a drama student, one is a school newspaper editor, one is a soccer player. Luis and the soccer player ride the same bus. Charles and the editor have the same lunch period. Luis is not a drama student. Who is the editor?

6. There are four children in the Levin family: Chris, Jon, Jeff, and Susan. Jeff is older than Susan. Jon is not the youngest. Jeff is older than Jon. Susan is older than Chris. Write in order from oldest to youngest.

CHAPTER 12

Lesson 12.1 (pages 384–385)

Measure each line segment, using the most appropriate metric unit of length. Include both the number and the unit in your answer.

1. —

2. _____

Choose the most appropriate customary unit of length for each situation. Write *in., ft, yd,* or *mi.*

3. length of a piece of fabric

4. Rita's height

5. distance between two cities

Choose the most appropriate metric unit of length for each situation. Write *mm, cm, m,* or *km.*

6. thickness of a credit card

7. length of a magazine cover

8. height of a street lamp

Lesson 12.2 (pages 386–387)

Write *exact* or *estimate* to describe each measurement.

1. height stated on a driver's license

2. length of a hiking trail

3. Which is the most reasonable estimate of a giraffe's height?

   a. 6 km   **b.** 6 mm   **c.** 6 cm   **d.** 6 m

4. Which is the most reasonable estimate of the door's height?

   a. 210 mm   **b.** 210 cm   **c.** 210 km   **d.** 210 m

Lesson 12.3 (pages 388–391)

Give the precision of each measurement.

1. 4 in.   **2.** $3\frac{1}{3}$ cm   **3.** 100 mm   **4.** $3\frac{1}{6}$ yd

5. 3.9 m   **6.** $11\frac{1}{4}$ mi   **7.** 9.81 km   **8.** 4 cm

Find the greatest possible error of each measurement.

9. 3 in.   **10.** 100 yd   **11.** 15 m   **12.** 9 in.

13. $3\frac{1}{2}$ ft   **14.** 0.4 km   **15.** $4\frac{1}{5}$ mi   **16.** 0.57 cm

17. 8.7 cm   **18.** $2\frac{5}{6}$ in.   **19.** 3 mm   **20.** $4\frac{1}{10}$ mi

More Practice

Lesson 12.4 *(pages 392–393)*

Find each sum or difference. Use rounding to express the answer with the correct number of significant digits.

1. 3.05 mm + 5 mm

2. 4.125 m + 5.1 m

3. 8.375 m − 4 m

4. 3.210 m − 1.02 m

Find each product or quotient. Use rounding to express the answer with the correct number of significant digits.

5. 4.3 m × 1.9 m

6. 2.85 m × 6.8 m

7. 8 m ÷ 3.42 m

8. 6.49 m ÷ 2.3 m

9. 6.059 cm · 2.1 cm

10. 55.81 m ÷ 6.84 m

Lesson 12.5 *(pages 394–395)*

Make a model.

1. How many 3-in. square tiles are required for making a 12-in. by 18-in. hot plate?

2. How many 1-ft square tiles are required for covering a 12-ft by 13-ft kitchen floor?

3. How many 2-in. equilateral triangular tiles are required for making a regular hexagon whose sides measure 6 in.?

4. How many 1-in. equilateral triangular tiles are required for making a 9-in. equilateral triangle?

5. How many 1-in. equilateral triangular tiles are required for making a regular hexagon whose sides measure 10 in.?

6. How many 2-in. equilateral triangular tiles are required for making a 12-inch equilateral triangle?

Lesson 12.6 *(pages 396–397)*

Find the perimeter of each regular polygon.

1.

3 in.

2.

1.5 in.

3.

2 in.

The perimeter of each polygon is given. Find the missing length.

4. *P* = 12 in.

5. *P* = 24 in.

6. *P* = 17.8 cm

4. 3 in., a, 4 in.

5. 6 in., w

6. a, 2 cm, 2.3 cm, 5.4 cm, 4.8 cm

Lesson 12.7 *(pages 400–402)*

Find the circumference to the nearest hundredth. Use 3.14 for π.

1. $d = 3.15$ m   **2.** $r = 0.28$ m   **3.** $d = 1.01$ m   **4.** $r = 0.89$ m

5. $d = 8.3$ m   **6.** $r = 2$ in.   **7.** $r = 4.75$ m   **8.** $d = 0.5$ m

9. $d = 78$ cm   **10.** $r = 102$ mm   **11.** $d = 38$ ft   **12.** $r = 42$ in.

Find the circumference. Use $\frac{22}{7}$ for π.

13. $r = 7$ in.   **14.** $r = 84$ m   **15.** $d = 35$ in.   **16.** $d = 105$ m

17. $d = 63$ cm   **18.** $d = 49$ mm   **19.** $r = 14$ cm   **20.** $r = 91$ cm

21. $r = 56$ cm   **22.** $d = 70$ m   **23.** $d = 91$ mm   **24.** $r = 21$ in.

Lesson 12.8 *(pages 402–403)*

Find the area of each rectangle.

1. $l = 4$ m, $w = 9$ m   **2.** $l = 6$ m, $w = 8$ m   **3.** $l = 0.5$ m, $w = 4$ m

4. $l = 1.2$ m, $w = 5$ m   **5.** $l = 4.9$ m, $w = 3.5$ m   **6.** $l = 6.1$ m, $w = 5.1$ m

Find the length of each rectangle.

7. $A = 192$ ft^2, $w = 12$ ft   **8.** $A = 43.2$ m^2, $w = 4.8$ m   **9.** $A = 840$ in.^{2}, $w = 40$ in.

Find the area of each parallelogram.

10. $b = 11$ m, $h = 12$ m   **11.** $b = 13$ m, $h = 20$ m   **12.** $b = 1.4$ m, $h = 2.2$ m

13. $b = 15$ m, $h = 18$ m   **14.** $b = 14.8$ m, $h = 3.9$ m   **15.** $b = 5.3$ m, $h = 9.4$ m

Find the height of each parallelogram.

16. $A = 143$ m^2, $b = 11$ m   **17.** $A = 800$ cm^2, $b = 25$ cm   **18.** $A = 171$ m^2, $b = 9.5$ m

Lesson 12.9 *(pages 404–405)*

Find the area of each triangle.

1. $b = 8$ cm, $h = 9$ cm   **2.** $b = 8$ in., $h = 11$ in.   **3.** $b = 6.5$ m, $h = 4.2$ m

4. $b = 7$ m, $h = 4.5$ m   **5.** $b = 19$ cm, $h = 17$ cm   **6.** $b = 9.1$ m, $h = 7.8$ m

7. $b = 3.6$ cm, $h = 2.9$ cm   **8.** $b = 14$ m, $h = 12.4$ m   **9.** $b = 21.3$ m, $h = 14.2$ m

Find the area of each trapezoid.

10. $h = 8$ m, $b_1 = 3$ m, $b_2 = 6$ m   **11.** $h = 10.6$ m, $b_1 = 4.5$ m, $b_2 = 4.7$ m

12. $h = 9$ cm, $b_1 = 2$ cm, $b_2 = 5$ cm   **13.** $h = 20$ cm, $b_1 = 10$ cm, $b_2 = 3.7$ cm

14. $h = 4.2$ m, $b_1 = 5.3$ m, $b_2 = 4.6$ m   **15.** $h = 9.2$ m, $b_1 = 10$ m, $b_2 = 7.4$ m

Lesson 12.10 *(pages 406–407)*

Find the area of each circle to the nearest hundredth.
Use 3.14 for π.

1.

15 m

2.

4 cm

3.

12.6 m

4. $r = 34$ m

5. $r = 8.2$ cm

6. $d = 22$ m

Find the area of the shaded region.

7.

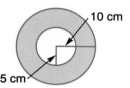

10 cm

5 cm

8.

8 m

9.

6 in.

Lesson 12.11 *(pages 408–409)*

Use the formula $R = \dfrac{Ph}{3} - w$ for Exercises 1–4.

1. A bedroom is 4 m wide and 6 m long, with a 3-m ceiling. There are 2 doors and 2 windows. How many rolls of wallpaper are needed?

2. A family room is 5 m wide and 7 m long, with a 2.5-m ceiling. There are 3 doors and 4 windows. How many rolls of wallpaper are needed?

3. An office is 3.5 m wide and 5.5 m long, with a 2.5-m ceiling. There are 2 windows and 1 door. One roll of wallpaper costs $12.99. What is the total cost for the wallpaper?

4. A bathroom is 2 m wide and 3 m long, with a 3-m ceiling. There is 1 door. One roll of wallpaper costs $14.99. What is the total cost for the wallpaper?

CHAPTER 13

Lesson 13.1 *(pages 418–419)*

Write the name of the polyhedron formed by the pattern.

1.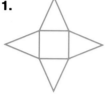

2.

3.

4.

5.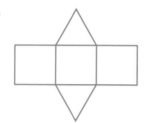

6.

Lesson 13.2 *(pages 420–421)*

Name each three-dimensional figure.

1.

2.

3.

4. grape   **5.** clown's hat   **6.** pen

Write *cylinder, cone,* or *sphere* for each description.

7. curved appearance from any view

8. two circular bases

9. one circular base

Lesson 13.3 *(pages 422–423)*

Use one-point perspective to draw each view.
Do not show hidden lines.

1. Draw a right view.   **2.** Draw a left view.

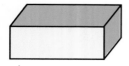 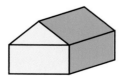

Lesson 13.4 *(pages 424–425)*

Paul makes specialty card boxes. Use the table on page 424 to solve
Exercises 1–4.

1. Paul makes a box that is shaped like a hexagonal prism. How many pieces of cardboard will he need?

2. Paul makes a box that is shaped like an octagonal pyramid. How many pieces of cardboard will he need?

3. Paul makes a box that is shaped like a septagonal prism. The bases have seven sides. If he seals all the edges except three at the top, how many edges does he seal?

4. Paul makes a box that is shaped like a nonagonal pyramid. The base has nine sides. If he puts a fastener on each vertex, how many fasteners will he need?

Lesson 13.5 *(pages 426–427)*

Find the surface area of each prism or pyramid.

1.
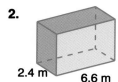
6 cm   12 cm
6 cm

2.
4.9 m
2.4 m   6.6 m

3.
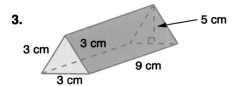
5 cm
3 cm   3 cm
9 cm
3 cm

Find the surface area. Round to the nearest tenth.

4. cube
   side = 9.8 cm

5. rectangular prism
   $l = 15$ in., $w = 12$ in., $h = 40$ in.

6. square pyramid
   side = 7 cm
   slant height = 12.3 cm

7. cube
   side = 6.25 cm

Lesson 13.6 *(pages 430–431)*

Find the surface area. Use $\pi = 3.14$.

1.
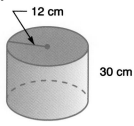
12 cm
30 cm

2.
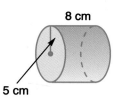
8 cm
5 cm

3.
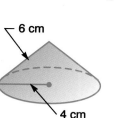
6 cm
4 cm

4.

8 cm
5 cm

Find the surface area. Use $\pi = 3.14$.
Round to the nearest tenth.

5. cylinder
   $r = 7$ in.,
   $h = 10$ in.

6. cylinder
   $d = 42$ m,
   $h = 4$ m

7. cone
   $r = 10$ m,
   $l = 7$ m

8. cone
   $r = 12$ m,
   $l = 30$ m

Lesson 13.7 *(pages 432–433)*

Find each volume.

1.

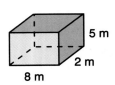
5 m
2 m
8 m

2.

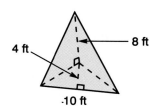
4 ft
8 ft
·10 ft

3.

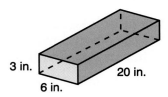
3 in.
6 in.
20 in.

4.

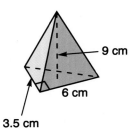
9 cm
6 cm
3.5 cm

5.

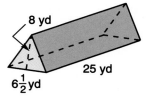
8 yd
25 yd
$6\frac{1}{2}$ yd

6.

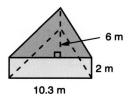
6 m
2 m
10.3 m

Lesson 13.8 *(pages 434–435)*

Find the volume. Use $\pi = 3.14$, and round to the nearest whole number.

1.

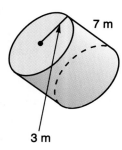
8 cm
18 cm

2.

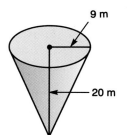
9 m
20 m

3.

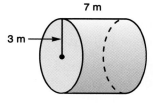
7 m
3 m

4.

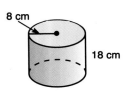
7 m
3 m

5.

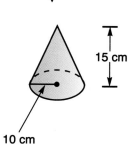
15 cm
10 cm

6.

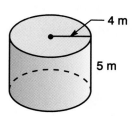
4 m
5 m

Lesson 13.9 *(pages 436–437)*

Copy and complete the table for each rectangular prism of water.

	Length	Width	Height	Volume	Capacity	Mass
1.	10 cm	8 cm	8 cm	■	■	■
2.	30 cm	40 cm	60 cm	■	■	■
3.	6 cm	10 cm	5 cm	■	■	■
4.	20 cm	30 cm	20 cm	■	■	■
5.	17 cm	10 cm	25 cm	■	■	■

Lesson 13.10 *(pages 438–439)*

Find the volume of each sphere to the nearest whole number.
Use the formula $V = \frac{4}{3}\pi r^3$. Use 3.14 for π.

1.
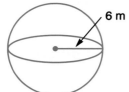
6 m

2.
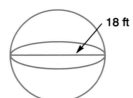
18 ft

3.
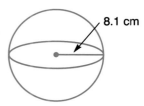
8.1 cm

Use the formula $V = \frac{4}{3}\pi r^3$ for Exercises 4–7. Round your answer
to the nearest whole number.

4. A beach ball has a 38-cm diameter.
What is the volume?

5. The new spherical water tank has a
radius of 50 feet. What volume of
water can it hold?

6. A world globe has a diameter of
200 cm. What is the volume?

7. A bowl has the shape of half a sphere.
Its diameter is 25 cm. What volume
of juice can it hold?

CHAPTER 14

Lesson 14.1 *(pages 448–449)*

Name the hypotenuse and the legs of each right triangle.

1.

2.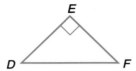

3.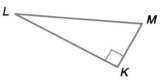

Decide whether the three sides form a right triangle. Write *yes* or *no*.

4. 10 m, 15 m, 18 m **5.** 25 m, 27 m, 37 m

6. 12 m, 16 m, 20 m **7.** 21 m, 28 m, 35 m

Lesson 14.2 *(pages 450–451)*

Find the unknown length to the nearest tenth.

1.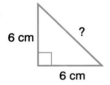

2.

3.

4.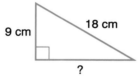

5.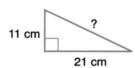

6.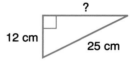

7.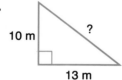

8.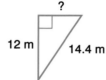

9.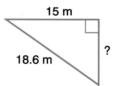

Lesson 14.3 *(pages 452–453)*

Use Figure A to find the unknown length.

1. $c = 16, a = $ ____?____

2. $a = 10, c = $ ____?____

3. $a = 9, c = $ ____?____

4. $c = 14, a = $ ____?____

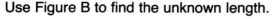

Figure A

Use Figure B to find the unknown length.

5. $c = 20, a = $ ____?____

6. $c = 26, b = $ ____?____

7. $c = 30, a = $ ____?____ , $b = $ ____?____

8. $c = 6, a = $ ____?____

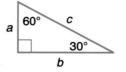

Figure B

Lesson 14.4 *(pages 454–455)*

Angela writes 20 checks a month. She has three choices of checking accounts. Use the choices for Exercises 1–4.

Choice 1: Cost is $8.00 per month with no check fee.

Choice 2: Cost is $3.00 per month and $0.20 fee per check written.

Choice 3: Cost is $4.50 per month and $0.15 fee per check written.

1. Which choice is the least expensive for Angela?

2. Angela now writes 50 checks per month. Which choice is the least expensive?

3. What is the difference between the cost of Choice 1 and Choice 3 if Angela writes 10 checks per month?

4. If Angela writes only 5 checks per month, which choice is the least expensive?

Lesson 14.5 *(pages 457–458)*

Tell whether the figures in each pair are similar. Write *yes* or *no*.

1.   **2.**   **3.**

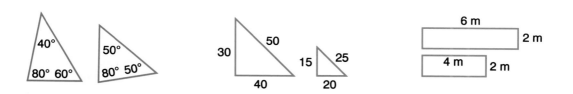

Each pair of triangles is similar. Find x.

4.   **5.**

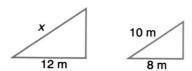   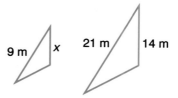

Lesson 14.6 *(pages 460–461)*

Find the trigonometric ratio to the nearest hundredth.
You may use a calculator.

1. $\tan 15° = \dfrac{1.98}{\blacksquare} = \blacksquare$

2. $\cos 15° = \dfrac{\blacksquare}{7.2} = \blacksquare$

3. $\sin 15° = \dfrac{\blacksquare}{\blacksquare} = \blacksquare$

4. $\tan 75° = \dfrac{\blacksquare}{\blacksquare} = \blacksquare$

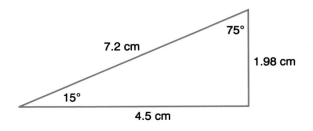

Lesson 14.7 *(pages 462–463)*

Find *x* to the nearest tenth. Use the table on page H104.

1.
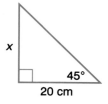

2.
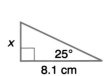

3.
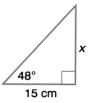

4.
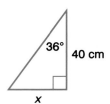

5.
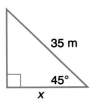

6.
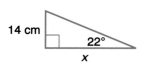

Lesson 14.8 *(pages 464–465)*

Find *x* to the nearest tenth. Use the table on page H104.

1.

2.
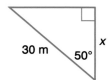

3.
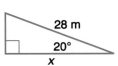

4.

5.
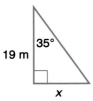

6.
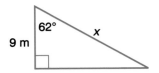

Lesson 14.9 *(pages 466–467)*

1. A square room has an area of 144 ft^2. Darlene drew a diagonal line through the room. How long is the line to the nearest foot?

2. Nadir's mainsail is 15 ft high, and his secondary sail is 9 ft high. The mainsail's shadow is 50 ft. How long is the secondary sail's shadow?

3. Jessica owns a 3-row beaded necklace. Each row has 9 beads. The first row pattern is red, white, red, ... The pattern in the second row is blue, white, blue, . . . , and the pattern in the third row is red, blue, red, ... How many red beads, white beads, and blue beads are in the necklace?

4. Arnold put a desk 4 ft long in front of a wall 12 ft long. The distance from the right end of the desk to the right end of the wall is 3 times the distance from the left end of the desk to the left end of the wall. How far is the right end of the desk from the right end of the wall?

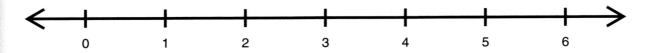

Learning Resources

The Learning Resources can be traced, colored, and cut out. These resources can be used as tools to help you understand math concepts and solve problems.

Number Lines

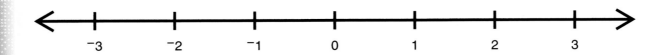

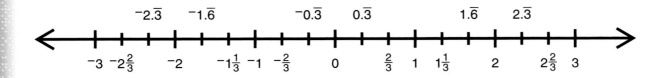

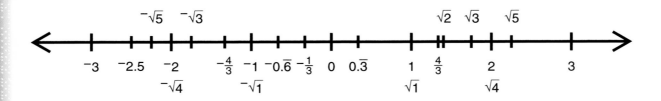

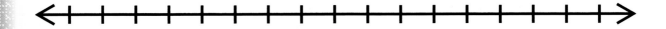

Fraction Circles

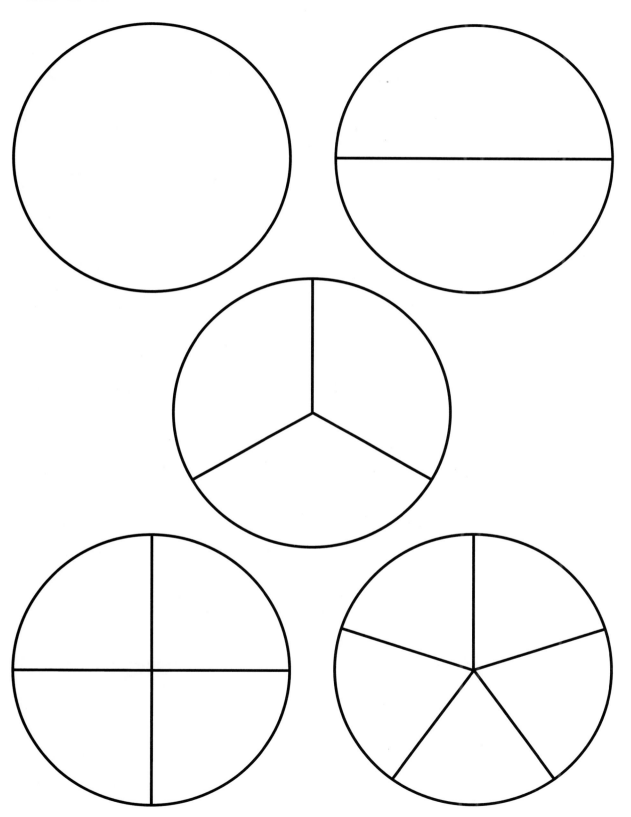

Fraction Circles

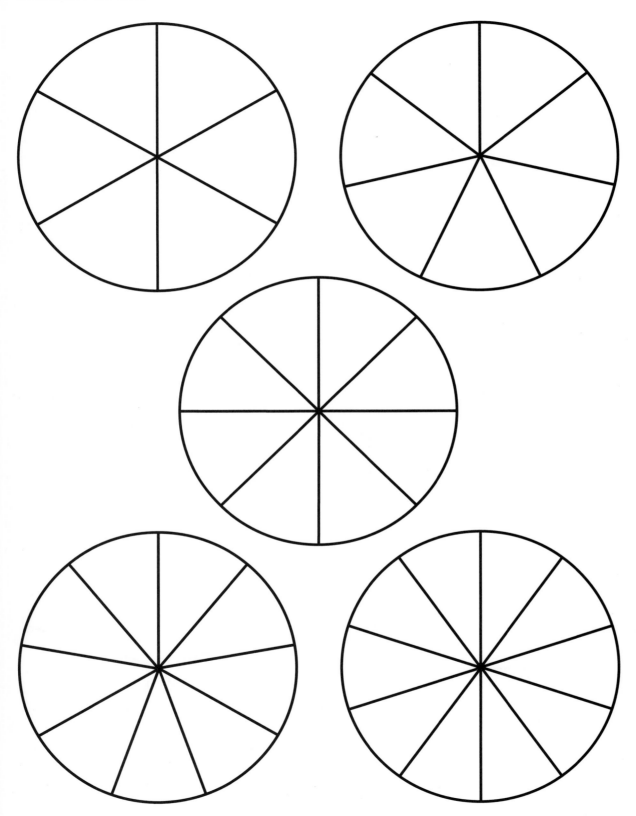

Fraction Bars

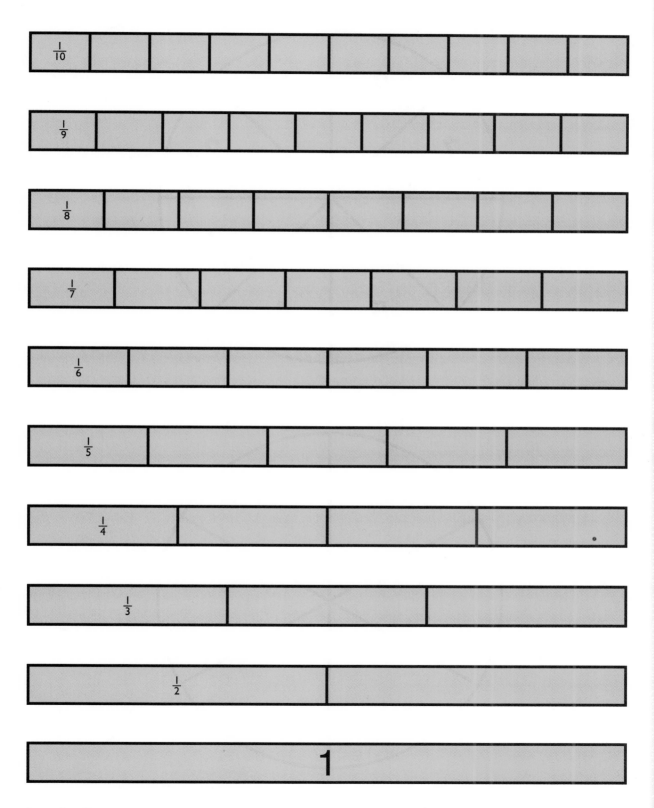

Spinners

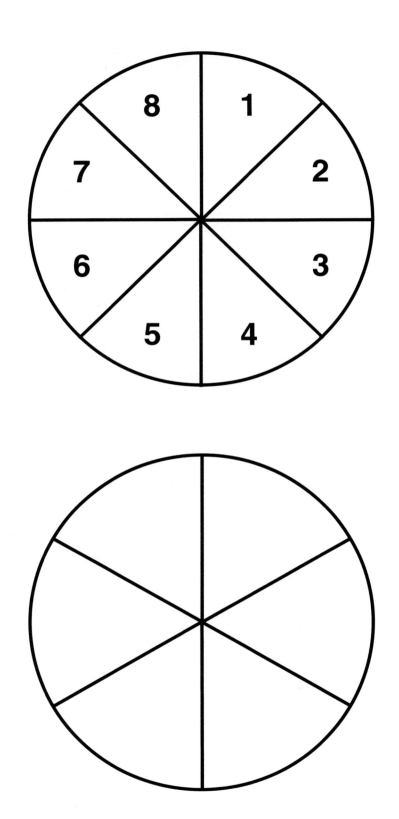

Solid Figure

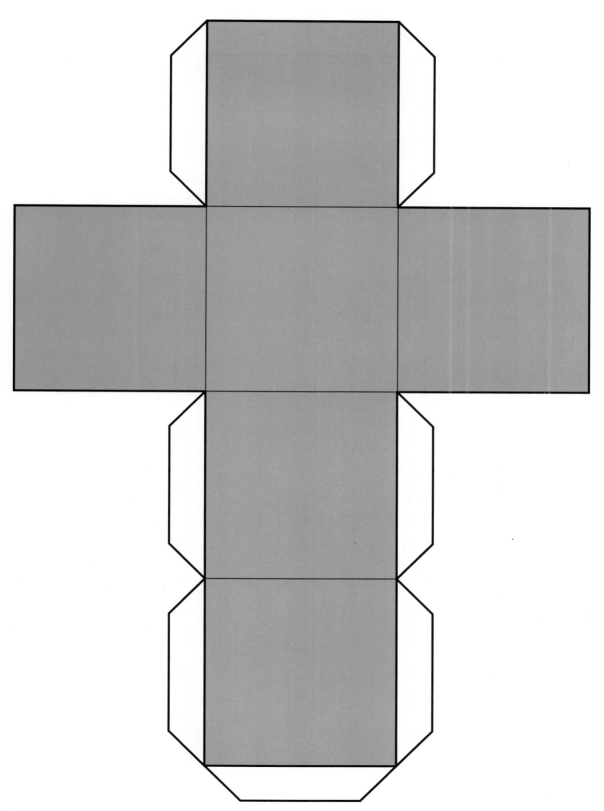

Solid Figure

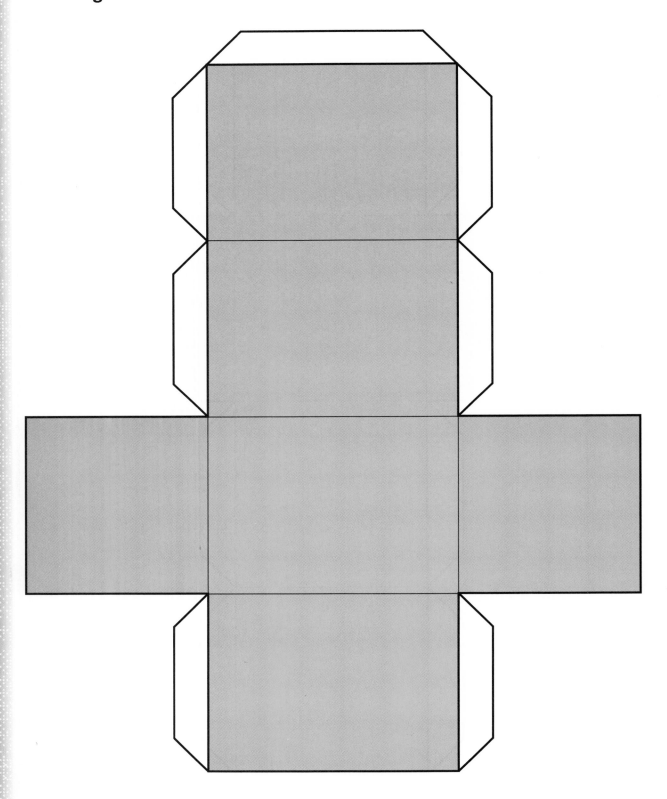

Solid Figure

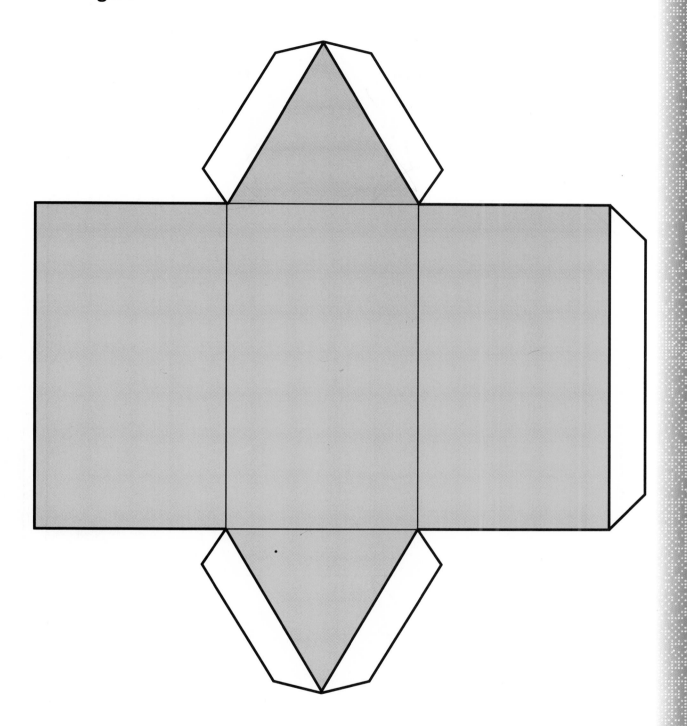

Solid Figure

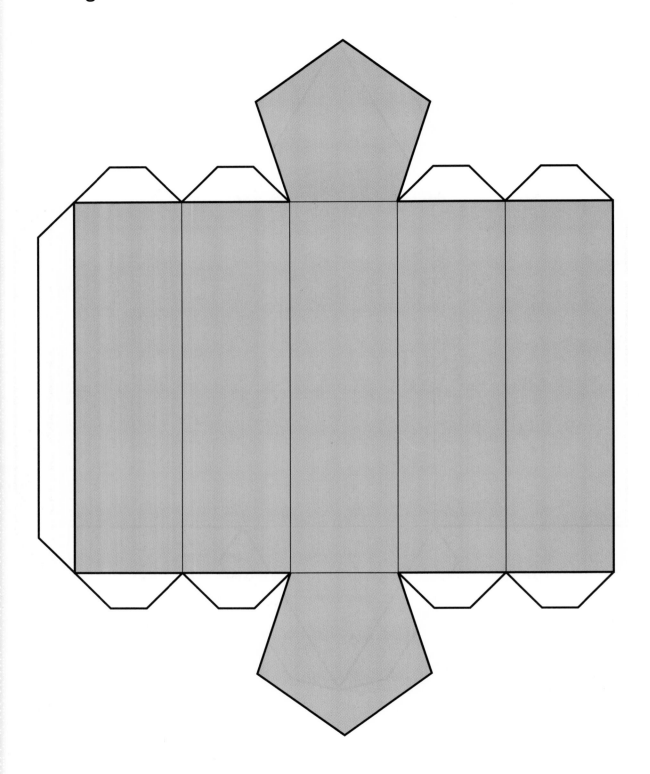

Solid Figure

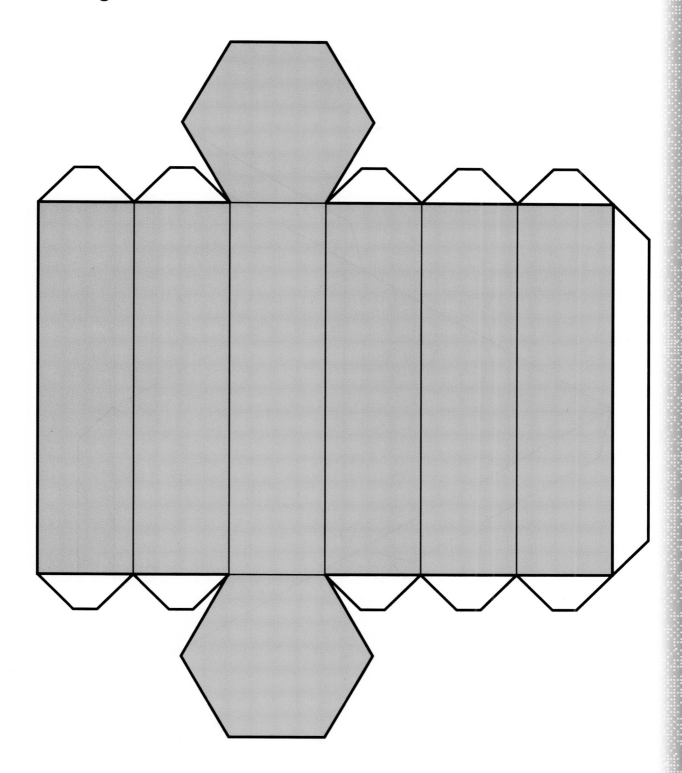

Solid Figure

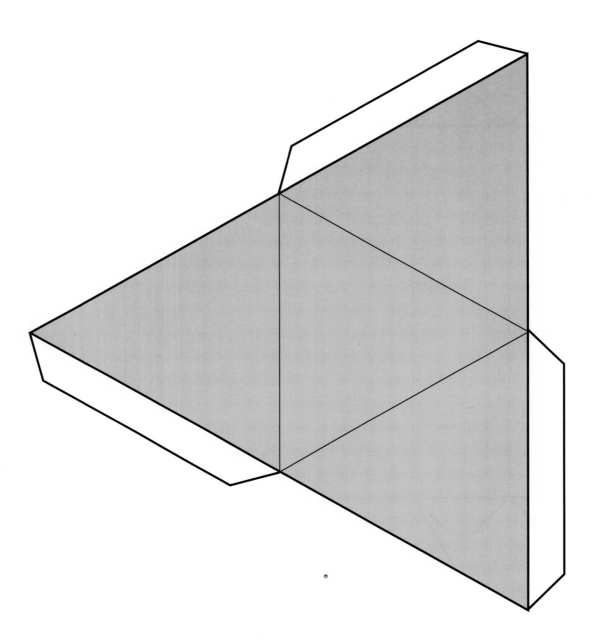

Solid Figure

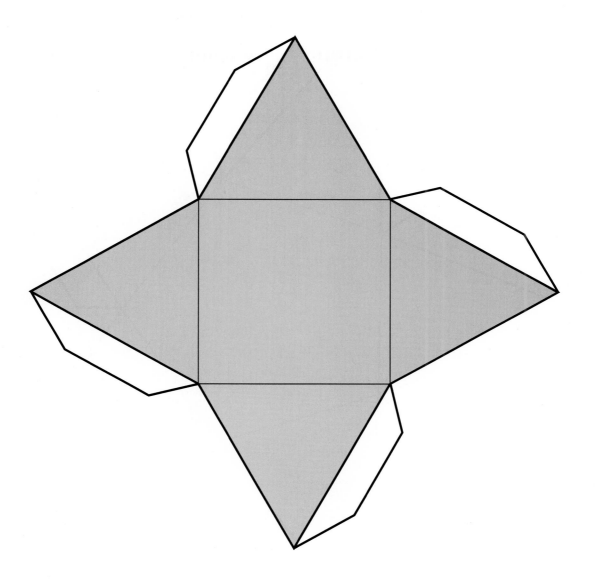

Solid Figure

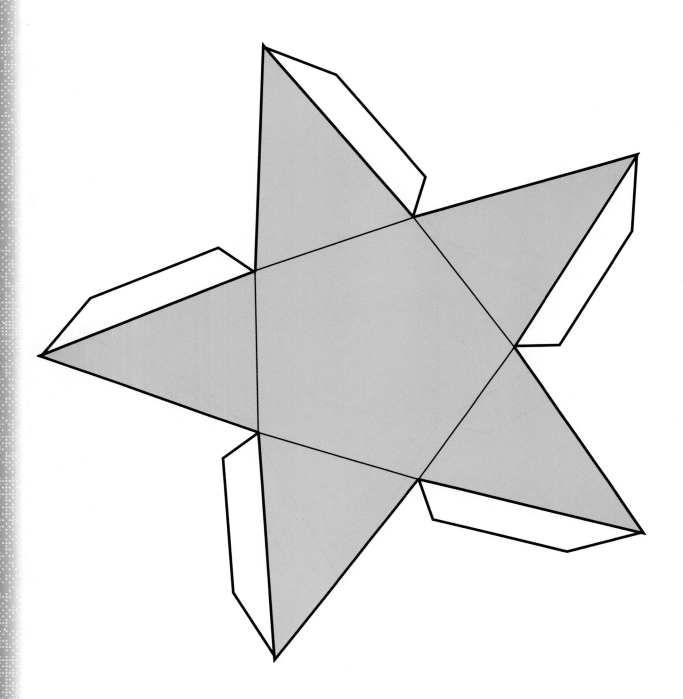

Solid Figure

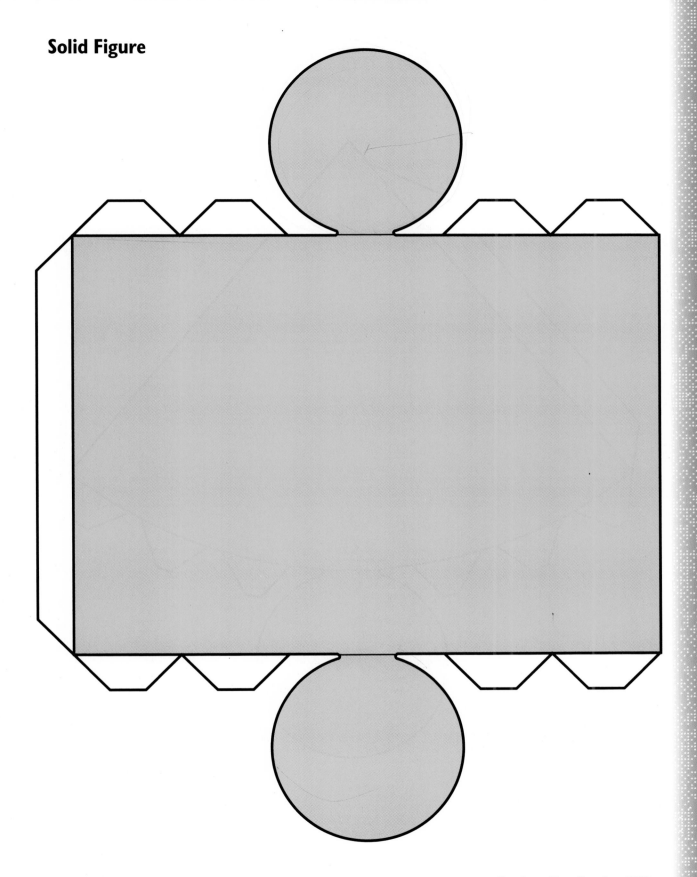

Solid Figure

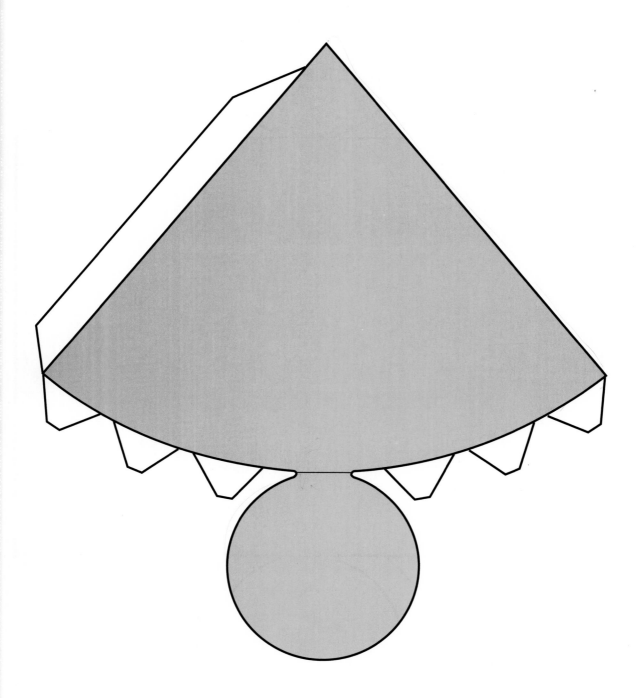

Table of Measures

Metric Units

LENGTH
1 millimeter (mm) = 0.001 meter (m)
1 centimeter (cm) = 0.01 meter
1 decimeter (dm) = 0.1 meter
1 kilometer (km) = 1,000 meters

MASS
1 milligram (mg) = 0.001 gram (g)
1 centigram (cg) = 0.01 gram
1 decigram (dg) = 0.1 gram
1 kilogram (kg) = 1,000 grams

CAPACITY
1 milliliter (mL) = 0.001 liter (L)
1 centiliter (cL) = 0.01 liter
1 deciliter (dL) = 0.1 liter
1 kiloliter (kL) = 1,000 liters

VOLUME/CAPACITY/
MASS FOR WATER
1 cubic centimeter (cm^3) → 1 milliliter → 1 gram
1,000 cubic centimeters → 1 liter → 1 kilogram

Customary Units

LENGTH
1 foot (ft) = 12 inches (in.)
1 yard (yd) = 36 inches
1 yard = 3 feet
1 mile (mi) = 5,280 feet
1 mile = 1,760 yards
1 nautical mile = 6,076.115 feet

WEIGHT
1 pound (lb) = 16 ounces (oz)
1 ton (T) = 2,000 pounds

CAPACITY
1 cup (c) = 8 fluid ounces (fl oz)
1 pint (pt) = 2 cups
1 quart (qt) = 2 pints
1 quart = 4 cups
1 gallon (gal) = 4 quarts

Time

1 minute (min) = 60 seconds (sec)
1 hour (hr) = 60 minutes
1 day = 24 hours
1 week (wk) = 7 days
1 year (yr) = 12 months (mo)
1 year = 52 weeks
1 year = 365 days

FORMULAS

PERIMETER	Polygon	P = sum of the lengths of the sides
	Rectangle	$P = 2(l + w)$
	Square	$P = 4s$
CIRCUMFERENCE	Circle	$C = 2\pi r$, or $C = \pi d$
AREA	Circle	$A = \pi r^2$
	Parallelogram	$A = bh$
	Rectangle	$A = lw$
	Square	$A = s^2$
	Trapezoid	$A = \frac{1}{2}h(b_1 + b_2)$
	Triangle	$A = \frac{1}{2}bh$
SURFACE AREA	Cone	$S = \pi r^2 + \pi rl$
	Cylinder	$S = 2(\pi r^2) + (2\pi rh)$
VOLUME	Cone	$V = \frac{1}{3}Bh$, or $V = \frac{1}{3}\pi r^2 h$
	Cylinder	$V = Bh$, or $V = \pi r^2 h$
	Cube	$V = e^3$
	Prism	$V = Bh$
	Pyramid	$V = \frac{1}{3}Bh$
	Sphere	$V = \frac{4}{3}\pi r^3$
OTHER	Diameter	$d = 2r$
	Pythagorean Property	$c^2 = a^2 + b^2$
TRIGONOMETRIC RATIOS	sine of $\angle A$	$\sin A = \dfrac{\text{length of side opposite } \angle A}{\text{length of hypotenuse}}$
	cosine of $\angle A$	$\cos A = \dfrac{\text{length of side adjacent } \angle A}{\text{length of hypotenuse}}$
	tangent of $\angle A$	$\tan A = \dfrac{\text{length of side opposite } \angle A}{\text{length of side adjacent } \angle A}$
CONSUMER	Distance traveled	$d = rt$
	Interest (simple)	$I = prt$

SYMBOLS

$<$	is less than		$\angle ABC$	angle ABC
$>$	is greater than		$m\angle A$	measure of $\angle A$
$\leq$	is less than or equal to		$\triangle ABC$	triangle ABC
$\geq$	is greater than or equal to		$\overset{\frown}{AB}$	arc AB
$\neq$	is not equal to		$\perp$	is perpendicular to
$\approx$	is approximately equal to		$\parallel$	is parallel to
2^3	2 to the third power		$\cong$	is congruent to
$0.\overline{16}$	repeating decimal $0.161616\ldots$			
7	positive 7		π	pi (about 3.14 or $\frac{22}{7}$)
$^-7$	negative 7			
$\sqrt{}$	positive square root		$(4,7)$	the ordered pair 4,7
$^-\sqrt{}$	negative square root		3^{-5}	3 to the negative fifth power
$\lvert^-4\rvert$	absolute value of negative 4		$5!$	factorial $5 \cdot 4 \cdot 3 \cdot 2 \cdot 1$
\$5/hr	the rate \$5 per hour		%	percent
$^\circ$	degree (angle or temperature)		$P(4)$	the probability of the outcome 4
$\overset{\leftrightarrow}{AB}$	line AB		$1{:}2$	the ratio 1 to 2
$\overset{\rightarrow}{AB}$	ray AB		$_6P_4$	permutation $6 \cdot 5 \cdot 4 \cdot 3$
$\overline{AB}$	line segment AB		$_5C_3$	combination $\dfrac{5 \cdot 4 \cdot 3}{3 \cdot 2 \cdot 1}$

Squares and Square Roots

Number	Square	Square Root	Number	Square	Square Root	Number	Square	Square Root
1	1	1.00	51	2,601	7.14	101	10,201	10.05
2	4	1.41	52	2,704	7.21	102	10,404	10.10
3	9	1.73	53	2,809	7.28	103	10,609	10.15
4	16	2.00	54	2,916	7.35	104	10,816	10.20
5	25	2.24	55	3,025	7.42	105	11,025	10.25
6	36	2.45	56	3,136	7.48	106	11,236	10.30
7	49	2.65	57	3,249	7.55	107	11,449	10.34
8	64	2.83	58	3,364	7.62	108	11,664	10.39
9	81	3.00	59	3,481	7.68	109	11,881	10.44
10	100	3.16	60	3,600	7.75	110	12,100	10.49
11	121	3.32	61	3,721	7.81	111	12,321	10.54
12	144	3.46	62	3,844	7.87	112	12,544	10.58
13	169	3.61	63	3,969	7.94	113	12,769	10.63
14	196	3.74	64	4,096	8.00	114	12,996	10.68
15	225	3.87	65	4,225	8.06	115	13,225	10.72
16	256	4.00	66	4,356	8.12	116	13,456	10.77
17	289	4.12	67	4,489	8.19	117	13,689	10.82
18	324	4.24	68	4,624	8.25	118	13,924	10.86
19	361	4.36	69	4,761	8.31	119	14,161	10.91
20	400	4.47	70	4,900	8.37	120	14,400	10.95
21	441	4.58	71	5,041	8.43	121	14,641	11.00
22	484	4.69	72	5,184	8.49	122	14,884	11.05
23	529	4.80	73	5,329	8.54	123	15,129	11.09
24	576	4.90	74	5,476	8.60	124	15,376	11.14
25	625	5.00	75	5,625	8.66	125	15,625	11.18
26	676	5.10	76	5,776	8.72	126	15,876	11.22
27	729	5.20	77	5,929	8.77	127	16,129	11.27
28	784	5.29	78	6,084	8.83	128	16,384	11.31
29	841	5.39	79	6,241	8.89	129	16,641	11.36
30	900	5.48	80	6,400	8.94	130	16,900	11.40
31	961	5.57	81	6,561	9.00	131	17,161	11.45
32	1,024	5.66	82	6,724	9.06	132	17,424	11.49
33	1,089	5.74	83	6,889	9.11	133	17,689	11.53
34	1,156	5.83	84	7,056	9.17	134	17,956	11.58
35	1,225	5.92	85	7,225	9.22	135	18,225	11.62
36	1,296	6.00	86	7,396	9.27	136	18,496	11.66
37	1,369	6.08	87	7,569	9.33	137	18,769	11.70
38	1,444	6.16	88	7,744	9.38	138	19,044	11.75
39	1,521	6.24	89	7,921	9.43	139	19,321	11.79
40	1,600	6.32	90	8,100	9.49	140	19,600	11.83
41	1,681	6.40	91	8,281	9.54	141	19,881	11.87
42	1,764	6.48	92	8,464	9.59	142	20,164	11.92
43	1,849	6.56	93	8,649	9.64	143	20,449	11.96
44	1,936	6.63	94	8,836	9.70	144	20,736	12.00
45	2,025	6.71	95	9,025	9.75	145	21,025	12.04
46	2,116	6.78	96	9,216	9.80	146	21,316	12.08
47	2,209	6.86	97	9,409	9.85	147	21,609	12.12
48	2,304	6.93	98	9,604	9.90	148	21,904	12.17
49	2,401	7.00	99	9,801	9.95	149	22,201	12.21
50	2,500	7.07	100	10,000	10.00	150	22,500	12.25

Trigonometric Ratios

Angle	Sin	Cos	Tan	Angle	Sin	Cos	Tan
1°	0.017	1.000	0.017	46°	0.719	0.695	1.036
2°	0.035	0.999	0.035	47°	0.731	0.682	1.072
3°	0.052	0.999	0.052	48°	0.743	0.669	1.111
4°	0.070	0.998	0.070	49°	0.755	0.656	1.150
5°	0.087	0.996	0.087	50°	0.766	0.643	1.192
6°	0.105	0.995	0.105	51°	0.777	0.629	1.235
7°	0.122	0.993	0.123	52°	0.788	0.616	1.280
8°	0.139	0.990	0.141	53°	0.799	0.602	1.327
9°	0.156	0.988	0.158	54°	0.809	0.588	1.376
10°	0.174	0.985	0.176	55°	0.819	0.574	1.428
11°	0.191	0.982	0.194	56°	0.829	0.559	1.483
12°	0.208	0.978	0.213	57°	0.839	0.545	1.540
13°	0.225	0.974	0.231	58°	0.848	0.530	1.600
14°	0.242	0.970	0.249	59°	0.857	0.515	1.664
15°	0.259	0.966	0.268	60°	0.866	0.500	1.732
16°	0.276	0.961	0.287	61°	0.875	0.485	1.804
17°	0.292	0.956	0.306	62°	0.883	0.469	1.881
18°	0.309	0.951	0.325	63°	0.891	0.454	1.963
19°	0.326	0.946	0.344	64°	0.899	0.438	2.050
20°	0.342	0.940	0.364	65°	0.906	0.423	2.145
21°	0.358	0.934	0.384	66°	0.914	0.407	2.246
22°	0.375	0.927	0.404	67°	0.921	0.391	2.356
23°	0.391	0.921	0.424	68°	0.927	0.375	2.475
24°	0.407	0.914	0.445	69°	0.934	0.358	2.605
25°	0.423	0.906	0.466	70°	0.940	0.342	2.747
26°	0.438	0.899	0.488	71°	0.946	0.326	2.904
27°	0.454	0.891	0.510	72°	0.951	0.309	3.078
28°	0.469	0.883	0.532	73°	0.956	0.292	3.271
29°	0.485	0.875	0.554	74°	0.961	0.276	3.487
30°	0.500	0.866	0.577	75°	0.966	0.259	3.732
31°	0.515	0.857	0.601	76°	0.970	0.242	4.011
32°	0.530	0.848	0.625	77°	0.974	0.225	4.331
33°	0.545	0.839	0.649	78°	0.978	0.208	4.705
34°	0.559	0.829	0.675	79°	0.982	0.191	5.145
35°	0.574	0.819	0.700	80°	0.985	0.174	5.671
36°	0.588	0.809	0.727	81°	0.988	0.156	6.314
37°	0.602	0.799	0.754	82°	0.990	0.139	7.115
38°	0.616	0.788	0.781	83°	0.993	0.122	8.144
39°	0.629	0.777	0.810	84°	0.995	0.105	9.514
40°	0.643	0.766	0.839	85°	0.996	0.087	11.430
41°	0.656	0.755	0.869	86°	0.998	0.070	14.301
42°	0.669	0.743	0.900	87°	0.999	0.052	19.081
43°	0.682	0.731	0.933	88°	0.999	0.035	28.636
44°	0.695	0.719	0.966	89°	1.000	0.017	57.290
45°	0.707	0.707	1.000				

Glossary

A

absolute copy   A copy of a cell or a group of cells in a spreadsheet; the computer makes an exact copy of the information *(page 481)*

absolute value   The distance from a point on the number line to zero *(page 216)*
  Examples: $|{}^-2| = 2$;
    $|2| = 2$

acute angle   An angle whose measure is greater than 0° but less than 90° *(page 134)*

Additive Inverse Property   The property which states that the sum of a number and its opposite is zero *(page 230)*
  Examples: ${}^-3 + 3 = 0$;
    $4 + {}^-4 = 0$

adjacent angles   Angles that share a common side, have the same vertex, and do not overlap *(page 135)*
  Example:

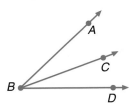

∠*ABC* and ∠*DBC* are adjacent angles.

algebraic expression   An expression that is written using one or more variables *(page 36)*
  Examples: $2x$; $x - 4$; $2a + 5$; $a + b$

alternate exterior angles   A pair of angles on the outer sides of two lines cut by a transversal, but on opposite sides of the transversal *(page 141)*
  Examples:

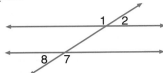

∠1 and ∠7; ∠2 and ∠8
are pairs of alternate exterior angles.

alternate interior angles   A pair of angles on the inner sides of two lines cut by a transversal, but on opposite sides of the transversal *(page 141)*
  Examples:

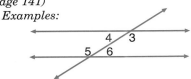

∠4 and ∠6; ∠3 and ∠5
are pairs of alternate interior angles.

angle   A geometric figure formed by two rays with a common endpoint *(pages 134, H14)*
  Example:

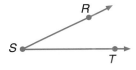

∠*RST* or ∠*TSR* or ∠*S*

angle bisector   A ray in the interior of an angle; its endpoint is on the vertex, and it divides the angle into two congruent angles *(page 144)*
  Example:

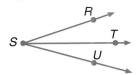

$\overrightarrow{ST}$ bisects ∠*RSU* because
∠*RST* ≅ ∠*TSU*.

arc   A part of the circumference of a circle *(page H16)*
  Examples:

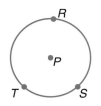

$\overset{\frown}{RS}$ and $\overset{\frown}{RT}$
are arcs
of circle *P*.

area   The number of square units needed to cover a region *(page 402)*

Associative Property of Addition   The property which states that when there are three or more addends, they may be grouped in any order without changing the total sum *(page 8)*
  Example:
  $(2 + 3) + 4 = 2 + (3 + 4)$

Associative Property of Multiplication   The property which states that when there are three or more factors, they may be grouped in any order without changing the product *(page 8)*
  Example:
  $(5 \times a) \times 6 = 5 \times (a \times 6)$

average   See *mean.*

base   The number that is used as a repeated factor *(page 22)*
  Example: $6^3 = 6 \times 6 \times 6$
    6 is the base; 3 is the exponent.

base   A side of a polygon or a face of a solid figure by which the figure is measured and/or named *(pages 402, 418)*
  Examples:

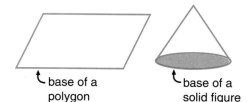

base of a polygon   base of a solid figure

bisect   To divide into two congruent parts *(page 144)*

box-and-whisker graph   A graph that shows how widely and how evenly the data is distributed; includes the lower and upper extreme values of data, the lower and upper quartiles of the data, and the median of the data *(page 332)*

capacity   The amount a container will hold when filled *(page 436)*

category (or field)   A type of information in a data base, such as names or phone numbers *(page 489)*

cell   In a spreadsheet, a block area in which data or formulas can be entered; the cell is located by an address consisting of a letter and a number *(page 480)*

chord   A line segment whose endpoints lie on a circle *(page H16)*
  Example:

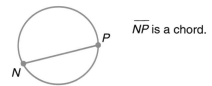

$\overline{NP}$ is a chord.

circle   A closed curve with all points an equal distance from a given point called the center *(page H16)*

circumference   The distance around a circle; $C = \pi d$ *(page 400)*

clipboard   An area in a computer's memory in which the program stores information to be moved or copied from one location or document to another location or document *(page 486)*

combination   An arrangement of items or events in which order does not matter *(page 354)*

Commutative Property of Addition   The property of addition that allows two or more addends to be added in any order without changing the sum *(page 8)*
  Example: $12 + 4 = 4 + 12$

Commutative Property of Multiplication   The property of multiplication that allows two or more factors to be multiplied in any order without changing the product *(page 8)*
  Example: $3 \times 6 = 6 \times 3$

complementary angles   Two angles whose measures have a sum of $90°$ *(page 134)*

composite number   A whole number that has more than two whole-number factors *(page 68)*

cone   A solid figure with one vertex and one circular base *(page 420)*

congruent   Having the same size and shape *(pages 135, 156)*

coordinate plane   A plane formed by two perpendicular number lines called axes; every point on the plane can be named by an ordered pair of numbers *(page 282)*

corresponding angles Angles that are in the same position; they are formed by a transversal cutting two or more lines *(page 140)*
Example:

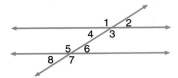

∠1 and ∠5 are corresponding angles.

cosine (cos) In a right triangle, the ratio of the side adjacent to an angle to the length of the hypotenuse *(page 460)*

cylinder A solid figure with two parallel, congruent, circular bases connected by a curved surface *(page 420)*

data base A computer program used to organize, sort, and find the kind of information that is normally kept in a list or on file cards *(page 488)*

decagon A ten-sided polygon *(page 148)*

degree The unit of measure for angles *(page 134)*

Density Property The property which states that between any two rational numbers there is always another rational number *(page 248)*

dependent events Events for which the outcome of one event is affected by the outcome of the other event *(page 370)*

desktop An area in a computer's memory in which to store documents or files *(page 486)*

diagonal A line segment that connects two nonadjacent vertices of a polygon *(page 148)*
Example:

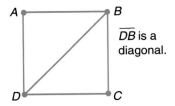

$\overline{DB}$ is a diagonal.

diameter A chord that passes through the center of a circle *(page H16)*

Distributive Property of Multiplication over Addition The property which states that multiplying a sum by a number is the same as multiplying each addend by the number and then adding the products *(page 8)*
Example:
$3(4 + 5) = 3 \times 4 + 3 \times 5$

domain The *x*-coordinates of the ordered pairs in a relation *(page 287)*
Example: In the relation (2,20), (3,30), (4,40), (5,50), the domain is 2, 3, 4, 5. *(page 287)*

edge The line segment along which two faces of a polyhedron intersect *(page 422)*

equation A mathematical sentence that uses an equals sign to show that two quantities are equal *(page 36)*

equivalent fractions Fractions that name the same number *(page 74)*

equivalent ratios Ratios that make the same comparison *(page 174)*

estimate An answer that is close to the exact answer and is found by rounding, by using front-end digits, or by using compatible numbers *(pages 6, 82)*

experimental probability The ratio of the number of times an event occurs to the total number of trials *(page 364)*

exponent The number that indicates how many times the base is used as a factor *(pages 22, 232)*

expression A mathematical phrase that combines operations, numerals, and/or variables to name a number *(page 36)*

exterior angle of a triangle An angle that is outside a triangle and is formed by extending one of the sides of the triangle *(page 152)*
Example:

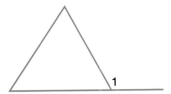

∠1 is an exterior angle of the triangle.

exterior angles Angles on the outer sides of two lines cut by a transversal *(page 141)*
Example:

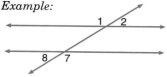

∠1, ∠2, ∠8, and ∠7
are exterior angles.

extrapolation An estimate or a prediction of an unknown value, based upon known values *(page 334)*

face A flat surface of a polyhedron *(page 418)*

factor A number that is multiplied by another number to get a product *(page 68)*

factorial The product of all whole numbers, except zero, less than or equal to a number *(page 351)*
    Example: 5! = 5 × 4 × 3 × 2 × 1 = 120

Fibonacci Sequence The infinite sequence in which each number, after two ones, is the sum of the two preceding numbers *(page 380)*
    1, 1, 2, 3, 5, 8, 13, 21, . . .

field (sometimes called category) A type of information in a data base *(page 489)*
    Example: ADDRESS could be a field for a data base that organizes information found in a phone book.

formula An equation that states a fact or rule *(page 272)*

function A relation in which no ordered pairs have the same *x*-value *(page 284)*

Fundamental Counting Principle If there are *p* choices for the way one thing can be done and *q* choices for the way another thing can be done, then together they can be done in *p* × *q* different ways *(page 348)*

greatest common factor (GCF) The largest common factor of two or more given numbers *(page 70)*

greatest possible error (GPE) One half of the precision of the units used in a measurement *(page 389)*

hexagonal prism A polyhedron whose bases are hexagons and whose other six faces are parallelograms *(page 436)*
    Example:

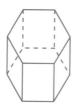

histogram A bar graph that shows the frequency of data within intervals *(page 316)*

hypotenuse In a right triangle, the side opposite the right angle *(page 449)*

Identity Property of Addition The property which states that adding 0 to a number does not change the number's value *(page 8)*
    Example: 3 + 0 = 3

Identity Property of Multiplication The property which states that multiplying a number by 1 does not change the number's value *(page 8)*
    Example: 6 × 1 = 6

independent events Events for which the outcome of one event is not affected by the outcome of another event *(page 368)*

inequality A mathematical sentence that shows quantities that are not equal, using <, >, ≤, ≥, or ≠ *(pages 36, 56)*

integer One of the set of whole numbers and their opposites *(page 216)*

interest The amount of money paid for borrowing or using money *(page 204)*

interior angle of a triangle Any one of the three angles inside a triangle *(page 152)*
    Examples:

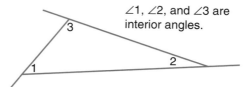

∠1, ∠2, and ∠3 are interior angles.

interior angles   Angles on the inner sides of two lines cut by a transversal *(page 141)*
   Example:

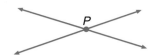

∠4, ∠3, ∠5, and ∠6 are interior angles.

interpolation   An estimated value between two known values *(page 334)*

intersecting lines   Lines that cross at exactly one point *(page 132)*
   Example:

P

inverse operation   An operation that has the opposite effect; addition and subtraction are inverse operations; multiplication and division are inverse operations *(pages 40, 50)*
   Examples:
   $20 - 5 = 15$; therefore $15 + 5 = 20$.
   $20 \div 5 = 4$; therefore $4 \times 5 = 20$.

irrational number   A number that cannot be expressed as a/b, where a and b are integers, and where $b \neq 0$; a number that is nonterminating and nonrepeating *(page 256)*
   Examples: $\sqrt{13}$
   $0.121121112\ldots$

isosceles triangle   A triangle with at least two congruent sides *(page 452)*

least common denominator (LCD)   The smallest common multiple of two or more denominators *(page 78)*

least common multiple (LCM)   The smallest number, other than zero, that is a multiple of two or more given numbers *(page 70)*

leg   In a right triangle, either of the two sides that intersect to form the right angle; in an isosceles triangle, one of the two congruent sides *(pages 449, 452)*

like terms   Expressions that contain the same variables; corresponding variables have the same exponent *(page 55)*

line   A set of points that extends without end in opposite directions *(pages 132, H14)*
   Example:

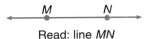

Read: line *MN*

linear equation   An equation whose graph is a straight line on the coordinate plane *(page 288)*

line of best fit   A straight line drawn through as much data as possible on a scattergram *(page 337)*

line of symmetry   A line that separates a figure into two congruent parts *(pages 150, 300)*
   Example:

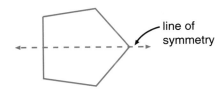

line of symmetry

line segment   A part of a line that has two endpoints *(pages 132, H14)*
   Example:

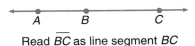

Read $\overline{BC}$ as line segment *BC*

$\overline{BC}$ is a part of $\overleftrightarrow{AC}$

LOGO   A computer language used primarily to draw graphic designs; it can also perform calculations *(page 476)*

lower extreme   The least number in a set of data *(page 330)*

lower quartile   The median of the numbers that are to the left of (less than) the median of an ordered set of data *(page 330)*

mathematical probability   The ratio of the number of favorable outcomes to the number of possible outcomes *(page 356)*

mean (average)   A number found by dividing the sum of a set of data by the number of items in the set *(page 314)*

measure of central tendency   A measure used to describe data; the mean, median, and mode are measures of central tendency *(page 314)*

median The middle number or the average of the two middle numbers in an ordered set of data *(page 314)*

mode The number or numbers that occur most frequently in a set of data *(page 314)*

negative correlation A relation in which one set of data increases as the other decreases *(page 337)*

negative integer An integer less than zero *(page 216)*

numerical expression An expression that contains numbers and operations *(page 36)*

obtuse angle An angle whose measure is greater than 90° but less than 180° *(page 134)*

octagon An eight-sided polygon *(page 149)*

octagonal pyramid A pyramid whose base is an octagon and whose other eight faces are triangles *(page 424)*
Example:

odds in favor The ratio of the number of favorable outcomes to the number of unfavorable outcomes *(page 357)*

opposites Two numbers represented by points on the number line that are the same distance from 0, but are on opposite sides of 0 *(page 216)*

ordered pair A pair of numbers used to locate a point on the coordinate plane *(page 282)*

order of operations The order in which operations are done within an expression; first, do the operations within parentheses or the computations above or below a division bar; also, find the value of any numbers in exponent form; then, do multiplication and division from left to right; finally, do addition and subtraction from left to right *(page 24)*

origin The point on a coordinate plane where the *x*-axis and *y*-axis intersect (0,0) *(page 282)*

parallel lines Lines in a plane that do not intersect *(page 140)*

parallelogram A quadrilateral in which opposite sides are congruent and parallel *(page 149)*

Pascal's Triangle A triangular arrangement of numbers in which each row starts and ends with 1, and each other number is the sum of the two numbers above it *(page 358)*

pentagon A five-sided polygon *(page 148)*

pentagonal prism A polyhedron whose two bases are congruent, parallel pentagons and whose other five faces are parallelograms *(page 418)*

pentagonal pyramid A polyhedron whose base is a pentagon and whose other five faces are triangles that share a common vertex *(page 418)*

percent Ratio of a number to 100; percent means per hundred *(page 184)*

perfect square A number that has an integer as its square root *(page 250)*
Example: 25 is a perfect square because $\sqrt{25} = 5$.

perimeter The distance around a polygon *(page 396)*

permutation An arrangement of items or events in which order is important *(page 350)*

perpendicular bisector A line or line segment that intersects a given line segment at its midpoint and forms right angles *(page 144)*

perpendicular lines Lines that intersect to form right angles *(page 136)*

pi (π) The ratio of the circumference of a circle to the length of its diameter;

$$\pi \approx 3.14 \text{ or } \frac{22}{7} \quad \text{(page 400)}$$

plane A set of points forming a flat surface that continues forever in all directions *(page H14)*

point of intersection The point where two or more lines intersect *(pages 132, 296)*

point of rotation A point around which a figure can be turned *(pages 150, 300)*
Example:

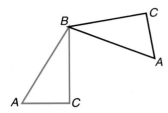

polygon A closed plane figure formed by three or more line segments *(page 148)*

polyhedron A solid figure in which all the sides, or faces, are polygons *(page 418)*

positive correlation A relation in which two sets of data increase or decrease at the same time *(page 337)*

positive integer A whole number that is greater than 0 *(page 216)*

precision A property of measurement related to the unit of measure used; the smaller the unit of measure used, the more precise the measurement is *(page 388)*

prime factorization A number written as the product of its prime factors *(page 68)*
Example: $24 = 2 \times 2 \times 2 \times 3$, or $2^3 \times 3$

prime number A whole number greater than 1 that has exactly two factors, itself and 1 *(page 68)*

principal The amount of money borrowed or saved *(page 204)*

prism A polyhedron whose bases are congruent, parallel polygons and whose other faces are parallelograms *(page 418)*

probability (P) The number used to describe the chance of an event occurring *(page 356)*

$$P = \frac{\text{number of favorable outcomes}}{\text{number of possible outcomes}}$$

proportion An equation which states that two ratios are equivalent *(page 176)*
Example:

$$\frac{5}{10} = \frac{1}{2} \quad \text{or} \quad 5{:}10 = 1{:}2$$

pyramid A polyhedron with one base that is a polygon and whose other faces are triangles that share a common vertex *(page 418)*

Pythagorean Property In a right triangle, if a and b are the lengths of the legs and c is the length of the hypotenuse, then $a^2 + b^2 = c^2$ *(page 449)*

quadrant One of the four regions of the coordinate plane *(page 282)*

radius A line segment with one endpoint at the center of a circle and the other endpoint on the circle *(pages 162, H16)*

random selection A selection that allows for each person or item to have an equal chance of being chosen *(page 362)*

range The difference between the upper extreme (greatest number) and the lower extreme (least number) in a set of data *(page 330)*

range The y-coordinates of the ordered pairs in a relation *(page 287)*
Example: In the relation (2,20), (3,30), (4,40), (5,50), the range is 20, 30, 40, 50.

rate A ratio that compares quantities of different units, such as miles per hour, price per pound, students per class *(page 174)*

ratio A comparison of two numbers *(pages 174, 186)*
Example:

6 to 7; 6:7; $\dfrac{6}{7}$

rational number Any number that can be expressed as a ratio $\dfrac{a}{b}$, where $b \neq 0$ and a and b are integers *(page 248)*

ray A part of a line that has one endpoint and extends in one direction without end *(pages 132, H14)*
Example:

Read: ray *AB*

real numbers The set of numbers that includes all rational and all irrational numbers *(page 257)*

reciprocal One of two numbers whose product is 1 *(page 100)*

record In a data base, information for one particular person or item *(page 488)*

rectangular prism A polyhedron whose parallel bases are rectangles and whose other faces are parallelograms *(page 418)*

rectangular pyramid A polyhedron whose base is a rectangle and whose other four faces are triangles that share a common vertex *(page 418)*
Example:

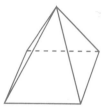

reflection (flip) The figure formed by flipping a geometric figure about a line to obtain a mirror image *(page 300)*
Example:

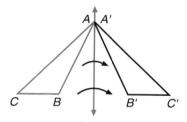

regular polygon A polygon in which all sides and all angles are congruent *(page 396)*

relation A set of ordered pairs *(page 284)*

relative copy A copy of a cell or a group of cells in a spreadsheet; the computer makes changes in the new cells to reflect their position in the spreadsheet *(page 481)*

repeating decimal A decimal in which one or more digits repeat infinitely *(page 118)*
Examples: 24.6666 . . . or 24.$\overline{6}$; 5.272727. . . or 5.$\overline{27}$

rhombus A parallelogram with four congruent sides and congruent opposite angles *(page 149)*

right angle An angle whose measure is 90° *(page 134)*

right triangle A triangle containing exactly one right angle *(page 449)*

rotation A type of transformation, or movement, that results when a geometric figure is turned about a fixed point *(page 300)*
Example:

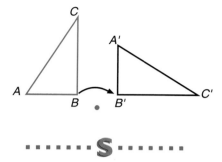

· · · · · · · **S** · · · · · · ·

sample space The set of all possible outcomes *(page 356)*

scale The ratio of the size of an object or the distance in a drawing or model to the actual size of the object or the actual distance *(page 178)*

scale drawing A drawing whose shape is the same as an actual object and whose size is determined by the scale *(page 178)*

scattergram A graph made by plotting points on a coordinate plane *(page 336)*

scientific notation A method of expressing a number as the product of two factors; one factor is greater than or equal to 1 and less than 10; the other factor is a power of 10 *(page 236)*
Example: $6,300,000,000 = 6.3 \times 10^9$

sequence An ordered list of numbers *(page 26)*

significant digits The number of digits used to express the accuracy of a measure *(page 392)*

similar figures Figures with the same shape but not necessarily the same size *(page 456)*

simple interest The amount obtained by multiplying principal by rate by time; $I = prt$ *(page 204)*

simplest form A fraction is in simplest form when the numerator and the denominator have no common factors other than 1 *(page 74)*

sine (sin) In a right triangle, the ratio of the length of the side opposite an angle to the length of the hypotenuse *(page 460)*

slope The steepness of a line; the ratio of vertical change to horizontal change

$$\text{slope} = \frac{\text{vertical change}}{\text{horizontal change}} \quad \textit{(page 292)}$$

solid figure A three-dimensional figure *(page 418)*

solution The value or values that make an equation, an inequality, or a system of equations true *(pages 40, 270, 296)*

sphere A solid figure with all points an equal distance from the center *(page 420)*
Example:

spreadsheet A computer program that organizes information in rows and columns and does calculations with numbers and formulas *(page 480)*

square To square a number means to multiply the number by itself *(page 250)*

square pyramid A polyhedron whose base is a square and whose other four faces are triangles *(page 418)*
Example:

square root One of two equal factors of a number *(pages 250, 252)*

stem-and-leaf plot A method of organizing intervals or groups of data *(page 328)*
Example:

Stem	Leaves					Set of data				
1	1	3	5	5	7	11	13	15	15	17
2	2	4	6	8	8	22	24	26	28	28
3	3	4	4	9	9	33	34	34	39	39

straight angle An angle whose measure is 180° *(page 134)*

supplementary angles Two angles whose measures have a sum of 180° *(page 134)*

surface area The sum of the areas of the faces or surfaces of a solid figure *(page 426)*

system of equations Two or more linear equations *(page 296)*
Example: $y = 10 - x$
$y = x + 2$

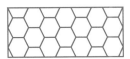

tangent (tan) In a right triangle, the ratio of the length of the side opposite an angle to the length of the side adjacent to the angle *(page 460)*

terminating decimal A decimal that terminates, or ends; a decimal for which the division operation results in a remainder of zero *(page 118)*

tessellation An arrangement of congruent plane figures that completely covers the plane with no gaps and no overlaps *(page 170)*
Example:

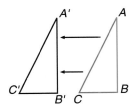

transformation A change in size, shape, or position of a geometric figure *(page 300)*

translation (slide) A movement of a geometric figure to a new position without turning or flipping the figure *(page 300)*
Example:

transversal A line that intersects two or more lines *(page 140)*

trapezoid A quadrilateral with only one pair of parallel sides *(page 149)*
Example:

triangular prism A polyhedron whose two bases are congruent triangles and whose other three faces are parallelograms *(page 418)*
Example:

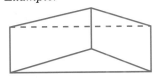

triangular pyramid   A polyhedron whose base is a triangle and whose other three faces are triangles that share a common vertex *(page 418)*
Example:

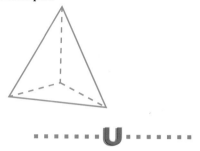

unit rate   A rate in which the second term is 1 *(page 174)*

upper extreme   The greatest number in a set of data *(page 330)*

upper quartile   The median of the numbers that are to the right of (greater than) the median of an ordered set of data *(page 330)*

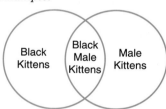

variable   A letter or symbol that represents one or more numbers *(page 36)*

Venn diagram   A diagram that shows relationships between groups *(page 372)*
Example:

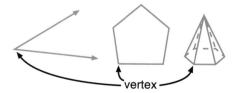

vertex   A point where two or more rays meet, where sides of a polygon meet, or where edges of a polyhedron meet *(pages 135, 424, H14)*
Examples:

vertical angles   Angles, formed by intersecting lines, that have a common vertex, are congruent, and are not adjacent *(page 135)*
Examples: ∠AHD and ∠CHB are vertical angles.

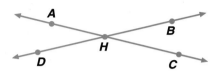

volume   The number of cubic units that can fit inside a solid figure *(page 432)*

word processor   A computer program used to write text, such as letters, reports, word problems, or memos *(page 504)*

x-axis   The horizontal axis on a coordinate plane *(page 282)*

x-coordinate   The first number in an ordered pair; tells whether to move right or left along the x-axis of the coordinate plane *(page 282)*

y-axis   The vertical axis on a coordinate plane *(page 282)*

y-coordinate   The second number in an ordered pair; tells whether to move up or down in the coordinate plane *(page 282)*

Answers to Selected Exercises

Chapter 1

Pages 2–3

1. 45 thousand, 6 hundred 78 point 8, or 45 thousand, 6 hundred 78 and 8 tenths **3.** 145 thousand, 8 hundred 97 point 69, or 145 thousand, 8 hundred 97 and 69 hundredths **5.** 4 hundred 32 point one two six, or 4 hundred 32 and 126 thousandths **7.** 2 million, 6 thousand, 4 hundred one **9.** 4,500,000 **11.** 22,100,000,000 **13.** thirty thousand, ninety-one **15.** three million, seventy-four thousand, three hundred eighty-nine and thirty-two hundredths **17.** ten thousands **19.** millions **21.** 24,560,000 **23.** 1,030 **25.** 13.456 million **27.** 124.06 million **29.** < **31.** > **33.** Answers may vary. Possible answer: 425.09 **35.** 11.7 million VCR's **37.** 13,425

Pages 4–5

1. tens **3.** ten thousands **5.** 34,499; 33,500 **7.** 605,499; 604,500 **9.** tens **11.** hundreds **13.** hundredths **15.** millions **17.** 124; 115 **19.** 16,499; 15,500 **21.** 4,549,999; 4,450,000 **23.** 94; 85 **25.** No; the number is 12.4999 . . . . The 9's repeat forever. **27.** 64,400,000; 64.4 million **29.** 1,434,700,000; 1,434.7 million **31.** 9,990,100,000; 9,990.1 million **33.** 4,499,999 **35.** 12.4

Page 7

1. overestimate **3.** c. **5.** b. **7.** a. **9.** 877 **11.** 345 **13.** 320 **15.** 77.5 **17.** overestimate **19.** $3.01

Pages 8–9

3. 20; 4 **5.** Associative Property of Addition **7.** Identity Property of Multiplication **9.** Commutative Property of Multiplication **11.** Distributive Property **13.** Distributive Property **15.** 0 **17.** 20; 6 **19.** 12; 1; 12; 372 **21.** $(6 \times 12) + (6 \times 8) = 6 \times (12 + 8) = 6 \times 20 = 120$; $1.20 **23.** Examples will vary. Possible examples: $32 \times 16 = 32 \times (10 + 6)$, $32 \times 16 = 32 \times (20 - 4)$ **1.** 1,600 **3.** 500,000 **5.** 235.2 **7.** 1.0 **9.** > **11.** <

Pages 10–12

1. subtract; $1,022.39 **3.** $59.47 **5.** $51,492,542,460 **7.** $189,742,000,000 **9.** 19,920,020,443 pennies **11.** No. The value of one $20 bill is twice the value of one $10 bill

Page 13

1. Add amounts for June; subtract $8.32; $32.89. **3.** $1.50 **5.** $270.47 **7.** $14.50

Pages 14–15

1. divide; $55.60 **3.** $9,045 **5.** $256.88 **7.** 384 gal **9.** first option: $129.90 + $27.50 + $27.50 **11.** $78,650.00 For Exercises 13–16, answers will vary. Possible answers are given. **13.** 124 + 1 + 340 + 10 + 421 + 100 **15.** You know $10 \times 12 = 120$, so use $42 \times 12 + 120$.

Page 16

1. 120 in. **3.** about 20 gal **5.** about 40 mi **7.** = **9.** < **11.** > **13.** > For Exercises 15–22, estimates will vary. Possible estimates are given. **15.** 250; 300 **17.** 480; 620 **19.** 10; 12 **21.** 5,000; 5,300 **23.** 3,192 **25.** 737.901 **27.** 3,618 **29.** 21

Page 19

1. $32\overline{)2,022.4}$ **3.** $43\overline{)1,108}$ **5.** 9.5 **7.** 54.8 **9.** 9 **11.** 1.35 **13.** 3.6 **15.** 0.52 **17.** 0.065 **19.** 25.4 **21.** 5.4 **23.** 7.5 **25.** 4.27 **27.** 0.05 **29.** 12 times greater **31.** 222.2; 2,222.2; 22,222.2

Page 21

1. 4 buses; remainder shows need for extra bus. **3.** $3; remainder is what is left. **5.** no **7.** 5 sections **9.** 9 banners; 10 in. **11.** $4\frac{1}{4}$ cookies **1.** = **3.** < **5.** 2.4 **7.** 0.5

Pages 22–23

1. 2 **3.** 6 **5.** 9 to the second power, or 9 squared **7.** 6.3 to the first power **9.** 7 to the fourth power **11.** 7^4 **13.** 3^4 **15.** 5^6 **17.** 343 **19.** 64 **21.** 1.69 **23.** 729 **25.** 0.0625 **27.** 9 **29.** 9 **31.** 4 **33.** 10 **35.** $1.23 **37.** 91.125 cm^3

Page 25

1. 30 + 35 **3.** 6 × 5 **5.** No. The calculator did not follow the rules for order of operations. **7.** 33 **9.** 10.8 **11.** 578 **13.** 54 **15.** 7.3 **17.** 7.98 **19.** 5 **21.** 25 **23.** 54 **25.** $5 \times 2.2 + 18 = 29$ **27.** $16.8 - 5 \text{ M}^+ 4.2 \times \text{MRC} = 49.56$ **29.** $6 \times 6 + 45 = 81$ **31.** $3 \times (14 - 8) = 18$ **33.** $5 \times 7 - 3 \times 9 = 8$

Page 27

1. 14, 16 **3.** 25, 50 **5.** 665 employees **7.** Jim **9.** 640 bolts

Pages 28–29

1. overestimate **3.** exponent, base **5.** ten thousands **7.** ten thousandths **9.** five hundred thousand, seven hundred twelve **11.** six hundred seventy-two thousand, eight hundred forty-one and twelve hundredths **13.** 3,200,000 **15.** 82,400,000,000 **17.** hundreds **19.** tens

21. underestimate **23.** overestimate
25. 3 times **27.** 1 time **29.** 3×4 **31.** 5^3
33. $18 - 3$ **35.** 124 thousand **37.** 1.25
thousand **39.** 454; 445 **41.** 71,499; 70,500
43. 171 **45.** 334 **47.** 0 **49.** 9 **51.** 20.15
53. 12.08 **55.** 81 **57.** 32,768 **59.** 71 **61.** 11
63. $91.16 **65.** $80.85

Page 33
1. A. **3.** C. **5.** D. **7.** D. **9.** A. **11.** A.

Chapter 2

Pages 36–37
1. t **3.** s **5.** inequality **7.** algebraic expression
9. numerical expression **11.** inequality
13. equation **15.** inequality **17.** equation
19. inequality **21.** inequality **23.** expression
25. expression **29.** > **31.** > **33.** = **35.** <
37. $225 + 15 = 240$ **39.** $34 \times 5 + 8 = 178$
For Exercises 41–44, equations will vary.
Possible equations are given. **41.** $x + 4 = 12$
43. $2t + 4 = 14$ **45.** $24 - 6 > 17$ **47.** $121 \times 12 \geq 1{,}400$ **49.** $b - 6 < 2$ **51.** $x + 7 \neq 11$
53. $7 + 7$ **55.** no; $13 + 25 = 38$ **57.** Values are
the same; 6.

Page 39
1. $n + 6$ and $6 + n$ **3.** $6 - n$ **5.** 26 **7.** 16.3 **9.** 4
11. $12 + b$, or $b + 12$ **13.** $t + 23$, or $23 + t$
15. $a - 30$ **23.** 12 **25.** 2.9 **27.** 9.5 **29.** 1.2
31. 6 **33.** 2.43 **35.** 7.5 **37.** $c - 1.50$
39. $-; -; +$

Page 41
1. 23; $b = 18$ **3.** 2.5; $x = 7.3$ **5.** no **7.** yes
9. $a = 15$ **11.** $y = 82$ **13.** $e = 4.7$ **15.** $x = 20$
17. $d = 12$ **19.** $r = 45$ **21.** $a = 3.5$
23. $t = 107$ **25.** c = cost of new car; $c + 630 = 9{,}875$ **27.** d = deposits; $d + 455.32 = 565.33$
29. $p + 2.13 = 22.80$; $p = 20.67$; $20.67

Page 43
1. 20 dimes **3.** $20.75 **5.** 4.3 lb **7.** $69.00
9. 52 compact cars

Pages 44–45
1. no **3.** yes **5.** $m = 39$ **7.** $n = 50$ **9.** $x = 32$
11. $z = 365$ **13.** $w = 12.99$ **15.** $u = 69.23$
17. $m = 6.8$ **19.** $y = 2.65$ **21.** $t = 86$
23. $b = 108$ **25.** $s = 18$ **27.** g = number of
gallons pumped; $4{,}333.7 - g = 3{,}687$
29. n = number of pounds; $n - 35.6 = 125.6$
31. $c + 8.45 = 38.00$; $c = 29.55$; $29.55
33. 45 years old **1.** 52 **3.** 7 **5.** $x = 12$
7. $t = 0.8$

Page 46
1. 3 weeks **3.** four 3-legged stools and three
4-legged stools **5.** 17 and 7 **7.** 3,200; 4,200
9. 90; 110 **11.** 4.23 **13.** 71.21 **15.** 1.2
17. 1.6 **19.** 16 **21.** 8 **23.** 1.44 **25.** 58 **27.** 4
29. 11.5 **31.** 7.27 **33.** $a = 5$ **35.** $c = 6.2$
37. $n = 6.3$ **39.** $n = 7.6$

Page 49
1. $5t$ **3.** $\frac{5}{t}$ **5.** 25 **7.** 140 **9.** 29 **11.** $2d$ **13.** $\frac{g}{12}$
21. 28 **23.** 12 **25.** 1 **27.** 650 **29.** 26 **31.** 65
33. $\frac{2}{5}$, or 0.4 **35.** 260 **37.** 15.5 **39.** 12
41. $0.35t$ **43.** $\frac{2n}{3}$, or $2(\frac{n}{3})$

Page 51
1. yes **3.** no; $y = 6$ **5.** $h = 15$ **7.** $a = 37$
9. $k = 2$ **11.** $w = 254$ **13.** $k = 0.5$ **15.** $n = 3$
17. $b = 26$ **19.** $p = 3$ **21.** $35.80m = 286.40$;
$m = 8$; 8 mo **23.** 16 **25.** $19.6 = 5.6t$; $t = 3.5$;
3.5 min

Pages 52–53
1. yes **3.** no **5.** $t = 120$ **7.** $s = 156.4$
9. division **11.** subtraction **13.** $a = 253$
15. $r = 360$ **17.** $n = 3$ **19.** $b = 558$ **21.** $r = 56$
23. $t = 7$ **25.** $t = 432$ **27.** $t = 65$ **29.** $\frac{c}{6} = 7.80$;
$c = 46.80$; $46.80 **31.** $p = c + 5$ **1.** $x = 14$
3. $b = 7.45$ **5.** $a = 2$ **7.** $t = 52.7$

Pages 54–55
1. subtraction; $x = 2$ **3.** addition; $c = 33.6$
5. subtraction, division **7.** subtraction,
multiplication **9.** $e = 45$ **11.** $m = 8$ **13.** $a = 4$
15. $r = 81$ **17.** $g = 6$ **19.** $n = 6$ **21.** $9d + 5 = 32$ **23.** $\frac{n}{2} + 12 = 50$; $n = 76$; $76 **27.** $r = 5$
29. $t = 3$

Page 57
1. yes **3.** yes **5.** $x > 7$; 8, 9, 10, ... **7.** $b \neq 64$;
all whole numbers except 64 **9.** $b \leq 5$; 0, 1, 2,
3, 4, 5, **11.** $k \geq 6$; 6, 7, 8, ... **13.** $s < 12$; 0, 1,
2, ... 11 **15.** $t > 14$; 15, 16, 17, ...
17. $w < 36$; 0, 1, 2, ..., 35 **19.** $n > 7$; 8, 9,
10, ... **21.** $s \leq 6$; 0, 1, 2, 3, 4, 5, 6 **23.** $t > 7$;
8, 9, 10, ... **25.** $5c < 795$; $c < 159$; no, each
paid less than $159. **27.** False; "more than 20"
means 21, 22, 23, or greater. **29.** Possible; see
Exercise 27.

Page 59
1. $r - 5 = 16$; $r = 21$; $21 **3.** 32 chairs
5. about 2,000 tickets **7.** 50 min

Pages 60–61
1. multiplication **3.** equation **5.** subtraction
7. $4n$ **9.** $\frac{n}{4}$ **11.** division **13.** addition
15. subtraction **17.** division **19.** yes **21.** no
23. no **25.** addition **27.** subtraction **29.** no

31. $n + 12$ **33.** $n - 9.5$ **35.** 12   **37.** 20
39. 12.8   **41.** 1   **43.** $n = 11$ **45.** $d = 0.5$
47. $g = 16$ **49.** $c = 18.7$ **51.** $n = 4$ **53.** $t = 3.3$
55. $n = 24$ **57.** $b = 13.5$ **59.** $t = 9$ **61.** $t = 4$
63. $p = 1$ **65.** $b \geq 113$; 113, 114, 115, . . .
67. three-speed: 40; ten-speed: 80
69. $w - 3.5 = 47.6$; $w = 51.1$; 51.1 kg

Page 65
1. B.   **3.** C.   **5.** D.   **7.** D.   **9.** B.   **11.** B.

Chapter 3

Page 69
1. 1, 2, 4   **3.** 1, 2, 4, 5, 10, 20   **5.** 1, 2, 4, 5, 10,
20, 25, 50, 100   **7.** composite   **9.** prime
11. composite   **13.** 3   **15.** 2; 3   **17.** composite
19. composite   **21.** composite   **23.** $2^2 \times 7$
25. $2 \times 3^2 \times 5$ **27.** $2^3 \times 11$ **29.** 5^3 **31.** $3^2 \times 5$
$\times 7$ **33.** $2^2 \times 3^2 \times 5^2$ **35.** 44   **37.** 1,573
39. 1,225   **41.** 2,499   **43.** 6 choices   **45.** 30

Page 71
1. GCF   **3.** 60 trees   **5.** 60 sec   **7.** $21.63

Page 73
1. $508.80   **3.** $57.80   **5.** yes   **7.** 33
photographs   **9.** about $85

Pages 75–76
1. 12   **3.** 4   **5.** 2; $\frac{7}{8}$ **7.** 5; $\frac{4}{5}$ **9.** 12; $\frac{3}{2}$ **11.** $2\frac{1}{3}$
13. 3   **15.** 6   **17.** $\frac{12}{5}$ **19.** $\frac{15}{8}$ **21.** $\frac{31}{7}$ **23.** $\frac{4}{10}$,
$\frac{6}{15}$, $\frac{8}{20}$ **25.** $\frac{3}{7}$, $\frac{6}{14}$, $\frac{18}{42}$ **27.** $\frac{14}{30}$, $\frac{21}{30}$, $\frac{28}{30}$ **29.** $\frac{2}{3}$
31. $\frac{7}{15}$ **33.** $\frac{5}{7}$ **35.** $\frac{12}{14}$ **37.** $\frac{3}{4}$ **39.** $\frac{2}{1}$, or 2   **41.** 2
43. $20\frac{1}{4}$ **45.** $7\frac{1}{2}$ **47.** $\frac{15}{2}$ **49.** $\frac{55}{6}$ **51.** $\frac{56}{5}$
53. $\frac{18}{30}$ **55.** $\frac{2n}{3}$ **57.** $\frac{2}{5b}$ **59.** $\frac{3}{x}$

Page 77
1. 11.4 mi   **3.** 4 cans   **5.** $26.65   **7.** 12 in.

Page 79
1. 18   **3.** 40   **5.** 24   **7.** $\frac{7}{8}$ **9.** $15\frac{2}{3}$ **11.** $\frac{2}{3}$ **13.** 60
15. 30   **17.** >   **19.** =   **21.** <   **23.** =   **25.** <
27. $\frac{2}{3}$, $\frac{7}{8}$, $\frac{5}{4}$ **29.** $3\frac{1}{10}$, $3\frac{2}{5}$, $3\frac{1}{2}$ **31.** business
33. Answers may vary. Possible answer: Write
2.4 as $2\frac{4}{10}$.   **1.** 5^2 **3.** $2^2 \times 3^2$ **5.** $2^2 \times 3^3$ **7.** $\frac{1}{3}$
9. $\frac{4}{11}$ **11.** $\frac{5}{6}$

Page 80
1. 4 cars   **3.** $10.65   **5.** $60.39   **7.** 6.1   **9.** 12.2
11. 12   **13.** 73.2   **15.** 61   **17.** $x = 21.6$
19. $n = 72.1$ **21.** $b = 4$ **23.** $m = 13$ **25.** prime
27. composite   **29.** composite   **31.** $\frac{53}{6}$ **33.** $\frac{24}{7}$
35. $\frac{21}{8}$ **37.** $1\frac{7}{8}$ **39.** $4\frac{1}{4}$ **41.** $2\frac{1}{2}$

Page 83
1. 0   **3.** 1   **5.** $\frac{1}{2}$ **7.** $\frac{1}{2}$ **9.** 2   **11.** b.   **13.** b.
15. $1\frac{1}{2}$ **17.** $1\frac{1}{2}$ **19.** 5   **21.** 11   **23.** $2\frac{1}{2}$ **25.** 7
27. about $1\frac{1}{2}$ oz   **29.** $\frac{5}{16}$

Pages 84–85
1. $\frac{5}{4}$, or $1\frac{1}{4}$ **3.** $\frac{22}{15}$, or $1\frac{7}{15}$ **5.** $\frac{19}{12}$, or $1\frac{7}{12}$ **7.** $6\frac{1}{2}$
9. $9\frac{3}{10}$ **11.** $\frac{3}{4}$ **13.** $\frac{13}{9}$, or $1\frac{4}{9}$ **15.** $\frac{15}{14}$, or $1\frac{1}{14}$
17. $\frac{7}{8}$ **19.** $\frac{31}{20}$, or $1\frac{11}{20}$ **21.** $6\frac{17}{30}$ **23.** $16\frac{5}{6}$
25. $4\frac{2}{35}$ **27.** $12\frac{1}{12}$ **29.** $5\frac{7}{30}$ hr   **31.** Answers
may vary. Possible answer: $3\frac{1}{2} + 4\frac{1}{2} = 8$,
$3\frac{5}{10} + 4\frac{5}{10} = 8$ **33.** put the fraction in simplest
form; renamed $1\frac{4}{3}$ as $2\frac{1}{3}$ **35.** Answers may
vary. Possible answers: 3 Unit 1 / 3 + 3 Unit 4 /
5 = Ab/c

Pages 86–87
1. no; 2   **3.** yes; $2\frac{13}{16}$ **5.** $\frac{1}{4}$ **7.** $\frac{7}{15}$ **9.** $\frac{3}{10}$ **11.** $5\frac{1}{4}$
13. $2\frac{7}{24}$ **15.** $2\frac{5}{12}$ **17.** $2\frac{3}{8}$ **19.** $20\frac{4}{7}$ **21.** 3
23. $\frac{1}{6}$ **25.** $\frac{1}{3}$ **27.** $\frac{7}{12}$ **29.** $\frac{5}{6}$ hr   **31.** about $792
1. <   **3.** <   **5.** 5,000   **7.** 6

Page 89
1. 36 in.   **3.** five 20-lb bags   **5.** about 14 hr
7. 15 blocks

Pages 90–91
1. prime   **3.** composite   **5.** simplest form
7. composite   **9.** composite   **11.** 2   **13.** 6   **15.** 3
17. $\frac{10}{16}$, $\frac{15}{24}$ **19.** $\frac{4}{5}$, $\frac{8}{10}$ **21.** 1   **23.** $\frac{1}{2}$ **25.** $\frac{1}{2}$
27. yes   **29.** no   **31.** 2×3^2 **33.** 3^4 **35.** $2\frac{2}{3}$
37. 2   **39.** $7\frac{3}{4}$ **41.** $\frac{35}{8}$ **43.** $\frac{16}{7}$ **45.** <   **47.** <
49. 1   **51.** 2   **53.** $\frac{14}{15}$ **55.** $2\frac{11}{24}$ **57.** $1\frac{5}{7}$ **59.** $3\frac{13}{20}$
61. 3 sisters   **63.** $390   **65.** 450 ft

Page 95
1. A.   **3.** B.   **5.** B.   **7.** D.   **9.** A.   **11.** D.

Chapter 4

Pages 98–99
1. $[\frac{1}{2}]$; overestimate   **3.** [6]; underestimate
5. [22]; close estimate   **7.** [2]; close estimate
9. $\frac{1}{2}$ **11.** 6   **13.** 35   **15.** 18   **17.** 2   **19.** 4
21. 112   **23.** 150   **25.** [1]; overestimate
27. [81]; close estimate   **29.** [36]; close estimate
31. [6]; underestimate   **33.** about 5 mo
35. $4 + 7 + 3 = 14$; about 14 hr

Pages 100–101
1. a.   **3.** $\frac{1}{4}$; $\frac{1}{2} \times \frac{1}{2} = \frac{1}{4}$ **5.** 1   **7.** $\frac{3}{5}$ **9.** $\frac{35}{4}$, or $8\frac{3}{4}$
11. $\frac{20}{9}$, or $2\frac{2}{9}$ **13.** $\frac{2}{27}$ **15.** $\frac{3}{44}$ **17.** $\frac{7}{8}$ **19.** $\frac{16}{45}$
21. $\frac{1}{9}$ **23.** $\frac{3}{10}$ **25.** $\frac{1}{2}$ and $\frac{2}{1}$, $\frac{3}{4}$ and $\frac{4}{3}$, $\frac{8}{9}$ and $\frac{9}{8}$
27. $\frac{3}{80}$ **29.** $\frac{31}{40}$ **31.** $\frac{1}{10}$ of the garden   **33.** The
product would increase.   **35.** $\frac{1}{4}$ of a beat

Pages 102–103
1. $\frac{39}{8}$, or $4\frac{7}{8}$ **3.** 30 **5.** $\frac{35}{6}$, or $5\frac{5}{6}$ **7.** $\frac{323}{32}$, or $10\frac{3}{32}$ **9.** $\frac{13}{8}$, or $1\frac{5}{8}$ **11.** $\frac{209}{6}$, or $34\frac{5}{6}$ **13.** $\frac{7}{3}$, or $2\frac{1}{3}$ **15.** $\frac{35}{6}$, or $5\frac{5}{6}$ **17.** $\frac{21}{10}$, or $2\frac{1}{10}$ **19.** $\frac{50}{27}$, or $1\frac{23}{27}$ **21.** 0.7, or $\frac{7}{10}$ **23.** 5.85, or $5\frac{17}{20}$
25. Answers may vary. Possible answers: $5 \times 2\frac{1}{8}$, $1\frac{1}{4} \times 8\frac{1}{2}$ **27.** $16\frac{2}{3}$ hr **29.** $6 \times 2\frac{1}{4} = 6 \times (2 + \frac{1}{4}) = (6 \times 2) + (6 \times \frac{1}{4}) = 12 + 1\frac{2}{4} = 13\frac{1}{2}$ **1.** 2,500 **3.** 77,000 **5.** 3 **7.** 3

Page 105
1. > **3.** < **5.** greater than 1 **7.** greater than 1 **9.** greater than 1 **11.** less than 1 **13.** 1 **15.** 2 **17.** 4 **19.** $\frac{1}{2}$ **21.** 9 **23.** 3 **25.** about 40 points; about 8 points **27.** $\frac{8}{27}$ **29.** $\frac{6}{27}$, or $\frac{2}{9}$

Page 106
1. 6 strips **3.** 56 passengers **5.** Judy **7.** $2h$ **9.** $\frac{d}{10}$ **11.** $n < 6$; 0, 1, 2, 3, 4, 5 **13.** $p > 9$; 10, 11, 12, . . . **15.** < **17.** = **19.** < **21.** > **23.** 1 **25.** 24 **27.** 3 **29.** $\frac{1}{2}$

Page 109
1. $\frac{24}{1} \times \frac{1}{3}$ **3.** $\frac{9}{1} \times \frac{2}{3}$ **5.** $\frac{7}{8} \times \frac{3}{1}$ **7.** $\frac{3}{14}$ **9.** $\frac{1}{16}$ **11.** $\frac{5}{6}$ **13.** $\frac{48}{49}$ **15.** $\frac{1}{4}$ **17.** 75 **19.** $\frac{7}{24}$ **21.** $\frac{20}{9}$, or $2\frac{2}{9}$ **23.** $\frac{25}{32}$ **25.** 18 **27.** $\frac{2}{8}$, or $\frac{1}{4}$ **29.** $\frac{19}{15}$, or $1\frac{4}{15}$ **31.** $4\frac{4}{5}$hr **33.** Answers may vary. Possible answers: $\frac{4}{9} \div \frac{1}{2}$, $\frac{2}{9} \div \frac{1}{4}$

Page 111
1. 35 diagonals **3.** 36 handshakes **5.** 29.8 m **7.** 26 days

Pages 112–113
1. $\frac{5}{9} \times \frac{4}{5}$ **3.** $\frac{23}{5} \times \frac{3}{5}$ **5.** $\frac{11}{5}$, or $2\frac{1}{5}$ **7.** $\frac{15}{28}$ **9.** $\frac{10}{7}$, or $1\frac{3}{7}$ **11.** $\frac{55}{14}$, or $3\frac{13}{14}$ **13.** $\frac{17}{11}$, or $1\frac{6}{11}$ **15.** $\frac{21}{50}$ **17.** $\frac{25}{18}$, or $1\frac{7}{18}$ **19.** $\frac{2}{7}$ **21.** $\frac{50}{21}$, or $2\frac{8}{21}$ **23.** 74 **25.** 2 **27.** $\frac{140}{99}$, or $1\frac{41}{99}$ **29.** $\frac{6}{17}$ **31.** $5\frac{3}{4}$ oz **33.** Sequences may vary. Possible answer: $7 \div 2 \times 9 \div 14$; Fraction calculator: 3 Unit 1 / 2 ÷ 1 Unit 5 / 9 = **35.** $\frac{3}{4}, \frac{7}{8}, \frac{1}{2}, \frac{7}{8}, \frac{1}{2}, \frac{3}{4}, \frac{3}{4}, \frac{7}{8}, \frac{1}{2}$

Pages 116–117
1. add $\frac{2}{3}$ **3.** divide by $\frac{3}{5}$ **5.** subtract $\frac{1}{2}$, divide by 2 **7.** subtract $2\frac{4}{5}$, multiply by 5 **9.** $b = 4\frac{1}{5}$ **11.** $n = \frac{15}{32}$ **13.** $m = 5\frac{1}{2}$ **15.** $r = \frac{1}{2}$ **17.** $p = \frac{1}{4}$ **19.** $c = \frac{7}{12}$ **21.** $n = 9\frac{1}{2}$ **23.** $m = \frac{2}{3}$ **25.** $t = 3$ **27.** $r = \frac{172}{5}$, or $34\frac{2}{5}$ **29.** $p = \frac{15}{2}$, or $7\frac{1}{2}$ **31.** $c = \frac{35}{2}$, or $17\frac{1}{2}$ **33.** $b + 3\frac{1}{2} = 12\frac{1}{4}$; $b = 8\frac{3}{4}$, $8\frac{3}{4}$ bushels **35.** subtract $\frac{1}{8}$, $2\frac{1}{8}$, 2, $1\frac{7}{8}$ **1.** < **3.** = **5.** > **7.** < **9.** $4\frac{1}{12}$ **11.** $3\frac{29}{30}$ **13.** $\frac{4}{9}$ **15.** $10\frac{7}{40}$

Page 119
1. $0.8\overline{2}$ **3.** $0.\overline{2}$ **5.** 0.5 **7.** $0.\overline{6}$ **9.** 3.25 **11.** 0.15 **13.** 0.25 **15.** 0.06 **17.** 0.1875 **19.** 1.3125

21. $0.\overline{8}$ **23.** < **25.** < **27.** > **29.** > **31.** 0.5 in.; greater than

Page 121
1. 10 **3.** 100 **5.** $\frac{2}{5}$ **7.** $\frac{3}{20}$ **9.** $2\frac{1}{10}$ **11.** $\frac{1}{3}$ **13.** $\frac{1}{6}$ **15.** $\frac{1}{2}$ **17.** $\frac{3}{4}$ **19.** $5\frac{4}{5}$ **21.** $\frac{3}{500}$ **23.** $8\frac{7}{250}$ **25.** $\frac{8}{9}$ **27.** $\frac{8}{11}$ **29.** $\frac{83}{99}$ **31.** $\frac{2}{5}$, $\frac{1}{2}$, 0.6, $\frac{3}{4}$ **33.** 0.24, $\frac{1}{4}$, $\frac{2}{5}$, $0.\overline{6}$ **35.** 0.125, $\frac{2}{8}$, 0.375, $\frac{5}{8}$ **37.** $\frac{5}{8}$ lb
39. \$2 per ft

Page 123
1. 12 oak plant stands **3.** 25 books **5.** 11:00 A.M. **7.** 6 mi

Pages 124–125
1. overestimate **3.** GCF **5.** underestimate **7.** underestimate **9.** $\frac{4}{3}$ **11.** $\frac{7}{6}$ **13.** $\frac{5}{14}$ **15.** greater than 1 **17.** less than 1 **19.** divide by $\frac{4}{5}$ **21.** multiply by 9 **23.** repeating **25.** terminating **27.** $\frac{1}{2}$ **29.** 12 **31.** 2 **33.** $\frac{1}{4}$ **35.** $\frac{65}{24}$, or $2\frac{17}{24}$ **37.** $\frac{2}{3}$ **39.** $\frac{169}{18}$, or $9\frac{7}{18}$ **41.** $\frac{57}{2}$, or $28\frac{1}{2}$ **43.** $\frac{8}{15}$ **45.** $\frac{1}{15}$ **47.** $\frac{60}{77}$ **49.** $\frac{75}{64}$, or $1\frac{11}{64}$ **51.** $b = \frac{15}{4}$, or $3\frac{3}{4}$ **53.** $t = \frac{19}{2}$, or $9\frac{1}{2}$ **55.** 0.875 **57.** $1.41\overline{6}$ **59.** $1\frac{3}{4}$ **61.** $2\frac{3}{50}$ **63.** 28 handshakes **65.** \$5

Page 129
1. B. **3.** C. **5.** D. **7.** D. **9.** C. **11.** C.

Chapter 5

Page 133
11. b, f **13.** d, g **15.** $\overrightarrow{QP}$, $\overrightarrow{QR}$ **17.** $\overleftrightarrow{RP}$, $\overleftrightarrow{QR}$, $\overleftrightarrow{PQ}$ **19.** true **21.** false **23.** $\angle XBS$, $\angle SBY$, $\angle YBT$, $\angle TBX$, $\angle XBY$, $\angle TBS$ **25.** Tilton

Pages 136–137
For Exercises 1–4, students' angle measures should be close to those given. **1.** 90°; right **3.** 120°; obtuse **5.** $\angle DBF$ and $\angle FBA$ **7.** $\angle ABF$ and $\angle FBC$ **9.** 50° **11.** 130° **13.** 180° **15.** 90°; perpendicular lines form right angles. For Exercises 16–19, students' angle measures should be close to those given. **17.** 90°; right **19.** 126°; obtuse **21.** 58° **23.** 129° **25.** m$\angle 1$ = 90°; m$\angle 2$ = 90°, m$\angle 3$ = 90° **27.** 10°; 100° **29.** 18°; 108° **31.** m$\angle 1$ = 70°; m$\angle 3$ = 70°; m$\angle 4$ = 110° **33.** 7,600 spectators

Page 139
17. 60°; 30°

Page 141
1. 60°; 120°, 60°; 120°, 60°; 120°, 60° **3.** They are the same. **5.** 110° **7.** 110° **9.** 110° **11.** 110° **13.** $\angle 1$ and $\angle 5$ are corresponding angles, or $\angle 3$ and $\angle 5$ are alternate interior angles.

Page 143
5. one line   7. They are parallel.   1. $\frac{8}{5}$ 3. $\frac{3}{1}$
5. $\frac{19}{2}$ 7. $\frac{3}{5}$ 9. $\frac{7}{20}$ 11. $\frac{1}{8}$

Page 145
15. They intersect at one point.   17. 4 m

Page 147
1. b.   3. a.   7. $17.22   9. $6.50

Pages 150–151
1. 180°   3. 720°   5. 2   7. 35   9. 4   11. 0
13. 540°   15. 3,240°   17. 0   19. 35
21a. parallelogram, rhombus, or trapezoid
b. parallelogram or trapezoid   c. parallelogram
23. 2   25. 0   27. 90°: none; 180°: rectangle,
rhombus, and parallelogram   29. trapezoid
31. 25 cm

Page 153
1. 180° − (m∠1 + m∠3)   3. 130°   5. ∠2 + ∠3
7. 100°   9. 125°   11. 55°   13. 360°

Page 154
1. 3 nickels, 3 dimes, and 7 quarters   3. no
5. 8   7. 7   9. 1   11. $d − 2.4$ 13. $\frac{d}{7}$ 15. $2^2 \cdot 11$
17. $2^2 \cdot 5^2$ 19. $\frac{7}{2}$ 21. $\frac{36}{5}$ 23. $\frac{17}{2}$ 25. $7\frac{1}{12}$
27. $\frac{14}{5}$, or $2\frac{4}{5}$ 29. $\frac{27}{5}$, or $5\frac{2}{5}$ 31. $\frac{14}{27}$

Page 157
1. $\overline{UV}$ 3. $\overline{ZX}$ 5. 38°   7. $\overline{AB} \cong \overline{PQ}$, $\overline{BC} \cong \overline{QR}$,
$\overline{CD} \cong \overline{RS}$; $\overline{DA} \cong \overline{SP}$, ∠A ≅ ∠P, ∠B ≅ ∠Q, ∠C
≅ ∠R, ∠D ≅ ∠S   9. $a = 50°$, $b = 8$, $c = 120°$
11. $a = 100°$, $b = 9$, $c = 100°$ 13. Yes. Opposite
sides and angles are congruent.

Pages 160–161
1. SAS   3. SSS   5. yes   7. ASA   9. SAS
13. $ST = 3$ cm; m∠T = 105°   15. 45°; ∠APD
and ∠BPC are vertical angles.   17. Yes; the
measure of each angle is 180° − (70° + 40°);
yes; ASA.   19. no

Page 163
1. quadrilateral   3. hexagon   5. quadrilateral
7. Answers for Exercise 7 may vary. Possible
answers are given. ∠1 and ∠3, ∠2 and ∠4; ∠1
and ∠2, ∠2 and ∠3; ∠1 and ∠2, ∠2 and ∠3
9. Yes. Each angle would have a measure of 90°.
1. $\frac{1}{2}$ 3. $\frac{3}{10}$ 5. $\frac{2}{25}$ 7. >   9. <

Page 165
1. $25,200   3. $525; $285   5. $21.50   7. 45 yd^2

Pages 166–167
1. bisect   3. transversal   5. supplementary
7. SAS For Exercises 12–15, answers may vary.
Possible answers are given.   13. ∠BGC and

∠FGE   15. trapezoid   17. pentagon   19. 68°
21. 112°   29. 9   31. yes   33. 120°   37. $5.50

Page 171
1. D.   3. B.   5. B.   7. C.   9. B.   11. B.   13. C.

Chapter 6

Page 175
1. $\frac{5}{4}$ 3. $\frac{4}{9}$ 5. $\frac{8}{15}$ 7. $\frac{5}{7}$ 9. $\frac{6}{7}$ 11. $\frac{2}{3}$ 13. $\frac{4}{5}$
15. yes   17. yes   19. =   21. =   23. $\frac{\$0.25}{1 \text{ orange}}$
25. $\frac{15 \text{ calories}}{1 \text{ oz}}$ 27. 33 cans   29. 9 lb of potatoes,
18 eggs, 12 cups of celery

Page 177
1. $d = 160$ 3. $b = 3$ 5. $\frac{\$0.70}{2} = \frac{n}{8}$; $2.80   7. 8;
12; 16; 36   9. $\frac{45}{63} = \frac{5}{7}$ 11. $\frac{9}{10} = \frac{108}{120}$ 13. $n =$
360   15. $100n = 600$ 17. $n = 21$ 19. $n = 143$
21. $n = 3$ 23. $n = 1$ 25. 10 students

Pages 180–181
1. 9   3. reduce   5. enlarge   7. reduce For
Exercises 9–12, answers will vary. One possible
answer is given.   9. 1 in.; 5 ft   11. 1 in.; 250 ft
13. 36   15. 5   17. 1.3   19. 2.5   21. 1.5   23. 12
25. drawing: 1 in. by $1\frac{1}{2}$ in.; actual: 50 ft by 75
ft   27. drawing: $\frac{1}{2}$ in. by $\frac{1}{2}$ in.; actual: 25 ft by
25 ft   29. $172.86   31. 9.8-cm by 7-cm
rectangle   33. circle with 2-in. radius

Page 183
1. 5 mi   3. $4\frac{2}{3}$ mi, or $4.\overline{6}$ mi   5. $2.40   7. 6

Page 185
1. 60%   3. 35%   5. 200%   7. 4%   9. 26%
11. 17%   13. 600%   15. 52%   17. 97%
19. 100%   21. 120%   23. 68%   25. 43.75%
27. 80%

Page 187
1. 0.45; 45%   3. 100%   5. $\frac{9}{100}$; 0.09   7. 0.28
9. 0.1   11. 0.89   13. 0.01   15. 81%   17. 53%
19. 72%   21. 1%   23. $\frac{1}{2}$ 25. $\frac{9}{10}$ 27. $\frac{9}{20}$ 29. $\frac{9}{4}$
31. 80%   33. $87\frac{1}{2}$%, or 87.5%   35. $62\frac{1}{2}$%, or
62.5%   37. 600%   39. 0.17   41. 0.2

Page 189
1. a.   3. b.

Page 191
1. $n = 0.1 \times 290$ 3. $n = 0.5 \times 4,800$ 5. $\frac{86}{100} =$
$\frac{n}{90}$ 7. 45   9. 36   11. 162.4   13. 10   15. 17.04
17. 0.0432   19. $57.96   21. 18   23. 0.5   25. =
27. 18 students   1. 5%   3. 30%   5. 7%   7. 0.3%

Page 192
1. 21 handshakes   3. 14 questions   5. 6,050,000
7. 4,350,000,000   9. Commutative Property of

Addition   **11.** $1\frac{1}{9}$ **13.** $10\frac{5}{8}$ **15.** $\frac{3}{5}$ **17.** $\frac{5}{42}$
19. $n = 8$ **21.** $k = \frac{1}{2}$ **23.** 0.12   **25.** 2.75
27. $4.\overline{3}$ **29.** 600%   **31.** 120%   **33.** 65°

Page 195
1. $9 = n \times 45$; 20%   **3.** $25 = n \times 50$; 50%
5. $\frac{n}{100} = \frac{24}{96}$; 25%   **7.** $\frac{n}{100} = \frac{8}{5}$; 160%   **9.** 60%
11. 20%   **13.** $83\frac{1}{3}$%   **15.** 80%   **17.** 100%
19. 10%   **21.** 125%   **23.** 52.5%   **25.** 1%
27. 400%   **29.** 20%   **31.** 1,000%   **33.** 75% of the
votes   **35.** 120°, 240°

Page 197
1. $0.25n = 41$; $n = 164$ **3.** $\frac{180}{100} = \frac{9}{n}$; $n = 5$ **5.** 300
7. 17   **9.** 55   **11.** 88   **13.** 290   **15.** 400
17. 450,000   **19.** 85   **21.** 360   **23.** $60.32
25. Day 5; $66\frac{2}{3}$, 80, 85, $95\frac{5}{21}$, $91\frac{2}{3}$

Pages 198–199
1. 100%   **3.** 1%   **5.** 10%   **7.** c.   **9.** c.   **11.** c.
13. b.   **15.** a.   **17.** $\frac{1}{4}$ **19.** $\frac{1}{10}$ **21.** about 75%
23. about 20%   **25.** about $66\frac{2}{3}$%   **27.** about 800
29. about 120   **31.** about 300   **33.** about 3,500
35. Estimates may vary; about 1,500 cases of
corn.   **37.** −; +

Page 201
1. 12.5%   **3.** 90%   **5.** 236%

Page 203
1. I; 5   **3.** I; 242   **5.** 100% increase   **7.** 25%
increase   **9.** 14% increase   **11.** 25% decrease
13. 6% decrease   **15.** $66\frac{2}{3}$% decrease   **17.** 50%
decrease   **19.** 20% increase   **21.** Jason: yes,
27.5%; Vicki: no, 33%

Page 205
1. I = $2,160; A = $6,660   **3.** I = $87,500;
A = $122,500   **5.** 72.00   **7.** $5.80   **9.** $143.00
11. $595.00   **13.** $324 interest; $1,524 total
amount   **15.** 10 hexagons, 10 trapezoids, 30
triangles   **1.** about 50   **3.** about 1,000   **5.** about
100%   **7.** about 1%

Page 207
1. about $6.00   **3.** about $4.50   **5.** about $0.75
7. about $1.50   **9.** about $3.00   **11.** Estimates
may vary. Possible estimate: about $230
13. $1,260   **15.** 5 quarters, 6 dimes   **17.** 12% of
the total area

Pages 208–209
1. ratio   **3.** proportion   **5.** divide   **7.** $\frac{3}{4}$ **9.** $\frac{4}{3}$
11. $\frac{7}{3}$ **13.** $\frac{46 \text{ mi}}{1 \text{ hr}}$ **15.** $\frac{1}{3}$ **17.** $\frac{52}{25}$ **19.** $\neq$ **21.** =
23. enlarge   **25.** enlarge   **27.** 384%   **29.** 52%
31. 0.12   **33.** 1.5   **35.** 0.375   **37.** D   **39.** $n = 4$
41. $n = 15.3$ **43.** $\frac{245}{45} = \frac{n}{40}$ **45.** 200%   **47.** 81

For Exercises 48–51, estimates may vary. One
possible estimate is given.   **49.** about 50%
51. about 5   **53.** 42% decrease   **55.** $10.40
57. 30 ft by 21 ft   **59.** 225 mi

Page 213
1. C.   **3.** B.   **5.** B.   **7.** D.   **9.** A.   **11.** D.

Chapter 7

Page 217
1. 2   **3.** ⁻2   **5.** ⁻6   **7.** ⁻23   **9.** ⁻112   **11.** 150
13. 18   **15.** 1   **17.** 253   **19.** 196   **21.** 12
23. 115   **25.** walking north 2 km   **27.** 4
29. 116   **31.** ⁻34   **33.** >   **35.** >   **37.** <   **39.** <
41. ⁻9, ⁻7, ⁻4, 4   **43.** ⁻7, ⁻6, 6, 7, 9   **45.** ⁻21,
⁻19, 10, 20   **47.** Ship B   **49.** 110° and 70°

Page 219
1. positive; 5   **3.** negative; ⁻3   **5.** negative; ⁻8
7. ⁻5   **9.** 29   **11.** ⁻10   **13.** ⁻2   **15.** 0   **17.** ⁻14
19. ⁻67   **21.** 14   **23.** 63   **25.** 42   **27.** 13   **29.** 16
31. ⁻12   **33.** ⁻37 m   **35.** ⁻7, ⁻4, ⁻1, 2, 5
37. ⁻22   **39.** 75

Pages 220–221
1. 10 + 3   **3.** 11 + ⁻3   **5.** ⁻1 + ⁻5   **7.** ⁻6 + 12
9. 21   **11.** ⁻3   **13.** 41   **15.** 12   **17.** 3   **19.** 35
21. ⁻9   **23.** ⁻23   **25.** 37   **27.** ⁻8   **29.** ⁻4   **31.** 0
33. ⁻136   **35.** 31   **37.** ⁻8   **39.** ⁻5   **41.** ⁻6   **43.** 8
45. ⁻2   **47.** ⁻3,150 ft   **49.** ⁻8 and ⁻5

Page 223
1. positive; 35   **3.** negative; ⁻40   **5.** negative;
⁻36   **7.** positive; 60   **9.** 18   **11.** 2   **13.** ⁻9
15. ⁻42   **17.** 88   **19.** ⁻90   **21.** 45   **23.** 16
25. 26   **27.** 77   **29.** 36   **31.** 60   **33.** ⁻30   **35.** 12
37. ⁻14   **39.** ⁻42   **41.** ⁻18 m   **43.** 9 dives

Page 225
1. space shuttle system.   **5.** $16.25; $18.75;
$21.25   **7.** $8.75   **9.** about 140 riders

Pages 226–227
1. negative   **3.** negative   **5.** positive   **7.** zero
9. ⁻5   **11.** 5   **13.** 9   **15.** ⁻3   **17.** 4   **19.** ⁻2
21. 50   **23.** ⁻5   **25.** ⁻14   **27.** ⁻40   **29.** Answers
may vary. Possible answers: ⁻25 and 5, 100 and
⁻20   **31.** ⁻11   **33.** ⁻5   **35.** 4   **37.** 6   **39.** 9
41. ⁻2   **45.** negative   **47.** zero   **49.** negative
51. positive   **1.** 1,477.44   **3.** ⁻192   **5.** $3\frac{1}{2}$ **7.** ⁻29

Page 228
1. about $1.35   **5.** 7 four-day experiments   **7.** 27
9. 1   **11.** 144   **13.** $b \geq 7$; 7, 8, 9, . . .   **15.** $x > 7$;
8, 9, 10, . . .   **17.** $2^2 \times 7$ **19.** $2^2 \times 5^2$ **21.** 0.3
23. 1.25   **25.** $0.\overline{7}$ **27.** 110°   **29.** 25%   **31.** 150%
33. 90%   **35.** 9.4   **37.** 163   **39.** inequality
41. equation

Page 231

1. $^-8$ 3. $^-7$ 5. 3 7. $^-13$ 9. Identity Property
11. Additive Inverse Property 13. Distributive
Property 15. $^-180$ 17. 276 19. 35 21. 365
23. $^-140$ 25. 2 27. $^-10$ m 29. No; Tim did
not use the $\pm$ key.

Pages 232–233

1. 3^{-2} 3. 10^{-5} 5. 6^{-10} 7. $\frac{1}{49}$ 9. $\frac{1}{64}$ 11. 10^{-1}
13. 4^{-2} 15. 10^{-3} 17. 5^{-2} 19. 4^{-2}, or 2^{-4} 21. 10^{-5}
23. $\frac{1}{100}$ 25. $\frac{1}{1,000}$ 27. $\frac{1}{2,401}$ 29. $\frac{1}{81}$ 31. $\frac{1}{4}$
33. 0.5 35. $0.1\overline{6}$ 37. 0.008 39. 0.01
41. negative exponent 43. negative exponent
45. 0.3125 47. 0.000064 49. 5,764,801

Page 235

1. $4 + 1$ 3. $4 + {}^-2$ 5. $4 - 2$ 7. $5 - 2$ 9. 2^8
11. 9^{16} 13. 10^9 15. 12^5 17. $(^-1)^8$ 19. $(2.4)^{-6}$
21. 2^4 23. 12^6 25. 10^3 27. 7^{-4} 29. $(^-6)^{-4}$

Page 237

1. 3 3. 3.1 5. 10,000 7. 1.64×10^5
9. 9.5×10^4 11. 1.6×10^{-3} 13. 5.2×10^{-6}
15. 5.2×10^9 17. 83,000 19. 0.000041
21. 0.0000000631 23. 2,150,000 25. 1.51288×10^8 km 27. Calculator answers may vary.
Possible answer: Error 0; 4.5×10^5; 3.7×10^5;
16.65; multiply by 10^{10}; 166,500,000,000
1. $^-96$ 3. $^-39$ 5. $^-20$ 7. $^-64$ 9. 324 11. $^-120$

Page 239

For Exercises 1–4, variables will vary.
1. $2n = {}^-934$; $n = {}^-467$; $^-467$ ft per min
3. $n + 45 = 35$; $n = {}^-10$; $^-10°$F 5. 4,355 ft
7. 275 gal 9. 15 in.

Pages 240–241

1. negative 3. opposite 5. negative 7. $^-5$
9. $^-14$ 11. 16 13. 37 15. $<$ 17. $=$
19. negative 21. positive 23. positive
25. negative 27. positive 29. positive 31. $^-8$
33. less than 1 35. less than 1 37. greater
than 1 39. less than 1 41. 33 43. 0 45. $^-4$
47. 17 49. 88 51. $^-216$ 53. $^-4$ 55. 4
57. $^-3$ 59. 576 61. 6^{-2} 63. 4^{-6} 65. 5^{-10}
67. 7^{-5} 69. 2.37×10^{11} 71. 0.000659
73. 0.0000000437 75. \$2.50 77. Table should
show 7 at \$27.50, 8 at \$30.00, and 9 at \$32.50.
79. 4 years old

Page 245

1. C. 3. C. 5. B. 7. B. 9. D. 11. B.

Chapter 8

Page 249

1. $\frac{4}{10}$ 3. $\frac{-5}{1}$ 5. $\frac{6}{10}$ 7. $\frac{7}{20}$ 9. 0.46 11. $\frac{16}{5}$
13. $\frac{-23}{4}$ 15. $>$ 17. $<$ 19. $<$ 21. $=$ 23. $^-1\frac{1}{2}$,
$\frac{1}{2}$, $2\frac{1}{2}$ 25. $\frac{-6}{3}$, $^-1.2$, $\frac{-4}{5}$, $\frac{1}{2}$, 3.5 27. $^-2.55$
29. $\frac{5}{10}$ 31. Possible answers: 10.05°F, 10.06°F,
10.07°F 33. true; $\frac{-4}{1} = {}^-4$

Page 251

1. 4 m 3. 7 cm 5. SR 7. S 9. N 11. 169
13. 144 15. 0.25 17. 1.44 19. $\frac{9}{49}$ 21. 10, $^-10$
23. 8, $^-8$ 25. $^-9$ 27. 6 29. $^-12$ 31. 0.8
33. 0.4 35. $^-0.1$ 37. 0.2 39. $\frac{8}{9}$ 41. 80 ft of
fencing 43. 9

Pages 254–255

1. $x = 9$; $y = 16$ 3. $x = 100$; $y = 121$
5. $x = 49$; $y = 64$ 7. 8.7 9. 15.1 11. 14.1
13. 6.93 15. 8.49 17. 4.58 19. 1.58 21. $^-0.89$
23. 8.8 25. $^-8.1$ 27. $^-7.5$ 29. 13.6 31. 12.0
33. 4.36 35. 9.70 37. 10.82 39. 9.38
41. 10.34 43. 0.39 45. 0.82 47. 2.8 49. 5
51. 4.7 53. 3.46 55. 5.20 57. 5 61. 11.0 mph
63. 34.6 mph

Page 257

1. Real Number; Rational Number; Whole
Number; Integer 3. Real Number; Rational
Number 5. Real Number; Irrational Number
7. Real Number; Irrational Number 9. Real
Number; Rational Number 11. $^-6.2$, $^-\sqrt{3}$, $\frac{3}{4}$,
$(1.2)^2$, $2\frac{1}{2}$, $2.6457513\ldots$, $\sqrt{25}$, $8.1240384\ldots$,
18, 182 13. 3.7416573; irrational number
15. $0.\overline{3}$; rational number 17. 1; rational
number; whole number; integer 19. $^-12$;
rational number; integer 21. $\frac{-5}{7}$; rational
number

Pages 258–259

1. positive; 21.9 3. negative; $^-8.7$ 5. negative;
$\frac{-5}{6}$ 7. positive; $\frac{1}{12}$ 9. $\frac{-1}{11}$ 11. $1\frac{9}{11}$ 13. $\frac{-11}{9}$, or
$^-1\frac{2}{9}$ 15. $^-0.7$ 17. $^-11.38$ 19. $^-17.29$ 21. $1\frac{5}{12}$
23. $\frac{-1}{2}$ 25. $\frac{-1}{6}$ 27. 3 29. $^-5.92$ 31. 1.76
33. $^-1.59$ 35. $^-4.97$ 37. $\frac{-7}{6}$, or $^-1\frac{1}{6}$
39. $^-2.6°$C 1. $\frac{5}{12}$ 3. 120 5. $3\frac{1}{2}$ 7. $^-24$
9. $18\frac{1}{5}$ 11. 1,127

Page 261

1. Alan 3. 8 student tickets 5. Mr. Kubach,
Ms. Baker, Mr. Smith, Ms. Thomas, or Ms.
Thomas, Mr. Smith, Ms. Baker, Mr. Kubach

Pages 262–263

1. $^-18.29$ 3. $^-8$ 5. $\frac{-10}{21}$ 7. $^-3\frac{3}{4}$ 9. $\frac{-5}{48}$ 11. $\frac{1}{4}$
13. $\frac{-1}{4}$ 15. $^-8$ 17. $^-1$ 19. $\frac{-9}{32}$ 21. $\frac{-1}{9}$ 23. $\frac{1}{18}$
25. $^-4.05$ 27. $^-3.28$ 29. $^-4.4$ 31. $\frac{-2}{3}$ 33. $\frac{1}{10}$
35. $^-4.8$ 37. 6 39. $\frac{1}{2}$ 41. $^-1$ 43. $x = 0.9$
45. 12 years 47. $^-0.9°$C

Page 264
1. $6.77 **3.** $320,275,000 **5.** $3.21 **7.** 12 **9.** 4
11. 6.5 **13.** 30 **15.** 3 **17.** $\frac{3}{2}$ **19.** $\frac{1}{8}$ **21.** $\frac{9}{10}$
23. $x = 24$ **25.** $x = 81$ **27.** $r = 24$ **29.** 60%
31. $66\frac{2}{3}$% **33.** 0.7%

Page 267
1. subtract $^-3.2$ **3.** subtract 9.2 **5.** divide by
$\frac{^-5}{6}$ **7.** $a = ^-10$ **9.** $x = 8.2$ **11.** $d = 3$
13. $a = ^-15$ **15.** $y = ^-6$ **17.** $m = 45$
19. $p = 17$ **21.** $q = 13$ **23.** $n = ^-20$
25. $n - 12.4 = ^-6.5$ **27.** $\frac{2}{3}n = 420$; $n = 630$;
630 people **1.** 2.94 **3.** 60

Pages 268–269
1. $n = ^-3$ **3.** $m = 21$ **5.** $h = ^-45$ **7.** $n = ^-3$
9. $n = 0.\overline{3}$, or $\frac{1}{3}$ **11.** $n = 20$ **13.** $c = ^-8$. **15.** $b = ^-4$ **17.** $n = ^-18$ **19.** $s = ^-12$ **21.** $u = 16$
23. $m = 3$ For Exercises 25–27, key sequences
may vary. Possible answers are given. **25.** 7 +
11 = × 3 ÷ 5 = **27.** 9 + 6 = × 2 ÷ 6 = **29.** $\frac{n}{4} -$
$5 = ^-2$; $n = 12$ **31.** $\frac{n}{3} + 10 = ^-17$; $n = ^-81$
33. $31.80

Page 271
1. $x > ^-2$ **3.** $n \le ^-5$ **5.** $c > 5$ **7.** $n > 2$
9. $n < 2$ **11.** $a > 9$ **13.** $c \le ^-5$ **15.** $s \ge 3$
17. $n \ge 3$ **19.** d **21.** c **23.** Variable will vary;
$n + 5 < 29$; $n < 24$; fewer than 24 persons.
25. $n < ^-1$ or $n \ge 0$; the numbers greater than
or equal to $^-1$ and less than 0.

Page 273
1. 65 mi **3.** 54.17 mph **5.** 82 pots **7.** 8 in.
9. One possible answer is given. Fill the 5 qt
container. Pour it into the 3 qt container.
Discard the 3 qt. Pour the remaining 2 qt from
the 5 qt container into the 3 qt container. Fill
the 5 qt container again and pour off 1 qt into
the 3 qt container. Now you have 4 qt left in the
5 qt container.

Pages 274–275
1. rational **3.** square **5.** perfect squares
7. square root For Exercises 8–12, answers will
vary. Possible answers are given. **9.** $\frac{5}{2}$ **11.** $\frac{^-17}{2}$
13. SR **15.** S **17.** S **19.** irrational
21. irrational **23.** positive **25.** positive
27. divide by 4 **29.** multiply by $^-5$ **31.** >
33. < **35.** $\frac{^-13}{20}$ **37.** $\frac{9}{12}$ **39.** 289 **41.** 12 **43.** $^-6$
45. 3.9 **47.** $^-8.4$ **49.** 10.2 **51.** $^-4$ **53.** $\frac{^-17}{12}$,
or $^-1\frac{5}{12}$ **55.** 2 **57.** $^-3.2$ **59.** $n = \frac{^-1}{2}$
61. $n = ^-7$ **63.** $n \le 6$ **65.** $n > ^-9$ **67.** 8 sec

Page 279
1. B. **3.** C. **5.** A. **7.** A. **9.** D. **11.** B.

Chapter 9

Pages 282–283
1. quadrant I **3.** quadrant II **5.** quadrant II
7. $(3,^-2)$ **9.** $(2,3)$ **11.** $(1,6)$ **13.** $(1,^-6)$
15. $(^-7,4)$ **17.** $(5,^-4)$ **19.** $(^-7,^-4)$ **21.** $(4,0)$
23. S **25.** P **27.** R **29.** 0 **31.** J **33.** quadrant
II **35.** quadrant I **45.** $(^-4, ^-5)$ **47.** 50%

Page 285
1. (5,2), (8,5), (10,7), (15,12) **3.** no **5.** yes
7. (1,3), (1,2), (1,1), (1,$^-1$), (1,$^-2$); no **9.** (1,$^-2$),
(2,1), (3,$^-1$), (4,2); yes **11.** Divide each total
score value by 5.

Page 287
1. (4,7) **3.** (4,12) **5.** ($^-2,^-8$), ($^-1,^-4$), (0,0), (1,4),
(2,8) **7.** ($^-2,^-5$), ($^-1,^-4$), (0,$^-3$), (1,$^-2$), (2,$^-1$)
9. ($^-2,0$), ($^-1,3$), (0,6), (1,9), (2,12) **11.** ($^-2,^-1$),
($^-1,\frac{^-1}{2}$), (0,0), (1,$\frac{1}{2}$), (2, 1) **13.** no **15.** yes
17. yes **19.** $y = 6 - 2x$ **21.** $y = x + 2$; Possible
solutions: (1,3), (2,4), (3,5) **23.** domain: 0,1,2;
range: 0,4,$^-4$ **25.** domain: 0,$^-1$,$^-2$; range:
$^-2$,$^-3$,$^-4$ **27.** domain: $^-3$, 0, $^-2$; range: $^-3$, 4, 8

Pages 288–289
1. $^-5$; $^-4$; $^-3$ **7.** ($^-3,^-2$) **9.** Answers may vary.
Possible answer: (1,6) **19.** $y = 2x$ **1.** $^-3$ **3.** 14
5. $x = 5$ **7.** $y = 51$ **9.** $x = 0.7$ **11.** $t = ^-1$

Page 291
1. about 3 km **3.** about 3.5 sec **5.** 2:45 P.M.
7. 60.025 m

Page 293
1. $\frac{3}{5}$ **3.** $\frac{1}{1}$, or 1 **5.** $\frac{3}{5}$ **7.** $\frac{^-1}{3}$ **9.** $\frac{^-1}{1}$, or $^-1$
11. positive **13.** negative

Page 294
1. 5 cassettes and 4 CD's **3.** 61 fish
7. 3,340,000,000 **9.** 99,400,000 **11.** $^-14$
13. 19 **15.** 0.779 **17.** $^-14.96$ **19.** $\frac{^-6}{4}$, $\frac{^-4}{5}$, $\frac{5}{4}$,
1.3 **21.** $^-1\frac{3}{4}$, 0.14, $1\frac{1}{8}$, 1.4 **23.** 55° **25.** 125°
27. 125° **29.** 75% **31.** 4% **33.** 20%

Page 297
1. ($^-1,^-3$) **3.** ($^-1,5$) **5.** (4,2) **7.** ($^-1,3$)
9. ($^-1,2$) **11.** (1,6) **13.** $x + y = 20$; $y = x + 4$;
(8,12); Jane: 12 papers, Eric: 8 papers **15.** 10
triangles **17.** (30°E, 30°N) **19.** (15°W, 15°N)
21. (30°E, 15°N)

Page 299
13. no **15.** Answers will vary. Possible answer:
(2,2) **17.** Answers will vary. Possible answer:
(4,2) **19.** no; no **21.** (0,6), (3,4), (6,2), (9,0)
23. 4 pairs for $32.40

Pages 302–303
1. translation **3.** rotation **5.** translation
7. A′(1,2), B′(5,2), C′(4,4) **9.** A′($^-$3,$^-$2),
B′(1,$^-$2), C′(0,$^-$4) **11.** reflection
13. translation **15.** rotation **17.** ($^-$2,1)
19. (1,5) **21.** ($^-$2,$^-$3) **23.** ($^-$4,5) **25.** ($^-$2,$^-$7)
27. (4,0) **1.** < **3.** < **5.** <

Page 305
1. 4 baseball cards; 6 football cards **3.** 3 adult
tickets and 1 student ticket **5.** 10 pie, 1 cake;
7 pie, 3 cake; 4 pie, 5 cake; 1 pie, 7 cake
7. 2,401 newsletters

Pages 306–307
1. origin **3.** slope **5.** transformation
7. ($^-$5,$^-$3); III **9.** (1,$^-$5); IV **11.** (4,$^-$3); IV
13. (2,4); I **15.** yes **17.** x-coordinates **19.** no
25. $\frac{1}{2}$ **27.** (3,1) **29.** (1,3) **35.** A′($^-$4,$^-$2),
B′($^-$4,$^-$7), C′($^-$1,$^-$9) **37.** about 55 ft
39. 5 dimes; 3 quarters

Page 311
1. B. **3.** C. **5.** A. **7.** B. **9.** A. **11.** B.

Chapter 10

Page 315
1. mode **3.** median **5.** 4.42; 4.7; no mode
7. 78.71; 77; 75 and 90 **9.** 7 ft 6 in.; 7 ft 10 in.;
5 ft 4 in. **11.** 75 and 90 **13.** 56, or 56, 75, and
90 **15.** true **17.** true **19.** $160

Page 317
1. 75.5% **3.** 75.5% **5.** 20 cm **9.** 84.5%
11. 5 girls **13.** about $0.40; about $4.50

Page 319
1. 10 members **3.** March to May 1991
5. Graph B **7.** no; 56 in. > $3\frac{1}{2}$ ft

Page 321
1. sufficient **3.** sufficient; 80–89°F
5. insufficient **7.** interest: $2,856; total
amount: $9,656 **9.** 4 times greater **11.** peat
moss: 13 bags; fertilizer: 11 bags

Pages 322–323
1. points scored; game number **3.** bars 3 times
longer; bars $\frac{1}{2}$ the size **5.** Chicago; 52°F
7. San Francisco, 13°F **9.** San Francisco
1. $d = 17.3$ **3.** $d = 1\frac{13}{20}$ **5.** $d = 113.4$

Pages 324–325
1. 20 ft **3.** $299 **5.** rhombus **7.** square
9. parallelogram; 360° **11.** octagon; 1,080°
13. ∠C **15.** 20° **17.** $\frac{3}{4}$ **19.** $\frac{9}{10}$ **21.** 9 **23.** 0
25. < **27.** < **29.** $^-$18 **31.** 6.1 **33.** $\frac{1}{6}$
35. $\frac{21}{20}$, or $1\frac{1}{20}$

Page 327
1. 12 games **3.** 33% or $33\frac{1}{3}$% **5.** 360° **7.** 120°
11. 33% or $33\frac{1}{3}$% **13.** 72° **15.** 169°
19. business

Page 329
1. $1.50; $2.25; $2.50; $2.75; $3.00, $3.00, $3.00,
$3.50, $3.50; $4.00, $4.50, $4.80, $4.90; $5.00,
$5.00, $5.50; $6.00, $6.50; $7.00, $7.50 **3.** cents
amount **5.** $3.00 range **7.** 53°F; 39°F, 51°F,
55°F, 81°F; 54°F **9.** 59 in.; 58 in. **11.** Plot A;
less snowfall

Pages 330–331
1. 76 **3.** 59; 93 **5.** 38; 27; 69 **29.** 5; 51.5
7. 4; 1; 9; 2; 6 **9.** Class 3 **11.** Class 2 **13.** No.
One very high score may not represent the data.
1. 9.2×10^3 **3.** 3.7×10^{-2} **5.** 1×10^{-2}
7. 6.853332×10^{12} **9.** 1×10^{-5}

Page 333
1. about 24 **3.** 21; 26.5 **5.** 25% **13.** National
League: 3.5; American League: 3.5; they are the
same. **15.** National League: 42 runs; American
League: 48 runs; 6 more runs

Pages 334–335
1. about 40,000 **3.** about 48,000 **5.** about
30,000 **7.** Weight increases as age increases.
9. about 140 lb **11.** decreasing over time
13. Less than 3%. **15.** about 40 million; about
90 million **17.** about 209.4 million

Page 337
1. negative **3.** no correlation **5.** no correlation
7. negative

Page 339
For Exercises 1–3, answers may vary. One
possible answer is given. **1.** circle graph
3. line graph **5.** 615.75 in.² **7.** boys: 95; girls:
103 **9.** 60 fence posts

Pages 340–341
1. median **3.** quartile **5.** mode **7.** mean
9. $250 **11.** negative correlation **13.** positive
correlation **15.** 23; 14; 11; 64 **17.** 66; 2; 40.5; 7
19. 24.5 **21.** increases with each consecutive
game **23.** comedy **25.** no; need the unit price
27. box-and-whisker graph

Page 345
1. C. **3.** D. **5.** D. **7.** C. **9.** A. **11.** D. **13.** C.

Chapter 11

Page 349
1. 6 **3.** 6 **5.** 10 **7.** 16 **9.** 36 choices **11.** 48
choices **13.** 840 ways **15.** 17,576,000 choices

Pages 352–353
1. 6 3. 40,320 5. 6,720 7. 120 9. 20
11. 6 ways 13. 30,240 ways 15. 720
17. 3,628,800 19. 56 21. 19,958,400 23. 48
25. 4! 27. $\frac{10!}{8!}$ 29. $\frac{20!}{17!}$ 31. 120 33. 380
35. 20,160 37. 5,040 39. 7,880,400 41. 24
43. 504 45. 60 47. 720 49. 210 ways 51. 6
three-digit numbers 53. 3,360 ways 55. 46, 64
1. $\frac{4}{5}$ 3. $\frac{8}{5}$ 5. $\frac{7}{10}$ 7. 35 9. 6

Page 355
1. 10 teams 3. 20 pizzas 5. 6 7. 28 9. 252
11. 6 13. 455 15. permutation; 60 ways
17. combination; 6 ways 19. 6,435 committees
21. 24 ways

Page 357
1. 3 blue, 1 green, 2 red, 2 black, or, blue, blue,
blue, green, red, red, black, black 3. $\frac{3}{8}$ 5. 0
7. $\frac{7}{8}$ 9. $\frac{3}{8}$ 11. $\frac{1}{4}$ 13. $\frac{1}{3}$ 15. $\frac{1}{2}$ 17. $\frac{2}{3}$ 19. $\frac{1}{3}$
21. $\frac{1}{2}$ 23. $\frac{1}{5}$ 25. $\frac{1}{1}$

Page 359
1. Same numbers in rows and table; total
outcomes same as sums of rows. 3. $\frac{6}{16}$, or $\frac{3}{8}$
5. 0 7. $\frac{10}{32}$, or $\frac{5}{16}$

Page 361
1. 165 combinations 3. 35 groups 5. 29 blocks
7. 52 mph 9. 16 quarters

Page 363
3. 16 spins 5. 4 times; 4 times greater
7. 2 tires

Page 365
1. $\frac{2}{5}$, or 0.4 3. $\frac{4}{5}$, or 0.8 5. 12 completed passes
7. $\frac{9}{20}$, or 0.45 9. 90 eighth graders 1. $\frac{1}{8}$ 3. $\frac{1}{4}$
5. mean: 80; median: 79

Page 366
1. $412.50 3. 7 spaces, 8 spaces, and 11 spaces
5. $266.00 7. $\frac{19}{15}$, or $1\frac{4}{15}$ 9. $8\frac{5}{8}$ 11. 10 13. 36
15. 5 17. 2 19. $\frac{15}{2}$, or $7\frac{1}{2}$ 21. $\frac{4}{5}$ 23. 24
25. 12 27. 6^6 29. 8^2 31. 9^{-8}

Pages 368–369
1. $\frac{1}{4}$ 3. $\frac{1}{8}$ 5. $\frac{3}{8}$ 7. $\frac{1}{4}$ 9. $\frac{5}{12}$ 11. $\frac{1}{6}$ 13. $\frac{1}{8}$
15. $\frac{1}{16}$ 17. $\frac{3}{16}$ 19. 0 21. $\frac{1}{8}$ 23. $\frac{1}{24}$ 25. $\frac{1}{12}$
27. $\frac{1}{8}$ 29. $\frac{1}{4}$ 31. 78 questions

Pages 370–371
1. $\frac{1}{90}$ 3. $\frac{2}{45}$ 5. $\frac{2}{45}$ 7. dependent 9. $\frac{2}{5}$ 11. $\frac{4}{15}$
13. $\frac{1}{5}$ 15. $\frac{1}{14}$ 17. $\frac{1}{26}$ 19. $\frac{6}{35}$ 21. a shirt
23. 25 white flowers

Page 373
1. false; true; false 7. 43 students; 23 students
9. 35 students 11. 50 students

Page 375
1. P Q N D: N D P Q: D N Q P: Q P D N
3. $432 5. $25.60 7. David

Pages 376–377
1. permutation 3. sample space
5. combination 7. dependent 9. 3 pairs
11. 120 13. 336 15. $\frac{1}{4}$ 17. $\frac{1}{2}$ 19. $\frac{3}{4}$ 21. 336
23. 70 25. 360 ways 27. 5 times 29. $\frac{1}{48}$
31. $\frac{4}{33}$ 33. 0 35. 15 students 37. 210
combinations 39. 1 way: 4 dimes, 2 nickels

Page 381
1. D. 3. B. 5. D. 7. C. 9. B. 11. A.

Chapter 12

Page 385
1. 4 in. 3. in. 5. ft or in. 7. km 9. 4 mm
11. Answers will vary. Possible answer: mi
13. yd or ft 15. cm 17. mm 19. Jill

Page 387
5. thumbnail width 7. Possible answer:
bookshelf 9. no 11. b. 13. about 75 mi
15. about 100 mi 17. about 10 mi 19. $3.75
21. $83.33 per second; $8.33 per foot

Pages 390–391
1. 4 cm; 44 mm 3. 48 in. 5. 12.0 m 7. $\frac{1}{2}$ mi
9. 0.005 km 11. 1 m 13. $\frac{1}{8}$ in. 15. 0.5 cm
17. $\frac{1}{2}$ yd 19. $\frac{1}{6}$ mi 21. 0.005 km 23. $54\frac{1}{2}$ mi;
$55\frac{1}{2}$ mi 25. 82.65 km; 82.75 km 27. 5 cm;
4.5 cm, 5.5 cm; 53 mm; 52.5 mm, 53.5 mm
29. $\frac{1}{4}$ in. 31. $36,197\frac{1}{2}$ ft; $36,198\frac{1}{2}$ ft 1. $\frac{1}{4}$ 3. $\frac{5}{4}$
5. $\frac{9}{29}$ 7. 4 9. $^-11$

Page 393
1. 1 3. 4 5. 6.429 m; has more significant
digits than the other measurements 7. 9.3 m
9. 1 11. 2 13. 2 15. 2 17. 30 m 19. 79 m
21. 3.2 m^2 23. 8 mm^2 25. 2 significant digits
27. 27.78 mph

Page 395
1. 20 tiles 3. 6 tiles 5. $22\frac{1}{2}$ lb 7. 4,380 mi
9. hexagonal 1-in. tiles

Page 397
1. 31 yd 3. 31 cm 5. 51 cm 7. 38 m 9. 5.4 m
11. n = 6.6 cm 13. Yes; 996-ft perimeter is less
than 1,000 ft. 15. 175 ft

Page 398
1. about 50 points 3. 7-yr-old: $3.50; 8-yr-old:
$4.50 5. 8 7. $^-6$ 9. $\frac{1}{10^8}$ 11. $\frac{1}{4^3}$ 13. 10^{-4}
15. 2^{-3} 17. 2^4 19. 5^{-9} 21. 4.4×10^{-4}

Answers to Selected Exercises

23. 7.4×10^{-6} **25.** 4 **27.** ⁻11 **29.** $\frac{-1}{2}$, $\frac{3}{4}$, 8
31. $n = 7\frac{1}{4}$ **33.** $n = 12$ **35.** $n > 18$

Pages 400–401
1. 12 m **3.** 14 in. **5.** 25.47 cm **7.** 1.51 m
9. 0.25 mm **11.** 256.85 cm **13.** 22 in.
15. 132 ft **17.** 110 yd **19.** 440 in. **21.** 8 km
23. 200 m **25.** 32 cm **27.** about 8 cm
29. 7,760.9 revolutions **31.** 3.125000
33. 3.142857

Page 403
1. 21 m² **3.** 50 mm² **5.** 104 ft² **7.** 336 ft²
9. 28.52 cm² **11.** 60 m² **13.** 36 m²; 11 m²
15. Area increases 1,500 cm² (225%); perimeter
increases 70 m (150%)

Page 405
1. 15 m² **3.** 126 cm² **5.** 10 cm² **7.** 5.22 m²
9. 90.62 m² **11.** 32 in.² **13.** 1,925 ft²
15. 528 ft² **1.** 70 **3.** 2 **5.** 12 **7.** 0.16 **9.** 0.1̄6̄

Page 407
1. 1 ft **3.** 4 ft² **5.** 254.34 cm² **7.** 171.95 m²
9. 1,256 in.² **11.** 206.02 m² **13.** $235\frac{1}{2}$ yd²
15. 28.26 m² **17.** $44\frac{1}{2}$ ft **19.** 43,000 ft

Page 409
1. 10 rolls **3.** $143.84 **5.** 803.84 ft² **7.** $0.60
per pound **9.** 8:30 A.M.

Pages 410–411
1. significant digits **3.** precision **5.** accuracy
7. area **9.** mm **11.** about 30 mi **13.** about
20 mi **15.** 18 in.; 1 in. **17.** $\frac{1}{2}$ yd **19.** 0.05 cm
21. 5.5 cm; 6.5 cm **23.** $8\frac{1}{8}$ ft; $8\frac{3}{8}$ ft **25.** 6.4 m²
27. 3 km² **29.** 78 mm; 368 mm² **31.** 44 yd
33. 264 in. **35.** 6.8 m² **37.** 113.04 cm²
39. 706.5 in.² **41.** $8\frac{1}{3}$ yd **43.** 1,274 yd²

Page 415
1. B. **3.** D. **5.** C. **7.** A. **9.** B. **11.** C. **13.** C.

Chapter 13

Page 419
1. no **3.** yes **5.** triangular pyramid
7. rectangular prism **9.** prism; triangular
prism **11.** pyramid; octagonal pyramid
13. 1 square base; other faces, triangles
15. 2 pentagonal bases; other faces,
parallelograms **17.** 1 triangular base; other
faces, triangles **19.** triangular pyramid
21. 200 ft **23.** Answer for 1992: 1,913 yr ago

Page 421
1. sphere **3.** cone **5.** cone **7.** sphere
9. sphere **11.** cylinder **13.** cylinder; stacks
well **15.** sphere; looks circular **17.** 28.26 ft

Page 423
9. $44,000 **1.** 1, 7 **3.** 1, 2, 3, 4, 6, 8, 12, 24
5. 1, 3, 7, 9, 21, 63 **7.** $\frac{3}{4}$ **9.** $\frac{3}{5}$

Page 425
1. 7 surfaces **3.** 18 bows **5.** 1.4 in. **7.** 21 birds
9. 50 pieces of glass

Page 427
1. 236 in.² **3.** 240 cm² **5.** 103.68 m²
7. 1,386.2 cm² **9.** 5,040 m² of shade material
11. 1,100 ft² **1.** 50 **3.** 170 **5.** 4 **7.** 20 **9.** $9\frac{1}{11}$

Page 428
1. 4 T-shirts; 2 sweatshirts **3.** 11 half dollars
5. IV **7.** I **9.** 9.57, or $9\frac{4}{7}$; 9; 11 **11.** $504
13. $792 **15.** 84 choices **17.** 56 **19.** 2,520
21. $\frac{1}{2}$ in. **23.** $\frac{1}{2}$ yd **25.** 22 in. **27.** 110 ft

Page 431
1. 602.88 cm² **3.** 113.04 cm²

Page 433
1. 18 in.³ **3.** 60 ft³ **5.** 360 cm³ **7.** 561 m³
9. 120 in.³ **11.** 408 cm³ **13.** 2,592,100 m³
15. 6 ft

Page 435
1. 1,130 cm³ **3.** 402 m³ **5.** 4 m³ **7.** 464 cm³
9. 565 cm³ **11.** 20 m **13.** 78,500 ft³

Page 437
1. 1 cm by 1 cm by 1 cm **3.** 1 g **5.** 4.5
7. 180 mL; 180 g **9.** 88 mL; 88 g
11. 1,040 mL; 1,040 g **13.** 55,264 mL; 55.264 L
15. 2,400,000 g **17.** 7,800 L

Page 439
1. 4.186.̄6̄ cm³ of helium **3.** 7,191.12 cm³
greater **5.** 7 slices of pizza and 5 drinks
7. 252 boxes **9.** 3 hr

Pages 440–441
1. polyhedron **3.** prism **5.** surface area
7. capacity **9.** square pyramid **11.** sphere
13. cone **15.** pyramid **17.** cylinder
21. 392 in.² **23.** 427 m² **25.** 88 in.³
27. 236 m³ **29.** 32 mL; 32 g **31.** 63 mL; 63 g
33. 15 edges **35.** 25.12 ft² of wrapping paper

Page 445
1. B. **3.** B. **5.** C. **7.** C. **9.** D. **11.** B.

Chapter 14

Page 449
1. hypotenuse: $\overline{PQ}$; legs: $\overline{PR}$, $\overline{QR}$
3. hypotenuse: $\overline{LM}$; legs: $\overline{LN}$, $\overline{MN}$ **5.** no **7.** yes

Page 451
1. 17 cm   **3.** 8 cm   **5.** 11.7 mm   **7.** 12.7 km
9. 11.5 m **11.** 34 m   **13.** 10 years old

Page 453
1. $b = 20\sqrt{2}$ cm   **3.** $c = 20\sqrt{2}$ m   **5.** $4\sqrt{2}$
7. $6\sqrt{2}$ **9.** $4\sqrt{3}$ **11.** 14   **13.** $21.50   **15.** $250

Page 455
1. Choice 1   **3.** $32   **5.** 2 or 3 presents   **7.** 7.5%

Pages 456–457
1. $\frac{2}{1}$, or $\frac{1}{2}$ **3.** no   **5.** yes   **7.** $x = 70$ mm
9. false   **11.** $\frac{5}{16}$ **1.** $n = 6$ **3.** $n = 3\frac{3}{4}$ **5.** 0.60
7. 0.53   **9.** 0.24

Page 458
1. 20 ways   **3.** $416.50   **5.** yes   **7.** yes
9. 282.6 m^3 **11.** 72 cm^3 **13.** $\frac{1}{12}$ **15.** $\frac{1}{6}$ **17.** 0
21. 0.6   **23.** $0.\overline{6}$ **25.** 0.375   **27.** $x = 46$
29. $c = 2.5$ **31.** $d = {}^{-}18$

Pages 460–461
1. FE **3.** $\frac{FE}{GF}$ **5.** BC **7.** AC **9.** $\frac{DE}{DF}$ **11.** 2.66;
0.42   **13.** $\frac{5.7}{2.66}$; 2.14   **15.** $\frac{2.66}{6.3}$; 0.42   **17.** They
are the same.

Pages 462–463
1. 0.754   **3.** 11.430   **5.** 1.327   **7.** 0.577
9. 57.290   **11.** 0.139   **13.** 20°   **15.** 45°   **17.** 28°
19. $x = 18.0$ cm   **21.** $x = 62.4$ m
23. $x = 25.2$ m   **25.** 24 m   **29.** 0.3249197
31. 6.3137515

Pages 464–465
1. $x = 38.1$ mm   **3.** $x = 6.4$ m   **5.** $x = 18.4$ m
7. $x = 10.3$ m   **9.** $x = 22.5$ m   **11.** 19.3 m
13. about 1.6 million   **1.** 36   **3.** 84.64   **5.** 40,000
7. 5.2   **9.** 9.3

Page 467
1. 8 red beads, 8 white beads, and 4 blue beads
3. 57 m   **5.** 1 set of batteries and 5 rolls of film
7. 61 tapes

Pages 468–469
1. isosceles   **3.** cosine   **5.** right   **7.** tangent
9. no   **11.** 45–45 right   **13.** 45–45 right   **15.** no
17. 12.8 cm   **19.** 10.0 in.   **21.** $x = 11$ cm
23. $x = 23.1$ m   **25.** about 107 cosmetic articles
27. 150 mi

Page 473
1. C.   **3.** B.   **5.** B.   **7.** A.   **9.** B.   **11.** C.

H126   **Answers to Selected Exercises**

Index

A

Absolute value, 216–218
Accuracy, 392–393
Acute angles, 134, 136
Addition
  Associative Property of, 8–9, 230–231
  with calculators, 12, 85, 219, 396–397
  Commutative Property of, 8–9, 230–231
  of decimals, H6–H7
  equations, 40–41
  estimating sums, 6–7, 10, 82–84
  expressions, 38–39
  of fractions, 82–85, 88, H23
  Identity Property of, 8–9, 230–231
  of integers, 218–220, 222, 230–231, H18–H19
  properties of, 8–9, 230–231
  of rational numbers, 258–259, H25
  using, 10–11
Additive Inverse Property, 230–231
Adjacent angles, 135–137
Algebra, 34–41, 44–62
  coordinate planes, 282–283, 285, 288–289, 292–293
  equations, 36–37, 40–41, 44–45, 50–55, 58–59, 114–117, 266–269, 286–289, 296–298
  expressions, 36–39, 48–49
  fractions, 76
  functions, 284–289, 296–297
  inequalities, 36–37, 56–57, 270–271, 298–299
  like terms, 55
  relations, 284–291, 296–299
  variables, 36
Algebraic equations, 36–37
  addition, 40–41
  checking solutions, 40–41, 44–45, 50–55, 114–117, 266–269

  division, 52–53
  with fractions, 114–117
  graphing, 288–289, 296–298
  linear, 286–289, 296–298
  multiplication, 50–51
  proportions, 176–179, 182, 184, 188–191, 194–197, 456, 462, 464, H28
  solving, 40–41, 44–45, 50–55, 58–59, 114–117, 120, 122, 176–179, 182, 184, 188, 194–197, 238, 266–269, 482–483
  subtraction, 44–45
  systems of, 296–297
  two-step, 54–55, 268–269
  with two variables, 286–289, 296–298
  writing, 58–59, 122, 238–239
Algebraic expressions, 36–39, 48–49
  addition, 38–39
  division, 48–49
  evaluating, 38–39, 48–49
  multiplication, 48–49
  subtraction, 38–39
Algebraic fractions, 76
Alternate exterior angles, 141
Alternate interior angles, 141
Analyzing data, 53, 191, 197, 229, 263, 314–315, 317, 323
Angles, 132–142, H14–H15
  acute, 134, 136
  adjacent, 135–137
  alternate exterior, 141
  alternate interior, 141
  bisecting, 144–145
  central, H16–H17
  complementary, 134–137
  congruent, 138–139, 141–142, 156–158
  corresponding, 140–141, 156–158, 456
  exterior, 141, 152–153
  interior, 141, 152–153
  obtuse, 134, 136
  of polygons, 148–153
  right, 134, 136

  supplementary, 134–137, 140–141, 152
  vertical, 135–137, 140–141
  vertices of, H14
Angle-side-angle, 158–161
Answers, H115–H126
Archimedes, 444
Arcs, H16–H17
  semicircles, H16–H17
Area, 402–407, 429, 448
  of circles, 406–407, 430–431, 434
  of parallelograms, 402–404, 406, 426, 430–431
  of rectangles, 402–403, 426–427, 430–431
  of squares, 23, 250, 253, 426–427
  surface, 426–427, 430–431
  of trapezoids, 404–405
  of triangles, 404–405, 426–427
Associative Property
  of Addition, 8–9, 230–231
  of Multiplication, 8–9, 230–231
Averages, 314–315
  batting, 185, 379

B

Back-to-back stem-and-leaf plots, 328–329
Bar graphs, 322–323, 325, 338, 480–481
  histograms, 316–317
Bases
  of powers, 22
  of solid figures, 418–419, 424
BASIC, 478–479, 490
Batting averages, 185, 379
Bisectors, 144–145
Box-and-whisker graphs, 332–333, 338–339
Bridge Lessons, H2–H21

Calculator Connection, 463
Calculators, 15, 55,
    408, 431–435, 437–439,
    450–451, 461
    and addition, 12, 85, 219,
    396
    change of sign key, 219, 222,
    233, 262
    and division, 14, 18, 50, 113,
    118, 186, H10
    fractions, 85
    memory keys, 24
    and multiplication, 23,
        102–103, 204, 222, 237, 252,
        262, 402
    order of operations, 24–25
    percent key, 202, 326–327
    for powers, 23, 233
    scientific, 233, 463
    solving proportions, 176
    square root key, 253–254, 256,
        450
    and subtraction, 10, 12,
        221
    trigonometric ratios, 463
Capacity, 436–437
    liters, 436–437
    milliliters, 436–437
Center
    of circles, H16–H17
    of spheres, 420
Centimeters, 384–385, 388–392
Central angles, H16–H17
Central tendencies, 314–315,
    H20–H21
    means, 314–315, 344,
        H20–H21
    medians, 314–315, 328–333,
        H20–H21
    modes, 314–317, 328–329,
        H20–H21
Challenges, 32, 76, 113
    Logical Reasoning, 3, 32, 64,
        170, 212, 278, 310, 472
    Number Sense, 15, 94, 128,
        170, 278, 310, 344, 414, 444
    Patterns, 128, 414
    Visual Thinking, 64, 212, 444,
        472
Change of sign key, 219, 222,
    233, 262
Chapter Reviews, 28–29, 60–61,
    90–91, 124–125, 166–167,
    208–209, 240–241, 274–275,
    306–307, 340–341, 376–377,
    410–411, 440–441, 468–469

Chapter Tests, 30, 62, 92, 126,
    168, 210, 242, 276, 308, 342,
    378, 412, 442, 470
Chords, H16–H17
    diameters, 162–163, 400–401,
        H16–H17
Circle graphs, 326–327,
    338–339
Circles, 162–163, H16–H17
    arcs, H16–H17
    area of, 406–407, 430–431,
        434
    center of, H16–H17
    central angles, H16–H17
    chords, H16–H17
    circumference of, 400–401,
        407, 430
    diameters, 162–163, 400–401,
        H16–H17
    radii, 400–401, 406–407,
        H16–H17
    semicircles, H16–H17
Circumference, 400–401, 407,
    430
Collecting data, 229
Combinations, 354–355,
    360–361
Common denominators, 78, 115
    least, 78, 84, 86
Common factors, 234, H12
    greatest, 70–71, 74, 100,
        H12–H13
Common multiples, H12
    least, 70–71, 78–79, H12–H13
Commutative Properties
    of Addition, 8–9, 230–231
    of Multiplication, 8–9
Comparisons
    of decimals, H2–H3
    of fractions, 78–79
    of rational numbers, 248–249
Compass, 138–139, 142–145,
    159, 326
Compatible numbers, 104–105,
    112
Complementary angles, 134–137
Complex fractions, 112–113
Composite numbers, 68–69
Computers, 474–491
    BASIC, 478–479, 490
    data bases, 488–489, 491
    ENIAC, 246
    LOGO, 476–479, 490
    for random numbers, 363,
        478–479, 490
    spreadsheets, 480–491
    word processors, 486–487,
        490–491

Cones, 420–421
    surface area of, 430–431
    volume of, 434–435, 437, 444,
        H28
Congruent figures
    angles, 138–139, 141–142,
        156–158
    line segments, 138–139,
        156–158
    polygons, 156–161
Connections
    Calculator, 463
    Computer, 474–491
    Everyday, 161
    Everyday Math, 185, 437, 461
    Geography, 297
    Health, 203, 269
    History, 401
    Math, 55, 76, 85, 219, 233, 287
    Music, 101
    School-Home, H22–H28
    Science, 51, 255, 371, 435
    Social Studies, 335, 407
Constructions
    bisecting angles, 144–145
    bisecting line segments,
        144–145
    of congruent angles, 138–139,
        142
    of congruent line segments,
        138–139
    of congruent triangles,
        159–160
    of parallel lines, 142–143
    of perpendicular lines,
        142–143
Continued fractions, 128
Cooperative Learning. See
    Exploring and Teamwork
    Projects
Coordinate planes, 282–283,
    285, 288–289, 292–293,
    296–303
    graphs of inequalities,
        298–299
    graphs of linear equations,
        288–289, 296–298, 483
    graphs of points, 282–285,
        288, 292
    graphs of relations, 284–285,
        288–291, 296–299
    graphs of systems of
        equations, 296–297
    quadrants, 282–283
    transformations, 300–303, 310
Correlations, 337
Corresponding angles, 140–141,
    156–158, 456

Corresponding sides, 156–159, 456
Cosine, 460–461, 464–465
Cross products, 174
Cubes, 432
    volume of, 23
Cumulative Reviews, 33, 65, 95, 129, 171, 213, 245, 279, 311, 345, 381, 415, 445, 473
Customary system
    feet, 384–385, 389–391, 414
    inches, 384–385, 389–391, 414
    links, 414
    miles, 385–387, 414
    rods, 414
    yards, 384–385, 414
Cylinders, 420–421
    surface area of, 430–431
    volume of, 434–435, 436–437, 444, H28

•••••• D ••••••

Data
    analyzing, 53, 191, 197, 229, 263, 314–315, 317, 323
    bar graphs of, 316–317, 322–323, 325, 338, 480–481
    box-and-whisker graphs of, 332–333, 338–339
    circle graphs of, 326–327, 338–339
    collecting, 229
    extremes of, 330–333
    finding, 3, 79, 119, 259, 317, 323
    frequency tables for, 316–317
    histograms of, 316–317
    insufficient, 320–321
    line graphs of, 318–319, 334–335, 338–339, H26
    mean of, 314–315, 344, H20–H21
    measures of central tendency, 314–315, H20–H21
    median of, 314–315, 328–333, H20–H21
    misleading graphs of, 325
    mode, 314–317, 328–329, H20–H21
    organizing, 191, 317, 323, 328–333
    predictions using, 334–335
    quartiles of, 330–333
    range of, 316–317, 329–333, H25

    scattergrams of, 336–337
    stem-and-leaf plots of, 328–329, 338, 344
    sufficient, 320–321
Data base, 488–489, 491
Decagonal pyramids, 425
Decagons, 476
Decimal points, 18, 236, H2, H6, H8
Decimals
    adding, H6–H7
    comparing, H2–H3
    dividing, 18–19, 32, H8–H9
    equivalent, H2, H6
    to fractions, 120–121
    fractions to, 118–119
    multiplying, 32, H8–H9
    ordering, H2–H3
    to percents, 186–187
    percents to, 186–187, 190
    place value, H2–H3
    repeating, 118–121, 256
    rounding, H4–H5
    scientific notation, 236–237
    subtracting, H6–H7
    terminating, 118, 256
    in words, H2–H3
Decimeters, 384
Decrease
    percents of, 200–203
Denominators, 74–75, 100, 102
    least common, 78, 84, 86
Density, 248–249
Dependent events, 370–371
Diagonals, 111, 148–150
Diameters, 162–163, 400–401, H16–H17
Differences
    estimating, 6–7, 10, 82–83
Discounts, 480–481, H24
Distributive Property, 8–9, 230–231
Dividends, 18, 104, H8
Divisibility, H10–H11
Division
    with calculators, 14, 18, 50, 113, 118, 186, H10
    of decimals, 18–19, 32, H8–H9
    dividends, 18, 104, H8
    divisibility, H10–H11
    divisors, 18, 104
    equations, 52–53
    estimating quotients, 7, 14, 18, 104–105, 112
    expressions, 48–49
    of fractions, 104–105, 108–109, 112–115
    of integers, 226–227

    and multiplication, 226
    of powers, 234–235
    quotients, 104, H8–H9
    of rational numbers, 262–263
    remainders, 20–21, 118
    using, 14–15
Divisors, 18, 104
Domains, 287
Double-bar graphs, 322–323, 325, 480
Double-line graphs, 318–319

•••••• E ••••••

Earnings, H22
Edges, 424
Endpoints, H14
ENIAC, 246
Enlargements, 472
Equally likely events, 356
Equations, 36–37
    addition, 40–41
    checking solutions, 40–41, 44–45, 50–55, 114–117, 266–269
    division, 52–53
    with fractions, 114–117
    graphing, 288–289, 296–298
    linear, 286–289, 296–297
    multiplication, 50–51
    pairs of, 278
    proportions, 176–179, 182, 184, 188–191, 194–197, 456, 462, 464, H28
    solving, 40–41, 44–45, 50–55, 58–59, 114–117, 120, 122, 176–179, 182, 184, 188, 194–197, 238, 266–269, 482–483
    subtraction, 44–45
    systems of, 296–297
    two-step, 54–55, 268–269
    with two variables, 286–289, 296–297
    writing, 58–59, 122, 238–239
Equilateral triangles, 155, 170, 394–397
    perimeter of, 396–397
Equivalent decimals, H2, H6
Equivalent fractions, 74–76, 78
Equivalent ratios, 174–179, H28
Estimation, 193
    of circumference, 419
    compatible numbers, 104–105, 112

of differences, 6–7, 10, 82–83
extrapolations, 334–335
with graphs, 290–291
interpolations, 334–335
of measures, 386–387
overestimates, 6–7, 98–99
with percents, 198–199,
206–207
of products, 6–7, 14, 98–99,
102
of quotients, 7, 14, 18,
104–105, 112
of reasonable solutions, 399
rounding numbers, 4–6, 98,
H4–H5
of square roots, 252–254
of sums, 6–7, 10, 82–84
underestimates, 6–7, 98–99
using, 206–207
Events
dependent, 370–371
equally likely, 356
independent, 368–371
probability of, 356–357, 359,
362–365, 368–371
Everyday Connection, 161
Everyday Math Connections,
185, 437, 461
Experimental probability,
364–365, H27
Exploring
irrational numbers, 256–257
parallel lines and transversals,
140–141
Pascal's triangle, 358–359
percent of increase and
decrease, 200–201
percent problems, 188–189
products and quotients of
powers, 234–235
right triangles, 448–449
scattergrams, 336–337
slope of a line, 292–293
surface area of cylinders and
cones, 430–431
triangles, 152–153
Exponents, 22–25
integers as, 232–237
one as, 22–23
zero as, 22–23
Expressions, 36–39, 48–49
addition, 38–39
algebraic, 36–39, 48–49
division, 48–49
evaluating, 38–39, 48–49
multiplication, 48–49
numerical, 36–37
subtraction, 38–39

Extend Your Thinking, 32, 64,
94, 128, 170, 212, 244, 278,
310, 344, 380, 414, 444, 472
Exterior angles, 141, 152–153
alternate, 141
Extrapolations, 334–335
Extremes, 330–333

Faces, 418–419, 424–425
Factorials, 351–355
Factors, 68–70, H8, H12–H13
common, 234, H12–H13
greatest common, 70–71, 74,
100, H12–H13
prime, 68–70
Factor trees, 68
Feet, 384–385, 389–391, 414
Fibonacci, 401
Fibonacci sequence, 380, 477
Finding data, 3, 79, 119, 259,
323
Formulas
for area of circles, 406
for area of parallelograms, 402
for area of rectangles, 402
for area of squares, 23, 250
for area of trapezoids, 404
for area of triangles, 404
for circumference, 400
for distance, 51, 272
for interest, 204
for perimeter of rectangles,
396
for perimeter of squares, 396
for rolls of wallpaper, 408–409
for speed, 255
in spreadsheets, 480–485
for surface area of cones, 431
for surface area of cylinders,
431
tables of, H102
using, 272–273, 408–409,
438–439
for volume of cones, 434, 444
for volume of cubes, 23
for volume of cylinders, 434,
444
for volume of prisms, 432, 436
for volume of pyramids, 432
for volume of spheres,
438–439, 444
Fractions, 74–76, 78–89,
98–109, 112–121, 232–233
adding, 82–85, 88, H23
algebraic, 76

with calculators, 85
comparing, 78–79
continued, 128
to decimals, 118–119
decimals to, 120–121
denominators, 74–75, 78, 100,
102
dividing, 104–105, 108–109,
112–113
equations with, 114–117
equivalent, 74–76, 78
least common denominators,
78–79, 84, 86
like, 78
mixed numbers, 75–76, 82–89,
98–99, 102–105, 112–117
multiplying, 98–103, H23
numerators, 74–75, 94, 100,
102, 128, 232
ordering, 78–79
to percents, 184–187, 201–202
percents to, 186–188, 190, 198
reciprocals, 100, 108, 115
rounding, 98
simplest form of, 74–76,
100–102, 234
subtracting, 82–83, 86–87
unit, 94
Franco of Liege, 401
Frequency tables, 316–317
Functions, 284–289, 483
Fundamental Counting
Principle, 348–349

Games, 32, 244
Geography Connection, 297
Geometry, 130–153, 155–163,
H24
angles, 132–142, 144–145,
H14–H15
area, 23, 250–251, 402–407,
429, 448
circles, 162–163, 400–401,
406–407, H16–H17
circumference, 400–401, 407,
430
cones, 420–421, 430–431,
434–435, 437, 444, H28
constructions, 138–139,
142–145, 159–160
cubes, 23, 432
cylinders, 420–421, 430–431,
434–435, 437, 444, H28
lines, 132–133, 135–136,
140–143, H14–H15

line segments, 132–133,
138–139, 144–145, H14–H15
parallelograms, 149–151,
402–404, 406
perimeter, 384, 396–397, 408
planes, 132, H14
points, 132–133, H14
polygons, 148–153, 155–163,
394–397, 476
polyhedra, 418–419, 422–427,
432–433, 436–437
prisms, 418–419, 422–427,
432–433, 436–437
pyramids, 418–419, 424–427,
432–433, 437
rays, 132–133, H14–H15
rectangles, 130, 148–151,
396–397, 402–403
rhombuses, 149, 151
similar figures, 456–457, 472
spheres, 420–421, 438–439,
444
squares, 23, 130, 149–151,
155, 250–251
surface area, 426–427,
430–431
symmetry, 150–151, 300–301,
303
tessellations, 170, 394–395
transformations, 300–303
trapezoids, 149–151, 404–405
triangles, 148–153, 155,
158–161, 170, 394–395,
404–405, 448–453, 456–457,
460–465, 472, 476
volume, 23, 432–439, 444
Glossary, H110–H116
Grams, 436–437
Graphs
bar, 316–317, 322–323, 325,
338, 480–481
box-and-whisker, 332–333,
338–339
choosing appropriate, 338–339
circle, 326–327, 338–339
coordinate planes, 282–283,
285, 288–289, 292–293,
296–303
of equations, 288–289,
296–297, 483
for estimation, 290–291
histograms, 316–317
of inequalities, 270–271,
298–299
line, 318–319, 334–335,
338–339, H26
of lines, 288–289, 292–293,
296–297

misleading, 325
of points, 282–289, 292–293,
296–303
of relations, 284–285,
288–291, 296–299
scattergrams, 336–337
slopes, 292–293
of square roots, 255
stem-and-leaf plots, 328–329,
338–339, 344
of systems of equations,
296–297
transformations, 300–303, 310
Greatest common factors (GCF),
70–71, 74, 100, H12–H13
Greatest possible error, 389–391
Guess and check, 42–43,
304–305

. . . . . . .H. . . . . . .

Health Connections, 203, 269
Hexagonal prisms, 419, 436
Hexagonal pyramids, 419
Hexagons, 148–150, 155, 394,
476
regular, 170, 394
Histograms, 316–317
History Connection, 401
Hours, 414, H23
Hypotenuse, 449–453, 460, 464

. . . . . . .I. . . . . . .

Identity Properties
of Addition, 8–9, 230–231
of Multiplication, 8–9,
230–231
Inches, 384–385, 389–391, 414
Incommensurable quantities,
212
Increase
percents of, 200–203, 485
Independent events, 368–369
Indirect measurement, 450–453,
456–457, 460–465, H28
Inequalities, 36–37, 270–271
graphing, 298–299
solving, 56–57, 270–271
Inferences, 334–335
Insufficient data, 320–321
Integers, 216–239, 244, 257
absolute value of, 216–218
adding, 218–220, 222,
230–231, H18–H19
dividing, 226–227
as exponents, 232–237

multiplying, 222–223, 226,
230–231
opposites, 216–217, 220, H18
properties of, 230–231
subtracting, 220–221,
H18–H19, H25
Interest, 204–205
Interior angles, 141, 152–153
alternate, 141
Interpolations, 334–335
Intersecting lines, 132–133,
135–137
perpendicular, 136–137,
142–143
transversals, 140–141
vertical angles, 135–137,
141
Inverse operations, 40, 50
Inverse Property, 230–231
Irrational numbers, 256–257
Irrelevant information, 81
Isosceles triangles, 452–453

. . . . . . .K. . . . . . .

Kilograms, 436–437
Kilometers, 385, 389–391

. . . . . . .L. . . . . . .

Learning Resources, H86–H100
Least common denominators
(LCD), 78, 84, 86
Least common multiples (LCM),
70–71, 78–79, H12–H13
Legs, 449–453
Length, 384–393
centimeters, 384–385,
388–393
customary units, 384–385
decimeters, 384
estimating, 386–387
feet, 384–385, 389–391, 414
inches, 384–385, 389–391, 414
kilometers, 385, 389–391
links, 414
meters, 384–385, 389–391
metric system, 384–385
miles, 182–183, 385–387, 414
millimeters, 384–385,
388–391
nautical miles, 407
perimeter, 384, 396–397, 408
rods, 414
yards, 384–385, 414
Like fractions, 78

Like terms, 55
Linear equations, 286–289, 296–297, 483
Line graphs, 318–319, 334–335, 338–339, H26
Lines, 132–133, 135–137, H14–H15
  of best fit, 337
  graphing, 288–289, 296–297
  intersecting, 132–133, 135–137
  number, 216–218, 270–271, 332–333, H4
  parallel, 140–143
  perpendicular, 136–137, 142–143
  slope of, 292–293
  of symmetry, 150–151, 300–303
  transversals, 140–141
Line segments, 132–133, H14–H15
  bisecting, 144–145
  chords, H16–H17
  congruent, 138–139, 156–161
  diagonals, 111, 148–151
  diameters, 162–163, H16–H17
  radii, 420, 430–431, 434, 438, 444, H16–H17
Links, 414
Liters, 436–437
Logic, 57
Logical Reasoning, 3, 19, 32, 39, 64, 85, 109, 145, 170, 203, 212, 227, 231, 278, 297, 299, 310, 319, 329, 349, 355, 371, 387, 401, 419, 427, 451, 461, 472
  challenge, 113
LOGO, 476–479
Lower extremes, 330–333
Lower quartiles, 330–333

······· **M** ·······

Magazine, M1–M16
Make up a problem, 11, 41, 55, 195, 331, 423
Make up a question, 373, 433
Making choices, 72–73, 113, 164–165, 221, 299, 385, 454–455
Making decisions, 385
Maps, 182–183, 297, 386–387
Mass
  grams, 436–437
  kilograms, 436–437

Math Connections, 55, 76, 85, 219, 233, 287
  challenge, 76
Math Fun, 32, 64, 94, 128, 170, 212, 244, 278, 310, 344, 380, 414, 444, 472
Math Fun Magazine, M1–M16
Mean, 314–315, 344, H20–H21
Measurement, 382–393, 396–397, 399–409
  accuracy, 392–393
  of angles, 134–137, 140–141, 152–153
  appropriate units, 384–385
  of area, 23, 250–251, 402–407, 429, 448
  centimeters, 384–385, 388–393
  of circumference, 400–401, 407, 430
  decimeters, 384
  estimating, 386–387, 419
  feet, 384–385, 389–391, 414
  grams, 436–437
  greatest possible error, 389–391
  hours, 414, H23
  inches, 384–385, 389–391, 414
  indirect, 450–453, 456–457, 460–465, H28
  kilograms, 436–437
  kilometers, 385, 389–391
  of length, 384–393
  links, 414
  liters, 436–437
  meters, 384–385, 389–391
  miles, 182–183, 385–387, 414
  milliliters, 436–437
  millimeters, 384–385, 388–391
  minutes, 414, H23
  nautical miles, 407
  of perimeter, 384, 396–397, 408
  precision, 388–391
  protractors, 134, 138–140, 152, 326–327
  rods, 414
  rulers, 138–139, 388–390
  seconds, 414
  significant digits, 392–393, 402
  of surface area, 426–427, 430–431
  table of measures, H101–H102
  tolerance, H27
  volume, 23, 432–444
  yards, 384–385, 414

Measures of central tendency, 314–315, H20–H21
  mean, 314–315, 344, H20–H21
  median, 314–315, 328–333, H20–H21
  mode, 314–317, 328–329, H20–H21
Median, 314–315, 328–333, H20–H21
Memory keys, 24
Mental math, 3, 19, 83, 99, 101, 137, 176, 349, 369, 453
Meters, 384–385, 389–391
Metric system
  centimeters, 384–385, 388–393
  decimeters, 384
  grams, 436–437
  kilograms, 436–437
  kilometers, 385, 389–391
  liters, 436–437
  meters, 384–385, 389–391
  milliliters, 436–437
  millimeters, 384–385, 388–391
Midpoints, 316–317
Miles, 182–183, 385–387, 414
  nautical, 407
Milliliters, 436–437
Millimeters, 384–385, 388–391
Minutes, 414, H23
Mixed numbers, 75–76
  adding, 82–85, 88
  to decimals, 118–119
  dividing, 104–105, 112–113
  multiplying, 98–99, 102–103, H23
  rounding, 82–83, 98–99
  subtracting, 82–83, 86–87
Mixed Reviews, 9, 21, 45, 53, 79, 87, 103, 117, 143, 163, 191, 205, 227, 237, 259, 267, 289, 303, 323, 331, 353, 365, 391, 405, 423, 427, 457, 465
Mode, 314–317, 328–329, H20–H21
Money
  discounts, 480–481, H24
  earnings, H22
  interest, 204–205
  sales tax, 190, 480–481
  stocks, H25
  tips, 206–207
More Practice, H30–H85
Multiples, H12–H13
  least common, 70–71, 78–79, H12–H13

Multiplication
   Associative Property of, 8–9,
      230–231
   with calculators, 23, 102–103,
      204, 222, 237, 252, 262,
      402–403
   Commutative Property of, 8–9
   of decimals, 14–15, 32, H8–H9
   and division, 14–15, 226
   equations, 50–51
   estimating products, 6–7, 14,
      98–99, 102
   exponents, 22–23
   expressions, 48–49
   factors, 12–13, 68–70
   of fractions, 98–103, 108–109,
      112, H23
   Fundamental Counting
      Principle, 348–349
   Identity Property of, 8–9,
      230–231
   of integers, 222–223, 226,
      230–231
   patterns, 222
   of powers, 234–235
   properties of, 8–9, 230–231
   of rational numbers, 262–263
   using, 14–15
Music Connection, 101

· · · · · · · N · · · · · · ·

Nautical miles, 407
Negative correlations, 337
Number lines
   for addition, 218
   box-and-whisker graphs,
      332–333, 338–339
   inequalities on, 270–271
   integers on, 216–218
   for rounding, H4
Numbers
   absolute value of, 216–218
   adding, 8–11, 82–85, 88,
      218–219, 258–259, H6–H7,
      H18–H19, H23, H25
   compatible, 14, 104–105, 112
   composite, 68–69
   decimals, 118–121, H2–H9
   dividing, 14–15, 18–21, 32,
      104–105, 108–109, 112–113,
      226–227, 234–235, 262–263,
      H8–H9
   factorials, 351–355
   fractions, 74–76, 78–89,
      112–121, 232–233

integers, 216–227, 229–239,
   257, H18–H19
irrational, 256–257
mixed, 75–76, 82–89, 98–99,
   102–105, 112–117
multiplying, 8–9, 14–15, 32,
   98–103, 222–223, 234–235,
   262–263, H8–H9, H23
opposites, 216–217, 220, 258,
   268, H18
ordered pairs, 282–289,
   292–293, 296–303, 483, H26
palindromic, 32
percents, 184–207, 326–327
pi, 400–401, 406–407,
   430–431, 434–435, 444
place value, 2–5, H2–H3
prime, 68–69
prime factorization of, 68–70,
   78
Pythagorean triples, 450
random, 362–363, 478–479,
   490
rational, 248–250, 257–259,
   262–273, 278
real, 257
reciprocals, 100, 108, 115
rounding, 4–5, H4–H5
scientific notation, 236–237
square roots of, 250–257, 450
squares of, 250–251
standard form of, 2–3,
   236–237
subtracting, 10–11, 82–83,
   86–87, 220–221, 258–259,
   H6–H7, H18–H19
triangular, 380
in words, 2–3, H2–H3
Number Sense, 5, 7, 9, 15, 39,
   69, 79, 94, 99, 103, 109, 113,
   119, 121, 128, 170, 199, 221,
   237, 251, 278, 310, 344, 369,
   405, 414, 421, 444
Numerators, 74–75, 94, 100,
   102, 128
Numerical expressions, 36–37

· · · · · · · O · · · · · · ·

Obtuse angles, 134, 136
Octagonal prisms, 419
Octagonal pyramids, 419, 424
Octagons, 149, 151, 476
Odds, 357
One
   as exponent, 22–23
   multiplying, 8–9

   Property of, 8
One-point perspective, 422–423
Operations
   addition, 8–11, 82–85, 88,
      218–219, 258–259, H6–H7,
      H18–H19, H23, H25
   division, 14–15, 18–21, 32,
      104–105, 108–109, 112–113,
      226–227, 234–235, 262–263,
      H8–H9
   inverse, 40, 50
   multiplication, 8–9, 14–15, 32,
      98–103, 222–223, 234–235,
      262–263, H8–H9, H23
   order of, 24–25
   subtraction, 10–11, 82–83,
      86–87, 220–221, 258–259,
      H6–H7, H18–H19
Opposites, 216–217, 220, 258,
   268, H18
Order
   of decimals, H2–H3
   of fractions, 78–79
   of operations, 24–25
   of rational numbers, 248–249
Ordered pairs, 282–289,
   292–293, 296–303, 483, H26
Organizing data, 191, 317, 323,
   328–333
Overestimates, 6–7, 98–99

· · · · · · · P · · · · · · ·

Palindromic numbers, 32
Parallel lines, 140–143
   constructing, 142–143
Parallelograms, 149–151
   area of, 402–404, 406, 426,
      430–431
   rectangles, 148–151, 395–397,
      402–403
   rhombuses, 149, 151
   squares, 23, 149–151, 155,
      250–257, 395–397, 476
Pascal's triangle, 358–361, 380
Patterns, 19, 128, 414
   finding, 26–27, 146–147
   in multiplication, 222
   Pascal's triangle, 358–361,
      380
   sequences, 26–27, 380, 477
Patterns for solid figures, 418,
   420, 430, H91–H100
Pentagonal prisms, 418–419,
   424–425
Pentagonal pyramids, 418, 424

Pentagons, 148–151, 476
  regular, 476
Percent key, 326–327
Percents, 184–207, 212,
  326–327
  calculators, 202, 326
  to decimals, 186–187, 190
  decimals to, 186–187
  of decrease, 200–203
  discounts, H24, 480–481
  estimating, 198–199, 206–207
  finding, 194–195
  of increase, 200–203, 485
  interest, 204–205
  of numbers, 190–191,
    198–199, 202
  to ratios, 186–188, 190, 198
  ratios to, 184–187, 201–202
  tips, 206–207
Perfect squares, 250–252
Perimeter, 384, 396–397,
  408–409
Periods, H2
Permutations, 350–355
Perpendicular lines, 136–137
  constructing, 142–143
Perspective, 422–423
Pi, 400–401, 406–407, 430–431,
  434–435, 444
Place value, 2–5, H2–H3
  charts, H2
  periods, H2
Planes, 132, H14
  coordinate, 282–283, 285,
    288–289, 292–293, 296–303
Points, 132–133, H14–H15
  centers, 420, H16–H17
  decimal, 18, 236, H2, H6, H8
  endpoints, H14
  graphing, 282–285, 288–289,
    292, 296–303, 483
  of rotations, 150–151,
    300–303
  vertices, H14
Polygons, 148–153
  angles of, 148–153
  congruent, 156–161
  decagons, 148, 476
  diagonals of, 111, 148–150
  hexagons, 148–150, 155, 170,
    394, 476
  octagons, 149–151, 476
  pentagons, 148–149, 151,
    476
  quadrilaterals, 149–151, 170,
    402–405
  regular, 170, 394–397,
    476

triangles, 148–153, 155–161,
  170, 394–395, 404–405,
  448–453, 456–457, 460–465,
  476
Polyhedra, 418–419
  prisms, 418–419, 422–427,
    432–433, 436–437
  pyramids, 418–419, 424–427,
    432–433, 437
Positive correlations, 337
Powers, 22–25, 232–237
  with calculators, 23, 233
  integers as exponents,
    232–237
  products of, 234–235
  quotients of, 234–235
  squares, 250–251
  of ten, 22–23, 236–237
Precision, 388–391
Predictions, 334–335, 362–365,
  371, 379
Prime factorization, 68–70
  in finding greatest common
    factors, 70, H12–H13
  in finding least common
    multiples, 70, 78, H12–H13
Prime numbers, 68–69
Prisms, 418–419
  cubes, 23, 432
  drawing, 422–423
  hexagonal, 419, 436
  octagonal, 419
  pentagonal, 418–419, 424
  rectangular, 418–419,
    422–424, 426–427, 432–433,
    436–437
  surface area of, 426–427
  triangular, 418–419, 424, 427,
    433, 437
  volume of, 23, 432–433,
    436–437
Probability, 346–365, 368–371,
  H27
  combinations, 354–355,
    360–361
  of dependent events, 370–371
  of events, 356–357, 359,
    362–365, 368–371
  experimental, 364–365, H27
  Fundamental Counting
    Principle, 348–349
  genetics, 371
  of independent events,
    368–369
  odds, 357
  Pascal's triangle, 358–361, 380
  permutations, 350–355
  predictions, 362–365, 371, 379

random numbers, 362–363,
  478–479, 490
tree diagrams, 348
Problem solving
  choose an appropriate graph,
    338–339
  choose a strategy, 77, 122–123
  making choices, 72–73,
    164–165, 454–455
  multistep problems, 12–13
  Spotlight on Problem Solving,
    17, 47, 81, 107, 155, 193,
    229, 265, 295, 325, 367, 399,
    429, 459
  sufficient and insufficient
    data, 320–321
  use a diagram, 360–361
  use a graph to estimate,
    290–291
  use a map, 182–183
Problem-solving strategies
  act it out, 374–375
  draw a picture, 88–89,
    466–467
  find a pattern, 26–27,
    146–147
  guess and check, 42–43,
    304–305
  make a model, 394–395
  make a table, 224–225,
    260–261, 424–425
  solve a simpler problem,
    110–111
  use a formula, 272–273,
    408–409, 438–439
  use estimation, 206–207
  work backward, 122
  write an equation, 58–59, 122,
    238–239
Products, 14–15, H8–H9
  cross, 78, 174, 176
  estimating, 6–7, 14, 98–99, 102
  of powers, 234–235
Projects
  Batting Averages, 379
  Choose a Field-Trip
    Destination, 343
  Design a Youth Center, 471
  Exercise and the Heart, 309
  Find Geometry in
    Architecture, 169
  Just the Facts Brainteasers,
    413
  Make a Scale Drawing, 243
  Make a Table, 211
  Make Movie Products, 31
  Plan a Garden, 127
  Recycle Containers, 443

Take a Survey, 93
Write an Article, 277
Write a Newsletter, 63
Properties
of Addition, 8–9, 230–231
Additive Inverse, 230–231
Associative, 8–9, 230–231
Commutative, 8–9, 230–231
of Density, 248–249
Distributive, 8–9, 230–231
Identity, 8–9, 230–231
of Integers, 230–231
of Multiplication, 8–9,
230–231
of One, 8–9
of Zero, 8–9
Proportions, 176–181, 456, 462,
464, H28
percent, 184, 188–191,
194–197
scale drawings, 178–183, 243,
386–387, 471
Protractors, 134, 138–140, 152,
326–327
Pyramids, 418–419
decagonal, 425
hexagonal, 419
octagonal, 419, 425
pentagonal, 418, 424
square, 418–419, 424,
426–427, 433, 437
surface area of, 426–427
triangular, 418–419, 424,
432–433
volume of, 432–433, 437
Pythagoras, 449
Pythagorean Property,
448–451
Pythagorean triples, 450

· · · · · · **Q** · · · · · · ·

Quadrants, 282–283
Quadrilaterals, 149–151, 170
parallelograms, 149–151,
402–404, 406
rectangles, 148–151, 395–397,
402–403
rhombuses, 149, 151
squares, 23, 149–151, 155,
250–251, 253, 395–397, 476
trapezoids, 149, 151,
404–405
Quartiles, 330–333
Quotients, 14–15, H8–H9

estimating, 7, 14, 18,
104–105, 112
of powers, 234–235

· · · · · · **R** · · · · · · ·

Radical symbol, 250–251
Radius, 400–401, 406–407,
430–431, 444, H16–H17
of spheres, 420, 438–439, 444
Random numbers, 362–363,
478–479, 490
Ranges
of data, 316–317, 329–333, H25
for relations, 287
Rates, 174
unit, 174–175
Rational numbers, 248–250,
257–259, 262–273, 278
adding, 258–259, H25
comparing, 248–249
dividing, 262–263
in equations, 266–269
in inequalities, 270–271
multiplying, 262–263
subtracting, 258–259
Ratios, 174–177, 211–212, 456
equivalent, 174–179, H28
percents, 184–191, 193–207
probability, 356–357
proportions, 176–181, 456,
462, 464, H28
scales, 178–183, 243, 386, 471
simplest form of, 174–175, 187
slopes, 292–293
trigonometric, 460–465
Rays, 132–133, H14–H15
Real numbers, 256–257
Reciprocals, 100, 108, 115
Rectangles, 130, 148–151
area of, 402–403, 426–427,
430–431
perimeter of, 396–397
squares, 23, 149–151, 155,
250–251, 253, 395–397, 476
Rectangular prisms, 418–419,
422–424, 426–427, 432–433,
436–437
cubes, 23, 432
Reflections, 300–303, 310
Regular polygons, 170, 394–397,
476
equilateral triangles, 155, 170,
394–397
hexagons, 170, 394
octagons, 396

pentagons, 476
perimeter of, 396–397
squares, 23, 130, 149–151,
155, 250–251, 253, 395–397,
476
Relations, 284–291, 296–299
domain, 287
functions, 284–291, 296–297
range, 287
Remainders, 20–21, 118
Repeating decimals, 118–121,
256
Reviews
Chapter, 28–29, 60–61, 90–91,
124–125, 166–167, 208–209,
240–241, 274–275, 306–307,
340–341, 376–377, 410–411,
440–441, 468–469
Cumulative, 33, 65, 95, 129,
171, 213, 245, 279, 311, 345,
381, 415, 445, 473
and Maintenance, 16, 46, 80,
106, 154, 192, 228, 264, 294,
324, 366, 398, 428, 458
Mixed, 9, 21, 45, 53, 79, 87,
103, 117, 143, 163, 191, 205,
227, 237, 259, 267, 289, 303,
323, 331, 353, 365, 391, 405,
423, 427, 457, 465
Rhind Papyrus, 94
Rhombuses, 149, 151
squares, 23, 149–151, 155,
250–253, 395–397, 476
Right angles, 134, 136
Right triangles, 448–453,
460–465
hypotenuse, 449, 452, 460, 464
isosceles, 452–453
legs, 449–450, 452
Pythagorean Property,
449–451
special, 452–453
trigonometric ratios, 460–465
Rods, 414
Rotations, 150–151, 300–303
Rounding
decimals, 4–5, H4–H5
fractions, 98
mixed numbers, 98
using number lines, H4
whole numbers, 4–5, H4–H5
Rulers, 138–139, 388–390

· · · · · · **S** · · · · · · ·

Sales tax, 190, 480–481
Sample spaces, 356

Scale drawings, 178–183, 243, 471
    maps, 182–183, 386–387
Scales, 178–183
Scattergrams, 336–337
School-Home Connections, H22–H28
Science Connections, 51, 255, 371, 435
Scientific calculators, 233, 463
Scientific notation, 236–237
Seconds, 414
Selected Answers, H117–H128
Semicircles, H16–H17
Sequences, 26–27
    Fibonacci, 380, 477
Side-angle-side, 158–161
Side-by-side frequency tables, 316–317
Side-by-side histograms, 316–317
Sides
    corresponding, 156–159
Side-side-side, 158–160
Significant digits, 392–393, 402
Similar figures, 456–457
    enlargements, 472
Simple interest, 204–205
Simplest form
    of fractions, 74–76, 100–103, 234
    of ratios, 174–175, 187
Sine, 460–461, 464–465
Slant height, 426, 430–431, 434
Slopes, 292–293
Social Studies Connections, 335, 407
Solid figures, 418–427, 430–439
    cones, 420–421, 430–431, 434–435, 437, 444, H28
    cylinders, 420–421, 430–431, 434–435, 437, 444, H28
    drawings, 422–423
    prisms, 418–419, 422–427, 432–433, 436–437
    pyramids, 418–419, 424–427, 432–433, 437
    spheres, 420–421, 438–439, 444
Solutions, 40, 56, 296
    checking, 40–41, 44–45, 50–55, 114–117, 266–269
Spheres, 130, 420–421
    surface area of, 444
    volume of, 438–439, 444
Spotlight on Problem Solving
    analyze information, 81

analyze misleading graphs, 325
    check the reasonableness of the solution, 399
    choose a method for solution, 429
    collect and analyze data, 229
    decide when to estimate, 193
    determine reasonable solutions, 265
    discuss the process, 107
    identify relationships, 47
    recognize multiple solutions, 295
    restate the problem, 17
    understand the question, 367
    visualize the results, 155, 459
Spreadsheets, 480–487, 490–491
Square pyramids, 418–419, 424, 426–427, 433, 437
Square root key, 253–254, 256, 450
Square roots, 250–257, 450
    tables of, H103
Squares, 149–151, 155, 476
    area of, 23, 250–251, 426–427
    of numbers, 250–251
    perfect, 250, 252
    perimeter of, 396–397
    tables of, H103
Standard form, 2–3, 236–237
Statistics, 312–323, 325–339
    analyzing data, 53, 191, 197, 229, 263, 314–315, 317, 323
    bar graphs, 316–317, 322–323, 325, 338, 480–481
    box-and-whisker graphs, 332–333, 338–339
    circle graphs, 326–327, 338–339
    collecting data, 229
    extremes, 330–333
    finding data, 3, 79, 119, 259, 323
    frequency tables, 316–317
    histograms, 316–317
    line graphs, 318–319, 334–335, 338–339, H26
    mean, 314–315, 344, H20–H21
    measures of central tendency, 314–315, H20–H21
    median, 314–315, 328–333, H20–H21
    misleading graphs, 325
    mode, 314–317, 328–329, H20–H21

organizing data, 191, 317, 323, 328–333
    predictions, 334–335, 362–365
    quartiles, 330–333
    range, 316–317, 329–333, H25
    scattergrams, 336–337
    stem-and-leaf plots, 328–329, 338–339, 344
    surveys, 93, 229, 488–489
Stem-and-leaf plots, 328–329, 338–339, 344
Stocks, H25
Straightedges, 135, 138–139, 142–145
Subtraction
    with calculators, 10, 12, 221
    of decimals, H6–H7
    equations, 44–45
    estimating differences, 6–7, 10, 82–83
    expressions, 38–39
    of fractions, 86–87
    of integers, 220–221, H18–H19, H25
    of rational numbers, 258–259
    using, 10–11
Sufficient data, 320–321
Supplementary angles, 134–137, 140–141, 152
Surface area, 426–427, 430–431
Surveys, 93, 229, 488–489
Symmetry, 150–151, 300–301, 303
Systems of equations, 296–297

• • • • • • • T • • • • • • •

Tables
    of formulas, H101–H102
    frequency, 316–317
    making, 211, 224–225, 260–261, 424–425
    of measures, H101–H102
    place value, H2
    of squares and square roots, 253–254, H103
    of symbols, H101–H102
    trigonometric ratios, 460–463, H104
Tangent, 460–463
Taxes, 190, 480–481
Teamwork Projects
    Batting Averages, 379
    Choose a Field-Trip Destination, 343

Design a Youth Center, 471
Exercise and the Heart, 309
Find Geometry in
   Architecture, 169
Just the Facts Brainteasers,
   413
Make a Scale Drawing, 243
Make a Table, 211
Make Movie Products, 31
Plan a Garden, 127
Recycle Containers, 443
Take a Survey, 93
Write an Article, 277
Write a Newsletter, 63
Terminating decimals, 118–119,
   256
Terms
   like, 55
Tessellations, 170, 394–395
Tests, 30, 62, 92, 126, 168, 210,
   242, 276, 308, 342, 378, 412,
   442, 470
Three-dimensional figures,
   418–427, 430–439, 444
   cones, 420–421, 430–431,
      434–435, 437, 444, H28
   cylinders, 420–421, 430–431,
      434–435, 437, 444, H28
   drawing, 422–423
   prisms, 418–419, 422–427,
      432–433, 436–437
   pyramids, 418–419, 424–427,
      432–433, 437
   spheres, 420–421, 438–439,
      444
Time
   hours, 414, H23
   minutes, 414, H23
   seconds, 414
Tips, 206–207
Tolerance, H27
Transformations, 300–303,
   310
   reflections, 300–303, 310
   rotations, 150–151, 300–303

translations, 300, 302, 310
Translations, 300, 302, 310
Transversals, 140–141
Trapezoids, 149–151
   area of, 404–405
Tree diagrams, 348
Triangles, 148–153
   angles of, 148, 150, 152–153
   area of, 404–405, 426–427
   congruent, 156–161
   equilateral, 155, 170,
      394–397, 476
   isosceles, 452–453
   Pascal's, 358–361, 380
   right, 448–453, 460–465
   similar, 456–457, H28
Triangular numbers, 380
Triangular prisms, 418–419,
   424, 427, 433, 437
Triangular pyramids, 418–419,
   424, 432–433
Trigonometric ratios, 460–465
   cosine, 460–461, 464–465
   sine, 460–461, 464–465
   tables of, 462–463, H104
   tangent, 460–463

U

Underestimates, 6–7, 98–99
Unit fractions, 94
Unit rates, 174–175
Upper extremes, 330–333
Upper quartiles, 330–333

V

Variables, 36
Venn diagrams, 372–373
Vertical angles, 135–137,
   140–141
Vertices
   of angles, H14

of solid figures, 424
Visual Thinking, 25, 37, 64, 83,
   103, 137, 157, 187, 205, 271,
   297, 323, 331, 421, 423, 444,
   453, 472
Vitruvius, 401
Volume, 432–440
   of cones, 434–435, 437, 444,
      H28
   of cubes, 23, 432
   of cylinders, 434–435, 437,
      444, H28
   of prisms, 432–433, 436–437
   of pyramids, 432–433, 437
   of spheres, 438–439, 444

W

Wang Fan, 401
Whole numbers
   rounding, 4–5, H4–H5
Word processors, 486–487,
   490–491
Work Together. See Exploring
   and Teamwork Projects
Write a problem, 285, 463
Write a question, 45, 185, 227,
   391, 421
Writer's Corners, 13, 43, 89, 111,
   147, 183, 225, 261, 291, 305,
   339, 361, 409, 439, 455

Y

Yards, 384–385, 414

Z

Zero
   adding, 8–9
   annexing, H2, H6
   in division, 226–227
   as exponent, 22–23
   Property of, 8

MATH FUN MAGAZINE

These brainteasers don't stump me!

Have fun solving these brain teasers!

▶ As you learn
▶ new things this year,
▶ you will be able
▶ to solve problems
▶ that might have
▶ stumped you at first.
▶ So, keep trying!

FUNNY MONEY

These four brain ticklers will cause you to think hard about money. See if you can supply answers that make dollars and sense!

1 Brett's mother said, "Brett, I'm going to pay you $6 an hour for the 6 seconds you spent washing your hands for dinner." How much money did Brett receive for the 6 seconds?

2 Three men checked into a hotel. Their room cost $30, so each man paid $10. Later, the hotel clerk realized he had overcharged the men by $5. He gave $5 to the bellhop and told him to return it to the men. The bellhop, knowing $5 could not be divided evenly among the 3 men, gave back only $3 and kept $2. Then each man paid $9, for a total of $27. The bellhop kept $2 making the total $29. Where was the missing dollar from the original $30?

3 Three sisters went to the store to buy new notebooks for school. Each sister bought 3 notebooks. All their notebooks were the same kind. One sister paid for the entire purchase with a $10 bill. She received less than $0.50 in change, all in nickels. How much did each notebook cost?

4 Neil went to the store to buy tomato sauce. For one brand the prices were $0.40 for a large can, $0.24 for a medium can, and $0.17 for a small can. Another brand of tomato sauce was $0.01 cheaper for each size. Neil spent exactly $1.00. Which cans did he buy?

M2

ALL IN THE FAMILY

How well do you know the members of a family? See how many of these family puzzles you can solve.

1 Julius is Dr. Baker's son. However, Dr. Baker is not Julius's father. How is this possible?

2 Rick, Ralph, and Robin are mountain climbers. Rick is Ralph's brother. Ralph is Robin's brother. Yet, Robin is not Rick's brother. How can this be?

3 Two mothers and two daughters went out to eat. Each person ate one hamburger. Yet, only three hamburgers were eaten in all. How is this possible?

4 Albert, Barry, and Chuck are married to Doris, Eunice, and Flo. Doris's sister is married to Chuck. Albert has never met Flo, who is an only child. Who is married to whom?

5 Gail and Martha have the same parents. The girls were born on the same date in the same year. They look alike yet they are not twins. How can you explain this?

6 If 6 brothers take 6 hr to cut down 6 trees, how long will it take 5 brothers to cut down 5 trees?

Magic Shapes

You can create something magical with each shape below!
Read each set of directions to learn how.

1. 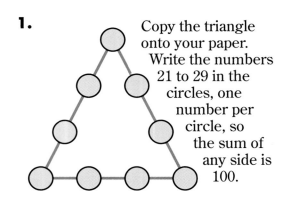 Copy the triangle onto your paper. Write the numbers 21 to 29 in the circles, one number per circle, so the sum of any side is 100.

2.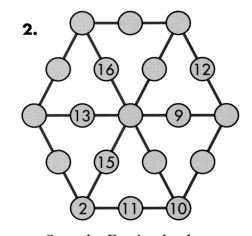

Copy the Ferris wheel and its numbers onto your paper. Fill in the remaining numbers so that each line of three numbers adds up to 23.

3. **Copy the square and its numbers onto your paper. In this magic square, multiplying the three numbers across, down, or diagonally will always give you a product of 1. Fill in the missing numbers.**

2	■	$\frac{1}{8}$
■	■	■
■	$\frac{1}{4}$	■

4. Copy the star and its numbers onto your paper. Fill in the remaining numbers so that each straight line of four numbers adds up to 40.

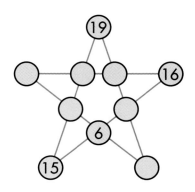

THE PLOT THICKENS

Copy the graph onto your paper.

Plot each set of coordinates. Then connect each pair of points with a line segment.

The first set has been done for you.

The message you will spell tells what time it is if you give 10¢ to one friend and 15¢ to another friend.

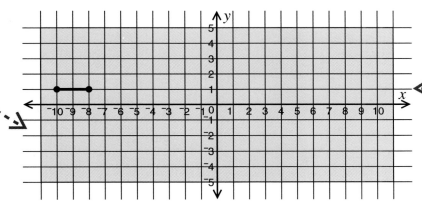

1. (⁻10,1) (⁻8,1)
2. (⁻10,1) (⁻10,4)
3. (⁻8,4) (⁻10,4)
4. (⁻8,4) (⁻8,1)
5. (⁻9,2) (⁻8,1)
6. (⁻7,4) (⁻7,1)
7. (⁻7,1) (⁻5,1)
8. (⁻5,1) (⁻5,4)
9. (⁻4,1) (⁻2,4)
10. (⁻2,4) (0,1)
11. (⁻3,2) (⁻1,2)
12. (1,1) (1,4)
13. (1,4) (2,3)
14. (2,3) (1,2)

15. (1,2) (2,1)
16. (4,1) (4,4)
17. (3,4) (5,4)
18. (6,1) (6,4)
19. (6,4) (8,4)
20. (6,2) (8,2)
21. (6,1) (8,1)
22. (9,1) (9,4)
23. (9,4) (10,3)
24. (10,3) (9,2)
25. (9,2) (10,1)
26. (⁻7,⁻4) (⁻7,⁻1)
27. (⁻8,⁻1) (⁻6,⁻1)
28. (⁻5,⁻1) (⁻5,⁻4)

29. (⁻5,⁻4) (⁻3,⁻4)
30. (⁻3,⁻4) (⁻3,⁻1)
31. (⁻3,⁻1) (⁻5,⁻1)
32. (0,⁻1) (2,⁻1)
33. (1,⁻1) (1,⁻4)
34. (3,⁻1) (4,⁻4)
35. (4,⁻4) (5,⁻1)
36. (5,⁻1) (6,⁻4)
37. (6,⁻4) (7,⁻1)
38. (8,⁻1) (10,⁻1)
39. (10,⁻1) (10,⁻4)
40. (10,⁻4) (8,⁻4)
41. (8,⁻4) (8,⁻1)

M5

Silly Situations

The word problems that follow contain true facts
put into silly situations.
See how many you can solve . . .
seriously!

1

A standard golf ball has 336 dimples. Suppose you wanted the kids in your town to pose as a "human golf ball" by pushing their faces together. However, only 1 out of every 8 kids has dimples! This being the case, how many kids must live in your town in order for you to succeed? (Remember, each eligible kid has two dimples!)

2

The country of Liechtenstein is the leading exporter of false teeth. It ships about 30 million sets of false teeth a year! If each set had 4 cavities in it, about how many cavities would be shipped on an average day? (HINT: Use compatible numbers.)

3

A sparrow's brain makes up 4.2% of its total body weight. If you met a sparrow that weighed 500 lb, you would likely step aside! You'd also know that the sparrow's brain weighed how many pounds?

4

The actress Tuesday Weld was born on a Friday. If January 1 that year had been a Friday and someone named Tuesday had been born every Friday of that year, how many people named Tuesday would have been born?

5

Suppose the state of Maine produced 24 billion toothpicks last year and each toothpick was 2 in. long. If you took the year's supply and placed it end to end, about how many times could you reach the moon and return to the earth? The moon is 238,857 mi from the earth. (HINT: To simplify computations, use compatible numbers for the distances.)

Believe it or not!

The following word problems all contain true information. You can solve each one with just a few simple facts— believe it or not!

1 In 1894 there were only 4 automobiles in the United States. Today there are 340 million passenger cars in the world, and 36% of them are in the United States. How many times the number of cars that were in the United States in 1894 are now there?

2 The largest iceberg on record was 208 mi long and 60 mi wide. It was first sighted on November 12, 1956. How many square miles was the iceberg on its top surface?

3 In 1913 the tax on an income of $4,000 was just 1 penny. Write a number that shows the percent of tax on $4,000.

4 One of the largest cakes ever baked weighed 25,000 lb and stood 25 ft high. If sliced horizontally into 1-ft layers, how much would each layer weigh?

5 A human heart pumps 4,320 gal of blood every day. How much blood does it pump every minute?

6 The largest living thing on Earth is the General Sherman Tree in California. It is 272 ft 4 in. tall. The tallest human in modern times was Robert Wadlow, who measured 8 ft, 11 in. How many Wadlows, standing on top of each other, would it take to reach the top of the General Sherman Tree?

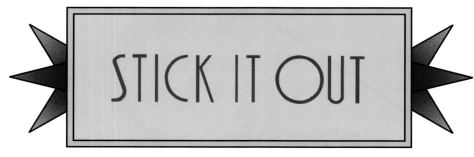

STICK IT OUT

You may find it helpful to use toothpicks,
other thin sticks, paper clips, or similar articles
to solve these puzzles.

1 Remove 3 of
these 6 sticks
to show
in Roman
numerals that
half of 9 equals
4!

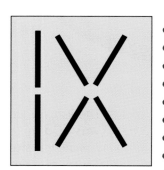

2 These 4 sticks
represent a
glass with a
stem. Can you
get the ice cube
into the glass
by moving only
2 sticks?

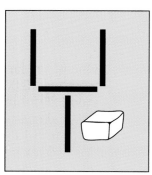

3 Remove
3 sticks
from
the 15
shown
so that
only
3 squares
remain.

4 Remove 4 sticks from the 24 shown
so that only 5 squares remain.

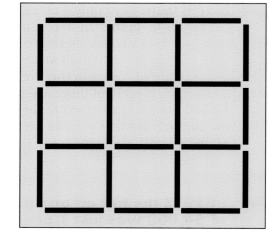

5 Remove 1 stick
from the 13
that are shown.
Then rearrange
the remaining
12 sticks so
that they form
6 triangles of
equal size.

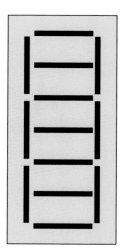

Reading
Between the Lines

To solve these puzzles, look closely at the lines. So, get into line now, and see where you end up!

1

Which of the long lines in this design are parallel?

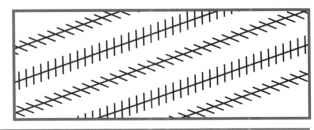

2 Jack wants to travel each road on the map only one time. He plans to leave from and return to point *A*. Copy the map onto your paper, and trace the route that he should follow.

B
A *C*
E *D*

3 Trace this shape onto your paper. Then see if you can divide it into two equal pieces by drawing just two straight lines.

4 Three houses are to have their utilities connected. Each house is to receive a gas line, a water line, and an electric line. The challenge is to hook up these utilities to the three houses *without any of the service lines crossing.* Copy the map onto your paper, and see if you can draw a line (not necessarily straight) from each utility to each house, with none of the lines crossing.

G W E
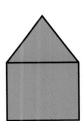 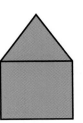 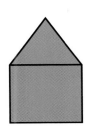

BREAKING THE CODE

How good are you at decoding secret symbols? See how quickly you can break the codes in these puzzles.

1 In this puzzle the key to the code is at the right. Numbers are represented by the shapes of the lines they are within. For example, the number 3 is represented as ⌞. Now solve the following problems. Write your answer in code and as a number.

1	2	3
4	5	6
7	8	9

(a) ⌈ × ☐ = ?

(b) ⌟⌐⌐ ÷ ⌟⌎ = ?

(c) ☐⌞⌐ + ⌎⌐⌐ = ?

(d) ⌐☐⌟⌟ − ⌐⌞⌐ = ?

(e) ⌐⌈⌎ ÷ ⌐ = ?

(f) ⌐⌐ × ⌟⌞⌈ = ?

2 Use the information in the box at the right to complete each statement. Use the correct symbol or symbols in your answers.

! + @ = ¢
* + & = *

a. ¢ − @ = ?

b. ! + @ + & = ¢ + ?

c. * − & = ?

d. @ + & = ?

e. ¢ − & = ?

f. & + & = ?

g. ! + & = ¢ − ?

h. * + * = ? + ?

3 Use the statements below to figure out the number that each symbol represents.

a. ■ + ● = 950

b. 950 − △ = ▬

c. ▬ + ■ = 1,500

■ = ?

● = ?

△ = ?

▬ = ?

M10

IN SO MANY Words

In each of these puzzles, every letter represents a number between 0 and 9. Figure out the number to replace each letter. The number for each letter varies from puzzle to puzzle.

1

```
        ANT
ITS)STING
    ITS
    RTSN
    RIEN
     ITCG
     IISV
      IVV
```

A = ?
C = ?
E = ?
G = ?
I = 4
N = ?
R = ?
S = 7
T = 9
V = ?

2

```
  CANADA
+NIGERIA
 FINLAND
```

A = 6   G = ?
C = ?   I = 1
D = ?   L = 7
E = ?   N = 4
F = ?   R = ?

3

```
 DANGER
- CROSS
  ROADS
```

A = ?   E = ?   O = ?
C = 9   G = ?   R = 6
D = ?   N = 8   S = ?

4

```
   NON
 ×FAT
  IMHT
  NON
 LHLT
 LAMENT
```

A = ?   L = 2
E = ?   M = 4
F = ?   N = 6
H = ?   O = ?
I = ?   T = 8

CHECKMATE

A checkerboard has 64 small squares with sides of 1 unit.
It has 1 large square with sides of 8 units.

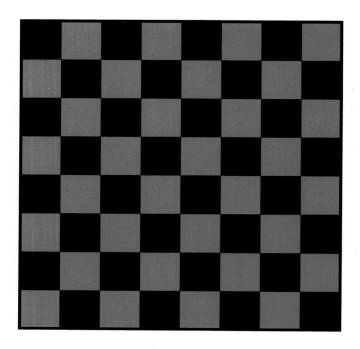

1 Copy and complete the table to show the number of squares on the checkerboard that have sides of 1 through 8 units.

Side of square	1	2	3	4	5	6	7	8
Number of squares	64	?	?	?	?	?	?	1

2 What is the total number of squares on the checkerboard?

3 How many times on the checkerboard does this pattern appear?

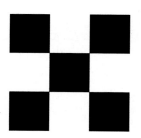

4 How many times on the checkerboard does this pattern appear?

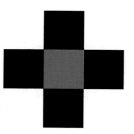

Who's Who?

Be a detective and use the clues to solve each puzzle.
You may want to make a table of choices.

1. The last names of three children are Cuevas, Duncan, and Moore. Their first names are James, Jonathan, and Maria. Their ages are 2, 3, and 4. Maria is two years older than the Moore child. The Cuevas child is 3 years old, and his name is not James.

What is each child's full name and age?

First Name	Last Name			Age		
	Cuevas	Duncan	Moore	2	3	4
James						
Jonathan						
Maria						

2. Ms. Adams, Mrs. Baldwin, and Miss Chen are neighbors. They all have interesting jobs. One is a social worker, one is a nurse, and one is a lawyer (but not in that order). The nurse has no brothers and earns the least money of the three. Mrs. Baldwin is married to Ms. Adams' brother, and she earns more money than the lawyer. Which woman has which job?

3. Four students live in the same apartment house. Tony, Susan, Oliver, and Rosa each live on a different floor of a four-story apartment house. Their ages are 14, 13, 12, and 10, but not necessarily in that order. Tony lives directly above the 13-year-old and directly below the 12-year-old. Susan has to pass by the 10-year-old's apartment. Susan is more than one floor away from Rosa, who is more than one year younger than Susan. How old is each student, and on which floor does each live?

The puzzles on this page are all about dots.
See if you can solve them without going "dotty" yourself!

A·M·A·Z·I·N·G·!

1 Copy this design onto your paper. See if you can fill in 6 dots, 1 dot per square, so that no 3 dots are in a straight line. One of the 6 dots has been put in for you.

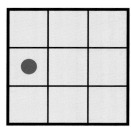

2 Now, copy this design. See if you can fill in 12 dots, 1 dot per square, so that no 4 dots are in a straight line.

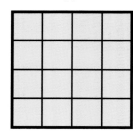

3 How many different routes can you take to get from dot A to dot D? There's only one catch: For each route that you plan, you cannot go over the same path twice. (HINT: "Same path" means total path, not simply a portion of it.)

A •——————• B
C •——————• D

4 Trace the dots below onto your paper. Draw a horizontal or a vertical straight line between the dots that show equivalent amounts in fractions or decimals. You will end up spelling a good name for a race-car driver!

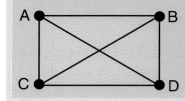

$\frac{4}{6}$	$0.\overline{66}$	0.125	$\frac{1}{2}$	$\frac{1}{8}$	0.25	0.375	$\frac{1}{4}$	$\frac{3}{4}$	$\frac{15}{20}$
•	•	•	•	•	•	•	•	•	•
•	•		•			•		•	•
$\frac{2}{3}$	$\frac{8}{12}$		0.5			$\frac{3}{8}$		$\frac{6}{8}$	0.75

What's Your SIGN?

The problems below are a challenge. The numbers are there, but the signs are missing! See if you can restore them.

1. Messy Bessie did her homework with a leaky pen. Each time that she wrote +, −, ×, or ÷, the ink ran and blotted out the sign. Can you help straighten out this mess? Write each problem on your paper, and fill in the signs that are blotted out.

Example: $8 \bullet 3 \bullet 4 \bullet 5 = 11$

$8 \times 3 \div 4 + 5 = 11$

a. $(16 \bullet 2) \bullet 2 \bullet 6 = 30$

b. $(100 \bullet 50) \bullet 3 \bullet 1 = 151$

c. $(41 \bullet 6) \bullet 2 \bullet 90 = 4$

d. $(3.6 \bullet 0.8) \bullet 3 \bullet 2 = 4.2$

e. $44 \bullet 11 \bullet (6 \bullet 2) \bullet 30 = 240$

f. $(33 \bullet 30) \bullet 5 \bullet 5 = 20$

g. $(\frac{2}{3} \bullet \frac{1}{3}) \bullet \frac{1}{2} \bullet \frac{1}{4} = \frac{1}{2}$

h. $(\frac{1}{4} \bullet \frac{1}{4} \bullet \frac{1}{4}) \bullet \frac{1}{4} = \frac{3}{16}$

i. $\frac{2}{5} \bullet 5 \bullet \frac{1}{2} \bullet 6 = 7$

j. $\frac{1}{2} \bullet \frac{1}{2} \bullet \frac{1}{2} \bullet \frac{1}{2} = 0$

k. $6 \bullet (1 \bullet 2) \bullet 2 = 36$

l. $100 \bullet (12 \bullet 2) \bullet 8 = 18$

2. Messy Bessie also created a magic square using signs that got blotted out. Will you help her fill in the correct signs? Copy the puzzle below onto your paper. Then fill in the right sign where each ink blot is so that the problems are correct going across or down.

4	●	12	●	8	=	6
●		●		●		●
16	●	16	●	2	=	2
●		●		●		●
8	●	6	●	14	=	34
=		=		=		=
8	●	32	●	2	=	38

Make a 100

There are many ways to write 100.

| one hundred | 100 | 10 × 10 | 10^2 |

| C Roman numeral | $(4 + 4 + 4 + 4 + 4 + 4) \times 4 + 4$ |

Try to find some other ways to write 100.

Make 100 by

1. using 1 five times.
2. using 3 five times.
3. using 2 seven times.
4. using 5 four times.
5. using 9 six times.
6. adding 2 square numbers.
7. adding 4 cube numbers.
8. adding 5 prime numbers (remember: 1 is not a prime number).
9. adding 9 prime numbers.
10. using each number from 1 to 9 once.

It's your turn!

I solved every problem! Did you?

Make up some interesting ways to make 100.
See if your friends can find the solutions.